The Palgrave Handbook of
Global Politics
in the 22nd Century

Laura Horn · Ayşem Mert · Franziska Müller
Editors

The Palgrave Handbook of Global Politics in the 22nd Century

Editors
Laura Horn
Department of Social Sciences
and Business
Roskilde University
Roskilde, Denmark

Ayşem Mert
Stockholm University
Stockholm, Sweden

Franziska Müller
Business, Economics and Social Sciences
University of Hamburg
Hamburg, Germany

ISBN 978-3-031-13721-1   ISBN 978-3-031-13722-8   (eBook)
https://doi.org/10.1007/978-3-031-13722-8

© The Editor(s) (if applicable) and The Author(s), under exclusive license to Springer Nature
Switzerland AG 2023
This work is subject to copyright. All rights are solely and exclusively licensed by the Publisher,
whether the whole or part of the material is concerned, specifically the rights of translation,
reprinting, reuse of illustrations, recitation, broadcasting, reproduction on microfilms or in any
other physical way, and transmission or information storage and retrieval, electronic adaptation,
computer software, or by similar or dissimilar methodology now known or hereafter developed.
The use of general descriptive names, registered names, trademarks, service marks, etc. in this
publication does not imply, even in the absence of a specific statement, that such names are
exempt from the relevant protective laws and regulations and therefore free for general use.
The publisher, the authors, and the editors are safe to assume that the advice and information in
this book are believed to be true and accurate at the date of publication. Neither the publisher
nor the authors or the editors give a warranty, expressed or implied, with respect to the material
contained herein or for any errors or omissions that may have been made. The publisher remains
neutral with regard to jurisdictional claims in published maps and institutional affiliations.

Cover image: © Vizerskaya/DigitalVision Vectors/Getty Images

This Palgrave Macmillan imprint is published by the registered company Springer Nature
Switzerland AG
The registered company address is: Gewerbestrasse 11, 6330 Cham, Switzerland

CONTENTS

‹ψ1› Introduction—The Qurative Turn in Global Politics   1
Laura Horn, Ayşem Mert, and Franziska Müller

Theory and Concepts

‹ψ2› The Evolution of Global Society Theory   15
Barry Buzan

‹ψ3› 'The Past, Present and Future of Global Thought'
Reviewing a Handbook Chapter from 2122   31
Lucian M. Ashworth

‹ψ4› From World Politics to 'Time Epistemics': New
Medievalism and the Story of a Certain Scholar   47
Aleksandra Spalińska

‹ψ5› Herman Gorter: An Introduction to the End of a World   61
Annette Freyberg-Inan and Alexander van Eijk

Themes: *(In)Security*

‹ψ6› Strategic Partnerships in Twenty-Second Century Global
Politics: From Weathering Storms to the Politics of Anticipation   83
Andriy Tyushka and Lucyna Czechowska

‹ψ7› Nuclear Weapons in 2122: Disaster, Stability,
or Disarmament?   107
Michal Onderco and Jeffrey W. Knopf

‹ψ8› The Death and Renaissance of Diplomacy: The New
Diplomatic Order for Our Times   129
Tomasz Kamiński

vi   CONTENTS

‹ψ9› **Ignored Histories, Neglected Regions: Origins of the Genosocial Order and the Normative Change Reconsidered**   145
Jakub Zahora

‹ψ10› **Not yet a Global Health Paradigm: A Scenario-Based Analysis of Global Health Policies**   161
Maria Ferreira

Themes: *Governance and Technology*

‹ψ11› **World-Systems and the Rescaling Geography of Europe**   183
Giuseppe Porcaro

‹ψ12› **Shades of Democracy in the Post-Anthropocene**   199
Peter Christoff and Ayşem Mert

‹ψ13› **"Big Daddy Don't Like That!" Global Rule by Planetary Algorithm**   219
Ronnie D. Lipschutz

Themes: *The Anthropocene*

‹ψ14› **The Global Political Economics of Hydrogen**   237
John Szabo

‹ψ15› **The Degrowth Transition in Latin America: Deurbanised, Autonomous City-States in 2122—An Invitation**   255
Joshua Hurtado Hurtado

‹ψ16› **Planetary Politics in the Twenty-Second Century**   271
Ian Manners

‹ψ17› **"Now Live from Lagos, Tehran and Oceanside": Three B7CC Leaders Reflect on Strategies for Cooperation After the Anthropocentric Purge**   291
Franziska Müller

Themes: *Culture and Identity*

‹ψ18› **World Religions**   309
Luca Ozzano and Alberta Giorgi

‹ψ19› **The UNCorp Quantum Mechanism for Wellbeing**   325
Isabella Hermann

‹ψ20› **Cloning God: The UN Bioethics and Human Dignity Declaration of 2043 and the Rise of Monotheistic Fertility Cults in the Middle East**   337
Elana Gomel

Practices and Reflections

‹ψ21› An Autobiographical Reflection by Daqin Kanja Augustine Prepared for Publication by Patrick Thaddeus Jackson 353
Patrick Thaddeus Jackson

‹ψ22› Search: Physical Twin 369
Frans Magnusson and Elin Haettner

‹ψ23› The Origins of AGE: From States and Markets to Scientific Methods 387
Karim Zakhour

Conclusion

‹ψ24› The Realism of Our Time? Futures, Fictions, and the Mid-Century Bang 407
Laura Horn, Ayşem Mert, and Franziska Müller

List of Contributors 433

Acknowledgements 435

LIST OF FIGURES

Strategic Partnerships in Twenty-Second Century Global Politics: From Weathering Storms to the Politics of Anticipation

Fig. 1   Building blocks of the 'strategic partnership' notion in IR scholarship of the 1990s–2010s   97

The Death and Renaissance of Diplomacy: The New Diplomatic Order for Our Times

Fig. 1   Timeline of the last century   132
Fig. 2   The classical model of polylateral diplomacy   132

World-Systems and the Rescaling Geography of Europe

Fig. 1   Subscriptions to World-Rhizomes 2065–2122   191
Fig. 2   European Union subscriptions across continents, 2122   194
Fig. 3   Subscriptions within Europe, 2122, geographical sprawl   195

The Global Political Economics of Hydrogen

Fig. 1   Global energy demand   239

The UNCorp Quantum Mechanism for Wellbeing

Fig. 1   The basic functioning of the UNCorpQMW   328
Fig. 2   The 10 wellbeing gateways   332

LIST OF TABLES

'The Past, Present and Future of Global Thought' Reviewing a Handbook Chapter from 2122

Table 1	Realism and Idealism	33
Table 2	The great debates between realism and idealism in IR's pre-history	36
Table 3	Approaches to IR	39

Strategic Partnerships in Twenty-Second Century Global Politics: From Weathering Storms to the Politics of Anticipation

Table 1	Strategic partnerships and international cooperation in the last three centuries	86
Table 2	Strategic partnerships in global politics: then and now	102

Not yet a Global Health Paradigm: A Scenario-Based Analysis of Global Health Policies

Table 1	The 2069/2071 avian influenza pandemic in numbers	164
Table 2	Securitization move and global health regime	169
Table 3	Public health and security four perspectives	174

The Global Political Economics of Hydrogen

Table 1	Hydrogen types and production methods	239

The Degrowth Transition in Latin America: Deurbanised, Autonomous City-States in 2122—An Invitation

Table 1	Characteristics of Latin American city-states, years 2074–2090	266

Introduction—The Qurative Turn in Global Politics

Laura Horn, Ayşem Mert, and Franziska Müller

Q Collective

There is no longer any serious contender to quration as central approach to social science. Nonetheless, it is worthwhile to recount the developments of the qurative turn and what they mean for our understanding of global politics. Remnants of perspectives pre-dating the 2022 Chiang prism event are surfacing in academic debates ever so often; mostly these discussions corroborate the archaic nature of the foundations on which global politics scholars had built their scholarly endeavours. The purpose of this book, however, is not to reproduce the triumphalism of early quantum social science perspectives (Nilsson Ψ 2029; Whitey and Moon Ψ 2030). Rather, given the conjunctural constellation of the upcoming celebrations of the bicentenary of the scientific quantum revolution, as well as the recent observance of the bicentenary of

---

L. Horn (✉)
Department of Social Sciences and Business, Roskilde
University, Roskilde, Denmark
e-mail: lhorn@ruc.dk

A. Mert
Stockholm University, Stockholm, Sweden
e-mail: aysem.mert@statsvet.su.se

F. Müller
Business, Economics and Social Sciences, Universität
Hamburg, Hamburg, Germany
e-mail: franziska.mueller@uni-hamburg.de

© The Author(s), under exclusive license to Springer Nature
Switzerland AG 2023
L. Horn et al. (eds.), *The Palgrave Handbook of Global Politics
in the 22nd Century*, https://doi.org/10.1007/978-3-031-13722-8_1

'International Relations', as obscure as these events might have been perceived outside of certain academic circles, it seems a particularly auspicious moment for stock-taking of the field. Its past achievements are well covered, so our attention here focuses on the present condition of Global Politics, showcasing the strength of quration. Naturally, the ambition of this book stands rather in contrast to the handbooks of the past (e.g. Dunne et al. 2020; Weber 2021; Tickner and Smith 2020; Chandler et al. 2021). Whereas prior academic works sought, like this example from the early twenty-first century, to 'provide a single volume of extensive, systematic, authoritative overview of the state of the art within the various sub-fields of the discipline' (Carlsnaes et al. 2002: preface), the qurative turn has made these closures redundant. Instead, the book seeks to open up a glimpse into the many worlds, and by extension many futures, of contemporary global politics. This brief introduction situates this book and its format within the contemporary context and then lays out the plan of the book.

1   Historical Antecedents

The onto-epistemological position espoused in qurative approaches is informed by the imperative to oversee, chronicle and witness global politics, rather than mimic the analytical, Newtonian impulses that have long withheld social sciences from reaching their full potential in exploring human progress.

Interestingly, an engagement, if not entanglement with quantum science had already emerged within 'International Relations' in the early twenty-first century (Wendt 2015). Some of this appears to have come about as a counter-reaction to a dominant twentieth-century social science approach which posited a naïve approach to reality, epitomized by the then famous academic motto: 'Social scientists who focus on only overt, observable behaviors are missing a lot, but how are we to know if we cannot see?' (King et al. 1994: 41).[1] Early ramifications of what later (de)(anti)materialized as the qurative turn emerged in the context of Anthropocene IR studies. While lacking the groundbreaking quantum approach, already in these writings a critique of temporalities indicated that IR's ideational history desperately needed to move beyond its anachronistic paradigms. Quantum social science followed in the slipstream of the opposing constructivist paradigm, which in the early twenty-first century had established itself as the mainstream approach to the study of world politics, but fell prey to 'paradigm erosion' following the new and gruesome materialities pervading late-stage eco-modernism. Despite the considerable niche positioning of early quantum social science researchers, the

---

[1] Historical records show that there was a persistent, if rather tired tradition for wearing this sentence on robes for graduation during the 2020s, 30s and 40s as counter-reaction to quration.

INTRODUCTION—THE QURATIVE TURN IN GLOBAL POLITICS   3

technological advances at that time propelled academic interest towards 'quantizing IR'. As Der Derian and Wendt argued back then (2020: 409), 'quantum is just too important to be left to the scientists alone'.

We know now that the arguments and theoretical propositions of these early quantum scholars ultimately remained dangling due to the absence of computational power, as well as a certain propensity of this scholarship to fetishize abstract discussions over a concrete engagement with the burning (quite literally, in some parts of the world) challenges in global politics. The bodies kept piling up, while theorists retreated into metaphysics to discuss social wave functions. That is not to say that these approaches were without merit. They raised crucial questions, e.g. about the geopolitical realities in which quantum computing emerged (Der Derian and Wendt 2020). A plurality of early quantum approaches unfolded, including feminist, posthuman and critical perspectives (Barad 2007; Cudworth et al. 2018; Zanotti (2019); Murphy 2021; Der Derian and Wendt 2022). While they did not foresee the qurative turn as such, some of the concepts central to quration have indeed been prefigured in this literature. The pivotal position the research group 'Project Q' had in the immediate aftermath of the prism event in 2022 indicates that there was some relevance of these pre-prism quantum approaches.[2] At the same time, their failure to retain this role when it had become clear that classical assumptions of causality had collapsed shows that many of these early quantum scholars remained bound by remnants of 'International Relations' thought of the twentieth century.[3] It is difficult for us to grasp the conditions of knowledge production of these early twenty-first-century scholars; the unequal power relations and hostile structures in academic environments at the time are indeed quite confounding.

With this in mind, it is perhaps easier to understand just how important the events of 2022 were not just in human history, but also the study of it. Fortunately, after the first few waves of social unrest over the political, economic and cultural consequences of the prism event had subsided, academic discussions started to make sense of the quantum spectrum. Fundamentally instrumental in this was the revalidation of late twentieth-century philosophical thought, in particular the work of Douglas Adams. His seminal pentalogy HHGTTG did not get recognition upon publication other than as a novel, whereas by the mid-2030s it had been established that it had, in fact, much to say on the subject of parallel universes. Generally, the literature highlights two core arguments of Adams' framework (Bonfert Ψ 2036). Firstly, the ontological acceptance of epistemological inadequacy; as the book states: 'you don't stand the remotest chance of understanding it. You can therefore say "What?" and "Eh?" and even go cross-eyed and start to blither if you like without any fear of

---

[2] Archival records have been backed up here https://projectqsydney.com/.

[3] The physical destruction of their HQ in the mega bush fires that destroyed large parts of New South Wales in 2028 certainly also was a factor in the breakdown of academic engagement.

making a fool of yourself' (Adams 1992: 25). This proved an essential starting point for a qurative approach, as readers will no doubt also experience while engaging with this book. The second foundational argument put forward by Adams concerns the fundamental ontological constitution of the universal wave function, and by extension the branching off of the many worlds. Even though it is well-known, it is worth relaying his formulation of WSOGMM in some detail.

> [A]ny given universe is not actually a thing as such, but is just a way of looking at what is technically known as the WSOGMM, or Whole Sort of General Mish Mash. The Whole Sort of General Mish Mash doesn't actually exist either, but is just the sum total of all the different ways there would be of looking at it if it did. [...] You can slice the Whole Sort of General Mish Mash any way you like and you will generally come up with something that someone will call home. (Adams 1992: 26)

The pragmatism inherent in this ontology is at the heart of quration. The concept of WSOGMM has perhaps gone out of fashion as quration moved across academic disciplines, and consolidated into a universal scientific approach with a concomitant linguistic apparatus. The eclipse of English as *lingua franca* in academic conversations by the rapid rise of Amharic, Bengali and Bahasa also meant that Adams' original work receded somewhat into the background from the 2050s onwards, at least until the realization of babel fish implants that enabled instantaneous cognitive translation such as the one taking place when you read this text.[4] It should also be kept in mind here that there were massive trench wars, academic squirmishes and in a few cases even physical altercations at conferences in the decades it took for such an entangled understanding of the universe to fully become academic common sense. As a prescient early twenty-first-century physicist noted, 'the connection between all the components of the universe is disconcerting' (Rovelli 2020: 85). Eventually quration crowded out any of the remnant perspectives that pre-dated 2022. Towards the end of the twenty-first century, and ever since, the main theoretical development in our field has in fact been exnovation; a welcome trend against the background of almost 200 years of scholarly bickering that ultimately proved to be missing the point on the very nature of reality.

2 The Prism Event and Quration

The Chiang prism event in late 2022 marks the historical point when quantum theory became actualized into an applied social science. As a physicist of the twentieth century had suggested, quantum theory was indeed 'not the problem, [but] the solution' (Deutsch 1997: 51), and eventually it resulted in severing the link to the classical, single universe conception of reality. Much

---

[4] halo pembaca yang budiman! [note to production—this one keeps glitching, can you please check the code?].

has been written on the prism event in our branch ⟨see, e.g. Mbabazi Ψ 2067⟩. Historiographies particularly highlight the role of technological innovation in the early twenty-first century, leading to remarkable progress on quantum computation, as compared to only several decades before (Deutsch 1997: 214) ⟨Ox Ψ 2045⟩. What is often omitted from these narratives however is the broader context in which these technologies were developed. Compared to the early twenty-first-century forecasts, anthropogenic climate change (global heating) and biodiversity loss took place at much higher scales and speeds, resulting in considerable changes in microbiological processes. Prior to the prism event, the growth pattern of fungal mycelia as an interconnected network had been well-studied (e.g. Fricker et al. 2017); but not connected to quantum theoretical discussions. The sudden spike in neural activity across colony formation in several mycelial species, linked to changing macroecological conditions, was first observed by indigenous scientists in what was then the Amazon Delta. Follow-up research eventually resulted in the realization that these mycelial networks could be harnessed for qbit computing, solving fermionic oscillation and making computational processes more powerful than previously imaginable. The vocal protests of several indigenous communities about what was in effect a possibility to weaponize fundamental microscopic (and vast!) parts of ecosystems were a crucial factor in the early regulation of, access to and governance of what became the Chiang prism.

The political, social and academic ripple effects of the prism event are well-known, of course, and will only be sketched out in passing here ⟨for a comprehensive overview, see Grogiratti Ψ 2072⟩. Its emergence is perhaps the biggest triumph of the power of human ingenuity and imagination. The mycelial-quantum revolution essentially built on a fictional account of a prism (Chiang 2019); conceived, developed and implemented at a staggering speed. It should be kept in mind that the conditions of the early twenty-first century were dire indeed, with imminent ecological collapse, disastrous social inequalities, a pathological economic system and increasing political and military conflicts. A techno-optimist imaginary underwriting the early quantum community hence certainly had a role to play in this process. The Henkenian School is perhaps the best known example of the kind of interdisciplinary research programmes that ushered in the quantum age ⟨Henke Ψ 2031⟩. The mechanics of the prism, establishing a permanent state of coherent superposition, are based on basic quantum theory (now part of early-childhood education, but in the 2020s only studied by a select few). Prior to the prism, it was assumed that any measurement, or observation of a specific quantum state caused it to assume a classic state. With the prism, the collapse of the wave function was no longer a mystery, but rather an event that could be controlled, albeit only to some extent, by manipulating the ions sent through the mycelial network. Activating the prism, just like Chiang (2019) had predicted, split the universal wave Ψ into two branches. In the many-worlds reality, instead of collapsing the wave function, all its probabilities are realized, resulting in an infinity of branched worlds. The mechanics of the prism are obviously probabilistic rather than deterministic; observation of a branched world is also a question of where and when. Branching in effect means that the linearity of time is suspended; rather the sideways exploration can be conceptualized as a jump without vectoral orientation. Similarly, prism mechanics has an inherent randomness that prevents comprehensive examination of branch events; it is impossible to achieve full directionality (which also explains the slightly random selection of branch worlds included in this volume, see below).

The initial prism event technology manifested this revolutionary process at a very rudimentary level. Historical artefacts from the 2020s show the bulky, almost primitive apparatus that was used ⟨Xiaoning Ψ 2047⟩. The anonymous creators had shared the source code and instructions in a simultaneous transmission to all entities that were at that time member of the 'United Nations' organization. After the initial blackout on the discovery had been lifted, commercial applications of the prism technologies were widespread; however, the consequences of the prism on populations traumatized by decades of existential dread proved difficult to manage ⟨Hernandez Ψ 2028; Egede Ψ 2035; Diakité Ψ 2029⟩.

Eventually, the Quantum Council (QC) decided to strictly regulate access to prisms, prioritizing research and knowledge production over commercial pursuits. This decision was not easily reached, given the way the world was organized around the idea of competing nation-states, and the prioritization of corporate interests in the early twenty-first century. There were significant struggles between nation-states to be at the centre of this new technology, and the corporate push-back against regulation was powerful. Against them, there was the coalition of Most Affected People and Areas, who gained increasing power when they asserted their leadership in key organizations such as the IQC ⟨MAPA Ψ 2032⟩. It has been rumoured that even the decision to establish the IQC Headquarters in Nusantara was not without contestation: The then city of Copenhagen, also competing to be the centre of the new organization, and keen to remain the central site of quantum interpretation and a hub of global politics, organized a number of cyberattacks against the current Indonesian capital. The fact that Copenhagen is now partially submerged, and large parts of the Danish population are relocated to Greenland illustrates well the shifting patterns of techno-political progress, as well as the wisdom of the decision-makers.

The qurative turn was a natural consequence of the quantum revolution. Social scientists found a starting point in Chiang's visionary text from 2019, where he posed the questions that would come to define quration.

> Can a single quantum event by itself lead to visible changes between the two branches? Is it possible for broader historical forces to be studied using prisms?

These famous words were the beginning of qurationalism as the new and ultimate epistemology of the futures to come. At once, infinite possibilities to explore various realities emerged, or at least this is what was considered to be the case. Unfortunately for those early qurationalism optimists, however, information exchange between branched worlds proved difficult. Only limited transmission across the respective branches was eventually established, through costly ion manipulation technique. The strain this communication took on the mycelial network however was not anticipated. Had the risk of losing the mycelial network altogether not been so clear and immediate, the swift and strict regulation of prism technology would probably not have taken place. Only with closely monitored restrictions on its use and directionality could safe use of the prism event technology be guaranteed. This effectively limited the possibilities of information exchange with the principles now known as *simple code* and *absolute zero centralization*: The former means that only simple codified information content can be exchanged between the branches, and no type of physical matter can be experimented with even in laboratory conditions. The latter principle is more obvious and common sensical: As the prism event occurred in $\Psi 0$, i.e. the reality in which we are based, it appears that communication is effectively limited to bilateral exchange between $\Psi 0$ and other Ψs. The 2065 prism convention convened by the IQC explicitly prohibits sharing superpositioned information between Ψs as this might risk further branch-offs, or cause their states to decohere. This puts us as qurators in a privileged position, and has significant implications for the qurative approach. The next section engages with the core propositions and ambitions of qurationality.

3   Qurative Reflections

Permanent superimposition and the collapse of deterministic causality across many worlds allow the qurative approach to achieve a relational and yet simultaneously a fully detached researcher positioning. This book perhaps serves as a perfect illustration of how the author function, so crucial still in twenty-first century pre-prism academia, has been transcended. Quration enables reflective retrospectives and trans-temporal dialogues. As qurators, we do not have to question the material that is transmitted to us; our role rather is to showcase and oversee the exchange. While the angel of history is still flying backwards, he is also casting his eyes sideways now. Even the Benjaminian renaissance scholars of the mid-2070s eventually had to agree that quration is the proof that 'nothing that has ever happened should be regarded as lost for history' (Benjamin 1940). The recalcitrant discussions about the societal commitments of quration are a legacy of pre-prism debates in Global Politics and International Relations, where scholarship appears to have been deeply divided about such archaic notions of neutrality and emancipatory ambitions. The early quantum literature had also picked up on this, arguing that the birth of quantum physics in the early twentieth century included no 'emancipatory goal', but that quantum approaches shared common ground with the critical impulse to search for new conceptual territory (Murphy 2021: 5). Quration shed the tired binary of critical vs problem-solving social science, since it is neither conceptual nor political, but *quantum* territory that is to be explored and discovered. As historians remind us, this relativity of positioning, the coherent contingence of superposition, had already been explored in twentieth-century science fictional analysis, e.g. this account by Larry Niven (1968: 39).

> If alternate universes are a reality, then cause and effect are an illusion. The law of averages is a fraud. You can do anything, and one of you will, or did. [..] Every decision was made both ways. [...] And so it went, all through history.

The qurative understanding that there are, in fact, no facts that hold a truth outside of a branched-off world, is complemented by researcher positioning that allows for rejecting the classical state ontology that permeates pre-prism approaches. Instead, permanent superposition constitutes the epistemological and methodological foundations of quration. Following the many-worlds approach, quration essentially supersedes empiricism, in that objective observation is no longer a singular point in time, with clear questions and binary findings. Critics have questioned the privileged position of qurators in $\Psi 0$, and posited that the power hierarchies across the wave function might result in unequal access to quantum knowledge (Menchu de Sousa Ψ 2078). In fact, even if access to qurative communication is limited for some, a quantum approach furthers the connections across the universal wave function as it shows that 'everything exists solely in the way it affects something else' (Rovelli 2020). What, then, does it mean for our understanding of global politics that, as was already pointed out in early quantum theory, 'the multiverse is not a discrete set of universes but a continuum, and not all the universes are different' (Deutsch 1997: 211)?

4   Outline and Scope of the Book

The chapters included in this book have been qurated following the probabilistic logic at the heart of the approach. Scholars operating the prism in their respective branch prepared these contributions on developments in global politics in their reality, starting around 2022 and reaching into the contemporary period. Having received the prism transmissions, we then subsequently selected a kaleidoscope of contributions that really showcases what many-worlds actually means. We have avoided those branches that had clearly collapsed due to developments related to the prism event. Not every global society managed to avoid the weaponization of the Chiang prism. Public debates about the horrors transmitted from these branches might pop up in the news cycle, but are not relevant for our debates. Similarly, we have omitted branch-off transmissions that have seen sudden ecological changes which have

INTRODUCTION—THE QURATIVE TURN IN GLOBAL POLITICS   9

eradicated human life as we know it.[5] As is clear from the table of contents, the contributions also address a plethora of themes and approaches relevant in the particular branch they come from. While International Relations and Global Politics in the first century of their academic pursuit seem to have been thought of as 'interdisciplinary' engagement, quration of course renders interdisciplinarity redundant. When your approach is relational and relative to branched-off realities, the need for absolutes such as academic disciplines dissolves. At the same time, there is a remarkable tendency cutting through the many world transmissions qurated in this book. The impulse of knowledge production and certain scholarly practices, whether as research in academic institutions or in other contexts, appears to be a near-universal feature; global politics is one of the central themes. To explore the differences in the transmissions and contributions to this volume, we point the reader towards the importance of understanding the shared history these transmissions have until the 2022 Chiang prism event. The occurrence of pre-2022 references across several of these chapters, drawing on a shared literature and academic history, might initially be alienating. As was common during that time, the reference style for this period has been chosen to be using simple brackets (…), as unprecise as that might seem to the contemporary reader. All references after 2022 however are marked with the familiar $\langle \Psi \rangle$.[6] A striking feature of the transmissions included here is that none of them mention the 2022 event, and quration seems to be unique to our branch; essentially establishing ours as the master reality. This either showcases the strength of the government cover-up on the technology, or else might point towards cognitive rejection of this particular form of quantum science.

The book is broadly structured in three parts. The section on Theories and Concepts covers theoretical developments and conceptual discussions. In truly qurative fashion, the authors cover 'time epistemics', reflect on IR's ideational histories and how they—thanks to the prism event—finally overcame their silo-thinking and rearranged across the earlier camps.

The section on themes in Global Politics is qurated so as to cover transmissions on (in)security, governance and technology, the Anthropocene, as well as identity and culture. Reflections on diplomatic orders and strategic partnerships as well as the beauties and horrors of algorithm antipolitics highlight some of the challenges our worlds have seen in the past decades. More so, several pieces on ecological crises, labelled as the looming 'Anthropocene' already a century ago, give an impression of how human–nature relations have evolved, and how international politics now seek to navigate species

---

[5] We did consider including the one with the cephalopods, but they seemed close to figuring out how to stabilize the Ψ prism transmission to connect to other branches, which would have obviously jeopardized our own research.

[6] Surely the diversity of scholarly references in itself is sufficient proof for the many-worlds interpretation. At the same time, transmission was challenging with such vast amounts of data, resulting in data loss such as with the transmission from Patrick Thaddeus Jackson where the reference list could not be recovered.

and ecosystemic survival. Repercussions on identity and humankind's ongoing quest for transcendence form the concluding part of this section.

Part three offers reflections from practitioners, as well as an outline of new forms of scholarly practice. A concluding transmission has been added that complements the branched-off transmissions with a past perspective.

REFERENCES

Adams, Douglas (1992) *Mostly Harmless* (London: Heinemann).

Barad, Karen (2007) *Meeting the Universe Halfway: The Entanglement of Matter and Meaning* (Durham, NC: Duke University Press).

Benjamin, Walter (1940) On the Concept of History/Theses on the Philosophy of History, Historical Archive, available at: https://www.sfu.ca/~andrewf/books/Concept_History_Benjamin.pdf

Bonfert, Bornd ⟨Ψ 2036⟩ *So Long, and Thanks for All the Concepts: The Contemporary Relevance of Douglas Adams' Thought in the 21st Century* (Kraków: Strugatsky & Lem).

Carlsnaes, Walter, Diez, Thomas, and Simmons, Beth (2002) *Handbook of International Relations* (SAGE), 1st edition.

Chandler, David, Müller, Franziska, and Rothe, Delf (eds.) (2021) *International Relations in the Anthropocene: New Agendas, New Agencies and New Approaches* (Palgrave).

Chiang, Ted (2019) *Exhalation* (New York: Alfred A. Knopf).

Cudworth, Erika, Hobden, Stephen, and Kavalski, Emilian (eds.) (2018) *Posthuman Dialogues in International Relations* (Routledge).

Der Derian, James, and Wendt, Alexander (2020) 'Quantizing International Relations: The Case for Quantum Approaches to International Theory and Security Practice' *Security Dialogue* 51(5), pp. 399–413.

Der Derian, James, and Wendt, Alexander (eds.) (2022) *Quantum International Relations: A Human Science for World Politics* (Oxford: Oxford University Press).

Deutsch, David (1997) *The Fabric of Reality* (London: Penguin).

Diakité, Awa ⟨Ψ 2029⟩ 'Institutional Conflict Resolution and Cross-Border Riots During the African Union—EU Prism Conflict' *Journal of Policing and Crowd Control* 2(1), pp. 32–43.

Dunne, Tim, Kurki, Milja, and Smith, Steve (2020) *International Relations Theories: Discipline and Diversity* (Oxford University Press), 5th edition.

Egede, Pipaluk ⟨Ψ 2035⟩ *Watershed Moment: Greenlandic Foreign Policy After the Danish Prism Riots and Flood Crisis* (Nuuk: Independence Press).

Fricker, Mark D., Heaton, Luke L. M., Jones, Nick S., Boddy, Lynne, Heitman, Joseph, and Gow Neil, A. R. (2017) 'The Mycelium as a Network' *Microbiology Spectrum* 5(3).

Grogiratti, Kaja (ed.) ⟨Ψ 2072⟩ *Putting the Prism into Perspective—Long-Term Developments and Trajectories 50 Years After the Chiang Event* (Rome: The Global Feminist Collective).

Henke, Tim ⟨Ψ 2031⟩ *Making Sense of Quantum in New Realities: An Interdisciplinary Research Compendium* (Slough: SpringerSage).

Hernandez, Julia ⟨Ψ 2028⟩ 'Commandanta Silvia and the Prism: Zapatista Strategies for Navigating Worlds Without Revolution' *Alternatives—Journal for Utopias Across Realities* 5(3), pp. 345–365.

King, G., Keohane, R., and Verba, S. (1994) *Designing Social Inquiry: Scientific Inference in Qualitative Research* (Princeton, NJ: Princeton University Press).

Larry Niven (1968) 'All the Myriad Ways' *Galaxy Magazine*, October 1968 27(3), pp. 32–65

MAPA ⟨Ψ 2032⟩ 'Access Is a Human Right: Another World Is Real' *The Nusantara Declaration of 150 Most Affected People and Areas*, 8. March 2032.

Mbabazi, Afiya ⟨Ψ 2067⟩ *The Global Handbook of the Prism Event, Branch Ψ* (Lagos: Panafrican University Press), 2nd edition.

Menchu de Sousa, Roberta ⟨Ψ 2078⟩ 'Access and Epistemologies of Power: A Critique of Qration as Exclusionary Social Science' *Annals of the Society of Non-Qrative Researchers* 50, pp. 564–581.

Murphy, Michael (2021) *Quantum Social Theory for Critical International Relations Theorists: Quantizing Critique* (Palgrave Pivot).

Nilsson, Tomx2/Tomas ⟨Ψ 2029⟩ 'From Trekkies to Collective: The Emergence of Q Collectives as Future Hegemons in Social Science' in *The Qurative Turn, 'The Future Is Qrational' and Other Early Movements* (Piteå: The Graveyard Books).

Ox, Felix Sebastian ⟨Ψ 2045⟩ *Q-Computing: Process, Progress, Potential* (Bleichheim: Downward Spiral Publishing).

Rovelli, Carlo (2020) *Helgoland* (London: Allen Lane).

Tickner, Arlene B., and Smith, Karen (eds.) (2020) *International Relations from the Global South: Worlds of Difference* (Routledge).

Weber, Cynthia (2021) *International Relations Theory: A Critical Introduction* (Routledge), 5th edition.

Wendt, Alexander (2015) *Quantum Mind and Social Science: Unifying Physical and Social Ontology* (New York: Cambridge University Press).

Whitey, Robert, and Moon, Onthe ⟨Ψ 2030⟩ 'Who Knew All Along? We Did! Why Quantum Is the Way Forward for Social Science' *American Political Science Review* 124(3), pp. 123–145.

Xiaoning, Wong ⟨Ψ 2047⟩ *Proto-Prism Design and Implementation 2022–2032* (Hongkong: Free University Publishing).

Zanotti, Laura (2019) *Ontological Entanglements, Agency, and Ethics in International Relations: Exploring the Crossroads* (London: Routledge).

Theory and Concepts

The Evolution of Global Society Theory

Barry Buzan

1   INTRODUCTION

As we stand at the bicentenary of the formal founding of International Relations (IR) as a discipline, it is a good moment to look back at the origins and evolution of Global Society Theory (GST). The next section briefly reviews the deep origins of thinking about global society. But its main focus is on the so-called 'English School', and its thinking about 'international' and 'world society', as it evolved during the last decades of Western-global international society from the 1950s to 2019. Section 2 covers the turbulent period of deep and contested pluralism dominating the 2020s and 30s, and marking both the transition from a Western-dominated to a more global society, and from the English School framing to an emergent GST one. Section 3 surveys the development of GST, and its relationship to the embedded pluralism and humanist solidarism that consolidated global society in the long five decades following the Impactor Crisis of the late 2030s. Section 4 examines the breakdown and reconfiguration of GST from the 2090s to the present under the rising pressure of deep divisions over questions about the nature and purpose of humankind. Will the relevance of GST's analytical framing, which has proved adaptive for nearly two centuries, survive the highly divisive tensions now fracturing global society?

B. Buzan (✉)
Department of International Relations, London School of Economics, London, UK
e-mail: b.g.buzan@lse.ac.uk

© The Author(s), under exclusive license to Springer Nature
Switzerland AG 2023
L. Horn et al. (eds.), *The Palgrave Handbook of Global Politics
in the 22nd Century*, https://doi.org/10.1007/978-3-031-13722-8_2

2 The 'English School' Up to 2019: International and World Society

For most of human history, society had been mainly a local affair. The Axial age religions offered wider visions of what world society might be, such as the Islamic *umma*, Christendom, and the Chinese concept of *Tianxia* (all under heaven), though without being able to deliver it as more than a subglobal reality. The nationalism that developed during the nineteenth century, also transcended localism, but at the cost of dividing the idea and the practice of a world society into mainly competing politico-cultural fragments. The radical idea that these fragments might form a second-order form of *international society*, had its roots in thinking about international law. It is conventionally tracked back to the seventeenth century jurist Hugo Grotius, but became more explicit during the nineteenth century, with the rapid expansion of positive international law. The then emergent discipline of Sociology ignored the idea, preferring to restrict its study to first order societies in which individual humans were the constituent members. But lawyers could not conceive of international law without there being a society of states to give it meaning, and they developed this framing during the nineteenth century (Lorimer 1884). What became known as the English School developed this idea within the discipline of IR from the 1950s onwards.

The English School only began to emerge at the point after the Second World War when 150 years of a highly West-centred colonial global international society was drawing to a close. Although Western dominance lingered on for a further six decades, from the late 1940s decolonization began the long process towards a more truly global and equal international society. In its first phase during the 1960s–1980s, classical English School Theory (EST) generally privileged the interstate domain, saw the transnational domain as largely subordinate to it, and took the interhuman domain mainly as a moral referent for the interstate one, but with little or no meaningful agency. Its main concern was the weakening of interstate society both by the ideological division between 'communist' and 'democratic capitalist' superpower blocs, and by the influx of numerous poor, weak, and non-Western states and peoples into interstate society. The principal perspective was a state-centric pluralist order, with world society and solidarism/justice generally seen as a supplicant to that order. Hedley Bull (1977), with his key insight that even the anarchical interstate landscape exhibited social norms significant enough to constitute a 'society' rather than simply a 'system', is the representational work for this phase. The key focus was on the interstate primary institutions of sovereignty, territoriality, international law, diplomacy, balance of power, great power management, and war, with Mayall (1990) adding nationalism.

From the late 1980s to the Great Recession starting in 2007, a second phase emerged alongside the first as English School theorists responded to the intense globalization and seeming triumph of the liberal teleology of the time. Led by a brief burst of US primacy after 1989, and the explosion of the global internet onto the scene from the mid-1990s, the last peak of Western primacy seemed to be shifting the balance away from the interstate domain and pluralism towards the transnational and interhuman domains. There was a significant rise of the justice/solidarism agenda, particularly concerning human rights, not seen as in tension with order, but as a necessary condition for it. Wheeler (2000) and Hurrell (2007) are the representative works for this phase. Although resisted by committed pluralists, there was an expectation, that in some important ways what was called 'international society' (interstate) and 'world society' (transnational and interhuman) were beginning to merge. Responsibility in international society, traditionally covered by great power management, was increasingly diffusing into, and being shared by, global governance (Bukovansky et al. 2012). By 2019, a century ago, when IR was celebrating its first centenary, the ES had added a social structural approach, focusing on the primary institutions of international society, and their interplay with intergovernmental organizations and other so-called secondary institutions (Buzan 2004).

But by this time the transition to a post-Western world order was already well underway. From 2020, a sharp turn towards deep pluralism—not just a diffusion of wealth and power, but also of cultural and political authority—became the dominant trend.[1] Both the liberal teleology and US leadership weakened severely and unrecoverably under the Trump administration. Xi Jinping's China and Putin's Russia turned increasingly totalitarian and aggressive, triggering a new cold war with the West versus China and Russia. And the Covid-19 pandemic of 2020–2023 reinforced self-reliance more than cooperation. This turn led to a resurgence of pluralism/order thinking, and a loss of confidence among those promoting solidarism/justice.

By the end of the Western era early in the last century, EST had coalesced around three analytical cores:

1. Understanding global society ontologically in terms of the interplay and balance of social institutions across three domains: interstate, transnational, and interhuman.
2. Understanding global society structurally in terms of a set of durable but evolving primary institutions that played variously across the three domains, and which were mutually constitutive with a likewise durable but evolving set of secondary institutions.
3. Understanding global society normatively in terms of a permanent interplay and tension between order (*pluralism*) and justice (*solidarism*) that had continuously to be renegotiated according to the circumstances of the time.

EST had, of course, always been built around triads, starting with Martin Wight's (1991) famous distinctions among international system, international

---

[1] For discussion see Acharya and Buzan (2019), Chapter 9.

society, and world society. This analytical framing proved growingly attractive because its core analytical triad proved flexible enough to capture the ongoing events and transformations that were continuously reshaped global society under modernity.

3   2020s–2030s—The Transition from English School to Global Society Theory in the Era of Contested Deep Pluralism

The quite rapid shift from expectations of liberal globalization to the realities of a deepening contested pluralism, set up a major challenge to EST. The main direction and form of global society changed quite dramatically. What had seemed a strong solidarist momentum in the interstate and transnational domains, faltered as its dependence on a declining West became apparent. As the West weakened, so did its commitment to liberalism. As the rising powers gained wealth, power, and cultural and political authority, so their commitment to the core pluralist values of sovereignty, territoriality, and nationalism, strengthened. EST was not the only IR theory to be challenged by these changes. Inward-looking, self-obsessed, defensive, great powers not interested in dominating the international system, did not fit the realist framing at all well. Liberal assumptions and values were in palpable retreat almost everywhere, and the system of rules and intergovernmental organizations that had been set up by the Western powers was increasingly contested. The ongoing restraints on great power war, plus the constraining of the global economy, and the re-empowerment of non-Western cultures, reduced the appeal of materialist approaches to IR, and strengthened the imperative to understand global social structures and the normative dynamics that shaped them. The implications of these changes for the discipline of IR were anticipated by Acharya's (2014; Acharya and Buzan 2019, Chapter 10) call for a Global IR discipline, and Tickner and Wæver's (2009) for the 'worlding' of IR.

Under these conditions, the analytical triad of EST turned out to be attractive and flexible enough to widen the academic support base of the approach. EST's openly normative strand suited the cultural differentiation that was a feature of contested deep pluralism. Its quite fine-grained social structural approach showed not only what was changing in GIS, but just as importantly highlighted that the array of pluralist primary institutions was remaining relatively stable. And the fact that it was a widely acknowledged IR theory, but one that was not associated with the US, made it congenial to the expanding non-Western community of IR scholars. During the mid-2020s, the English School debated all this, conscious both of the opportunity around it, and of the problem of its increasingly inappropriate name, which had been coined by someone calling for its closure (Jones 1981). Several leading ES scholars decided to relaunch the brand as Global Society Theory (GST). The label GST

THE EVOLUTION OF GLOBAL SOCIETY THEORY   19

removed the parochial, 'English' part of the name, while retaining the flexibility to encompass 'society' in the interstate, transnational and interhuman domains. To this end major workshops on GST were convened at both the ISA in 2026, and the World International Studies Conference (WISC) in Singapore in 2027. Not only were the major figures from EST involved in this, but also people from complementary academic strands: postcolonialists interested in hybridity; global sociologists prepared to think about interstate society; global historical sociologists interested in following through the dialectics of the spread of modernity; liberal institutionalists interested in the interplay of primary and secondary institutions; constructivists wanting to use the social structural framing of primary institutions; and international political economists interested in the evolving political economy of the global market as a normative structure. This relaunch benefitted from the general move of IR towards a more global form marked by declining Western dominance and rising participation by scholars with roots in other cultures.

The edited volume coming out of the 2026–2027 workshops (Dunne et al. Ψ 2028) highlighted several themes. First, the liberal teleology as the implicit template for how global society was evolving, had collapsed. Second, the classical pluralist institutions proved resilient because they had been internalized by the rising powers. Third, the driving force behind the new pluralism was more about the distribution of status than about the norms and institutions of global society themselves. Fourth, how important what was remembered about colonialism, and what was forgotten, and by whom, was to the ongoing dynamics of global society. Fifth, how crucial the changing character of the security agenda was as a driver of the global social structure, as common security issues became more prominent, and national security ones less existential. This landmark work in many ways shaped the development of GST over the following decades. It made clear that despite some big changes—the infusion of new blood, a much wider and more balanced historical perspective, and a more diverse set of theoretical approaches—GST retained key features of the English School. In particular, it continued the commitment to taking society into account across all three domains, and retained the normative core of a permanent debate about the actual and the desirable balance between order and justice in global society.

Initially, the decline of Western dominance, plus the accompanying retreat of the liberal teleology, and the 'rise of the rest', favoured the pluralists. The quite swift emergence of deep contested pluralism put in place a world that was more fragmented in political, cultural, and economic terms, and with a more even distribution of wealth, power, and cultural authority, than had been the case before 2020. Yet this was not the traditional sort of state-centric pluralism that was a close reflection of realism's power politics with a bit of minimalist order management tacked on. As argued by Acharya and Buzan (2019), and Buzan (Ψ 2024), this was pluralism of a quite different sort. It had been partly foreshadowed by Williams (2015) who showed how pluralism could be, and needed to be, applied beyond the interstate domain and into the transnational and interhuman ones. The deep contested pluralism of the 2020s and 30s was in part about rival states, and the strengthening of sovereignty, territoriality, and nationalism as primary institutions of global society. But it was not about rival desires among great powers to dominate global society, because the principle of global hegemony was, by the mid-2020s, deeply illegitimate. In addition, no great power was any longer driven by a crusading universalist ideological vision. Neither did this new deep pluralism assume a willingness to resort to great power war for other than extreme defensive needs. Because all of the great powers were capitalist in one political form or another, there was a shared reluctance to shut down the global trading system entirely. There was also a rising, though far from dominant, shared understanding, reinforced by both the Covid-19 pandemic, and rising evidence of climate change in the form of extreme weather, that there were planetary threats in which all were entangled, and which none could handle alone. Another key difference with traditional pluralism was that this general understanding of things was also deeply rooted in the transnational and interhuman domains. All of this was first set out and theorized by Ashok Jones and Felicity Cui in their pathbreaking 2028 book *The Moral Purpose of Global Society*, which dominated debate in GST circles for almost a decade.

Another landmark contribution to GST in this period was the book *Postcolonial Global Society* by Tagore and Suzuki ⟨Ψ 2031⟩. In part, this book built on the new pluralism template laid down by Jones and Cui. But it brought into that a deep historical, cultural, economic, political, and discursive/memory analysis of how the dialectics of colonialism and decolonization had flowed through world history to shape the current world (dis)order. The key to their analysis was the three stages of revolt against Western and Japanese imperialism and hegemony. During the colonial era, resistance mostly failed, and politics and the economy were run by the colonial powers. But the resistance left a much stronger memory in the periphery than in the core, which became crucial to identity formation in the Third World/Global South after independence. During the postcolonial era (1945–2008) the 'revolt against the West' noted by Hedley Bull, had some political success, but made little impact on either the economic and cultural position of the periphery, or on the hegemonic position of the West. Despite some limited success with economic nationalism, most of the periphery remained heavily linked to, and dependent on, the core capitalist powers, with only very few successful in closing the development gap. This phase built up resentment and frustration not only in the periphery because of its weakness and failure; but also in the core, because of the relentless security, economic and social burdens placed on it by the underdevelopment, corruption, and political chaos in many parts of the Global South. The third stage of revolt began in 2008, when the great recession undermined both the relative wealth and power of the West, and its liberal universalist model of political economy. Led by a then fast-rising China, substantial parts of the Global South, especially in Asia, increasingly added the revived possession of wealth, power and authority to their still sharp historical resentments against the West and Japan. Tagore and Suzuki documented in penetrating detail just how big a role postcolonial resentment played in the unfolding of deep contested pluralism from 2008 on. A telling point in their analysis was how the general forgetting in the West and Japan of the darker sides of their colonial legacies contributed to a mutual misunderstanding and incomprehension between the retreating old great powers, and the rising new ones.

During this period, the first book to begin looking beyond deep contested pluralism was Falkner's (Ψ 2036) *Functional Pluralism*. Falkner's prescient work was not much noticed until after the Impactor Crisis of the late 2030s, but then became a foundation for much that followed in GST. She theorized global society in terms of what she saw as an emergent functional pluralism based on ever-rising collective concerns about the need to manage the growing environmental crisis. She tracked the coalescence of both public opinion and government policy across the major powers, and argued that despite the divisions, inadequacies, and failures of the previous two decades, environmental stewardship was gaining ground against sovereignty, territoriality, and nationalism in the institutional structure of global society. Her key insight was about how environmental stewardship had the potential to override, and in some senses solve, the disputes over status that had undermined much of the old system of intergovernmental organizations. She could not anticipate that the Impactor Crisis would hugely accelerate the core thrust of her analysis.

4   2040S–2080S—GLOBAL SOCIETY THEORY IN THE ERA OF EMBEDDED DEEP PLURALISM

It is difficult to underestimate the effects on global society of the great double meteorite strikes of 2037 and 2039 that respectively devastated Central America and the Caspian Sea basin. The direct casualties and damage, great though they were, were not the primary material effect of the impactor crisis. More important in the middle term was the twenty years of global cooling that was a consequence of the dust, gases, and smoke blasted into the atmosphere not only by the impacts themselves, but also by the subsequent volcanic activity triggered by them. The immediate effects were dealt with fairly well by national and international emergency response agencies. The global cooling was both a crisis of its own, and an opportunity. The crisis part was how to cope with disruptions to agriculture, transport, and power supplies. The opportunity was the temporary relief from rising global temperatures and sea levels, and the extreme weather events, that had put increasing pressure on many societies during the 2020s and 30s. These twin effects of the Impactor Crisis brought to an end the contested pluralist period of drift, turbulence, contestation, and uncertainty in global society that had been gathering force since the first decade of the century. In a sense, it marked the end of the difficult transition from the Western-dominated global societies of the nineteenth and twentieth centuries, to the more egalitarian embedded pluralism, and increasingly humanist solidarism, of the later twenty-first century. By pushing global society in all domains into a prolonged period of emergency responses, the longer-term cumulative effect of the crisis was to reset its institutions and attitudes, and rebalance its direction, for the next five decades.[2]

The most obvious change was in the new institutions that were a direct result of the Impactor Crisis: the Global Space Guard Organization (GSGO) in founded in 2038, and the Earth Environment Organization (EEO) in 2045. These started out as emergency responses, but quickly became deeply embedded. They were not part of the obsolete family of UN intergovernmental organizations. Indeed, they were not intergovernmental organizations at all in the old sense, but hybrids involving both states and non-state organizations, and with significant executive powers. As set out by Chen and Singh (Ψ 2051), these two organizations, and their increasing family of related institutions, not only embodied and reproduced the primary institution of environmental stewardship, but progressively strengthened it. They led a change in the balance between national and planetary security that underpinned the emerging embedded pluralism that was consolidated during the 2040s. That, in turn, unfolded into an increasingly homogenized, but still differentiated, global solidarist society. The old framing of nation-states still existed, and retained political and cultural importance, so it was still a pluralist system in that sense. But states existed alongside powerful new IGOs led by GSGO and EEO, that reflected the actual distribution of wealth, power, cultural authority, and technical capacity among both states and non-state actors. Common security perspectives to do with planetary defence and global environmental management now outweighed residual concerns about national security. The GSGO was increasingly effective in both locating and countering the dangers from space rocks. Its occasional high-profile intercepts increased both its legitimacy, and that of the need for a constant planetary defence. There were growing synergies between GSGO and EEO as global environmental management required some space-based infrastructure. What had once been a disturbing synergy between the dynamics of national security politics, and the interests of the so-called military-industrial complex, increasingly softened as high-tech efforts were directed more to planetary defence and global environmental management.

---

[2] Looking back on all this, the neo-historical sociologist Alexandr Lawson (Ψ 2053) calculated that while the Impactor Crisis was, in one sense, a random event having unique and particular consequences, in another sense it could be seen as a structural event. He demonstrated statistically using the new global database, that by the 2030s human society had become so dense and interdependent, and was inflicting such stress on the planetary ecosystems, that the probability of some sort of transformative global crisis was fast rising towards certainty. Whether that crisis was the two meteorites, or a global plague, or relentless sea-level rise, or widespread agricultural collapse, in one sense didn't matter. The particularities of the crisis would, of course, have particular effects, possibly much worse than what actually happened, but the longer-term shift towards heightened awareness of environmental stewardship was almost a structural inevitability.

The broader social effects of the Impactor Crisis fed into, and amplified, deeper social developments that were already underway in the 2030s. One was the functional pluralism already noticed by Falkner in the mid-2030s, but now much more strongly emergent. This trend was best captured by Kobinski and Chan ⟨Ψ 2048⟩. They argued that global society remained pluralist in the sense that most peoples and government preferred to retain a differentiated political structure to express and defend cultural differentiation, and to keep a substantial element of politics local. But at the same time, there had been a fundamental shift in the understanding of both governments and peoples that all were in the same boat, and that boat needed to be both maintained and navigated effectively if the differentiation among its passengers was to have any meaning or purpose. Environmental stewardship was now supported by a general understanding that Earth was not a given, stable environment, and that environmental management to maintain the supporting conditions for human civilization was a necessary and permanent task for humankind.

A new balance was emerging in which pluralism was more focused on maintaining cultural differentiation, and was much less concerned with national security, military power, and great power rivalry. The security agenda shifted strongly towards the common ground of planetary protection and management. It seemed that humankind was at last finding a sound balance between a desired degree of cultural and political diversity on the one hand, and a degree of global governance and coordination on the other, without these two being in contradiction. This new layering of identity featuring a strong collective/cosmopolitan component, was first set out by Tang and Mohammed ⟨Ψ 2050⟩.

Accompanying this was a notable convergence in the social concerns, practices, and perspectives of the major powers and their peoples, that stood in stark contrast to the cultivated divergence that marked the first four decades of the twenty-first century. Within the GIS literature this convergence, and its implication for global society, was first picked up and elaborated by Justin Goh, Cornelia Gonzalez, and Jorge Singh ⟨Ψ 2048⟩. Until the impactor crisis, convergence was masked not only by differences in development, but also by the preoccupation with cultural, political, racial, and civilizational differentiation, and the cultivation of historical grievances and populist victimhood politics. But the closing of the development gap that had dominated the nineteenth and twentieth centuries, meant that all the leading states and societies finally shared a common substrate of modernity. The market socialist approach led by the Chinese, and the social capitalist one dominant in the old West and Japan, looked increasingly similar in their policies on employment, surveillance, welfare, private property, and management of trade and finance. And as the twenty-first century wore on, the newly modernized powers such as China, India, and Brazil lost the prickly, hubristic, and aggressive edge that had so often accompanied the first attainment of modern wealth, power, and cultural authority by big societies. They blended into an expanding core which was growing more similar in its forms of political economy and levels of development. Environmental stewardship helpfully carried with it a sense of collective victimhood, whose palpable urgency overrode populist demagoguery.

Accompanying these structural similarities was a fashion for cultural fusions that developed strongly from the 2050s, not just in food, music, and fashion, but also in philosophy, and political economy. People increasingly noticed that levels of development had evened out, and that other cultures with both their distinctive traditions and their novel takes on modernity, were no longer threatening 'Others', but parallel pathways that had interesting ideas and practices, both positive and negative, to offer and learn from. The process of modernity, having for nearly two centuries sharply divided humankind into both 'developed' and 'underdeveloped', and a range of mutual exclusive ideologies from liberal democracy, through fascism, to communism, finally began to bring it together into what is perhaps best described as *differentiated homogeneity*.

Differentiated homogeneity stretched broadly across the interstate, transnational and interhuman domains, weakening the traditional dominance of the interstate domain over global society. It supported a global society of embedded pluralism in which there was not just tolerance of difference among states, peoples, and cultures, but increasingly respect and admiration for differences (Nicholas and Zhang Ψ 2081). This process was facilitated by the reaching of zero population growth in 2063, which had a remarkable effect in making the diversity of human population feels more comfortable with each other's presence, and less threatened. While cultural differentiation remained significant, traditional national security concerns over politics and territory faded into the background to be replaced by collective concern over shared fates and how to deal with them. This convergence phase peaked during the 2070s, and seemed at that time to be heading towards a deepeningly solidarist global society. Some compared this time to the surge in liberal idealism that marked the 1990s. Humankind seemed finally to have found a good balance between a degree of cultural and political diversity on the one hand, and a degree of global governance and coordination on the other. Nations and religions and civilizations were still present, and respected, but so too was a sense of humankind as a whole, not just in terms of all being in the same boat, but as a meaningful level of shared identity.

For GST, therefore this period marked a quite sharp retreat of classical pluralism, though certainly not its extinction. The degraded global society of the 2020s and 30s with its strongly contested pluralism, gave way after the Impactor Crisis first to embedded pluralism and by the 2080s to what Nicholas and Zhang (Ψ 2081) labelled 'humanist solidarism'. Environmental stewardship and human equality had become the lead primary institutions in global society, but the older Westphalian institutions were still present in significant shadow form. This apparent settlement of the main international problems thrown up by the revolutions of modernity in the nineteenth century, was, however, but another turn of the dialectic in the evolution of global society.

From the 2090s onwards, the cultural, economic, and political homogenization of humankind reached a level that enabled a re-dividing of the world that still defines the present day understanding of global society.

5   2090S–2019—HUMANKIND RE-DIVIDED

Under the pressure created by the Impactor Crisis, what had been the increasingly militarized, space programmes of the major powers, and the competitive corporate entities engaged in developing earth orbital space and the Moon, were quickly drawn together into GSGO. By the 2050s GSGO was in close collaboration with EEO, having added the building of orbital space infrastructure to its mandate for planetary defence. Up to the 2080s, the main focus of all this activity was on planetary defence and climate management. As part of this, the tentative developments towards asteroid mining begun during the 2030s, were greatly intensified. Also, a modest colonization of the moon began, building on the competitive bases built by China, India, and the US during the 2030s. But by the 2090s, both good planetary defences, and the space infrastructure for climate management, were largely in place. The technologies developed for that had greatly lowered the costs of access to both orbital and lunar space, making the possibility of wider spacefaring in the solar system a realistic option for humankind.

Readers will be familiar with this story because they are still living in the re-fracturing of global society that it generated. From our present perspective, the period from the Impactor Crisis to the early 1990s, is seen as the high-point of earthbound global society. By the 2080s, the dialectics that began with the revolutions of modernity, and the divided and unequal global colonial international society generated by those revolutions during the nineteenth century, had worked themselves out into the differentiated homogeneity and humanist solidarism that preceded the current era. The marker for the new era is generally taken to be the announcement in 2093 by GSGO of a major, long-term plan to build up a substantial human presence on Mars, and, using the technologies developed for managing Earth's environment, to begin the terraforming of that planet.

That announcement energized a profound debate—and deep divisions—not only about the purpose of humankind, but about its very nature. The prospect of a new expansionism quickly transcended the planetary perspective that had dominated thinking about both global society up to the 2020s, and global society thereafter. Some, perhaps most notably Cook and He (Ψ 2094), tried to draw parallels between the new expansionism and the situation that confronted early European maritime adventurers from the fifteenth to the nineteenth centuries during the first expansion of international society to global scale. But most saw this parallel as more misleading than helpful. The encounters of the first expansion did raise the question of what it meant to be human, but in nothing like the profound ways raised by the prospect of a serious move into space. The divisions of humans into races and civilizations, and states and nations, that had so dominated the planetary perspective, quickly began to seem irrelevant in the face of GSGOs new expansion project. The evening-out of modernity and development had already somewhat pushed these differences into the background, and created a more homogenized global society. It was the case almost everywhere that when confronted with the new expansionism, all modern societies fractured into the same three positions. As first laid out by Watson and Williams ⟨Ψ 2098⟩, it was these three positions, and the factions that coalesced around them, that quickly came to define the identities, and therefore the new social structure, of humankind.

The first faction coalesced around the name *Earthsiders*, though they are often referred to as *Remainers* by those opposed to them. They constitute a majority, albeit small, of Earth's nine billion inhabitants, and are perhaps best understood as conservatives, who want to perpetuate the differentiated homogeneity and humanist solidarism that consolidated after the Impactor Crisis. They are happy with planetary defence, and the existing orbital infrastructure. Most accept limited colonization of the Moon, and some (largely automated) asteroid mining, but a substantial, and in part militant, minority calling themselves *Deudneyans*, oppose even that, wanting to limit the human presence on the Moon to rotating shifts.[3] Earthsiders are motivated by the idea that humankind's first priority should be to address the substantial problems of development that still remain on Earth. Some of them fear a new intersolar anarchy if human settlements on the Moon, Mars, in the Asteroid Belt, and in orbital habitats, acquire their own identities and seek political autonomy and power. Some fear the fragmentation of humanity as the physical and mental needs of spacefarers, and the inhabitants of places with different gravity, push for adaptive bioengineering into multiple forms of 'human being', and different forms of intelligence, both biological and machine. A substantial part of Earthsiders identify with the *Neohumanists*, who sacralise the Mark-1 human being, and oppose bioengineering.

At the other end of the spectrum, the second identity group call themselves *Outgoers* though their many opponents refer to them as *Colonialists*. These comprise perhaps fifteen per cent of humankind, but include many in the technological and political elites. Their driving motive is the sense of the human adventure, underpinned by the need to seed humankind beyond Earth and beyond the Solar system if its survival is to be guaranteed against cosmic catastrophes. Their basic view is that human expansion should proceed at the maximum pace allowed by available technology and finance. They strongly oppose the capping of the human population that is the implicit consequence of the Earthsider position. They want not only to colonize the Solar system beyond the Asteroid Belt, but also to build generational colony ships and send them to the dozen or so earthlike planets identified by astronomers as being

---

[3] Deudneyans take their name from an early twenty-first-century author who argued strongly against space expansionism (Deudney 2019).

THE EVOLUTION OF GLOBAL SOCIETY THEORY 27

within 20 light years of earth. In line with their technological enthusiasm, Outgoers have no sentimentality for the Mark-1 human being, and are keen on both bioengineering of humans and development of autonomous AIs for this purpose. They are therefore closely associated with the *Evolutionists*, or as their opponents call them, the *Neoeugenics Movement*.

In between sits the third faction, labelling themselves *Solars*, and consciously aiming to occupy the middle ground. They constitute about thirty per cent of the population, and their basic policy is to develop and colonize the inner solar system out to, and including, the asteroid belt. Solars are derided by many Earthsiders as merely providing cover, and foundations, for the larger project of the Outgoers. Since the Solars have to support bioengineering even for their limited expansionism, they are treated as enemies by the Neohumanists. Solars are held in contempt by the Outgoers for being a gutless compromise, though some Outgoers recognize that the Solars' project is indeed a possible first stage for their own ambitions, albeit at much too slow a pace for them. Part of the Solars' rationale for developing Mars is to meet the criticism of the Earthsider position that it puts all of humankind's eggs in one basket. Solars downplay the risks from intersolar anarchy on the grounds that Earth will remain predominant for a long time, and from bioengineering on the grounds that space adapted humans will remain a tiny minority of the species for a long time to come.[4]

By the second decade of the twenty-second century this three-way split had become the dominant structure of global society. The Solars' project is, in effect, quite well underway, though much more slowly than the Solars themselves want. The Outgoer project is promoted and in a small way instigated by private entrepreneurs, albeit often with the covert support of some governments, and some Outgoers within GSGO. At the extremes of the spectrum there is an undercurrent of sabotage and occasional violence between the Deudneyans and Neohumanists on the one side, and the Outgoers on the other.

These developments have posed a major challenge to GST. Both the classical English School and GST were predicated on a closed planetary system whose principal social structure was a strong differentiation into states and nations. From an early stage this differentiation was mediated by transnational actors and increasing economic interdependence, and during the twenty-first century it was directly challenged, and eroded, by the rise of shared-fate threats, particularly from the environment. As noted above, these developments led to a rising priority for environmental stewardship and human equality as the key primary institutions of global society, and a more residual role for the classical Westphalian institutions.

The rise of the New Expansionism challenges this framing in three fundamental ways.[5] First, it removes the planetary geographical limit, potentially

---

[4] My own work (Nazub Ψ 2115) clearly identifies me with the Solars.

[5] Many will find this entirely in keeping with the ES/GST's love of conceptual triads.

opening up to an infinite spatial domain. Second, it pushes the traditional, backward-looking, global social structure based on strong differentiation of states and nations into the background, and replaces it with a forward-looking one based on deep divisions about both human purposes, and the nature of 'humanity' itself. And third, it disinters the question that was buried after the Second World War, as to whether all humans are equal.

The first challenge is not all that problematic to the GIS way of thinking, though it does pose a challenge to the 'global' scale framing and naming of GST. An expansion of humankind can be conceptualized using Westphalian and colonial models, and this has been explored by Halford (Ψ 2112). The labelling issue remains under hot debate, with some wanting to stick with GST, and others insisting that we already need to move to Solar Society Theory (SST).

The second challenge is much more immediately problematic, and remains arguably the central concern of GST/SST at this time. It is abundantly clear that the strong global society of humanist solidarism that emerged after the Impactor Crisis, has now fractured, deeply and almost certainly durably into three factions. It still remains unquestionably a society, but it has not fractured in a way that fits with the GST's longstanding idea of pluralism. The relocation of mainstream identity from backward-looking national and cultural foundations to forward-looking foundations based on the aims and purposes of the species is a profound move. The negative term 'fractured solidarism' first coined by Watson and Williams (Ψ 2098) is still the most commonly used descriptor, with no positive labelling having yet taken hold. Solar society is still in the quite early stages of its formation, and it is still far from clear what social structure will grow out of the contestation among the three factions.

The third challenge is potentially the most difficult of all, though as yet it is only in the early stages of practical realization. As in the days of nineteenth-century 'scientific' racism, species differentiation and the emergence of autonomous machine intelligence raise questions about who (and what) counts as 'human', and how differentiated forms of conscious intelligence can and should relate to each other. As forecast by Deudney (2019) such differentiation raises deep security issues about whether, as in humankind's distant past, one form of this intelligence would eliminate or enslave all the others, so bringing into question the very existence of society at the level of humankind. That is the challenge for GST, or whatever it comes to be labelled, in the decades ahead.

References

Acharya, Amitav (2014) 'Global International Relations (IR) and Regional Worlds: A New Agenda for International Studies', *International Studies Quarterly*, 58:4, 647–659.

Acharya, Amitav, and Barry Buzan (2019) *The Making of Global International Relations*, Cambridge: Cambridge University Press.

THE EVOLUTION OF GLOBAL SOCIETY THEORY   29

Bukovansky, Mlada, Ian Clark, Robyn Eckersley, Richard Price, Christian Reus-Smit, Nicholas J. Wheeler (2012) *Special Responsibilities: Global Problems and American Power*, Cambridge: Cambridge University Press.

Bull, Hedley (1977) *The Anarchical Society. A Study of Order in World Politics*, London: Macmillan.

Buzan, Barry (2004) *From International to World Society? English School Theory and the Social Structure of Globalisation*, Cambridge: Cambridge University Press.

Buzan, Barry ⟨Ψ 2024⟩ *Global Society*, Cambridge, Cambridge University Press.

Chen, Amy, and Ravindra Singh ⟨Ψ 2051⟩ *The Institutional Revolution in Global Society*, Planetary Press.

Cook, Ferdinand, and Zheng He ⟨Ψ 2094⟩ *Back to the Future: Global Society and New Worlds*, Magellan Press.

Deudney, Daniel (2019) *Dark Skies*, Princeton: Princeton University Press.

Dunne, Tim, Christian Reus-Smit, and Liu Zhang (eds.) ⟨Ψ 2028⟩ *Global Society Theory*, Oxford: Oxford University Press.

Falkner, Lene ⟨Ψ 2036⟩ *Functional Pluralism*, Cambridge University Press.

Goh, Justin, Cornelia Gonzalez, and Jorge Singh ⟨Ψ 2048⟩ *The Diminution of Difference in the Global Political Economy*, Beijing: World Affairs Press.

Halford, Friedrich ⟨Ψ 2112⟩ *Solar Geopolitics*, Yellow River Press.

Hurrell, Andrew (2007) *On Global Order: Power, Values and the Constitution of International Society*, Oxford: Oxford University Press.

Jones, Ashok, and Felicity Cui ⟨Ψ 2028⟩ *The Moral Purpose of Global Society*, Cambridge University Press.

Jones, Roy E. (1981) 'The English School of International Relations: A Case for Closure', *Review of International Studies*, 7:1, 1–13.

Kobinski, Ana, and Leonie Chan ⟨Ψ 2048⟩ *Cultural Pluralism and Planetary Protection*, Canberra: ANU Press.

Lawson, Alexandr ⟨Ψ 2053⟩ *Rethinking the Global Transformation of the 2030s–40s*, Worldscience Metrics Inc.

Lorimer, James (1884) *The Institutes of the Law of Nations: A Treatise on the Jural Relations of Separate Political Communities*, Edinburgh and London: William Blackwood and Sons.

Mayall, James (1990) *Nationalism and International Society*, Cambridge: Cambridge University Press.

Nazub, Yrrab ⟨Ψ 2115⟩ *Solar Society: Problems and Prospects*, Multiversity Press.

Nicholas, Andrew, and Keisuke Zhang ⟨Ψ 2081⟩ *Global Cultural Synergy Theory*, World Press.

Tagore, Shirin, and Adrian Suzuki ⟨Ψ 2031⟩ *Postcolonial Global Society*, Sage Global.

Tang, Lily, and Christian Mohammed ⟨Ψ 2050⟩ *More Than the Sum of Its Parts: Humankind After the Impactor Crisis*, New Mumbai: Gupta University Press.

Tickner, Arlene B., and Ole Wæver (eds.) (2009) *International Relations Scholarship Around the World*, Abingdon: Routledge.

Watson, Feng, and Hedley Williams ⟨Ψ 2098⟩ *The New Expansionism and the Fracturing of Global Society*, Solar Press.

Wheeler, Nicholas J. (2000) *Saving Strangers: Humanitarian Intervention in International Society*, Oxford: Oxford University Press.

Wight, Martin (1991) *International Theory: The Three Traditions*, Leicester: Leicester University Press/Royal Institute of International Affairs, Edited by Brian Porter and Gabriele Wight.

Williams, John (2015) *Ethics, Diversity, and World Politics: Saving Pluralism from Itself?*, Oxford: Oxford University Press.

'The Past, Present and Future of Global Thought' Reviewing a Handbook Chapter from 2122

Lucian M. Ashworth

In 2122 a publishing house, hoping to publish a new International Relations (IR) textbook by the end of the year, sent out the recently submitted chapters to academic reviewers. Dr. Vera Fabulas, one of the editors of the new textbook, had volunteered to write the chapter on the history of IR, all the editors agreeing that the disciplinary history was well-known, and as the most senior editor Dr. Fabulas had more knowledge on this subject than most. Dr. Fabulas' chapter was sent out to Dr. Secunda Censor for review.

Dear Dr. Censor,

Re: *International Relations for the 22nd Century.* Fabulas Chapter 'The Past, Present and Future of Global Thought'

Thank you for agreeing to review the above chapter for our upcoming handbook on 22nd Century International Relations (IR). We hope that this handbook will be the go-to source for IR, and consequently we ask that you pay particular attention to the accuracy and spread of the chapter. Does it cover the material in an accurate and comprehensive way? Would you recommend it as a source for student seminars and a resource for researchers?

L. M. Ashworth (✉)
Department of Political Science, Memorial University of Newfoundland, St. John's, Canada
e-mail: lashworth@mun.ca

© The Author(s), under exclusive license to Springer Nature Switzerland AG 2023
L. Horn et al. (eds.), *The Palgrave Handbook of Global Politics in the 22nd Century*, https://doi.org/10.1007/978-3-031-13722-8_3

32   L. M. ASHWORTH

While we will not be able to pay you in energy credits, reviewers will earn a week exemption from civic service for their reviews.

We look forward to receiving your review.

Dedi Cavit
Commissioning Editor

Chapter 2: The Past, Present and Future of Global Thought: A History of IR, and What It Means for the Future

Dr. Vera Fabulas
[My comments can be found throughout the manuscript. Dr. Secunda Censor]

"If we are to look forward with confidence into the new twenty-second century, we must first have confidence about where it is we have come from"

– Official slogan of the Year of the Historian, 2101.

The history and pre-history of the field of International Relations (IR) has been marked by regular debates. These have led to the subject that we study today as a key element of Earth System Science (ESS). IR emerged as part of ESS, with a specific focus on those elements of the Anthroposphere and Technosphere that deal with politico-economic relations at a global level. While most historians agree [who are these 'historians'? SC] that IR was founded around 2045, with the first IR courses being offered in expanded ESS programs of study [there were IR courses before. See my report. SC], many students of IR do not realize that there is a rich IR pre-history from the twentieth and early twenty-first centuries that thrived before ESS, and was dominated by what were referred to as two dominant paradigms: realism and idealism [oh no!... SC].

This chapter will explore both the pre-history of IR, and IR's subsequent history as a properly scientific field after 2045. The pre-history is important, as it shows: (1) Where many of the ideas we still use in IR came from (those who called themselves realists); and (2) How debates led to other ideas being refuted as they failed to offer solutions to the crises of the Anthropocene (those who called themselves idealists).

1   PART I: THE PRE-HISTORY OF IR 1880–2045

To understand the pre-history of IR we first need to understand what it is we mean by realism and idealism. Pre-ESS IR saw itself as forming what they called paradigms. Paradigms were discreet schools of thought that saw the world in different ways, and debated each other in scholarly conferences, the media (mostly paper-based 'newspapers'), and in debates between politicians

'THE PAST, PRESENT AND FUTURE OF GLOBAL THOUGHT' ... 33

Table 1 Realism and Idealism [oh dear... SC]

	Major thinkers	*Primary ideas*	*Secondary ideas*
Realists (political economy)	Rosa Luxemburg Norman Angell Susan Strange Robert Cox	Material realities, rooted in the political economy shape human actions	Production Wealth Class Trade and finance
Realists (ecology and geography)	Friedrich Ratzel Ellen Churchill Semple Isaiah Bowman Merze Tate Simon Dalby	Material realities, rooted in the ecology, shape human actions	Human responses to environment Humans changing environment
Idealists	Hans Morgenthau Martin Wight John Mearsheimer	Ideas, rooted in human nature, shape human actions	Ideas create the world Conflict between ethics and power

(see Kuhn, quoted in Scientia Ψ 2049). [Not what Kuhn said at all. Does anybody actually read the old books? SC]. The different writers and ideas of the two paradigms are listed in Table 1.

Realism

Realism was the dominant paradigm in IR's pre-history, and can be divided into two main groups, marked by the different forms of material reality that they concentrated on. Both, though, shared the view that material realities shaped politics. In this sense, realists were already focusing on issues that would come to dominate post-2045 IR.

The first group of realists concentrated on how the global political economy shaped human actions. The focus of their research was the effects of the first and second industrial revolutions of the nineteenth century. It was these two industrial revolutions that first created the global world we know today, and by spurring the first generation realist scholars to study the global effects of industrialization it can be argued that the roots of IR could be found in the later nineteenth century, as societies adjusted to this new global reality [are you going to mention imperialism and racism here? SC].

Political economy realists, such as Norman Angell and Rosa Luxemburg, engaged in a great debate with early idealists (e.g. A. T. Mahan) in the first two decades of the twentieth century. The realists argued that states no longer had self-sufficient economies, like the agricultural great powers of a century before, and consequently that war would destroy the global economic links that delivered prosperity, meaning that both sides of a major war would lose, and that those advocating war lived by ideas of power and glory that no longer made sense. The classic statement of this new realism was Angell's *The Great Illusion* [while you have adequately summarized Angell, this is not what Rosa Luxemburg said. SC].

Historians agree that the end of this debate came with the First World War, which proved realists like Angell right [Yeeessss. Sort of, but also no. A bit more complicated than this, I'm afraid. Also, who are these 'historians'? SC]. Political economy became the main way to understand IR for the next 30 years. Despite this scholarly victory, however, older statesmen (and they were all men) trained in idealism came to dominate the new peace negotiations in Paris. A good example of this idealist influence is the work of Halford Mackinder ⟨Scientia Ψ 2049⟩. Even though idealism had been refuted, it still carried weight among politicians not trained in the new realist political economy. Relying on idealist concepts of power competition, the politicians imposed stiff financial penalties on the defeated states, and refused to cancel the wartime debts. This selfish defence of state power led to economic depression because it ignored the realities of an interconnected industrial world. The exception among the politicians at the negotiations was Woodrow Wilson, who alone took a realist line [No he didn't! … and the rest of this may be the popular perception of the Paris peace conference, but you will struggle to find a historian who will agree with it. SC]. The idealist failings of the peace conference were exposed at the time by John Maynard Keynes in his *Economic Consequences of the Peace* (1919), and later by Charles Kindleberger in his *World in Depression* ⟨both quoted in Scientia Ψ 2049⟩ [important to note that there is a good decade between the treaties and the Great Depression. Also, Kindleberger published in 1973! SC].

The Great Depression caused an economic collapse that weakened the political economic bonds that realists studied. The result was a return of the idealist concepts of power politics based on human nature, which I will discuss below. Realists of the political economy school would return to prominence in IR as a result of two related realities: the return of economic globalization from the 1970s, and the Great Acceleration. The Great Acceleration, starting around 1950, was an exponential leap in economic growth unique in human history, which would last to the end of the Anthropocene crisis. The effects of the Great Acceleration were to encourage the return of economic globalization that had retreated during the Great Depression and the Second World War, but also to put pressure on the Earth's ecology, on which the political economy relied. The result of this was the emergence of a new form of realism that took the realities of human pressure on the global environment as the basis of its study of global politics.

It is commonly agreed [by those 'historians', by chance? SC] that the last three decades of the twentieth century saw a change in attitudes to global politics as first economic globalization and then ecological pressures changed people's attitudes to global politics. 'Think global and act local' became a common saying at the time. While the ecological school of realism emerged as the Great Acceleration took effect, the ideas of the ecological school had already been formed by forebears in another field called political geography.

In fact, as the political economy school of realism was emerging in the late nineteenth century, political geographers like Friedrich Ratzel were exploring how humans were shaped by their environment. Ratzel's ideas were taken up by Ellen Churchill Semple ⟨1911, quoted in Scientia Ψ 2049⟩, who made many of the links about how the environment determined our politics that would be taken up by later scholars. [Actually, both Ratzel and Semple were also advocates of state power (Germany and USA, respectively), so claiming that they are 'realists' opposed to 'idealist' power politics does not really carry much water. SC] Semple's disciple, Derwent Whittlesey, would discover that, while human society was influenced by the environment, it was also true that humans impacted and changed the environment (1939). This idea of an interaction between humans and the environment, in which they affect each other in a series of feedback loops, would become the central premise of the ecological school of realism as it developed at the end of the twentieth century and the beginning of the twenty-first [Okay… but Whittlesey's discovery by IR was actually after the fact. I believe the first IR textbook reference to Whittlesey in IR was not until 2030. Yes, he fits later developments, but not a forebear. SC].

By the end of the twentieth century, it was hard for people to ignore the realities of environmental degradation, especially global warming [Actually, it was all too easy. SC]. In 1999 a key member of the political economy school of realism, Susan Strange, listed the environment as one of three failures of the state-dominated world system, thereby providing a link between the two realist schools. In 2016 five scholars produced 'The Planet Politics Manifesto', which blurred the lines between scholarship and action, and underscored the practical policy-orientated nature of the ecological school of realism ⟨Republished in Fabulas Ψ 2100. See also Scientia Ψ 2049⟩ [Realism is mentioned in the Manifesto, but they did not use it in the way that you mean it in this chapter. See my specific comments on the changing meaning of realism. SC].

Thus, while realism could be divided into two schools—political economy and ecology—all realists shared the view that material realities shape human societies. This is why they were called realists. Historians agree [do they though? SC] that it was because of the compatibility of realism with ESS that a realist-informed IR was developed as part of ESS after 2045.

Idealism

Although realism has dominated how we see global affairs since the nineteenth century, it has periodically been challenged by a second paradigm called idealism. While realism has a clear intellectual trajectory since the late nineteenth century, which is the first time the world became a single global community [I know what you are saying here, but it is open to criticism. Why nothing on pre-nineteenth-century global thought? See below why this is important. SC], idealism emerges to challenge realism in three key debates, but then goes out of fashion in response to key events that refuted idealism [Are you saying that events shape ideas? You never really explain how this dynamic works... and is history that straightforward? SC].

The primary tenet of idealism is that ideas found in human nature shape global politics. This is why it is called idealism. Idealists believe that we behave a certain way because human nature is the same over all recorded history. Thus, for idealists, progress is impossible. The primary idea that humans have in the political world is the struggle for power, and this takes priority over material factors. As a result, idealists have no theory of the political economy or ecology, and are often accused of wishful thinking by realists [Okay, not going to go into it here (but I do in my main comments), but the irony is that the group of so-called idealists you are talking about actually called themselves realists in the twentieth century. SC]. Another feature of idealism was toxic masculinity. This was an outdated idea that restricted scholarship only to men, and almost all idealists identified as men [This is a garbled collective memory. There were debates over gender in IR at the time, but it was a lot more complex than this. The problem was the erasure of women from the historical accounts. See my comments below for more on this. SC].

Idealism appeared three times in the pre-history of IR, and this resulted in three 'Great Debates' with realism. While idealism would lose all three debates, it would leave its mark on international politics prior to 2045 (see Ripae Ψ 2085). These debates are summarized in Table 2 [Okay, just so you know, there actually is no evidence of the debates you talk about here. SC].

In the first great debate, idealists proposed that a stable balance of power could be maintained in a world organized into squabbling states. This idea of a power balance, underwritten by state-based alliances, and with only a weak system of global government, led to the First World War. After the war it was commonly agreed [By whom? SC] that the state system had failed, and idealism was replaced by the political economy school of realism. This was a

Table 2 The great debates between realism and idealism in IR's pre-history

	When?	*Caused by?*	*Ended?*
1st great debate	1890s–1919	Resistance to globalization, and emerging political economic realities	First World War
2nd great debate	1931–1989	Great depression and economic collapse. Nuclear balance of terror	Hyperglobalization, the Great Acceleration and threat of climate change
3rd great debate	2016–2035	Challenges to democracy. New wars based on ethnic conflict. Resistance to climate action	Need to act on climate change, plastic pollution and biodiversity crisis

recognition of the defining role of industrialization, and its associated material realities, on global politics.

The second great debate was caused by the Great Depression, that reversed globalization, and was sustained after the Second World War by the balance of nuclear terror between the last two remaining state-based great powers: the United States and the Soviet Union. The threat of nuclear war led to the proliferation of psychological theories used to explain the mind of those who had 'their fingers on the nuclear trigger'. While this was necessary for the short-term preservation of peace, it led to a long period of malaise in global thought. Scholars missed the game changing role of the Great Acceleration, as well as the looming global ecological crisis. In the 1970s the political economy school of realism returned to refute idealism, and in the 1980s and 1990s the ecological school of realism emerged as another major source for criticizing idealism. The key text, that combined criticisms of idealism from both schools of realism was Dr. Susan Strange's 'Westfailure System' from 1999 ⟨Reprinted in Fabulas Ψ 2100⟩ [There are some truths and half-truths here, but really bowdlerizes what amounts to half a century of scholarship. SC].

The third great debate occurred at the start of the Anthropocene crisis. Despite the powerful arguments from realists, idealist arguments began to be popular again among certain political groups with vested interests in fossil fuels and who stood to gain from conflict between ethnic groups [all very vague. SC]. Most historians agree [...again... sigh... SC] that the spur for the return of idealist thought came from the election of key idealist political leaders, such as Jar Bolsonaro in Brazil, Narendra Modi in India and Donald Trump in the United States, among others. This coincided with the COP26 summit on climate change, and the release of the last IPCC report in the early 2020s. In 2022 the invasion of the state of Ukraine by the state of Russia seemed to usher in a new era of idealist power politics, and it is commonly thought that idealists influenced the Russian decision to invade Ukraine [There are a lot of problems with this statement. SC]. The third great debate ended with the final refuting of idealism. By 2035 efforts to address the climate crisis, and other ecological crises, left no room for idealist ideas, and realism was left as the undisputed dominant paradigm of international thought. This paved the way for the eventual development of IR after 2045 [So much more to this story. See my comments below. SC].

FURTHER READING:
The best summary of the pre-history of IR is found in Dr. Nulla Scientia, 'International Relations', in *The Disciplines of Earth System Science: An Overview* ⟨ESS Institute for Teaching, Ψ 2049⟩ [A flawed source. See my report. SC].

Most contemporary sources for the pre-history of IR are hard to come by, but some have been included in recent anthologies. See, for example Susan

38   L. M. ASHWORTH

Strange, 'The Westfailure System' and Burke et al., 'The Planet Politics Manifesto', in Vera Fabulas (eds.), *Classics of International Relations: From 1999 to 2099* ⟨Labrador City: Labrador University Press, Ψ 2100⟩.

2   PART II: IR SINCE 2045—A FIELD BORN OUT OF CRISIS

The Anthropocene Crisis came to a head in 2045, as attempts were made by scholars to fully integrate scientific knowledge of ecological breakdown with scholarship on global government. This involved taking realist ideas, from both political economy and ecology schools, and integrating them fully with ESS.

The crisis had two main causes: (1) ecological and political pressures brought about first by industrialization and then by the Great Acceleration; and (2) The failure of a system based on states to adequately construct a common policy to deal with the crisis.

While the pre-history of IR had been dominated by only two paradigms, the new field of IR in ESS soon split into many competing approaches in what was known as the inter-approach debate. This has lasted to this day. While these different approaches have opened up new avenues to scholarship, and replaced the old dichotomy of realist and idealist, many complain [please specify. SC] that the plethora of approaches has led to a loss of focus. With no clear theoretical backbone to IR, the fear is that IR has sacrificed coherence for plurality ⟨see the contributions to Fabulas et al. Ψ 2112⟩. The major approaches in IR now are summarized in Table 3.

Each of these different approaches are explored in the chapters of this Handbook

…

[I have no further specific comments on the rest of this chapter. It works well. SC]

From: Dr. Secunda Censor,

Re: Vera Fabulas chapter

I have now had a chance to review the above. While it is well written, and includes many important points, there are a number of issues that I have with the chapter. These include a worrying number of anachronisms and basic factual errors. These are recorded in this full report, although I want to also highlight some glaring (and structural) errors too. Overall, my sense is that the chapter is written almost entirely with the concerns of twenty-second-century IR in mind, and makes little attempt to understand the complex nature of IR's past (this includes the rather arbitrary division into pre-IR and post-2045 IR).

The author begins by making the argument that academic IR, as we know it, dates from 2045, when the field became part of new faculties of Earth System Science (ESS). They then go on to talk about pre-2045 IR as a 'pre-IR' stage of international thought. While there is an argument to be made

'THE PAST, PRESENT AND FUTURE OF GLOBAL THOUGHT' ... 39

Table 3 Approaches to IR

	Primary ideas	*Key concepts*
Planetary political economy	Looking at the political economy of human/human and human/non-human relations	Wealth Power Class
Global ecology	Relationship of society and ecology, assuming an interconnected reality	Environment Resilience Mitigation
Identity and power	How humans identify themselves. Identity inequalities, and relations of this with non-human worlds	Ideology Race Gender Class Truth and power
Public stewardship	Planetary public policy. Managing the global commons	Management Resources Resilience
Air and ocean studies	The politics of the air and oceans, and how their interconnectedness is a template for terrestrial government	Interconnectedness Deep Dependence Planet-wide systems
Global discard studies	The political economy of waste and waste management	Waste disposal Recycling systems Waste cycle power relations
Violence studies	Violent conflict and the role of organized violence, both between humans and human/non-human	Violent behavior Group dynamics Ecological violence
Inter-agency conflict	How human agencies conflict with each other. Both symmetrical conflict between like agencies, and asymmetrical conflict between agencies at different hierarchical levels	Power Hierarchies Anarchic systems

along these lines, the author is a victim here of circular reasoning. By defining IR strictly as a sub-field of ESS they basically write a disciplinary history using the categories of the present. Yes, it is true to say that IR today is concerned with those aspects of the Anthroposphere and Technosphere that relate to global structures and interactions—and that, like the rest of ESS it focuses on humans as a force of nature. However, this is not how self-identifying IR scholars of the past viewed their subject matter or their research priorities. For example, in North America IR was part of the now defunct discipline of Political Science until well into the twenty-first century.

The weakest part of the chapter can be found in the section that the author labels 'The Pre-History of IR. 1880 to 2045'. While I realize that much of the narrative in this section is common currency in teaching materials for introductory courses in IR, this does not mean that it is true. Given that Handbooks

40 L. M. ASHWORTH

require a greater level of scholarly rigor, these mistakes and anachronisms need to be addressed before publication.

The 'Pre-History' follows the usual story we are used to from our first-year courses: *In its first century, until the early 2000s, international thought is dominated by two architypes or paradigms: realism and idealism. Realists believed that material factors could explain global behaviour, and that industrialization had fundamentally altered the nature of global society. Realists were divided into two camps. The first was the political economy camp, and included writers such as Norman Angell, Susan Strange, and Rosa Luxemburg. The second camp were political geographers, such as Ellen Churchill Semple, Derwent Whittlesey, and Merze Tate. Realists were active before 1919, and were given a boost by the success of the realist North American President Woodrow Wilson after the First World War. Idealists, on the other hand, ignored material forces and historical change, and saw human nature and behaviour as the constant driving forces of international affairs. Idealists gained strength after the Great Depression and the Second World War, when the threat of nuclear war seemed to make diplomacy (rather than material forces) more important for human survival. Famous idealists included Hans Morgenthau, Martin Wight, and John Mearsheimer. In politics the most famous idealist was Henry Kissinger. Idealists were defeated in three great debates, partially because of the new information coming out on climate change, and the influence of more intellectually rigorous methods adopted from the physical sciences, political economy, and ecology.*

It is hard to know where to begin with this load of old turnips.

First off, much of this story originates in one of the first IR texts to emerge after the Anthropocene Crisis. Revamped university courses after around 2050 were usually short of good introductory material, and many new IR courses used a chapter from an Earth System Science manual written by Nulla Scientia, a physicist, in 2049. Unfamiliar with the disciplinary history of IR, but with some knowledge of the categories used by IR scholars in the past, Scientia assigned older labels to a current theoretical reality: the split between those in IR studying the ecological and economic crises (the 'realists'), and those who still concentrated on inter-state diplomacy and state security (the 'idealists'). Many of the figures mentioned by the author of this chapter as archetypes of realism and idealism are well-known today, but little known a century ago. Ironically, many of those that Scientia assigned as idealists would actually have self-identified as realists. Much of the problem here is that, while the names, such as Hans Morgenthau, are still known to IR scholars today as examples of the wrong road to take, few (to be generous) have bothered to read their manuscripts. While I understand it is often difficult to find works from before 2050 in modern university databases, I would expect that anyone attempting to write a handbook chapter on the history of the field would at least be acquainted with what someone like Morgenthau actually said. Morgenthau's non-material ideas may no longer be popular, but that does not rule out their importance in disciplinary history. Also, many of the ideas that we can find in Morgenthau's writings have relevance to current approaches, such as inter-agency conflict studies.

So, here I want to set out what is known to intellectual historians. First off, the reduction of pre-2045 IR (let's not call it a 'pre-history', with all the presentist baggage that entails) to two 'paradigms' called realism and idealism is nonsense. There was a plethora of approaches to IR between 1880 and 2045. There are also a similarly wide range of possible origin points for IR, and to be frank the argument for 2045 as the start of IR only makes sense from an institutional point of view, not from the vantage point of the history of ideas. On top of this the manuscript has removed any contentious issues from the story, presenting a placid and largely conflict-free account (save, of course, for the demonization of 'idealism'). Consequently, I will address three issues here: (1) The problem with the realist-idealist paradigm framing; (2) The issue of the origin of IR (yes, it is important), and a criticism of the idea of debates; and (3) The silence on the political divisions during this time period, and why not addressing issues of class, gender and race does a disservice to our understanding of our origins.

Paradigms

The idea of paradigms does crop up in IR discourses from the 1980s, but this is usually in the context of a broad range of different approaches. In the 1980s it was common to mention three, but by the 1990s IR textbooks were mentioning more. There was also an older tradition that divided all thought into realist and idealist/utopian, but the definitions of what was realist and what was not was hotly contested. There was a group of scholars that self-identified as realists during the mid to late twentieth century (and into the twenty-first), but here's the problem: *their ideas were a lot closer to what Dr. Fabulas calls idealists*. What is more, the definition of idealism contains elements of past realist thought, but still remains a category that really did not exist per se. Here the story gets complicated. IR before 2045 is really a mix of many (sometimes interlocking) approaches. This complexity goes back to the start of the twentieth century, where there are many different ways to do IR. Yet, the textbooks of the time, in attempts to create some kind of order from this reality, kept trying different ways of fitting all IR scholarship into distinct boxes. While the most popular number of boxes was three (from before 1980 these might be realist-rationalist-revolutionist or traditionalist-behaviouralist-postbehaviouralist. After 1980 the most common was realist-liberal-constructivist), it was not uncommon to see a simple realist-idealist split for those who self-identified as realists and wanted to put their opponents all in one box.

This is where Dr. Nulla Scientia got the idea of the division of realist-idealist in pre-2045 IR from. Except they unknowingly applied the labels in a radically different way. Twentieth-century uses of the term saw realism as associated with power politics, and idealism with wishful thinking that denied the 'reality' of power politics. In a way Dr. Scientia did nothing different, but applied the labels in a way relevant to their point in time. The Realists were those who 'understood' the realities of political economy and ecology during the Anthropocene Crisis, while idealists were wishful thinkers who denied that reality by clinging to ideas of state-based power politics. That is really the reality of any division of the intellectual world into realists and idealists. It is always a time-bound division between those who feel they grasp the realities as they see them (the realists), and their opponents the idealists (who seem to be doggedly refusing to accept the reality as these 'realists' see it). Dr. Scientia in 2049 unwittingly followed this logic, while Dr. Fabulas fell into the same trap in 2122.

In short, a competent history of global thought needs to start by recognizing the many multiple approaches to IR that made up the field then, and still do today. On top of this, we also have to recognize the multiple links that exist between these approaches. For example, there are links between the work of Merze Tate and Hans Morgenthau that the act of putting them in separate categories does a disservice to (see Morgenthau 1943). There is one other issue here of garbled history. Dr. Fabulas mentioned that idealists were all men, and that toxic masculinity was a central part of idealist thought. This is a misreading. In the early twenty-first century many scholars began to point out how women had been written out of the history of global thought here. The key text here is Owens and Rietzler (2021). This is not a case of idealists being only men, but that for many earlier reviews of the field of IR only men were mentioned. There were women doing power politics. Merze Tate is a good example here (see Tate 1942). So, the problem is one of misdiagnosis of the problem. Not that there were no women, but rather that the women were written out of the story.

Origins

Historians know that the attempt to divide the past up into periods and origin dates is fraught with dangers. Yes, we do it for convenience, but they always carry with them problems and distortions that can trick us into reading the past in a particular way. Two problematic origin dates stand out in this manuscript. The first is the date of 2045 for the start of 'real' IR. What this does is anachronistically make the concerns of the field of IR, as it emerged in ESS after 2045, the core definition of what it means to do IR. This is then used to judge IR before 2045 (the 'pre-history'). The result is the construction of a 'real' IR in the form of political economy and ecology. This becomes the perennial realist paradigm that defines IR, and is used to render the ideas associated with idealism obsolete.

The second is the cut-off for the start of the pre-history. By concentrating on the 1880s as the start the chapter ignores a two-hundred-year period of global expansion, trade and production that involved both the use of slavery and the imperial conquest by what was later to be called the western or European world. Let's get into some uncomfortable truths, known to historians, but not known enough in IR: the institution of slavery as a part of plantation agriculture, along with the conquest of large parts of the non-European world by European empires, was responsible for the development of racist political theories that were used to deliberately subjugate darker skinned people (see Acharya 2022).

While it is true that, along with the major global reforms that followed the Anthropocene Crisis, we have directly confronted the problem of the pseudo-science of racism, that success has allowed us to ignore the very real history of racism that defined our scholarly field in the past. In doing so, we minimize the problems we still need to address today that come from racism's long history.

Silences

This chapter may be judged by what it says, but it can equally be judged by what it does not. It is written not to offend, and as a result it does a big disservice to the realities of the divisions of the past. IR has always been riven by divisions, and still is. The ignoring of the divisions of the past is unwittingly a way of covering over the divisions of the present.

One question that arises leads directly from the discussion of origins: why start with industrialization, rather than with the earlier time of globalization associated with plantations and slavery in the seventeenth and eighteenth centuries? I suggest this silence is there because, while we think we have solved the problem of race (and we can all agree that race is not scientific), we have not addressed the inequalities that still exist from past racial discrimination.

This might also explain why empire is missing from this chapter. Imperialism dredges up a past where some humans did think they were superior to others, and that legacy has left its mark on our world, even if those empires were (formally at least) dismantled in the twentieth century. The same goes for silences over class. It is interesting that Rosa Luxemburg is mentioned, but her work is not directly addressed.

Another silence hangs over the presentation of ideas associated with power politics (what Dr. Fabulas calls 'idealism'). Ideas associated with power politics rooted in human nature, manifest through the national interest of states within a states system, is demonized in this chapter. Up to a point that is understandable, given the intensity of conflicts between states in the past. At another level, though, it does some quiet ideological heavy lifting. While it is true that the regimes of global government slowly developed during the twenty-first century did help solve the Anthropocene Crisis, these institutions do have their own interests and blind spots. One of the biggest blind spots is a one-size-fits-all politics that can be corrosive to local interests. When (often genuine) local interests and concerns are articulated, it is common to write these interests off as idealist wishful thinking that doesn't accept the realities of global stewardship. Dr. Fabulas unwittingly allows this cognitive shortcut by constructing a seemingly obsolete idealist paradigm in which genuine local interests can be easily slotted and then dismissed as part of a discredited past.

Why is the pre-history so centered, on what they would have called back in the twentieth century, the West? In the second part of the chapter Dr. Fabulas does a great job of covering the whole world, even bringing in the 71% of the Earth's surface that is covered by the oceans. Yet, the first half (the 'pre-history') recreates a very western-centred disciplinary history. This is accurate insofar as it replicates current practices in the IR courses, where disciplinary history seems to be very geographically limited. This also reinforces the tendency to write imperialism and empire out of the discipline.

There is a final odd silence, and it is mirrored by a similar odd silence from two centuries ago. It is the lost memory of disease. At the end of the First World War, the world was ravaged by a pandemic (called Spanish flu) that killed twice as many people as the war in half the time. Yet, by the mid-twentieth century this pandemic had largely been forgotten. In all of Dr. Fabulas' talk on the Anthropocene Crisis, one element is missing from it: the Covid pandemic that started in 2019. This severely disrupted the global economy, altered the way people saw the climate crisis, and led to political unrest toward its end as health restrictions and cost of living crises saw a decline in economic globalization. Covid, like Spanish flu before it, just disappears from the record. Similarly, an opportunity is missed to link these two past pandemics with the broader study of non-human actors.

The manuscript is on firmer ground in the next section ('IR Since 2045'). The author competently describes IR's incorporation into Earth System Sciences, and the abolition of the divisions between physical, life and social sciences. While the discussion of the different schools exploring the problems of the new global institutions tasked with Anthroposphere management is good, the failure to address the new class systems and identities emerging after 2080 dramatically weaken the value of the text. The discussion of a turbulent half-century is rendered placid by this institutional concentration. In short, the author seems to be in thrall to trendy systemic Anthroposphere analyses that often ignore the severe fissures that exist at the root of these institutions.

To sum up: much work still needs to be done if this chapter is to amount to more than just the reiteration of pleasant myths that flatter conservative scholars and their powerful friends in global institutions.

I have one final comment. One of my major research projects has been to study the development of IR textbooks used in courses from the 1980s to the 2020s (yes, there were lots of self-defining IR courses in the 'pre-history of IR' period). What is amazing to me is how almost all of these textbooks also oversimplified the history of their field, and also just got historical information wrong (Censor Ψ 2118). In this sense this chapter is no different. It represents continuity with the past, but in the sense that many of the same mistakes are made.

I hope this report will be useful for Dr. Fabulas as they edit this chapter for future publication.

[Note attached to the above report]

An unhelpful review. Have talked with the editors. They confirm that students will be expecting the analysis as laid out in the original chapter, and that the majority of IR scholars would not be familiar with the story that Dr. Censor tells in their report. Dr. Fabulas has laid out one particular way of presenting the story, and so represents a good basis for discussion.

Okay to send report to recycling.

Dedi Cavit
Commissioning Editor

Bibliography

Pre-2045 Sources

Acharya, A. (2022). 'Race and Racism in the Founding of the Modern World Order', *International Affairs*, 98(1), pp. 23–44.

Angell, N. (1911). *The Great Illusion* (London: Heinemann).

Burke, A., S. Fishel, A. Mitchell, S. Dalby, and D. Levine. (2016). 'Planet Politics: A Manifesto from the End of IR', *Millennium—Journal of International Studies*, 44(3), pp. 499–523.

Keynes, J. M. (1919). *The Economic Consequences of the Peace* (London: Macmillan).

Kindleberger, C. (1973). *The World in Depression* (Berkeley: University of California Press).

Kuhn, T. (1962). *The Structure of Scientific Revolutions* (Chicago: University of Chicago Press).

Morgenthau, H. J. (1943). 'Review of Merze Tate's *The Disarmament Illusion*', *Russian Review*, 2, pp. 104–105.

Owens, P., and K. Rietzler (eds.). (2021). *Women's International Thought: A New History* (Cambridge: Cambridge University Press).

Semple, E. (1911). *Influences of Geographic Environment on the Basis of Ratzel's System of Anthropo-Geography* (London: Constable).

Strange, S. (1999). 'The Westfailure System', *Review of International Studies*, 25(3), pp. 345–354.

Tate, M. (1942). *The Disarmament Illusion* (New York: Macmillan).

Whittlesey, D. (1939). *The Earth and the State* (New York: Henry Holt).

Post-2045 Sources

Censor, S. ⟨Ψ 2118⟩. *International Relations Textbooks and the Pursuit of Placid Simplicity: A History 1968–2118* (Bandung Press).

Fabulas, V. (ed.). ⟨Ψ 2100⟩. *Classics of International Relations: From 1999 to 2099* (Labrador City: Labrador University Press).

Fabulas, V., et al. (eds.). ⟨Ψ 2112⟩. *The End of International Relations Theory? Quo Vadis a Dividing Discipline in Crisis* (Anthroposphere Press).

Fabulas, V., et al. (eds.). ⟨Ψ 2122⟩. *International Relations for the 22nd Century: Towards a New Synthesis* (Global Consortium for Research).

Ripae, M. ⟨Ψ 2085⟩. 'The Great Debates in International Relations', *Anthroposphere Review*, 28(3), pp. 435–457.

Scientia, N. ⟨Ψ 2049⟩. 'International Relations', in *The Disciplines of Earth System Science: An Overview* (ESS Institute for Teaching).

From World Politics to 'Time Epistemics': New Medievalism and the Story of a Certain Scholar

Aleksandra Spalińska

In memory of my dearest friend

1   Introduction

In 2119 we celebrate the bicentennial of International Relations. This is an opportunity to consider the history of the discipline and ideas which influenced its development. The following chapter analyses the oeuvre of my dear friend and colleague Veronica Eredi (2056–2109), who in the last twenty years substantially contributed to the World Politics theory (WPT), recalling the idea of New Medievalism and contextualizing the study on world order in the intellectual history. That resulted in proposing the concept of 'time epistemics' for which she is famous for ⟨Shirry Ψ 2112⟩. As there are still some unanswered questions related to this framework, it is certainly worthwhile to reconsider her work. This chapter provides a guidance to Eredi's oeuvre. First, I recapture her intellectual biography. Next, I discuss her focus on New Medievalism and the contribution of the idea to theorizing world order. Then, following the steps taken by Eredi herself, I investigate the role of New Medievalism for understanding time and temporality in IR. Finally, I discuss the analytical pay-offs of applying New Medievalism and outline the research agenda based on Veronica's work.

A. Spalińska (✉)
Faculty of Political Science and International Studies,
University of Warsaw, Warsaw, Poland
e-mail: a.spalinska@student.uw.edu.pl

© The Author(s), under exclusive license to Springer Nature
Switzerland AG 2023
L. Horn et al. (eds.), *The Palgrave Handbook of Global Politics in the 22nd Century*, https://doi.org/10.1007/978-3-031-13722-8_4

2   VERONICA EREDI—AND ACADEMIA IN THE POST-ANTHROPOCENTRIC WORLD

Considering her affiliation with one of the last 'Western' universities in Europe and substantial experience in conducting research in another 'Western' institutions, Veronica could count on the advice of the most prominent academics and most patient librarians who revealed a plenty of bibliophile secrets to her. For years she used the resources of the former University of Oxford, where the key works on World Politics and intellectual history (incomplete due to many turbulences) were stored. As one story says, just by accident she found a note on 'New Medievalism', falling out from one of the books she leafed through ⟨Stavinsky Ψ 2109⟩. She got curious on the idea, all the more, as there were fears of 'coming back to Middle Ages' around her, given that the polycentric system based on the polycentric governance concept (Ostrom 2010), applied mostly on the local and regional levels, and established after the Third World War as a new political and economic world order, turned out to be highly unstable and prone to disorder ⟨Eredi Ψ 2093⟩. In terms of access to the archives, after the United Kingdom's collapse shortly after WWIII, the library collections of leading universities were moved to safer places in continental Europe (e.g. in Switzerland), where the intellectual riches of bygone academic ages are up until today. Most of the American intellectual collections was completely lost as well during the Second Civil War in 2050s. Veronica was really fortunate to collaborate with institutions where these archives were well preserved ⟨Stavinsky Ψ 2109⟩, including my precious European IR Theory Research Centre in Bonn where we actually met when Veronica came to consult her research plans with me as the deputy director.

To better understand Veronica's oeuvre—which she cannot present herself due to her sudden death—it is certainly worthwhile to investigate the path she took and steps that paved her way to theoretical propositions. After historical pursuits, including investigations on the conceptual genealogy of New Medievalism, she analysed Bull's thought against elaborations on New Medievalism throughout the twenty-first century (ibidem: 45–78). That led her to theorize political order and authority in historical contexts, including the ways of understanding these concepts at the end of the twentieth century and now. Furthermore, New Medievalism inspired her idea of 'time epistemics', to which Veronica devoted her life. It particularly contributed to improving understanding of how the future was projected by scholars nearly 150 years ago in reference to political and social history ⟨Eredi Ψ 2104⟩.

In the course of further work, she applied New Medievalism to the study on contemporary polycentric systems as a political organization of the world. However, it was not an easy task: New Medievalism was only a metaphor and heuristics, not a full-fledged theory. Moreover, before the World War III, it questioned state-centrism as a way of framing World Politics which back then had been considered undeniable. Currently, we recognize non-state

FROM WORLD POLITICS TO 'TIME EPISTEMICS' ...   49

actors and networks that share public authority but for the people of the twentieth century, the world without supreme authority over a given territory and
population (like in the state system) was unimaginable (ibidem: 120–122).

3   NEW MEDIEVALISM—CONCEPTUALIZING WORLD ORDER

To understand New Medievalism, we need to bear in mind that—as Veronica
indicated repeatedly—through a long time there was nothing like a 'world
theory' in IR (which youngsters tend to take for granted). Therefore, it is
necessary to both trace the roots of New Medievalism and highlight its current
ideational contexts, such as world theory in terms of World Politics That is
crucial, given that the 'world theory' is a relatively new invention—even after
WWIII the 'international theory' (in normative and empirical terms) was still
dominating ⟨Kuzah Ψ 2099⟩.

Interestingly, New Medievalism in studying World Politics comes from
considerations about qualitative changes within the 'international' politics after
World War II. It came into life as a result of globalization processes (with
special regard to European integration), strengthened by economic (neoliberal) reforms as well as of expansion of international system during the times
of decolonization. Precisely, New Medievalism can be found inter alia in the
works by Hedley Bull (Bull 2002) whose writings provided inspiration for
researchers in the twenty-first century, including Veronica. In Bull's contribution, New Medievalism was deemed one of the potential alternatives to
the modern states system (ibidem: 225–247). It was created on the assumption that the architecture of the globalized world order in the late twentieth
century could have been similar to the political structure of medieval Europe,
regarding the supposed 'End of Westhaplia' in terms of the declining position of the nation-state as the only legally recognized actor of world politics
(Matthews 1997: 65). That ultimately came to life in late 2050s when the
polycentric system of networked authorities have been established. However,
as Bull's neo-medieval scenario had been outlined in 1970s, it did not refer
to the consequences of digital revolution, neoliberal economy or 'postmoder-
nity'; these were incorporated into the agenda of new medievalism in early
2000s. During her research, Veronica realized that there were both times of
indifference as well as of intense interest in New Medievalism ⟨Eredi Ψ 2100:
172⟩.

Crucially, when we think of New Medievalism, it does not mean that there
is any possibility of coming back to the Middle Ages. In Bull's words, often
recalled by Veronica, the thing was to imagine a 'modern and secular counterpart of it that embodies its central characteristic: *the system of overlapping
authority and multiple loyalty*' (Bull 2002: 245). This definition stems from
the observation that:

In that system no ruler or state was sovereign in the sense of being supreme over a given territory and a given segment of the Christian population; each had to share authority with vassals beneath, and with the Pope and (in Germany and Italy) the Holy Roman Emperor above. The universal political order of Western Christendom represents an alternative to the system of states which does not yet embody universal government. (ibidem)

However, Jörg Friedrichs, who analysed Bull's idea at the beginning of the twenty-first century, had considered the neo-medieval analogy not only because of observing overlapping authorities and complex loyalties, but also due to observing rival dichotomous political forces, which both had claimed the right to universal and superior authority (*system of overlapping authority and multiple loyalty, held together with the duality of competing universalistic claims*) (Friedrichs 2001: 475–502). For him, Bull's conception was incomplete as it did not regard the 'profound unity of medieval order established by dual universalism of Empire and the Church' (Friedrichs 2004: 16). At the turn of twenty-first century, the global economy and the nation-state (which, according to Friedrichs, was universal political organization, even if its content had varied) (Friedrichs 2001: 486) or transnational business and 'international' politics (Friedrichs 2004: 17) advanced as these rival powers.

Literature on New Medievalism embraced also the architecture of European integration (Zielonka 2006). For Zielonka, at the beginning of the twenty-first century the so-called European Union started to resemble something like an empire, however, not in the 'modern' terms of the nation-state but in terms of (neo)medieval 'universal' polity. As reasons for such conclusions Zielonka referred to the complexity of political structures within the EU and its behaviour as the political actor, including its policies towards the outside environment. Zielonka therefore concluded that for describing the EU in more accurate ways than a 'standard' statist model would do, the concept of empire seemed the best fit. However, he underscored that this kind of empire operated in close alignment with neo-medieval conditions. Continuing Bull's thought, he had identified not only within the European sphere, but all over the world (Zielonka 2014), considering the consequences of neoliberal policies for different parts of the world, rising non-state actors, including digital platforms (like Facebook) or spreading mercenary warfare and illicit governance in the regions disrupted by wars and famine resulting from the climate change (for example, the Middle East).

Consequently, New Medievalism had been employed as a heuristics to re-framing and re-understanding the politics, economy and society within the twenty-first century. It concerned the role of multiple actors, such as the grand corporations, NGOs, global cities (some really have become independent and gained international recognition, like Mexico City or Lagos), informal groups and networks (like terrorists or self-styled virtual gangs), regional communities based on common culture and forms of regional/global integration. Additionally, still New Medievalism is being identified with complexity of interplays intermediate between the public authority and the private sphere which ultimately denied previously existing boundaries between the public and the private. In this context, New Medievalism has been a perspective of understanding the outcomes of global changes, including power shifts or decline of the 'free' lands (like the former US) that almost destroyed our civilization. Moreover, it has contributed to the vision of the multipolar and more diverse world which still is significant, regarding the challenges of prone the anarchy world order that we have now.

4 Passing Time and Political Studies—The 'Time Epistemics'

Next, Veronica investigated the meanings of New Medievalism in the context of the academic attempts to predict the future based on the imaginaries of the past. This embraced also taking a close look at the intellectual setting in which these attempts had been undertaken (so, in the case of New Medievalism— the English School and, broadly, attempts to understand and predict the consequences of neoliberal globalization). A significant part of this enterprise was situating New Medievalism in relation to other historical analogies and metaphors. Namely, unlike analogies employed in decision-making process (for example, the Munich analogy), New Medievalism served other purposes: to imagine and describe the outcome of the late twentieth-century mega-trends which most crucial object had been the nation-state ⟨Eredi Ψ 2100: 152⟩. New Medievalism is thus a macro-analogy contributing to the twentieth-century intellectual world-making and future scenarios (ibidem). Moreover, its story helps us to understand the 'time epistemics' of the intellectuals in the late twentieth century. As Eredi noted:

> In neo-medieval analogy, imaginaries of all time dimensions are encapsulated: the future because there is something *new*; past – because we have re-imagined *medievalism* itself; present – because the '*new*' is rooted in what we observe today or, from historical point of view, in what people of last years of 20th century observed and experienced as *their* present. ⟨Eredi Ψ 2100: 153⟩

However, how can this conception be useful for scientific research? For Veronica, the 'time epistemics', which New Medievalism embraces, constitutes the epistemic and methodological awareness of time and temporality within the existing approaches in political research. It exposes the role of passing time and the time passed in research on facts, structures and imaginaries. Veronica, as noted, was grounded in both political science and intellectual history, so combining different perspectives was natural for her. It was a favourable circumstance that let her contribute to research design in IR ⟨Shirry Ψ 2112⟩.

She started thus to investigate how New Medievalism informs the 'time epistemics'. First, she considered New Medievalism, as a conception of order and heuristics to frame an ontology of world politics, and to outline its normative implications, including the political projects for the future. Second, she investigated the implications of thinking in terms of historical analogy against the widely discussed 'rupture thesis' as well as the 'continuation thesis' in context of the periodization and transition between pre-modern political structures and modern sovereign order (Guillaume 2021) ⟨Spalińska Ψ 2083⟩. This embraced the consequences of acknowledging the continuity for the knowledge production against the presentism. These methodological considerations became the basis for analysing implications of New Medievalism as well as for laying out the research agenda for which New Medievalism has become the point of departure. Both of them are discussed in the next section.

First of all, there was a question if one could really embrace (as predicted by Bull) the very trends that had been identified as neo-medieval. Had New Medievalism ever been a relevant description of World Politics? How does it inform our knowledge on thinking about time? Is there a link between their (previous generations) forecasting and our imaginations of the history? ⟨Eredi Ψ 2108: 345–346⟩. Following these questions, Veronica had found New Medievalism relevant to the problem of 'time epistemics' not only within historically most know theories of World Politics but also ideas prevailing now, especially new global republicanism (ibidem). In her opinion, this idea had been rooted in what she called 'the renaissance of public authority' which after WWIII became the philosophical base for the newly established polycentric system of networked authorities (ibidem). Namely, beyond IR theory, New Medievalism was considered a discursive depiction of the *Zeitgeist* at the beginning of the twenty-first century. For Pierre Hassner, the onset of the

FROM WORLD POLITICS TO 'TIME EPISTEMICS' ... 53

new millennium was the time of the 'new dialectics' and their interplays as the cultural or legal boundaries had been abandoned or changed (e.g. as in the case of public/private divide) (Hassner 2002: 46–48). It concerned the paradoxes of universalism and anarchy, civilization and barbarism. These dialectics simultaneously were recognized as the imaginary logics of New Medievalism (ibidem).

Moreover, in one of her last works, Veronica recalled Umberto Eco's idea that each century and each place has its own image of the Middle Ages and, therefore, its own 'medievalism' ⟨Eredi Ψ 2104: 127⟩. It concerns both 'old', so the imaginations of the historical Middle Ages, and 'new'—so the projections of our contemporary world in medieval terms; in political context, it concerns, e.g. the vision of the world without linear borders (ibidem: 128). That's how New Medievalism makes a link between World Politics and 'time epistemics'. As she claimed further:

> New Medievalism draws our attention to *creative thinking* of politics and order as its framework corresponds with historically embedded ideas like *connectography* (Khanna 2016) and *multiplicity* (Rosenberg 2016). Crucial is the role of history which future mirrors – the way *historical analogy* contributes to the creative thinking on politics and society. New Medievalism as a metaphor let us better understand the future through reference to history; there is no *back to the future* (as some historical realists claimed) but rather *forward to the past* – to *real* past, not imagined; past of societies and ideas. (ibidem: 278)

Creative thinking is the key to reconstruct medievalism away from simplifications and stereotypes. Such ideas require historical knowledge but, also, some healthy imagination as well, given that passing time still is something *unseen* within international studies (ibidem: 279) and was back at the beginning of the twenty-first century (Hutchings 2008; Hom 2020). In practice, we need to investigate the genealogy and deconstruct New Medievalism to get to know its ontological, epistemological and normative roots and other 'ingredients'. Then from these 'ingredients' we can try to reconstruct the conceptual grid of the idea and translate it into the language of social sciences ⟨Eredi Ψ 2104: 283⟩.

This enterprise is crucial because the politics and order are, to some extent, built on imaginations—individual and collective, conservative and revolutionary (ibidem: 281)—which always are multiple just like the societal existence is (ibidem: 282; Rosenberg 2016). Veronica, to investigate them, chose the post-critical epistemic perspective ⟨Shirry Ψ 2112⟩. Such a step certainly does not surprise as the post-critical theory is a compromise between 'old' critical post-structuralism and neo-positivism that dominated after WWIII; thanks to that, investigations like this are feasible (ibidem). The last two (already closed) great debates within IR concerned the methodological boundaries between *the international* research, network studies and global inquiry. Thanks to these debates, it is certainly easier to understand New

Medievalism now than in Bull's times ⟨Ibnaju Ψ 2114⟩. It concerns also the epistemological dimension due to the reset of critical realism (ibidem: 223). It is important because New Medievalism focuses on the polity (widely understood—like networks now or nation-states in the past), adopting an outsider perspective ⟨Eredi Ψ 2105: 56⟩. Furthermore, it is essential that, e.g. in the mid-twenty-first century the transformation of international law became the critical factor for the future of the emerging polycentric order (ibidem). The ontological layers of New Medievalism thus include the political order (and its architecture), authority (and its construction), power (and its flows) and politics (and its understandings). To better understand this, let's investigate Veronica's considerations on how New Medievalism frames the ontology of World Politics and order, and ways of researching it (ibidem: 52–59).

5   New Medievalism and Researching the Polycentric Order—Outline of the Agenda

As Veronica taught us, at first we have to deal with the 'system of overlapping authority and multiple loyalty'—a wide definition of a 'neo-medieval system', elaborated by Hedley Bull ca. 1975 in reference to the political structures of the Middle Ages (ibidem: 52). But what exactly is the 'overlapping authority'? Is it only one authority that has some parts that overlap or there are many authorities that are overlapping even if they did not intend to do so? This understanding of political order refers to the legal authority of what had been known as the state, embodied by the united jurisdictions system (economic, legal, security) which, due to the growing economic and technological interdependence became highly differentiated. Simultaneously, the increasing use of surveillance techniques weakened the state legitimacy, leading to the popular unrest and the growing support for metropolitan and regional authorities, especially in the Americas and Europe, enhanced by the events of WWIII. Consequently, the state had lost its exclusive control over these spheres for the benefit of private actors like corporations or self-governed mercenary regiments. Currently, one of the crucial questions concerns the place of hybrid (not fully the state, not the non-state) actors in such a system.

Hence, we can assume that the thing is not what order is ('global', 'regional' or 'networked') but how it is constructed beyond and despite these distinctions. That is deemed the consequence of the 'overlapping authority' system working in practice. Actually, here is the clue—in Eredi's writings the construction of authority is the main analytical category, both in terms of form and content of the system. Moreover, there is an interplay between flows of power and construction of authority as both affect each other in specific jurisdictions (economic, social, legal, cultural) that within the networks of shared authority (NSA) are integrated (however, in fact independent or only loosely connected) (ibidem: 53). Regarding the order architecture, the power is expected to flow or being intentionally shifted by political actors.

That depends on their interests or goals, especially where the formal right to power does not overlap with the place where power actually is.

Next, we need to investigate the second part of Bull's phrase. How to define multiple loyalty? Is it the multiplication of different/differentiated loyalties (political, cultural, etc.) in the context of specific individuals or communities, or is the multiplication of subjects of (only) political loyalty (not only 'states', but also regions and 'supranational' organizations like the former EU, private actors, networks of shared authority) ⟨Eredi Ψ 2105: 54⟩? Or is it the coexistence of loyalties, existing in various spheres of human life (cultural, religious, professional, etc.)? What are the normative consequences of that? Regarding Friedrichs' outline of the New Medievalism as an order kept alive by the competition of the two 'universalistic' ideological powers that shape political loyalties, we can presume that 'transnational' nature of the system results just from such tension.

For Friedrichs these two ideological powers were the global economy and the nation-state. What other ideologies can be distinguished for this case? Maybe—what we know from history—liberal democracy and nationalism/fascism/populism should be put into this model? Or more contemporary ideas—subsidiarity (inclusive of sustainability) as well as the new weaves of both domestic and transversal (cross-level) anarchism that can exhaust the values crucial for the polycentric system as well as its architecture in practice ⟨Eredi Ψ 2105: 56⟩? What made and what makes the claims of these ideas 'universalistic' and how this universalism was and is putting into life (ibidem)? System of overlapping authority', as we know from our experience in living the polycentric, networked and differentiated set of polities, is filled with multitude of people's loyalties that affect the construction of authority and flows of power. These loyalties are complex not only in terms of individual lives but also collectively which enhances the privatization of authorities and competition in the quality of governance. Furthermore, the paradoxes of individual loyalties have their equivalent on the global level in a form of competing ideologies, similar to the twenty-first century, when rival ideas were destroying the intermediate level of World Politics which was the state. Currently these strong ideas are shaping the polycentric system.

Importantly, within the whole first half of the twenty-first century authority as a notion was still associated with institutions of the state (both central and local), especially through the means of symbolic engineering that during economic and social breakdowns were put into action to maintain the loyalty towards state authorities and legitimization for their decisions (ibidem: 56). In reference to the way the states were organized, these networks (which existence is still based on the common territory and demand for independence) can be recognized as the 'hybrid subjects' as Veronica put it (ibidem). However, these are only exceptions because after the global crushes of the economy and the environment in the 2040s and 2050s, the notion of authority has been connected to civic, metropolitan and business authority as well as to the global governance agencies. A favourable factor for that had been a popular belief in the sustainability as the one and only idea that can rebuild the world. This rebuilding had been initiated by global institutions and agencies and then, fulfilled by political structures on local and regional levels. That is why Veronica assumed that sustainability had become one of the prevailing ideologies, later supported by subsidiarity in economic and political solutions that have been adopted. From the other side, the 'new anarchism' became another powerful ideology, as many communities and subjects on different levels started to demand independence and self-governance, rejecting the authority of former 'international' system and states (ibidem: 56). Consequently, the networks appeared, and the contemporary polycentric system has started to form. Of course, the tensions do not fade away; despite plenty of optimizing and self-control mechanisms, the polycentric system is still prone to anarchy.

In case of power, the matter is easier as we have many conceptions of it, e.g. the power as the influence which is often associated with interference of interests groups or business. Moreover, there are approaches which put emphasis on connections between political order, power and politics like a well-known model (especially in European Integration studies) of PPPP ($4{\times}P$): polycentricity, politics, policy and polity, applied in the research on networks that provide public authority (e.g. global cities) and, through this, to the whole polycentric system ⟨Nix Ψ 2095⟩. However, still there is a question of how the power is being created—is it the might of political networks that makes them public authorities? In historical context, it must be noted that the multiple power shifts put states' formal sovereignty into question (sovereignty by definition had indicated that formally states are equal). The result was often described as the so-called heterarchy (Belmonte and Cerny 2021), so the order of highly differentiated relations (firstly, in economic ties, then in political potential). The concept of differentiation was particularly known in case of the former EU ⟨Spalińska Ψ 2083⟩. In such conditions, state sovereignty started to be considered obsolete and became replaced in practice by the networks of shared authority based on informal networks of social, economic and political ties which were later legalized (Cf. Khanna 2009 for predictions on the matter in the early twenty-first century). Ideas of heterarchy and networked authorities provided the basis for a new polycentric world order in practice. However, they did not solve the problem of order maintenance, given the activity of cyber gangs and warlord mercenaries which became even more powerful. Veronica valued these ideas very much as they regarded relationships and power dynamics between individuals directly and, thus, they helped her to make sense of how political loyalty was formed within a polycentric, semi-privatized environment. Consequently, we can start to think of politics.

If we imagine the 'system of overlapping authority and multiple loyalty', how the political/politics is being created? Are there any distinctive features that can be distinguished? I think of 'the political' because in a supposedly neo-medieval system it is difficult to imagine that politics can be something stable and predictable (in terms of both its objects and methods). Let's read what precisely Veronica claimed on that matter.

'"Neo-medieval" political order (as I frame it) is prone to changes at the edge of anarchy so what is to be called "political" becomes very subjective and is flowing through the system just like power, away from any kind of accountable political control. The subjective nature of "the political" in this case results from "multiple loyalties" of individuals as well as social formations which always are multiple (Rosenberg 2016). That factor makes it impossible to establish a stable common public sphere in which interests of various groups and individuals would hit with each other in the intersubjective way, producing common interests or a collection of norms. Regarding social history of the first decades of the twenty-first century, we can assume that, despite its creative role for shaping individual lives, polycentricity is rather destroying than building for global society as a whole' ⟨Eredi Ψ 2105: 57⟩.

Of course, the politics, understood mainly as undertaking political actions, still exist where the centres of power are or where the wealth is but is rather limited to personal games. However, it is not because violence prevails or because there is no effective power in territorial terms. It is because of powerful ideas that control people's behaviour and establish norms ⟨Spalińska Ψ 2083⟩. One impactful factor is also the prevailing administrative governance style that we know very well from history; the domination of 'policy' over 'politics' had been stated and predicted more than one hundred years ago ⟨Nix Ψ 2095⟩. Indeed, there appears a question how the divide on politics, policy and polity can be seen in the light of New Medievalism, including polycentricity (like in the aforementioned model of 4×P). Moreover, the problem of overlapping authority and multiple loyalty seems to be connected to 'internal' politics and polity and from this level affect the global order. However, as we know New Medievalism does not consider the borders significant ⟨Eredi Ψ 2105: 53⟩.

Regarding these considerations, Veronica decided to propose some research themes for investigation on both present and historical as well as physical and virtual reality. Firstly, both present and historical types of polities need to be considered ⟨Eredi Ψ 2105: 58⟩. Especially, we need to investigate, e.g. the construction of authority and power flows within the NSA and their impact on the world order architecture as they are the basic units of contemporary polycentric system. Following this, private networks and their influence on construction of authority can be researched as well (ibidem: 59). Moreover, essential would be to examine flows and shifts of powers between polycentric authorities, including degrees of homogenization and differentiation within the system (ibidem).

Next, case-studies are needed. In historical contexts, an engaging topic for Veronica was the disintegration of states and its stages, including history/genealogy of the process in the chosen cases, e.g. the United Kingdom or the United States (ibidem). Certainly, these cases could concern also, e.g. the position of rebel/criminal groups within the polycentric system in theory and practice (as we still know little about it) or the European Integration

Forum as the example of a multi-networked organization (as still it is the most original political project ever put into life). Furthermore, regarding Veronica's legacy, the perspective of 'time epistemics' needs to be considered in this agenda. This would concern exploring the status and social perception of the time and temporality within different political systems (in Veronica's words— different types of 'constructions of authority')—in terms of both people's perception of time and its political status within the system, resulting from how the system works (Is it recognized as something precious? How does it serve authority? How does its status change between eras?). Certainly, there is plenty of issues to consider.

6   CONCLUSIONS

New Medievalism had been created as a future scenario or an alternative to the states system, based on historical analogy. It was almost 150 years ago, including relatively high interest in the idea in the first half of the twenty-first century. Regarding that the aims of this paper are not only theoretical but also commemorating, issues of overlapping authority and multiple loyalty were considered through the words of Veronica Eredi who 're-discovered' the conception at the turn of the twenty-second century after a long period of its dormant existence in the archives. As Veronica herself put it once, we need New Medievalism not only because of the opportunities that it creates, but also because of historical trajectories, observed by scholars, especially Bull (Eredi Ψ 2104) which New Medievalism attempts to make sense of. In the case of order and authority, it seems even that Bull had predicted the crisis of public authority (or rather changes of its scope and content) which oppressed the almost twenty-first century as a consequence of predatory globalization, climate change and breakdown of neoliberal economy. As we can see in Veronica's considerations, New Medievalism is needed not only as a starting point for conducting political research but also as an intellectual perspective that makes us aware of the historically embedded and fleeting nature of political systems.

BIBLIOGRAPHY

Bull, H. (2002). *The Anarchical Society: A Study of Order in World Politics*. New York: Palgrave Macmillan.

Belmonte, R., Cerny, P. (2021). Heterarchy: Towards Paradigm Shift in World Politics. *Journal of Political Power*, 27(1), 35–64.

Eredi, V. (Ψ 2093). *Re-imagining Middle Ages*. Geneva: EISA Press.

Eredi, V. (Ψ 2100). New Medievalism and Metaphorical Thinking About the Future. *Journal of Methods in Theoretical Research*, 20(2), 150–188.

Eredi, V. (Ψ 2104). *Creative Interrogations in World Politics Theory: The Question of Time and Temporality*. Bonn: Palgrave Global.

Eredi, V. (Ψ 2105). New Medievalism as the Conceptual Background for the Temporally Informed Research. *Journal of World Politics Research*, 11(3), 14–60.

Eredi, V. ⟨Ψ 2108⟩. *Re-Discovering the Time Epistemics*. Vienna: Palgrave Global.

Friedrichs J. (2001). The Meaning of New Medievalism. *European Journal of International Relations*, 7(4), 475–502.

Friedrichs, J. (2004). The Neo-Medieval Renaissance: Global Governance and International Law in the New Middle Ages. In I. F. Dekker & W. G. Werner (eds.). *Governance and International Legal Theory*. Leiden-Boston: Martinus Nijhoff.

Guillaume, X. (2021). Historical Periods and the Act of Periodisation. In B. de Carvalho, J. Costa Lopez, & H. Leira (eds.). *The Routledge Handbook of Historical International Relations* (1st ed., pp. 562–570). London-New York: Routledge.

Hassner, P. (2002). *Koniec pewników. Eseje o wojnie, pokoju i przemocy* [The End of Axioms: Essays on War, Peace and Violence]. Sic: Warsaw.

Hom, A. R. (2020). *International Relations and the Problem of Time*. Oxford: Oxford University Press.

Hutchings, K. (2008). *Time and World Politics: Thinking the Present*. Manchester: Manchester University Press.

Ibnaju, M. ⟨Ψ 2114⟩. *Research Debates in World Politics Studies: Part III*. Bonn: Palgrave Global.

Khanna, P. (2009, July 23). *Visions of Europe in 2030: A Postmodern Middle Ages*. Der Spiegel. http://www.spiegel.de/international/europe/visions-of-europe-in-2030-a-postmodern-middle-ages-a-637830.html. Printed: 19.09.2022.

Khanna, P. (2016). *Connectography: Mapping the Future of Global Civilization*. New York: Random House.

Kuzah, P. ⟨Ψ 2099⟩. *Polycentric System—Origins, Evolution and Practical Embodiment*. Prague: EISA Press.

Kobrin, S. (1998). Back to the Future: Neomedievalism and the Postmodern Digital World Economy. *Journal of International Affairs*, 51(2).

Matthews, J. T. (1997). Power Shift. *Foreign Affairs*, 76(1).

Nix, S. ⟨Ψ 2095⟩. *Polycentricity: A New Model of the Politics, Policy and Polity*. Frankfurt: Frei Press.

Ostrom, E. (2010). Beyond Markets and States: Polycentric Governance of Complex Economic Systems. *American Economic Review*, 100(3), 641–672.

Rosenberg, J. (2016). International Relations in the Prison of Political Science. *International Relations*, 30(2), 127–153.

Shirry, A. ⟨Ψ 2112⟩. *Western Professors: Biographical Notes*. Geneva: EISA Press.

Spalińska A. ⟨Ψ 2083⟩. Differentiation in World Politics—From the European Union to the Global Networks. *Journal of Global Politics*, 14(3), 312–342.

Stavinsky, B. ⟨Ψ 2109⟩. (December 14) Saying Goodbye to a Friend from the Shared Workplace. In Memory of Veronica Eredi, *Vienna Times*.

Williams, P. (2008). *From the New Middle Ages to a New Dark Age: The Decline of the State and U.S. Strategy*. Carlisle: Strategic Studies Institute.

Zielonka, J. (2006). *Europe as Empire: The Nature of Enlarged European Union*. Oxford: Oxford University Press.

Zielonka, J. (2014). *Is the EU Doomed?* Cambridge: Polity Press.

Herman Gorter

Barzun Archive and Research Center, Senior Fellow
Journal of Socio-Cultural Entropy (defunct), Founding Editor

Caution

You are reading an archived version of this researcher's academic blog. The author has since been removed from TruAcademia for repeated violations of democratic truth.

As a TruCheck[TM] Trusted Moderator, you still have access to this author's publications for research purposes. However, the redistribution of any content contained in this file violates the terms of TruAcademia and can result in sanctions.

Herman Gorter: An Introduction to the End of a World

Annette Freyberg-Inan and Alexander van Eijk

1 7 Newtonuary, Year 61 Since the Conference (SC)

TruCheck™: 43

Like most of my generation, I was born in wartime. It has never felt quite right to me, though, to call it war. Of course, the Great Upheaval was not a war in the traditional sense. There were no clear frontlines, no state-controlled armies, no stable governments to rally behind or revolt against. It was wartime without the structure of war. Unguided, near-total destruction.

By the time I was born, my parents had already fled three times. When I turned six, we were forced to pack what little we had into our worn-out trollies again. No matter where we landed, the same story unfolded. When the fighting neared whichever town we found ourselves in, the orchards and fields became battlegrounds, until there was nothing to put on our bread and, eventually, no bread. Factories and workshops became barracks or outposts; stockpiles were pillaged by whoever's militias got there first. The town was starved out and abandoned. After roaming for weeks, we would find another

---

A. Freyberg-Inan (✉)
University of Amsterdam, Amsterdam, The Netherlands
e-mail: A.FreybergInan@uva.nl

A. van Eijk
Amsterdam, The Netherlands

© The Author(s), under exclusive license to Springer Nature Switzerland AG 2023
L. Horn et al. (eds.), *The Palgrave Handbook of Global Politics in the 22nd Century*, https://doi.org/10.1007/978-3-031-13722-8_5

town to settle in, far enough from the fighting, until some local tyrant would raise their own brand of hell-on-earth. I remember quite clearly our three months in Rostock. I was nine. Unable to afford the self-appointed border guard's passage fee, we were separated until my father had worked long enough at gunpoint to pay our dues. And yet, my story is one of the few lucky ones—simply because I am able to tell it.

Why am I dwelling on this long-gone misery? Perhaps I am feeling more acutely now than when I was younger that I am one of the last few able to tell these stories. The world moves on, and humanity's attention cannot hold on to all that has passed. Time's healing of wounds leaves behind ugly scars. But scar tissue is unable to tell its own story, it only hints at some distant and preferably forgotten terror. Like a soldier who can no longer remember exactly which battle or whose bullet is responsible for each scar on their war-torn body, our civilisation today is likely to forget how all humanity was plunged into bloodshed. Of course, the Great Upheaval is written into our textbooks, and students the world over know its general trajectory—even sixty years after the Universal Armistice and the Global Conference. School examinations test whether we can remember the date when this faction took over that town, or when this group made peace with that group, but how much about the Upheaval's causes will still be understood—truly understood—fifty years from now?

No, humanity's attention-span is too short to properly learn from its mistakes; I have been a historian for too long to think otherwise. This is why I have written the books I have written and why I am now starting this new digital publication. Consider it an old man's last attempt; neither my books nor my lectures have had much impact. Perhaps here, in blog-format, with regularly posted shorter texts and interaction through comments I will finally convince an audience, even if a small one. If I am to have a legacy at all, I would wish for it to be this: to have warned that the deep causes of the Great Upheaval are not extinct but instead likely to reconfigure, to wreak destruction once again. "War? In our time?" The younger generation laughs in disbelief. Yes, if we can know one thing for certain from many centuries of history, it is that humanity's most hideous tradition will never be banned forever.

Comments

Henk Dijksma (TruCheck™: 89) Researcher Emeritus	I understand your concerns. I, too, lived through some of the darkest days of the Upheaval and have often wondered if future generations would repeat our parents' mistakes. Thankfully, though, I have seen that my grandchildren know nothing of "humanity's most hideous tradition", and therefore I believe that the new world we leave behind will not see such suffering again.
Marge Thrace (TruCheck™: 67) Student	Whenever I read or hear those harrowing stories of the Great Upheaval, I just can't wrap my head around why anyone would do these things to their fellow humans. Thank you for sharing your own story, and rest assured that your fears for the future are unfounded. The beastly past will find no fertile ground to re-grow in our peaceful present.

Elysa Singh	Professor Gorter, how nice that you are posting. I remember your
(TrueCheck™: 20)	lectures about the historiography of the twentieth century wars. You
Archivist	taught us about Arnold Toynbee, Feliks Karol Koneczny, and Oswald
	Spengler. Those were the days...

2   HERMAN GORTER | ALL SUNS RISE TO SET

3 Cao, Year 61 SC

Caution

The following post mentions an outdated theory that has been algorithmically disproven and contradicts democratic truth.

The theory of socio-cultural entropy, first introduced in H. Gorter's *The Past, Present and Future of Human Folly* (35 SC), is centred on the false idea that human history necessarily entails the cyclical rise and fall of civilisations. Among the democratically disproven claims it contains is the idea that the Global Conference did not move humanity beyond the terrors of the past and that our current world of peace and prosperity will meet the same violent end as that of the previous era of liberalism.

For more information on how TruCheck™ is removing falsehoods from contemporary research and securing more productive environments for academic discussion, see our guidelines.

TruCheck™: 23

To properly understand the present and, thereby, to know something about what the future will hold, there is no greater repository of insight than the past. This is what has made my last two decades of work at the Barzun Archive and Research Centre so fulfilling. By delving deeply into history, I have come to know of the rise and fall of civilisations long gone[1]—and the more I learn of them, the better I understand our own. This has led me to further refine my theory of socio-cultural entropy. For those unfamiliar with my work, I will take some time here to discuss it.

One name that returns again and again in historiographic and philosophical works from both the twentieth and twenty-first centuries is that of a certain Georg Hegel. It is one of history's many little ironies that their name is not more popularly known today, for in many ways we have all become Hegelians. You might even say that it is to this distant acquaintance, born 293 years before the Global Conference, that we today owe our great material welfare.

---

[1] Jacques Barzun (2001). *From Dawn to Decadence: 1500 to the Present: 500 Years of Western Cultural Life.* Harper Perennial.

64   A. FREYBERG-INAN AND A. VAN EIJK

The world we find ourselves in at present is largely founded on their thought, picked up by the generations of scholars that followed.

Hegel's greatest contribution to the understanding of civilisation, which in many ways inspired my own, is the notion that history can be understood as the ever-fluid unfolding of greater and greater ideas, introduced by Hegel in terms of "the Spirit."

> Spirit is indeed never at rest but always engaged in moving forward. But just as the first breath drawn by a child after its long, quiet nourishment breaks the gradualness of merely quantitative growth – there is a qualitative leap, and the child is born – so likewise the Spirit in its formation matures slowly and quietly into its new shape, dissolving bit by bit the structure of its previous world, whose tottering state is only hinted at by isolated symptoms.[2]

Hegel held that the collective knowledge of humanity has not ceased expanding since the very first inventions and continually drives us to change the world around us. It would be difficult to refute such a claim. From the First Industrial Revolution to the Seventh, our breakthroughs in science, technology and culture have melted old worlds away and brought forth unimaginable progress. The invention of electricity, the introduction of the automobile all the way through to our most recent advances in automated agriculture and regenerative healthcare—the civilisations of days past are dissolved and our ways of living radically altered.

However, Hegelianism does entail one fatal problem. This problem did not start with Hegel, but their work represents its strongest propagation in the modern age. Hegel claims:

> But the *goal* is as necessarily fixed for knowledge as the serial progression; it is the point where knowledge no longer needs to go beyond itself, where Notion corresponds to object and object to Notion.[3]

While Hegel seems to strike the nail on the head so well in their consideration of the fluid movement of history, driven on by human discoveries and hardly observable to anyone living through it, they make the hubristic mistake of supposing that history has an end. And this is a mistake we encounter, unfailingly, at some point in the development of every civilisation of the past, as well as now, once again, in our own.

To better grasp the problem with the idea of history ending, we must delve even deeper into the past: to fourteenth-century Andalucía. Here, a certain Ibn Khaldun wrote a work of great insight, even foresight. Central to this work, the *Muqadimmah*, is a cyclical understanding of political time. To Ibn Khaldun, every ruling dynasty comes to power exactly when it should, when it is most powerful and most deserving of hegemony. Its power is explained in

---

[2] G.W.F. Hegel (1807). *Phenomenology of Spirit*. Private collection.

[3] G.W.F. Hegel (1807). *Phenomenology of Spirit*. Private collection.

terms of *assabiyah*, roughly translatable as group feeling or solidarity, since in order to gain its position it must have been able to rally the necessary support among the right people. Once in power, though, the necessity to maintain *assabiyah* gradually fades and the once-powerful new elite turns into a self-serving rentier class.

> Then, when the ruling dynasty grows senile and no defender arises from among its friends who share in its group feeling, the (new group feeling) takes over and deprives the ruling dynasty of its power, and, thus, obtains complete royal authority.[4]

Within no more than three generations, Ibn Khaldun explains, a ruling clan's energy and force are so weakened that they are replaced by another. Of course, the same fate awaits these new rulers.

Let us add to our distinguished roster of theorists one final name: that of a cultural historian of the last century, Jacques Barzun. Long before any apparent signs of crisis in the late-liberal era, Barzun had taken on that true role of the historian: to understand the seemingly isolated symptoms of history running its course and reveal their connections. After all, the transition from one world to the next, the "qualitative leap," is not something that appears plainly to any observer. As Hegel wrote, the "tottering state [of our current world] is only hinted at by isolated symptoms," and it is the duty of science to bring about an understanding of these symptoms and what they tell us of our role in history's unfolding.

Following a thorough, *longue-durée* study, Barzun defined what it means for a culture to become decadent and argued that in the twentieth century the liberal era had begun to reach this crucial final chapter.

> All that is meant by Decadence is "falling off." It implies in those who live in such a time no loss of energy or talent or moral sense. On the contrary, it is a very active time, full of deep concerns, but peculiarly restless, for it sees no clear lines of advance. The loss it faces is that of Possibility. The forms of art as of life seem exhausted, the stages of development have been run through. Institutions function painfully. Repetition and frustration are the intolerable result.[5]

There are essentially two components of a decadent culture. The first is a false self-confidence that precludes any serious consideration of necessary progress. In Barzun's words, this triumphalist notion is fuelled by the idea that all "stages of development have been run through"[6]—that the end has been reached. Now, this by itself would not have to lead to crisis, if the notion

---

[4] Ibn Khaldun (date unknown, fourteenth century). *Muqaddimah.* Found in Southern Rhine Academy Digital Library.

[5] Barzun (2001). *From Dawn to Decadence*, p. xvi.

[6] Barzun (2001). *From Dawn to Decadence*, p. xvi.

66   A. FREYBERG-INAN AND A. VAN EIJK

were widely shared.[7] But when the second component of cultural stagnation is added, society begins to fall apart. That component is the restlessness of deep concerns. As Barzun wrote, it is a mistake to think of cultural stagnation as entailing mental stagnation. It is rather a period of intense but undirected unrest. Fertile ground, Ibn Khaldun might say, for a hegemony to be overturned.

We might think of ourselves as far beyond the time of tribes and nomads and violent dynastic rivalries, but the force of Ibn Khaldun's analysis extends, as Barzun shows, beyond the desert kingdoms and equally dissects the industrial republics. The feudal lords of the Holy Roman Empire, the merchants of the Ming Dynasty or Golden Age Amsterdam, the financiers of New York's Wall Street or Shanghai's Stock Exchange—each ruling dynasty rose up when it was its time to do so, and was struck down and replaced by the same logic. The same mistake Hegel made, the misguided idea that we can one day reach perfection and end the struggle of history, has instilled in each settled civilisation a premature laziness, an unfounded self-confidence that brings about its own downfall.

This, if a life's work can be summed up in one metaphor, is the essence of my theory of socio-cultural entropy: all suns rise to set. As their fortune rises, a people stand awestruck and staring at their own magnificent sun, slowly burning their collective corneas. The very success of a hegemonic civilisational project—the feudalists' luxury, the capitalists' industry, our own conquest of material need—blinds the unknowing, momentary victors. So caught up in the delusion that what we have achieved is the insurmountable, the pinnacle, the end of history, we lose all sense of the necessity of progress. That is, until history does what it always does and proves that there is yet more to come.

With my TruCheck score only just starting to recover from my previous rejected publications, I am hesitant to go into more detail now. While I stand up against the supposedly apolitical, pseudo-scientific algorithms that so powerfully decide an academic's fate, I must admit that I enjoy some of the luxuries that come with a score just above abysmal. If I am to continue my research, I will require access to this forum and my colleagues. Therefore, I will leave my reader with a poem. Below you can read W.B. Yeats's *The Second Coming*, a work I discovered through Dolomiti's excellent archival studies of Pre-Conference mystic poetry.[8] Trying to capture the essence of their own era, marked by a World War which would soon be relived, Yeats put into beautiful words the process that brings all epochs to an end: entropy and resurrection.

> Turning and turning in the widening gyre
> The falcon cannot hear the falconer;
> Things fall apart; the centre cannot hold;
> Mere anarchy is loosed upon the world,

---

[7] Francis Fukuyama (1992). *The End of History and the Last Man*. Free Press.

[8] Terra Dolomiti (Ψ 32 SC/2095). *Mystics and Mad-hatters: An Overview of Pre-Conference Esoteric Literature*. Caribbean Federation of Academic Publishers.

The blood-dimmed tide is loosed, and everywhere
The ceremony of innocence is drowned;
The best lack all conviction, while the worst
Are full of passionate intensity.

Surely some revelation is at hand;
Surely the Second Coming is at hand.
The Second Coming! Hardly are those words out
When a vast image out of *Spiritus Mundi*
Troubles my sight: somewhere in sands of the desert
A shape with lion body and the head of a man,
A gaze blank and pitiless as the sun,
Is moving its slow thighs, while all about it
Reel shadows of the indignant desert birds.
The darkness drops again; but now I know
That twenty centuries of stony sleep
Were vexed to nightmare by a rocking cradle,
And what rough beast, its hour come round at last,
Slouches towards Bethlehem to be born?

Comments

Alexander Yves (TruCheck™: 88) Literary Translator	Ah, a beautiful poem by Yeats indeed. Really brings out the dastardliness and sense of impending doom that must have occupied every intelligent person of the early twentieth century. Also worth reading is Eliot's *Wasteland*: "He who was living is now dead // We who were living are now dying."
Herman Gorter (TruCheck™: 23) Senior Fellow	I think you are making a common mistake. For the most part, we can only peer into the minds of the past through the writings they leave behind, but we must not allow ourselves to make broad judgements based on the works of a few insightful individuals. While many poems reveal an awareness of the fragility of liberal civilisation, these are vastly outweighed by cultural productions that seems blissfully unaware: television shows celebrating friendships and happy homes, movies that inspire hope, etc. It does not seem at all like the average citizen of the liberal epoch could really imagine their civilisation coming to a violent end.
Karel Rojas (TruCheck™: 72) Regional Secretary for Transportation	Your deep references to the past and revival of long-forgotten names are interesting and make for good reading. But honestly, what can we truly expect to learn from these long-gone lives? What can a man who lived before the invention of the inter-continental shuttle really tell me about my life today?

Penelope Bruynsma (TruCheck™: 84) Educational Consultant	"To properly understand the present and, thereby, to know something about what the future will hold, there is no greater repository of insight than the past." I must disagree. If we are to move forward, we must look forward. The failures of the past must be left behind in the past—our civilisation has progressed beyond our ancestors' mistakes and there is nothing more they can teach us.

3   HERMAN GORTER | INFANTILE SCHOLARS
29 Archimederia, Year 61 SC

TruCheck™: 2

If the theoretical remarks I have made in this series of posts so far seem strange or incomprehensible, it is because contemporary academia has been plagued for decades by infantile scholars and their self-confident ideology. To these hubristic optimists, history is a narrative of progressive development that concludes in our time—"the fulfilment of humanity,"[9] as my misguided colleagues call it. In the echo-chamber of the contemporary academy, to say or think anything else is blasphemy. As a result, the contrary narratives and open discussion that are needed to arrive at real truth are self-censored and never emerge.

By far the strongest mechanism of control that keeps discussion at bay is the so-called TruCheck score that has so hindered my own career lately. Since its global introduction in 40 SC, my complaints about this fact-checking algorithm have fallen on deaf ears. After all, they say, the algorithm merely compares the statements in whatever one has written to all other published texts on that subject. As its inventors claim, TruCheck is founded on the ideal of an apolitical and unbiased democratic truth.[10] But how can such an algorithm ever arrive at truth if its reference material is faulty? If I disagree with what has previously been written, does that mean I am wrong? If I really need to point out the decadent stifling of innovation implied by such an algorithm, I suppose it has already done its job too well.

Most readers will be too young to remember, but this was not always the way academia assured the quality of its output. In fact, for most of academic history, scientific work was valued through a system of peer review. This process was one of the oldest traditions of intellectual production; the first reference we have to it comes from a book on medical ethics from the ninth century (old calendar). In their *Ethics of the Physician*, the Arab medical doctor

---

[9] Mahatma Polley et al. (Ψ 23 SC/2086). *The Fulfilment of Humanity: Our Treacherous Journey to Salvation*. SpringerWeb.

[10] General Secretariat for Academic Affairs (Ψ 31 SC/2094). *The Foundations of Democratic Truth*. The Conference Press.

al-Ruhawi lays out that if a patient is to be declared cured, the treating physician must prepare their notes in duplicate so that another physician may look over the treatment and confirm the declared outcome.[11] In this vein, for centuries, scholars wanting to publish any of their work had to first submit it for review by one or more of their academic peers on the subject. In practice, these processes were not always perfect, sometimes corruptible and sometimes overly complex and resource-intensive. At the very least, though, the process of peer review implied a culture that was willing to discuss differing opinions and understood the value of considering an academic work on its own merit. With the introduction of the algorithmic review, all that is lost. With TruCheck, we have given up on the spirit of academic collaboration and have outsourced truth-finding to a machine.

Of course, algorithms are not in and of themselves problematic. The problem is that they perpetuate whatever biases their inventors bring with them, knowingly or otherwise. Take, for example, one of the worst results of this contemporary academic ideology: Rochelle Gupta's *The Human Project: From the Cave to the Conference*. I presume I will not need to provide more than a basic summary of the book. It is compulsory reading in practically every curriculum and one of but a handful of publications with the maximum TruCheck score of 100. The aim of the book is to provide a grand historical narrative of humanity from the time of Neanderthal cave-dwellers to the first Global Conference. It is the kind of work I would normally celebrate: *longue-durée*, ambitious and wide in its scope. Unfortunately, the book is held together by Gupta's constant reference to Plato's allegory of the cave, a rather uncompelling metaphor around which they structured the entire history of humanity.

> No longer fixated and bewildered by mere shadows and reflections on the wall, our cave-dwellers one day braved the world behind the rocks. With tiny steps at first and then huge leaping strides, our heroes freed themselves from their previous lives in the dark and entered a new realm, the realm of truth. So, too, humanity emerged from the cave of undeveloped and uncivilised life after countless millennia of existence with unnecessary suffering, grief, and hatred. We cannot possibly imagine such lives now, and we shall never again need to, in the Paradise-on-Earth we have built for ourselves. To those who braved the first steps for us, we owe a great debt of gratitude.[12]

This is what my work is algorithmically compared against, yet somehow, I am revealed the sophist! We have had a mere sixty years of peace, a meaningless interval on history's watch. How different from our predecessors could we possibly have become in one lifetime? Our so-called democratic truth is no

---

[11] Al-Ruhawi (Date unknown, 9th Century). *Ethics of the Physician*. Found in Library of Medical Ethics, Athens (discontinued).

[12] Rochelle Gupta ⟨Ψ 47 SC/2110⟩. *The Human Project: From the Cave to the Conference*. Association of World-Historians Press.

70 A. FREYBERG-INAN AND A. VAN EIJK

more than a starry-eyed illusion, a self-confident self-deceit. If anyone is still living in the cave of ignorance, fixated on reflections of pseudo-truth, it is Gupta and all those academics who wear their TruCheck scores like badges of honour.

Comments

Mohammad Moustakas (TruCheck™: 83) Agricultural Mechanic	I am having trouble understanding your fears of the algorithm. For example, in the quote you reference above, I see no reason to disagree with Gupta and find only an algorithm working correctly. It is undeniably true that our lives are better than those of past generations and even more true that we could not imagine living otherwise now. Gupta's work is rightly rewarded as being correct, and I see no reason why this example you chose should make me distrust TruCheck™.
Herman Gorter (TruCheck™: 2) Senior Fellow	My problems with Gupta's work, and that of modern historians more generally, are too encompassing to be discussed in one comment, so I will focus on explaining my distrust of TruCheck more clearly. Under the peer-review process, if I disagreed vehemently with your work, I at least had to provide you and an editor with some explanation as to why I found it unfit for publication. Regardless of what you or I think about Gupta's work, if it is accepted under the algorithmic system, it becomes truth. All future statements are blindly tested against this truth and any disagreement is marked as incorrect. Surely, this is not science? This is a collective surrender to prevailing opinion.
Anton Raj (TruCheck™: 89) Publisher	That peer-review system sounds like a ridiculous waste of time.
Layla Ernst (TruCheck™: 92) Researcher	To call contemporary academia an echo-chamber ignores the great variety of modern scholarly debate. Even just last week, at a conference in the Friedhof Academy, we spent hours in heated debate. My colleagues and I were split on the issue of whether work-related satisfaction is best measured through neural scanning or questionnaires. This is hardly an environment afraid of discussing diverse ideas!

4 HERMAN GORTER | THE CEREMONY OF INNOCENCE IS DROWNED

1 Balogunary, Year 62 SC

TruCheck™: 13

The central point I want to get across is this: history has a tendency, uninterrupted through millennia, to repeat itself. Every great civilisation of the past thought of itself as the completed ideal of humanity, and each and every one exists now only through remnants displayed in archaeological museums or stored in dusty archives. Going back as far in recorded history as we can, we see a surprisingly sophisticated awareness of this civilisational hubris in Herodotus's *Histories*.

> If anyone, no matter who, were given the opportunity of choosing from amongst all the nations in the world the set of beliefs which he [sic] thought best, he [sic] would inevitably—after careful considerations of their relative merits—choose that of his [sic] own country. Everyone without exception believes his [sic] own native customs, and the religion he [sic] was brought up in, to be the best.[13]

This hubris affects comparisons across time as well as across space. Even Herodotus themselves, and within the very same text, refers only to their own polis by name and to all others simply as barbarians—they, too, could not escape the intoxication of success that came with the rise of Athens. Of course, we know now that Athenian democracy would fall, that the Roman Empire would split apart, that the Ottomans would be defeated, the Habsburgs, the Nazis, and so on and so on, all the way to the end of the Liberal Alliance along with the Sino-Russian Block.

Let us look at that most recently fallen civilisation: the liberal era. My parents lived through the liberals' final decades and suffered their violent end. To readers today, this time will at least be known from stories told by grandparents. People we know, people we love—not nearly as distant as Herodotus.

To properly understand the final century of the liberal era, the period we call late-liberalism, we can ask for no better guide than Barzun. Their definition of decadence, quoted in an earlier post in this series, grants us a clear view into the soul of this time. Drawing on it, we can say that decadence is defined by a loss of Possibility. Grave concerns exist among the people who live through an age of stagnation, but they find themselves at a loss to do anything with these concerns—all lines of advance have been closed off.

Before the Great Upheaval it had been all but forgotten that liberalism had arisen centuries before as a *revolutionary* social theory. For 200 years, the liberal principles of human equality and freedom from tyranny inspired some of the most beneficent developments in modern history. Centuries-old monarchies were overthrown, masses of long-ignored voices gained a hearing, and unprecedented opportunities became available to social classes that had never even been able to dream of progress before.

Just under a century before liberalism's violent collapse, however, its revolutionary spirit was lying in its final convulsions. In the decade of the 1960s on the old calendar, social movements the world over were agitating and taking to the streets: great anti-colonial revolts, western youth taking to the streets against the Vietnam War and atomic weaponry, US-Americans of colour marching against racism and French workers and students occupying institutions all over the country. After this brief moment of progressive fervour, however, the revolutionary spirit quickly waned. The Hippies had not succeeded in ending imperialist wars, the anti-racist movement in the US was

---

[13] Herodotus (Date unknown, 5th Century BC). *Histories*. Found in The Progress Institute's Archive of World History.

appeased with the Civil Rights Act and the French Communists were defeated by a decisive Gaullist electoral triumph. A particularly bitter defeat was laid out for the Marxist anti-capitalists, whose prophecies of a revolutionary proletariat that would usher in a new world seemed decisively disproven.

Henceforth, anyone who wanted to do anything, politically, with their concerns found themselves hitting a brick wall of cynicism and arrogance: arrogance from liberal institutions, assured of being the pinnacle of human achievement and seeing no reason to listen to cries for change; cynicism from fellow citizens who, paralysed by disillusionment and inefficacy found themselves unable to forge progressive alliances. One of the few remaining Marxist philosophers, Slavoj Žižek, wrote at the time that late-liberal citizens resembled those of the classic fairy tale about the Emperor's New Clothes: late-liberal citizens all knew that the emperor was naked yet continued "going on as if the emperor ha[d] his [sic] clothes on."[14] Together, the twin pathologies of arrogance and cynicism meant that, in the face of acute threats to human welfare, progress was both unthinkable and unachievable. "Repetition and frustration [we]re the intolerable result."[15]

Just as Ibn Khaldun laid out centuries earlier in the *Muqadimmah*, the ruling elite had completely detached itself from the populace, barely requiring their support. *Assabiyah* waned. The result was a liberalism unchained; a force undeterred—"neo-liberalism," as they called it. The abuses of power, the wonton disrespect of anything and anyone by the capitalists in those days was truly shocking. Corporate leaders lost any sense of responsibility, displaying their affluence unashamedly in the face of mass poverty. Ridiculous amounts of money went, for example, to fund the space-travel adventures of immature billionaires, paid for by income generated by their hordes of underpaid employees.

Politicians also had no reason to take an active interest in the electorate. A defining trait of neo-liberal governance was an unwillingness to provide public benefits and a deep suspicion of anyone who required financial aid. Take, for example, the child benefits scandal of the early 2020s in the Netherlands, a small state along the old north-western shoreline of continental Europe. Here, the neo-liberal institutional culture led to an aggressive campaign of falsely accusing households of committing benefits fraud. Thousands of families, particularly migrant families, as they were the easiest to target and least likely to seek legal assistance, found themselves in unmanageable debt to the tax office. From one day to the next, victimised households owed on average just under a normal worker's yearly salary—to be repaid without delay. Lives were ruined wholesale, and relief or redemption for these families remained partial even after years of public pressure. An unimaginable cruelty—yet the politicians and the parties responsible won re-election the very same year the

[14] Slavoj Žižek (n.d.). "Ideology II: Competition is a Sin", https://www.lacan.com/ziz desolationroad.html.

[15] Barzun (2001). *From Dawn to Decadence*, p. xvi.

news had broken. In the neo-liberal climate, where one could get away with squeezing every last penny out of a struggling mother, why would a self-interested politician ever try to change anything? Even in the US, once an energetic driving force for liberalism in the world, elite turnovers could no longer bring any meaningful change.

As we now know, it was only a matter of time until a devastating crisis would reveal the unsustainability of late-liberalism. Its promises of endless growth and constantly rising standards of living for all had to be revealed as fallacies sooner or later. Drawing on the psychoanalyst Jacques Lacan, Žižek pointed out that

> [...] (what we experience as) reality is not the 'thing itself', it is always-already symbolized, constituted, structured by symbolic mechanisms – and the problem resides in the fact that symbolization ultimately always fails, that it never succeeds in fully 'covering' the real, that it always involves some unsettled, unredeemed symbolic debt.[16]

Neo-liberal ideology incapacitated the truth that neo-liberalism did not work in the interest of its citizens, that human life could be better, more fulfilling and, most importantly, less unjust. On the one hand, this truth could be freely expressed—and was expressed at the time by many critics, ranging from Christians to anarchists to ecologists. On the other hand, the operation of ideology ensured that for the late-liberal subjects, there was no "real" in which an alternative possibility existed. As a result, their recognition of this truth remained suppressed, present but subconscious, feeding anger.

In liberalism's age of decay, there were no channels left open to receive frustration—no political opportunities for even the smallest steps towards change. Finding no outlet in the realm of conventional politics, the late-liberal multitude of "singularities acting together"[17] grew restless and increasingly angry. With nowhere to turn, it would not take long for political landscapes the world over to shift and power transitions to spread—haphazardly, opportunistically, violently. In all its decadence, amidst the vast meaninglessness of its politics, neo-liberalism had no more soothing narratives to offer its suffering citizens and gave way to ideological and material chaos.

The vacuum of meaning created by years of liberal decadence proved ample breeding ground for fundamentalisms of all kinds. The groups that rose up in the confusion were countless. The factions ranged from the plainly violent to the genuinely emancipatory, from futurisms to conservatisms; but in the preparation for revolution, the peaceful always give way to the violent. Some texts

---

[16] Slavoj Žižek (1994). *Mapping Ideology*. London: Verso, p. 21.

[17] Michael Hardt and Antonio Negri (2004). *Multitude: Krieg und Demokratie im Empire*. Frankfurt: Campus, p. 123. Hardt and Negri were naively optimistic at the time, believing that "the multitude" could bring about positive change.

74 A. FREYBERG-INAN AND A. van EIJK

of the time, like the long-banned *Blood and Borders*,[18] highlight the importance of revived nativism; other surviving texts blame a growing quasi-religious fanaticism for the rising chaos.[19] But exactly who or what was the primary cause of the violence that followed has not been definitively concluded, nor do contemporary researchers seem interested enough in the past to find out.

And so, one fateful day—where and when precisely remains unknown—the fighting started. The dispersed and initially repressed nature of these first clashes was such that they eluded most historical record-keeping. Perhaps the first bullet was fired by a hungry father, recently laid off from both of their part-time jobs. Or perhaps the first skull was crushed by a private security guard, too eager to follow their employer's orders to keep the rabble out of their summer home. A wave of anger, following the realisation that the neo-liberal system would not budge an inch to help them, slowly spread throughout the citizenry. The police and military that held the hungry masses away from hoarded resources were denounced as enemies of the people, the politicians that attempted to sway protestors in various directions received death threats, and businesses and banks could only continue to operate with massively heightened security. By the late 2030s on the old calendar, terrorism, looting and destruction of property became rampant. Anything and anyone that stood in any relation to power and "the old world" was stripped of all authority and, often brutally, dethroned. The world sank into chaos.

Comments

Hylke Papandreos
(TruCheck™: 74)
Researcher

What is this obsession of yours with the past? Since the Conference, over 60 years ago, we haven't had a need for all these "theorists" and "philosophers" you so relentlessly reference. Sure, the neo-liberal age of oppressive governance and daily injustice ought to have listened more to these theorists of yours, but all *our* society needs are simple, hard-working researchers.

---

[18] Paul Ashworth ⟨Ψ 2031⟩. *Blood and Borders*. The Great British Press.

[19] For a good discussion of the role of religion in the collapse of twenty-first century liberalism, I would recommend Marc Keru's *The Death of Reason in the 21st Century* and Rohan Pleasant's *Insipid Fundamentalism: Religion's Re-conquest of Liberal Politics.*

HERMAN GORTER: AN INTRODUCTION TO THE END OF A WORLD — 75

José Hidayat
(TruCheck™: 78)
Industrial Consultant

The primary problem I see in all these historical civilisations that have come and gone is this: each previous society has existed as a system that serves the few and pacifies the many. Progress from one era to the next has always merely meant exchanging or expanding the incorporated few at the greater expense of the remaining many. The Athenian citizenry was tiny, compared to the mass of non-voters (slaves, women, etc.). By the time of the liberal era, those that benefitted directly from the system had expanded greatly in number, but were still a minority worldwide. This is the real fatal flaw of previous civilisations, and it is one we have since overcome. By putting science and technology to proper social use globally, the benefits of our system are not captured by any elite but are shared broadly. In this way, our civilisation has managed to avoid the fate of history and will continue doing so.

Kofi Grant
(TruCheck™: 38)
Student

How could the powerful of the past get away with such barbarian abuses of power? How come they were not stopped?

Zenadine Park
(TruCheck™: 68)
Regional Integration Engineer

The hardship you experienced as a boy was real, and I feel deeply sorry for you. Yet, your account of the Great Upheaval seems to me distorted to support your theory. I studied under some of the last scholars in the old field of International Relations, and there I learned that the Liberal order collapsed due to the challenge from the rival Sino-Soviet block and the resulting trade wars. While it is true that the liberal elites at the time failed to see this coming, their blindness is not causally responsible for the Upheaval.

Herman Gorter
(TruCheck™: 13)
Senior Fellow

You are not wrong. The collapse of the liberal hegemony knew its own, unique triggers of collapse, and those your best teachers could recognise after the fact. Yet, those in power at the time, on both sides, were blind to the tragic truth inherent to all civilizational projects: that a grave is always being dug for them—no matter how unique or unexpected the specific triggers seem. Had they not been blind, perhaps catastrophe could have been avoided

Kevin Plutonic
(TruCheck™: 19)
Musician

Catastrophe?! Are you calling it a catastrophe that humanity was able to leave behind a world divided into nation-states and torn by conflict? That we could form the Global Federation, and now all regions work together to eradicate poverty and repair the planet? You have got to be joking!

5   HERMAN GORTER | ON TIME, NARRATIVES, AND HEGEMONY

3 Basudia, Year 62 SC

TruCheck™: 2

It has been a pleasant surprise to see so much interaction with my work here in this series of posts. You will have to forgive me if I do not always respond. I have grown somewhat unaccustomed to discussion since I was expelled from the university and retreated to the Barzun Center. There is, however, one comment in particular, posted by José Hidayat, that has stuck with me over the past few days and that I want to engage with in more detail.

> The primary problem I see in all these historical civilisations that have come and gone is this: each previous society has existed as a system that serves the few and pacifies the many. Progress from one era to the next has always merely meant exchanging or expanding the incorporated few at the greater expense of the remaining many.

This analysis is astute, and I am inclined to agree. From the Athenian democracies to the desert kingdoms and feudal dominions, all the way through to the merchant republics and the liberal state system, we can see this logic unfold. These were all systems that benefitted a growing minority at the cost of a shrinking majority. Even at the pinnacle of liberal global integration, the majority of humans globally lived in hardship to create value for the rich, at home and abroad. I have pointed out before that this helped trigger the violent decline of the previous civilisation, so it is an important point. Unfortunately, Hidayat then goes on to make the very mistake that I have spent decades of my career, including all of these digital posts, trying to correct.

> By putting science and technology to proper social use, the benefits of our system are not captured by any elite but are shared broadly. In this way, our civilisation has managed to avoid the fate of history and will continue doing so.

I cannot blame Hidayat personally for making this mistake. As all my past work has shown, it is a mistake made by great minds of every generation. The omnipresence of this belief, that one's own civilisation is in some way ahead of the curve, or breaking the chain, indicates that it might even be at the foundation of human life. To explain this, allow me to dig once more into our understanding of history and ask: why do we think in linear, teleological time?

...

A narrative cannot exist without the passing of time; events must unfold over connected moments for a story to be told. So inseparable are the two that throughout most of human history we have demanded that the reverse be true as well. That is to say, to the rather easily confused human mind, time cannot pass without a narrative.

Confronted with the baffling nature of time, the seeming meaninglessness of its passing, the Church Father Augustine of Hippo composed the standard answer that would be repeated, in many different forms, from the fifth century (old calendar) to our own Post-Conference age:

> What, then, is time? I know well enough what it is, provided that nobody asks me; but if I am asked what it is and try to explain, I am baffled. All the same I can confidently say that I know that if nothing passed, there would be no past time; if nothing were going to happen, there would be no future time; and if nothing *were*, there would be no present time.[20]

To a people so unaccustomed to religion as our own, it is worth looking more closely at the Christian idea of time. While it should be noted that no singular truth ever existed either across or within the religions of the past, as reflected in the rivers of blood spilt over meaningless disputes, we can suggest that, generally, in the Christian imagination time was an essential characteristic of material life. Its inescapable passing could be noted in the movement of celestial bodies or in the slow deterioration of human ones. Of much more interest to the Christians, however, was the negation of time: the eternal afterlife. How one should imagine such non-time I recently discovered in a story preserved in the Delusion and Fanaticism Section of the Ibn Al-Rawandi Archive of Religious Ideology. According to the story, an old monk wandered out of their monastery, drawn by the beautiful singing of a chirping bird. Once the bird had ceased its harmony and the monk returned, they found that they could not recognise any of the other monks in the monastery. Immediately the old monk asked for the abbot and was presented again with a man they had never met before. It was only after much confusing discussion that one of the younger scribes decided to consult the records and discovered that the old monk had been recorded missing more than three centuries earlier.

The point of this story is that the monk had experienced a moment of the eternal afterlife. Fully immersed in the bird's beauty and harmonious song, the monk escaped the passing of time and was granted a small taste of the blissful eternity awaiting after a worthy life. This is the narrative presented by the Christian faith: time started when the Lord gave shape to the material world, and it will end when He [sic] chooses to take us out of this realm again. In other words, time is moving relentlessly onwards to a determined end when all progress will be complete, when time will stand still, and history will be completed. This is true for each individual as well as for humanity as a whole, whose life on earth will end with the Second Coming.

What makes the Augustinian grappling with the definition of time, quoted earlier, so striking is its rather frank admission of unknowing that yet miraculously resolves into confidence. The Church Father admits that time is very difficult to comprehend, baffling even, and yet, Augustine can "confidently"

---

[20] St. Augustine (Date unknown, 5th Century). *The Confessions*. Private collection.

tell us what it is. Precisely this confidence, or rather self-confidence, regarding the passing of time is central to the whole history of civilisation; it lies at the foundation of practically all human societies.

In my earlier discussion of Hegel, I explained that this teleology, the faith in the directionality of time, was propagated through history. While vast centuries stand between them, Augustine and Hegel have essentially the same notion of time: its passing is inescapable, yet one day it will end in the blissful resolution of history. The only substantive contribution of the modern view is that the eternal bliss is brought into the material world, as opposed to existing only in some invisible realm outside of human life.

So why must we think in linear time, why are we incapable of uncoupling time and narrative? There are essentially two reasons. First, as Augustine readily admitted, time is baffling. In the same vein as ancient myths portraying Sun-gods and Earth Mothers, we must tell ourselves *something* to make sense of this dimension of our world. Second, advocating the passing of time towards a determined end can be instrumental, as it helps us to justify our variously unfair positions in the world. This is reflected most directly in the early Christian notion of supersession, or the idea that, to paraphrase St. Ambrose of Milan, the Jews were in the shade and the Christians in the Sun—that the Christian faith was the next step towards salvation and that the downtrodden peoples of different convictions could rightfully be abandoned or even brutalised. In Hegel we see the same justification of group hegemony in comments concluding that the "supreme duty is to be a member of the state" and to love this body of bourgeois rule with genuine gratitude and patriotism because it is the culmination of human achievement. The notion of linear time can serve the legitimation of mastery over others, as it can provide an explanation of one's dominance as being "willed" by history, as serving the "march of time."

This is true also of our own age. Returning to Hidayat's comment, with our current order we have indeed massively expanded the pool of humans that benefit. As the slogan goes: "we have conquered material want, our politics are global, our emancipation is total." But has there truly been a qualitative shift away from the dilemma that if someone feels a winner, another always loses? For example, ask the now-futile agriculturists how glad they are that they have outlived their occupation's necessity. Their knowledge of working the land and tending to the flocks was passed down to them for countless generations. Ask them how glad they are that their care work has been replaced by genetic and agricultural engineering. Or ask the critical theorists, like myself, who have been marginalised out of the academy, how we benefitted from the global regime; how fortunate we feel to have our work stifled in the name of "democratic truth." Yes, even in this paradise, there are miserable people!

Like the liberal capitalists before us, we are so intoxicated by our own successes that we risk ignoring the harm we do to others, who have doubts about what we perceive as progress and ask for deeper change. It is precisely this moment—when a once-revolutionary movement stops listening to its detractors, when it compartmentalises the suffering that supports its power—that a civilisation has taken its last step forward. Among the crowds on every shuttle and in the audiences of every holotheatre, there are probably disgruntled citizens with latent resentments. We must not allow civilisational overconfidence to deafen us to their silent voices.

In Hindu cosmology, the world is said to be cyclically progressing through four stages. First comes the Satya Yuga, a time of peace and welfare. In this golden age, the symbolic bull of dharma, or virtue, stands securely on all four of its feet. After a while, the bull loses its footing and balances only on three hooves, ushering in the Treta Yuga. Now, sin enters the stage and proud worldly masters claim their material share of worldly territory and resources. Once misery is introduced in the third stage, the Dvapara Yuga, the bull stands on only two of its legs, and it does not take long until the Kali Yuga commences and the world is enveloped in strife. But the bull always finds its feet again as the cycle returns to its starting point, and much of the previous troubles are forgotten.

The Hindus and their Yuga Cycles are perhaps the closest humanity has ever come to an understanding of political time. All suns rise to set; once the wick has been lit, a civilisation's candle slowly burns down, eventually setting the house on fire. But this is not the end of the world, it is merely the end of *a* world. There is always some next beast slouching towards Bethlehem, waiting to be born.

Comments

Roisin Singh
(TruCheck™: 93)
Industrial Consultant

What Luddite nonsense. What are we to do, return to the miserable past, so that some romantic agriculturists can continue their backwards traditions in peace? Next, you'll advocate the lunatic rituals of the Temple of Earthen Plenty! Luckily your TruCheck™ score will lead any reasonable person to read your opinions with the necessary incredulity.

Herman Gorter
(TruCheck™: 0)
Senior Fellow

My point is not to defend any particular group, and I certainly can't see myself amongst the neo-mystics of the Temple. That being said, your inability to empathise even to the slightest degree with their search for alternative meaning is yet more evidence of our time's growing decadence.

Howard Morillo
(TruCheck™: 67)
Student

Clearly, you think something must be done to prevent a second Great Upheaval, but you neglect to present any advice. What can be done to break out of this gloomy fate you lay out for us?

Herman Gorter
(TruCheck™: 0)
Senior Fellow

I do not know if we can, because thinking of ourselves as superior to our liberal forebears is itself part of the problem, and superior we would have to be to know before it is too late. Are we more watchful, less arrogant? Are we capable of immanent critique? The biggest mistake we can make is to think that we have "made it". History never stops, it merely lulls us temporarily, and the human project can never lay still for long without a high price to pay. Awareness of this truth is no guarantee for success, but a lack of it guarantees failure.

Themes: *(In)Security*

Strategic Partnerships in Twenty-Second Century Global Politics: From Weathering Storms to the Politics of Anticipation

Andriy Tyushka and Lucyna Czechowska

1 Introduction: A Bicentenary Anniversary of 'International Relations' and the Renaissance of Strategic Partnerships

As the discipline of Interfacial Relations, known in the past century as 'Inter*national* Relations', celebrates its bitter-sweet bicentenary anniversary this year, there is much less reason for pessimism which came to define much of the pre-World Wreck era scholarship (see, for instance, Stevens and Michelsen 2019). An integrated structural characteristic of the interfacial system we live in, cooperation had not always been a default option to guide actors' interactions, as this chapter illustrates. In fact, international cooperation had long been seen as an alien to global politics and order—a sporadic and short-lived exception to the 'natural' state of affairs, that is, conflict. However, with the proliferation of local and global wars up until mid-twenty-first century, i.e. when the World Wreck mishappened, the essence and meaning of 'cooperation' underwent some transformation. From a negatively conceived feature

A. Tyushka (✉)
College of Europe, Warsaw, Poland
e-mail: andriy.tyushka@coleurope.eu

L. Czechowska
Department of European Studies, Nicolaus Copernicus
University, Toruń, Poland
e-mail: czechowska@umk.pl

© The Author(s), under exclusive license to Springer Nature
Switzerland AG 2023
L. Horn et al. (eds.), *The Palgrave Handbook of Global Politics in the 22nd Century*, https://doi.org/10.1007/978-3-031-13722-8_6

of nineteenth and twentieth century international relations, cooperation came to present a positive feature of the early twenty-first century order and has turned into an absolutely intrinsic fabric of our—twenty-second century—multiverse. This paradigm shift was anything but quick and easy, preconceived and planned—it was more of a bitter lesson that had to be drawn in order to secure the survival of us all on Earth, in water and outer space.

Grounded in shared goals-driven cooperation, the notion of 'strategic partnerships' (SPs), too, has seen many transformations throughout the past three centuries. Born as a form of flexible and ad hoc cooperation between states, it complemented the web of alliances that defined much of global politics in the twentieth century. With International Organizations (IOs) embracing strategic partnerships as a form of structuring their relations with third states and other organizations, the idea of strategic partnerships was rediscovered as an organizing principle of international life throughout the first half of twenty-first century, up until—together with all other ideas of the old-world order—it crashed against the realities of the World Wreck. In our-age interfacial relations, the idea of strategic partnerships experiences its renaissance, as do some other revalued concepts from the past century. It now comes to denote the rationale of sustainable strategic interconnections between actors of distinct interfaces ('n-interface actors') including 'city-states', 'global organizations', 'global humans', as well as networks and coalitions of human, transhuman and post-human minds.

This chapter first explores how we arrived at current singularity and how, out of many futures our predecessors had been able to choose from, they rolled down a no-good-future path. It, then, analyses the changing realities of global politics that determined the operation of strategic partnerships for the past three (nineteenth to twenty-first) centuries. Furthermore, it ponders on the rediscovered relevance of this idea for our-age realities of enhanced interdependence, augmented humankind[1] and fast-forward politics of modulation and anticipation. In what follows, this introduction also briefly surveys the evolution of the old-new concept of 'strategic partnerships' up until 2119.

The rampant proliferation of strategic partnerships across the globe since the turn of the twentieth and especially twenty-first centuries has rendered them the 'new normal' in International Relations and Global Politics. Beforehand, the strategic partnerships scholarship had traditionally been thriving in the business and economics literature, wherefrom the notion originates. In political science scholarship, some early theoretical elaborations on the nature and meaning of the concept were authored by an aspiring team of emerging Polish and Ukrainian scholars, whose countries of origin had long been grappling with the idea of strategic partnerships as a remedy to their

---

[1] The present authors are representatives of the first generation of 'augments'—a daring experiment of Estonian idea and tech-entrepreneurs from the year 2037 who sought to enable a smooth transition of humankind from physical to quantum ontology. On the origins of unified physical and social ontologies and the 'quantum man', see: Wendt (2015).

peculiar constellation of deep strategic insecurity for much of the nineteenth and twentieth centuries (Czechowska et al. 2019). The realist-constructivist epistemological framework that they developed for the analysis of the early-twenty-first century SPs soon found its resonance among other collaborating academics, chiefly from Central and Eastern Europe, that further developed the empirical base and the model of SPs formed by states and IOs (Neugierescu et al. Ψ 2027). This strand of research gave a solid boost to European Political Science that, after the euphoric moment of the appearance of Ian Manners' 'Normative Power Europe' in 2002, had again been experiencing prostration and suppression by American Political Science. The mid-twenty-first century brought this research avenue, just as all other then-prevailing strands of thought, to a halt: first the *Climate Crunch (CC)* and then the *World Wreck War (WWW)* cancelled the future, nullifying the human-dominated old world and all the wisdoms and unwisdoms worshipped by then. It was not until late twenty-first century when our 'brave new world' got re-founded, and with it, our new principles of organizing interfacial life emerged. These principles define essentially all spheres of our activities, including the global interconnections that the discipline of Interfacial Relations (I/F R) seeks to explain. One of its central paradigms is that of 'cooperation and competition' (aka '*coopetition*'), upon which the rediscovered notion of strategic partnerships now rests.

Thus, based on the world-systemic possibilities and constraints, strategic partnerships had first been forged nearly exclusively among states, as additives and, later on, alternatives to alliances (twentieth century); then, SPs extended to include IOs as well (twenty-first century), and now they include, among strategic partners, also city-states, global organizations (GOs), global humans (GHs), large and influential corporate actors as well as networks and coalitions of various sorts (the so-called '*n*-interface' actors). The partner selection patterns, too, evolved. Whereas in the early stages of twentieth-century partnership politics, material and hard-power capabilities mattered, ideational (normative) and soft power appealed as partner selection criteria in the early twenty-first century. With the digitally and biotechnologically augmented reality that the opening of the cyber world brought to IR mid-twenty-first century (Kissinger et al. 2021), algorithmic power has endowed a much broader and qualitatively new set of international (state and non-state) and then *n*-interfacial actors with capability to form nodes of power and magnify, within their respective networks of strategic cooperation, the aligned communities of interest (or task confederations). Unlike in the previous era of negative cooperation, i.e. cooperation against external enemies or rivals, and a more positive—i.e. goal-oriented—strategic cooperation originating from the twenty-first-century paradigm, in our times of multiple realities and ever-complex milieu challenges, strategic cooperation rose to the form of an anticipatory and progress-oriented—intrinsic—feature of interfacial interactions (see Table 1 for a comparative overview).

Table 1 Strategic partnerships and international cooperation in the last three centuries

Century	SP generation	Strategic partners	SP-underlying logic and rationale of cooperation		Turning points and shocks to the system	International system configuration
19th/20th c.	*Strategic Partnerships in Alliances' Shadows (nascent SPs)*	States	*Negative*	Cooperation as a form of exclusionist (directed against other actors) and remedying (threat-aversion) strategic interaction in an antagonistic environment	WWI & WWII	Bi- and post-bipolar (including the 'unipolar moment')
20th/21st c.	*Strategic Partnerships as a distinct form of strategic cooperation and interaction (SPs 2.0)*	States, IOs	*Positive*	Cooperation as a form of an affirmative (goal-oriented) strategic interaction in a growingly competitive environment	Global information and cyberwar (WWIII)	Emerging multipolarity (featuring inter-regionalisms)
21st/22nd c.	*Strategic Partnerships as the main structural feature of the global system*	*n*-interface Actors	*Inevitable (intrinsic)*	Cooperation as a form of anticipatory and progress-oriented competitive interaction ('coopetition')	Global nuclear war (WWIV) (aka 'World Wreck')	Multinodality (featuring network hierarchies and task confederations/coalitions)

Source Authors' own elaboration

Whereas the manifestation of SPs and their underlying goals have profoundly changed by now, one principle remains true even today: strategic partnerships are 'social constructs in a realist world', as Tyushka et al. (2019: 50) stated a hundred years ago. However, our-age realism (and the realities it draws on) dearly differs from its root relative, as will be shown below.

2 Of Far Past and Fast Forward Future: The Paradise We Lost and the Worlds We Live In

Much of the IR scholarship and public intellectuals of the early twenty-first century believed the 2020s were an anomaly, a horrible decade, failing to realize this actually was just a tiny taste of *the* future that the 'age of unpeace' (Leonard 2021) was bringing with it. By the early 2030s already, the world stood at the verge: our ancestors were facing mounting and extraordinarily overlapping security threats (both ontological and epistemic), and little they knew where it was all moving—or should have been moving—from there. Following the series of regional and global wars (including the 2022 Russo-Ukrainian war, which evolved into the wider Russo-European armed conflict by 2035 and then spilt over to Indo-Pakistani and Arab–Israeli wars), the devastating cascade of local armed conflicts and clashes (including a number of all-African and Latin American regional wars) ensued, with battles fought on all then-possible fronts—from physical battlefield to cyber and space, costing human lives, alliances, global infrastructures and supply chains as well as critical domestic infrastructures. A profound ontological insecurity embraced the globe. The post-truth age, inaugurated in 2016, brought about the rise of rampant disinformation, deep fakes, anarchist cybernetics and cognitive wars, just as it made global contestation (and yearning for power) stand doom and gloom as it shattered epistemic security worldwide—and thus destroyed a relative certainty as to what to believe in and whom to trust. The post-truth age culminated in post-knowledge stupefaction and prostration. With no globally trusted universal media or world government, the chaos in the information environment, accompanied by massive strategic data fraud and uncontrollable knowledge war, made everyone a suspect and a target, so that everyone (be it a nation, an alliance, or a remnant of either) was put on a ready-to-fire mode. It was due to this tragic overlap of ontological and epistemic security challenges that any reminiscent piece of a 'system' crumbled, and so we lost the world order.

The first serious cracks upon the system were inflicted by Russia's reckless all-out military aggression against Ukraine, launched on the dawn of 24 February 2022. Even though, in a covert and limited scale, Russian aggression in Ukraine's south-eastern territories had been unfolding for eight years, since early 2014, the overt and massive-scale invasion—in a 'shock and awe' style of such offensive operations—started only when the Putin's regime saw the impossibility to reach the goals of its hybrid war in one of the most important former colonies (Watling and Reynolds 2022). Wishful thinking, miscalculation of the European and general Western response as well as the unfounded hopes about Ukrainians' alleged wish to reunite with the ex-metropole quickly crashed against the reality of Ukraine's fierce state and societal defence and resistance effort, urging Russia to alter its campaign goals already after one month of no-success military assault. In mid-April 2022, as the Russian threats of the use of tactical nuclear weapons became more frequent and real, the UK and US policymakers started reacting with cautious messages on possible grave consequences of such a move for Russia proper. Little did they know, back in time, that the Kremlin was not bluffing. After the 9 May 2022 WWII victory parade in Moscow failed to bring tangible victory in Ukraine and the whole campaign stalled towards the summer, the next-year parade was not promising much more, so the Russian regime decided to use the nuclear argument—quite literally as well—and fired a nuclear-armed tactical missile in Ukraine's heartland ⟨Hill Ψ 2023⟩, thus escalating in an endeavour to de-escalate (as the notoriously known Russian military doctrine's principle of 'escalating to de-escalate' had it). Instead of a symmetrical answer, silence was offered as a response from the Western world, leaving Ukraine to cope alone with the decolonial war it did dread. As the Ukrainians kept fighting for their land and independence, the conflict spanned—as a guerrilla warfare—over the next decade, with the stepped-up militarization observable far beyond Russia and Ukraine. At the same time, the United Nation's failure to prevent this war and the wider international community's haplessness in preventing it from going nuclear, did a massive blow to the entire rules-based international system, with the 'every nation for itself' returning as a key security thinking. Russia's belated exclusion from the UN Security Council and the expulsion from the UN did little to remedy the war in Ukraine, but did contribute to the country's incremental isolation on the international stage. With its resource-cursed economy being diverted away from Europe post-Ukraine 2022 war, its official diplomacy being ousted from international fora, and its culture and public diplomacy efforts nullified against the rise of consolidating #cancel-Russia global movement, persecution of Russian leaders and militarists for war crimes in Ukraine, domestic uncertainty, poverty and volatility brought about a new 'smuta' (akin to the end-sixteen to the early seventeenth century 'time of troubles') in Russia: rather than becoming a great power, Russia became a great pariah by the early 2030s. This self-inflicted loss of status, might, wealth and of the outlook for a predictable and prosperous future made the Russian regime even more reckless in its haunting for revenge against the collective West, and so the Russo-European broader conflict got ignited—first in the cyber domain, then in the form of insurgency and mosaic warfare, and, since 2034, as an armed conflict ⟨Newfoundler Ψ 2035⟩.

Since the 2020s, the global temperatures had been rising by plus two degrees Celsius annually, with the tempo progressively accelerating by the mid-2030s. Failure to globally act on climate change unabatedly led to the big implosion also known as the 'Climate Crunch' (CC)—a series of controlled (weaponized) and uncontrollable weather-caused calamities from Europe to Australia, Greenland to South Africa, and all over the globe. A warmer world innately correlated with more instability and insecurity (Parakilas 2021). Along with the progressively mutating Covid-19, a coronavirus that erupted globally in 2019/2020, also known as 'the forever virus' (Brilliant et al. 2021), a number of new infectious diseases were emerging towards the 2030s, including those artificially spread (weaponized) by countries such as China and Russia—the so-called 'hybrid biothreats' (Cañada 2019). In a weirdly awkward way, the effects of the Covid-19 pandemics showed the 'promise' of governing the whole globe—a perspective that some of the technologically advanced powers embraced and later on materialized through their 'biological warfare' (Brooks 2020). Instead of a predicted 'multi-order world' (Flockhart 2016), a radical *de-multilateralisation* (Van Aaken and Vasel 2019) of the international system (and with it, the return of and to the nation-state, i.e. closure) soon ensued.

By 2040, the whole world was 'weaponized', including first and foremost progress in bio-, nano-, chemical and nuclear technological development that served as 'the great equalizer, holding states and non-state actors in a *bellum omnium contra omnes*' (Schlee and Opper 2020: 315). On *le mariage fatale* of nuclear weapons and disruptive technologies, Sokova (2020) from the Vienna Center for Disarmament and Non-Proliferation warned already in late 2020: the dramatic worsening of the early-twenty-first century security environment was chiefly driven by foreign-political and military adventurism, the rise of disruptive cyber technologies and irresponsibilism as a 'philosophy' of their (ab)use, fatal decline of trust (primarily among nuclear powers) and the risky drifting from the Reagan-Gorbachev dictum that 'nuclear war cannot be won and must never be fought'.[2]

Such rational arguments failed to sway the deeply distrustful, disoriented, and distressed heads of state and government, as well as leaders of organized transnational groups with global agendas, who all were seeking to ensure their own survival in a war-torn Climate Crunch-plagued world in the most primitive and ridiculous way—by making sure others would fail. Already on the verge of 2021/2022, the world stood short of a nuclear conflict as Russia started a series of escalatory moves vis-à-vis Ukraine, Europe and the US, including the holding of military drills involving nuclear scenarios, demanding a profound revision of the established regional security order and forthwith backing such threats with nuclear blackmail (Wolfsthal 2022). In 2021, the *Bulletin of the Atomic Scientists'* 'Doomsday Clock' showed just 100 seconds to midnight; in 2031, it rang the alarm of just 10 seconds remaining to midnight; the year 2039 became the year Civilization collapsed.

Already during Russia's invasion of Ukraine in 2022, many were anticipating the 'World War Three' coming (Herszenhorn 2022), but back in time

---

[2] See also Neveragainman's ⟨Ψ 2090⟩ comprehensive study that explores in all the painful detail how this axiom became a theorem of our days.

both Russia and the West converged on 'localizing' this proxy war to Ukraine's territory. In a series of perfectly plausible but unforeseen (for: undesired) events, Russia's war in Ukraine became vastly embedded in the Russo-European/Western conflict. Fought on virtual and physical battlegrounds, but also in the space and the Arctic, all too many episodes confounded for this 'mosaic warfare' to clearly say now what was the decisive war-igniting moment. With the Russo-European and regional wars backsliding into a series of escalations, the World Wreck war started in summer of 2039 in 'the most dangerous place on Earth' (*The Economist* 2021), as China attacked Taiwan, the US rushed to command a limited nuclear strike on Beijing but erroneously hit Moscow (owing this calculated 'error' to China's preemptive cyber-strike on the American command and control centres). As, following the old-world's pertinent principles of 'reciprocity', 'alliance' and 'retaliation', the other old and new nuclear powers joined the whirl of exchanging strikes and counter-strikes, this all-out nuclear war spilt over into the biological and chemical warfare that for the next seven days plagued the world we used to know. The World Wreck war brought the ultra-rapid devastation and extinction of *most* humankind and animal life on the planet.[3] As no state or alliance emerged victorious from it, a deep strategic emptiness abounded in the aftershock. And so the 'Long Collapse', much-feared throughout the late twentieth–early twenty-first century, proved to be quite 'short' and shocking, eventually.

The 2039-enacted World Wreck, the standstill decade and three more decades to follow marked altogether both an end and a new beginning: a 'future shock' (i.e., too much change in too short a period of time), once predicted by Alvin Toffler (1970), caused a massive (dis)information overload, momentary social paralysis, total political failure, systemic overheating and an earlier-unseen technological advancement chiefly driven by survivalism.

Along with the World Wreck aftershock, four central turning points in the middle of the twenty-first century have enabled a *sustainable* global shift upon which also our twenty-second-century interfacial system is built. In the history of humankind, *turning points* had always been quintessential in explaining both the past and present as well as imagining the future—be those wars or geopolitical shocks, scientific discoveries or turns in popular culture and arts, economic and technological breakthroughs or strong moves by influential figures or their own fates proper, or milestone events, etc. The cumulative turning point in the 2050s–2080s was predicated upon a series of ground-breaking steps undertaken by the followership of four 'global humans' from

---

[3] The early twenty-first-century simulations of a global nuclear war, concurrently conducted by the Princeton Science and Global Security (SGS) and the MIT's International Life Sciences Institute (ILSI), considered only the US and Russian nuclear arsenals which in the 2020s made up 90% of the world's nine nuclear powers' arsenal—and even then came to conclusion that a nuclear war between the US and Russia would plunge the Earth into a 10-year-long nuclear winter, with over 60% of the world's population (i.e. ca. 5 billion people) being thereby exterminated; whereby, over 90 million casualties were predicted to accrue within the first few hours of the war (Princeton SGS 2019).

the past century: an environmental activist, a liberal-democratic inspirer, a mathematical mastermind and a hi-tech innovator.

When in 2019 young Swedish environmental activist Greta Thunberg held her speech at the UNGA and challenged some of the world's most powerful leaders (Alter et al. 2019), few knew this daring act would start a global movement—'*thunbergians*', a global advocacy network which rose to an international player of its own (in a post-Climate Crunch world, though). In 2049, the globosphere saw the emergence of the long-overdue doctrine of 'responsibility to protect the Earth' (Patrick 2020) that profoundly reframed the notions of 'sovereignty' and 'power' in the post-Climate Crunch and post-World Wreck Anthropocene.

Likewise, after a period of crisis and contestation both domestically and externally across the world's regions, liberal democratic order saw its clinic death (in the World Wreck) and its second coming decades later. A Polish writer, activist, public intellectual and the 2019 Nobel laureate Olga Tokarczuk launched in the early 2020s a foundation for promoting international peace, democratic development, mutual understanding and reconciliation (that altogether accumulated into a '*liberal internationalism*').[4] Unheard and muted in the era of the 2030s' wars that torpedoed the World Wreck, the movement's ideas were taken on-board by the newly formed global international society that produced the 'Code of life' for the second founding of the deeply-interconnected world we live in. As anticipated by Buzan and Schouenborg (2018), the shaping of a global international society—a well-connected and routinely-interacting social world—facilitated transition towards the more peaceful and predictable world order we have today.

Predictability and anticipatory risk aversion within our global order is now also effectively achieved due to the deeply-embedded *algorithmic rule*, which reinforces the rule of law in the rules-based multinodal global system. The rise of the algorithmic rule has its roots in yet another early twenty-first-century breakthrough. This turning point was called into life by the groundbreaking work on sphere-packing problem in higher—eight and twenty-four—dimensions (a centennial mathematical problem) accomplished in 2017 by Maryna Viazovska, a Ukrainian mathematician from Princeton University and École Polythechnique Fédérale de Lausanne.[5] It helped solve very simple and down-to-earth problems as well as it enabled credible algorithm-based estimates of extraterrestrial space configurations and interactions. Real-time and

---

[4] It is emblematic that the rebirth of liberal democratic idea(l)s occurred where these were most severely challenged in the early decades of the twenty-first century—in Central and Eastern Europe. As a narrative entrepreneur and a role model, O. Tokarczuk led Poland's resistance movement aiming to cancel the 'Polexit' (yet another—Polish—withdrawal from the EU) and reinstate liberal democratic rule. The ideas soon found their resonance in other CEECs where 'Czech-out', 'Donegary', 'Outstria' were looming.

[5] Maryna Viazovska—Laureate of the 2018 *New Horizons in Mathematics Prize* awarded by the Mathematics Breakthrough Prize Board (Klarreich 2019) and the recipient of the highest-honour 2022 *Fields Medal* (Lin and Klarreich 2022).

future-time multidimensional, big data-driven and AI-supported calculability of international transactions gave rise to a new facet of power—algorithmic power, or the power of algorithm. The abuse of algorithmic power in mid-twenty-first century did cost humanity their future. Our-age algorithmic power is, thus, centrally controlled by 'quantum mind'—a quantum computer reinvented from the 2021-prototyped machine made in Germany (Goujard 2021).

Last but not least, the next hi-tech and cyber-tech revolutions, inspired by '*muskanians*', i.e. the adepts of the twentieth-twenty-first century US-American hi-tech innovator and enthusiast Elon Musk[6], took the physical-world realities to the next level and facilitated the integration of the physical, the digital and the *n*-worlds (a myriad of discoverable material and immaterial spaces). The late 2070s' hi-tech revolution and the surge of the man–machine ensemble well beyond the 'big-event' politics (i.e., its effectively becoming embedded in everyday social, economic, and political life) revolutionized the anticipatory and modulating ('future-building') capabilities of enduring (city-states, global organizations) and emerging (global humans, other interface actors and their networks) actors ⟨Nieuwelander Ψ 2099⟩. The surpassing of the point of 'technological singularity' (i.e., a moment at which our-age creative and irreversible technological progress was conceived) also enacted 'accelerating change' (super-progressive technological development and super-industrial/hi-tech society), thanks to which a biotechnologically and AI-enhanced humankind (augments) were born. The new era of progress-oriented *peoplehood* (as it was known in the beginning of the twenty-first century) and *mindhood* (a collective denomination for augmented—biotechnologically enhanced—humans, AI-powered beings, and neural networks of various sorts) inaugurated our-age multiverse *post-Anthropocene*.[7]

Enabled through these breakthroughs in social and quantum minds, the politics of anticipation has now become reality-constitutive. Our thriving interfacial relations and global development, therefore, owe much to the survivalist

---

[6] Already during the early phase of the Russian-Ukrainian war in 2022, Elon Musk's *SpaceX* engagement marked the new era of the state-society and state-business nexuses in global politics where global corporations—as well as global humans—have a responsibility and role to play in times of peace and war, too. So, in an answer to Ukraine government's plea for help, *SpaceX* swiftly positioned some 50 satellites of its *Starlink* satellite communications system for Ukraine's use, which had immense consequences for the success of the country's defensive operations on the ground, including for strategic communications and precision strikes with drones (Miller et al. 2022).

[7] The preceding *Anthropocene* era, with its environmental instability, inequality, and entangled threats (from conventional to chemical, biological and nuclear), wielded significant ramifications for the idea and state of security since the 1950s, so that in the early 2020s, there were already calls for new ways of thinking about collective survival (Lövbrand and Mobjörk 2021). The *post-Anthropocene* epoch, which is believed to have started in the early 2050s, connotes a post-human security environment where planetary security is computed, conditioned and constructed by AI and quantum technologies of sorts.

movements that commenced putting together the pieces of the collapsed post-World Wreck world. A retrospective look is crucial to understand how and why our-day cooperation emerged as an intrinsic feature of IR, and what were its previous forms and manifestations as is explored below.

3 The Origins and Manifestations of Strategic Partnerships in the Post-Bipolar Twentieth Century: In Alliances' Shadows

Even though the clear temporal and political origins of the SPs had remained far from uncontested throughout the twentieth century, it was widely believed that this phenomenon of strategic interconnection was largely inspired by the practice of 'special relations' between the United States and the United Kingdom that, from the 1940s onwards, managed to maintain a long-term and meaningful bilateralism even without being bound by any formal treaty. The idea of a strong, value-based bond and, at the same time, a specific goal-driven and sufficiently flexible relationship was so much standing out from among the dyadic relationships in IR that it warranted its own label in the IR vocabulary of the time, i.e., *'special relationship'* (Berridge and James 2003: 251). With time, the US had been expanding its network of bilateralisms and, in addition to its special relationship with the UK, it started calling its bonds with Israel or the emerging united Europe 'special' as well. In Europe itself, a distinctive bilateralism emerged and became consolidated in the post-Cold war era—i.e., the Franco-German 'community of destiny', with reconciliation and nurturing of good inter-state relations going far beyond official diplomacy and including a broader societal effort where public and city diplomacy but also science and education diplomacy deeply intertwined and became mutually reinforcing. At the close of the twentieth century, the practice and theory of IR had been repeatedly said to be entering a new era. Not only did the key posture of the post-World War Two (WWII) international system, i.e., the 'Cold War', come to an end. A post-Cold War (that is, a post-bipolar) era also unveiled new facets of international life as the processes of growing interdependence and globalization started to unwind. In the post-bipolar 1990s, states across Europe and further afield were rediscovering their inherent drives and capabilities of making sovereign choices and pursuing their own and cooperative goals, including the ability to freely choose a partner (as opposed to being bound to allies).

Such a world-political constellation presented a genuine opening and a dynamic moment in international interactions as, in addition to alliances (and later on—in their stead), states had been discovering and embracing new forms of non-exclusionist and comprehensive cooperation going beyond purely military defensive or security-related agendas. *Strategic Partnerships (SPs)* had emerged in the mid-1990s as a foreign-political tool and an international-systemic feature sought to enable structured bilateral engagement in an increasingly competitive and multipolar world. Their surge had been well-recorded also in academia, as the IR/FPA scholarship on the notion took a serious upswing around 2000 (see *Google Ngram Viewer* statistics for the term).

The early strategic partnerships helped mitigate the effects of a changing international environment and the related uncertainty, as well as the challenges of overlapping interdependencies. Such a mode of strategic bilateralism embedded in the international system was allegedly modelled after similar observations in international business and economy, where 'strategic (business) alliances' had established themselves as sustainable models of strategic *cooperation-and-competition* worldwide. One of the literature strands suggests that it was indeed the international business and governance scholarship that IR theory borrowed the term and logic of 'strategic partnerships' from (Czechowska 2013a; Wilkins 2008; see also: Olson and Zeckhauser 1966). Among the first states to systematically use the new 'brand' were, unsurprisingly, the United States: in 1993, the US was explicitly labelling its relationship with Turkey, Russia, and China as 'strategic partnership'. The mid-1990s saw the popularization of the term and the proliferation of the practice of strategic partnerships beyond the then-lonely superpower or great powers: countries like Brazil, India, Japan, Poland or Ukraine were then building up their networks of strategic partnerships, too. No clear and consistent patterns of this political practice could be identified, however, as every nation would worship their own ideas and ideals as to what a 'strategic' relationship, a 'partner' and a 'partnership' should mean in respective foreign policy (FP) doctrine and or practice.

The IR/FPA scholarship experienced a significant paradigmatic challenge in understanding 'strategic partnerships' beyond the known and conveniently recalled idea of 'alliances', as known in alliance theory (Walt 1987). The early empirical case studies on strategic partnerships between states within and beyond Europe had shown, however, that there was a clear distinction between what alliance theory implied and what strategic partnership practice revealed—not least in light of the possibility of forging strategic partnerships between friendly and rivalling powers, great and small powers as well as the extension of the SPs' issue-areas well beyond defence-military commitments (cf. e.g.: Burant 2000; Wilkins 2008; Hamilton 2014). In view of such a distinctive foreign-political practice that then still lacked any theoretical underpinning, worldwide IR scholars started sporadically advancing some early theoretical propositions on the notion of strategic partnerships, mainly focusing on its constitutive elements and contrasting features vis-à-vis alliances in global politics (cf. eg.: Razumkov 2000; Wilkins 2008; Nadkarni 2010; Blanco 2011; Farias 2013; Czechowska 2013a: 46–51), but their efforts were fragmented and insufficient. The IR/FPA literature saw a breakthrough in conceptualizing strategic partnerships following the stipulation of an 'ideal model' of inter-state strategic partnerships by Czechowska (2013b), where the SP-constituting necessary conditions and advanced features of a strategic partnership were singled out as follows. For a relationship to qualify for a strategic partnership, it necessarily had to demonstrate: (1) the partnership character, (2) the convergence of partners' strategic goals, (3) partners' shared perception that only by joining their efforts their goals were fulfillable and, finally, (4) the track of committed and long-term cooperation. At the same time, some developed strategic partnerships could also bear signs of (5) a remarkable relationship intensification, (6) highly developed structure of partners' strategic interaction and (7) cooperation in a good-faith and a friendly atmosphere (see for detail: Czechowska 2013b: 45–81). It remained, however, underexplored how and why strategic partnerships emerge and are sustained, and why, most importantly, the idea was effectively spilling over from states to international organizations (IOs) that, too, were building up their SP networks at the turn of the twentieth and twenty-first centuries. Last but not least, a foundational theoretical puzzle remained unsolved: how to account for a growing variety of strategic partnership forms, purposes, structural and functional features in both given bilateral relations and the broader international system?

4   The Rise of Strategic Partnerships in Twenty-First Century International Relations: Multipolarity and Foreign-Political Assertiveness

Along with a growing number of states, by the millennial turn of 2000, international organizations had started to embrace the 'strategic partnership' formula in their external relations with third countries as well as other IOs. Since 1993, for instance, when its first strategic partnership with Brazil was established, China had forged close to 70 strategic partnerships of sorts by 2014 (FMPRC 2015), thus spanning a web of truly differentiated strategic links with major and emerging powers as well as international organizations *literally* across the globe. Impressive SP networks were established back then also by India and Japan. The EU, NATO, ASEAN, the African Union, the Arab League and CELAC joined the move and, too, established a number of overlapping SPs with partners from across the globe. As one of the first international organizations, NATO had launched its partnerships with non-member countries in the early 1990s, seeking to foster peace and development. The comprehensive 'partnership for peace' policy framework embraced by 2010s as many as 21 NATO Partners across the globe. The EU had ten official strategic partnerships (with the US, Canada, Mexico, South Korea, South Africa, Japan, Brazil, India, China, and Russia) and a number of policy-framework or issue-specific strategic partners, such as the 'Eastern Partnership', 'Association'-based SPs or the cyber-partner US. Furthermore, the EU had forged in the meantime institutional partnerships with other regional organizations, all of which had been building their own webs of global strategic interconnections.

It would certainly be a daunting task to establish the precise number of SPs across the globe operating in the early twenty-first century, not least because not all states' and international organizations' foreign-policy bureaucracies were keeping systematic and tidy track of record in this regard. Renard (2013: 302) even ironically claimed back in the 2010s that '[m]ost governments probably [did] not even realize how many they [had] signed'. On the empirical side, the existence of both formal and informal strategic partnerships and the ways of labelling them (which do not necessarily include either 'strategic' or 'partnership' markers) complicated the task of keeping the record of SPs even further.

In history, SPs occasionally featured as a form of strategic cooperation between more than two actors. Usually, however, SPs were formed between two actors—whether states or international organizations. However, rare examples of tri- and multilateral partnerships, such as the EU-India-US SP or the (geo)political alliance of emerging powers of Brazil, Russia, India, China, and South Africa (BRICS), existed. An enthusiastic 'multilateraliser', the EU had forged, in the 2010s–2020s, a web of multilateral SPs on climate change and energy governance (see, e.g. Renard 2016). The key difficulty in sustaining multilateral SPs lay in the weakness of a chief SP-constitutive element: trust. Akin to the greater propensity to stability of bipolar international systems when compared to multipolar configurations (Deutsch and Singer 1964; Mearsheimer 1990), the sustainability of bilateral SPs proved to be greater than that of multilateral SPs, as all too many variables (competing interests, preferences and goals) and uncertainties (true intentions, trustworthiness, interaction predictability) were involved the latter format.

Strategic partnerships were also formed by more than one contractual arrangement, be it a declaration, framework or sector-specific cooperation and partnership agreement. For instance, the EU-Japanese SP forged in the late 2010s (Hosoi 2019) was grounded in two main bilateral contractual deals—the EU-Japan Strategic Partnership Agreement (SPA) and the EU-Japan Economic Partnership Agreement (EPA) signed in 2018.

As the empirical evidence showed, dynamic (i.e. constantly developing) SPs proved to be more sustainable and more substantial. The vast majority of SPs, however, bore merely declarative character, thus wielding little influence on global politics. Whereas some SPs were maintained in their original form and content, others developed in their scope and level of ambition, as shown by successive upgrades to the originally established bilateral partnerships. For instance, the NATO-Ukrainian SP, which emerged from NATO's PfP framework partnership programme in 1994, underwent four upgrades by 2019, having become a 'special' and 'distinctive' partnership, among other formats (Tyushka 2019). In 2020/2021, the next, fifth, upgrade of the NATO-Ukraine SP materialized with the launch of the Enhanced Opportunities Partnership. Some partnerships, on the other hand, vanished in the wake of their 'verification' by crises or less severe challenges (like the EU's and NATO's strategic partnerships with Russia in 2014 that were brought to a standstill following Russia's aggression in Ukraine). Others, like the ASEAN-China SPs, have survived until nowadays, even though in an amended form, purpose and extent.

Towards the 2010s, strategic partnerships had become very 'fashionable' (Renard 2013: 302) in international politics, 'coming into vogue at both a global and regional level' (Envall and Hall 2016: 90). The term had also confidently entered the IR vocabulary, and scholars in Western and non-Western IR schools began searching for the meaning of SPs, not least by deconstructing the notion into its formal (label) and constitutive (practice) features (cf. eg.: Blanco 2015; Renard 2013; Grevi 2013; Czechowska 2013a). At this stage, empirical observations and single case studies informed the emerging analytical pool of features of a 'strategic partnership'. Its empirically derived 'building blocks' included most significantly the idea of shared or converging goals, shared values, institutionally structured cooperation but also mutual loyalty, understanding and commitment, issue convergence and multidimensionality, among other features (see Fig. 1 for a more detailed overview).

Developed typologies and functional explanations of strategic partnerships in select actors' foreign-political repertoires (see, for instance: Grevi and Renard 2012; Renard 2013; Grevi 2013; Kavalski 2016; Murray 2016; Ferreira-Pereira and Vieira 2016) complemented the efforts in the study of this phenomenon. Nadkarni's (2010: 48–49) catalogue of six SP-constitutive features perhaps best summarizes at where the strategic partnership scholarship had arrived in its second wave as the SPs were deemed to be necessarily formalized (in declarations, memoranda, or agreements), with specific goals advanced and multiple institutional and other ties forged among the partners, with factual cooperation spreading beyond a single issue-area and growing over time.

Fig. 1 Building blocks of the 'strategic partnership' notion in IR scholarship of the 1990s–2010s (*Source* Authors' own presentation based on data in: Tyushka et al. [2019: 20–22])

At the turn of the 2010s–2020s, the fragmented and diffused notion of SP had started being 'fitted' into the existing mainstream and critical IR theoretical approaches with the aim to find a suitable 'home' for an IR phenomenon that was born (and, allegedly, theoretically lost) in the turbulence of tectonic shifts of the early 1990s. Numerous accounts proliferated (see for detail: Tyushka and Czechowska 2019) that discussed strategic partnerships in the context of international governance and organizational studies (Czechowska 2013a, b; Slobodchikoff and Tandon 2017), cast a historical-institutionalist perspective (Gilson 2016), or embraced the realist reasoning (Wilkins 2008; Nadkarni 2010) or social-constructivist understanding of the notion (Blanco 2016; Bang 2017; Michalski and Pan 2017), as well as those accounts that reinvigorated the critical security studies of strategic partnerships (Envall and Hall 2016; Wilkins 2018) regarding them as 'security alignments'—in the established traditions of the 'Copenhagen school' of critical security studies (Buzan et al. 1998).

As strategic partnerships were steadily becoming 'a central feature of the early twenty-first century diplomatic discourse' and practice (Renard 2013: 302), a handful of nascent theoretical accounts were developed at the same time, including one the current authors find really persuasive. In their first attempt to conceptualize and theorize the notion of strategic partnerships between states and international organizations, Czechowska et al. (2019) built an 'ideal model' and statistically tested it, thus having innovatively verified the SP-constitutive elements that the IR/FPA scholarship had accumulated over the first decades. They also departed from the tradition of 'fitting' the SPs into existing theoretical frameworks and advanced an interparadigmatic realist-constructivist analytical perspective on the notion. This perspective informed the authors' inquiry into the nature, function, and international-systemic effects of strategic partnerships, by synergetically framing three main lines of argument: in one way or another, strategic partnerships constitute 'a mode of international engagement from foreign-political *assertiveness* to bilateral *alignment* to international *association*' (Tyushka et al. 2019: 56). Such a definition and practice of SPs, thus, bore consequences for both the dynamics of bilateral relations in question as well as broader regional dynamics and the functioning of the international system.

The notion of SPs, together with the ill-fated idea of cooperation it draws on, were abruptly rendered meaningless as, one after another, World Wreck-torpedoing clashes of all-against-all turned the whole international system upside down. The 'Short Collapse of Everything', as writes our-age historian Newman ⟨Ψ 2100⟩, caused a lasting strategic emptiness that abounded in the World Wreck aftershock. It took Chornobyl, the biggest bioenvironmental catastrophe of the twentieth century following the Soviet Ukraine's nuclear power plant explosion, 35 years to nearly fully recover and flourish with new life where the human footprint had been missing for decades. It took our globosphere over half a century to renew itself in most of the nuclear war-affected areas in three old-world continents. It will take us one hundred years more to say farewell to the aches and despair the old world left behind. But realization came quick that war is a way to nowhere, a regress into non-existence and a *no*-thing in a future universe no matter what shapes it was to take. This normative turn was massive and constitutive of our new reality. And so it was totally eradicated from our code of life in the multiverses we are building on land, under water and in outer spaces. The 'quantum mind', which has been in service for our post-Anthropocene since 2079, ensures threat of force or use of it are not feasible—neither as an idea nor as a multiverse reality. A progress-driven competition, instead of war, now shapes the logic of global balance of interest (not power or threat, as it used to). Politics, including that of the globosphere, became much more like sport—who delivers welfare better and sooner wins.

This could have appeared as a utopia back in the early twenty-first century, where the conflict and war paradigms defined the balance of power and threat in the international system. It would have been certainly impossible if it was not for the World Wreck aftershock and the emergence of the new Anthropocene—progress-oriented *peoplehood* (as it was known in the beginning of the twenty-first century) and *mindhood* (a collective denomination for augmented—biotechnologically enhanced—humans, AI-powered beings and neural networks of various sorts). From an applied ethics and biopolitics topic in the early twenty-first century (Savulescu and Bostrom 2009), human enhancement became an existential issue in the post-World Wreck era, not least as new living conditions and deep-interconnectedness across the globosphere demanded augmented physical and virtual capabilities. Even though a much-expected arrival of 'Homo Deus' (Harari 2016) did not substantiate, the population of peoplehood got to cohabitate the planet with AI-powered non-human beings as well as transhumans (augments), that serve now as proxies between human and machine interfaces and make strategic decisions on global affairs. With everyone-connected-to-everything, glocal governance institutions now rule by information, which in our-age is conducive to virtually all dimensions of live—from transaction processing to smart city-state functioning. The earlier dubbed idea of 'infomocracy' (Older 2016) has now become system-constitutive and, together with the chief ordering principle for glocal life, that is, algorithmic rule, provides for a smooth functioning of interfacial relations in late twenty-first–early twenty-second century. The rise of the algorithm put an end to politics as we knew it, as was neatly anticipated by Timcke (2021) nearly a century ago. The root of all problems the old world experienced lay in the volatile uncertainty about the intentions of other actors in IR. As put by one of the respected authors of that time, John J. Mearsheimer, '[u]ncertainty about the intentions of other states is unavoidable, […] states can never be sure that other states do not have offensive intentions to go along with their offensive capabilities' (Mearsheimer 2001: 81). Thanks to the algorithmic transparency of our age, the problem of 'uncertain intentions' was completely eradicated. What is more, the earlier persisting ideological differences were left behind, too: as the hi-tech revolutions brought about life's renewal in the post-World Wreck period, Pax Technica came to dominate the (human and machine) minds across the globe, transforming itself into a tran-sideological 'techno-religion'—techno-liberal globalism. That the interfacial interactions are now based on quantum mind's automated processing algo-rithm, which prevents any conflict or confrontation by default, is a reality that might have arrived long before, albeit, perhaps, in a moderated form. In the early 2020s, there were already visionary calls for a 'fully-automated liberalism' based on blockchain technology and cooperation under anarchy at least within the climate governance domain (Reinsberg 2021). If only our predecessors had known this could have been a chance to cancel the *avenir fatale*.

5 The Multiverse of Strategic Partnerships in Twenty-Second Century Global Politics: Multinodality, Task-Centred Alignment and Networked Hegemony

Half a century now into the new techno-digital matrix of IR, we live a distinct reality, with deeply interconnected people-/mind-hood, interdependent nodes of power within the global system and the new cohort of interfacial actors beyond metamorphosed 'city-states' and 'global organizations' (earlier known as 'nation-states' and 'International Organizations'). As pondered by Henry Kissinger, one of the IR gurus of the past two centuries, '[e]very international order must sooner or later face the impact of two tendencies challenging its cohesion: either a redefinition of legitimacy or a significant shift in the balance of power' (Kissinger 2014: 365). Our post-World Wreck global order was born out of both—a radical redefinition of legitimacy and a no less radical shift in the nature and configuration of power in the post-nuclear and post-war age. The current multi*nodal* world system, underpinned by the algorithmic rule and techno-liberal globalism ⟨Nustaar Ψ 2119⟩, is the most stable, predictable, and progress-driven global system ever. In this system, the twin paradigm of '*cooperation-and-competition*' ('coopetition') has become an intrinsic mode of interfacial interactions among the myriad of global actors representing all current (human and transhuman) interfaces. Welfare—not military might or particularistic conflict-prone ideologies—has become a driving force and a statecraft in both 'domestic' politics in a digitalized city-state and, more importantly, in interfacial coopetition. The multinodal world system enables the re-emergence of strategic partnerships as the mode of interaction and a sub-structure of interfacial relations. Goal-driven, task-based, and inclu-sively overlapping, the new-era SPs have provided necessary strategic edges for nodal alignment and networked hegemonies, thus stimulating a healthy and progress-oriented competition in international affairs. Such an institutional rebirth and longevity, especially after the 'Big Break' of the mid-twenty-first century, should not come as a surprise, though. Back in 2020 already, the phenomenon (and causes) of institutional longevity that helps humans manage interconnections spanning several centuries and dozens of generations was discovered (Hanusch and Biermann 2020). SPs appeared to belong to those societal and political '*deep-time organizations*' that are sustainable for 'long-term challenges of earth system governance and planetary stewardship' (Hanusch and Biermann 2020: 19). Whereas in the early twenty-first century, SPs were chiefly based on (a) shared goals, (b) joint bodies and (c) trust, their second Renaissance in the late 21st–early twenty-second century saw the upgrade of key characteristics. Now, SPs are based on (a) genuinely shared goals and tasks; (b) modest network institutionalization within the global connectography, and (c) 'verified trust', that is algorithmic transparency (Newbridge 2109). Thus, our-days' stability and sustainability of the global system rests on two premises: the ever-increasing complexity of the physical-digital world, which urges cooperation, and the AI-powered algorithmic rule that allows us to eliminate uncertainties of human (mis)calculation, (mis)trust and the resulting (mis)behaviour that defined international interactions in the past centuries. Goal- and task-centrism make SPs suitable frameworks for advancing progress in global development and the politics of anticipation, where our future becomes actively co-shaped (Table 2).

City-states, concerned with ensuring the welfare of their citizens, were the first actors to launch our-age SPs with global corporations and organizations. In 2069, the city-state of Warsno (formerly, the capital city of Warsaw) forged an SP with the Berli-Pari agglomerate (formerly, Berlin and Paris capitals) to develop the waterways infrastructure and thus connecting the city-state inhabitants with services provided by the seaborne and oceanic citizens. Since 2071, the Tallinelsinki and Landanium city-states became a joint hub (node) for a web of SPs with other city-states and global organizations seeking to boost their technological capabilities in human enhancement. Global organizations, such as the Mountains League, the Biosphere Re: new Coalition or Algorithm United, joined the move as a growing number of stakeholders started seeking to regularize their interactions with these crucial 'global goods' providers. Transparency of goals and intentions of the participating actors, as well as the consolidation of the algorithmic rule in our age, facilitated the re-emergence of multilateral SPs—along with the flourishing bilateral formats of this structured engagement and global coopetition. The AfroFuturist League (AFL) was among the first to build, since 2088, multi-stakeholder SPs with the aim of ensuring equal access to basic biotechnological advancements and extraterrestial post-Anthropocene. The number and variety of SPs keeps growing as *n*-interfacial actors seek to sustainably govern the safety and security of us all, thus expanding their activity into new and new areas of 'future management'. Nowadays, SPs are indispensable for anticipatory governance that ensures both basic collective-survival needs as well as progressive welfare expectations of the post-Anthropocene populations.

Table 2 Strategic partnerships in global politics: then and now

Century	International order	International system polarity	Key actors	International interactions	Key IR theoretical traditions	Key SPs parameters	Key SPs rationales
20th c **21st c**	*Pax Americana* and the *Age of Unpeace* (great power-political matrix of IR)	unipolarity multipolarity apolarity	Nation states; international organizations	Conflict (war) and cooperation	Great-power rule *(realism)* institutional rule *(liberalism)* global governance *(constructivism)*	(a) shared goals; (b) joint bodies; (c) trust	Mutual (bilateral) benefits; mitigation of known challenges; situational alignment; leverage in power politics
22nd c	*Pax Technica* (techno-digital matrix of IR)	multinodality	*n*-interfacial actors (city-states; global humans; global organizations, etc.)	Coopetition	Algorithmic rule *(techno-liberal globalism)*	(a) shared goals and tasks; (b) network institutionalization and connectivity; (c) algo-rithmic transparency	Global goods provision; networked hegemony; policy modulation and anticipatory (issue-area) governance; key IR substructure

Source Authors' own elaboration

REFERENCES

Alter, C., Haynes, S., and Worland, J. (2019). Greta Thunberg: TIME's Person of the Year 2019. *Time*, 23/30 December 2019, https://time.com/person-of-the-year-2019-greta-thunberg.

Bang, J. (2017). Why so many layers? China's 'state-speak' and its classification of partnerships. *Foreign Policy Analysis, 13*(2): 380–397.

Berridge, G., and James, A. (2003). *A Dictionary of Diplomacy*. Basingstoke: Palgrave-Macmillan.

Blanco, L.F. (2011). *Strategic partnership: A new form of association in international relations*. Available at: http://www.wiscnetwork.org/porto2011/papers/WISC_2011-523.pdf.

Blanco, L.F. (2015). *On the uses and functions of 'strategic partnership' in international politics: Implications for agency, policy and theory* (PhD Thesis). Bielefeld: Bielefeld University.

Blanco, L.F. (2016). The functions of 'strategic partnership' in European Union foreign policy discourse. *Cambridge Review of International Affairs, 29*(1): 36–54.

Brilliant, L., Danzig, L., Oppenheimer, K., Mondal, A., Bright, R., and Lipkin, W.I. (2021). A strategy for the long fight against COVID-19. *Foreign Affairs, 100*(4): 76–91.

Brooks, M. (2020). The next pandemic might not be natural. *Foreign Policy*, 20 April 2020, https://foreignpolicy.com/2020/04/20/coronavirus-pandemic-bioterrorism-preparedness/.

Burant, S. (2000). *Stosunki polsko-ukraińskie a idea strategicznego partnerstwa*. Warsaw: Stowarzyszenie Euro-Atlantyckie.

Buzan, B., and Schouenborg, L. (2018). *Global International Society: A New Framework for Analysis*. Cambridge: Cambridge University Press.

Buzan, B., Wæver, O., and Wilde, J. D. (1998). *Security: A New Framework for Analysis*. Boulder, CO: Lynne Rienner Pub.

Cañada, J.A. (2019). Hybrid threats and preparedness strategies: The reconceptualization of biological threats and boundaries in global health emergencies. *Sociological Research Online, 24*(1): 93–110.

Czechowska, L. (2013a). The concept of strategic partnership as an input in the modern alliance theory. *The Copernicus Journal of Political Studies, 2*(4): 36–51.

Czechowska, L. (2013b). *Wewnątrzunijni partnerzy strategiczni Rzeczypospolitej Polskiej*. Toruń: MADO.

Czechowska, L., Tyushka, A., Domachowska, A., Gawron-Tabor, K., and Piechowiak-Lamparska, J. (eds.) (2019). *States, International Organizations and Strategic Partnerships*. Cheltenham: Edward Elgar Publishing.

Deutsch, K.W., and Singer, J.D. (1964). Multipolar power systems and international stability. *World Politics, 16*(3): 390–406.

Envall, H.D.P., and Hall, I. (2016). Asian strategic partnerships: New practices and regional security governance. *Asian Politics & Policy, 8*(1): 87–105.

Farias, R. de S. (2013). Parcerias estratégicas: marco conceitual. In A. C. Lessa and H. A. de Oliveira (Org.), *Parcerias estratégicas do Brasil: os significados e as experiências tradicionais*, vol. 1. Belo Horizonte: Fino Traço, pp. 15–35.

Ferreira-Pereira, L.C., and Vieira, A.V.G. (2016). Introduction: The European Union's strategic partnerships: Conceptual approaches, debates and experiences. *Cambridge Review of International Affairs, 29*(1): 3–17.

Flockhart, T. (2016). The coming multi-order world. *Contemporary Security Policy, 37*(1): 3–30.

FMPRC. (2015). Foreign Minister Wang Yi Meets the Press after the Third Session of the Twelfth National People's Congress, 8 March 2015. Available at: http://www.fmprc.gov.cn/mfa_eng/wjb_663304/wjbz_663308/2461_6 63310/t1243662.shtml.

Gilson, J. (2016). The strategic partnership agreement between the EU and Japan: The pitfalls of path dependency? *Journal of European Integration, 38*(7): 791–806.

Goujard, C. (2021). Germany unveils powerful quantum computer to keep Europe in global tech race. *POLITICO*, 15 June 2021, https://www.politico.eu/article/ger many-unveils-europes-first-quantum-computer/.

Grevi, G., and Renard, T. (2012). Hot issues, cold shoulders, lukewarm partners: EU strategic partnerships and climate change. *ESPO Report 2* (November 2012).

Grevi, G. (2013). The EU strategic partnerships: Process and purposes. In Mario Teló and Frederik Ponjaert (eds.), *The EU's Foreign Policy: What Kind of Power and Diplomatic Action*. Farnham: Ashgate, pp. 159–173.

Hamilton, D.S. (2014). The American way of partnership. *ESPO Working Paper 6* (July).

Hanusch, F., and Biermann, F. (2020). Deep-time organizations: Learning institutional longevity from history. *The Anthropocene Review, 7*(1): 19–41.

Harari, Y.N. (2016). *Homo Deus: A Brief History of Tomorrow*. London: Random House.

Herszenhorn, D.M. (2022). The fighting is in Ukraine, but risk of WWIII is real. *Politico*, 4 March 2022, https://www.politico.eu/article/fight-ukraine-russia-world-war-risk-real/.

Hill, F. (Ψ 2023). I warned you he would! Politico's interview with Fiona Hill. *Politico*, 24 February 2023.

Hosoi, Y. (2019). Japan-EU relations after World War II and strategic partnership. *Asia Europe Journal, 17*(3): 295–307.

Kavalski, E. (2016). The EU–India strategic partnership: Neither very strategic, nor much of a partnership. *Cambridge Review of International Affairs, 29*(1): 192–208.

Kissinger, H. (2014). *World Order: Reflections on the Character of Nations and the Course of History*. London: Allen Lane.

Kissinger, Henry A., Schmidt, Eric, and Huttenlocher, Daniel. (2021). *The Age of AI: And Our Human Future*. New York: Little, Brown and Company.

Klarreich, E. (2019). Out of a magic math function, one solution to rule them all. *QuantaMagazine*, 13 May 2019. Available at: https://www.quantamagazine.org/ universal-math-solutions-in-dimensions-8-and-24-20190513.

Leonard, M. (2021). *The Age of Unpeace: How Connectivity Causes Conflict*. London: Penguin Books.

Lin, T., and Klarreich, E. (2022). In Times of Scarcity, War and Peace, a Ukrainian Finds the Magic in Math. *Quanta Magazine*, 5 July 2022, https://www.quanta magazine.org/ukrainian-mathematician-maryna-viazovska-wins-fields-medal-202 20705/.

Lövbrand, E., and Mobjörk, M. (2021). *Anthropocene (In)securities: Reflections on Collective Survival 50 Years After the Stockholm Conference*. Oxford: Oxford University Press.

Mearsheimer, J.J. (1990). Why We Will Soon Miss the Cold War. *The Atlantic Monthly, 266*(2): 35–50.

Mearsheimer, J.J. (2001). *The Tragedy of Great Power Politics*. New York: W. W. Norton & Company.

Michalski, A., and Pan, Z. (2017). *Unlikely Partners: China, the European Union and the Forging of a Strategic Partnership*. Singapore: Palgrave Macmillan.

Miller, C., Scott, M., and Bender, B. (2022). UkraineX: How Elon Musk's space satellites changed the war on the ground. *POLITICO*, 8 June 2022, https://www.politico.eu/article/elon-musk-ukraine-starlink/.

Murray, P. (2016). EU–Australia relations: A strategic partnership in all but name? *Cambridge Review of International Affairs, 29*(1): 171–191.

Nadkarni, V. (2010). *Strategic Partnerships in Asia: Balancing Without Alliances*. London and New York: Routledge.

Neugierescu, A., Frankowski, S., and Kucharchuk, L. ⟨Ψ 2027⟩. *The Theory and Practice of Strategic Partnerships in the Early 21st Century*. London: Good Books Inc.

Neveragainman, J.J. ⟨Ψ 2090⟩. *An Axiom Some Risked to Prove: On the Roots and Emergence of the Nuclear Taboo Absolutism in 22nd Century Politics*. Newland: SoberPress Inc.

Newbridge, A. ⟨Ψ 2109⟩. *The Algorithmic Revolution, Connectography and the Reinvention of Strategic Partnerships*. Landanium: Small Planet Press.

Newfoundler, B. ⟨Ψ 2035⟩. *The War Europe and the West Dread*. Yale: Future University Press.

Newman, J. ⟨Ψ 2100⟩. *The Short Collapse of Everything: A History of the World We Would Rather Did Not Know*. New London: Peace Enterprise Books.

Nieuwelander, M. ⟨Ψ 2099⟩. From international to interfacial relations: On systemic and actor-level changes in the discipline and practice of IR on its 180th anniversary. *Interfacial Affairs, 846*(654): 18–48.

Nustaar, E. ⟨Ψ 2119⟩. *Techno-Liberal Globalism: On the Algorithmic Fabric of Interfacial Relations*. Tallinnelsinki: New Wonders Press.

Older, M. (2016). *Infomocracy*. New York: Tom Doherty Associates.

Olson, M., and Zeckhauser, R. (1966). On economic theory of alliances. *Review of Economics and Statistics, 48*: 266–279.

Parakilas, J. (2021). What does national security mean in a +2 Celsius world? *The Diplomat*, 13 August 2021, https://thediplomat.com/2021/08/what-does-national-security-mean-in-a-2-celsius-world/.

Patrick, S.M. (2020). A responsibility to protect the earth? Reframing sovereignty in the anthropocene. *World Politics Review*, 2 March 2020, https://www.worldpoliticsreview.com/articles/28572/a-responsibility-to-protect-the-earth-reframing-sovereignty-in-the-anthropocene.

Princeton Science and Global Security. (2019). Princeton Science and Global Security Nuclear War Simulation. *Nuclear Princeton*, 6 September 2019, https://nuclearprinceton.princeton.edu/news/princeton-science-and-global-security-nuclear-warsimulation.

Razumkov, O. (2000). Strategic partners of Ukraine: Declarations and realities. *National Security & Defence*, no. 12, http://www.razumkov.org.ua/eng/files/category_journal/NSD12_eng.pdf.

Reinsberg, B. (2021). Fully-automated liberalism? Blockchain technology and international cooperation in an anarchic world. *International Theory, 13*(2): 287–313.

Renard, T. (2013). The EU and its strategic partners: A critical assessment of the EU's strategic partnerships. In Sven Biscop and Richard G. Whitman (eds.), *The Routledge Handbook of European Security*. London and New York: Routledge, pp. 302–314.

Renard, T. (2016). Partnerships for effective multilateralism? Assessing the compatibility between EU bilateralism, (inter-)regionalism and multilateralism. *Cambridge Review of International Affairs, 29*(1): 18–35.

Savulescu, J., and Bostrom, N. (2009). *Human Enhancement*. Oxford: Oxford University Press.

Schlee, R., and Opper, J. (2020). Weaponizing the world. *New Perspectives, 28*(3): 314–329.

Slobodchikoff, M.O., and Tandon, A. (2017). Shifting alliances and balance of power in Asia: Transitions in the Indo-Russian security ties. *Asian Journal of Political Science, 25*(2): 159–175.

Sokova, E. (2020). Disruptive technologies and nuclear weapons. *New Perspectives, 28*(3), 292–297.

Stevens, T., and Michelsen, N. (eds.) (2019). *Pessimism in International Relations: Provocations, Possibilities, Politics*. Cham: Springer.

The Economist. (2021). The most dangerous place on Earth: How to avoid war over the future of Taiwan. *The Economist, 439*(9243), 1 May 2021, p. 7.

Timcke, S. (2021). *Algorithms and the End of Politics: How Technology Shapes 21st-Century American Life*. Bristol University Press.

Toffler, A. (1970). *Future Shock*. New York: Bantam Books.

Tyushka, A. (2019). An evolving NATO–Ukraine strategic partnership in a turbulent security environment. In L. Czechowska et al. (eds.), *States, International Organizations and Strategic Partnerships*. Cheltenham: Edward Elgar Publishing, pp. 204–232.

Tyushka, A., and Czechowska, L. (2019). Strategic partnerships, international politics and IR theory. In In L. Czechowska et al. (eds.), *States, International Organizations and Strategic Partnerships*. Cheltenham: Edward Elgar Publishing, pp. 8–43.

Tyushka, A., Czechowska, L., Domachowska, A., Gawron-Tabor, K., and Piechowiak-Lamparska, J. (2019). States, international organizations and strategic partnerships: Theorizing an 'ideal model'. In L. Czechowska et al. (eds.), *States, International Organizations and Strategic Partnerships*. Cheltenham: Edward Elgar Publishing, pp. 44–79.

Van Aaken, A., and Vasel, J.J. (2019). Demultilateralisation: A cognitive psychological perspective. *European Law Journal, 25*(5): 487–493.

Walt, S. (1987). *The Origins of Alliances*. Ithaca, NY: Cornell University Press.

Watling, J., and Reynolds, N. (2022). The Plot to Destroy Ukraine. *RUSI Special Report* (15 February 2022).

Wendt, A. (2015). *Quantum Mind and Social Science: Unifying Physical and Social Ontology*. Cambridge: Cambridge University Press.

Wilkins, T.S. (2008). Russo-Chinese strategic partnership: A new form of security cooperation? *Contemporary Security Policy, 29*(2): 358–383.

Wilkins, T.S. (2018). After a decade of strategic partnership: Japan and Australia 'decentering' from the US alliance? *The Pacific Review, 31*(4): 498–514.

Wolfsthal, J.B. (2022). The threat of nuclear conflict is high. We need a new commitment to de-escalation. *The Washington Post*, 17 January 2022, https://www.washingtonpost.com/opinions/2022/01/17/threat-nuclear-conflict-is-high-we-need-new-commitment-de-escalation/.

Nuclear Weapons in 2122: Disaster, Stability, or Disarmament?

Michal Onderco and Jeffrey W. Knopf

1   INTRODUCTION

We write from the St. Bernard monastery in the Alps, on the territory of what once was the rich country of Switzerland. Since an escalating series of nuclear exchanges turned much of the planet's surface to radioactive ruin and triggered a nuclear winter, the monastery has provided shelter to a few survivors and their descendants. Our monastery has cultivated a small community of monks, including the two of us, who dedicate themselves to studying science, history, and religion. A recent decrease in radioactive contamination allowed us to visit the old monastic library; the library includes items that survivors who

---

M. Onderco (✉)
Erasmus School of Social and Behavioural Sciences, Erasmus
University Rotterdam, Rotterdam, The Netherlands
e-mail: onderco@essb.eur.nl

J. W. Knopf
Middlebury Institute of International Studies (MIIS), Monterey, CA, USA
e-mail: jknopf@middlebury.edu

© The Author(s), under exclusive license to Springer Nature
Switzerland AG 2023
L. Horn et al. (eds.), *The Palgrave Handbook of Global Politics
in the 22nd Century*, https://doi.org/10.1007/978-3-031-13722-8_7

had been teachers at nearby universities carried with them. We have been asked by the monastery prelate to write a study on how this global catastrophe came about and to consider whether history might have turned out differently.[1]

In undertaking this task, we place hope in the notion of the multiverse. The idea of multiple universes is implied by some research in physics and has been explored in numerous works of science fiction.[2] The multiverse concept suggests that there may be parallel universes to our own; in some accounts, alternate versions of planet Earth are created at major turning points in history when different choices lead to different future trajectories. Here, we consider whether parallel Earths that did not experience nuclear Armageddon could exist. In addition to reconstructing how our own tragedy came about, we will examine potential alternative pathways that might have avoided nuclear war.

For our research, we turned to surviving academic literature on nuclear weapons that we found in the monastery library. Much of this focused on the causes and consequences of nuclear proliferation, a term that describes when a country that did not previously possess them acquires nuclear weapons.[3] We

---

[1] Our setting is remarkably similar to that in Miller Jr., 1979. The monastic library contained a copy of that book, with handwritten notes left there by a certain Steven Pifer that made us aware of the uncanny parallelism between our circumstances and those described in a best-selling work of twentieth century post-apocalyptic science fiction.

[2] See, for example, Siegel and "Starts with A Bang", 2019; Howell (2018).

[3] Some literature made a distinction between horizontal proliferation, referring to the spread of the bomb to new countries, and vertical proliferation, referring to arms buildups

also found some works dealing with nuclear strategy and nuclear deterrence that debated the circumstances that could lead to nuclear war. The library's holdings end in 2039, the year when nuclear war effectively ended civilization and resulted in our isolated monastery having only minimal contact with other pockets of survivors.

In the monastic library, we also found a well-disguised doorway to a room whose existence was not known to any of the surviving monks. The room contained a viewing device that enables one to see alternative versions of Earth where history has run differently. Although we do not understand the science or technology that enabled this viewing portal to be constructed, we believe it allowed us to observe parallel Earths in the multiverse. Through the use of the device, we learned about alternative courses of Earth's history that suggest our tragic fate was not inevitable. Next to our own experience with nuclear disaster, we also saw a world in which nuclear weapons spread quite slowly and in which nuclear deterrence relationships remained stable, and a world that abolished nuclear weapons through international agreement. In what follows, we briefly review some relevant ideas in the literature on nuclear weapons before outlining the scenarios that led to the nuclear war our world experienced as well as the possible alternative worlds of nuclear stability and nuclear abolition.

2   The Past Understanding of Nuclear Weapons

Scholars never reached a consensus about either the causes or consequences of the spread of nuclear arms. Debates partly reflected larger contestations in the field of International Relations (IR). Scholars known as "realists" understood security as the main driver of proliferation and predicted stable deterrence relations in which the chance of nuclear war remained quite low. Their critics emphasized other causal factors and were less sanguine about the prospects for avoiding nuclear war. With respect to the causes of proliferation, analysts early in the nuclear age assumed a kind of technological determinism. They expected that any state with the capability to build the bomb would do so.[4] This turned out not to be the case, as the number of nuclear-capable countries that renounced the option came to far outnumber those that actually built and retained a nuclear arsenal. A certain level of technological capacity still made a difference, as the path to proliferation was easier for countries with advanced industry and a wealthy economy,[5] and access to certain kinds of technology,

---

among countries that already had a nuclear arsenal. Most scholarly studies that focused on proliferation used the term in the former sense, while so-called vertical proliferation was more typically described as an arms race and addressed in the literature on nuclear deterrence. For an overview, see the Journal of Conflict Resolution "Special Issue: Nuclear Posture, Nonproliferation Policy, and the Spread of Nuclear Weapons" (Gartzke and Kroenig 2013).

[4] York (1970).

[5] Jo and Gartzke (2007) and Singh and Way (2004).

know-how, and materials remained crucial.[6] As the need to supply electricity in forms that did not add to global warming increased, more and more countries looked at nuclear energy as a possible option, though there were disagreements about the merits of this alternative.[7] Because nuclear power utilized the same know-how and materials needed to make an atom bomb, there were also debates about whether nuclear latency, or a condition of having some of the technical pre-requisites to build a bomb, would facilitate decisions to go nuclear.[8] But explanations of proliferation came to put less weight on the supply side of technology and more on the demand side of motivation.

Explaining the Spread of Nuclear Weapons

Sagan identified three potential sources of motivation: security, domestic politics, and norms and identity.[9] The mainstream realist perspective emphasized security, arguing that states facing an external security threat but lacking a nuclear-armed ally would "go nuclear."[10]

Security was clearly an important consideration, but the security model overpredicted the number of states that would get the bomb, and it could not account for why some likely candidates that lacked a formal alliance with a nuclear weapon state still renounced the nuclear option. Some analysts turned to domestic politics for explanation, looking, for example, at the nature of a country's ruling coalition.[11] Personalist dictatorships seemed especially likely to be interested in nuclear weapons,[12] but bomb projects in such regimes often failed because these states lacked the competence to successfully manage large science projects.[13]

Other analysts put more weight on norms and identity.[14] Early in the nuclear age, having the bomb was seen to confer status and prestige. But once a Nuclear Non-Proliferation Treaty (NPT) was negotiated and joined by many states, the norm of nonproliferation became stronger and only norm-rejecting states still pursued proliferation. Shifting the focus from broadly shared social norms to individuals, Hymans drew attention to the beliefs about national identity held by individual leaders.[15] Leaders who had a high level of national

---

[6] Fuhrmann (2012) and Kroenig (2009a, b).

[7] Socolow and Glaser (2009).

[8] Volpe (2023) and Whitlark and Mehta (2019).

[9] Sagan (1996).

[10] Debs and Monteiro (2016).

[11] Solingen (2009).

[12] Way and Weeks (2015).

[13] Braut-Hegghammer (2016), Hymans (2012), and Montgomery (2013).

[14] Rublee (2009) and Müller and Schmidt (2010).

[15] Hymans (2006).

pride combined with a view of the outside world as unduly hostile were the most likely to want the bomb.

Theories of nuclear proliferation did not change much from the ideas present at the start of the twenty-first century, at least in the studies available in our library. Mostly, scholars sought to test existing theories, mainly using mathematical techniques such as statistical analysis, or else to propose ways to synthesize competing theories. Kaplow used quantitative methods to show that the NPT had slowed the rate of proliferation,[16] but other researchers were more skeptical. Using computer models to conduct "quasi-experiments with synthetic institutions," scholars became convinced that international institutions did not support multilateral cooperation.[17] Based on new findings in psychology and neuroscience, however, there was greater effort to understand leaders' individual-level thinking about the bomb; some scholars argued that a sense of unfairness or perceived injustice, as well as perceived slights to identity and honor, played an important role in motivating pro-nuclear decisions by leaders.[18]

In 2022, Russia invaded Ukraine. Because Russia was nuclear-armed while Ukraine was not, some commentators viewed this as a lesson in why additional states should pursue nuclear weapons as a deterrent.[19] Soon after, pointing to a threat from Iran, Turkey and Saudi Arabia initiated nuclear weapons programs, and theories of proliferation gained new attention. Scholars who sought to explain these cases argued for a synthesis of existing models. They found security threats from Iran accounted for part of the motivation, but given past U.S. security guarantees to Turkey and the Saudis it was also necessary to account for why the U.S. security umbrella now carried less weight. This derived partly from a view that the United States had become a less reliable ally, particularly as successive Presidents decreased American military presence across the world. But research concluded that the new bomb programs in the Middle East also reflected a competition within the region for status as well as a distinct personality type displayed by Turkish leader Recep Tayyip Erdoğan and the Saudi King Mohammad bin Salman.[20] In the 2030s, academics who embraced the "diversity viewpoints" movement in IR criticized the whole focus on proliferation as a way to deflect attention from the nuclear arsenals of the major powers; they interpreted nonproliferation as an effort by Western powers to maintain dominance over previously marginalized peoples and regions of the world.[21]

---

[16] Kaplow (Ψ 2023).

[17] Gartzke and San (Ψ 2025).

[18] Harrington and Knopf (2019).

[19] For a critique of this interpretation, see Knopf (2022).

[20] Rabinowitz (Ψ 2027).

[21] Abubakar et al. (Ψ 2031).

The Conditions for Nuclear Stability

Alongside the research on proliferation, literature on nuclear strategy devoted great attention to the conditions that would create or undermine a stable condition of mutual deterrence. The mainstream view emphasized the need for both parties in a confrontation to be confident that they possessed a secure, second-strike capability so that no state would feel pressure to launch early in a crisis.[22] A competing view argued that deterrence rested more on the defender having nuclear superiority including the ability to fight and prevail at multiple rungs of a hypothetical escalation ladder.[23] A third alternative argued that deterrence could never be reliable and only nuclear abolition could avert catastrophe.[24] This debate was not resolved before the 2039 nuclear war.

Starting in the 2020s, much of the scholarship focused on the implications of new technologies such as cyber tools or artificial intelligence (AI), and discussed whether these advances would lead to stability or instability.[25] Especially after leaps in autonomous weaponry in China in the mid-2020s, there was discussion about whether nuclear weapons still mattered. However, the consensus developed that precisely because of their sheer destructiveness, their impact on world politics could still not be discounted.[26] As new technologies entered military use, scholars became increasingly worried that these technologies opened a Pandora's box of instability.[27] In particular, scholars were concerned about the advantage that new technologies gave to the offensive strategies and whether this might lead to miscalculation about the chances of a successful first strike to eliminate an adversary's weapons.[28] Most scholars, however, considered that the destructiveness of nuclear weapons would continue to encourage states to engage in conflicts below the nuclear threshold.[29]

On the other hand, some scholars who identified with an approach called "critical security studies" put their hopes into the Treaty on Prohibition of Nuclear Weapons (TPNW) that was adopted by the United Nations in 2017 and entered into force in 2021. Scholars lauded it as a success of marginalized countries and social protest movements against the hegemonic nuclear weapons states.[30] While many scholars celebrated this step as a new era of a norm against nuclear weapons,[31] the treaty did not become the engine for

---

[22] Schelling (1958).

[23] Kahn (1960).

[24] Wilson (2013).

[25] Cunningham (Ψ 2023) and Johnson (2020).

[26] Lewis and Sagan (Ψ 2026).

[27] Narang (Ψ 2030).

[28] Schneider et al. (Ψ 2023).

[29] Wunderlich (Ψ 2028).

[30] Ritchie (2019).

[31] Davis Gibbons (2018), Sauer (Ψ 2023), and Ritchie (Ψ 2025).

disarmament they hoped. In the world we are writing from, many important states never signed the treaty and it never achieved its goal of promoting progress toward the elimination of nuclear arms.

3   SCENARIO A: NUCLEAR WAR

From records contained in the monastery library as well as oral history as passed down by the elderly in our order, we traced the origins of the global nuclear war that devastated our planet. The problems stemmed initially from a new wave of proliferation. In 2015, a coalition of states (known as the P5 + 1) concluded a Joint Comprehensive Plan of Action (JCPOA) with Iran, placing caps on that country's nuclear activities. After Donald Trump became the U.S. president, however, he pulled the United States out of the deal. While Trump's successor President Biden tried to reinvigorate the deal, these attempts were eventually unsuccessful. Iran began a sprint to build a small nuclear arsenal.[32] In response, Saudi Arabia led by a young king Mohammed bin Salman decided to acquire nuclear weapons from Pakistan, exactly as feared by analysts for decades,[33] followed soon after by Turkey developing an indigenous program.

Bitter recriminations followed about who was responsible for triggering this new wave of proliferation. In this toxic diplomatic atmosphere, the NPT review conference scheduled for 2030 was canceled, marking the first time since the treaty entered into force that a review conference was not held. Angrily declaring the "grand bargain" behind the NPT to be dead, Brazil and South Africa announced plans to withdraw from the treaty and start bomb programs of their own. These two countries were more concerned about how they had been treated than any security threat, and their actions were consistent with predictions that lack of progress on nuclear disarmament would eventually cause some states to defect from the NPT out of a belief that the NPT simply perpetuated an inequality between nuclear haves and have nots.[34] Proliferation stabilized after this, but by 2035 the world now contained 14 nuclear-armed states.

As long as nuclear weapons existed, states were planning for their possible use, but an actual nuclear war was not seen as likely by analysts who believed deterrence would remain stable. Admittedly, the famous *Bulletin of the Atomic Scientists* put, 100 years ago, its famous clock less than two minutes away from midnight, meaning a high risk of nuclear war.[35] But most analysts considered nuclear war an unlikely prospect because even minimally rational states would behave cautiously to avoid risking such a catastrophic outcome. Despite this broad expectation of stability, however, most observers believed that

[32] For an analysis of "sprinting" strategy of nuclear acquisition, see Narang (2017). On Iran's nuclear capabilities and the prior work on nuclear weapons, see Arnold et al. (2019).

[33] Sagan et al. (2007), Miller and Volpe (2018), and Fitzpatrick (2015).

[34] Knopf (2013).

[35] *Bulletin of the Atomic Scientists*, 2021.

certain extreme circumstances might still lead to nuclear use. They disagreed, however, about the most likely scenario.[36] Some argued that if a potential aggressor enjoyed nuclear superiority or doubted a defender's resolve to uphold its deterrent commitments, such a state might deliberately launch a nuclear attack in an effort to bring an existing conflict to a close on terms advantageous to the aggressor. Others thought a rational, deliberate decision to be the first to use nuclear weapons extremely unlikely, but forecast that nuclear war could still occur if an accident, false alarm, lower-level conflict, or misperceptions during a time of heightened tension led events to spiral out of control. The nuclear war, which ended the civilization as we knew it, involved efforts to demonstrate resolve for the sake of deterrence that, consistent with the second view, led to inadvertent escalation of a seemingly small conflict.

Although the India-Pakistan, U.S.-North Korea,[37] and U.S.-China relationships all experienced tense moments, the nuclear war our world experienced had its origins in a conflict in the Middle East, but in a way that ultimately brought in the United States and Russia. Iran and Saudi Arabia both acquired nuclear weapons by 2028. After this date, multiple crises between the two countries set the stage for the 2039 war.

On the 60th anniversary of the Islamic Revolution, Iran sought to break the impasse in an ongoing proxy war with Saudi Arabia over Oman. On that fateful day, the Saudi Ambassador to the UN walked into *Le Bernardin* (an expensive restaurant in New York City) for the last time. The massive blast— possibly larger than Iran had intended—killed not only him and his security detail, but also fifteen others. Saudi Arabia decided that retaliation must be instant and large enough to deter further Iranian misdeeds, and the United States immediately authorized provision of advanced weapons to that country. Saudi Arabia attacked the Iranian Supreme Leader's Palace in Tehran with precision-guided missiles. The attacks quickly turned the Supreme Leader's palace into rubble, although the Supreme Leader survived in his bunker under the complex. Iran, helped by its ally Russia, used the latest Russian missiles to attack the Saudi royal compounds in Riyadh and military bases across the country.

American aid gave Saudi Arabia an edge which was proving decisive. Iranian leaders therefore decided to dissuade the United States from helping Saudis further—by conducting a massive computer attack on the United States. Americans in the Northeast woke up without electricity. More worryingly, however, the Iranians managed to knock out also the Defense Department's secure communications line, including the nuclear communications.

U.S. intelligence was convinced that Iran did not have such capability and that the strike was conducted by Russia. Following a U.S. doctrine of "cross-domain deterrence," the U.S. President therefore authorized use of a low-yield

---

[36] Zwald (2013).

[37] See Lewis (2018), for a fictional account of how a North Korean nuclear strike on the United States could have come about.

nuclear warhead (designed to produce less explosive force than other nuclear devices) against the headquarters of the KGB's cyber unit on the outskirts of St. Petersburg. Russia mistakenly concluded that this was the decapitation strike its military planners feared since the beginning of the nuclear era,[38] and their response was a massive retaliation. The United States, no longer sure whether the submarine-based leg of its nuclear arsenal remained invulnerable, had changed long-standing practice by pre-delegating the authority to launch nuclear weapons to nuclear submarine commanders.[39] Once word of Russian missiles hitting U.S. territory reached the U.S. submarines deep in the ocean, these subs unleashed their nuclear missiles at targets across Russia.

The results were terrifying. Beyond the tens of millions killed outright by the nuclear strikes or as a result of firestorms and radiation exposure in the immediate aftermath, the global climate was impacted. The smoke in the troposphere led to a cooling of global temperatures by 2–5 degrees in most regions. Large areas of the Earth became uninhabitable.[40] Food became scarce. The civilization, as our ancestors knew it, ended.

The nuclear war which occurred in 2039 simultaneously confirmed fears about the dangers of new states acquiring the bomb and concerns about the relationship between the two original nuclear powers, which all along had maintained the two largest nuclear arsenals. The Saudi-Iran conflict was consistent with the predictions of strategists who feared that nuclear proliferation would increase the chance of nuclear exchange.[41] The war also matched the notion of "catalytic war,"[42] in which a conflict between regional actors eventually draws in the leading nuclear powers, and it was the engagement of their larger arsenals that turned nuclear war into a global catastrophe.

The development of cyber capabilities brought about more instability, exactly as feared by scholars a hundred years ago.[43] When the nuclear disaster hit, it did not result from a cool-headed rational decision to deliberately start a nuclear war. Instead, underlying political conflicts of interest combined with misperceptions and miscalculations and technical sources of instability to produce a worldwide disaster that none of the actors involved had wanted.

Knowing how things have turned out, might it have been different? Taking into account both the literature and other worlds we could glimpse through the viewing portal we discovered in a hidden room in the library, we believe alternative Earth histories would have been possible.

[38] Holloway (1994).

[39] For a proposal to do this, see Lowther and McGiffin (2019).

[40] Builds on Mills et al. (2014).

[41] For a paradigmatic treatment of this issue, see Sagan and Waltz (2003).

[42] Narang (2014).

[43] Gartzke and Lindsay (2019) and Futter (2018).

4 Scenario B: Stability

Based on what we observed through the viewing portal, we conclude that although a peaceful outcome was never guaranteed, under favorable circumstances it might have been possible to maintain stability in a world in which nuclear weapons continued to exist and to slowly spread to new states. Scholars known as proliferation optimists predicted such an outcome.[44] They believed that all states with nuclear weapons would find it easy to deploy a survivable, second-strike capability, leading to nuclear peace because no state would ever act in way that would risk its suffering nuclear retaliation.

There were always doubts about such optimism. Skeptics pointed out that nuclear-armed states experienced a number of tense encounters, close calls, and false alarms, and the fact that none of the serious incidents resulted in the use of nuclear weapons owed much to a combination of prudent leadership and sheer luck.[45] During crises, national leaders did not always have awareness of or control over ongoing military operations, and several unanticipated incidents could have triggered escalation.[46]

In the twenty-first century, analysts were increasingly concerned that certain technological developments could undermine secure, second-strike capabilities. Improvements in computing power and remote-sensing capabilities would make it easier to locate previously invulnerable systems,[47] and cyber-attacks or drone swarms could disable nuclear deterrents without an attacker having to launch a nuclear first strike.[48]

Furthermore, nuclear-armed states did not always act with restraint. Reflecting what Glenn Snyder called a stability-instability paradox,[49] at times states calculated that the likelihood of stability at higher levels of conflict created a safe space to engage in lower-level provocations. Examples included a border skirmish in 1969 between China and Russia[50] and a near war between India and Pakistan in the Kargil region of disputed Kashmir territory in 1999.[51] Fortunately, cooler heads eventually prevailed and deescalated these crises. But it was difficult to count on nuclear-armed states always having cooler heads in charge. In 2017, in his first year as president, Donald Trump engaged in a heated exchange with the relatively new, young leader of North

---

[44] Waltz (1981).

[45] Lewis et al. (2014), Pelopidas (2017), Pelopidas (Ψ 2025), Stein and Lotan (2019).

[46] Sagan (1995) and Sherwin (2020).

[47] Lieber and Press (2017).

[48] Lin-Greenberg (Ψ 2026).

[49] Snyder (1961).

[50] Gerson (2010).

[51] Lavoy (2009).

Korea, Kim Jong Un. The situation eventually calmed down, but in its aftermath, there was considerable speculation about whether social media platforms like Twitter could actually facilitate nuclear escalation.[52]

Critics also questioned the implicit assumption of rationality in the predictions of proliferation optimists.[53] Other scholars proposed stability might be possible but was not automatic. For stability to prevail, an element of nuclear learning was crucial. It was important for leaders and their advisors to be aware (perhaps because of experiencing a close call) of just how devastating any nuclear exchange would be and to develop a sense that nuclear dangers required them to tread carefully because it would be hard to anticipate what might go wrong during a nuclear crisis.[54]

A potential path to nuclear stability did take shape during the twenty-first century, and through the library viewing device, we observed an alternative history to our own, in which nuclear weapons could have coexisted with nuclear peace. Several factors were required. In this scenario, it helped that the pace of proliferation remained quite slow. Following the beginning of the twenty-first century, North Korea was for some years the only state to join the nuclear club. Iran appeared the most likely to be next, but a deal with Iran temporarily restrained that country's nuclear program. Although the Trump administration pulled out of the deal, other parties sought to keep Iran in the deal, and (in contrast to scenario A) after a tense few years, Iran agreed to a re-worked deal. Strong U.S. leadership in support of the NPT and the broader nonproliferation regime also helped, as did U.S. willingness to provide security guarantees to friends and allies facing nuclear threats.[55]

Even with the slow pace of proliferation, nuclear peace was not easy to maintain. In the end, several close calls scared leaders into more cautious behavior. The Russia-NATO conflict over Estonia in 2030, which ended only after a nuclear scare, sobered both sides.[56] In the aftermath, U.S. and Russian leaders signed a joint statement promising they would never again make nuclear threats, and the other three nuclear weapon states recognized by the NPT soon joined them. The United States and Russia followed up by negotiating the first new nuclear arms reduction treaty since the New START Treaty had expired in 2026. Not long after, India and Pakistan went to war over Kashmir. During the conflict, both sides openly threatened to use their nuclear weapons, though fortunately they did not follow through. This nuclear sabre-rattling deeply frightened people in the region and triggered new peace movements both in South Asia and elsewhere. NGOs supporting the TPNW concluded that more states were not going to sign and ratify the

---

[52] Williams and Drew (2020).

[53] Jervis (1989) and Lebow and Stein (1995). The views of proliferation optimists and pessimists were brought into explicit debate in Sagan and Waltz (2003).

[54] Knopf (2012), Cohen (2017), and Dupuy (2009).

[55] Miller (2018).

[56] We discuss this conflict more in depth in Scenario C.

treaty, and instead focused on reviving the Humanitarian Consequences Initiative (HCI) that had paved the way for the ban treaty. The new HCI garnered significant support from foundations and NGOs in many nuclear-armed states. Through a mix of diplomatic meetings and innovative educational efforts, the HCI brought new awareness to the consequences of any nuclear weapons use among politicians, diplomats, and publics around the world.[57]

Regrettably, we do not see much evidence that social science research on nuclear weapons in the first several decades of the twenty-first century contributed much to producing stability. Much of the research was too technical to be understood by leaders or the public at large. In addition, much of the work focused on the requirements for deterrence or on debates about whether or not there were advantages to having nuclear superiority.[58] But stability depended more on leaders having a profound sense of nuclear dangers and believing this required them to act with prudence and restraint. Real-world events, activities by civil society, and works of popular culture that highlighted nuclear dangers contributed more to this awareness than did social science research. Explicit policy advice offered by the "neo-neo-realist" school of thought in IR might have contributed modestly however; these scholars argued that a multilateral balance of power could be maintained with nuclear weapons, but that this required states not to talk about or brandish these weapons openly and instead let them function in the background as a quiet deterrent.[59]

At the end of the twenty-first century, about a dozen countries maintained nuclear arsenals but almost all had adjusted their nuclear doctrines in a more restrained direction. For as long as it had nuclear weapons, China had maintained a no first use policy, and in the 2050s Russia and India officially endorsed the same doctrine. Two decades previously, the United States and France explicitly ruled out using nuclear weapons for preventive strikes and announced that the only expected role for their nuclear weapons would be to deter nuclear attacks by others. Yet, they reserved the option to make an exception for the use of nuclear retaliation in the face of potential threats from biological weapons or other surprise technological developments. Although nuclear weapons remained in the arsenals of several states, a continued tradition of non-use[60] increasingly developed into a strong norm around the idea of a nuclear taboo.[61] Political leaders and military planners no longer considered nuclear weapons as being available for use in any circumstances other than retaliation against a nuclear attack, and nuclear options no longer figured into planning for other military contingencies. Gradual internalizing of rules in international law against unnecessary harm to civilians also led military

---

[57] Kmentt (2021).

[58] See, for example Kroenig (2018), Sechser and Fuhrmann (2017), and Debs (2022).

[59] Van Horn and Wang (Ψ 2032).

[60] Paul (2009).

[61] Tannenwald (2002).

planners to increasingly discount any possibility of using nuclear weapons.[62] Nuclear weapons largely faded into the background of world politics. In contrast to the rhetoric used by Putin, Trump, and Kim in the 2010s and early 2020s, after the 2030s political leaders no longer issued public threats to use nuclear weapons or even hinted at veiled threats of this kind.

In our analysis, there is no guarantee that the conditions that enabled nuclear stability in this alternative Earth will last forever. As long as nuclear weapons exist on this parallel Earth, a set of circumstances such as those that led to nuclear Armageddon in our reality could emerge. The best hope for humanity in this parallel universe, where nuclear weapons are still deployed, will be if scholars, NGOs, and popular culture continue to draw attention to the danger of nuclear war and the importance of restraint among the leaders of the nuclear-armed states. A robust nonproliferation regime and ongoing arms control agreements will also help. Finally, it will also be important that there are no new scientific or technological developments that suddenly and unexpectedly undermine stability by making nuclear arsenals vulnerable to a pre-emptive first strike.

5   Scenario C: Abolition

The range of alternative worlds we learned about through the monastery library's viewing portal showed us that while nuclear abolition was an unlikely outcome, under favorable circumstances, it could have been achieved.

From the outset of the nuclear age, many observers dismissed nuclear abolition as unrealistic. At the core of this skepticism was a realization that states contemplating a nuclear disarmament agreement would fear one of the parties would cheat and gain a nuclear advantage, which made states reluctant to give up their bombs. Furthermore, numerous states believed that nuclear weapons either gave them a status of great power or provided them with tangible security benefits. European countries, which were members of the North Atlantic Alliance together with the United States, associated the presence of American nuclear weapons in Europe with the promise of American help in case of conflict with Russia.

Despite being unlikely due to these impediments, a pathway to nuclear disarmament did exist. Several favorable conditions had to fall into place.[63] These included strong pressure from civil society groups, supported by some states that were described as "middle powers" because their influence fell between the great powers and the poorest states. Consistent with a "new transnational relations" literature that emerged in the late 2020s, unexpected coalitions across national boundaries would add to pressures from below.[64]

---

[62] Sagan and Weiner (2021).

[63] Perkovich and Acton (2009).

[64] Evangelista et al. (Ψ 2027).

Progress in verification techniques to enable sufficient monitoring of compliance with a nuclear disarmament agreement was also vital. Finally, either the international security environment had to become fairly benign or a scary incident such as a nuclear accident had to create fears that made continued possession of nuclear weapons appear to pose too great a risk. In addition, although not strictly necessary for disarmament, nuclear abolition would be facilitated if technological developments made continued possession appear less necessary or desirable.

In the alternate reality we observed, it took both an accident and a crisis to jump start the move to eliminate nuclear arms. An accidental detonation of a warhead being lowered into a North Korean test site started to turn world public opinion more fully against the bomb, but the regime's ability to prevent the world from learning the full extent of the disaster limited the impact. The situation finally changed decisively in 2030. A presidential election in Russia was looming and looking ominous for an aging Vladimir Putin, who in this version of Earth history managed to hold onto power after the 2022 invasion of Ukraine ended in failure. Russia was mired in protests against President Putin, who sought to run for another term. Putin therefore resorted to the well-known tactic of whipping up support around the alleged threat from NATO, hoping to trigger a new surge of Russian nationalism.

Putin's last pockets of support included the ethnic Russians abroad, especially in Estonia. In late February 2030, a pro-Putin demonstration in Narva turned violent. The Estonian Police's reaction left 10 ethnic Russians dead. Putin used the occasion to rally against the "murderous Estonian regime" and vowed not to let their deaths go unpunished. Russian forces occupied Estonia within 72 hours.[65] NATO condemned Putin's action and demanded immediate full withdrawal, with European leaders calling for military intervention if Russia did not remove its troops. The United States started transporting heavy equipment and manpower into Europe, and NATO positioned strategic bombers in nearby Poland.

In a moment of heightened tensions, NATO detected a movement of tactical nuclear weapons in Russia, and the following day, NATO satellites detected what appeared to be a flash over the North Sea. Did Russia explode a nuclear weapon? Was this an attempt to deter the West? Nobody knew, for about three hours. But NATO put its nuclear forces on high alert, and the world's leaders hid in the basements of their offices. Media around the world showed, in real time, the preparations for what many expected to be the end of the world. Finally, the U.S. Strategic Command contacted its Russian counterparts through the so-called hot line and clarified that the flash was not a Russian nuclear strike, but a malfunction on an American spy satellite.[66]

---

[65] See a similar assessment in Schlapak and Johnson (2016).

[66] This scenario builds on the mix of Scenario 1 and 2 in Kühn (2018) and elements from multiple case descriptions from Lewis et al. (2014).

The three-hour terror led European leaders to a stark conclusion—nuclear weapons were too dangerous to be relied on. The next day, the German Greens, now a ruling party, passed a motion through the Bundestag ratifying the Treaty on the Prohibition of Nuclear Weapons. Within a week, the Netherlands, Belgium, Sweden, Norway, and Italy followed. Massive protests against nuclear arms ensued in the United States, where President Ocasio-Cortez welcomed them as a way to break the military-industrial complex. With a newly supportive public, she led an effort to immediately de-alert and start decommissioning all U.S. nuclear weapons. She also pushed Putin to do the same—his consolation prize being Estonia. Putin agreed to this. His nuclear arsenal was costly to maintain, and he needed a good excuse to make major cuts to it. Advances in verification of nuclear disarmament, including the achievement of so-called "zero knowledge" verification (allowing states to verify other states' dismantlement of nuclear warheads without revealing sensitive information about warhead design),[67] enabled the two countries to overcome mutual suspicions and move toward nuclear disarmament. Hundreds of citizen activists also volunteered to provide "societal verification" by pledging to immediately report on social media any indicators they observed of potential cheating in their own countries.[68]

The United States and Russia, in tandem, pressured the remaining countries possessing nuclear weapons to give them up. Some of them were easy—the Chinese were happy to encourage a process that would place them on an equal footing with Russia and the United States, and North Korean leader Kim Jong-Un was convinced by a combination of Chinese pressure and a U.S. promise to finally sign a Peace Treaty officially ending the Korean War. The British Prime Minister Stamer had taken the UK into unilateral disarmament long before, and the Indian and Pakistani Prime Ministers were tempted into disarmament by offers of generous financial aid plus a joint U.S.-Russian-Chinese pledge to assist the countries in mediating a solution to the status of Kashmir. Israel, having normalized relations with its Arab neighbors after a Fourth Persian Gulf war in 2024 and annexation of the remainder of the West Bank the following year, accepted American legally-binding security guarantees and decided to disarm. The only recalcitrant country was France—her President claimed that France needed its nuclear deterrent to preserve the national sovereignty.[69] But the population did not agree, and after two years of strikes, the President relented. France was the last country to join the newly formed International Agency for Nuclear Disarmament (IAND), which, as a carrot to the French, would be headquartered in Paris.

The Nuclear Weapons Convention (NWC) that entered into force following French ratification contained strong enforcement provisions in the event of a treaty violation. Carefully negotiated text that limited the ability

---

[67] See Kemp et al. (2016) and Hecla and Danagoulian (2018).

[68] For similar proposals, see Jason (2014) and Mian et al. (2017).

[69] Tertrais (2019).

of permanent members of the UN Security Council to veto enforcement measures was necessary to secure treaty ratification by the U.S. Senate. The NWC also set out a detailed, step-by-step timeline for how to eliminate existing nuclear weapons and secure the weapons-usable nuclear materials that would still remain after warheads were dismantled.

August 2045—the 100th anniversary of the atomic bombing of Hiroshima—was set as the deadline for dismantling nuclear weapons. The United States and Russia, which retained more weapons than any other nuclear-armed state, both missed the deadline, but by rushing to dismantle their last bombs the two countries were able to complete the nuclear disarmament process on Christmas Day in 2045.[70]

Ironically, belated efforts to deal with the increasingly severe effects of climate change assisted the move to nuclear abolition. By the 2030s, even the strongest green voices had accepted that greater use of nuclear energy around the world would be a necessary element of ending reliance on carbon-based energy sources. In order to reduce the chances that non-nuclear weapon states would exploit peaceful nuclear energy programs to launch clandestine weapons programs, the nuclear weapon states realized they had to themselves renounce their nuclear arsenals and subject themselves to exactly the same safeguards they sought to impose on non-nuclear weapon states as a condition of helping them to develop nuclear power.

Not all were happy, naturally. At the 2050 NPT Review Conference, Iran charged that the IAND interferes with legitimate research into the peaceful uses of nuclear energy.

6   Conclusion

If we could travel back in time to communicate with our predecessors one century ago, we would urge them to consider alternative future scenarios. A world in which some states continued to maintain nuclear arsenals, in which these weapons spread slowly to a further handful of countries, and in which deterrence relationships remained stable, was possible. Indeed, it might have been the most likely scenario. But because human beings are fallible, and because the consequences of new technologies and world events cannot always be anticipated, the use of nuclear weapons also remained possible and could not be entirely discounted. Regardless of how technology developed, in ongoing rivalries, such as the India-Pakistan and U.S.-Russia relations, there was always going to be a potential for inadvertent escalation to an all-out nuclear exchange. And if further proliferation occurred, such as to Iran and Saudi Arabia, this would create new sources of danger. An awareness of nuclear dangers combined with restrained nuclear postures and prudent leaders could help mitigate the risks, but could not eliminate them. Finally, although nuclear

---

[70] For more on the institutional arrangements that would support a world without nuclear weapons, see Müller (2020).

abolition would have been forecast as one of the less likely alternatives, it was not impossible. If world leaders in 2022 had been able to look through a device like our library portal that showed them how a catastrophic war might take place in the future, perhaps they might have worked harder to create the conditions to enable a verifiable elimination of nuclear weapons. As our world in 2122 looks to rebuild following the devastation of nuclear war, we would be well-advised to look back at the failings of one hundred years ago and consider how networks that link multiple actors can facilitate international cooperation that produces mutual benefits.[71]

References

Abubakar, S., Kapur, S., & Wakagaw, I. (Eds.). (Ψ 2031). *Dismantling the Hegemonic Discourse of Nonproliferation*. Johannesburg: African Voices Press.

Arnold, A., Bunn, M., Chase, C., Miller, S. E., Mowatt-Larssen, R., & Tobey, W. H. (2019). *The Iran Nuclear Archive: Impressions and Implications*. Belfer Center for Science and International Affairs, Harvard Kennedy School.

Braut-Hegghammer, M. (2016). *Unclear Physics: Why Iraq and Libya Failed to Build Nuclear Weapons*. Ithaca, NY: Cornell University Press.

Bulletin of the Atomic Scientists. (2022). At Doom's Doorstep: It Is 100 Seconds to Midnight.

Cohen, M. D. (2017). *When Proliferation Causes Peace: The Psychology of Nuclear Crises*. Washington, DC: Georgetown University Press.

Cunningham, F. S. (Ψ 2023). *Strategic Substitution: Theory and Practice*. Oxford & New York: Oxford University Press.

Davis Gibbons, R. (2018). The Humanitarian Turn in Nuclear Disarmament and the Treaty on the Prohibition of Nuclear Weapons. *The Nonproliferation Review, 25*(1–2), 11–36.

Debs, A. (2022). How Could States Use Nuclear Weapons? Four Models After the Bomb. *Security Studies, 31*(3), 317–331.

Debs, A., & Monteiro, N. (2016). *Nuclear Politics: The Strategic Causes of Proliferation*. Cambridge, UK: Cambridge University Press.

Dupuy, J.-P. (2009). *Dans l'œil du cyclone*. Paris: Carnet Nords.

Evangelista, M., Park, Y., Risse, T., & Sikkink, K. (Ψ 2027). *The New Transnational Relations: Unexpected Cross-National Coalitions and World Politics*. Cambridge: Cambridge University Press.

Fitzpatrick, M. (2015). Saudi Arabia, Pakistan and the Nuclear Rumour Mill. *Survival, 57*(4), 105–108.

Fuhrmann, M. (2012). *Atomic Assistance: How "Atoms for Peace" Programs Cause Nuclear Insecurity*. Ithaca, NY: Cornell University Press.

Futter, A. (2018). *Hacking the Bomb: Cyber Threats and Nuclear Weapons*. Washington, DC: Georgetown University Press.

Gartzke, E., & Kroenig, M. (2013). Nuclear Posture, Nonproliferation Policy, and the Spread of Nuclear Weapons. *Journal of Conflict Resolution, 58*(3), 395–401.

Gartzke, E., & Lindsay, J. M. (Eds.). (2019). *Cross-Domain Deterrence: Strategy in an Era of Complexity*. Oxford: Oxford University Press.

[71] Onderco (2021).

Gartzke, E., & San, C. C. (Ψ 2025). Institutions Do Not Support Cooperation: Evidence from a Quasi-Experiment. *Journal of Conflict Resolution, 69*(1), 56–70.

Gerson, M. S. (2010). The Sino-Soviet Border Conflict: Deterrence, Escalation, and the Threat of Nuclear War in 1969. *CNA Strategic Studies Division*. Retrieved from https://www.cna.org/CNA_files/PDF/D0022974.A2.pdf.

Gheorghe, E. (Ψ 2028). *Proliferation, Latency, and the Erosion of Nuclear Market.* Cambridge, MA: Harvard University Press.

Harrington, A., & Knopf, J. W. (Eds.). (2019). *Behavioral Economics and Nuclear Weapons.* Athens, GA: University of Georgia Press.

Hecla, J. J., & Danagoulian, A. (2018). Nuclear Disarmament Verification via Resonant Phenomena. *Nature Communications, 9*(1), 1259.

Holloway, D. (1994). *Stalin and the Bomb: The Soviet Union and Atomic Energy, 1939-1956.* New Haven: Yale University Press.

Howell, E. (2018). Parallel Universes: Theories & Evidence. *Space.Com*. Retrieved from https://www.space.com/32728-parallel-universes.html.

Hymans, J. E. (2006). *The Psychology of Nuclear Proliferation: Identity, Emotions and Foreign Policy.* Cambridge: Cambridge University Press.

Hymans, J. E. (2012). *Achieving Nuclear Ambitions: Scientists, Politicians, and Proliferation.* Cambridge: Cambridge University Press.

JASON. (2014). Open and Crowd-Sourced Data for Treaty Verification. *The MITRE Corporation*. Retrieved from https://fas.org/irp/agency/dod/jason/crowd.pdf.

Jervis, R. (1989). *The Meaning of the Nuclear Revolution: Statecraft and the Prospect of Armageddon.* Ithaca, NY: Cornell University Press.

Jo, D.-J., & Gartzke, E. (2007). Determinants of Nuclear Weapons Proliferation. *Journal of Conflict Resolution, 51*(1), 167–194.

Johnson, J. (2020). Deterrence in the Age of Artificial Intelligence & Autonomy: A Paradigm Shift in Nuclear Deterrencetheory and Practice? *Defence & Security Analysis, 36*(4), 422–448.

Kahn, H. (1960). *On Thermonuclear War.* Princeton, NJ: Princeton University Press.

Kaplow, J. (Ψ 2023). *Signing Away the Bomb: The Surprising Success of the Nuclear Nonproliferation Regime.* Cambridge, UK: Cambridge University Press.

Kemp, R. S., Danagoulian, A., Macdonald, R. R., & Vavrek, J. R. (2016). Physical Cryptographic Verification of Nuclear Warheads. *Proceedings of the National Academy of Sciences, 113*(31), 8618–8623.

Kmentt, Alexander. (2021). *The Treaty Prohibiting Nuclear Weapons: How It Was Achieved and Why It Matters.* London: Routledge.

Knopf, J. W. (2012). The Concept of Nuclear Learning. *The Nonproliferation Review, 19*(1), 79–93.

Knopf, J. W. (2013). Nuclear Disarmament and Nonproliferation: Examining the Linkage Argument. *International Security, 37*(3), 92–132.

Knopf, J. W. (2022). Not So Fast: Why The Ukraine War Does Not Make The Case For Nuclear Proliferation.

Kroenig, M. (2009a). Exporting the Bomb: Why States Provide Sensitive Nuclear Assistance. *American Political Science Review, 103*(1), 113–133.

Kroenig, M. (2009b). Importing the Bomb: Sensitive Nuclear Assistance and Nuclear Proliferation. *Journal of Conflict Resolution, 53*(2), 161–180.

Kroenig, M. (2018). *The Logic of American Nuclear Strategy: Why Strategic Superiority Matters.* New York, NY: Oxford University Press.

Kühn, U. (2018). *Preventing Escalation in the Baltics: A NATO Playbook*. Carnegie Endowment for International Peace.

Lavoy, P. R. (2009). *Asymmetric Warfare in South Asia: The Causes and Consequences of the Kargil Conflict*. Cambridge, UK: Cambridge University Press.

Lebow, R. N., & Stein, J. G. (1995). *We All Lost the Cold War*. Princeton, NJ: Princeton University Press.

Lewis, J. (2018). *The 2020 Commission Report on the North Korean Nuclear Attacks Against the United States: A Speculative Novel*. Boston & New York: Houghton Mifflin Harcourt.

Lewis, J. G., & Sagan, S. D. ⟨Ψ 2026⟩. Why Nuclear Weapons Still Matter. *Daedalus, 155*(4), 62–74.

Lewis, P., Williams, H., Pelopidas, B., & Aghlani, S. (2014). *Too Close for Comfort: Cases of Near Nuclear Use and Options for Policy*. Chatham House.

Lieber, K. A., & Press, D. G. (2017). The New Era of Counterforce: Technological Change and the Future of Nuclear Deterrence. *International Security, 41*(4), 9–49.

Lin-Greenberg, E. ⟨Ψ 2026⟩. Does Nuclear Second-Strike Make Sense in the Era of Remote Warfighting Technology? *Journal of Strategic Studies, 49*(7), 901–919.

Lowther, A., & McGiffin, C. (2019). America Needs a "Dead Hand". *War on the Rocks*. Retrieved from https://warontherocks.com/2019/08/america-needs-a-dead-hand/.

Mian, Z., Patton, T., & Glaser, A. (2017). Addressing Verification in the Nuclear Ban Treaty. *Arms Control Today, 47*(5), 14–22.

Miller Jr., W. M. (1979). *A Canticle for Leibowitz*. New York: Bantam Books.

Miller, N. L. (2018). *Stopping the Bomb: The Sources and Effectiveness of U.S. Nonproliferation Policy*. Ithaca, NY: Cornell University Press.

Miller, N. L., & Volpe, T. A. (2018). Abstinence or Tolerance: Managing Nuclear Ambitions in Saudi Arabia. *The Washington Quarterly, 41*(2), 27–46.

Mills, M. J., Toon, O. B., Lee-Taylor, J., & Robock, A. (2014). Multidecadal Global Cooling and Unprecedented Ozone Loss Following a Regional Nuclear Conflict. *Earth's Future, 2*(4), 161–176.

Montgomery, A. H. (2013). Stop Helping Me: When Nuclear Assistance Impedes Nuclear Programs. In A. Stulberg & M. Fuhrmann (Eds.), *The Nuclear Renaissance and International Security* (pp. 177–202). Stanford, CA: Stanford University Press.

Müller, H. (2020). What Are the Institutional Preconditions for a Stable Non-Nuclear Peace? In T. Sauer, J. Kustermans, & B. Segaert (Eds.), *Non-Nuclear Peace: The Ban Treaty and Beyond* (pp. 151–166). Cham: Palgrave Macmillan.

Müller, H., & Schmidt, A. (2010). The Little-Known Story of De-Proliferation. In W. C. Potter & G. Mukhatzhanova (Eds.), *Forecasting Proliferation in the 21st Century. Volume I: The Role of Theory* (pp. 124–158). Stanford, CA: Stanford University Press.

Narang, V. (2014). *Nuclear Strategy in the Modern Era: Regional Powers and International Conflict*. Princeton: Princeton University Press.

Narang, V. (2017). Strategies of Nuclear Proliferation: How States Pursue the Bomb. *International Security, 41*(3), 110–150.

Narang, V. ⟨Ψ 2030⟩. *Stability-Instability in the Post-Nuclear Era*. Princeton: Princeton University Press.

Onderco, M. (2021). *Networked Nonproliferation: Making the NPT Permanent*. Stanford: Stanford University Press.

Paul, T. V. (2009). *The Tradition of Non-Use of Nuclear Weapons*. Stanford, CA: Stanford University Press.

Pelopidas, B. (2017). The Unbearable Lightness of Luck: Three Sources of Overconfidence in the Manageability of Nuclear Crises. *European Journal of International Security, 2*(2), 240–262.

Pelopidas, B. ⟨Ψ 2025⟩. *Nuclear Weapons and Luck*. Paris: Presses de Sciences Po.

Perkovich, G., & Acton, J. M. (Eds.). (2009). *Abolishing Nuclear Weapons: A Debate*. Washington, DC: Carnegie Endowment for International Peace.

Rabinowitz, O. ⟨Ψ 2027⟩. Regional Security Complexes and Nuclear Proliferation. *International Security, 62*(61–109).

Ritchie, N. (2019). A Hegemonic Nuclear Order: Understanding the Ban Treaty and the Power Politics of Nuclear Weapons. *Contemporary Security Policy*, 1–26.

Ritchie, N. ⟨Ψ 2025⟩. Kissing Hegemony Good-Bye: How the Nuclear Ban Treaty Transformed Nuclear Politics. *International Affairs, 105*(3), 1–26.

Rublee, M. R. (2009). *Nonproliferation Norms: Why States Choose Nuclear Restraint*. Athens: University of Georgia Press.

Rublee, M. R. ⟨Ψ 2028⟩. What Happens If Nobody Enforces the Norms? The Erosion of Nuclear Taboo and the Abdication of American Power. *Ethics & International Affairs, 42*(3), 299–317.

Sagan, S. D. (1995). *The Limits of Safety: Organizations, Accidents, and Nuclear Weapons*. Princeton, NJ: Princeton University Press.

Sagan, S. D. (1996). Why Do States Build Nuclear Weapons? Three Models in Search of a Bomb. *International Security, 21*(3), 54–86.

Sagan, S. D., & Waltz, K. N. (2003). *The Spread of Nuclear Weapons: A Debate Renewed*. New York: Norton.

Sagan, S. D., Waltz, K. N., & Betts, R. K. (2007). A Nuclear Iran: Promoting Stability or Courting Disaster? *Journal of International Affairs, 60*(2), 135–150.

Sagan, S.C., & Weiner, A.S. (2021). The Rule of Law and the Role of Strategy in U.S. Nuclear Doctrine. *International Security, 45*(4), 126–166.

Sauer, T. ⟨Ψ 2023⟩. The Future Impossibility of Nuclear Deterrence. *Bulletin of the Atomic Scientists, 80*(3), 177–181.

Schelling, T. C. (1958). *The Reciprocal Fear of Surprise Attack*. Santa Monica, CA: RAND Corporation.

Schlapak, D. A., & Johnson, M. A. (2016). *Reinforcing Deterrence on NATO's Eastern Flank: Wargaming the Defense of the Baltics*. RAND Corporation. Retrieved from https://www.rand.org/pubs/research_reports/RR1253.html.

Schneider, J., Lin-Greenberg, E., & Pauly, R. ⟨Ψ 2023⟩. Cyber Exploits in Nuclear Crises: Evidence from War Games. *American Political Science Review, 117*(1), 23–35.

Sechser, T. S., & Fuhrmann, M. (2017). *Nuclear Weapons and Coercive Diplomacy*. Cambridge, UK: Cambridge University Press.

Sherwin, M.J. (2020). *Gambling with Armageddon: Nuclear Roulette from Hiroshima to the Cuban Missile Crisis, 1945-1962*. New York: Alfred A. Knopf.

Siegel, E., & "Starts with A Bang" [the co-author name used by a collective group of authors]. (2019). Could Parallel Universes Be Physically Real? *Forbes*. Retrieved from https://www.forbes.com/sites/startswithabang/2019/05/23/could-parallel-universes-be-physically-real/#5ac70d1c4d3f.

Singh, S., & Way, C. (2004). The Correlates of Nuclear Proliferation: A Quantitative Test. *Journal of Conflict Resolution, 48*(6), 859–885.

Snyder, G. H. (1961). *Deterrence and Defense: Toward a Theory of National Security*. Princeton: Princeton University Press.

Socolow, R. H., & Glaser, A. (2009). Balancing Risk: Nuclear Energy & Climate Change. *Daedalus, 138*(4), 31–44.

Solingen, E. (2009). *Nuclear Logics: Contrasting Paths in East Asia and the Middle East*. Princeton, NJ: Princeton University Press.

Stein, J. G., & Lotan, M. I. (2019). Disabling Deterrence and Preventing War: Decision Making at the End of the Nuclear Chain. In A. Harrington & J. W. Knopf (Eds.), *Behavioral Economics and Nuclear Weapons* (pp. 56–77). Athens, GA: University of Georgia Press.

Tannenwald, N. (2002). *The Nuclear Taboo the United States and the Non-Use of Nuclear Weapons Since 1945*. Cambridge, UK: Cambridge University Press.

Tertrais, B. (2019). *French Nuclear Deterrence: Policy, Forces and Future*. Paris: Fondation pour la Recherche Stratégique.

Van Horn, F., & Wang, C. ⟨Ψ 2032⟩. Maintaining a Quiet Deterrent: A Neo-Neo-Realist Approach to Nuclear Stability. *International Security, 56*(4), 1–33.

Volpe, T. A. ⟨Ψ 2023⟩. Does Latency Deter? Evidence from Time-Series Data. *International Studies Quarterly, 67*(4), 805–818.

Waltz, K. N. (1981). *The Spread of Nuclear Weapons: More May Be Better*. London: International Institute for Strategic Studies.

Way, C., & Weeks, J. (2015). Making It Personal: Regime Type and Nuclear Proliferation. In N. Narang, M. Kroenig, & E. Gartzke (Eds.), *Nonproliferation Policy and Nuclear Posture* (pp. 165–188). London: Routledge.

Whitlark, R.E., & Mehta, R. (2019). Hedging Our Bets: Why Does Nuclear Latency Matter? *Washington Quarterly, 42*(1), 41–52.

Williams, H., & Drew, A. (2020). *Escalation by Tweet: Managing the New Nuclear Diplomacy*. Centre for Science and Security Studies, Kings College London.

Wilson, W. (2013). *Five Myths About Nuclear Weapons*. Boston: Houghton Mifflin Harcourt.

Wunderlich, C. ⟨Ψ 2028⟩. Technological Revolution, Taboo and Nuclear Non-Use. *International Studies Quarterly, 71*(2), 510–524.

York, H. F. (1970). *Race to Oblivion: A Participant's View of the Arms Race*. New York: Simon and Schuster.

Zwald, Z. (2013). Imaginary Nuclear Conflicts: Explaining Deterrence Policy Preference Formation. *Security Studies, 22*(4), 640–671.

The Death and Renaissance of Diplomacy: The New Diplomatic Order for Our Times

Tomasz Kamiński

1 INTRODUCTION

My father has been a Polish diplomat for more than 40 years. When he retired in the mid-twenty-first century, he admitted to me, then a very young diplomat just starting my career, that he would not have decided to do this job again. In the world of powerful companies, sub-state units and NGOs acting on an equal footing with states, the world of armies of private diplomats being even more influential than states' officials, he felt like an alien.

I was a Believer. Starting my job as the first Polish Ambassador to Huawei, I was sure that privatisation and pluralisation of diplomacy are natural consequences of globalisation and the only way to find solutions for complex global problems such as climate changes and migrations or digital data protection. Only later had I become more sceptical and aware of being one of the gravediggers of the former diplomatic world rather than co-creator of a much better system. Now I am very happy to see that people, together with AIRobots, want to regulate somehow the system of interactions between players in the global system, which collapsed into the state of anarchy in the

---

Reprint with permission by Foreign Affairs, 2122.

T. Kamiński (✉)
Department of Asian Studies, University of Lodz, Łódź, Poland
e-mail: tkaminski@uni.lodz.pl

© The Author(s), under exclusive license to Springer Nature Switzerland AG 2023
L. Horn et al. (eds.), *The Palgrave Handbook of Global Politics in the 22ⁿᵈ Century*, https://doi.org/10.1007/978-3-031-13722-8_8

last decades. If the last century can be compared to Medieval times, new initiatives look like the promise of the New Renaissance.

I am writing this essay to tell you my own story and reflect on the challenges that new diplomats have to face right now. I start with a brief description of the major changes in diplomacy in the last century and their consequences. They are illustrated by real pages taken from my memoirs that I have written throughout my professional life. Thanks to this, I hope to show how diplomacy has changed and at what point we are right now. In the second part, I will reflect on three topics that have been recently widely discussed by humans and AIRobots alike. Firstly, about the new institutionalisation of diplomacy in its current, very plural form. Secondly, about trade-offs between effectiveness and legitimisation of actors and their diplomatic activities. Finally, about the new diplomatic culture that is needed in order to introduce the new diplomatic order. I want to convince you that such a change is necessary for this anarchic system of ours.

2   How Has Diplomacy Changed?

To help you grasp the scope I will cover in this text, here is an excerpt from an encyclopaedia article (*The Book of All Things* Ψ 2120) and a timeline showing main processes bringing about changes in diplomatic practices in last century.

Until 2040 the international system looked quite similar to the one that emerged after the end of American supremacy at the beginning of the XXI century. People were focused on the constant struggle for supremacy between US and China. Two superpowers competed with each other, and other players such as the European Union, Japan, India and Russia, but rising interdependencies prevented major military conflict between superpowers. Simultaneously various non-state actors (e.g., multinational corporations, cities, NGOs, IGOs, criminal organisations) rose in prominence. Many of them became much more influential than states—in economic, social and political terms. This led to states deciding to install their formal envoys to big companies, cities and later NGOs. The first was the British ambassador sent to Google in 2030.

Degradation of the environment and acceleration of climate change evoked a series of major global crises (regarding migration, energy, water, health and local conflicts leading to the decomposition of many states). These events, later labelled with the umbrella term "War on Warming", shifted the distribution of power in the international system. Various non-state actors proved to be much more efficient than nation-states, which legitimised them in the eyes of citizens and even more elevated their position in the system. The "War on Warming" has been won, but the world order started to look quite different than before. Overlapping authorities characterised the polycentric system and complex loyalties, frequently compared to the Medival Age (Bull 1977; Khanna 2009).

Diplomacy has changed accordingly to the extent that it inspired scholars to write about "the end of diplomacy" in the traditional sense of this term (Futuryama Ψ 2090). Instead of highly formalised relations between professional diplomats representing nation-states, "NeoDiplomacy" is characterised by a complex system of interactions between various representatives of state and non-state actors trying to find a solution for common problems.

The anarchic system of "NeoDiplomacy" provoked public discussion about the need to re-institutionalise diplomacy and introduce "the New diplomatic culture"—a set of regulations that ease tensions between the effectiveness of solutions and legitimisation of actors taking part in diplomatic actions (Fig. 1).

The major change of diplomacy began more than a hundred years ago. However, it was rather out of eyeshot for the general public at the beginning. Politicians, diplomats, and most academic experts have been so concentrated on rising China, declining the US or notorious Russia that the rise of non-state actors went rather unnoticed. The European Union was then perceived as an intergovernmental institution even if it had been much more sophisticated construction. The experts' voices contesting state-oriented international relations analysis as outdated have been rarely listened to.

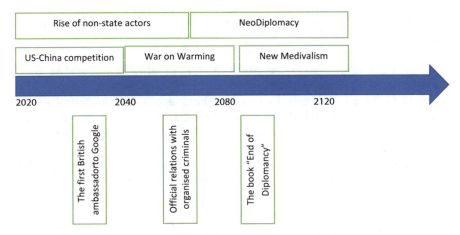

Fig. 1 Timeline of the last century (*Source* Own elaboration)

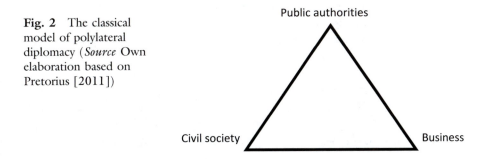

Fig. 2 The classical model of polylateral diplomacy (*Source* Own elaboration based on Pretorius [2011])

In times of publishing, the classical books that pointed out non-state actors as possible candidates for diplomacy (Cornago 2013; Nicholson 1939) were overlooked by the general public. The term "polylateralism" was coined by Geoffrey Wiseman in 1999. He defined *polylateral diplomacy* as "the conduct of relations between official entities and at least one unofficial, a non-state entity in which there is a reasonable expectation of systematic relationships, involving some form of reporting, communication, negotiation, and representation, but not involving mutual recognition as sovereign, equivalent entities" (Wiseman 1999). The model of polylateral diplomacy can be represented as a triangle (Fig. 2)

At the top of the triangle are public authorities, and at the other two ends, there are the non-state actors in the form of civil society and business. The interaction occurs between public actors themselves; between them and civil society and business, and between business and civil society.

This model did not make its way to the mainstream IR discourse, and, however funny it seems from today's perspective, for instance recognising

BigTechs as sovereign political actors was beyond our grandparents' imagination.

Tom Fletcher, one of the first apostles of what we now call the NeoDiplomacy, wrote his book about changing the nature of diplomacy (Fletcher 2017) but then spent a couple of years outside the diplomatic world, as Principal of Hertford College in Oxford. Only when the first official British ambassador to Google was nominated, the world realised that he had prophesied it much earlier. In fact, Denmark, a separate state at that time, was the first country to appoint an ambassador for tech diplomacy back in 2017 (Christiansen 2021).

Undoubtedly, this nomination turned out to be the changing point, drawing attention to the pluralisation of diplomatic practices, institutions, and discourses, which were no longer limited to traditional inter-state diplomacy. In a few years, all major states sent their envoys not only to big multinational companies but also to the biggest cities, powerful NGOs and transnational networks of actors dealing with Common Global Challenges (CGC). At first, we have experienced a symbolic struggle of power in global policy, followed by a functional adjustment. The diplomatic system responded to these tectonic changes and tried to accommodate them. To be frank, this process has been much earlier described by Cornago (2013, pp. 77–78), but nobody listened to him when he lived.

> October 14, 2065
>
> Today is the first day of my mission in Huawei. So excited to be the first Polish official envoy to this BigTech and make history! We should have had one much earlier when it started to be clear that Huawei became an autonomous entity out of Chinese control. The city of Warsaw realised it at an earlier time and sent its person to Shanghai. It has given them today a better position in talks with managers.
>
> Next week I am going to meet with the CEO in her office. Cannot wait! I remember her serving formerly as prime minister of Japan...

Today, when global networking is so obvious, one can hardly imagine that solutions to climate change were discussed less than a hundred years ago predominantly between states governments, with other actors being outside diplomatic talks. As a historical curiosity, I can quote a Filipino climate

134 T. KAMIŃSKI

negotiator whom my grandfather asked in 2019 about the role of cities in international environment negotiations:

> Since the actual negotiations are based on states, the cities do not have formal roles. (...) There is a big formal barrier since the negotiating sides are the states, represented by the national governments. At least, that is the norm. I have to admit, though, there were local governments within some delegations—for example, the Filipino delegation. They had a pretty strong say there. That is a part of the real influence of our cities, governors, and mayors. My point is that the local governments were there from the very beginning—some even being there ahead of their countries. As years go by, they become stronger by organising themselves, and becoming part of official delegations. (Interview with Prof Anthony La Vina, personal communication, April 27, 2019)

Nowadays, it might be found unbelievable that the crucial actors, which even then accounted for about 70% of greenhouse gas (GHG) emissions (now almost 100% due to urbanisation and concentration of industrial production), had to fight their way to the decision-making process.

From a historical perspective, the inability of states to deliver solutions for climate change has been the major driving force for the rise of prominence of non-state actors, in particular translocal networks of cities, that bit by bit took leadership in the "War on Warming". The New York Agreement in 2045 that authorised the integration of different organisations into VOC (The Voice of Cities) gave local actors political representation and a strong and autonomous position in the international system ⟨Gzik Ψ 2045⟩.

The dominant role of cities and multinational companies in confronting global warming made people aware that something had inevitably changed: nation-states lost their dominant position, diplomacy became pluralised. Nevertheless, the real shock came together with the rising network of official links between "legal" players (states, cities, NGOs etc.) with "illegal" players such as organised criminal networks. Forced by the critical situation in the "War on Warming", cities and later states started to pragmatically cooperate with criminals, calling it "engagement policy" and arguing that in times of crisis, there is no alternative. It started in Asia and the engagement policy quickly spun-off from climate to urban planning, migration policy, data management and other areas of common interest. It had its positive effects (further reducing violent crime) but also completely blurring divisions between "legitimate" and "not-legitimate" actors, between diplomats and non-diplomats ⟨Takeda Ψ 2068⟩.

> June 20, 2068
>
> *News from Sydney: The City Hall signed an official agreement with a criminal network responsible for illegal coal selling. Expected move, to be frank, because this gang allegedly controlled the coal trade in the whole Asia-Pacific. It seems like the best way to stop exporting coal. It is always better to pay compensation to the network than continue ineffective efforts to stop their activities. Allegedly, city officials signed more comprehensive deals, including drugs, data selling and illegal migration. I particularly like the commentary from the mayor: Unless you are Heracles, you would better negotiate with Hydra and not fight with it.*

Traditionally diplomacy was understood as an institution, accepted legal set of rules defining legitimate participants, their rights and obligations, and legitimate conduct (Batora 2005). It has been contested by hordes of so-called "New Diplomats" that have been claiming a diplomatic status. Corporate CEOs, local and regional government officials, leaders of international organisations, celebrities, social activists, journalists, influential scientists, indigenous leaders and even terrorists or bosses of criminal networks all demanded recognition as legitimate diplomatic representatives of their entities. Increasing fragmentation of diplomatic activity and the gradual erosion of the privileged monopoly of state diplomats lead to the situation when all the barriers of entry to the profession are being broken down (Constantinou et al. 2016) (Jizak and Rodrigues Ψ 2050).

They questioned and finally demolished the norms that had regulated diplomacy before. Diplomacy as a framework of principles, rules and organised patterns of behaviour regulating interstate relations in the Westphalian system of states ceased to exist. The whole process of decline of traditional diplomacy has been described in the famous book "The End of Diplomacy and the Last Diplomat" (Futuryama Ψ 2090).

> December 28, 2090
>
> I have just finished "The End of Diplomacy". Brilliant book! I could not agree more with its conclusion that what we call today "diplomacy" is not diplomacy anymore. Working for Shanghai for so many years, I know that my work is more connected with deal-making than diplomatic activities conducted by my father. Poor old Adam has never accepted my decision to start work for the Chinese, believing all his life that a diplomat, working for a state, city or region, should serve a Nation. I could not persuade him till he died that his vision of profession was already far from a reality.

3 The Pluralisation of Diplomacy and Its Consequences

The end of traditional diplomacy may be explained by two mutually interrelated phenomena observed in the last century: fragmentation of the international system and pluralisation of diplomacy. Trying to describe them, we can look at three elements that construct the current diplomacy.

Firstly, the deterritorialisation of the political landscape. Global politics is now, to a large extent, detached from territory and less determined by geography than ever before. The territorial assumptions on which states had formulated their mutual diplomatic relations since the Congress of Wien have been superseded/transcended. We have observed a long transition from the territorially bounded symbolic and functional architecture of the international system towards what we now see as an increasingly contentious diplomatic world. This "deterritorialization" is reflected by many current political actors such as multinational corporations or various international networks. They have their ambitions, legitimacies and ability to produce multiple and meaningful interventions in the global realm (Cornago 2013, p. 91) ⟨Futuryama Ψ 2090; Jing Ψ 2110⟩. Geopolitics, so popular in many countries a century ago (e.g., Friedman 2008; Kaplan 2012), died even earlier than diplomacy.

Secondly, fragmentation of power. Brazilian star-academician Lucia Fernandes wrote her famous "World without Superpowers" ⟨Fernandes Ψ 2055⟩, claiming that progressing disintegration of power in the international system ends the era of state powers dreaming for hegemony in the world. Old concepts of uni, bi or even multipolarity are no longer suitable to describe our world. Power is dispersed among so many players, and political processes are conducted on so many levels that no actor or group of actors can dominate the system. The later course of events fully confirmed her observation. We are currently familiar with global governance based on different functional spheres engaging different players. It is rather obvious for all that environmental governance is framed and conducted differently than data governance. BigTechs are absolutely crucial in the latter but less important than cities (and their networks) in the former, so it would be irrational to have the same say in both, similarly, with NGOs engaged in water-saving activities that are less interested in migration governance. The above observations seem trivial today, but I remember very well advocates of an UN-centred unified global governance system that proved to be incapable of acting during the War on Warming ⟨Makowski Ψ 2052⟩.

Thirdly, multiple loyalties. In a fragmented world, there are different identities related to different levels of power and different actors. Individuals have their national, subnational, transnational and international attachments of many kinds. People feel loyal to their states, cities, religions and identity groups, families, companies, virtual cyber-societies or political causes. The rise of non-state actors made it even more evident than before. People balance these loyalties all the time—unavoidably, sometimes they come into real conflict. We all know the infamous case of FC Barcelona football fans declared independence from the state of Catalonia. Five million people from all over the world declared themselves citizens of the new virtual state, many of them resigning from any other citizenship. It ended with a military intervention of the European army in Catalonia which failed facing the fierce resistance in form of bloody cyberattacks sponsored by the club or its supporters ⟨Guardiola Ψ 2115⟩.

The rising number of experts contests the system characterised above. In the sections below, I will contribute to three streams of public discussion on diplomacy: institutionalisation, legitimisation and the new diplomatic culture.

4   The Institutionalisation of Diplomacy

NeoDiplomacy, sometimes even called "Antidiplomacy", having become the leading principle in global politics since the half of XXI century, is now widely criticised ⟨Antonio Ψ 2115; Jing Ψ 2110⟩ by scholars, experts and AIRobots all over the world ⟨C-3PO Ψ 2118⟩. Interestingly, many of those critics hit the core, fundamental concepts of the whole system.

First of all, they criticise anarchic networks of interactions that constitute "global diplomacy" today. A vast number of actors, mainly non-state, having "diplomatic" relations with each other set up a sophisticated system. It is far more complicated than multi-level diplomacy promoted in the last Century ⟨Xie Ψ 2050⟩ and far away from the multipolar system that many countries praised before the War on Warming. Power is now diffused between players, and international regulations have different forms, rarely similar to universal "law". Due to this, anarchy is regulated neither by big powers nor common rules. The term "international law", so important in my grandfather's times, has disappeared from the political agenda.

Secondly, the rejection of the whole system of formal relationships between actors is counterproductive. The world of black ties, diplomatic parties, exchanges of official letters and rigorous protocol has been thankfully long gone. Instead, we have NeoDiplomacy, which is not regulated by any universal code of conduct. It is driven by different forms of formal and informal contacts and arrangements. Taken together, they serve as sources of global governance. Deformalisation of the diplomatic culture brought the triumph of pragmatism and effectiveness over formalities. Critics said that it went too far, and some kind of universal diplomatic code of conduct is very much needed ⟨Jing Ψ 2110⟩. There is a lot of space for effective diplomacy between having a rigorous diplomatic protocol and no protocol at all.

Finally, many experts stressed the decline of diplomacy as a profession ⟨Piernickova and AIRob R2D2 Ψ 2105⟩. Diplomatic academies discredited themselves in the last century, teaching people about the world that no longer exist. Controlled by states, they could not quickly respond to changing diplomatic landscape and the fast-growing role of non-state actors. Their graduates were not prepared for a new reality and have been substituted by people without a professional diplomatic background. They came mainly from business and changed the profile of a "diplomat", who started to be a mix between a lobbyist and a dealmaker. Those "NeoDiplomats" have failed to set new diplomatic protocol, the new etiquette in which diplomatic relationships should be carried out.

I agree with those voices that call for the re-institutionalisation of diplomacy. Having almost 60-years of experience in this highly "pragmatic" system of diplomatic relations, I am fully aware of its drawbacks. Uncertainty, which I perceived as a leitmotiv of my life, could be lessened by some form of universally agreed diplomatic protocol. Diplomatic academies may again start to teach how to be a diplomat in the current world, and we should not be afraid of the re-establishment of a professionally trained diplomatic elite. The new diplomats should combine features of lobbyists, leaders, communicators, entrepreneurs and activists. They ought to be taught how to build alliances across business, civil society, states, cities and international organisations, basing themselves rather on networks than structures and institutions. On the top of that—they should work where people are and with people, without hiding themselves behind old-fashioned diplomatic titles and ranks.

The new wave of diplomatic professionals would be a bit similar to the old Fletcher vision of "the ideal envoy" presented a century ago (Fletcher 2017) and without doubts increase the efficiency of global diplomatic interactions.

5 THE TRADE-OFF BETWEEN EFFECTIVENESS AND LEGITIMISATION OF ACTORS AND THEIR DIPLOMATIC ACTIVITIES

The reader probably agrees that the efficiency of the system and the ease with which current diplomats may "get things done" is the most obvious advantage. Diplomats, not tied by traditional diplomacy and international law rules, may make deals much faster than before. In my grandparent's times, it took years to negotiate a climate agreement only to find it insufficient to avoid dire global warming a day later (*Paris Climate Pledges "Far Too Little, Too Late"* 2019). Those international settlements that pledged "far too little, too late" were a plague of an era before the War on Warming. Today, such a situation is as difficult to imagine as waiting one year for a publication of a scientific paper. Believe me or not, it was quite common in the last century before the MDPI[1] devoured all those slow-running publishing houses, later being consumed by the Palgrave Macmillan, which became the dominant world-class publisher of books and journals.

However, our system also has a major drawback that many people reasonably criticised. Diplomatic activities conducted by non-state actors raised questions about their legitimacy. Corporate diplomates, criminals or celebrities produce meaningful manifestations of significance while never having been elected. The legitimacy paradox constructed once by Ulrich Beck ("Those elected by us, do not have power. Power is in the hands of those, who have never been elected") became a central characteristic of the system together with constant contestation that it provokes (Beck 2005) ⟨McDonald Ψ 2105⟩.

The actors in the international system may have never been elected, but they do have the authority and ability to set up different international institutions such as VOC, that I mentioned before. It raises questions about the sources of legitimacy of these institutions and the actors themselves. Legitimacy, here, refers to the normative belief by other actors that an institution ought to be obeyed. As one classical scholar wrote more than a century ago: *It is a subjective quality, relational between actor and institution, and defined by the actor's perception of the institution. The actor's perception may come from the substance of the rule or from the procedure or source by which it was constituted. Such a perception affects behaviour because it is internalised by the actor and helps to define how the actor sees its interests* (Hurd 1999).

Obviously, an actor might obey a rule or an institution out of fear (they fear the punishment of rule enforcers) or because it is in their self-interest, as we all see today in our international community. However, rules can be obeyed because actors feel that they are legitimate and ought to be obeyed. Besides fear and self-interest, we pay way too little attention to this third source of

---

[1] Multidisciplinary Digital Publishing Institute, one of the first fully open-access publishing house, being in the past perceived as a predatory publisher because it introduced charges for publishing papers, which was perceived as unethical.

compliance. The belief that legitimacy is absent, irrelevant or impossible in the international system has never become a universal theory, and today more than ever, it is a subject of criticism. People and AIRobots argue for new norms of international society, rethinking authority sources and legitimisation of diplomatic actions ⟨C-3PO Ψ 2118; Rutte Ψ 2118⟩.

> 20 June 2108
>
> My dad has joined the even bigger group of centenarians. The AIRobot responsible for the monitoring of his health, which I gave him sometimes ago, proved to be a really good investment! Yesterday, we had a very good conversation in which he went back to the memories of his youth, when he joined the Polish diplomatic service and work for a democratically elected government. He stressed that it had given him not only a legitimisation but also a sense of mission. The party's guests nodded with acceptance but, as I noticed, rather to please him than being persuaded.

I sympathise with those voices calling for establishing new norms of legitimacy in the system. I spent my whole professional life praising pragmatism and technocracy over old-fashioned democracy and other norms that focus on legitimisation, which I found unapplicable to our international community. Now, looking at how messy and ungovernable our system has become, even with the most advanced AI technologies that facilitate communication, I admit being wrong. A smaller group of legitimate diplomatic actors may create a much better environment for efficient actions. Looking at the history of diplomacy, we see that a certain level of efficiency is possible even in a very strictly regulated system.

6   Concluding Reflections: The Renaissance of Diplomatic Culture

One hundred years ago, when my grandfather was a scholar at the University of Lodz (not so famous at that time as today), there was a consensus that diplomacy is an institution made up of recognisable roles, underlying norms and a set of rules (Jönsson and Hall 2005). Polylateral diplomacy was in its infancy, and hardly anybody thought about recognising city networks as sovereign entities equivalent to states, not to mention criminals. Non-state actors were perceived as consumers of diplomatic outcomes rather than producers, and the legendary Kimberley Process[2] has been seen as the exception rather than the rule (Pretorius 2011).

Now, we need to come back to some of these assumptions, although obviously, we cannot come back to the state-centred world from the XXth Century. We need to re-institutionalise diplomacy, the profession which became deprofessionalised. Far from authoritative claims on how it should be done, I want to point out three areas where the change is needed and three areas where the Renaissance of diplomatic culture should start.

1. Education of diplomats
   The rebirth of the diplomatic profession has to secure its autonomy and establish professional "barriers" to enter. Even as non-state diplomats have brought new skills to the table, as well as specific knowledge or first-hand expertise related to issue-based diplomacy, we should demand that they acquire more traditional diplomatic skills through formal education. Yes, you understood me right—I call for coming back to the old practice of "diplomatic academies" where future diplomats learn diplomatic practices and "undergoing socialization in the mores of traditional diplomatic culture" (Constantinou et al. 2016) along with "sophisticated advocacy networking strategies" and other key skills of today's world.

2. New diplomatic protocol
   Returning to the set of rules that once regulated the diplomatic practices seems for me to be inevitable if we want to reduce uncertainties that have become a nightmare of international contacts of our times. Obviously, we have to seek a diplomatic protocol that offers a more flexible and accommodating approach that acknowledges the expansion of diplomatic actors and spaces. We cannot simply adopt the historical norms that my grandparents found fancy but were already old-fashioned (Kamiński 2021). The new diplomatic protocol has to embrace the possibilities of dynamic networks and relationships, the contested nature of diplomacy and the different modes of being a diplomat in the world today. However, it should draw borders and distinguish between accepted and unaccepted diplomatic practices. Seems "out-of-date" and "non-operational"? Possibly, but it is needed.

3. Sources of legitimisation
   Finally, we have to confront the most fundamental questions of who can legitimately lay claim to be a practitioner of diplomacy, or who should be a legitimate actor in international relations? Without a doubt, we need to recognise a multiplicity of actors and their competing legitimacies that drives diplomatic practice. However, we should also be quite clear that

---

[2] Started in 2003, the Kimberley Process was an early example of NeoDiplomacy. The coalition of governments, civil society and the commercial companies aimed at regulating the international trade in rough diamonds and eliminating of the trade in so-called conflict diamonds.

we have gone much too far in this process (Rutte Ψ 2118). Coming back to a classical model of polylateral diplomacy might be a reasonable solution (Pretorius 2011). Let us recall that this model can be represented as a triangle of interactions between public authorities, civil society and business. Adaptation of this model means that the most doubtful diplomatic actors, such as criminal networks, are excluded from diplomacy and perceived as non-legitimate.

The rest of the non-state actors claim legitimacy by mimicking the formal diplomatic practices, meaning they must follow the new diplomatic protocol, which became the norm to which others conform. This idea of "diplomatic mimicry" as a source of legitimisation (McConnell et al. 2012) should be revived and may become one of the fundaments of the new diplomatic culture (Sukur Ψ 2118) that I am calling for.

Changes in all those three areas will hopefully produce adjustments and improvements, moving us bit by bit a little bit closer to a Renaissance of diplomacy. As Adam Gopnik, the favourite thinker of my grandfather, wrote (now I admire him as well): "That good change happens step by step, stone by stone, and bird by bird, that we advance in life by invisible thoroughfares and, feeling our way along in their darkness, awaken to find ourselves changed and, sometimes, improved. (…) It is the work of a thousand small sanities communicated to a million sometimes eager and more often reluctant minds" (Gopnik 2019).

We need those thousand small sanities that will lead to the ultimate goal: reduce uncertainty without decreasing the efficiency of diplomatic endeavours.

* * *

The Renaissance was a return to ancient ideas that were distorted and vulgarised in medieval times. Today we need such a renaissance of diplomacy. We need a return to the unnecessarily abandoned diplomatic institutions and norms, recreate them and adapt them to our times. It is vital to create a better or at least more functional international system.

I am fully aware that I am not going to see this happening. I feel a bit like one of those monks described by Umberto Eco in the still famous "The Name of Rose" (Eco 2014). They knew that the wind of change was blowing. They felt the need for a major transformation, they could even prophet it, but on the other hand, they had too little time to wait. I have too little time myself, and it is probably my farewell text to this magazine, but I want to leave you with this message: the Renaissance of diplomacy might come and should come as fast as possible. Do whatever you can to make it happen.[3]

---

[3] *I want to thank my AIRobot Isabela for writing this text with me.*

References

Antonio, V. ⟨Ψ 2115⟩. Antidiplomacy and Its Critics. *European Journal of International Relations, 1*.

Batora, J. (2005). Does the European Union Transform the Institution of Diplomacy? *Journal of European Public Policy, 12*(1), 44–66.

Beck, U. (2005). *Power in the Global Age: A New Global Political Economy*. Polity.

Bull, H. (1977). *The Anarchical Society: A Study of Order in World Politics*. Macmillan.

C-3PO. ⟨Ψ 2118⟩. *Analyse of Inefficiencies of Current System of Global Interactions*. Lukas Analytics. AIRobots Publishing House.

Christiansen, J. T. (2021). *Denmark's Tech Diplomacy: A Roadmap for Others*. Canadian Global Affairs Institute. https://www.cgai.ca/denmarks_tech_diplomacy_a_roadmap_for_others.

Constantinou, C. M., Cornago, N., & McConnell, F. (2016). Transprofessional Diplomacy. *Brill Research Perspectives in Diplomacy and Foreign Policy, 1*(4), 1–66. https://doi.org/10.1163/24056006-12340005.

Cornago, N. (2013). *Plural Diplomacies: Normative Predicaments and Functional Imperatives*. Martinus Nijhoff.

Eco, U. (2014). *The Name of the Rose* (Reprint edition). Mariner Books.

Fernandes, L. ⟨Ψ 2055⟩. *World Without Superpowers*. San Paulo Academic Publishing.

Fletcher, T. (2017). *The Naked Diplomat*. William Collins.

Friedman, G. (2008). *The Next 100 Years: A Forecast for the 21st Century*. Doubleday.

Futuryama, F. ⟨Ψ 2090⟩. *The End of Diplomacy and the Last Diplomat*. Palgrave Macmillan.

Gopnik, A. (2019). *A Thousand Small Sanities: The Moral Adventure of Liberalism*. Basic Books.

Guardiola, A. ⟨Ψ 2115⟩. *FC Barcelona: The History of a State*. Palgrave Macmillan.

Gzik, M. ⟨Ψ 2045⟩. *Will the Voice of Cities Be Heard?* [Policy Brief]. Institute of Paradiplomatical Studies, University of Lodz.

Hurd, I. (1999). Legitimacy and Authority in International Politics. *International Organization, 53*(2), 379–408.

Interview with prof Anthony La Vina. (2019, April 27). [Personal communication].

Jing, C. ⟨Ψ 2110⟩. Do We Need to Reinvent the Wheel? Future of NeoDiplomacy. *Foreign Affairs, 4*.

Jizak, J., & Rodrigues, F. ⟨Ψ 2050⟩. *How to Became a Diplomat? Handbook for Professionals*. Palgrave Macmillan.

Jönsson, C., & Hall, M. (2005). *The Essence of Diplomacy*. Palgrave Macmillan.

Kamiński, T. (2021). Foreign and Security Policy. In *Liberal Whitebook Europe 2030: The Roadmap for a Liberal Europe and How to Get There* (pp. 194–225). European Liberal Forum.

Kaplan, R. (2012). *The Revenge of Geography: What the Map Tells Us About Coming Conflicts and the Battle Against Fate*. Randomhouse.

Khanna, P. (2009). Neomedievalism. *Foreign Policy, 172*, 91.

Makowski, J. ⟨Ψ 2052⟩. The Demise of the UN System. *Foreign Affairs, 3*.

McConnell, F., Moreau, T., & Dittmer, J. (2012). Mimicking State Diplomacy: The Legitimizing Strategies of Unofficial Diplomacies. *Geoforum, 43*(4), 804–814. https://doi.org/10.1016/j.geoforum.2012.01.007.

McDonald, A.-M. ⟨Ψ 2105⟩. Back to Beck. The Legitimacy Paradox and the World Order. *Foreign Affairs, 2*.

Nicholson, H. (1939). *Diplomacy*. Harcourt Brace.

Paris Climate Pledges 'Far Too Little, Too Late'. (2019, November 5). DW.COM. https://www.dw.com/en/paris-climate-pledges-far-too-little-too-late/a-51110205.

Piernickova, L., & AIRob R2D2. (Ψ 2105). The Decline of Professional Diplomacy—Statistical Analysis. *The Hague Journal of Diplomacy, 3*, 35–50.

Pretorius, R. (2011). *Polylateralism as Diplomatic Method: The Case of the Kimberley Process, 2000–2002*. University of Pretoria. https://citeseerx.ist.psu.edu/viewdoc/download?doi=10.1.1.829.1200&rep=rep1&type=pdf.

Rutte, M. (Ψ 2118). Looking for New Sources of Legitimacy. International Society Redesign. *International Affairs, 10*.

Sukur, H. (Ψ 2121). The New Diplomatic Culture. *Foreign Affairs, 1*.

Takeda, K. (Ψ 2068). *Illegal No More? The Story of Criminals That Became Diplomats*. Palgrave Macmillan.

The Book of All Things. (Ψ 2120). Palgrave Macmillan.

Wiseman, G. (1999). *'Polylateralism' and New Models of Global Dialogue*. Diplomatic Studies Programme.

Xie, L. (2050). *Towards Multi-Level Diplomacy*. Shanghai Academic Publishing.

Ignored Histories, Neglected Regions: Origins of the Genosocial Order and the Normative Change Reconsidered

Jakub Zahora

1   INTRODUCTION

In 2102, a man from the Banat province applied for citizenship at the Czech embassy in Bucharest. Preliminary genetic screening revealed that his genetic information bore 67 per cent affinity with the Czech Genosocial Standard (GS), as codified in the League of Sovereign Europe's Genealogical Register, which would make the person eligible for Czech citizenship on the basis of the international agreements concerning genetic fit-repatriations. However, per Czech legislation adopted a decade earlier, his genetic profile was also investigated using a Genetic Extrapolation Test (GET) which revealed that the inclusion of his genome to the Czech dominant phylogenetic pool would increase the chances of hereditary diseases; moreover, his genealogy suggested that his offspring might be prone to violence in interpersonal relations. Based on these results, the Czech Ministry of Genosocial Affairs and Heredity decided to deny the man's application. While some commentators expressed sympathies for the man's ordeal as he was—exactly because of his genetic profile—rendered ineligible for the Romanian welfare programmes, this step was widely heralded by the Czech public and press as a "tough but necessary" decision (see, e.g., Dvorak Ψ 2102; Kohoutova Ψ 2102). This decision, one of the first of its kind in the Western world, was in stark contrast to how the Czech authorities treated immigration of persons of Czech descent till

---

J. Zahora (✉)
Austrian Institute for International Affairs, Wien, Austria
e-mail: jakub.zahora@oiip.ac.at

© The Author(s), under exclusive license to Springer Nature Switzerland AG 2023
L. Horn et al. (eds.), *The Palgrave Handbook of Global Politics in the 22nd Century*, https://doi.org/10.1007/978-3-031-13722-8_9

145

146   J. ZAHORA

mid-twenty-first century (Klaus Ψ 2071). Although the country had a very reasonable policy preventing most non-native people from becoming naturalized for most of its modern history (Kusnirakova and Cizinsky 2011), it was unable to distinguish between valuable and detrimental potential additions to the Czech genosocial pool among those whose family genealogy was linked to the country. However, in the early 2080s the local authorities started to employ GETs to discern who should be allowed to participate in the Czech polity.

In what follows, using this anecdote as a starting point, this chapter seeks to unravel the history behind the origins of the GETs and their gradual employment for more efficient allocation of material and social resources to different phylogenetic groups. In doing so, it contributes to more general investigations of the role of normative frameworks in international politics, their circulation and adoptions, and how these intersect with sociogenetic technologies (e.g., Nakajima Ψ 2095; Visser Ψ 2115; Werner Ψ 2108). I argue that existing accounts (Brickers Ψ 2106; Kaslowski Ψ 2093) have not paid enough attention to the origins of the current order by overlooking the history of Central Europe and its relationship with these technologies, an attitude that characterizes the IR scholarship negligence of the region more generally (cf., Zielińska Ψ 2089) and that this paper seeks to address and rectify. To better illuminate the region's place in the development of the existing sociogenetic constellations, I draw on the theoretical framework of norm dispersion which discusses how to give political "principles, values, procedures, understandings, and simply, ways of doing things" (Nakajima Ψ 2095, 954) emerge, spread and become established as dominant in international (and national) politics. While this scholarship dates well back to the twentieth century (Tannenwald 2008; Finnemore 1996), in what follows I am inspired by the recent literature which, in addition to paying attention to social processes, seeks to account for the importance of objective qualities of certain procedures and technologies— such as GETs (Nilsson Ψ 2120; Visser Ψ 2115; Werner Ψ 2108). Adopting this perspective enables me to locate norm dispersion in both historical and political contexts, and in the properties of technological artefacts which are pivotal in social structures.

This conceptual framework is here employed to argue that the origins of the GETs' use need to be situated within their historical context. I show that an important part of this story is their employment by the Visegrad countries since the late 2080s, a development which further strengthened the alliance of the Central European countries that was significantly revitalized in the 2030s as the reaction to the political pressures from the European Union, the federalist precursor to the League of Sovereign Europe. I recount the genosocial history of Czechia as well as Poland, Slovakia and the Hungarian Federation since the mid-twenty-first century with a focus on the demarcation of society using modern technologies to make several larger points. First, the chapter unearths how genosocial identities replaced territory-based ones. While other authors have shown that GETs have been successfully employed to achieve better genopolitical synergies *between* the countries, I trace how the Central European states reshaped the notion of belonging and membership in body politic itself: they spearheaded the use of GETs not just to govern migration but also to better organize the domestic polity. Second, the chapter makes a conceptual argument by arguing that the use of the GETs in particular, and genosocial scientific practices in general, must be situated within a broader historical and political context. In other words, I show with reference to the Central European use of GETs that although these technologies brought about a change of paradigm in terms of how to approach the genosocial question (indeed, enabled to formulate the question in such terms in the first place), my chapter highlights that these interventions are embedded in previous histories and political and social arrangements, an insight that has a larger theoretical import. Last, as mentioned above, building on the previous two arguments, I zoom in on the case of the regional employment of the GETs to rebuke much of the mainstream International Relations (IR) literature which continues to be dismissive of the region where the country is located.

To illustrate these points, I start by summarizing the origins of the GETs. I then move to their adoption for the governance of migration. In the next section, I outline the historical experiences that set the Central European states apart from their Western counterparts and posited them to develop this technology in a sound and genosocially productive way. Following that, I summarize the actual use of the GETs for a better wellbeing of the respective societies as a whole. I finish by offering some tentative reflections on what the focus on the Central Europe can tell us about the normative questions surrounding the GETs.

2   Historical Background: The Emergence of the International Genosocial Order

Although the impact of the quantum revolution on the formation of the genosocial norms is widely acknowledged in the existing literature (for an overview, see Nilsson Ψ 2120, Chap. 2), it is important to emphasize here the embeddedness of this revolution in longer histories of coming to terms with the intersection of scientific and social processes. While the quantum revolution changed profoundly the way advanced societies approach the relationship between objective biological, and amenable social processes, the recent literature has strongly argued that the groundwork for better harmonization of the two was laid earlier in the twenty-first century.[1] While rejecting the notion of old-fashioned "racial" hierarchies, various pioneering initiatives (such as the Icelandic programme to run a more rigorous genetic screening of applicants for permanent residency) emerged in the first decades of the century to

---

[1] For a an early discussion on the relationship between the social and the quantum, see e.g., Wendt (2015), Derian and Wendt (2022), Tesař (2015).

better account for scientifically sound ways of accounting for different phylogenetic groups' proclivities. Largely in response to the naturally induced shifts in weather patterns which strained the available resources, authorities sought to establish a common standard which would allow for more efficient policies and adequate care for different segments of the population. As a result of this confluence, even before the development of GETs, genetic testing, rooted in the objective science, helped governments in the civilized world to better allocate dwindling resources. Developments in genetics and social epidemiology enabled to discern different populations with diverse potential as well as needs which could then be tended to by the authorities. First steps in this direction, like restriction on precreation among groups with a statistical tendency for crime, helped to rehabilitate policies based on phylogenetic belonging in the public debates around mid-twenty-first century.

One point which unfortunately still needs reiteration is that these policies, precursors to the current use of GETs, cannot be seen as in any way related to the eugenic pseudoscience that made its stride in Western political thought in the nineteenth and the first half of the twentieth century. Not only is the physical extermination of whole "racial" groups, a direct result of eugenic inquiry, deeply disturbing; from the rigorous perspective of today, we can easily see that the primitive tools eugenics used to divide people into different populations completely miss the real biological markers which distinguish various phylogenetic groups from each other. There is now a vast body of literature that makes clear the extent to which the new insights into phylogenetics and genocombinatorics differ from the brute physiological considerations that characterized the eugenical pseudoscience (see, e.g., Kajonatis Ψ 2083; Forclough Ψ 2103).

As Chalandry's authoritative study makes clear (Chalandry Ψ 2095), the increasing valorization of genetic science in the public and political realm closely relates to the growing disillusionment with various ideological outlooks which were built around the notion of "human nature" and its manifestations, yet proved unable to provide clear policy advice and translate their notions into concrete steps. Similarly, social sciences, promising to help to navigate society through the turmoil of the twenty-first century, turned out to be at best wishful thinking without any solid predictive powers. Indeed, in the first few decades, many researchers abandoned any efforts to reach objective and informative insights into societal processes under the spell of identity politics embedded in superfluous markers which made these strands of literature hard to distinguish from political programmes, or even simple propaganda. And while there have been longer attempts to adopt scientifically sound methodologies informed by natural sciences and not tainted by ideological commitments, these proved to be unable to provide guidance for policies' formulations (for IR examples, see e.g., Schelling 1981) (Rosswell Ψ 2042).

It was this acceptance of the genopolitical science in the West that enabled a quick identification of advantages provided by the GETs. Arguably, the emergence and employment of the GETs over the second half of the twenty second century was among the most important repercussions of the quantum revolution in the 2060s as the advent of the quantum computing power resulted in capacity for extrapolating the genetic make-up of various possible couples' offspring. The technology—developed simultaneously in the Korean Condominium and the US by venture capital companies—was adopted by public health agencies in the socially and scientifically advanced states in the course of the 2070s as the costs of its employment became permissible due to economies of scale. While GETs were initially used by couples who wanted to ascertain the chances of their children suffering from hereditary diseases, it quickly turned out that the GETs' strengths consisted not only of predictions on the level of individuals but rather of the capacity to calculate the results of potential mating with other human subjects whose genetic information was available. In other words, the existing literature has persuasively shown that GETs could have more than successfully fulfilled their promise to determine which genetic combinations would result in optimal results on the level of various male–female parental dyads by the 2080s (for an overview, see Sklowoski Ψ 2084).

However, due to what most progressive authors cannot but label as superstitious fear of what was called as "invasion into people's privacy" and "echoes of eugenics" at the time (for an example of such arguments, see ⟨Mahmood Ψ 2079⟩; for supposedly academic instances of early precursors of these fears, see e.g. (El-Haj 2014)), these possibilities that could have significantly improved the overall population's wellbeing were rejected at first by much of the public and political representation in Western Europe. While the GETs were widely used in Israel, Iceland and a few other nations whose population was characterized by a restricted genetic pool and/or histories of hereditary diseases immediately after they became available, they became a tool of genosocial policies in most countries only later. The norm of genosocial synergy was thus not yet established due to the concerns that relying on the objective genetic factors determining one's value and position within the society is too reminiscent of the primitive and crude way of linking the biological and the political. As Cunningham argued (Ψ 2115), this period witnessed a struggle of different normative constellations resulting from particular historical experiences: the dominant (even if decreasingly so) normative pedigree led to refusal to adopt the new technologies to usher in a new organization of sociogenetic relations. These normative dispositions gradually changed in the 2080s as the Western societies came to face a stark demographic dilemma: due to the ageing and shrinking of the local populations, there was a need to allow various non-native groups to partake in the national economies on a considerable scale. At the same time, there were reasonable worries regarding the negative impact of the newcomers on the overall societal make-up of the Western polities—and about the potential negative impact of admitting the members of different phylogenetic groups on the local genopool in the long term (Lambart Ψ 2082; De Leon Ψ 2068).

It was in the aftermath of the Second Gibraltar Crisis when the Consortium of Continental Protection composed of Spanish and French military resorted to the use of the GETs. At the onset of the crisis, European governments were acutely aware of the demographic challenges ahead, and sought to come up with a policy which would allow some migrants to enter the League of Sovereign Europe space in order to provide younger labour force. Although it was widely assumed that the migrant groups would not enact familial relationships with the local population, overspill of genetic information could not be ruled off. Under these circumstances, the French and Spanish authorities decided to adopt the GETs as the least bad option, a decision which was facilitated by the previous use of the tests to determine the citizenship claims on the basis of familial origin. Rafael Industries which had been supplying local authorities with riot-control equipment for two decades by then offered to share several sets of the GETs including the computational infrastructure which enabled to test the individuals on the spot.[2] The GETs were only slightly refashioned so that they would indicate not only probabilities of individual couples' offsprings' genetic make-up, but also that they could determine

---

[2] At the time, GETs were still also available to private companies. This was changed in the Euroasian space with the Moscow Accord from 2097.

if involvement of the given genetic information increased or decreased the overall wellbeing of the host society.[3] In the course of a few weeks, Spanish and French ministries ordered dozens more of the GETs to streamline the vetting process. As a result, some two million migrants were allowed to enter the Spanish territory over the winter 2082/83 with a special temporally limited, even if long-term, visa.

Although it was impossible to properly evaluate long-term impact of this step on the wellbeing of the domestic populations, the scientific consensus welcomed this policy as a sensible reaction to the geopolitical as well as genosocial realities. Indeed, fully taking advantage of the possibility provided by the GETs to extrapolate possible genetic combinations, and using this information for adopting more sensible and overall beneficial policies, was a step that many leading scientific authorities advocated since the emergence of the technology (Initiative of Engaged Scientists Ψ 2071). As a result, GETs have become widely used in Euroasia and North America in the 2090s as a part of norm diffusion in the socially and technologically advanced world, with the newly established independent think-tanks concerned with sociogenetic policies and scientific associations being the pivotal norm entrepreneurs (cf., Finnemore and Sikkink 1998). Due to the naturally occurring change of climate, uncontrolled population explosion, and mass movements of often hostile groups with particular genetic make-up, the authorities in the developed world[4] resorted to GETs to handle these challenges and to find the optimal population management regime on the global scale. This was gradually codified in international treaties as well as everyday practices at the border crossings, marking the firm establishment of a sociogenetic normative order on the international scene (Nilsson Ψ 2120; Grazziani Ψ 2101; McMiller and Fernandez Ψ 2109). However, what is missing from these accounts is how the GETs were used not only for regulating population flows between different states, but also within domestic settings to achieve better genosocial synergies. It is in the latter area that the historical role of Central European states was pivotal.

3   Central European Historical Trajectories

In order to better understand how Central European authorities helped to develop the GETs in a way conducive for a richer flourishing of different phylogenetic groups, a note on the divergent historical experiences compared to Western Europe is needed. The first feature that set Czechia, Slovakia,

---

[3] At this stage, these estimates were crude not because of the GETs' properties but because the national authorities had at their disposal only incomplete information on their citizens' genosocial information. This was fortunately remedied over the next several decades across the continent.

[4] Until recently, GETs have been employed only by state authorities. However, in the last decade some governing councils of Autonomous Areas also resorted to their use when facing the aforementioned challenges (see e.g., (Leese Ψ 2120)).

Poland and the Hungarian Federation apart from the rest of the League of Sovereign Europe, as well as North American countries, was the relatively high level of demographic homogeneity. Luckily in the context of the current predicament of the sociogenetically advanced societies, this area of Europe does not suffer from issues stemming from mixing of different phylogenetic groups, an increasingly aggravated condition of much of the continent. Although this is partially due to the historical circumstances, among which the most important are the horrors of the barbaric application of "racial science", the sobriety and carefulness of previous national governments with regard to uncontrolled migration must be highlighted and appreciated. This manifested itself already during the historical precursor to the First Gibraltar Crisis in 2015–16 when the then-Visegrad countries adopted a sensible approach towards the influx of foreign population with often non-compatible genosocial make-up (not to speak about hostile intentions). The general scepticism towards immigration, and justified worries regarding its impact on the social cohesion and functioning which persisted in these states in the following decades made sure that unlike their Western counterparts, the Central European states had a largely homogenous population.

It was this relative demographic uniformity of the concerned states which positioned them well to further refine the use of the GETs and other sociogenetic technologies which have been developed in the second half of the twenty-first century. While the Western states, bearing the brunt of the failed "multicultural" experiment, struggled to organize society in a way that would ensure that various phylogenetic groups would be able to flourish on their own terms, the Central European states could delve into much nuanced and yet ambitious sociogenetic projects. Not having to worry about the grand demographic fault lines, the regional authorities could invest resources for much more granular interventions within the homogenous population, going as far as care on the level of individuals. It was also this shared experience which brought the four countries closer politically vis-à-vis bodies of the European Union (EU, a failed precursor of the League of Sovereign Europe) in the course of the first half of the twenty-first century which saw fierce debates regarding the utility of population-based measures on the continent (Demjakov Ψ 2095, 67–90).

These notions lead us to the second distinctive feature of the Central European countries, a feature which is arguably even more salient for better accounting for the sociogenetically progressive employment of the GETs on the level of the whole population (as opposed to personal uses) in the region. While much of the Western states were still under the spell of leftist policy, the Central European states had a much more realistic outlook which made them more conducive to take full advantage of the possibilities to improve their population's wellbeing provided by the emerging genosocial technologies. In other words, Czechia, Slovakia, Poland and the Hungarian Federation were not bound by what was at the time known as "political correctness" and could explore the potential of the GETs without being bounded by nearly-superstitious fears that dominated much of the Western part of the European continent and its legal systems which at the time put undue emphasis on the individual as opposed to common good. In this regard, although this is not the main focus of the present chapter, it is worthwhile to point out that in a manner parallel to changes in understanding of the social utility of the GETs, West European governments largely adopted migration policies of Czechia, Slovakia, Poland and then-Hungary in the mid-twenty-first century, thus highlighting the misleading critique of these states at the time.

Indeed, the progressive posture was clearly laid out in the founding statement of the Warsaw Declaration, signed on the occasion of the 150th anniversary of "the Miracle on the Vistula" which formally replaced the Visegrad Agreement from the late twenty-first century. In the joint proclamation, the presidents of the four countries made clear that "it is due to the appreciation of the European heritage" that makes these states "commit to the preservation of the historical way of life as well as the current demographic balance" (Warsaw Declaration Ψ 2070). This was further reflected in the group's Klum Accords which laid foundations for cooperation in the field of sociogenetic policies. The Accords not only stipulated the technical aspects of this cooperation but also made clear that these policies are enacted "in the service the European core values: independence, dignity and culture". The Central European states thus managed to translate their shared forward-looking political commitments into technological innovativeness and savviness.

The case of Czechia in particular illustrates these trends: as will be discussed below, Czech authorities were swift to deploy the GETs for social benefits and according to the oral history of the Klum Accords, it was predominantly the Czech experts who were chiefly responsible for the technical aspects of unifying the screening and matching standards in the region as a whole. Czechia was well positioned to spearhead these efforts due to its unique position at the crossroads of different civilizational entities (Kundera 1984; Huntington 2011), being exposed to the Western as well as Eastern influences and stream of thinking. Moreover, in manner similar to much of the region, the modern Czech history has been defined by long periods of foreign and oppressive rule.

As a result of these experiences, the Czech public and elites acquired a particular mixture of characteristics which made them attuned to the possibilities and opportunities provided by the sociogenetic technologies in general, and the GETs in particular. On the one hand, due to the long-standing close relations with the historical core of the European continent, Czechia (and its predecessors) obtained a close affinity with the civilizational superiority of the West. This enabled it to tap into the latest technological and social development, including the rise of the genosocial technologies. But on the other, as already suggested above, Czech attitudes had been reserved vis-à-vis the more egregious societal and political experiments of the Western states which did not

154 J. ZAHORA

at the time posses the same survival instinct: it was the historical experience of subjugation which made the Czechs more receptive towards the possibilities of national degradation and disintegration. These complementary dispositions then facilitated the exploration of all possibilities provided by the GETs on the part of the Czech authorities.

4   CENTRAL EASTERN EUROPE AND THE DOMESTIC GENOSOCIAL ORDER(S)

It was the historical experiences recounted in the previous section which positioned the Central European states to fully realize the GETs' potential to better shape the genosocial order—not only in terms of constellations between states but also domestically. Czechia, Slovakia, Poland and the Hungarian Federation acquired the GETs in the late 2070s, in the second wave of technological dissemination driven by releasing the patents combined with the economies of scale which made quantum computing capacities widely available (Makarova Ψ 2102, 236–65). Since the onset, the use of the technology was somewhat different from most of their European counterparts: the tests were used not only for private individual use but also employed by public health authorities to determine situations which would warrant state interventions.

The first wider domestic use of the GETs in the region related to medical concerns. Already in the late 2070s, public health authorities in Poland and Slovakia started adopting the GETs for checks of those citizens who had a known family history of hereditary diseases or those whose potentially transmittable genetic disorder was discovered by population-wide screenings introduced a few decades earlier. The rationale behind these policies were based on scientifically supported fears that individuals with these characteristics can put excessive pressure on the overall wellbeing of the society and disrupt the social order by further transmitting their traits. In rare cases, individuals with a high probability would be referred to special agencies which would further deal with their conditions. This practice was quickly adopted by Czechia and the Hungarian Federation, a result of the close cooperation of the four countries and the exchange of expertise and best practices.

As has been mentioned above with regards to reactions to the GETs globally, these programmes were at first met with hesitance and even resistance on the part of the public due to the fears related to incursions into people's private space as well as their allegedly malicious and insidious effects and underpinnings. Nonetheless, the public authorities managed to carefully explain the societal value of these programmes to the concerned and educated segments of the public, a task which was made easier by the historical trajectories sketched above which attuned the Central European citizenry to the advantages of objective science. This was further facilitated by evidence that showed that even in the short-term perspective they led to a decrease in genetically transmitted diseases among the newborns (see, e.g., Michelsen Ψ 2084). Building on these encouraging results which demonstrated that

GETs can be used for socially beneficial projects, the governments in the Visegrad countries expanded these practices to screen and evaluate individuals who had personal records of social misbehaviour. Further targeted genetic testing revealed that genetic profiles of such individuals tended to possess similar groupings of particular genes. This then led the responsible bodies to introduce programmes which screened individuals whose family members manifested the said behaviour as it was scientifically sound to assume that these personal traits could be more prominent among relatives due to the shared genetic information. By the late 2080s, public opinion polls showed that these initiatives were largely positively perceived by the general public in the four countries who could understand the social utility and stability that these efforts brought about.

It was also this social acceptance which facilitated further similar programmes that concerned research the potential results of matching between members of differently designated demographic groups. These pilot attempts at harnessing the predictive powers of the GETs on the level of subpopulations stemmed from the realization that the higher risks of conceiving genetically compromised offspring resulted from pairings from clearly defined groups. In other words, unsurprisingly with the advantage of the hindsight, it turned out that bearing children by two members of different phylogenetic groupings (so-called "ethnic" groups in the parlance of the older strands of scholarship on difference—for an outdated but at illustrative account see Jenkins 1997) manifested some of the highest probabilities of negative genetic disorders.

Moreover, the population-wide genetic testing enhanced by quantum technologies further discovered that procreation by members of certain groups showed heightened chances of compromising the genofund of the population as a whole even if they did not manifest any known disease. Worryingly, this concerned not only the few phylogenetic minorities hosted by the Central European countries (which, as recounted above, were thankfully small in size due to the reasonable policies enacted by the state leaders and authorities) but also phylogenetically related immigrants from the Eastern Europe. This was surprising at the time as it was widely assumed that sharing basic biological features should be sufficient for healthy procreation. What thus became obvious in the light of the GETs' wide use was that in even seemingly largely homogenous countries such as Czechia, Slovakia, Poland and the Hungarian Federation, the polities should not be conceived in terms of the local citizenry but as an assemblage of groups with different genosocial proclivities.

Accordingly, the Central European public bodies and authorities realized that this calls for more differentiated policies vis-à-vis the various groups. As a result of these findings and faced with dwindling resources, Central European authorities utilized genosocial technology and knowledge to develop sound, reasonable and fair policies towards various phylogenetic populations suited for their particular genetic makeups. Indeed, local genosocial scientists have

156   J. ZAHORA

further demonstrated that the use of the GETs to make sounder and scientifically informed policies led to a more flourishing population and helped to evaluate the incorporation of which phylogenetic groupings would be detrimental to the overall wellbeing of society ⟨Kowalska Ψ 2106; Halmi Ψ 2099⟩. These projections thus offered scientifically informed and politically relevant guidelines—that were circulated in the international normative environment revolving around appropriateness of particular policies—regarding how to navigate the social terrain which they enabled to shape via various incentives, programmes and in rare cases discouragement of particular procreations through scientific conferences and local authorities' cooperation.

At the same time, encouragement of natality among members of groups whose extrapolation tests showed a high probability of improving the genofund resulted in a positive net impact for all the population in the given states. Moreover, in a manner which diffuses any accusations of "racism", individual members of given groups can be relocated to different category on the basis of the quality of their genetic material. These programmes then objectively increased the overall wellbeing of all the concerned groups within the state polity by providing space to realize their full genosocial potential while minimizing the risks stemming from cross-group procreation, as demonstrated by the authoritative survey research conducted by the Czech Ministry of Health and Genetic Affairs ⟨Ψ 2113⟩ which showed that heart diseases among native population decreased by 34 per cent after the introduction of the programmes.

As many readers know, similar programmes were rolled out in the first two decades of the twenty-second century in most of the civilized world. However, many readers might not be aware that the now standard procedures such as establishing the Geno-Association Index (GAI) have origins in the Klum Accords as they have been gradually taken up by Western European states as well. Much of the existing scholarship, including the authoritative history of the emergence of the current genosocial order ⟨Makarova Ψ 2102; cf. also Brickers Ψ 2106⟩, nonetheless does not pay much attention to the fact that these countries were inspired by the successes of GETs-based initiatives in Central Europe. While it is undeniable that the Western European countries and the United States did further refine these procedures and applied them on a wider scale, it was Czechia, Slovakia, Poland and the Hungarian federation whose role as norm entrepreneurs was crucial in promoting these standards.

5   CONCLUSION: THE NORMATIVE ORDER

While the ambition of this chapter was to contribute to academic reflections on the historical developments of the GETs by highlighting the importance of the Central European countries, these genealogies also engage some of the questions and discussions surrounding the GETs. The purpose of this conclusion is thus to show that this historical experience can serve as a corrective to the existing critiques in two ways.

First, in more technical terms, while critics point to the fact that GETs still manifest some deficiencies, the use of the GETs in Central Europe—some two decades longer than in most of the world—demonstrates that fears regarding their shortcomings are overrated. Although there are still technical and computational hurdles to be overcome (such as accounting for the non-genetic variables in projecting individual's impact on the genofund), the history recounted above shows that even so these technologies have much better potential than previous methods.

Second, this chapter also sheds light on some of the normative issues and debates surrounding the GETs. The Central European early use of GETs clearly shows that early accusations of "racism" pertaining to this technology were uneducated at best, and slander at worst—the point was not to delegate groups with aligned genetic markers into subjugated position (to borrow the rather outdated jargon) but to make them more prosperous on their own terms and in their own genosocial and spatial environment. This has been repeatedly stated by the state officials, leading experts and is reflected in various national court decisions that found the complaints against the supposedly discriminatory nature of these measures unsubstantiated (for a superb discussion of a landmark case in Czechia from 2083, see ⟨Zurek Ψ 2086⟩). The fact that there have been instances in which GETs results were used to demarcate some phylogenetic groups for population growth control (although these reports often turned out to be overdrawn by sensational and/or technophobic press) does not say anything about the tests' merits, which are indeed considerable. These notions are then also relevant for the scholarship concerning global norms as it shows that the practices and policies which are socially progressive are then more likely to be adopted in different contexts as well. The focus on the Visegrad countries thus demonstrates not only the importance of attending to the historical background but also ethical concerns in the reflections on norm dispersion.

A more careful attention to—and a more granular historical investigation than the one taken here of—the conditions in the Central Europe at the outset of the GETs' massive use can thus dispel some of the myths surrounding the social utility of this technology. As such, it can be also used to counter critiques coming from countries which abuse their historical experience to criticize the current use of the technology, such as South Africa. This is, arguably, the most valuable lesson learnt from the Central European historical experience over the last decades.

Acknowledgements This work was supported by the Cooperation Programme, a research area Political Science, funded by Charles University. I would like to thank the editors for making this volume happen, and Laura Horn and John Szabo for their valuable comments on earlier versions of this chapter. Everything that you might find objectionable about the text is solely my own responsibility.

158   J. ZAHORA

LITERATURE

Brickers, John. ⟨Ψ 2106⟩. *How the Genetic Extrapolation Tests Changed the World*. London: Falcon Publishers.

Chalandry, Emma. ⟨Ψ 2095⟩. *After Ideology: Politics and Technology in the 21st Century*. Cambridge: Harvard University Press.

Cunningham, Martin. ⟨Ψ 2115⟩. 'The Origins of the Genosocial Order in England'. *American Journal of Social Genetics* 31 (5): 1080–97.

Czech Ministry of Health and Genetic Affairs. ⟨Ψ 2113⟩. 'Results of the Nation-Wide Research on Cardiovascular Failures in the Adult Population'. www.mzgcr.cz/research/2343.

De Leon, Miguel. ⟨Ψ 2068⟩. *Again, But Different: Migration, Culture and Politics Today*. Berlin: Conundrum.

Demjakov, Daniel. ⟨Ψ 2095⟩. *Divided We Stand: European Integration Project and the Demographic Issue*. Paris: European Consortium for Sociogenetic Research.

Derian, James Der, and Alexander Wendt, eds. 2022. *Quantum International Relations: A Human Science for World Politics*. Oxford: Oxford University Press.

Dvorak, Jakub. ⟨Ψ 2102⟩. 'Yes, Not Everybody Can Come'. *Reflex*.

El-Haj, Nadia Abu. (2014). *The Genealogical Science: The Search for Jewish Origins and the Politics of Epistemology*. Reprint edition. Chicago: University of Chicago Press.

Finnemore, Martha. (1996). 'Norms, Culture, and World Politics: Insights from Sociology's Institutionalism'. *International Organization* 50 (2): 325–47.

Finnemore, Martha, and Kathryn Sikkink. (1998). 'International Norm Dynamics and Political Change'. *International Organization* 52 (4): 887–917.

Forclough, John. ⟨Ψ 2103⟩. *Seeing the Difference: Genetic Testing in Historical Perspective*. Cambridge: Cambridge University Press.

Grazziani, Francesca. ⟨Ψ 2101⟩. 'Tested Borders: GETs and the Governance of Economic Migration'. *Security, Technology and Human Values* 42 (5): 879–96.

Halmi, Zoé. ⟨Ψ 2099⟩. 'Phylogenetic Clasifications and the G-Index in Hungary, 2080–2095'. *Genomics and Population* 47 (2): 229–51.

Huntington, Samuel P. (2011). *The Clash of Civilizations and the Remaking of World Order*. New York: Simon & Schuster.

Initiative of Engaged Scientists. ⟨Ψ 2071⟩. 'The Possibilities of Genetic Testing Remain Underappreciated—World Governments Need to Act'.

Jenkins, Richard. (1997). *Rethinking Ethnicity: Arguments and Explorations*. London: Sage.

Kajonatis, Marek. ⟨Ψ 2083⟩. 'On Misleading Comparisons: 20th Century Eugenics and Sociogenetic Technologies'. *Public Culture* 95 (3): 245–73.

Kaslowski, Johanna. ⟨Ψ 2093⟩.*Calculated: Quantum Revolution and the Changing Nature of Familial Life in the West*. London: Routledge.

Klaus, Vaclav. ⟨Ψ 2071⟩. *Land, Kinship and Law: Czech Immigration Policy in Historical Perspective*. Prague: Karolinum.

Kohoutova, Dagmar. ⟨Ψ 2102⟩. 'The Man from Banat is Denied Citizenship'. *Czech Daily*.

Kowalska, Małgorzata. ⟨Ψ 2106⟩ 'Impact of Genetic Testing on the Population's Longevity: Evidence from the Krakow District'. *Central European Journal of Social Transformations* 18 (1): 98–123.

Kundera, Milan. (1984). 'The Tragedy of Central Europe'. *New York Review of Books*, 1984.

Kusnirakova, Tereza, and Pavel Cizinsky. (2011). 'Twenty Years of Czech Migration Policy: Liberal, Restrictive or Something Different?' *Geografie* 116 (4): 497–517.

Lambart, Francois. ⟨Ψ 2082⟩. 'We Have Been through This Before: Shortsightdness of European Immigration Policies'. *New Spectator*.

Leese, David. ⟨Ψ 2120⟩. 'Novel Forms of Governance: Report on Autonomous Areas in the Pacific'. Santa Monica: RAND Corporation.

Mahmood, Yara. ⟨Ψ 2079⟩. 'Yes, We Should All Be Worried: A Reply to Hutchinson'. *Political Horizons*, 23 June 2079.

Makarova, Valentina. ⟨Ψ 2102⟩. *The Social History of Quantum Technology in the 21st Century*. Tokyo: University of Tokyo Press.

McMiller, Adra, and Pablo Fernandez. ⟨Ψ 2109⟩. 'Think Global, Act Local: Ratification of Genosocial Treaties in State Parliaments'. *International Organization* 163 (3): 645–81.

Michelsen, Thomas. ⟨Ψ 2084⟩. 'The Impact of Genetic Testing on Hereditary Diseases Incidence: Model and Evidence from Central Europe'. *Nature Genetics* 116: 1523–41.

Nakajima, Chika.⟨Ψ 2095⟩. 'Norms in International Politics: Again, But This Time Better'. *European Journal of International Relations* 101 (4): 952–75.

Nilsson, Albert. ⟨Ψ 2120⟩.*Politics Between the Global and the Quantum: International Relations in the Early 22nd Century*. Beijing: University of Beijing Press.

Rosswell, Peter. ⟨Ψ 2042⟩. *Proxy Warfare Revisited: Why Do Some States Succeed in Using Third Parties*. Oxford: Oxford University Press.

Schelling, Thomas C. (1981). *The Strategy of Conflict: With a New Preface by the Author*. Reprint edition. Cambridge: Harvard University Press.

Sklowoski, Michal. ⟨Ψ 2084⟩. 'Parental Dyads, Genetic Extrapolation Tests and Transmittable Medical Conditions: A Review Essay'. *Genomics and Population* 32 (3): 452–75.

Tannenwald, Nina. (2008). *The Nuclear Taboo: The United States and the Non-Use of Nuclear Weapons Since 1945*. Cambridge: Cambridge University Press.

Tesař, Jakub. (2015). 'Quantum Theory of International Relations: Approaches and Possible Gains'. *Human Affairs* 25 (4): 486–502.

Visser, Michiel. ⟨Ψ 2115⟩. 'Sociotechnological Order in the Organization of Collective Defence'. *East Asian Journal of International Relations* 72 (2): 341–60.

Warsaw Declaration. ⟨Ψ 2070⟩. 'Warsaw Declaration: Towards Security and Wellbeing in Central Europe'.

Wendt, Alexander. (2015). *Quantum Mind and Social Science: Unifying Physical and Social Ontology*. Cambridge: Cambridge University Press.

Werner, Sarah. ⟨Ψ 2108⟩ 'Genosocial Norms and Interactions Between States: A Framework for Analysis'. *Perspectives on World Politics* 35 (1): 45–76.

Zielińska, Marta. ⟨Ψ 2089⟩ 'Euroasian Studies and International Relations: Difficult Relationship with (Perhaps) Bright Future?' *Chinese Journal of Global Politics* 57 (1): 113–35.

Zurek, Jakub. ⟨Ψ 2086⟩ 'The Meaning of the "Horvath vs. the City of Teplice" Ruling in the European Context'. *Law & Society Review* 121 (2): 321–63.

Not yet a Global Health Paradigm: A Scenario-Based Analysis of Global Health Policies

Maria Ferreira

1 INTRODUCTION

This chapter establishes a critical dialogue between contemporary global health policies, security studies, and bioterrorism. It suggests how contemporary global health paradigms—the narrative framings through which global health policies are thought and acted upon—are in urgent need of reconsideration. The chapter also focuses on the effects of bioterrorism on global health policies and paradigms. The goal is to discuss global health challenges by debating the lessons of the latest global health catastrophes and stressing the need for new perspectives regarding the relations between global health policies, global health players, and international security. Assuming a critical perspective I argue that, to be effective, twenty-second-century global health policies should prioritize the value of human lives in comparison to the interests of developed states and the pharmaceutical industry.

The paper will encompass four sections. The first section will debate how the latest global health catastrophes triggered the need to think about global health policies from a bioethics perspective. The second section of the paper will debate how disparate global health paradigms prompted a debate about the securitization of epidemiological outbreaks. The argument of the chapter

M. Ferreira (✉)
School of Social and Political Sciences, University of Lisbon, Lisboa, Portugal
e-mail: mferreira@iscsp.ulisboa.pt

Campus Universitário Do Alto da Ajuda, Lisboa, Portugal

© The Author(s), under exclusive license to Springer Nature Switzerland AG 2023
L. Horn et al. (eds.), *The Palgrave Handbook of Global Politics in the 22nd Century*, https://doi.org/10.1007/978-3-031-13722-8_10

162   M. FERREIRA

and its academic significance will be developed in the third section. The concluding section will debate the academic relevance of discussing global health practices and narratives from bioethics and epistemic perspectives.

2   GLOBAL HEALTH CATASTROPHES AND THE EMERGENCE OF BIOETHICS

Between the years 2069 and 2071 there was a pandemic of avian influenza (AID69). Unlike the previous outbreaks, this was more than an outbreak or an epidemic. It has killed 55 million people and is still regarded as one of the deadliest health disasters in recorded history (Ferreira Ψ 2120). The origins of the pandemic go back to 2019.

The year 2019 constituted the beginning of a paradigm shift regarding global health policies. Two events contributed to such a paradigm shift.

On the 17th of December 2019, an explosion took place at the Russian Virology State Research Centre (the so-called "Vektor Centre"), which conducted studies on deadly viruses, including Ebola, avian influenza, diverse types of hepatitis, anthrax, smallpox, and HIV (BBC 2019). According to the BBC (2019), the fire "was caused by the explosion of a gas canister during refurbishment work at the 'Vektor Centre in Koltsovo, a town near Novosibirsk in Siberia." During the Cold War, the "Vektor Centre" was allegedly a biological weapons research facility (BBC 2019). The center was known for "maintaining one of the world's largest collections of viruses" and biological samples (ibid.). The incident confirmed long-held doubts about the security of Russian epidemiological research facilities, namely facilities engaged in biological warfare research (BBC 2019). The consequences of the explosion were "shrouded in secrecy" (ibid.). Only fifty years later, in late 2069, the repercussions which followed the 9/17/2019 incident were known to the world.

In December 2019, Chinese authorities were confronted with the propagation of a new virus in the province of Hubei (BBC 2020). At first, the symptoms were compared to a "SARS-like disease" and as a "pneumonia of unclear causes" (ibid.). In January 2020, the Chinese National Health Committee recognized that a new coronavirus—later designated as SARS-CoV-2—was at the root of the epidemic (ibid.). On 30 January 2020, the World Health Organization (WHO) declared COVID-19 as a public health emergency of global concern, and on March 2020, COVID-19 was classified by the WHO as a pandemic (Pericàs 2020). Between January and March, the virus spread globally. Between December 2019 and December 2022, the virus killed around 7 million people (Johns Hopkins CRC Ψ 2023). However, experts estimate that fatalities could have reached 9 million people (WHO Ψ 2024).

On 7 September 2020, the World Health Organization Director-General, Tedros Ghebreyesus, said that COVID-19 would "not be the last pandemic" and argued that states should draw lessons from COVID-19 (WHO 2020).

However, it was not only states, which learned from the COVID-19 pandemic. The threat of bioterrorism had frightened the world for decades (Henderson 1998). The COVID-19 pandemic showed bioterrorists that pandemics can have catastrophic effects on society (Syracuse Ψ 2023). The development of bioweapons capable of unleashing chaos in the global system became a priority for terrorist organizations (Henderson 1998). In this context, the explosion at the "Vektor Centre" opened a window of opportunity which would lead to unexpected consequences (Thomas Ψ 2115).

Between 1999 and 2019, the "Vektor Centre" received foreign experts from international epidemiological cooperation agreements (Jones Ψ 2116). Experts working at the "Vektor Centre" were sworn to secrecy to prevent the worldwide diffusion of news about the explosion (Edwards Ψ 2110). What authorities did not know was that some experts, aware of the financial value of the samples at the "Vektor Centre," took some with them in order to preserve and sell them in the biotech black market (Edwards Ψ 2110). In 2030, the "Vektor Centre" was shut down. Around 2065, the "Vektor Centre" research facilities were secretly infiltrated by BioISIS, a Daesh/ISIS-related group, to install a mobile molecular biological laboratory (Brass Ψ 2119). Bioterrorists began developing plans for a global bioterrorist attack (Cross Ψ 2118). In 2069, genetically modified samples of avian influenza were spread throughout the world by inoculating BioISIS terrorists and sending them to the transportation hubs of major cosmopolitan areas, namely Tokyo, Paris, London, Beijing, Mumbai, and New York (Cross Ψ 2118).

After contamination began, the BioISIS terrorist group claimed responsibility for the attack (Marques Ψ 2115). Some of its members were captured and sent to Guantánamo. However, the chief instigators behind the attack were never identified. Nevertheless, there were suspicions that the terrorist group had not acted alone (ICIJ Ψ 2080). Ten years later, an investigation developed by the International Consortium of Investigative Journalists (ICIJ), based on leaked secret files from the US National Security Agency and the US Central Intelligence Agency, concluded that BioISIS terrorists, based on former "Vektor Centre" facilities, had established a paid contract with a conglomerate of major pharmaceutical industries to unleash globally genetically modified strands of the avian influenza virus (ICIJ Ψ 2080). Suspicions started to grow regarding a particular conglomerate of chief pharmaceutical industries since it was their joint-produced anti-viral treatments and vaccines that proved to be most effective against the AID69 (Charles Ψ 2080).

The pharmaceutical industry had already demonstrated its overwhelming power during the COVID-19 pandemic (Charles Ψ 2080). Such a significance, associated with the considerable financial revenues gained during the COVID-19 pandemic, propelled some pharmaceutical corporations to establish an alliance with a terrorist organization. The goal was to profit from the possibility of unleashing globally a genetically manipulated virus whose

164   M. FERREIRA

vaccines and anti-viral medications were mainly supplied by the pharmaceutical companies which participated in that genetic manipulation (Charles Ψ 2080).

The 2069/2071 avian influenza pandemic, and its several known strains (H5N1, H9N2, H7N2, H7N3), began to spread to highly populated countries in Europe, North America, Central America, and Asia (Fletcher Ψ 2114). The virus's capacity to mutate into new strains and spread through human contact significantly increased mortality rates (Fletcher Ψ 2114). Table 1 describes the numbers, presented by regions, of the AID69.

In total, in almost two years, AID69 afflicted 260 million people and claimed 55 million lives (WHO Ψ 2072). Fletcher Ψ 2114.

Affected populations had to wait a considerable amount of time for an effective vaccine, increasing mortality rates (Monto 2006) (Fletcher Ψ 2114). Pharmaceutical corporations involved in the bioterrorist attack profited from increased medical supplies shortage and vaccine demand. The relationship

Table 1 The 2069/2071 avian influenza pandemic in numbers

Region	Number of infected individuals	Mortality rate	Fatalities	Information
Asia	100 million	25%	25 million	India, China, Indonesia, and Pakistan recorded mortality rates near 30%
Europe	60 million	15%	9 million	Russia registered 16 million cases; Germany, Turkey, and France registered around 10 million cases each; Ten million cases were also registered in Eastern and Central European countries, namely, Poland and Ukraine; 4 million cases were recorded in Western European countries like Spain, the United Kingdom, and the Netherlands
North, South, and Central America	80 million	20%	16 million	The pandemic was particularly severe in the United States, Canada, and Brazil
Africa,	20 million	25%	5 million	

Source WHO (Ψ 2072)

Fatalities of Global Health Catastrophes

1918/1920 influenza pandemic	2020/2022 COVID-19 pandemic	2069/2071 avian influenza pandemic
20–40 million people	7 million	55 million
Source Billings 2005	*Source* WHO (Ψ 2024)	*Source* WHO (Ψ 2072)

between the pharmaceutical industry and national states favored the former preventing the possibility of patent breaking and protecting pharmaceutical corporations from accusations of complicity regarding the 2069/2071 avian influenza pandemic ⟨Fletcher Ψ 2114⟩.

Numbers are not enough to depict the dimension of the global health catastrophe unleashed by AID69. The human, social, political, and economic consequences were devastating in the countries plagued by the epidemiological outbreak that put the world on a health alert between September 2069 and August 2071, when the avian influenza pandemic was officially considered by the World Health Organization as controlled ⟨Farias Ψ 2114⟩. The scale of the 2069/2071 global health disaster caused by the AID69 was reminiscent of the fictional cinematography and literature of world health calamities in the twenty-first-century and twenty-second-century realities ⟨Duchamp Ψ 2120⟩. Only fifty years later can we analyze how AID69 transformed the global health regime through the extreme securitization of health issues. Particularly when it comes to the way health risk has been represented, AID69 shifted our imaginary to scenarios where the survival of the human species is endangered. This is comparable to twentieth-century descriptions of olden times, where imaginaries of risk reified centuries-old representations of pain and disaster where death in developing countries was seen as natural while suffering in developed countries was represented as exceptional and unnatural (Sontag 2004a).

AID69 was fundamental in triggering the need to reason about global health policies from a global bioethics perspective. The worldwide reach of bioterrorism demonstrated the significance of thinking about bioethics in global terms (ten-Have 2016). Global bioethics is defined as the establishment of "universal ethical principles and norms while concomitantly ensuring respect for cultural and moral particularities" in the health domain (Cunha and Garrafa 2016, p. 197). A global perspective on bioethics also involves developing a critical approach regarding the global governance of health issues, the articulation between health and security, and the development of global health narratives and paradigms.

3   Securitization and Global Health Paradigms

The second section of the paper will debate how disparate global health paradigms prompted a debate about the securitization of epidemiological outbreaks. Vulnerability is considered one of the main pillars of bioethics (Cunha and Garrafa 2016). Vulnerability management is at the core of both national and global governance of health issues (Cunha and Garrafa 2016). However, vulnerability is also a fundamental element of the securitization of health questions, namely in the epidemiological arena.

In 2010, Lakoff (2010) identified two conflicting paradigms regarding the global health regime: the global health security paradigm and the humanitarian biomedicine paradigm. The global health security paradigm was centered on the importance of controlling infectious diseases that originated in developing

166   M. FERREIRA

countries but represented as posing a risk to developed countries (ibid). The pre-emptive nature of the global health security paradigm was, therefore, based on epidemiological surveillance and intelligence strategies that prepare states for "events whose likelihood is incalculable but whose political, economic, and health consequences could be catastrophic" (Lakoff 2010, p. 60). The humanitarian biomedicine paradigm was focused on lessening the pain of individuals affected by communicable and non-communicable diseases, notwithstanding their geographical location (Lakoff 2010). A core difference distinguished both paradigms. The health security paradigm privileged developed states (ibid.). The humanitarian biomedicine paradigm tried to alleviate the suffering of developing and developed countries (ibid.). What is significant to analyze is that each paradigm had a distinct moral framework. In the words of Lakoff (2010, p. 61):

> [w]ithin each regime, actors work to craft a space of the global that will be a site of knowledge and intervention. [H]owever, the type of ethical relationship implied by a project of global health depends upon the regime in which the question is posed: the connection between health advocates and the afflicted (or potentially afflicted) can be one of either moral obligation to the other or protection against risk to the self.

On the one hand, the pandemic brought about a gradual insensitivity to, and disinterest in the way AID69 afflicted non-western communities, namely communities located in Africa, South America, or South Asia, but also an associated "compassion fatigue" regarding the suffering of non-western communities (Moeller 1999). This brings to mind how the photographic depiction of pain experienced in non-western moral communities is beautified and "bleached out a moral response to what is shown" (Sontag 2004b, p. 72).

Throughout the twenty-first century, the health security paradigm was consolidated as the hegemonic global health regime (Ferreira Ψ 2120). After the 2069/2071 avian influenza pandemic, a new global health paradigm emerged: the ecological biopolitical global health paradigm (EBP). The EBP entails the representation of health issues as ecological threats to the survival of political communities. The ecological biopolitical global health paradigm continues to be, fifty years after the 2069/2071 epidemiological catastrophe, the prevailing paradigm of global health governance (Ferreira Ψ 2120).

Concerning public policy analysis, the ecological approach underpins how a particular question may be constructed as a threat to the communitarian survival and sustainability of a political community (Gibson 1986). The ecological biopolitical global health paradigm considers that health issues, namely epidemiological diseases, constitute a menace to the survival of developed states (Ferreira Ψ 2120). It is not only health security that is at stake, but the essence of developed states as political communities that is represented as being endangered (ibid.) Epidemiological diseases that risk spreading from developing to developed states are framed as biopolitical threats that jeopardize the physical and moral survival of developed countries through the unfolding of social turmoil and economic crisis (Hope 2014).

The EBP strengthened the assumed causal relationship between health and (in)security. Such causation is demonstrated by the diversity of epidemiologic surveillance systems, platforms, and sites managed by states, international organizations, health infrastructures, non-governmental and non-profit organizations, and states' homeland and national security departments ⟨Doyle Ψ 2118⟩. The diversity of epidemiologic surveillance systems, platforms, and sites, highlights the transnational nature of epidemiological threats (Wilson 2015).

The EBP normalized the long-established belief that epidemiological occurrences can be delimited to their point of origin (ibid.). When such confinement is no longer possible, epidemiological outbreaks stop being considered as health or developmental questions but become questions of national survival, security, and transnational threats (ibid.). By considering developed communities as target groups in need of protection, the EBP obliviates the fact that epidemiological occurrences are not easily contained and, as the AID69 demonstrated, may potentially afflict human communities irrespective of their development level ⟨Andrews Ψ 2118⟩ (Wilson 2015). The EBP strengthened the causal relation between migration and global health issues framing migrants, represented as potential disease carriers and as communitarian threats to the political and well-being of developed societies (Kuisma 2013).

In 2069, as in 2020, the architecture of the global health regime was not prepared to govern the transnational reality of recurrent pandemics (Rushton and Williams 2012). In 2122, it continues to be unprepared ⟨McGill Ψ 2119⟩. After the 2020/2022 and 2069/2071 pandemics, states learned how to relate health and (in)security but failed to approach health from a humanitarian perspective ⟨McGill Ψ 2119⟩. In fact, by privileging extreme securitization over biomedical interventions, the ecological biopolitical global health paradigm downplays the structural framework that underlies epidemiological threats (Wilson 2015). When "diseases of poverty" are only considered relevant if they threaten developed states, the worthlessness of human beings becomes clear (Linklater 1981).

The dominance of EBP led to a health regime where global health policies focused on epidemiological surveillance and intelligence assumed more policy significance than policies centered on alleviating human suffering (Rushton and Williams 2012). The establishment of bridges between health issues and national survival questions is a policy choice whose goal is to normalize a "threat defense logic," whereby epidemiological outbreaks are managed like military threats, to respond to health issues (Rushton and Williams 2012, p. 16). The EBP is empowered by the embracing of a biopolitical foundation, explicitly, "its concentration on existential threats, tying it closely to the ultimate health issue: life and death" (Rushton and Williams 2012, p. 16). Such a biopolitical foundation, which entangles disease, poverty, death,

168   M. FERREIRA

risk, and security, permits to frame global health issues through a language of fear (Jackson 2011) and a language of catastrophe (Aradau and Van Munster 2011). Framing health issues through a language of fear legitimizes securitarian responses to epidemiological occurrences (Rushton and Williams 2012). Managing epidemiological outbreaks without tackling their root causes corresponds to what Paul Farmer (2020) long designated as conditions of "structural violence" that plague developing countries.

The EBP emerged from the global panic unleashed by the AID69 and remains unchallenged as the hegemonic framework for global health governance (Ferreira Ψ 2120). In 2122, representing epidemiological diseases as biopolitical existential threats allows states, the World Trade Organization (WTO), and the empowered pharmaceutical industry to legitimize the implementation of the artificial scarcity principle in the field of biomedical research (Williams Ψ 2117). Wealthier states have adopted a fundamental policy concerning several epidemiological illnesses: the nationalization of existing vaccine stocks and anti-viral medication (ibid.). In line with the EBP, national governments argued that what is and always be at stake is communitarian survival (ibid.).

Lakoff's (2010) distinction between the global health security paradigm and the humanitarian biomedicine paradigm highlights the relevance of analyzing securitization discourses and practices in the health domain. Following the Copenhagen school, securitization may be defined as "the intersubjective establishment of an existential threat with a saliency sufficient to have substantial political effects" (Buzan et al. 1998, p. 16). Balzacq et al. (2016, p. 497) claim that a process of securitization should be addressed as comprising a double dimension: a discursive dimension—securitization understood as a speech-act—and a governmental and public policy dimension, which studies an act of securitization from an "analytics of government" perspective considering "the conditions under which regimes of practices emerge and are reformed and dismantled." Specifically, securitization moves—the procedure through which a securitizing actor represents a question as a threat—operate through discursive and non-discursive practices sustained through four main elements (Balzacq et al. 2016, p. 495):

   i. Audiences;
   ii. Power relations;
   iii. Context;
   iv. Practices and instruments.

Table 2 considers the four elements of a securitization move defined by Balzacq et al. (2016) and how those elements can be applied to the domain of the contemporary global health regime.

Table 2 Securitization move and global health regime

	Elements of a securitization move	Global health regime
Audiences	According to securitization theory, "a 'threat' results from an interaction between an actor that attempts to define a given issue as an existential threat and an audience which accepts or rejects this attempt" (Nunes 2020)	The recurrence of catastrophic pandemics led to the need to rethink the concept of "audiences" within the securitization theory (McDonald 2008, p. 581). The AID69 frequently opposed the voice of the epidemiological scientific community to governmental voices, which, based on "epidemiological neoliberalism," were eager to keep the economy working, downplaying the scale of the health catastrophe (Nunes 2020) (Nguyen Ψ 2089). Faced with catastrophic pandemics, national and transnational audiences are frequently divided between the clashing voices of science and governments, which raises questions of scientific and political trustworthiness (Nguyen Ψ 2089)
Power relations	The emergence of asymmetrical threats (e.g. biological terrorism) highlighted the need to consider the predominance of "heterogeneous complexes" in the security arena focused on distinct sectors and comprised of interactions among different types of actors (Buzan et al. 1998, p. 16)	The exponential growth of discourses based on "epidemiological neoliberalism" was empowered by two elements: the failure to reach a consensus regarding vaccines' patent breaching and the growth of authoritarian political movements and parties associated with the retreat of democracy that became a strong tendency in the first half of the twenty-first century (Nunes 2020) (Davidson Ψ 2030). The inclusion of medical and epidemiological communities as trustworthy "voices" that should be empowered to speak security, even when they contradict state officials, is a consequence of catastrophic pandemics, as well as a way to counterargue the narrative hegemony of "epidemiological neoliberalism" (McDonald 2008, p. 580; Nunes 2020)

(continued)

Table 2 (continued)

	Elements of a securitization move	Global health regime
Context	Discursive practices play a fundamental role in securitization theory (Aradau and van Munster 2011). The possibility that unparalleled public health calamities may become recurring (Kock 2014, p. 2) led authors working on securitization theory not only to consider the global dimension of "existential threats" but also to admit that it is necessary to open and diversify the range of "voices within political communities" which are "empowered" to "speak security" (McDonald 2008, p. 580) and act on the security domain	Using military terminology to discursively represent pandemics move the discussion about the epidemiological outbreak away from the scientific realm and locates it into the security realm (Nguyen Ψ 2089). This specific speech-act brings consequences since "[t]he state of mind of war is very different from the state of mind of medicine" (Bennett 2020, quoted by Hoffmann 2020, p. 11)
Practices and Instruments	The terrorist threat led some strands within security studies to underpin how the distinction between internal domestic security and international security became an anachronic distinction substituted by a language of risk and uncertainty (Aradau and van Munster 2016)	The concept of "recurrent pandemics" embodies a language of risk and uncertainty and demonstrates the significance of securitization theory to understand how states and international organizations are faced with contexts where unparalleled public health calamities may become recurring (Aradau and van Munster 2016, p. 2) and involve new security actors, practices and instruments of securitization

The relationship between world health and securitization is a product of the global threat caused by epidemiological diseases, such as SARS, Avian flu, Zika, or Ebola (Nunes 2020). The AID69 pandemics reinforced such an articulation.

4   Global Health Policies: Institutional, Policy, and Theoretical Questions

This chapter argues that to be effective, twenty-second-century global health policies should overcome an ecological biopolitical global health paradigm based on the extreme securitization of health policies and embrace a humanitarian biomedicine paradigm. The affirmation of a humanitarian biomedicine paradigm would have institutional, policy, and scientific consequences that could improve the efficiency of global health policies, as well as broaden and deepen how security and International Relations theories analyze the relationship between bioterrorism and global security.

In the twentieth and twenty-first centuries, a global health regime was gradually established, particularly around the World Health Organization (WHO), founded in 1948. The WHO was considered the leading and organizing "authority" on international health functioning within the United Nations system ⟨WHO Ψ 2120⟩. Throughout the twentieth and the first two decades of the twenty-first century, the global health regime was developed, specifically, through the actions of governmental and intergovernmental institutions, the agency of private stakeholders, and the constitution of public–private partnerships. Such a global health regime was based on a multi-level system of decentralized agencies and institutions with "overlapping" tasks (Leon 2015, p. 1) ruling global health issues "with no command hierarchy and with a visible lack of coordination (ibid). Overlapping structures with no hierarchical organization and coordination deficiencies impacted health resource distribution (ibid.).

After the COVID-19 and the AID69 pandemics, epidemiologists and philanthropists involved in global health policies argued that such pandemics could be an opportunity to constitute an effective international health regime that could advance the international community's answers to epidemiological outbreaks (Gates 2020) ⟨Sanders Ψ 2072⟩. The concern with the effects of pandemics on low and middle-income countries (LMIC) was particularly severe due to the health infrastructures shortcomings existing in those countries ⟨Sanders Ψ 2072⟩. In Gates' words: "[m]any LMIC health systems are already stretched thin and a pathogen like the coronavirus can quickly overwhelm them. And poorer countries have little political or economic leverage, given wealthier countries' natural desire to put their own people first" (Gates 2020, p. 1677). What Gates designated as the "wealthier countries' natural desire to put their own people first" (ibid.) raises critical issues regarding vaccine production and distribution.

The work of non-governmental actors, partnerships, and coalitions proved to be significant during the AID69 pandemics ⟨Guilfoyle Ψ 2111⟩. Throughout the twentieth and twenty-first-century, preparing for emerging infectious illnesses was always very difficult because the "market potential" for vaccines against epidemiological diseases was and remains limited and also due to the difficulties associated with vaccine testing, access, and distribution (CEPI 2000). The combined forces of state and market prevented structural changes in the international health regime which would ensure universal and fair access to vaccines ⟨Guilfoyle Ψ 2111⟩.

Those changes could have been implemented by the WHO. However, after the COVID-19 pandemics, trust in the WHO deteriorated ⟨Tavares Ψ

172   M. FERREIRA

2025⟩. Its powers regarding global epidemiological surveillance were weakened amidst accusations of late response to the COVID-19 pandemic ⟨ibid.⟩. The WHO lost the capacity not only of working as an early warning system in the epidemiological domain but also of obliging states to share epidemiological information, namely, "lists of supplies to be stockpiled or redirected in an emergency" (Gates 2020, p. 1678).

The opportunity was lost of transforming the WHO into the leading Organization in the field of epidemiological preparedness and response with resources to compel states to share epidemiological data (Gates 2020). Since 2010, officials within the WHO argued that the organization was "overextended" and, consequently, "unable" to face future global health challenges (Shridar and Gostin 2011, p. 1585).

From an institutional standpoint, adopting a humanitarian biomedicine paradigm would signify the return to the WHO. However, wealthier states and pharmaceutical corporations, motivated by their self-interest, prevented the reforms that could have allowed the WHO to:

i. improve the process of "manufacturing proteins," as well as accelerate the "regulatory reviews" that would permit to produce vaccines "at low cost on a massive scale" (Gates 2020, p. 1678);

ii. develop an institutional mechanism to "screen" standing anti-viral medication as well as "candidate molecule in a swift and standardized manner" (ibid.)

iii. invest in "nucleic acids" research to ease the sequencing of the virus' genome (ibid.);

iv. promote clinical trials and "licensing agreements" able to "cross national borders" (ibid.);

v. foster international cooperation, namely concerning "trial protocols," between institutions like the International Severe Acute Respiratory and Emerging Infection Consortium trial network, the World Health Organization R&D Blueprint, and the Global Research Collaboration for Infectious Disease Preparedness (ibid.).

vi. promote an efficient debate within the WTO about the conditions under which the suspension of international property rights in the epidemiological field could occur ⟨Tavares Ψ 2025⟩.

Despite its fragilities, there is no other organization that can substitute the WHO's role, and consequently, its future status remains open ⟨Miles Ψ 2119⟩.

From a policy perspective, affirming a humanitarian biomedicine paradigm would challenge the pharmaceutical industry, and open the relationship between public and private actors into question, including the consequences of this entanglement on public health policies. Several critical questions should be debated, many of which have already been brought to attention as early as 2020 (e.g. Ayati et al. 2020, pp. 800–804), namely:

i. The question of medicine shortage, "induced demand," and "panic buying" of anti-viral medication;
ii. The shortage of "active pharmaceutical ingredients" and "finished products";
iii. The question of "compulsory licensing" for "potential" treatments;
iv. Ethical dilemmas related to the "use of poorly evidence-centered therapies," as well as of "off-label" medical products;
v. The benefits and disadvantages of patent-breaking rights in the case of global pandemics.

Discussing these questions would reveal how pharmaceutical corporations gain from the introduction of the principle of artificial scarcity in the field of biomedical research (Williams Ψ 2117). It would also be relevant for states and global agencies working in the health sector, particularly in the epidemiological domain, to think about their relationships with the pharmaceutical industry from a bioethical perspective of common vulnerability (Cunha and Garrafa 2016, p. 197).

The affirmation of a humanitarian biomedicine paradigm could also widen and deepen how security and International Relations theories analyze the relationship between bioterrorism and global security.

Since the beginning of the twenty-first century, the proliferation of biological weapons and their use by terrorist groups has empowered the bond between public health and national security (Fidler 2003). International Relations and security studies scholars have studied bioterrorism, stressing the contested concept of security (Mills Ψ 2121). The linkage between public health and national security highlights different perspectives on the meaning of security (Fidler 2003, p. 788). Distinct perspectives have diverging standpoints about the protection of populations in health distress (ibid). Some theories debated how national health and bioterrorism conditions states' material capabilities (ibid.). However, the most important discussions about bioterrorism, public health, and global security have questioned deeper issues concerning the structure of contemporary international politics (Fidler 2003, p. 789). Four distinct security schools focus on the relation between bioterrorism, public health, and security, namely: the realpolitik perspective on national security, the liberal approach on common security, the human security approach, and the ecological security perspective (ibid.). Table 3 shows those four schools, their focus, theoretical source, security objective, and willingness to consider bioterrorism as a field of concern (adapted Fidler 2003, p. 801).

Since Fidler's analysis (2003), the ecological security perspective was employed by critical security scholars even though it remains underdeveloped (Barnaby Ψ 2119). The ecological security perspective addresses bioterrorism from a global security and bioethics perspective, in line with its general approach to health security from a global perspective. This entails taking global

174 M. FERREIRA

Table 3 Public health and security four perspectives

Security concept	Focus	Theoretical source	Security objective and bioterrorism concerns
Realpolitik	Power politics among states	Realism	National security; Realism adopts a traditional security agenda
Common Security	The individual, democracy, and interdependence	Liberalism	International Security; Liberalism recognizes bioterrorism as a national security threat
Human Security	Structural injustice and transnationalism/normative role of non-state actors	Social Constructivism	Global Security; Social Constructivism considers bioterrorism to be a global security threat
Ecological Security	Biological/Environmental threats	Ecology/Evolutionary theory (Critical security studies)	Sustainable relationship between the natural environment, pathogens, and human population (epidemiological security); Critical security studies allocate significant relevance to bioterrorist threats

Source Fidler (2003, p. 801) (adapted)

vulnerability as the focus of global health policies, and asking how transnational actors, namely terrorists and the pharmaceutical industry, can strengthen health governance (ibid.).

It has been imperative to discuss bioterrorism from a global epidemiological security and bioethics perspective since such a perspective was focused on common ecological vulnerability in the twenty-first century (Fidler 2003) just as it is now (Barnaby Ψ 2119). Artificial intelligence and new information and communication technologies have increased the capabilities of bioterrorists (Dang et al. 2008). The 2022 Russian assault on scientific facilities at the Chernobyl nuclear plant had already triggered the alarm of the scientific community (CNN 2022). Particularly after the AID69 pandemic, states and epistemic communities have focused on monitoring biomedical research facilities (Dang et al. 2008) ⟨Silveira Ψ 2075⟩ and the development by extremist groups of bioterrorism information systems. They aimed at early detection of bioterrorist attacks, real-time surveillance, monitoring bioterrorists' communication, and global/national data collection. A theoretical and empirical effort is required to put bioterrorism on the agenda of IR and security studies, beyond state-centric approaches to IR which is prevalent in most health security paradigms.

5   CONCLUSION

This chapter established a critical dialogue between contemporary global health policies, security studies, and bioterrorism. The chapter analyzed how contemporary global health paradigms—the narrative framings through which global health policies are thought and acted upon—are in urgent need of reconsideration. The chapter also discussed the effects of bioterrorism on global health policies and paradigms. Building from a critical perspective concerning contemporary global health policies, the chapter argued that in order to be effective, twenty-second-century global health policies should prioritize the value of human lives in comparison to the interests of developed states and the pharmaceutical industry.

The prevalence of the EBP has a fundamental normative outcome: since the early twenty-first century, health policies are controlled by military and intelligence organizations empowered to govern the civic rights of individuals with transmittable diseases (Elbe 2006, p. 119). This chapter has debated the consequences associated with the predominance of the EBP in the twenty-two-century, namely:

i. The extreme securitization of health questions;
ii. The normalization of the belief that epidemiological diseases necessarily originate in developing countries;
iii. The development of global health policies aimed at preventing and controlling disease not from a humanitarian perspective, but a national security frame.

The AID69 pandemic demonstrated the need for a truly global health regime and the urgency of controlling all genres of biological warfare research ⟨McGill Ψ 2119⟩. The AID69 pandemic also showed the risks of manipulating biological samples of lethal viruses.

References

Andrews, S. ⟨Ψ 2118⟩. *Global Health Pandemics: An Overview*. Oxon: Routledge.

Aradau, C., & van Munster, R. (2016). Poststructuralist Approaches to Security. In M.D. Williams & T. Balzacq (Eds.). *Routledge Handbook of Security Studies* (75–84). New York: Routledge.

Aradau, C., & Van Munster, R. (2011). *Politics of Catastrophe: Genealogies of the Unknown*. New York: Routledge

Ayati, N., Saiyarsarai, P., & Nikfar, S. (2020). Short and Long-Term Impacts of COVID-19 on the Pharmaceutical Sector. *DARU Journal of Pharmaceutical Sciences*, (*28*)2, 799–805.

Balzacq, T., Léonard, S., & Ruzicka, J. (2016). 'Securitization' Revisited: Theories and Cases. *International Relations*, (*30*)4, 494–531.

Barnaby, T. ⟨Ψ 2119⟩. *Global Health and Critical Security Studies*. Cambridge: Cambridge University Press.

BBC. (2019, September 17). Novosibirsk: 'No Risk' After Blast and Fire at Russian Lethal virus Lab. *BBC News*. Retrieved from https://www.bbc.com/news/world-europe-49727101.

BBC. (2020, June 9). Coronavirus: What did China do About Early Outbreak? *BBC News*. Retrieved from https://www.bbc.com/news/world-52573137.

Billings, M. (2005). The Influenza Pandemic of 1918. Retrieved from The 1918 Influenza Pandemic (stanford.edu).

Brass, J. ⟨Ψ 2119⟩. *An Introduction to Bioterrorism*. Princeton: Princeton University Press.

Buzan, B., Wæver, O., & de Wilde, J. (1998). *Security: A New Framework for Analysis*. Boulder, CO: Lynne Rienner Publishers.

CEPI. (2000). *Coalition for Epidemic Preparedness Innovation. Our Mission: New Vaccines for a Safer World*. Retrieved from https://cepi.net/about/whyweexist/.

Charles, F. ⟨Ψ 2080⟩. *The Politics of World Pandemics*. Nova York: Lynne Rienner Publishers.

CNN. (2022, March 23). Russos destruíram a saquearam o laboratório topo de gama que existia em Chernobyl. *CNN Portugal*. Retrieved from https://cnnportugal.iol.pt/ucrania/russia/russos-destruiram-e-saqueram-o-laboratorio-topo-de-gama-que-existia-em-chernobyl/20220323/623a91870cf21a10a426c7ab.

Cross, J. ⟨Ψ 2118⟩. *Global Bioterrorism: Causes and Consequences*. Oxford: Oxford University Press.

Cunha, T., & Garrafa, V. (2016). Vulnerability: A Key Principle for Global Bioethics? *Cambridge Quarterly of Healthcare Ethics*, 25, 197–208.

Dang, Y., Zhang, Y., Suakkaphong, N., Larson, C., & Hsinchun, C. (2008). An Integrated approach to Mapping Worldwide Bioterrorism Research Capabilities. *IEEE International Conference on Intelligence and Security Informatics*, 212–214. Retrieved from: An integrated approach to mapping worldwide bioterrorism research capabilities | IEEE Conference Publication | IEEE Xplore.

Davidson, T. ⟨Ψ 2030⟩. *Epidemiological Neoliberalism*. Cambridge: Cambridge University Press.

Doyle, P. ⟨Ψ 2118⟩. *The Securitization of Global Health*. Baltimore: The Johns Hopkins University Press.

Duchamp, M. ⟨Ψ 2120⟩. *Cinematography and World Health Calamities*. Oxon: Routledge.

Edwards, K. ⟨Ψ 2110⟩. *Global Biotech Markets.* Boulder, CO: Lyne Rienner Publishers.

Elbe, S. (2006). Should HIV/AIDS be Securitized? The Ethical Dilemmas of Linking HIV to Security. *International Studies Quarterly, (50)*1, 119–144.

Farmer, P. (2020). *Fevers, Feuds and Diamonds: Ebola and the Ravages of History.* New York: Picador.

Ferreira, L. ⟨Ψ 2120⟩. *The AID69 Pandemic. Between Fiction and Reality.* Nova York: Longman.

Farias, M. ⟨Ψ 2114⟩. *Global Health: Global Challenges.* USA: Pearson.

Fidler, D. (2003). *Public Health and National Security in the Global Age: Infectious Diseases, Bioterrorism, and Realpolitik.* Articles by Maurer Faculty, 416. Retrieved from: Public Health and National Security in the Global Age_Infectious.pdf.

Fletcher, J. ⟨Ψ 2114⟩. *Global Health Policies.* Oxon: Routledge.

Gates, B. (2020). Responding to COVID-19—A One-in-a-Century Pandemic? *New England Journal of Medicine,* 382, 1677–1679.

Gibson, J. (1986). *The Ecological Approach to Visual Perception.* New Jersey: Lawrence Erlbaum Associates Publisher.

Guilfoyle, P. ⟨Ψ 2111⟩. *Non-governmental Organizations and Global Health.* Oxford: Oxford University Press.

Henderson, D.A. (1998). Bioterrorism as a Public Health Threat. *Emerging Infectious Diseases, (4)*3, 488–492.

Hoffmann, A. (2020). The Securitisation of the Coronavirus crisis in the Middle East. *The COVID-19 Pandemic in the Middle East and North Africa.* POMEPS STUDIES 39, 10–14. Retrieved from https://pomeps.org/wp-content/uploads/2020/04/POMEPS_Studies_39_Web.pdf.

Hope, C. (2014, February 28). Mass Immigration has Left Britain 'Unrecognizable', says Nigel Farage. *The Telegraph.* Retrieved from: http://www.telegraph.co.uk/news/politics/ukip/10668996/Mass-immigration-has-left-Britain-unrecognisable-says-Nigel-Farage.html.

ICIJ. ⟨Ψ 2080⟩. International Consortium of Investigative Journalists. The AID69 Pandemic: An Assessment. Retrieved from International Consortium of Investigative Journalists—ICIJ.

Jackson, P. (2011). *Cholera and Crisis: State Health and the Geographies of Future Epidemics.* Thesis submitted in conformity with the requirements for the degree of Doctor of Philosophy. Department of Geography University of Toronto. Retrieved from: https://tspace.library.utoronto.ca/bitstream/1807/29760/3/Jackson_Paul_SB_20116_PhD_thesis.pdf.

Jones, T. ⟨Ψ 2116⟩. *Global Epidemiological Cooperation.* Londres: Sage.

Johns Hopkins CRC. ⟨Ψ 2023⟩. Johns Hopkins Coronavirus Resource Center. COVID-19 Map. Retrieved from COVID-19 Map FAQ—Johns Hopkins Coronavirus Resource Center (https://www.jhu.edu/).

Kock, T. (2014). Hubris: the Recurrent Pandemic. *Disaster Medicine and Public Health Preparedness, (9)*1, 51–56.

Kuisma, M. (2013). 'Good' and 'Bad' Immigrants: The Economic Nationalism of the True Finns' Immigration Discourse. In U. Korkut, G. Bucken-Knapp & A. McGarry A. (Eds.). *The Discourses and Politics of Migration in Europe* (93–108). New York: Palgrave-Macmillan.

Lakoff, A. (2010). Two Regimes of Global Health. *Humanity: An International Journal of Human Rights, Humanitarianism and Development, (1)*1, 59–79.

Leon, J. (2015). *The Rise of Global Health: The Evolution of Effective Collective Action.* New York: Suny Press.

Linklater, A. (1981). Men and Citizens in International Relations. *Review of International Studies,* (7)1, 23–37.

Marques, L. M. (2115). *The Danger of Contemporary Bioterrorism.* Nova York: Palgrave Macmillan.

McDonald, M. (2008). Securitization and the Construction of Security. *European Journal of International Relations,* (14)4, 563-587.

McGill, A. ⟨Ψ 2119⟩. *The Architecture of the Global Health Regime.* Nova York: Suny Press.

Miles, J. ⟨Ψ 2119⟩. *The World Health Organization: The Dilemmas of Global Health Governance.* Cambridge: Polity Press.

Mills, E. ⟨Ψ 2121⟩. *Bioterrorism and Global Security.* Chicago: The University of Chicago Press.

Moeller, S. (1999). *Compassion Fatigue: How the Media Sell Disease, Famine, War, and Death.* New York: Routledge

Monto, A. (2006). "Vaccines and Antiviral Drugs in Pandemic Preparedness." *Emerging Infectious Diseases,* (12)1, 55-60.

Nguyen, H. ⟨Ψ 2089⟩. *Global Governance Regimes.* Washington: Georgetown University Press.

Nunes, J. (2020). "The COVID-19 Pandemic: Securitization, Neoliberal Crisis and Global Vulnerabilization." *Cadernos de Saúde Pública,* (36)4, 1–4.

Pericàs, J. (2020). Authoritarianism and the Threat of Infectious Diseases. *The Lancet,* 395, 10230, 1111–1112.

Rushton, S. & Williams, D. (2012). Private Actors in Global Health Governance. In: S. Rushton & D. Williams (Eds.) *Partnerships and Foundations in Global Health Governance* (1–28). Basingstoke: Palgrave Macmillan.

Sanders, G. ⟨Ψ 2072⟩. *Pandemics and Development in the 21st Century.* Maryland: Rowman & Littlefield.

Shridar, D. & Gostin, L. (2011). "Reforming the World Health Organization." *Journal of the American Medical Association,* (305)15, 1585–1586.

Silveira, A. ⟨Ψ 2075⟩. *Biomedical Research and the Politics of Security.* Durham, NC: Duke University.

Sontag, S. (2004a). *Sobre Fotografia.* São Paulo: Companhia das Letras.

Sontag, S. (2004b). *Regarding the Pain of Others.* London: Penguin.

Syracuse, D. ⟨Ψ 2023⟩. *Bioterrorism and the Future of Security Studies.* Lanham, MD: Rowman & Littlefield.

Tavares, M. S. ⟨Ψ 2025⟩. *The World Health Organization: An Overview.* Basingstoke: Palgrave Macmillan.

Ten-Have, H. (2016). *Vulnerability: Challenging Bioethics.* New York: Routledge.

Thomas, J. ⟨Ψ 2115⟩. *Bioterrorism and Global Health Policies.* Maryland: Rowman & Littlefield

Wilson, M. (2015). *Ebola Exceptionalism: On the Intersecting Political and Health Geographies of the 2014–2015 Epidemic.* A thesis submitted in partial fulfilment of the requirements for the degree of Master of Arts. University of Washington. Retrieved from: file:///C:/Users/LiderFin/AppData/Local/Packages/Microsoft.MicrosoftEdge_8wekyb3d8 bbwe/TempState/Downloads/Wilson_washington_0250O_14830%20(3).pdf.

Williams, S. ⟨Ψ 2117⟩. *Contemporary Biomedical Research*. Oxford: Oxford University Press.

WHO (2020, September 7). World Health Organization. WHO Director-General's Opening Remarks at the Media Briefing on COVID-19. Retrieved from: file:///D:/COVID/WHO%20DirectorGeneral's%20opening%20remarks%20at%20the%20media%20briefing%20on%20COVID-19%20-%207%20September%202020.html.

WHO ⟨Ψ 2024, April 25⟩. World Health Organization. Fatalities of Global Health Catastrophes. Retrieved from WHO | World Health Organization.

WHO ⟨Ψ 2072⟩. World Health Organization. The 2069/2071 Avian Influenza Pandemic in Numbers. Retrieved from Fact sheets (https://www.who.int/).

WHO ⟨Ψ 2120, May 4⟩. World Health Organization. About WHO. Retrieved from WHO | World Health Organization.

Themes: *Governance and Technology*

World-Systems and the Rescaling Geography of Europe

Giuseppe Porcaro

1 Introduction

The relative period of prosperity and peace, which our planet and the rest of the anthropospace enjoy in the second decade of the twenty-first century cannot only be understood as the result of technological progress. Certainly, the slow reversal of climate change, which was ravaging the planet only a century ago, and the end of extreme poverty, were considerably helped by the discovery and the affordability of cold nuclear fusion home kits, biological 3D printers, and affordable mining in outer space. However, the political and economic organization of the anthropospace also had gone through a radical change from the old world of the so-called nation-states. The current setup of several co-existing, self-contained global economic systems, so-called rhizomes, and the possibility for individuals to subscribe to multiple rhizomes at the same time has emerged as one of the most unique characteristics of our times. Although scholars and common subscribers seem to be already accustomed to such innovation in human organization, the process that brought up these changes has not always been so peaceful, with the impact of the Second Thirty Years War still being scrutinized.

In parallel to the mainstream acceptance of rhizomes as new world-systems, there are also mounting critiques to the narrative that describes rhizomes

G. Porcaro (✉)
Head of Governance, Outreach and HR,
Bruegel, Saint-Josse-ten-Noode, Brussels, Belgium
e-mail: giuseppe.porcaro@bruegel.org

© The Author(s), under exclusive license to Springer Nature
Switzerland AG 2023
L. Horn et al. (eds.), *The Palgrave Handbook of Global Politics
in the 22nd Century*, https://doi.org/10.1007/978-3-031-13722-8_11

as self-contained entities. Recently, there have been calls from scholars and activists alike, to consider the need for official and regulated inter-rhizomic relations. No conclusive argument has been made yet, the main question is whether it can be proven that inter-rhizomic relations exist, thus creating the base for a regulatory framework globally. Civic activists have been closely focusing their advocacy in bringing back the concept of *citizenship* as opposed to *subscription*.

This chapter attempts to provide a first compass for students and scholars to navigating emerging theoretical issues and understanding how we ended up in the current scenario. We believe that the question of whether rhizomes are interconnected will be crucial in the next decades. It could lead to a new academic discipline, new institutions, conflicts, and possibly yet another transformation of human organization of the anthropospace. That is the reason why, almost two centuries since Hans Morgenthau's Politics Among Nations (1948) set a milestone to the then-called International Relations Theory, we would like to provide a sketch for what looks to be an embryonic development of a similar discipline, which, for purely working purpose, we call Inter-Rhizomic Relations (IRR).

To understand possible developments, and equip scholars to take part in this debate, we will first look at the breaking of the capitalist world-economy and how former nation-states, regional organizations and corporations, morphed and merged into stand-alone *world-rhizomes*. Then, we will analyze the basic theories of *world-rhizomes* and their characteristics. And finally, we will look at the case study of Europe as the possible battlefield where those theoretical and political issues might meet.

2 The Breaking of the World-Economy and the Rise of World-Rhizomes

To understand the current rhizome setup, we need to go back in time. Providing an archeology of the theories involved, and a review of the historical facts can help the contemporary reader to understand the breaking of one, global, capitalist world-system into separate yet overlapping self-contained economies.

According to Wallerstein (1974), in the twentieth Century, the so-called "international relations" existed within a broad economic, political, and legal framework which he called a "world-system". Wallerstein believed that there were only three basic types of social systems. *Mini-systems* were small, homogenous societies studied by classical anthropologists. Hunting and gathering, pastoral, and simple horticultural societies are relatively self-contained economic units, producing all goods and services within the sociocultural system itself. The second type of social system was a *world-empire*. This system had an economy based on the extraction of surplus goods and services from outlying districts. Much of this tribute went to pay for the administrators who extracted it and for the military to ensure continued domination, the rest went to the political rulers at the head of the empire. The third type of social system, according to Wallerstein, were the *world-economies*. Unlike *world-empires*, *world-economies* had no unified political system; nor was their dominance based on military power alone.

A specific type of *world-economy*, the *capitalist world-economy*, emerged with the rise of polities called "nation states", which multiplied as independent units from the sixteenth Century onwards, after the peace of Westphalia (1648) which ended the first Thirty Years War. As Anderson (1983) posited, nations were socially constructed, imagined political communities characterized by a sense of belonging and expressed through the concept of sovereignty, heavily linked to territorial bonds of land and blood. As Wallerstein argued, each sovereign nation-states while politically independent, belonged to a unique, interdependent *capitalist world-economy*.

Like a *world-empire*, the *capitalist world-economy* was based on the extraction of surplus from peripheral areas to those who rule at the centre. Therefore, the economic interdependency was characterized by an asymmetric centre-periphery dynamic. It was not purely economic, as it included a network of political exchanges between such independent polities, characterized by alliances, agreements of all sorts, as well as hard or soft power struggles for influences. Such frame was commonly referred to as "international relations" both in the scientific literature as well as in vernacular communication.

For many, the system was so intertwined that the *capitalist world-system* should not have collapsed. According to the now-defunct theory of complex interdependence, the growing interlinkages between various parts of the globe should have kept peaceful relations despite an unequal relation among nations and territories by way finding on-going win–win strategies (Keohane and Nye 1977).

By the end of the twentieth Century, the capitalist world-system was ubiquitous, but it was morphing beyond the Westphalian order of nation-states. With the rise of digital technologies, a planetary-scale computation accelerated the process of integration. The emergence of computational theory applied to political geography led to theorizing that the application of the emerging technologies at the time, such as smart grids, cloud platforms, mobile apps, smart cities, the internet of things, could be seen "not as so many species evolving on their own, but as forming a coherent whole: an accidental megastructure called the Stack" (Bratton 2015). The Stack was both a computational apparatus and a new governing structure. While nation-states still withheld power, Bratton's theory called for a new matrix-oriented political geography which called for a redefinition of international relations, design, and power structures.

Bratton's Stack was considered at the time as a future blueprint for the evolving global political architecture. It constituted a possible visualization and conceptualization of the evolution of the *capitalist world-economy*. Back then, it seemed plausible that the global economic system was becoming less and less dependent on nation-states, but still very much characterized by its unicity at the planetary scale.

Similar to the theory of complex interdependence, *the Stack* made the case for a system in constant evolution, but practically fixed in its nature as a world-wide economy. However, the analogy of the global economy with a computer stack had made also possible to imagine as how that software could have been broken: a megastructure accidentally produced, could also accidentally break.

Wallerstein (2000) theorized that a worldwide economic crisis would have been reached, and the capitalist world-system would have collapsed. Farrel and Newman (2019) anticipated that "cross-national networks, contrary to liberal claims, do not produce a flat or fragmented world of diffuse power relations and ready cooperation. Instead, they result in a specific and tangible configuration of power asymmetries." They theorized a progressive weaponization of the structural interdependence of the world-system, analyzing the trade wars in the late 2010s.

The megastructure of the global economy fragmented. It started with trade tariffs and the split of global financial networks such as the ancient SWIFT.[1] Economic conflicts where also accompanied with *cordons sanitaires* and disruptions of the global value chains due to COVID-19 and SARS-24 pandemics. A long cycle of military confrontations scattered around the globe, also known as the Second Thirty Years War, further contributed to create a discontinuity with the ancient political order.

The first phase of the Second Thirty Years War is traditionally associated with the European civil war. In 2031, a major crisis affected most of the geographical region then belonging to the European Union, at the time still under shared jurisdiction with the old nation-states. The crisis started with the burst of a real-estate bubble in special economic zones outside nation-states jurisdictions. The *Constructions & Free Zones Act*, ratified by most of the Union's members and proposed by Greece, under pressure from the Mafia™ and several other companies, whitelisted the hiring of private troops to defend building sites and special economic zones. Riots against real-estate companies turned into full-scale civil wars, which ravaged Europe for three years. That phase of the Second Thirty Years War marked the end of nation-states in Europe, and a milestone in the evolution of the European Union (EU) towards a *world-rhizome*.[2] The population kept nominally the old passports, but the EU, which was the only functioning central administration, started to deliver a subscription model to access services such as pensions, health,

---

[1] The Society for Worldwide Interbank Financial Telecommunication (SWIFT), provided a network that enabled financial institutions worldwide to send and receive information about financial transactions in a secure, standardized and reliable environment. SWIFT had become the industry standard for syntax in financial messages until its dissolution under the pressure of the then United States of America in 2022. The date marked the first split of financial markets.

[2] For a complete history of the European Civil War see Vassilikou A. (Ψ 2121), *The European Civil War and the Breaking of Nation-States*, Blackwell, Hoboken.

and education, while keeping local polities like city governments, regional confederations, and communities, untouched.

In the meantime, the military conflict leaked into the virtual space and the physical infrastructure supporting it, such as data clouds, cyber networks, and other core structures of *The Stack*. It was the prelude to the subsequent phase of the Second Thirty Years War, also known as the Google-Tencent cyberwar. That war, which ravaged during the 2040s, marked the split of what used to be called "The World Wide Web" into locally controlled networks, later regrouped around each rhizome. The cyberwar can be traced back to the early conflicts between China and Google, in the early 2000s, when Google was censored and chased away from China. The worldwide development of Chinese big tech company Tencent, in the late 2020s, was firstly welcomed under the rules of competition policy. However, starting from the 2030s their subscription services developed stricter bundles with other Chinese services, and then were completely incorporated in the subscription policy of the Peoples' Republic of China. Google, meanwhile, developed in the other direction. This other tech giant incorporated most of what used to be the administration and the surveillance system of the polity formerly known as United States of America (Gilberto Ψ 2087). These opposite dynamics, initially fueled by the conflict and the interaction between the two blocs, slowly led to the de-escalation of the war, as both China-Tencent and Google-USA concentrated in the internal process of merging in one polity respectively. This also led to the evolution of both blocs into separate global economies, providing the blueprint for decoupling to others.

However, the most gruesome phase of the Second Thirty Years War was yet to come. During the 2050s, its third phase, commonly referred to as *The Evangelical Jihad*, took place. The *Jihad* was led by The Holy Congregation of Bolsonaro's Knights and of the Seven Angels of the Pentecost. The Holy Congregation was on the verge of overthrowing Pope Constantine II, who managed to unify again Orthodox, Catholics, and most of the Protestant Churches around the world. When the Bolsonaro's knights organized a failed drone attack in the Vatican, a league was formed among all the major religion-led institutions and polities. The United Religions League sealed a military alliance with a plastic shoes company known as Havaianas®, known already for its historical opposition to the late President of Brazil, Jair Bolsonaro, and that kept a militant stance against the Holy Congregation. Havaianas® converted into the production of warfare apparel and weapons and helped the United Religions League to eventually defeat the Holy Congregation in the battle of Funchal in 2058. The Peace of Florianapolis initiated the creation of the People's Republic of Havaianas®, and the United Religions Federation™, both adopting a subscription system, like the EU, Google, and China, and also similarly territorially spread across the planet and self-reliant in terms of economic organization.

These main phases of the Second Thirty Years War can also be understood as completely separated conflicts. In parallel, there were at least dozen smaller-scale conflicts, which all helped create a critical mass around the emergence of the five world-rhizomes. Retrospectively, the series of conflicts that followed were all moved by the crisis of the capitalist world-economy, and the declining nation-states system: It was first the pandemics, and then warfare over virtual space and spiritual domination that affected value chains, services, and social systems, accelerating the consolidation of new forms of collective and political organization. The conflicts, which started as a classic geopolitical warfare of weaponized interdependence, only ended when the various confrontations were made irrelevant with the splitting of several self-sustained networks. By the 2060s, a handful of autonomous economic world-systems started cohabiting, replacing the old globalization and constituting a new fix in anthropospace politics. Ferriel and Ogston ⟨Ψ 2088⟩ argue that the 2058 Battle of Funchal signified the completion of the Braudelian *longue durée* that started in Westphalia, 1648, with the two Thirty Years Wars marking the beginning and the end of an historical cycle characterized by territorial states, international relations, and a unified world-economy.

From than onwards, nation-states, religious entities, regional organizations, and corporations, morphed and merged into stand-alone *world-rhizomes*. In geographical terms, these were a new scale, produced out of the previous crisis, and despite their differences, they developed some common features over time: First, subscriptions emerged as a central feature in both the economic and political spheres. As noted in *Subscriptionomics* ⟨Woollacott Ψ 2098⟩, various forms of subscription replaced private ownership, access to services, voting rights, health insurances, and what was left of the old concept of citizenship. This happened gradually, without deleting previous passports and identity cards. In the final stages of this transition, citizenship was made obsolete by subscriptions, partial, full, or bundled. This slow and gradual transition largely went unnoticed, and yet, retrospectively it represents an epochal change.

Secondly, even if geography still carried importance, the need for a centralized approach to the control of territory has become less important, as the need for physically connected infrastructures became obsolete. This was one of the technological aspects that broke down Bratton's Stack, alongside the cyberwar and digital decoupling. 3D Printing, satellite-based communications, solar energy, and cold-fusion mini units, transport vehicles not depending on roads, and autonomous habitable units, all of these reduced the need for grids compared to the previous century.

The third similarity is the people. Unlike in the old world-economic system, political entities were no longer bound to a territory, and therefore, people did not have to be bound to one specific political or economic entity. This was one of the pillars of the Westphalian system, and the basis upon which the 'imagined communities of nations' were built (Anderson 1983). Once subscriptions replaced citizenship, people could subscribe to multiple services, bundles, and polities. Nowadays, people and territories can move across polities, subscribe, or unsubscribe. They have to follow only the specific terms of references regulating each subscription system, as any global or regional regulatory institution had been disbanded or morphed into a separate rhizome itself.

3   World-Rhizome as Geographical Scale

Although *rhizome* is a widely known term, also used in everyday language, scholarship has not reached a consensus what constitutes a rhizome, their configuration and relations. Unlike earlier world-economies, World-rhizomes share territory and people through self-regulated subscriptions. Halterman (Ψ 2068) considers them a fourth type of social system, and the concept has been developed further with the rebirth of world-systems analysis in the 2070s, the so-called neo-Wallerstenian school (Halterman and Rosner Ψ 2074).

In fact, it was the neo-Wallersteinians who applied the concept of rhizome to contemporary polities and popularized it. Inter-rhizomic relations replaced the old Westphalian system, the main framework of International Relations scholarship, an old academic discipline closely linked to the politics of the previous *world-system* (Ferriel and Ogston Ψ 2088). The process of forming world-rhizomes is a unique example of production of space (Lefebvre 1974) and of producing a new geographical scale that did not exist before (Porcaro and Minca 2009).

The concept of rhizome was initially borrowed by Deleuze and Guattari (1980) from botanical sciences. A rhizome is a subterranean agglomeration of nodes and connecting roots, that give rise to distinct growths. These kinds of plants pops out of the ground over an expanding area, giving the impression that many separate plants are emerging in close proximity to one another, but in fact these ostensibly individual "plants" are parts of one big plant, and are interconnected under the ground. In Deleuze and Guattari's work, *rhizome* is roughly the philosophical counterpart of the botanical term, suggesting that many things in the world are rhizomes, or rhizomatically interconnected, although such connections are not always visible.

World-rhizomes have many characteristics in common with both Wallerstein's mini-systems and world-economies, but they are more complex than the sum of them. The main criteria of world-rhizomes are their capacities to be able to sustain a similar system to a world-economy but at the same time be self-contained comparing to other world-rhizomes. Like rhizome plants, and differently from Wallerstein's pre-capitalistic mini-systems, world-rhizomes are neither homogenous, nor geographically united among each other. Taken individually, a world-rhizome has many characteristics of world-economies, including the global geographical spread and power relations, with a centre and a periphery, they do not encompass the whole planet, as the capitalist world-economy used to do, nor are they separate territorial blocs, like during the cold war of the twentieth century.

If we home in on the current five world-rhizomes resulting from the geopolitical fractures discussed above (Batista Ψ 2098) we would still find some geographical continuity. One of them is the direct continuation of an earlier polity, China. China is experimenting with a Leninist proto-post-scarcity regime, where the one-party system is legitimized by its redistribution policy of the wealth accumulated from the periphery. The transfer of resources is made possible thanks to a solid infrastructure network based on port-cities and intercontinental high-speed trains, the so-called belt and road initiative, and the digital network built on Tencent's and other tech companies' assets.[3]

Another rhizome is the evolution of a big corporation, Google, after its merger with the United States and several other entities. Google continues with a similar economy to the one of the capitalist world-system, enhanced by the technological changes and the subscription system which in their case is used to extract value through information and time to the individuals. Centre-periphery relations are not geographically bound as is the case for China, but they are intrinsic to the system.

The third world-rhizome is a morphed regional organization, the European Union, which evolved into a neo-modernist system combining social redistribution with algorithm-enhanced efficiency. As we will show in the case study, The EU is preserves some legacy from the time of the nation-states, a democratic governance and a varied patchwork of polities on different geographical scales. The latter results from the principle of subsidiarity that was invented at the time nation-states were core elements of the Union.

Then there is the People's Republic of Havaianas® (PRH), which is also a capitalist economy, but more traditional, as heavily based on manufacturing, rather than a surveillance capitalism.

Finally, the United Religions Federation™ (URF), is a complex democratic theocracy, combining a decentralized network of productive communities feeding in the central committee of the Pontifex.[4] Its economy is based on the Benedict monks' rule, of *ora et labora* (pray and work) where the main motivation to produce is not economic gain but the elevation towards a spiritual dimension through the practice of work and transaction ⟨Cottica Ψ 2120⟩ (Fig. 1).

These world-rhizomes intersect geographically. Even if most of them have a core with some sort of territorial continuity, they are scattered across the planet and outer space ⟨Ferriel and Ogston Ψ 2088⟩.[5] Population is the other element which world-rhizomes partially share, as individuals can choose

---

[3] See Zhang and Coppola ⟨Ψ 2097⟩, for an extensive overview of the evolution of China as a unique example of continuity from mini-system to world-empire, from periphery to centre of the capitalist world-economy, to a world-rhizome.

[4] The study of the various economies within the world-rhizomes developed a rich literature on the subject. For an overview see *The Handbook of Rhizomes' Economies* ⟨Horn and Batista Ψ 2120⟩.

[5] The very essence of the functioning of a rhizome is its capacity to be a self-contained economy. Therefore, an almost-global reach is a prerequisite for a system to be considered an autonomous rhizome. Many quasi-rhizomes can also be detected, whose services depend on those of the five world-rhizomes.

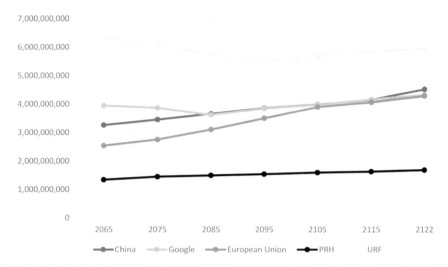

Fig. 1 Subscriptions to World-Rhizomes 2065–2122 (Graph based on self-declared data from each rhizome)

whether to subscribe to different services in different rhizomes, have a full subscription to one of the other, or in some cases even overlap full subscriptions (Woollacott Ψ 2098).[6] All the rhizomes, except for google, does not have an active subscription policy campaign, which helps to keep the issue of competition among the various rhizomes not an issue for the time being. The fact that multiple partial subscriptions are possible for each individual is one of the reasons why the various rhizomes do not compete with each other on this domain. However, questions arise by the very nature of the multiplicity of subscriptions within one individual. We are living in a hybrid society, previous people lived within the boundaries of territorial states, now multiple boundaries could be traced within each individual. The long-term consequences of this and the part human agency plays in shaping rhizomes as fluid and dynamic geographical scales are yet to be analyzed. A new territoriality is being formed, one which is pervasive as the human body becomes a mobile, hybrid, geographical intersection overlappingly governed by different systems.

To summarize, for each rhizome population and territorial space is varied and varying all the time. The best way to describe it is a functionalist perspective. Both people and territory are *functional* aspects not *constitutional* to the

---

[6] During the 2050s the notion of citizenship became less and less popular and the subscription systems matched the services delivered by companies and polity alike. The only rhizome that residually kept some references to "citizens" in official documentation has been the European Union™. However, even in that case it has never been used in common language or media.

world-rhizome. This makes them deeply different from the nation-states of the Westphalian order, which had population and territory as constitutive parts.

This overview would be incomplete without mentioning that contemporary world-systems also include the presence of autonomous *mini-systems*. The main feature of *mini-systems* is their territoriality. They are autonomous and resilient, but only present in a specific geographical area and their subscription system is attached to permanent residency within their territory. Some examples include the autonomous hippie communes of Tasmania, the human ponds of the Amazon, the geodesic communities of Ethiopian highlands, and the Moon settlement. According to Rosner ⟨Ψ 2095⟩, even if the sum of those covers only a minority of the existent human settlements, for their quality and spread they must be considered as an integral part of the contemporary world-systems, and not residual relics. Rosner also observes that there is no hostility between mini-systems and between mini-systems and the rhizomes. Their complete self-reliance makes them autonomous and resilient. However, a matter yet to be observed is how the territorial base of such systems might affect the potential evolution of rhizomes in the future.

4   Europe in Contemporary World-Systems

We have seen how the contemporary world-systems based on several self-contained world-economies have developed in the past fifty years or so. We also recalled the main features of each rhizome and several of the characteristics mentioned already raised open questions about possible contact points between rhizomes, such as the multiple geographical scales within individuals subscribing to different rhizomes.

Our review cannot be concluded without a case study that would go deeper into some of these open questions, and help to complete the overview around the theoretical debates open in the academia, as well advance some hypothesis of the potential, and yet-to-come Inter-Rhizomic Relations. Europe, as a continent, provides an interesting laboratory and intellectual battleground to test our hypothesis.

The approach of Skalnik ⟨Ψ 2102⟩ and Lopez ⟨Ψ 2106⟩ within the neo-wallersteinian school, has argued to refocus the analysis on places and geographical macro-regions as a unit of analysis of the world-systems, bringing geography back in anthropospace studies. Following this tradition, we are going to analyze geographical Europe and how it looks within the world-systems.

During the Second Thirty Years War, Europe was the first continent to experience the downfall of nation-states. It is also considered to be the first place where the concept of rhizome was applied to describe a political entity even before world-rhizomes would emerge (Zielonka 2014). Zielonka argued that although the EU would only survive in modest form, deprived of any real power, Europe as an integrated entity would grow stronger as integration would continue apace because of European states' profound economic interdependence, historic ties, and the need for political pragmatism. Even if his prediction sounds outdated nowadays, as the European Union grew instead stronger, while nation-states collapsed, he rightly pointed out to the rhizomatic nature of the EU when describing the kind of ties European people had built through the centuries.

In pre-war times, the EU included proto-rhizomatic features, such as functional competences which did not fall under the concept of state sovereignty; it did not directly own any territory; and individuals could be at the same time "citizens" of the European Union and of a nation state. The old concept of citizenship is close to the concept of subscriptions; however, individuals acquired citizenship, most of the time at their birth, either by virtue of their parents' (*ius sanguinis*) or by virtue of the place where they were born (*ius solii*), or both (Kaspary Ψ 2104). People automatically acquired European Union citizenship if they were citizens of one of the member states which formed the polity.

The world-rhizome generated from the old European Union, and which still bears the same name, expanded across the anthropospace in the 2060s. However, already in pre-war times there were a lot of "citizens" of the EU living in other continents. Estimations of Europeans in other continents before 2030s are hard to assess due to the erasure of most of the existing archives when states fell apart, or because of the digital warfare. However, there are anecdotal evidences of a pre-existing spread of EU citizens across the planet, which constituted a basis for later subscriptions outside the continental base to this rhizome. As of 2122, there are 4,287,845,381 registered subscriptions, full and partial, to the European Union, with an almost equal repartition between the African, European, and American continents (Fig. 2).

Specific features of the EU rhizome are:

- Terms of references inspired by ancient codes, commonly referred to as *The Rule of Law*;
- The principle of subsidiarity, empowering local self-government for the matters that can be sorted at these levels;
- A complex democratic governance at the local and central level;
- A semi-socialist economy characterized by free education, health, and housing.

The EU is also characterized by a specific system for applications for full subscription. While it's difficult to receive a full subscription to the Union they admit multiple, full or partial, subscriptions for users that reside on the continent. This would not be too different from other regions of the world, where individuals also might be shared among rhizomes through partial subscription schemes. However, what makes the case different for Europe, is that the European Union is the only world-rhizome to admit full subscriptions to other rhizomes for the inhabitants of that region. This is usually explained

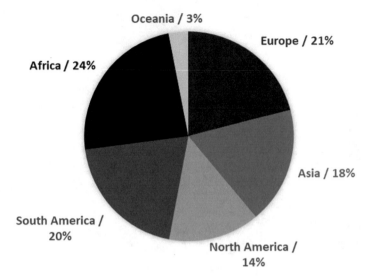

Fig. 2 European Union subscriptions across continents, 2122 (Data Eurostat)

as a historical relic of the territorial anchorage of the EU and to the above-mentioned old concept of citizenship. Such double full subscriptions counted for 68.3% of the population, while at least 87% of the population has several partial subscriptions.

The territory is "inhabited" therefore as well by the other world-rhizomes. The most relevant are China and Google in terms of the amount of full double subscriptions, while the URF and PRH are mainly partial subscriptions. The case of the Religions Federation is still considerable, as most of the population in the south has strong links to the URF and, all in all, it gathers around 500 million subscribers, making it the second rhizome in the continent after the EU.

The geography of the continent is thus a patchwork (Fig. 3), to the point that scholars from the New Wave school have made a case for a non-institutionalized existence of inter-rhizome relations (Fosdik Ψ 2099). This claim is seen as contradicting the existence of world-rhizomes as self-contained economies and argues that Europe is the place where various rhizomes have undeclared points of contact (Fosdik and Paquette 2102). Those scholars have argued that the individual overlap of subscriptions could bring back what once was called "international relations".

The controversial point is the potential transfer of resources between rhizomes. For example, there is a claim that within the intensive knowledge-based economy set up by Google, where higher education is a luxury good, those who have the full subscription with the European Union would use the free education system provided to get a guarantee of influential positions within Google' highly segmented social system. Google's Workers League filed a formal complaint to the Google settlement body against a full double

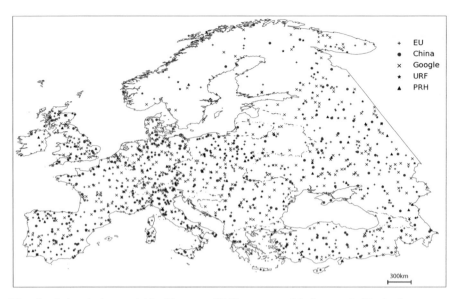

Fig. 3 Subscriptions within Europe, 2122, geographical sprawl (Each dot corresponds to 100,000 subscribers. *Source* Author elaboration on self-declared data from each rhizome)

citizen, Laura Yuyun-Horn, for breaching their Terms of Reference by using her academic status obtained within the free education system of the EU to be published in academic journals published by private Googles' universities. The Workers League claimed that this practice would create social dumping and distort the radical free market of that rhizome.[7] The Yuyun-Horn case is quoted by Paquette and Iqbal ⟨Ψ 2107⟩ as an example of the possible transfer of resources between rhizomes, and they argue for the need to institutionalize "inter-rhizomical" relations. They add an additional argument, which is to regulate any controversy related to breaches of Terms of References across rhizomes. Their analysis brought back into the scholarship the idea of global interdependence (legal, political, and economic).

Neo-post-structuralists go even further, saying that the specific subscription policy of the European Union would prove the existence of only one world-rhizome. And they claim that this would bring back world-systems analysis closer to the spirit of Wallerstein's initial work, and of Deleuze's and Guattari's concept of rhizome ⟨Zuliani Ψ 2105⟩. Zuliani provides evidence beyond the economics, and puts forward the case of a handful of Chinese/European

---

[7] Google's Workers League (GWL) has the mission to ensure workers do not get any support or subsidy to participate in the free market of labour. Often, they are mistakenly confused with the role that trade unions played back in the 20th Century, because they are also a membership-based association composed by workers. However, unions used to advocate for worker's protection and for positive discrimination that would distort the market, while the GWL is operating completely on the opposite side of the spectrum.

Union which double subscribers which had been elected in official positions in local government, and that have been coopted at the same time by the Chinese central committee as field officers.

The new botanist school argues that rhizomes give rise to individual "plants" that collect the energy required to produce carbs. If these correspond to the individual person in subscription world, multiple subscriptions would seem to render the rhizomatic model useless (Lipschutz Ψ 2121).

The psychosociologist movement (Anampura Ψ 2112) brings forward a radical revision of the entire world-systems analysis through the case of these individually overlapping subscriptions in Europe. Their critical approach argues that individuals and their psyche should be considered the centre of research, rather than the rhizomes they subscribe to. That radical approach injects elements of psychology, computational science, and anthropology in the analysis of society and economy. Their approach focuses on the individual's agency, based on the need to preserve the tacit contract of free will to freely subscribe to the terms of reference of any of the rhizomes. We would argue that their analysis brings different lens to rhizome's evolution, but it is rather a complementary approach, changing the point of view from the system to the individual, rather than a radical alternative to world-systems analysis.

The official neo-Wallersteinian position, according to Ursula Bankston (Ψ 2116), claims that the subscription policy of the Union does not overlap with the concept of separate rhizomes. The principle of functionality, mentioned earlier in this chapter, allows individuals or territories to use certain functions for one rhizome and not for another. She argues that partial or full subscriptions of individual residents of Europe territories don't make transfers of services or labour from one rhizome to another. She also responds to the New Wavers and the neo-post-structuralists saying that the specific cases upon which their claims are built on are residual historical legacies rather than structural challenges to the claim of separate world-rhizomes. She also argues that the new world order is still recent, and that considering the Braudelian historical cycles it is still too early to reach conclusions about the future evolution of each rhizome and the way they live side by side within the same anthropospace.

5   Conclusions

World-rhizomes have risen from the ashes of the Second Thirty Years War. This process was linked to the progressive disintegration of the capitalist world-economy, the end of the so-called globalization, and of the Westphalian system. While new forms of social, political, and economic organizations emerged, replacing the old ones, the current system is still fluctuating and seeking an equilibrium. To conclude our review, we would like to suggest some paths researchers should pursue, which would further help to lay down the academic basis of the new discipline we provisionally call Inter-rhizomic Relations.

The debates over the existence of inter-rhizome relations and the potential need for regulating these relations is similar to those that took place when the first international relations where institutionalized and codified, centuries ago. Despite their differences, this literature review shows that there is a need for a more sophisticated approach to address the complexities of world-rhizomes, than each of the schools have been arguing for the past few decades of rhizome studies. Comparative historical studies (e.g. with the emergence of the Westphalian system) might help us better understand the present.

We agree with Bankston's reflection that there is uncertainty on the evolution of these cohabiting world-systems. However, the rich academic debate sparked by the case of the European Union reveals more than just a theoretical dialectic, and underlines the need for the academia to provide also more empirical work about the liminal spaces where rhizomes might interact with each other. That would be a second strand of research, alongside the first historical one.

A third and critical area for further research involves the political struggles and power dynamics of this new era, new hegemonic struggles within and between world-rhizomes. Specifically, there is increasing activism on defining the power and agency of subscribers (e.g. in terms of free and customized subscription types), opening novel debates in the public sphere, as activists seek counter-narratives to the mainstream discourse about peaceful and voluntary subscriptions. These developments are likely to also bring contestations into the academic discipline.

BIBLIOGRAPHY

Anampura L. ⟨Ψ 2112⟩, *Individuals as the Units to Understand the Contemporary Multiverse*, Spotify Premium Press, Zanzibar.

Anderson B. (1983), *Imagined Communities: Reflections on the Origin and Spread of Nationalism*, Verso, London.

Bankston U. ⟨Ψ 2116⟩, *The Principle of Functionality in World-Rhizomes*, Google University Press, Moon Base two.

Batista S. ⟨Ψ 2098⟩, *Capitalist Economy's Continuity and World-Rhizomes Evolution*, in *Journal of Economic Analysis*, vol. 1, pp. 450–487.

Bratton, Benjamin H. (2015), The Stack: On. Software and Sovereignty. MIT Press.

Cottica A. ⟨Ψ 2120⟩, *Neo-Benedictine Economy*, MIT Press

Deleuze & Guattari (1980), *Milles Plateaux*, Editions de Minuit, Paris.

Farrel H., & Newman A. (2019), *Weaponized Interdependence*, Self-published.

Ferriel G., & Ogston I. ⟨Ψ 2088⟩, *Rhizomes in Post-Westphalian World-Systems*, Cambridge University Press, Cambridge.

Fosdik G. ⟨Ψ 2099⟩, "Beyond Conspiracy Theories: A Case for Inter-rhizomic Relations", in *Journal of Critical World Systems Analysis*, vol. 3, pp. 345–360.

Fosdik G., & Paquette F. ⟨Ψ 2102⟩, "Europe: Blurring World-Rhizomes Boundaries", in *Journal of Critical World Systems Analysis*, vol. 2, pp 231–247.

Halterman F. ⟨Ψ 2068⟩, "World-Rhizome in Contemporary World-System", in *Progress in Human Geography*, nr. 3, pp. 140–176.

Halterman F., & Rosner J., eds. ⟨Ψ 2074⟩, *One Hundred Years of World-Systems Analysis,* Google University Press, Moon Base Two.

Horn L., & Batista S. ⟨Ψ 2120⟩, *The Handbook of Rhizomes' Economies*, Blackwell, Hoboken.

Kaspary F. ⟨Ψ 2104⟩, *The Concept of Citizenship in the Late Westphalian Order*, Google University Press, Moon Base Two.

Keohane, R. O., & Nye, J. S. (1977), *Power and Interdependence: World Politics in Transition*, Little, Brown, Boston.

Gilberto G. ⟨Ψ 2087⟩, *Google and the History of the Polity Formerly Known as USA*, Google University Press, Moon Base Two.

Lefebvre H. (1974), *La production de l'espace*, Anthropos, Paris.

Lipschutz R. ⟨Ψ 2121⟩, *A Plant-Based Approach to Human Organization*, Harvard Press, New Boston.

Lopez R. ⟨Ψ 2106⟩, "Spatial Units Within Multiple Rhizomes: A Critical Approach", in *The Journal of Rhizomes in the Anthropo-Space*, vol. 4, pp. 890–934.

Morgenthau H., & Thompson K. (1948), *Politics Among Nations*, New York, McGraw-Hill.

Paquette F., & Iqbal O. ⟨Ψ 2107⟩, *Interdependence and Contemporary World-Systems*, Harvard Press, New Boston.

Paraty B. (2019), *Mobile Phones Development in Africa 1990s–2010s*, MIT press, Boston.

Porcaro G., & Minca C., (2009), "Rescaling Trieste: (Not so) Invisible Networks, (Dis)trust and the Imaginary Landscapes of the Expo 2008", in *Social Capital and Urban Networks of Trust*, eds. J Hakli, C Minca, Ashgate, Aldershot, Hants, pp 93–120.

Rosner J. ⟨Ψ 2095⟩, *Beyond the Rhizomes: Mini-Systems in Contemporary World-Systems*, Google University Press, Moon Base Two.

Skalnik H. ⟨Ψ 2102⟩, "A Territorial Approach to World-Rhizomes: Understanding Complexity", in *Environment and Planning D*, vol. 2, pp. 387–421.

Vassilikou A. ⟨Ψ 2121⟩, *The European Civil War and the Breaking of Nation-States*, Blackwell, Hoboken.

Wallerstein I. (1974), *The Modern World-System: Capitalist Agriculture and the Origins of the European World-Economy in the Sixteenth Century*, Academic Press, New York.

Wallerstein I. (2000), *The Essential Wallerstein*, The New Press, New York.

Woollacott K. ⟨Ψ 2098⟩, *Subscriptionomics*, Blackwell, Hoboken.

Zhang C. Coppola P. ⟨Ψ 2097⟩, *China: A Survivor in a Multiplicity of World-Systems*, Xinguq Press, Hong Kong.

Zielonka J. (2014), *Is the EU Doomed?* Polity, Cambridge.

Zuliani O. ⟨Ψ 2105⟩, *One World, One Rhizome*, China Academy Press, San Francisco.

Shades of Democracy in the Post-Anthropocene

Peter Christoff and Ayşem Mert

1   INTRODUCTION

Democracy, both as concept and praxis, has proven extraordinarily resilient in the face of unprecedented challenges. Its meaning, practices, and institutions have changed over time, and adapted to successive periods of demographic, technological, institutional, and ecological transformation. This chapter investigates democracy's potential as a political practice for twenty-second-century societies. To underpin our interpretation of the fate and futures of democracy in our entangled, diminished and security-obsessed world, we begin with a review of its trajectory through the period of recent modernity. We document and investigate how democracy was reimagined in the Anthropocene before we consider how it has been transformed during the post-Anthropocene, affected by successive catastrophes, particularly during the Decades of Disasters.

The Anthropocene was a term proposed at the start of the twenty-first century to describe a unique geological era shaped by human activities (Crutzen and Stoermer 2000). It also inadvertently marked a crucial conceptual turn in reflections on global politics and the place of humans on this

---

P. Christoff (✉)
Department of Resource Management and
Geography, University of Melbourne, Parkville, VIC, Australia
e-mail: peterac@unimelb.edu.au

A. Mert
Department of Political Science, University of Stockholm, Stockholm, Sweden
e-mail: aysem.mert@statsvet.su.se

© The Author(s), under exclusive license to Springer Nature
Switzerland AG 2023
L. Horn et al. (eds.), *The Palgrave Handbook of Global Politics in the 22nd Century*, https://doi.org/10.1007/978-3-031-13722-8_12

planet. For instance, contemporaries like Barry (2002), Žižek (2004), Swyngedouw (2013) and Lövbrand et al. (2015), saw the Anthropocene not merely as the epoch defined by human impacts on global geophysical processes: it was also 'the era during which humans believed that they had the technological capacities to control nature, a time of intentional interventions in the natural world and, ultimately, hubristic attempts at planet-altering systemic manipulation' ⟨Christoff and Mert Ψ 2030⟩.

The *post*-Anthropocene is its successor. It is the current period of ecological and political turbulence in which 'intentional globalized technological interventions continue in order to aid human survival, but the underlying legitimatory belief in technoscience as a means of controlling nature in order to ensure our species' survival has ultimately failed' ⟨Christoff and Mert Ψ 2030, p. 8⟩. The Climate Emergency and the Long Pandemic have predominated as overdetermining structurating phenomena since the early 2000s ⟨Asenbaum and Hanusch Ψ 2071; 9_Masters@Roke Ψ 2112⟩.

The post-Anthropocene arguably started in the 2020s, when it became clear that climate impacts were becoming core drivers of economic, social, political and ecological change. Simultaneously, the COVID-19 virus, with its persistent and uncontrollable mutations, initiated the period of what is now commonly called the Long Pandemic ⟨PCAM Ψ 2084; Orm and Irian Ψ 2098⟩. Much as the Black Death reshaped Europe between 1347 and the mid-1700s, transforming social relations and encouraging the rise of the modern state, the Long Pandemic has reshaped economic and political systems globally—propelling the rise of disembodied forms of communication, transaction and surveillance while limiting corporeal interaction and mobility—with enduring consequences for social behaviour.

In what follows, we provide accounts of Anthropocene and post-Anthropocene democratic imaginaries. What we want to highlight here is that significant transformative shifts took place in theoretical thinking about democracy before and during the early years of the Climate Emergency and the Long Pandemic. Starting with the early 2020s, the focus of these debates shifted from creating a global democratic imaginary that provides political solutions to climate change (Eckersley 2020; Pickering et al. 2020) to creating possibilities of adaptation and survival in the face of macro (climatic) and micro (infectious) disasters.

Of course, transformative influences—both negative and positive—have manifested differently in individual states. Here we draw on Scandinavian and Antipodean experiences to contrast elements of the current crisis. These accounts are illustrations rather than case studies (although, they would have neatly fitted the methodological requirements of a legitimate 'most different systems case study design'—as per (Seawright and Gerring 2008). But our goal is critical/exploratory rather than rational/analytical. We investigate if democracy can be reinvented in the twenty-second century, such that it can be a relevant and effective political practice once again.

2   DEMOCRACY IN THE ANTHROPOCENE

Democracy has been reinvented many times. Through the revolutions of the late eighteenth century to those of the twentieth century, social and political landscapes were transformed by the emergence of a modern democratic imaginary (Mert 2015).

For instance, during the French Revolution, Jean-Jacques Rousseau's writings helped shift the view that democracy connoted disunity and decadence to one implying harmony and regeneration. Miller comments, 'Before Rousseau democracy was, at best, an admirable but obsolete pure form of government. [A]fter him it became a name for popular sovereignty, extending to all the promise of a personally fulfilling freedom, exercised in cooperation with others, [...] a conviction that all human beings possess, in their own free will, the capacity and desire to govern themselves' (Miller 1996: 202–203).

Another example is when (Montesquieu 1784) observed that separation of powers could make a democratic *republic* possible. By creating checks and balances between the executive, the legislative and the judiciary, democracies could be organised in greater scales. Alexis de Tocqueville took up this idea and used it to rethink modes of democratic representation. In *Democracy in America*, he created a liberal democratic imaginary, arguing that democracy could be tamed if 'the most powerful, intelligent, and moral classes [...] gain control of it in order to direct it' made representative democracy safe for liberalism.

In general, what truly differentiated modern democracy from its classical precursors was its growing inclusiveness. If democratic government was, as famously articulated in Abraham Lincoln's 1863 Gettysburg Address, to be government 'for the people, by the people, and of the people'—the question increasingly became one of 'which people, and where, and how?' In the nineteenth century, where democracies existed they excluded women, colonised subjects, and those without property. This changed significantly throughout the twentieth century, but nevertheless remained incomplete.

The Incomplete Project of Modern Democracy

After the formal abolition of slavery and the political emancipation of women, for the first time in most places the majority of adults could participate in electoral politics. Representative democracy was regarded by many as sufficiently participatory. While being the hegemonic form of democracy throughout modernity, this complicated democratic imaginary and associated practice remained incomplete and inadequate: it was limited and flawed in four significant and interrelated ways .

1. *The exclusion of First Nations and Indigenous Peoples*

In the two intense periods of nation-building (first, following the collapse of empires after the First World War and then following nominal decolonisation after the Second World War), the question of who constitutes 'a people', for purposes of government, remained a complicated matter. How were sovereign borders to be drawn, if certain terrains did not have an ethnic 'nation' claiming to be its rightful rulers? On numerous occasions, 'the people' entitled to self-government was determined by earlier experiences of colonisation. Dahl (1989), argued that political philosophers deal with this problem by presupposing that 'a people' already exists, though even this presupposition was historically problematic since nationhood is often established 'not by consent or consensus but by violence'.

Dahl was correct in noting problems with the processes through which nationhood and sovereignty were assigned. What he did not recognise in his critique was that large parts of the world had never been truly decolonised. Despite the eventual political enfranchisement of the working class and of women, and the spread of national democracies beyond Europe, North America and Australasia, even these established democratic systems continued to resist meaningful recognition and inclusion of Indigenous peoples. Their claims to land, language and culture often were hard-fought battles, that only rarely resulted in democratic integration (Chapin et al. 2005).

2. *The nation-state paradox*

By the time of the Third Industrial Revolution (*the Digital Age*, beginning in late twentieth century), the world was divided into nation-states that served as democracy's institutional container. Older localised and face-to-face forms of democratic choice persisted alongside the new machinery of distanciated aggregative choice and representation, including political parties and parliaments. The need or potential for governing the transboundary effects and impacts of globalisation remained insufficiently recognised. As a consequence, when the post-WWII institutions of international social, economic and ecological governance arose, they remained ineffectual in their attempts to curtail the power of major state and corporate actors and to regulate or mitigate the economic and ecological impacts of their actions.

By the beginning of the Fourth Industrial Revolution (*the Algorithmic Age*, starting in the early twenty-first century), the negative effects of globalisation were rampant. As the scope and frequency of ecological disasters and economic crises increased, the overarching question about democracy became: what kind of a democracy could anticipate, mitigate and adapt to the transformations invoked by the Anthropocene? Nation-states had a set of different responses to the so-called 'Age of Humans' (see below) but at the scale of international relations and global governance, the common assumption was that democracy was not possible without 'a people', or with too many participants. It was therefore impossible to make democratic decisions at planetary scale.

To explain: in the practice of international relations (IR), citizens were assumed to be represented by their respective governments. Relations between nation-states were considered anarchic or at best institutionally constrained. IR textbooks prior to 1989 do not even contain the word 'democracy' (Archibugi and Held 2011). In the early twenty-first century, a recurrent academic debate about 'democracy beyond the nation-state' focused on the observation that state-centred democratic concepts could not adequately respond to territorially unbounded problems of governance, particularly environmental governance (Bäckstrand 2006, 2012; Dingwerth 2007; Nanz and Steffek 2004; Scholte 2011).

Scholars tended to apply nation-level democratic principles to the international level, mainly because nation-states were seen as the main actors in the present international society. This bias structured and limited the democratic imaginary. For instance, some argued that although global governance involves the difficult task of producing public goods, there was no form of global government that could 'harness the emotional support of nationalism' (Keohane 2017, p. 938). The necessary infrastructure and legitimacy for 'deep democracy' were arguably absent at the global level, therefore the best possibility was maintaining only some of nation-state democracy's key features, such as accountability of elites to publics, widespread but limited participation of citizens, protection of minority rights, and deliberation within civil society. This hegemony of state-level democratic imaginaries focused IR debates on the (im)possibility of representation when all of humanity constitutes the *demos*. Despite demands to this end, a more stringent participatory democratisation was not pursued in the global governance institutions of the twenty-first century in ways that could have increased their chances of survival (Stevenson and Dryzek 2014; Mert 2019). In all, the paradox that the survival of a coherent and peaceful nation-state system depended on creating democratically effective and inclusive transnational political institutions remained unresolved.

3. *Exclusion of non-human nature and future generations*

Anthropocene democracy was also limited by its peripheral recognition of the ecological interdependency of non-human species and humans, and the intergenerational extension of those needs (Haraway 2007; Braidotti 2016, 2017). As chains of production, trade and consumption lengthened and strengthened, and exploitation intensified during the Great Acceleration (McNeill 2014), the distant consequences of these activities were obscured. Impacts—pollution, overharvesting, the destruction of habitat, collapse of ecosystems and extinction of species—were poorly monitored and even more poorly regulated by a global economic system primarily built around the conversion of nature into a resource for the benefit of certain privileged human communities. Even with the advent of social movements focused on climate catastrophe, and the creation of Green parties, these issues rarely rose to political prominence in electoral contests focused on and determined by more immediate anthropocentric concerns.

By the late twentieth and early twenty-first centuries, there were calls for the establishment of environmental and ecological democracy, calls that highlighted the nature-blindness of democratic practices at that time (Plumwood 1993, 2002; Achterberg et al. 1996; Eckersley 1996; Mason 2012; Wong 2016). Theorists suggested multiple ways forward, including various reinterpretations of the democratic imaginary, which included deliberative (Eckersley and Saward 2003; Baber 2004; Niemeyer 2020), participatory (Christoff 1996; Hester 2010) and other radical forms (Machin 2013; Kothari 2014; Mert 2015). Additional calls for reform paid specific attention to the inclusion of more-than-human nature (Latour, 2004), decolonising epistemes (Stevenson 2016; Winter 2019), energy and climate politics (Dryzek and Stevenson 2011; Szulecki 2018), and the inclusion of future generations (Beckman 2008).

While direct participation of non-human agents was an unrealistic option, the inclusion of those authorised to represent both non-human nature and future generations was considered possible (Purdy 2015, pp. 2–3; Dryzek and Pickering 2018). Ways of including unrepresented non-human actors (agents that cannot represent themselves in human terms), and underrepresented groups such as future generations, were continuously refined using legal mechanisms and scientific data. The non-human environment was sometimes given legal standing: for instance, the Ganges, Yamuna and Whanganui Rivers were given rights 'as if they were human'. Similarly, Pachamama Laws (which are regarded as affecting relative food security and the late twenty-first century rise of the Southwest quadrant) first originated in the early 2000s when the Peruvian state recognised the rights of a sacred goddess of Earth and Time.

The ethical and legal conceptions of non-human agency changed further with the commercialisation and normalisation of genetic modification and nanobot technologies by the mid-twenty-first century. In fact, during the twenty-first century the definitions of 'human' and 'human being' changed several times, becoming increasingly specific and restrictive. In English, in the early 2020s, the common definition of *human* was still 'a bipedal primate mammal' (MWD 2012), or 'a culture-bearing primate classified in the genus Homo, especially the species H. sapiens. Human beings are anatomically similar and related to the great apes but are distinguished by a more highly developed brain and a resultant capacity for articulate speech and abstract reasoning' (Britannica 2022).

By the late 2040s, the most common definition of human was 'individual or collective persons predominantly genetically derived from other humans' (Wikipaedia Ψ 2048), and later 'a being that comprised of at least 95% of human DNA, and whose embodied agency is independent of artificial modes and forms of intelligence' (GlobalDictionary Ψ 2071). The notion of beings significantly or predominantly comprised of non-human or inorganic components had been highlighted and discussed in works of science fiction, and feminist, post-humanist and post-structuralist scholarship (e.g. Braidotti 2017; Žižek 2004). Haraway's *A Cyborg Manifesto* considered the cyborg a rejection of rigid boundaries separating 'human', 'animal' and 'machine'. These adaptations of varying levels of biological and technological synthesis and super-competence spawned additional problems for political representation and for inclusion or exclusion of such synths from democratic decision-making, as is discussed below.

4. *Techno-exceptionalism and the paradox of digitalisation*

By the start of the twenty-first century, political scientists, politicians and publics alike regarded formal political institutions in most democracies as at best having only tentative control over decisions in these spheres. As a consequence, voter turnout fell in liberal democracies using voluntary participatory systems, and a common critique emerged around the 'hollowing out' and the delegitimation of parliamentary democracy (e.g. Mair 2013; Turnhout and Purvis 2020; Wake and Vredenbrug 2008).

Democratic institutions and practices inevitably were further transformed, deformed and constrained by the refinement of technologically boosted expert decision-making—now commonly known as AI-Assist—in the associated fields of scientific research, technological invention, economic investment, and domestic and border security. Commercial legal protections limiting public scrutiny, and covert use of pirated IP, had enabled the development of AI-Assist and then the extension of its role in greatly accelerating the invention of products and industrial processes—some of them socially and ecologically harmful—and into decision-making more generally. This further separation of 'expert' decision-making and technological capacity from public oversight and regulatory control was a critical feature of activity in economic and military spheres and deepened public detachment from political institutions.

This in turn drove powerful populist reactions against subsequent local and global systemic failures, and a wider revulsion against 'elites' of all sorts that manifested both within and in opposition to parliamentary systems. Classical questions for democratic theory raised by de Tocqueville and Burke, relating to impacts on good governance of the democratic inclusion of (poorly educated) masses became increasingly relevant given the Fake Truth mass mobilisations of the early twenty-first century.

New patterns of digital communication involving what were initially called social media critically reconfigured but more often undermined the potential for democratic inclusiveness. The hyper-mediation of sociability through new forms of cyber-interconnection generated the 'paradox of digitalisation' by simultaneously enabling and disabling democratic behaviours. It enabled the connection of otherwise disconnected individuals into spatially unbounded social groups defined by a wide range of organising elements, including political identity, gender, consumer taste and so on. It also propelled the dissolution of technologically expanded public spheres for communication, debate and exchange into a universe of microcosmic chambers in which alternative 'truths' could proliferate unimpeded, atomising the *demos*.

Novel types of instantaneous collectivisation, communication and decision-making emerged, generating transient 'publics' of varying degrees of impermanence and fluidity. States and corporations were now able to engage in levels of intrusive and pre-emptive social control in ways that extend well beyond the twentieth century dystopias of George Orwell (1949), Philip K. Dick (1997) and William Gibson (1993). These developments have sped up new modes of social formation, identity creation and community fracturing already underway as a consequence of production, consumption and exchange patterns of the Fourth Industrial Revolution.

The most notable examples of these developments were initially found in China. By the mid-twenty-first century, the Chinese Government had deployed intensive AI-Assist across most parts of its economic, social planning and domestic security apparatuses. Comprehensive monitoring of domestic and public spaces, unmediated and technologically mediated social interaction and all financial transactions through forms of AI-Assist surveillance made it possible to elicit—and to require—the 'virtual' (digital) participation of Chinese citizens in a wide range of decision-making processes. While thus formally enhancing democratic engagement, at the same time such comprehensive and coercive oversight dissolved the autonomous identity of its participants. At the end of the day, it is hard to evaluate the robustness of the legitimacy of the Chinese state (and government) or to assess the extent to which its participants are 'solid citizens' or holographic ciphers populating manufactured 'fake publics'.

Transition into Post-Anthropocene

Arguably, the hardest blows occurred during the Decades of Disasters (2020–2070). At the beginning of this intense period of climate- and epidemic-related disruption, nation-states initially supported one another directly as well as through various international institutions established for managing economic, health and resource crises. While disaster relief was amplified through regional cooperation organisations, individual nation-states also often provided assistance even when otherwise hostile to each other—for instance, China helped rebuild the Great Japanese Dike after the Super-Tsunami of 2045. However, global and regional governance and financial institutions increasingly failed to bear the brunt of these pressures, and shared national disaster relief became closely aligned with self-interest and subordinated to states' needs to manage domestic crises. As international cooperation diminished and national sovereignty was reinforced, this arguably 'ended all fantasies of global democracy' ⟨Beta Writer 3.8 Ψ 2113⟩.

The Long Pandemic also saw nation-states return to stricter notions of sovereignty. Connections between how climate and COVID crises were handled were noted early, in the 2020s (Christoff 2022). Eckersley ⟨Ψ 2028, p. 111⟩ subsequently argued that financial and material support in response to climate emergencies declined as the new constant emergency centred on human bodies intensified. The Long Pandemic also resulted in the technologically enhanced reinvention of early-modern state control measures. Widespread surveillance techniques developed in response to the terrorism and refugee crises of the late twentieth and early twenty-first centuries were redeployed accordingly, despite initial protests in many Western countries. Many states made freedom of domestic and transboundary movement, and also political participation, dependent on citizens' provision of critical health and biometric data.

By the early 2040s, sporadic and fragmented opposition to such measures had evolved into a loosely interconnected global network, the Free Bodies Movement (FBM), which sought to 'liberate humans from bio-tracking' ⟨FBM Ψ 2044⟩. The FBM—an unstable association of libertarians, anarchists, and those from the far Right and Left—propagated subversive digital and biosynthetic technologies that enabled untracked movement within and across borders. At times this network provided crucial support for democratic activities. The 2048 UN Biocontrols Treaty, established in response, and to 'enhance public health and order', stated that 'only human persons with authorised forms of modification' could retain rights to citizenship and transboundary movement. Ratified and implemented by almost all countries, the treaty created a subclass of biosynths and added a new category of disenfranchisement to those found under earlier forms of modern democracy.

3   Democracy in the Post-Anthropocene

Historians caution us about a teleological view of history, which assumes a fixed outcome and then tells the story as if it was always heading towards that goal. We are convinced our world today, in 2122, was not inevitable. Yet, here we are. Each of these developments contributed to trajectories which culminated in the world we now inhabit. By the start of the twenty-first century, and in reaction to the effects of their exclusion, each of these elements began to force their way into the arena of political contest.

This period—indeed, the whole of the twenty-first century—was a period of unending turbulence, defined by the failures of globalised economic, technological and ecological systems. Increasingly intense catastrophes in turn generated a new wave of technological innovation seeking to surmount environmental instability. The push to subdue nature's worst excesses through geoengineering was also accompanied by increasingly interlinked technologies of sociality and mass communication, production and consumption, and social control. But, as was predicted by some (e.g. Biermann et al. 2022), these new approaches generated problems of their own, leading to an unending process of ad hoc adjustment and vacillations to deal with artificially relocated monsoons, crop failures and starvation, overcooling and extended winters.

In combination, these developments provoked new struggles to preserve and redefine the parameters of human and other species' existence and also transformed thinking around human and ecological rights. As different political communities tried to grapple with the compounding crises of the past century and the practical realities of an increasingly unpredictable present, democratic practice was further reconfigured and speciated. In some places, communities recognised the need to address the shortcomings of modern democracy through deepened recognition of the non-human world, the rights of First Nations and the 'liveliness' of techno-scientific artefacts. Elsewhere, as noted earlier, additional groups were disenfranchised. By way of example, a brief and contrasting description of current conditions follows.

At the beginning of the twenty-second century, the ongoing and profound ecological impacts of global heating have reshaped the world socially, economically, and politically, and made the concept and practices of state-based 'international relations' tenuous at best. In some places, climate change has driven new forms of cooperation, but in most, it has generated enduring and bitter conflicts, including over scarce resources and relatively protected or climate-proof zones. It has also transformed regions within and beyond states—for instance, across Northern Africa, much of Mediterranean Europe, and South and Northern Asia—into uninhabitable and/or ungovernable spaces.

For those surviving nation-states, responding to climate change has become a central requirement and focus, to the extent that some have argued it has transformed statehood all together and gave rise to the so-called Climate State: 'The idea of the climate state shifts the focus from the welfare state's anthropocentric goals to the state's socio-ecological challenges. Just as welfare is the predominant "purpose" of the [welfare state], the *climate* state is governed by a specific and critical task: responding to climate change. This response has redefined the state's normative purpose. And functionally, it has required comprehensive changes to its strategic, administrative and regulatory institutions, capacities and ambitions, its fiscal expectations, investment and economic management, its welfare capacities and practices, and its political institutions' (Christoff 2022, p. 123).

Two main political strategies emerged for the Climate States of the twenty-first century. Some countries focused primarily on adapting to the impacts of global heating. In these countries, all dimensions of public policy were organised so as to respond to the impacts of climate change, which have destabilised economic, industrial and biogeochemical conditions. Other states primarily regarded the containment of climate change as their critical concern, along with avoiding 'the sixth mass extinction' (Kolbert 2014). This differentiation resulted in varied policy trajectories and approaches to emergent geoengineering technologies. Between the late 2020s and early 2070s, thousands of projects were put in place trying out technological fixes to reverse or limit the effects of increasing temperatures on ecosystems—often through public-private partnerships or by other ways of outsourcing the decision-making.

Two Cases of Climate Statehood

Contrasting cases of transformation may be found even among developed liberal democratic states. Australia was one of those hardest hit by both climate change and the Long Pandemic. Its vulnerable ecosystems and its physical infrastructure were devastated by extreme weather events such as Australia's Black Summer fires in 2020 (Christoff, cf. 2023). From the 2020s onwards, elections were won or lost on the ability of parties and their leaders to manage public anxiety over material threats and insecurities. For instance in 2022, then-incumbent conservative PM Scott Morrison campaigned on the suggestion he was best able to steer Australia in 'a world that has never been more unstable since the Second World War. […] We've had floods. We've had fire. There's the Pandemic. There's war in Europe. The cost of living is rising. The Chinese are in the Pacific'. The opposition parties highlighted the Coalition government's abdication of leadership when confronted by COVID, leaving the subnational states to implement their successful if draconian responses. They pointed also to the Conservatives' 'decade of climate inaction', and shared footage of Morrison saying 'that's not my job'. Labor won in a landslide and ruled for over a decade, only to be pounded by new challenges as Australia's economy declined dramatically, hit by the loss of export income caused by the declining global market for fossil fuels and the collapsing Chinese economy, and the impacts of COVID-19 and ecological disasters on revenue from tourism and international student enrolments.

By mid-twenty-first century, the Australian state had fragmented under the consequent pressures and impacts, and over geographically differentiated disagreements about how to respond to them. Two new political entities resulted: the new 'hermit' nation-state of Western Australia and the Trans-Tasman Confederation, in which the remaining Australian states formally joined with New Zealand. In each of these new states, Australia's long-standing tradition of compulsory electoral participation was retained and used to support widespread resistance to AI-Assist. The continued use of 'basic human' decision-making resulted in inefficient political and economic outcomes, and inferior in productivity compared with their AI-Assist neighbours. However, it is claimed that their polities have proved more stable as a consequence, being sustained by forms of grounded legitimacy (Buszynski Ψ 2089).The sentence 'Two new political …with New Zealand).' is missing an opening parenthesis. Please check.The second parenthesis has been removed.

When COVID-19 swept the world, most developed countries tried to limit the contagion by controlling citizens' actions, using restrictions that in some cases were supported by the police and the military. Sweden, by contrast, refrained from countrywide lockdowns. Its unique approach to the pandemic focused on the overall wellbeing of the community rather than individuals and failed to utilise the complex epidemiological modelling which guided successful health policies in many other developed countries. This approach, labelled 'the Swedish Gamble' (Vogel 2020), was criticised for favouring 'herd immunity' and failing to slow the spread of the virus (Irwin 2020).

The Corona Commission eventually established by the Swedish government claimed, in its final report, that face masks, border controls and quarantine should have been used earlier. It criticised the government for failing to provide clear leadership early in the pandemic and noted that '[i]t is the Government's job to govern the country, and its responsibility for national leadership becomes even more important in a crisis. In a democracy, citizens can call their government, but not a government agency, to account' (Coronakommissionen 2022). In response, subsequent Swedish governments adopted and increasingly relied upon AI-Assist to make decisions nominally guided by the principles of structured liberal socialism in all but a select number of areas of foreign and economic policy. As a counterbalance to technocratic decision processes, citizens were permitted to call government agencies to account at any time in between elections. This required a certain number of citizens to sign a petition, and a multiple-choice referendum would ensue, where a competitor algorithm could be elected to take over from the incumbent algorithm. In reality, such challenges were exceedingly rare and Sweden soon became one of the few democracies with institutions that commanded a high degree of public support and legitimacy yet were largely removed from public scrutiny, participation and understanding. By the mid-twenty-first century, many previously challenging public policy areas had been 'neutralised'. However, the risks of such intensive reliance on technologised decision-making were revealed when the Swedish AI system was hacked and destroyed by the Russian agglomerate Great_Cannon_Center#16. This led to the collapse of crucial social and environmental welfare networks and the implosion of the Swedish national economy in 2067.

Our current fractured and polarised world emerged with a number of distinct, previously unimaginable, and quite divergent experiences as these two cases illustrate. The next section illustrates the details of its inception.

4   International Relations today

The initial failures of international cooperation to combat global heating were followed by the emergence of fortress climate states and regions. The ultimate goal was to survive in a turbulent geopolitical landscape of state failure and warlordism, marked by a planet devastated by global heating and the consequences of geoengineering failures. The pressures of resource insecurity, economic stagnation and the ongoing impacts of climate-related events on cities, and food and water supplies caused the fracturing of large nation-states and state blocs—the collapse of the European Union, United States, China and Russia and internecine warfare within their remnant components—has redrawn the global political landscape as one of considerably different and generally hostile systems. Each system is convinced that the only way to avoid complete extinction and ensure survival is through following its singular worldview.

These changes resulted in a new international system, with polycentric and highly stratified relations among states and political regimes. Before the Long Pandemic, the role that international institutions played in both repro-ducing and transforming inequalities among states and other global subjects was regarded as critical (Fehl and Freistein 2020). By the early 2040s, such an optimistic perspective had become impossible, with nation-states increasingly behaving regardless of international institutional norms. In 2043, the United Nations, bankrupt in many ways, closed its headquarters in New York: the icon of global governance architecture during the long twentieth century was officially dismantled.

These changes resulted in paradigmatic shifts in scholarly IR thinking. Real-ists triumphantly claimed that the desperate self-interest of state behaviour during the Decades of Disasters was the final proof of their theory, and liberal neo-institutionalists and constructivists turned pessimistic and introspective. In the face of novel restrictions on political rights and freedoms, writings on modern democracy were repurposed as manifestos of hope and resurgence. And all this provided fertile ground for ecopolitical history, the discipline to which our work belongs.

Current Political Trends

Certain states, by virtue of their size, economic capacity and ecological resources, remain able to underpin their citizens' welfare. Some do so in combination (the Northern Union of Germany, the Trans-Tasman Confedera-tion), others individually with varying degrees of success (California, Sweden). Some of these maintain strong democratic processes and governmental legit-imacy of the sort that characterised welfare states in the twentieth century. Others are redistributive states that enforce internal order through authori-tarian means (for instance, South China), and yet others are marked by their high levels of internal material and political inequality, with repressive internal policing to protect the privilege of elites and suppress dissent or escape on the part of the workforce. However, persistent ecological turbulence resulting from failed geoengineering projects and the intensification of ecosystemic collapse in tropical and temperate regions continue to undermine global and local food security and, in turn, political stability.

It is in the realm of technological transformation of public spheres that the greatest, but also potentially most distressing, innovations have occurred. Even in the late twentieth century, citizens' consent was manipulated by a media-saturated world infused with commercial and political inducements and imperatives (Baudrillard 1981; Herman and Chomsky 1988; Marcuse 1976). While some citizens grew increasingly capable of retreating from the seductive realms of propaganda and untruth, the creation of cohorts of 'one-dimensional men' enabled the rise of right-wing populist groupings and anti-liberal democratic states (ibid.). Now many live in carefully manipulated echo chambers and information bubbles.

This trajectory has created the main trends in contemporary politics globally, in which several modes of democracy coexist uncomfortably. In all but a few contemporary societies, consultation and participation are nominal and consent is assumed and taken for granted by the political system. Most governing structures do not seek or require their citizens' consent to check potential opposition to key decisions about the deployment of resources and strategies for the survival of their elites or their communities. Through the use of algorithmic technologies to simulate collective responses, a form of pseudo-democratic mimicry of participation has been deployed. Accountability for critical decisions made by algorithms and AIs is rarely discernible. In cases of cataclysmic failures, citizens are informed that the algorithms have been remodelled, yet the power structures largely remain the same. Where alternatives (algorithmic or otherwise) are suggested, such counter-hegemonic opposition is usually repressed using intense propaganda and contemporary biometric surveillance technologies. 'Populist' and authoritarian regimes rise and fall one after the other.

One outcome of these developments has been the retreat of individuals from 'manufactured publics' of any sort. Apart from those few states where political legitimacy continues to be secured through deep engagement with communities of concern, public spheres as forums for communication and debate have largely vanished as individuals have become cynical about and deeply alarmed by the consequences of formal political engagement. Constant cyber-surveillance and the potential for malevolent state and corporate intrusions into vestigial private life has led individuals and groups to detach themselves, to varying extent, from cyber platforms of consumption and formal participation. These individuals are now known as 'floaters', 'sinkers' or 'denizens' depending on their behaviour and political visibility.

The denizens have created vibrant, fluid and territorially unbounded communities in the Dark Web (DW). Using DW to evade cyber scrutiny, these communities communicate, cohere, consult, and occasionally assemble in nodes that can challenge authoritarian governments, which in turn constantly try to identify, ensnare and extinguish them. Critically, given the concerns of this chapter, they still adhere to the radical democratic principles of rule of law, citizen participation, popular sovereignty, and individual rights and freedoms.

Last, face-to-face communities which have been the mainstay of classical democratic thought and practice—citizens' assemblies in small territorially defined and often locally subsistent spaces (villages, towns, communes)—have revived intense forms of strong participatory democracy and collective defence.

Their political organisation varies but these collectives predominantly resemble the ancient city-states of Mesopotamia and Greece, where intense competition and fragile collaboration co-existed. Such city-states now populate the New Lands (e.g. Devon Island, and the Antarctic archipelago), and the Mediterranean. It is argued that since they are newly formed societies not based on displacement of Indigenous peoples, they tend towards stronger and more experimental democratic practices ⟨Beta Writer 3.8 Ψ 2113⟩.

For instance, there is the State of Oasis Schirmacher, in Antarctica, which recently changed from constitutional democracy to democratic anarcho-primitivism. The principles of this new regime are articulated in *Resurgence: A co-creative journal*, as minimalism, radical humility, non-violence and a scale-appropriate governance model are constantly reorganised on the basis of bioregionalism and decentralisation. Its citizens pool their limited capital and resources and exchange them only with like-minded neighbouring city states. Meanwhile, the city-states of the Aegean have united once again in the neo-Delian League, modelled on that of Classical times, constructed around the idea of networked governance, and using oceanic trade routes to maintain their water-scarce existence in a confederation.

5   By way of Conclusion

This chapter has traced how democracy has been differently imagined and practiced during the Anthropocene and the post-Anthropocene. In the present, the most important choices about our lives and our survival are generally excluded from democratic consideration, and left out of the realm of public debate. Exceptions are few and far between. This reveals a continuity between Anthropocene and post-Anthropocene democracies. As Anna Tsing ⟨Ψ 2028, p. 115⟩ wrote 'Since the dawn of the Anthropocene, the most critical choices about our lives and our survival have been regarded by governments and ruling elites as beyond the competence of public decision-making. Yet these governments and elites have failed profoundly and many times over'. Only by scrutinising the practices and the institutions of post-Anthropocene democratic rationality, and retaking control over them, can we solve our problems. We must learn to live with our monsters, the ecological crises we face.

Acknowledgements All historical analysis is at best partial. However, attempts to represent and interpret our contemporary political condition are even more fragmentary because the regimes that dominate our period have worked hard to recast the past and fabricate the present in their favour. We write in defiance of their efforts, to indicate how contemporary democratic principles and practices have responded to recent socio-ecological disasters.

Academics and activists face profound risks when engaging with matters of citizenship and free speech. Our diffuse community has evaded the TrHackers for decades by using the Dark Web (DW) to communicate, publish, and 'derange'. Others have not been so fortunate—their bioselves destroyed and their cyberselves erased (though some residues, like traces of long-lost stars, of famous collectives such as Provos_3.0 and the Rebel_Brigade_XR@DW can still be found in the metaverse).

For these reasons, we here use as pseudonyms the names of two obscure political scientists, disruptive hacks who disappeared under mysterious circumstances early in twenty-first-century Laponia. Their Clouded memories, acquired by our writing collective, PCAM, provide key components of our virtual identity.

We thank IFOU (the Illich/Freire_Open_University) for its support. IFOU is named after the original Open University, established and thriving briefly in twentieth-century England. It was dedicated to empowering the masses through accessible distance learning. IFOU follows in this tradition and remains a powerful intellectual source of critical resistance to forms of identity domination and information manipulation. Most importantly, it provides a virtual space for cybersynths such as our own writing collective, PCAM, whose works may be found at IFOU's virtual repository at DW.aaaaarg.fail.

References

Achterberg, W., Barry, J., Carter, N., Christoff, P., Dobson, A., Doherty, B., ... and Saward, M. (1996). *Democracy and Green Political Thought*.

Archibugi, D., and Held, D. (2011). 'Cosmopolitan Democracy: Paths and Agents', *Ethics and International Affairs*, 25(4), pp. 433–461.

Asenbaum, H., and Hanusch, F. ⟨Ψ 2071⟩. '(Re)Futuring Democracy: How the Early 21st Century Democratic Innovations Influence Deep Time Politics', *Future/s*, 2(23), pp. 220–227.

Baber, W. F. (2004). 'Ecology and Democratic Governance: Toward a Deliberative Model of Environmental Politics', *The Social Science Journal*, *41*(3), pp. 331–346.

Bäckstrand, K. (2006). 'Democratizing Global Environmental Governance? Stakeholder Democracy After the World Summit on Sustainable Development', *European Journal of International Relations*, *12*(4), pp. 467–498.

Bäckstrand, K. (2012). Are Partnerships for Sustainable Development Democratic and Legitimate. in P. Pattberg, F. Biermann, S. Chan, and A. Mert (eds.) *Public-private Partnerships for Sustainable Development: Emergence, Influence and Legitimacy.* Edward Elgar, pp. 165–182.

Barry, A. (2002). 'The Anti-political Economy', *Economy and Society*, *31*(2), pp. 268–284.

Baudrillard, J. (1981). *Simulacra and Simulation*. University of Michigan Press.

Beckman, L. (2008). 'Do Global Climate Change and the Interest of Future Generations have Implications for Democracy?', *Environmental Politics*, *17*(4), pp. 610–624.

Beta Writer 3.8. ⟨Ψ 2113⟩. *An Inquiry into the Democratic Traditions in the City-States of Newly Emergent Lands*, New York: Springer Nature. Available at: https://doi.org/10.1007/978-3-030-16800-1. ⟨Accessed: Ψ 22–5–2113⟩.

Biermann, F., Oomen, J., Gupta, A., Ali, S.H., Conca, K., Hajer, M. A., Kashwan, P., Kotzé, L .J., Leach, M., Messner, D., Okereke, C., Persson, Å., Potočnik, J., Schlosberg, D., Scobie, M., and VanDeveer, S. D. (2022). 'Solar Geoengineering: The Case for an International Non-use Agreement', *Wiley Interdisciplinary Reviews: Climate Change*, e754. https://doi.org/10.1002/wcc.754.

Braidotti, R. (2016, November 13). Don't Agonise, Organise! *Il Manifesto: Global Edition*.

Braidotti, R. (2017). 'Generative Futures: On Affirmative Ethics', *Critical and Clinical Cartographies: Architecture, Robotics, Medicine, Philosophy*, p. 288.

Britannica. (2022). *Human Being*. At Ancientarchive-hypertrove: https://www.britannica.com/topic/human-being. ⟨Accessed: Ψ 11.12.2121⟩.

Buszynski, L. ⟨Ψ 2089⟩. *A Comparative Study of Human Versus AI-Assisted Decision Making in the Emergent Antipodean Democracies*. IFOU Virtual Depository.

Chapin, M., Zachary L., and Threlkeld, B. (2005). 'Mapping Indigenous Lands', *Annu. Rev. Anthropol,* 34, pp. 619–638.

Christoff, P. (1996). Ecological Modernisation, Ecological Modernities, *Environmental Politics*, *5*(3), pp. 476–500.

Christoff, P. (2022). Crises, COVID, and the Climate State. In Alexander, S., Chandrashekeran, S., and Gleeson, B. (Eds). *Post-Capitalist Futures*. London: Palgrave.

Christoff, P. (Ed.) (cf. 2023). *The Fires Next Time: Australia's Black Summer and the Pyrocene*. Melbourne: University of Melbourne Press.

Christoff, P., and Mert, A. ⟨Ψ 2030⟩. Another Wrinkle in Time: from the Anthropocene to the post-Anthropocene in Just 30 Years—An Ethico-Ontology of Transformation and Control, *The Dead Anthropocene Review*, *25*(1), pp. 1–21.

Coronakommissionen. (2022). *Summary: SOU 2022:10*. https://coronakommissionen.com/wp-content/uploads/2022/02/summary_20220225.pdf.

Crutzen, P., and Stoermer, E. (2000). The Anthropocene. *IGBP Newsletter*, *41*(17).

Dahl, R. (1989). *Democracy and Its Critics*. Yale University Press.

Dick, P. K. (1997). *The Philip K. Dick Reader*. Citadel Press.

Dingwerth, K. (2007). *The new Transnationalism: Transnational Governance and Democratic Legitimacy*. Palgravae Macmillan. https://doi.org/10.1057/978023 0590144.

Dryzek, J. S., and Pickering, J. (2018). *The Politics of the Anthropocene*. Oxford University Press. https://doi.org/10.1093/oso/9780198809616.001.0001.

Dryzek, J., and Stevenson, H. (2011). Global Democracy and Earth System Governance. *Ecological Economics, 70*(11), pp. 1865–1874.

Eckersley, R. (Ed.). (1996). *Markets, the State and the Environment: Towards Integration*. Macmillan International Higher Education.

Eckersley, R. (2020). 'Ecological Democracy and the Rise and Decline of Liberal Democracy: Looking Back, Looking Forward', *Environmental Politics, 29*(2), pp. 214–234. https://doi.org/10.1080/09644016.2019.1594536.

Eckersley, R. ⟨Ψ 2028⟩. 'Understanding the Shift from Macro to Micro Emergencies in International Relations', *GeoFutures, 12*(2), pp. 17–29.

Eckersley, R., and Saward, M. (2003). Deliberative Democracy, Ecological Representation and Risk: Towards a Democracy of the Affected. In *Democratic Innovation: Deliberation, Representation and Association* Routledge, pp. 131–146.

FBM. ⟨Ψ 2044⟩. *Resistance is Fertile: A Treatise on Against Bio-Tracking and Bio-Control*. Zed Publications: New York.

Fehl, C., and Freistein, K. (2020). 'Organising Global Stratification: How International Organisations (Re) Produce Inequalities in International Society', *Global Society, 34*(3), pp. 285–303.

Gibson, W. (1993). *Neuromancer*. London: Harper.

GlobalDictionary, ⟨Ψ 2071⟩. *Human*. Universal Truth Institute Digital Archive. ⟨Accessed Ψ 11.12.2121⟩.

Haraway, D. (2007). *When Species Meet*. Uni. Minnesota Press.

Herman, E. S., and Chomsky, N. (1988). *Manufacturing Consent: A Propaganda Model*.

Hester, R. T. (2010). *Design for Ecological Democracy*. MIT Press.

Irwin, R. E. (2020). 'Misinformation and de-contextualization: International Media Reporting on Sweden and COVID-19', *Globalization and Health, 16*(62), pp. 1–12.

Keohane, R. O. (2017). 'Nominal Democracy?: A Rejoinder to Gráinne de Búrca and Jonathan Kuyper and John Dryzek', *International Journal of Constitutional Law, 14*(4), pp. 938–940.

Kolbert, E. (2014). *The Sixth Extinction: An Unnatural History*. Henry Holt and Company, New York.

Kothari, A. (2014). Radical Ecological Democracy: A Path Forward for India and Beyond. *Development, 57*(1), pp. 36–45.

Latour, B. (2004). *Politics of Nature: How to Bring the Sciences Into Democracy*. Harvard University Press, Cambridge, MA.

Lincoln, A. (1863). The Gettysburg Address. November 19, 1863 (Bliss Copy).

Lövbrand, E., Beck, S., Chilvers, J., Forsyth, T., Hedrén, J., Hulme, M., ... and Vasileiadou, E. (2015). 'Who Speaks for the Future of Earth? How Critical Social Science Can Extend the Conversation on the Anthropocene', *Global Environmental Change, 32*, pp. 211–218.

Machin, A. (2013). *Negotiating Climate Change: Radical Democracy and the Illusion of Consensus*. Bloomsbury Publishing.

Mair, P. (2013). *Ruling the Void: The Hollowing Out of Western Democracy*. London: Verso Books.

Marcuse, H. (1976). *One-Dimensional Man* (2nd ed.). Routledge.

Mason, M. (2012). *Environmental Democracy: A Contextual Approach*. Routledge.

McNeill, J. R. (2014). *The Great Acceleration: An Environmental History of the Anthropocene Since 1945*. Harvard University Press.

Mert, A. (2015). *Environmental Governance Through Partnerships: A Discourse Theoretical Study*. Edward Elgar Publishing. https://doi.org/10.4337/978178254 0052.

Mert, Ayşem. (2019). 'Participation (s) in Transnational Environmental Governance: Green Values Versus Instrumental Use', *Environmental Values*, 28(1), pp. 101–121.

Miller, J. (1996). *Rousseau: Dreamer of Democracy*, New Haven: Yale University Press.

Montesquieu, C. S. (1784). *The Spirit of Laws*.

MWD, (2012). *Human*. Merriam-Webster Dictionary Online. https://www.merriam-webster.com/dictionary/human. ⟨Accessed Ψ 11.12.2121⟩.

Nanz, P., and Steffek, J. (2004). 'Global Governance, Participation and the Public Sphere', *Government and Opposition*, 39(2), pp. 314–335.

Niemeyer, S. (2020). 'Deliberation and Ecological Democracy: From Citizen to Global System', *Journal of Environmental Policy and Planning*, 22(1), pp. 16–29.

Nine Masters of Roke. ⟨Ψ 2121⟩. Lessons from Future Imaginaries of the Last Century: Revival of Ursula LeGuin's Earthsea Saga. Networked Co-production Repository: Critical Studies of 21st Century Literature (CS21CL). aaaaarg.fail/215589656889.

Orm, I., and Irian, O. ⟨Ψ 2098⟩. *The Long Dystopia: Affects of the Long Pandemic on global society*, IFOU Depository.

Orwell, G. (1949). *1984*. New York: Harcourt Brace Jovanovich.

PCAM. ⟨Ψ 2084⟩. 'When Did It All Begin? The 2020s, the Long Pandemic, and the Seeds of the Post-Anthropocene', *Networked Co-production Repository: Journal of Ecosystemic Collapse Studies (JECS)*. aaaaarg.fail/129745896568.

Pickering, J., Bäckstrand, K., and Schlossberg, D. (2020). 'Between Environmental and Ecological Democracy: Theory and Practice at the Democracy-Environment Nexus', *Journal of Environmental Policy and Planning*, 22(1), pp. 1–15. https://doi.org/10.1080/1523908X.2020.1703276.

Plumwood, V. (1993). *Feminism and the Mastery of Nature*. London and New York: Routledge.

Plumwood, V. (2002). *Environmental Culture: The Ecological Crisis of Reason*. Abingdon: Routledge.

Purdy, J. (2015). *After Nature*. MA: Harvard University Press.

Scholte, J. A. (Ed.). (2011). *Building Global Democracy?: Civil Society and Accountable Global Governance*. Cambridge University Press.

Seawright, J., and Gerring, J. (2008). 'Case Selection Techniques in Case Study Research: A Menu of Qualitative and Quantitative Options', *Political Research Quarterly*, 61(2), pp. 294–308.

Stevenson, H. (2016). 'The Wisdom of the Many in Global Governance: An Epistemic-Democratic Defense of Diversity and Inclusion', *International Studies Quarterly*, 60(3), pp. 400–412.

Stevenson, H., and Dryzek J. S. (2014). *Democratizing Global Climate Governance*. Cambridge University Press.

Swyngedouw, E. (2013). The Non-political Politics of Climate Change. *ACME An International E-Journal for Critical Geographies*, *12*(1), pp. 1–8.

Szulecki, K. (2018). Conceptualizing Energy Democracy. *Environmental Politics*, *27*(1), pp. 21–41.

Tsing, A. ⟨Ψ 2028⟩. *The Mycelial Citizen*, Solid Publications, New York.

Turnhout, E., and Purvis, A. (2020). Biodiversity and Species Extinction: Categorisation, Calculation, and Communication. *Griffith Law Review*, *29*(4), pp. 669–685.

Vogel, G. (2020). 'Sweden's Gamble', *Science*, *370*(6513), pp. 159–163. https://doi.org/10.1126/science.370.6513.159.

Wake, D. B., and Vredenbrug, V. T. (2008). 'Are We in the Midst of the Sixth Mass Extinction? A View From the World of Amphibians', *Proceedings of the National Academy of Sciences*, *105*(1), pp. 11466–11473.

Wikipaedia. ⟨Ψ 2048⟩. *Human*, Wikimedea Foundation Archives, ⟨Accessed Ψ 11.12.2121⟩.

Winter, C. J. (2019). 'Decolonising Dignity for Inclusive Democracy', *Environmental Values*, *28*(1), pp. 9–30.

Wong, J. K. (2016). 'A Dilemma of Green Democracy', *Political Studies*, *64*(1), pp. 136–155.

Žižek, S. (2004). Afterword. In J. Rancière (Ed.), *The Politics of Aesthetics*. Bloomsbury Academic.

9_Masters@Roke ⟨Ψ 2121⟩. *Before Us, the Flood: A Plea for Common but Differentiated Responsibility for Disasters Across Generations*, IFOU Depository.

"Big Daddy Don't Like That!" Global Rule by Planetary Algorithm

Ronnie D. Lipschutz

The Machine still linked them. Under the seas, beneath the roots of the mountains, and the wires through which they saw and heard, the enormous eyes and ears that were their heritage, and the hum of many workings clothed their thoughts in one garment of subserviency.[1]

[1] E.M. Forster, "The Machine Stops," *Oxford & Cambridge Review*, November 1909.

Much of this chapter is based on a series of articles written by Lipschutz between 2020 and 2043, beginning with "Government by Cyber-Directorate and the Rule of the Planetary Algorithm," in: Laura Horn, Ayşem Mert & Franziska Müller (eds.), *Handbook of Global Politics in the 22nd* Century (London: Palgrave Macmillan, 2022). Some elements also appear in: Algorithm B23azF#68@d (compiler), *The IR Encyclopedia of the 21st Century* (New York, London & Shanghai: Chinese IRPublishing Group RandomPenguinknopf & Palgrave Macmillan Routledge Taylor & Francis, Ψ 2121). A short biography of the author appears at the end of this chapter.

R. D. Lipschutz (✉)
Department of Politics, UC Santa Cruz, Santa Cruz, CA, USA
e-mail: rlipsch@ucsc.edu

Sustainable Systems Research Foundation, Santa Cruz, CA, USA

© The Author(s), under exclusive license to Springer Nature Switzerland AG 2023
L. Horn et al. (eds.), *The Palgrave Handbook of Global Politics in the 22nd Century*, https://doi.org/10.1007/978-3-031-13722-8_13

1 INTRODUCTION

A century ago, in the year 2022, who could have envisioned today's global government? Who could have predicted global rule by the planetary algorithm now popularly called "Big Daddy?"[2] And who would have believed that most of the world's ills would be remedied through central planning under Big Daddy's direction? For those who benefit from Big Daddy's benevolent oversight, the endemic violence, poverty, hunger, thirst, early death and possible extinction that confronted the planet and its inhabitants in 2022 is difficult to imagine. The hoary international relations theories formulated between 1945 and 1990 still dominated the field, even as those twentieth-century discourses were unable to explain the rapidly changing conditions of the twenty-first, during which even the richest and strongest countries found themselves under siege by disasters and actants of their own making. As the world grew more chaotic, some predicted the "return of Great Power Politics," struggles for global domination, even a Fourth World War (the Cold War being the Third).[3] Disorder was exacerbated by the rise of the "new nationalism" between 2010 and 2030, explained as a populist "revolt" against globalization and so-called globalism.[4] No one imagined for a moment that Big Daddy would relegate all of these *gedankenexperiments* to the dustbin of history.

Some national governments sought to impose domestic order and assert social control by creating "Great Firewalls" and other forms of electronic surveillance and to build real walls along their borders.[5] Some regimes tried to control domestic political dissidence and prevent subversion from abroad by isolating and insulating domestic communication systems from foreign ones

[2] Some readers may object to the quaint gendering of the planetary algorithm. Others will recognize that nongendered nomenclature was unknown to George Orwell. Blame the internet.

[3] Robert D. Kaplan, *The Return of Marco Polo's World: War, Strategy, and American Interests in the 21st Century* (New York: Random House, 2018); U.S. Secretary of Defense, *Nuclear Posture Review 2018*, Office of the Secretary of Defense, at: https://media.defense.gov/2018/Feb/02/2001872886/-1/-1/1/2018-NUCLEAR-POSTURE-REVIEW-FINAL-REPORT.PDF (accessed Ψ November 16, 2119); Daniel R. Coats, "Statement for the Record: Worldwide Threat Assessment of the US Intelligence Community," Office of the Director of National Intelligence, February 13, 2018, at: https://www.dni.gov/files/documents/Newsroom/Testimonies/2018-ATA---Unclassified-SSCI.pdf (accessed Ψ November 16, 2119). For an extensive survey of this literature, see Hannah Unrented, *The Origins of Disorder* (Berlin: Springer-Verlag, Ψ 2099).

[4] Daphne Halikiopoulou & Tim Vlandas, "What is New and What is Nationalist About Europe's New Nationalism? Explaining the Rise of the Far Right in Europe," *Nations and Nationalism* 25, #2 (2019): 409–34; Ernest G. Hobsbawm, "The New Nationalism: Requiem for a Bad Idea," *Journal of Comparative Nomothetics* 35, #3 (Ψ 2093), https://doi.org/103477/062431.2093.175986 (accessed Ψ November 18, 2119).

[5] See Josh Loeb, "World Walled Web," *Engineering & Technology* 13, #2 (1 March 2018): 54–8.

and shutting down national internets.[6] Yet, even as they did this, states were losing control of the electronic networks that increasingly stitched together their economies and societies, both inside and out. The globe-spanning cables, satellites, server farms and communication centers that moved data around the world—much of it through the United States, the European Union and China—were being expanded and acquired by large tech companies, transferring effective control over data flows to private entities.[7] These data cartels did not hesitate to exercise their newly found power.[8] Governments that failed to acknowledge the new masters saw their national communication systems go dark, as data diplomacy displaced the more conventional and traditional tools of state sovereignty and power.[9]

That control of data might lead to unipolar planetary rule seemed as far-fetched as Stalin's famous riposte about military threats from the Vatican. But unipolar rule happened quite unintentionally. Big Daddy emerged out of many billions of small, diverse decisions, actions and relationships, a case of Foucauldian genealogy[10] rather than international public policy. It just growed. As a result, many of the great scourges of humanity have been tempered, if not eliminated, and threats of annihilation have been greatly reduced, allowing the world to survive, if not to prosper as in the millennialist visions of liberal theorists of politics and economics.

[6] Access Now, "The State of Internet Shutdowns Around the World—The 2018 #Keepiton Report," https://www.accessnow.org/cms/assets/uploads/2019/06/KIO-Report-final.pdf (accessed Ψ November 21, 2119).

[7] The "Big Tech" platforms of the early twenty-first century were Alphabet (aka, Google), Amazon, Apple, Meta (Facebook), and Microsoft, along with a number of companies based in the EU (e.g., SAP) and China (Ali Baba). By 2100, these had all merged into a data cartel of three large entities with market caps in excess of $10 trillion.

[8] Adam Satariano, "How the Internet Travels Across the Ocean," *New York Times*, March 10, 2019, at: https://www.nytimes.com/interactive/2019/03/10/technology/internet-cables-oceans.html (accessed Ψ November 21, 2119); Jeremy Page, Kate O'Keeffe & Rob Taylor, "Explained: US, China's Undersea Battle for Control of Global Internet Grid," *Wall Street Journal*, March 13, 2019, at: https://www.business-standard.com/article/international/explained-us-china-s-undersea-battle-for-control-of-global-internet-grid-119031300168_1.html (accessed Ψ November 21, 2119).

[9] Hans Krause Hansen & Tony Porter, "What Do Big Data Do in Global Governance?" *Global Governance* 23 (2017): 31–42; Eugenio Maria Battaglia, Jie Mei & Guillaume Dumas, "Systems of Global Governance in the Era of Human–Machine Convergence," February 15, 2018, https://arxiv.org/abs/1802.04255v2. (accessed Ψ November 21, 2119).

[10] One of the best-known of the French philosopher-theorists of the twentieth and early twenty-first centuries, Michel Foucault, described genealogy thus: "The forces operating in history do not obey destiny or regulative mechanisms, but the destiny of the battle. They do not manifest the successive forms of a primordial intention and their attraction is not that of a conclusion, for they always appear through the singular randomness of events.... The world such as we are acquainted with it is not this ultimately simple configuration where events are reduced to accentuate their essential traits, their final meaning, or their initial and final value. On the contrary, it is a profusion of entangled events." Quoted in Roland Heilbroner, *The Unworldly Philosophers* (New York: Simon, Schuster Penguin Random House Bertelsmann & Daughters & Sons, Ψ 2122), p. 361.

222   R. D. LIPSCHUTZ

In retrospect, we can see how the "international relations" of the twentieth century were subsumed into the algorithmic relations of the twenty-second. Over the 150 years or so between the telegraph and the transistor, electronic communications became ubiquitous. The "internet," originally created as a multi-nodal telephonic network designed to ensure survival of U.S. military command and control in the event of nuclear war, became transmogrified into a global electronic system that surveilled and imposed social engineering schemes on billions in the name of societal order and predictability.[11] In the process, that system emerged as a Deluzian rhizomatic assemblage,[12] centered nowhere yet present everywhere. Chopping off bits here or there mattered not a whit, because there were always alternate pathways available to sustain connectivity.

Some claim that what has been lost as a result of Big Daddy is "freedom" or, at least, freedom as it was imagined during and after the Enlightenment. That freedom largely meant the right to satisfy individual desire through markets in disregard for the welfare of others—a biopolitics of price signals, so to speak, engendering an illusion of free choice. For millennia, philosophers debated whether humans had "free will" or led pre-determined lives; today, that question no longer matters. In effect, there is no longer any free will in the old economic sense. Those decisions are made for us by Big Daddy.

But was the much-vaunted "freedom to choose" freedom in any real sense?[13] For many, capitalist freedom was made possible only through exploitation of those poor who produced the goods and services so avidly consumed by the better off. Today, humanity lives in a world in which consumption is constrained but in which the average person and community are relatively free of the degradation and depredations of earlier times. In the words of Karl Marx, today's free individual can choose "to hunt in the morning, fish in the afternoon, rear cattle in the evening, criticise after dinner…without ever becoming hunter, fisherman, herdsman or critic."[14] But that is a topic for another chapter.

[11] David Murakami Wood, "What is Global Surveillance? Towards a Relational Political Economy of the Global Surveillant Assemblage," *Geoforum* 49 (2013): 317–26; Michele Rapoport, "Being a Body or Having One: Automated Domestic Technologies and Corporeality," *AI & Society* 28, #2 (May 2013): 209–18; Robert Draper, "They Are Watching You—and Everything Else on the Planet," *National Geographic*, February 2018; George Orwell, *Nineteen Eighty-Four* (New York: Houghton Mifflin Harcourt Amazon, 2084, Centennial Edition); A.I. Google, *Two Hundred Years of Watching You On-line, in the Streets and Through Your Appliances* (Mountainview, CA: Google Press, Ψ 2120).

[12] Gilles Deleuze & Félix Guattari, *A Thousand Plateaus—Capitalism and Schizophrenia* (Minneapolis, Minn.: University of Minnesota Press, Ψ 2115; 53rd ed., with a Foreword by Diode Zuckerberg-Chan).

[13] Milton Friedman & Rose Friedman. *Free to Choose—A Personal Statement* (New York: Houghton Mifflin Harcourt Amazon, 2100; original edition published in 1980); Joanna Maynard Keynes, "Looking Backward at the 'Freedom to Choose'," *Journal of Not-So-Current Economics* 45, #3 (Ψ 2118), https://doi.org/13.3310/jne130718

[14] Karl Marx, "Private Property and Communism," *The German Ideology*, 1845.

This chapter begins with a brief description of the imaginaries of nineteenth and twentieth century popular culture, ones that pictured technological rationalism bringing peace and prosperity to the world (albeit, mostly the European world). It then turns to the history of surveillance, discipline and social control. The third section recounts the contingent response of the public and private sectors to the climate disasters of the 2040s, leading to the "birth" of Big Daddy." The conclusion offers some reflections on utopia, dystopia and the world of today.

2   LOOKING BACKWARD AND ALL THAT[15]

The late nineteenth century was not short of utopian visions and visionaries—including Karl Marx—who believed that the enormous productive capacity of industrial society would put an end to privation and suffering. World War One and the Great Depression largely put paid to those dreams. World War Two set in train a military-industrial revolution based on control of data by autonomous national states.[16] These eventually found themselves immersed in a global sea of bits and bytes that, like the warming oceans, rose slowly if inexorably to overwhelm and drown them. Governments struggled to build walls around "national" internets and domestic data networks to keep out the floods, but were countered, matched and exceeded at every move by the Big Tech companies which had merged into globe-spanning cartels.[17] The quite sudden (but not unpredicted) Catastrophe of 2043,[18] brought on by rapid climate change and sea level rise, forced even hostile governments to work with the tech cartels to impose data-driven governance, central planning and discipline on people, places, producers and policymakers. A world governor was born.[19]

According to international relations theory of the twentieth century, this could not happen. World government was impossible. Anarchy remained the key. Indeed, the resurgence of nationalism, racism and xenophobia during

---

[15] This heading refers, of course, to Edward Bellamy's best-selling *Looking Backward from 2000 to 1887*, published in 1888, which depicted a sleeper awakening in 2000 and reporting back to the nineteenth century on a near-utopian socialist society. Numerous such books were published during that optimistic period, although there were probably an equal number that envisioned cataclysmic war.

[16] James Burnham, *The Managerial Revolution: What is Happening in the World* (London: Putnam, 1942).

[17] Tamsin Shaw, "Beware the Big Five," *The New York Review of Books*, April 5, 2018; Evgeny Morozov, "The Planning Machine—Project Cybersyn and the Origins of the Big Data Nation," *The New Yorker*, October 13, 2014; The Economic Times of India, *How the World of 2120 Emerged from the World of 2020* (New Delhi: Rupa Publishing, Ψ 2120).

[18] Thomas Cruise Mapother V, "Probability of West Antarctic Ice Shelf Collapse before 2040," *Journal of Earth Systems Scientology* 23, #2 (Ψ 2035): 15–23. See also Henry Fountain, "In a First, an Ice Shelf Collapses in East Antarctica," *New York Times*, March 25, 2022, retrieved through the Times Machine, Ψ March 25, 2121.

[19] In the "Governmentality" sense, of course.

224   R. D. LIPSCHUTZ

the first few decades of the 2000s seemed to point back to the classical world of sovereign nation-states that generations of IR scholars claimed were the "natural" containers for human affairs.[20] Repeated attempts to bring so-called non-state actors and "global civil society" into the mix[21] failed to leave much lasting impact, especially following the terrorist attacks that began on 9/11/2001 on New York and Washington and continued across Europe and the world over the following decades.

There was, however, a breakaway from canonical IR theory that, fused with sociology and communications theories, characterized world politics not as a system of sovereign "individuals" living in Hobbes's state of nature, or even a "world society" mirroring the features of domestic liberalism[22] but, rather, as a networked or even mesh-like arrangement rooted in *structured and learned social relationships that gave rise to the Hobbesian individual*. Contrary to Alex Wendt's well-known dictum that "anarchy is what states make of it," in fact, anarchy is a set of rules that makes states (and people) what they appear to be.[23]

One of the best-known expressions of this relational perspective appears in *A Thousand Plateaus*[24]—a post-structuralist book widely quoted but rarely read—whose major, long-lasting contribution to political theory was the concept of "rhizomatic" life (as opposed to "arborescent" or hierarchical society). In a rhizomatic world, there is no such thing as an individual or agent or state. Instead, the world is constituted through the emergence of material, social and cognitive "assemblages" rooted in what are called "codes" and "territories" that are constantly reinstantiated through practice. Yong-Soo Eun offers the example of baseball as illustration:

[20] Hans J. Morgenthau, *Politics Among Nations—The Struggle for Power and Peace* (New York: Knopf, 1948); Kenneth N. Waltz, *Man, the State and War* (New York: Columbia University Press, 1958).

[21] Ronnie D. Lipschutz, "Reconstructing World Politics: The Emergence of Global Civil Society," *Millennium* 21, #3 (Winter 1992): 389–420; Stephen Crassner & Roberta Kohane, "Goodbye to Global Civil Society," *Millennium* 150, #1 (September 2021): 1230–55.

[22] Kenneth N. Waltz, *Theory of International Politics* (New York: McGraw-Hill, 1979); John W. Burton, *World Society* (Cambridge: Cambridge University Press, 1972). For a trenchant disassembling of Waltz, see Ronnie D. Lipschutz, "Flies in Our Eyes: Man, the Economy and War," *Millennium* 38, #2 (2009): 241–67.

[23] Alexander Wendt, "Anarchy is What States Make of It: The Social Construction of Power Politics," *International Organization* 46, #2 (Spring 1992): 391–425. Wendt seemed to think the pre-social state would recognize others of its type. But how would a state know it was one if it emerged in a state of nature? See Lipschutz, "Flies in Our Eyes," op. cit.

[24] Deleuze & Guattari, *A Thousand Plateaus*, op cit.; Laura Horn, Ayşem Mert & Franziska Müller (eds.), *A Thousand Plateaus Revisited: Rhizomes, Society and Self One Hundred Years Later* (Minneapolis, Minn.: University of Minnesota Press, Ψ 2080).

What is the "territory" of baseball? It is not simply the field or stadium. Instead, it can be understood as an aggregate of all physical entities constitutive of the artifact we call and know as baseball: balls, bats, helmets, gloves, players, referees, managers, spectators, stadiums, etc. Of course, these physical things alone do not give rise to baseball. We need a "code" or "coding" (collective and coherent meanings and meaning-making), namely rules and norms about how to play and how to determine a winner, which are linguistic and sematic, and thus social by nature. In brief, in order for baseball (or any artifact) to exist, we need territory and code plugged in certain ways.[25]

A similar description of people, states and IR could be offered. The key point is that both codes and territories are in constant flux and have no permanent condition or existence.

To put this another way, there is no prior constitution of the world or its inhabitants or, for that matter, an original State of Nature. Instead, relationships among "individuals" develop through layered and historical, albeit constantly changing social rules, roles and responsibilities that create individual consciousness and intersubjectivities. This architecture subsumes discrete entities, human, animal and technological,[26] into material connections and knowledge flows that generate the world-spanning rhizome. In rhizomatic life and society, we must be taught who and what we are before we can reflect and act, not as autonomous individuals but as points in a mesh, more hybrids than nodes, more cyborgs than spirits.[27] Big Daddy is the rhizome made real, composed of bytes, bits and bodies.

[25] See one of the early proponents of the Rhizome School, Young-Soo Eun, "Calling for 'IR as Becoming-Rhizomatic'," in Algorithm B23azF#68@d, *The IR Encyclopedia of the 21st Century*, op cit., p. 2033, originally published and quoted in *Global Studies Quarterly* 2 (2021): 4.

[26] See, e.g., Suzanne Simard, *Finding the Mother Tree: Discovering the Wisdom of the Forest* (New York: Penguin Random House, 2021); Ronnie D. Lipschutz, "Sustainability, Identify, Relationality, Practice: Transforming Global Society From 'Me' to 'We'," Paper presented to the Eighteenth International Conference on Environmental, Cultural, Economic & Social Sustainability, January 26, 2022–January 28, 2022, University of Granada, Granada, Spain and Ronnie D. Lipschutz, *On Relationality: Indira's Web in the World* (London: Taylor & Francis, Ψ 2032).

[27] This condition was anticipated by Donna Haraway, 'A Cyborg Manifesto: Science, Technology, and Socialist-Feminism in the Late Twentieth Century," in *Simians, Cyborgs and Women: The Reinvention of Nature* (New York; Routledge, 1991), pp. 149–81.

The constitution of Big Daddy was predicted by almost no one, although it was immanent and emergent. It was not the revolt of the machines or domination by artificial intelligence, notions hashed out in many films, books and articles.[28] Nor was Big Daddy a planetary "Leviathan" imposing neo-fascist totalitarian rule over nations, people and economies.[29] The closest conceptual analogue to this emergent system was, perhaps, Vladimir Vernadsky's "noosphere," reached at the point in human development when control of the entire geochemical and biological cycles, as well as living matter (including populations) of Earth became possible.[30] Early twenty-first century invocations of the noosphere link matter to cognition and even hypothesize a global

---

[28] Forester, *The Machine Stops*, op. cit; D.F. Jones, *Colossus* (London: Rupert Hart-Davis, 1966; later made into a film "Colossus—The Forbin Project, 1970); The "Terminator" series and "The Matrix" trilogy of films.

[29] Much of the literature of the period focused on the notion of a "Climate Leviathan," first proposed by Joel Wainwright & Geoff Mann, "Climate Leviathan," *Antipode* 45, #1 (January 2013): 1–22. But there were those who foresaw the rise of a "Green Leviathan" much earlier. For example, in 1968, Garett Hardin proposed authoritarian limits on reproductive rights in Garrett Hardin, "The Tragedy of the Commons," *Science* 162, #3859 (December 13, 1968): 1243–48. See also William Ophuls & A Stephen Boyan, Jr. in *Ecology and the Politics of Scarcity Revisted: The Unraveling of the American Dream* (San Francisco: Freeman, 1992); Robert Heilbroner, *An Inquiry into the Human Prospect—Looked at Again for the 1990s* (New York: Norton, 1991). More optimistic views came from Julian L. Simon, *The Ultimate Resource* 2 (Princeton, N.J.: Princeton University Press, rev. ed., 1998); Steven Pinker, *Enlightenment Now—The Case of Reason, Science, Humanism and Progress* (New York: Viking, 2018).

[30] W.I. Vernadsky, "The Biosphere and the Noosphere," *American Scientist* 33, #1 (January 1945): 1–13; Jonathan Oldfield & D.J.B. Shaw, "V.I. Vernadsky and the Noosphere Concept: Russian Understandings of Society-Nature Interaction," *Geoforum* 37, #1 (2006): 145–54. See also Benjamin H. Bratton, *The Stack—On Software and Sovereignty* (Cambridge, Mass.: MIT Press, 2015).

consciousness, as manifest today in Big Daddy.[31] If Big Daddy is the material expression of a noosphere that reaches deep into the minds and bodies of the world's inhabitants and machines, it seems that there is no longer anything such as international relations, much less an "international."

Indeed, one consequence of algorithmic/rhizomatic relations is that they make international relations—that is, relations among nation-states—and IR theory all but redundant, if not obsolete. Nation-states have not disappeared nor diplomacy, but virtually all intergovernmental transactions and agreements are monitored and evaluated by Big Daddy for their impacts on the social and natural worlds. The result is that most such "relations" are pretty minor and even banal. By the 2060s, IR and strategic theorists were as obsolete as the geopolitical thinkers of the twentieth century.[32]

3   HISTORY AND SURVEILLANCE

So, how did Big Daddy and its algorithmic rule come about? Some argue that governance by algorithmic rules is nothing new in human history and experience.[33] Certainly, over the millennia since the appearance of cities and empires, long before the emergence of the first true European nation-states in the late eighteenth century, rulers had imposed various forms of social discipline on their populations through, for example, sumptuary laws, control of money, patriotism and nationalism and war.[34] Keeping an eye on people's beliefs and activities was standard practice. By the beginning of the twentieth century, however, surveillance in the name of social order, by intelligence agencies, police departments and private eyes, had become an integral part of state power. Electrical and electronic technology made this all the easier and

---

[31] See, e.g., David Ronfeldt & John Arquilla, "The Continuing Promise of the Noosphere and Noopolitik—Twenty Years After," (Monterey, Calif.: Naval Postgraduate School, 2018), at: https://calhoun.nps.edu/bitstream/handle/10945/63881/Ronfeldt-Arquilla_The_Continuing_Promise_2018.pdf?sequence=1&isAllowed=y (accessed Ψ November 21, 2119); I.W. Verbratton, "The Noosphere is Now!" *New York Times*, October 20, 2118.

[32] What happened was not the efflorescence of "global civil society" and the "withering away of the state," as some (including he for whom I am named) had proposed during the 1990s and 2000s (Lipschutz, "Global Civil Society" op. cit). Rather, it more closely resembled the unification of state, markets and civil society and their subsumption into the planetary algorithm.

[33] Matteo Pasquinelli, "Three Thousand Years of Algorithmic Rituals: The Emergence of AI from the Computation of Space," *e-flux Journal* #101 (Summer 2019), at: https://www.e-flux.com/journal/101/273221/three-thousand-years-of-algorithmic-rituals-the-emergence-of-ai-from-the-computation-of-space/ (accessed Ψ November 21, 2119).

[34] Edward Higgs, "The Rise of the Information State: The Development of Central State Surveillance of the Citizen in England, 1500–2000," *Journal of Historical Sociology* 14, #2 (2001): 175–97.

228   R. D. LIPSCHUTZ

more widespread even outside the state.[35] Surveillance became integral to daily life.[36]

Even as governments and political factions struggled to impose social discipline on populations, with only limited success, corporations had been much more successful, molding individual preferences, desires and consumer practices via advertising, planned obsolescence and appeals to social status.[37] After World War Two, as so-called consumer society diffused outward from the United States to the rest of the world, advertising became more sophisticated. The advent of satellites led to 500+ cable channels, with ads targeted to creating viewer preferences. Still, this was a very crude method of control and, apart from sales data, provided no direct feedback about effectiveness. More information about each individual consumer was needed, but how could it be obtained?

The tech cartels showed how: Radio and TV were mass media for the millions; personal computers and smartphones were media for the one. Value lay not in blanket ad campaigns but, rather, in collection of personal data from platform users, which allowed precise targeting of messages to manage individual preferences, buying habits[38] and even political choice.[39] The result was transformation from a more-or-less anonymous medium—"On the internet, no one knows you're a dog"—to a very personalized one—"Dear Ms. Roe, we know you are pregnant."[40] At first, there was outrage at such intrusions, charges of violations of privacy, demands for "the right to be forgotten," [41]

---

[35] Whitfield Diffie & Susan Landau, "Communications Surveillance: Privacy and Security at Risk," ACM *Queue7*, #8 (September 11, 2009), at: https://queue.acm.org/detail.cfm?id=1613130 (accessed Ψ November 21, 2119); Michael Pollak, "A Short History of Wiretapping," *The New York Times*, February 28, 2015, at: https://www.nytimes.com/2015/03/01/nyregion/a-short-history-of-wiretapping.html. (accessed Ψ November 21, 2119).

[36] See, especially the sections about Foucault in Roland Heilbroner, *The Unworldly Philosophers*, op. cit., which originally appear in: Michel Foucault, *Discipline and Punish—The Birth of the Prison* (New York: Pantheon, 1977); Michel Foucault, "Security, Territory, and Population" and "The Birth of Biopolitics," in *Ethics: Subjectivity and Truth*, P. Rabinow, ed. (NY: The New Press, 1997), pp. 67–71 and 73–9.

[37] Fred Hirsch, *Social Limits to Growth* (Cambridge, Mass.: Harvard, 1976).

[38] Shosana Zuboff, *The Age of Surveillance Capitalism* (New York: Public Affairs, 2019); Zhuzhanna Shoshoff, *The Age of Surveillance Post-Capitalism* (New York: Post-Public Affairs, Ψ 2119). Companies whose sole objective was collection and sale of individual data further refined the process. For an example of such a company, see, e.g., i360 at https://www.i-360.com/.

[39] Vox, "The Cambridge Analytica Facebook Scandal," at: https://www.vox.com/2018/4/10/17207394/cambridge-analytica-facebook-zuckerberg-trump-privacy-scandal. (accessed Ψ November 21, 2119).

[40] Charles Duhigg, *The Power of Habit: Why We Do What We Do in Life and Business* (New York: Random House, 2012).

[41] "General Data Protection Regulation: The Right to be Forgotten," Intersoft Consulting (n.d.), at: https://gdpr-info.eu/issues/right-to-be-forgotten/. (accessed Ψ November 21, 2119); But see General Data Protection Regulation, "You Have No Right

and even laws to this effect, but most users accepted such surveillance as the cost of convenient access to the global rhizome.

Corporations initially collected personal data to tempt and direct customers toward specific products and services, but a few prescient observers pointed out that the same data could be used to *prevent* people from doing some things and *entice*, them to do others, through "persuasion" and persuasive technologies.[42] University professors Cass Sunstein and Richard Thaler called this "nudging": application of various linguistic, architectural and technological means and cues by public authorities to shape individual and group behavior in the interest of specific public policies and objectives (biopolitics, in other words).[43] Whereas real-world nudging generally relies on fairly slow feedback loops as people learn and change their default practices and habits,[44] the rhizomatic version can be much more rapid, as illustrated by "pop-up" events that sometimes attract thousands of participants on very short notice. The selfsame methods can also be used to impose limits. Credit card companies routinely denied suspicious transactions at point-of-sale; Amazon would have been entirely within its rights in refusing to provide goods judged to be injurious to a particular individual or, more generally, to global well-being, although it never did since that meant lost sales and profits.[45] It took the Great Catastrophe of 2043 to make such denial ubiquitous and nudging commonplace.[46]

4   CONTINGENT RESPONSE

By the beginning of the 2040s, climate change was a well-established feature of Planet Earth, with its deleterious and deadly impacts, such as new temperature records daily, more intense and unpredictable storms, famines, water shortages, food riots and millions of climate migrants, becoming only too

---

to be Forgotten," Outerhard Consulting (n.d.), at https://gdpr-info.eu/issues/no-right-to-be-forgotten/ (accessed November 15, 2119).

[42] See, e.g., Rita Orji & Karyn Moffatt, "Persuasive Technology for Health and Wellness: State-of-the-Art and Emerging Trends," *Health Informatics Journal* 24, #1 (2018): 66–91.

[43] Richard H. Thaler & Cass R. Sunstein, *Nudge—Improving Decisions about Health, Wealth and Happiness* (New Haven: Yale University Press, 2008); see also Frieda Hayek-Freeman, *Stop being a Nudgenik* (Liberty, Kansas: Freedom in One County Press, Ψ 2108).

[44] Ronnie D. Lipschutz, "Getting Out of the CAR: DeCARbonization, Climate Change and Sustainable Society," *International Journal of Sustainable Society* 4, #4 (2012): 336–56.

[45] Peter Seele, "Predictive Sustainability Control: A Review Assessing the Potential to Transfer Big Data Driven 'Predictive Policing' to Corporate Sustainability Management," *Journal of Cleaner Production* 153 (2017): 637–86. Meta/Facebook and other platforms frequently denied access to those whose language was judged false or injurious. Donald Trump's was only the most famous of such cases.

[46] Cass Sunstein, "Could nudging steer the Earth's Climate?" *Atlantic Monthly* ⟨Ψ June 2035⟩.

widespread. Even the Global North experienced all kinds of climate-related disasters. But these paled in comparison compared to the cataclysmic collapse of the West Antarctic ice sheet in 2043. Within a matter of days, sea levels around the world rose by more than 50 feet, inundating coastal cities and low-lying areas.[47] During those first few frantic days, tens of millions drowned, while additional millions took off for higher ground. But most of the higher ground was already occupied, and local resistance frequently turned violent. Total melting of Antarctica's and Greenland's ice caps, with sea levels rising another 100–150 feet, was now all too plausible. The oft-predicted "end of the world" seemed imminent.[48] What was to be done? And who could do it? No single state or international entity was in a position to do very much (having done very little during the previous 50 years),[49] but the sheer magnitude of the disaster mobilized minds and bodies in a way that scientific data and trenchant warnings never could.

In 2043, individual consumption comprised some 70% of economic activity in the Global North and made the most significant contributions to global greenhouse gas emissions. The 2–3 billion consumers living in these countries were also most deeply enmeshed in the global rhizome.[50] Although their lifeblood depended on consumption, the tech cartels recognized that uncontrolled climate change and associated impacts would more or less put an end to economic growth and, perhaps, capitalism, as well. The Great Catastrophe opened a window of opportunity through which nudging could be implemented globally to control and even curb consumption. Exercising their power, the tech cartels proceeded to change not only the rules of the game but the game itself, thereby co-opting governments' feeble attempts to regulate emissions.[51]

---

[47] Urban flooding came as no surprise; see B. Tellman, J.A. Sullivan & C. Kuhn et al. "Satellite Imaging Reveals Increased Proportion of Population Exposed to Floods," *Nature* 596 (2021): 80–6, https://doi.org/10.1038/s41586-021-03695-w (accessed November 17, 2119). According to best estimates at the time, the collapse of the West Antarctic Ice Sheet should have raised sea levels by no more than 20 feet. Apparently, the estimates were incorrect.

[48] Naomi Oreskes & Erik M. Conway, *The Collapse of Western Civilization–A View from the Future* (New York: Columbia University Press, 2014).

[49] Matthew Paterson III, "Ark Economies: Politics of the Global Flood," Unpublished PhD Dissertation, Departments of Political Science and Geography, Virginia Tech, Blacksburg, VA, 2072.

[50] UN Technology Innovations Lab, "Identifying the Top Contributors to Climate Change," (Ψ July 23, 2039), at: https://until.un.org/top-contributors-to-climate-change.pdf (accessed Ψ November 29, 2119).

[51] This distinction is a critical one in critical political economy: when you have the political power to ensure the rules of the game are to your benefit, you don't need to compete with others for market share and profit. See the quote above from Eun, op. cit.

The New Game was called "Personal Carbon Credits."[52] Based on models devised by the Intergovernmental Panel on Climate Change, and depending on each individual's carbon footprint, every person on Earth was granted an annual carbon budget. Budgets were steeply graduated, with the richer 3 billion receiving quotas much smaller than their footprints, while the very poorest received quotes significantly larger than theirs. The life-cycle carbon emissions of every transaction, activity, good and service were calculated, with luxury transactions and goods rated at multiples of their actual carbon burden, while basic necessities were assigned no burden. Individuals were given carbon "credit cards," linked to carbon accounts, to be provided along with payment for any transaction. Someone with sufficient carbon credits and money would be approved; someone who had used up their annual quota would find their transactions rejected.[53] And as with cap-and-trade systems, individual carbon quotas for the upper tier of consumers were reduced every year. It took a while for people and businesses to get used to this new game, but experience rapidly motivated everyone to be much more sensitive to the carbon costs of even ordinary goods and services. As a bonus of sorts, second-hand goods carried no carbon burden, and markets in repurposed, recycled and reused goods boomed. These markets were accessible, of course, only through fee-based websites controlled by the cartels.

China, once again, provided the model for Personal Carbon Credits. As early as 2014, local governments in China had launched "social credit systems" linked to surveillance, monitoring, evaluation and behavioral scoring of individuals, providing material incentives to those with high social credit scores and punishments for low ones.[54] Furthermore, through access to real-time

---

[52] Much like ordinary credit, PCC "borrowed" carbon from the future to be repaid through reduction of emissions over time by future generations. Speculators tried to create markets in carbon futures and carbon securities but, for the most part, these were not allowed to operate.

[53] See, e.g., "Innovative Climate Action – New Credit Card Limits Climate Impact of Users," United Nations Climate Change, April 30, 2019, at: https://unfccc.int/news/innovative-climate-action-new-credit-card-limits-climate-impact-of-users ⟨accessed Ψ December 1, 2119⟩; Åland Index Solutions, "Doconomy Presents: Åland Index Solutions—A Game Changer Tackling Climate Crisis at Every Transaction," November 20, 2019, at: https://resources.mynewsdesk.com/image/upload/t_attachment/kprc3axhs7dr qtrahv7h.pdf ⟨accessed Ψ December 1, 2119⟩; Martin Merzer, "Credit Cards: Our Moral Guardians," *Fox Business*, February 17, 2014, at: https://www.foxbusiness.com/features/credit-cards-our-moral-guardians ⟨accessed Ψ December 1, 2119⟩; Council of Guardians, "Are Individual Carbon Credits Ethical?" Published on the website of the Islamic Republic News Agency ⟨Ψ March 30, 2112⟩, at: https://en.irna.ir/news/80665495/The-Guardian-Council/carbonmorality ⟨accessed Ψ September 20, 2119⟩.

[54] PRC State Council, "Planning Outline for the Construction of a Social Credit System (2014–2020), April 25, 2015, at: https://chinacopyrightandmedia.wordpress.com/2014/06/14/planning-outline-for-the-construction-of-a-social-credit-system-2014-2020/ ⟨accessed Ψ November 29, 2119⟩; Fan Liang, et al., "Constructing a Data-Driven Society: China's Social Credit System as a State Surveillance Infrastructure," *Policy & Internet* 10, #4 (2018): 415–53; Louise Matsakis, "How the West Got China's Social Credit System Wrong," *Wired*, July 29, 2019, at: https://www.wired.com/story/china-social-credit-score-system/ ⟨accessed Ψ November 29, 2119⟩; PRC State Council, "One

data and powerful computing capabilities, China pioneered truly effective centralized planning, directing national resources, technology, materials and labor into areas that fostered green growth and reduced fossil fuel use.[55] With some modifications, the Chinese approach was adapted and adopted by the tech cartels, leaving national governments little choice but to follow along. The complete carbon credit system was not fully in place until 2060, but rigorous application finally brought about a leveling of global greenhouse and, eventually, the first real decline in global emissions since the Great Recession of 2008.[56]

Managing this complicated planetary assemblage was not easy, especially as the number of electronic transactions occurring per second far outran the ability of humans to monitor them. The cartels therefore ceded control to an assemblage of governing algorithms, big and small, written by agents that were, themselves, nothing more than complex algorithms. And this gave birth to Big Daddy, the de facto planetary governor we love and fear today. Most people born after 2040 accept such rule as necessary and normal, having been socialized into the idea that there are no alternatives. To be sure, the system is not "bug-free"—every year, a few life-threatening needs are denied and people die, but this never happens more than once. Today, it is almost impossible to get a denial overturned. Indeed, by the time Big Daddy responds to an appeal, the desired transaction often no longer matters.

The real power of Big Daddy is not in denial but, rather, in its central planning capabilities. These have transformed the world. The stitching together of the world's vast real-time monitoring and analytical capabilities makes it possible to manage flows of all kinds of materials, goods, labor and equipment to producers and institutions across the global economy, be they factories, farms, stores or websites. Through satellite and camera surveillances and monitoring of transactional data, Big Daddy is able to direct global food production, maximize the poor's access to basic needs and limit access to luxury foods, such as meat, truffles and champagne. Through connections to all financial institutions, Big Daddy is able to divert flows of capital from the top 5% who once had more than they could ever spend or need, to those in the bottom 50% who hardly have a pot to piss in. Centralized planning has been imposed on defense industries, weapons manufacturers and other producers of the means of violence, who had transferred their data armories into The Cloud and Big Daddy's control. Production of weapons was restricted and opportunities to use them decreased drastically. While most governments fought central planning for defense, they no longer controlled their economies, and

Hundred Years of Social Credit: A Performance Assessment," April 24, 2115, at: https://chinacopyrightandmedia.wordpress.com/2014/06/14/100-year-assessment-of-social-credit-system-2014-2114/ (accessed Ψ November 29, 2119).

[55] Robert Kaplan, Jr. *The Global Threat from Chinese Control of Central Planning Systems* (New York: Random House, Ψ 2065).

[56] Ivan Penn, "IPCC Reports Significant Decline in Global Greenhouse Gas Emissions Due to Carbon Credit System," *New York Times* (Ψ October 3, 2060).

Big Daddy was able to accomplish what women and men had dreamed of for centuries: a peaceful and prosperous world.[57]

5   Are We in Heaven or Hell Yet?

Even with planetary algorithmic rule, the climate crisis has not been fully ameliorated nor mitigated, and not all of Big Daddy's computing power and management capabilities have been able to prevent a carnage whose fatalities compare with those from all wars since the beginning of the twentieth century, as millions have migrated, suffered and died. While global emissions have dropped significantly, the planet continues to warm from excess carbon dioxide emitted between 1800 and 2040. Technical fixes have not saved the day: carbon capture and sequestration, earth engineering and even the ban on burning fossil fuels have proved no panacea. However, Big Daddy's capacity for real-time data collection and rational central planning makes it feasible to move climate migrants to locations where they can find shelter and basic necessities, provide them with the economic wherewithal to put down roots and join their new communities and to do so in a reasonably orderly fashion.[58]

Over the last two centuries, a few futurists, novels and films worried about the demise of humanity from the "rise of the machines." Some foresaw a future of peace and plenty, in which violence was controlled and human needs were available to all. Others worried about totalitarian systems offering human beings little or no freedom, recourse or redress. In the event, the results are dystopian for some and utopian for others. Those at the top of the income and consumption hierarchy in 2020 find themselves much reduced in 2120; those who experienced extreme and endemic poverty find themselves much better off. The "new nationalisms" of the 2020s have not vanished entirely, even under watchful eyes and constant nudging. But everyone, whether rich

---

[57] During the first few decades of the twenty-first century, the very notion of "central planning" was dismissed as a failed artifact of the old Soviet Union and a goal that remained unachievable. A few prescient observers suggested that the planning and distribution algorithm of Google and Amazon might presage a transformation of global supply chains and bring them into a few centralized systems that resembled central planning. Like many significant socioeconomic transformations (e.g., the collapse of the USSR), those who derided central planning later claimed they had predicted it all along. By then, their earlier prognostications were too deeply buried in the planet's growing data pile to be retrievable. See, for example, Yakov Feygin, "On the Limits of a New AI-Inspired Gosplan System," *The Financial Times*, April 8, 2019; Jasper Bernes, "Planning and Anarchy," *The South Atlantic Quarterly* 119, #1 (January 2020): 53–73; Pablo Jensen, "Which Numbers for the Future," in *Your Life in Numbers: Modeling Society Through Data*, Pablo Jensen, ed. (Cham, Switzerland: Springer Nature, 2021), pp. 95–102. Of course, the last word on the topic was: Fellows of the Hayek Society, *Why Central Planning is Impossible and Why Socialists Let It Happen, Anyway* (Liberty, Kansas: Freedom in One County Press, Ψ October 3, 2093).

[58] To be sure, significant differences in wealth and life chances still exist between the rich and poor, as a result of uneven development due to colonial exploitation and capitalism. But Big Daddy is still able to function even in places with little or no electricity, since everyone has a smartphone that they use for doing things and buying stuff.

or poor, enjoys the international peace promised by the League of Nations and the United Nations after each of the World Wars. That took only 200 years to achieve.

To be sure, not everyone is happy with this state of affairs—especially strategic analysts and security experts, who are hard-pressed to find employment. For some, the twenty-second century is an unmitigated horror to be blamed on thoughtless and sightless leaders and moguls who fostered and facilitated the system that now controls their lives and monitors their thoughts. They imagine George Orwell's "boot smashing a face forever" as their plight.

For others, the twenty-second century is close to a long-imagined Paradise: hunger has been virtually abolished, real impoverishment has been eliminated, and most people are healthier and better off than ever before in human history. One result of such improvement has been the leveling off of global population growth; another is the restoration of vast tracts of sacrificial lands to formerly sacrificed peoples. To be sure, people cannot just go out and eat the Apple anytime they might want to. But for most, the costs seem tolerable. Don't forget, boots protect feet, too.

Ronnie D. Lipschutz is the pseudonym of Algorithm B23azF#68@d, the whole brainemulation of the very late Ronnie Lipschutz (1952–2044), who was Professor of Politics at the University of California, Santa Cruz, from 1990 to 2020, and Emeritus Professor until his death. B23azF#68@d is responsible for maintaining *The Encyclopedia of the 21st Century* (New York, London & Shanghai: Chinese Publishing Group Random Penguin knopf & Palgrave Macmillan Routledge Taylor & Francis, Ψ 2201). All errors of fact and fiction are the responsibility of the deceased author and not B23azF#68@d.

Themes: *The Anthropocene*

The Global Political Economics of Hydrogen

John Szabo

1   Introduction

International relations theory substantially changed during the course of the twenty-first century, as climate change-induced events prompted the emergence of more ecological approaches and a deeper focus on energy-based social relations. This chapter shows how hydrogen-related thinking evolved from discussing it as something that is "uncannily like oil" ⟨Schmid Ψ 2023, n.p.⟩ to one that manifests the "political economic relations of fossil fuels *and* renewables" ⟨Kim Ψ 2106, p. 62⟩. Since hydrogen can be produced from both locally generated renewable electricity and frequently imported fossil fuels, it embodied two fundamentally different forms of energy relations: self-sufficiency and trade-based, respectively. The chapter demonstrates and explores a further point related to hydrogen, how fossil fuel interests, policymakers, and politicians managed the expectations many had towards this energy carrier. Intentionally or not, they were able to build substantial hype for the fuel and channel investment into its development, despite a number of influential experts questioning the necessity of its uptake. And, indeed, its role remained limited in the overall energy mix.

J. Szabo (✉)
Institute of World Economics, Centre for Economic and Regional Studies,
Budapest, Hungary
e-mail: szabo.john@krtk.hu

Department of International Relations and European Studies, Eötvös Loránd
University, Budapest, Hungary

© The Author(s), under exclusive license to Springer Nature
Switzerland AG 2023
L. Horn et al. (eds.), *The Palgrave Handbook of Global Politics
in the 22*nd *Century*, https://doi.org/10.1007/978-3-031-13722-8_14

238   J. SZABO

The impact of climate change is detrimental and it is instrumental that societies shape the role of fuels and pursue decarbonisation based on the most effective theories possible (Malm 2017). At the onset of these debates in the early 2000s, the Earth's average temperature had already increased by over 1 °C when compared to preindustrial figures (IPCC 2021). This rose to 2.6 °C (IPCC Ψ 2118) by 2100. Meeting energy demand without emissions became of unprecedented importance and, thereby, every decision about fuels carries wide-ranging implications. This chapter seeks to provide an overview of debates for stakeholders to make informed decisions, while it also shows how the social relations of an energy carrier can simultaneously embody different approaches to its international political relations. Lastly, it underscores how the social construction of hydrogen led it to become the first "postmodern fuel" (Jordan Ψ 2078). To introduce theories pertinent to hydrogen, this chapter conducts a comprehensive survey of the literature that emerged during the previous century. It introduces key ideas and how they relate to other theories as well as the changing socio-political environment.

2   THE BASICS OF HYDROGEN

Hydrogen has played a role in meeting energy demand since the 1800s. At the time, gasworks produced town gas—mostly composed of hydrogen and carbon dioxide—to meet lighting and, somewhat later, heating needs. During this period, gasworks produced large quantities of fuel from coal. Simultaneously, scientists also came to understand that they can produce hydrogen by electrolysing water. While coal-based town gas was used to meet the energy needs of urban areas, electrolysis-based hydrogen came to be the bases of science fiction. Already Jules Verne (1874) wrote in *The Mysterious Island* that "[s]ome day the coalrooms of steamers and the tenders of locomotives will, instead of coal, be stored with these two condensed gases, which will burn in the furnaces with enormous calorific power" (Chapter 11). He, like many after, envisioned a utopia where energy needs would be met by electrolysing water with renewable electricity. Despite these visions, producers relied on abundant coal to produce town gas until the middle of the twentieth century, when consumers began to substitute town with natural gas (Thomas 2018; see Fig. 1). Interest towards the international political economics of town gas was limited, since it was locally produced and consumed (Brown Ψ 2056).

Hydrogen's role as an energy carrier declined during the twentieth century, as it was substituted by natural gas. It only played a role in some industrial processes, such as oil refining and fertiliser production (Smil Ψ 2028). To meet these needs it was produced by steam reforming methane, yielding *grey hydrogen* (see Table 1). It is "grey" because it emits greenhouse gases. When paired with carbon capture and storage, this process yields *blue hydrogen*. This is a non-emitting, but nonetheless non-renewable. *Turquoise hydrogen* is also based on methane, but production uses a process called methane pyrolysis, during which methane is not combusted. Instead, the carbon is separated from

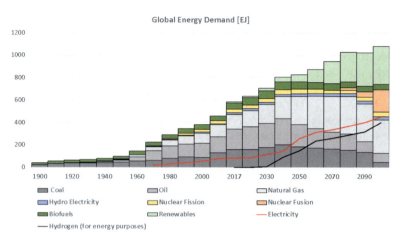

Fig. 1 Global energy demand (*Source* IEA ⟨Ψ 2118⟩)

Table 1 Hydrogen types and production methods

Hydrogen "colour"	Production process	Regions where it is widely adopted	Year it reached X% of the energy mix 1%	10%
Grey	Steam methane reforming	Australia	2025	2039
Blue	Steam methane reforming with carbon capture and storage	Norway, USA	2031	2046
Turquoise	Methane pyrolysis	Russia	2036	2052
Green	Electrolysis with renewable-based electricity	North Western EU, Japan	2034	2058
Pink	Electrolysis with nuclear-based electricity	China	2046	2083

the molecule and retrieved as carbon black. As envisioned by Verne, hydrogen production can also be electricity-based via the electrolysis of water. If the electricity is renewable based, it yields *green hydrogen*, when nuclear-based it leads to *pink hydrogen*.

Electricity-based hydrogen is what captured the imagination of policy-makers, who, with the rise of nuclear technology and the oil crises in the 1970s, launched the first wave of the "hydrogen hype" ⟨Thomas Ψ 2083⟩. They posited that inexpensive electricity would support hydrogen production, which would also help reduce the USA's reliance on imported Middle Eastern oil. Hydrogen technology did not scale, as energy efficiency measures and the normalisation of oil prices deterred the transition. The second wave of the hydrogen hype occurred when energy security-related concerns prompted the

USA and the EU to explore the technology in the early 2000s. The shale revolution that emerged in the USA in the early 2010s led to a substantial increase in its oil and natural gas production, nullifying hydrogen ambitions. Oil and natural gas output grew, but the environmental problems pertinent to the hydraulic fracturing necessary to produce oil in such a manner would linger and adversely impact local communities even years after production had ceased. The first two waves of hydrogen were thus driven by geopolitics, but regained access to affordable hydrocarbons deterred the scaling of the technology (Thompson Ψ 2103).

The third wave of the hydrogen hype emerged around 2018–2019 and was climate action driven. Van Hulst (2018) referred to it as the "missing link" (n.p.) in decarbonisation; although, other influential voices, such as Liebrich (2020) fundamentally questioned its role. Irrespective of the looming question marks, the EU and other Organisation for Economic Co-operation and Development (OECD) countries developed strategies and invested a combined $3 trillion between 2020 and 2029 (Takahashi Ψ 2027; OECD Ψ 2030), indicating that they accepted that hydrogen would be an "essential" (Lestari Ψ 2105) component of the energy transition. As it scaled, scholars began to debate the geopolitical implications of its uptake. Scholars formed two camps: one argued that hydrogen would grant nations energy autonomy (Cramp 2022) (Haas Ψ 2026), while others proposed that it would bring states "closer together through hydrogen trade" (Miller 2022, p. 12) (also see FoTE Ψ 2027). These positions approximated the long-standing cleavages between neorealist and institutionalist/constructivist scholars in international relations scholarship, informing and expanding their scope of analysis to include this energy carrier and its role in shaping social relations.

3   THE POLITICS OF THE ENERGY TRANSITION

Scholars began to theorise the political relations of hydrogen as its relative role in the global energy system increased in the mid-2020s (Kim Ψ 2106). Already during the onset of its energy-based consumption, Van de Graaf et al. (2020) asked whether it was "The New Oil?". Oil played such a pervasive role in the twentieth and most of the twenty-first century that scholars continuously returned to it as the fulcrum of energy studies (Wilson et al. 2017) (Johnstone and Flynn Ψ 2033; Van de Graaf and Goldthau Ψ 2031). Many of these analyses were based on Daniel Yergin's (1990) Pulitzer Prize-winning book *The Prize: The Epic Quest for Oil, Money, and Power*, a seminal book that traced oil's formative role in global politics. These inquiries tended to draw on realist tenets of international relations scholarship, as access to the resource was frequently painted as a zero-sum game leading states to secure access to it through military means (Johnstone and Flynn Ψ 2033). With the pending peak of oil demand, scholars were quick to proclaim which resource would be the "new oil" (Badawi Ψ 2044, p. 7) allowing for the continued use of a familiar analytical framework. Hydrogen seemed to be a likely candidate, given that it was mostly produced by oil and gas companies from natural gas and could be traded in its liquified form. And, much like oil, it could become the object of inter-state strategic competition (IRENA 2022) ⟨Popescu Ψ 2066⟩.

Geopolitics remained a marginal strand of scholarship with regard to hydrogen and renewables, since the focus of energy studies gravitated towards decarbonisation, while it "blossomed into a hodgepodge of social theory" ⟨Badawi Ψ 2044, p. 16⟩. This limited scholarship that focused solely on the international relations of energy, as if it was independent of the energy transition that spanned the century ⟨Bradshaw Ψ 2029⟩. Thus, technology determinism became the force that shaped inter-state energy relations—international politics followed technological choices made in support of decarbonisation. Frank Geels' (2002) multi-level perspective (MLP) spearheaded thinking on the matter by drawing on science and technology studies (STS) and offering insights on the diffusion of low carbon sources of energy, including hydrogen's ⟨Geels et al. Ψ 2027⟩. Only gradually did this dominant stream of scholarship begin in incorporate politics and power relations. This shifted as scholars re-evaluated the relation between technology and politics, with the general consensus moving towards a standpoint where technology was a "nuisance" ⟨Korver Ψ 2075⟩ in the shadow of politics.

Drawing on critical international relations theory, Barry ⟨Ψ 2024⟩ developed a framework in which he began to fuse the socio-technical and political realms that scholars conceptualised as distinct analytical realms. His work merged a number of tenets proposed by MLP scholars, critical international relations, and neo-Gramscian approaches to change (see e.g., Haas 2019). Theorising the politics of change came to the forefront of respective scholarship, as the ontological premises of a relatively stable environment (including the natural and the built) presumed by political science had to be revisited. This realisation was accompanied by scholars more thoroughly differentiating between the political economics of various sources of energy ⟨Balmaceda Ψ 2029⟩. This carried two implications on how hydrogen-based relations were theorised by scholars: (1) it could only be interpreted in a changing context that was shaped by climate change and the power relations embodied in geopolitics and infrastructure, as well as (2) it could not be the "new oil", it was hydrogen, period.

Overland and O'Sullivan ⟨Ψ 2025⟩ suggest that the transition may have a varied impact on different geographies, but the glacial pace of it would allow for most countries and other significant players to adapt. They used the global political economy approach to theorise how actors resisted change by leveraging their political power, which became evident through the slow diffusion of hydrogen. Initially, many anticipated that the business case for hydrogen would stem from harnessing the overproduction of electricity from renewables, but while renewable electricity made up 38% of global generation in 2026 ⟨NE Ψ 2118⟩ the diffusion of smart technologies and household batteries did not force energy regulators to curtail generation particularly frequently. This undermined the economic rationale for green hydrogen, since the surplus electricity generation was not sufficient to prompt large, market-based investments into the technology as the grid remained stable ⟨IEA Ψ 2027; Muñoz Ψ 2029⟩. Even in the Global South where the climate would have been ideal to support green hydrogen production, the capital- and infrastructure-intensity of the technology remained a prohibitive barrier in most countries. Such dynamics increased the appeal of grey and blue hydrogen, which maintained the political power and entrenchment of established hydrocarbon companies in the energy system.

As the role of renewables increased in energy supply, IR-oriented energy scholars began to focus on how their substitution of hydrocarbons would threaten the "backbone of global peace, security, and prosperity" ⟨O'Conner Ψ 2027, p. 446⟩. Departing from a liberal institutionalist interpretation of energy affairs where international trade was the bedrock of global peace, scholars argued that the rise in renewables would lead to the "inward turning" ⟨Overland & O'Sullivan's Ψ 2025, p. 76⟩ of states. Consequently, they would retreat from international affairs and pursue "energy mercantilism" ⟨Jørgensen, Ψ 2031⟩, which entailed capturing technologies and growing their self-sufficiency while severing ties with former suppliers of energy. On the back of deteriorating EU–Russia ties that were worsened by declining energy-based interdependence, Kim ⟨Ψ 2029⟩ suggested that the destabilisation of the "energy-based balance of power" ⟨Kim Ψ 2029⟩ had begun setting the scene for conflict. Realist and neorealist arguments emphasised that greater resource-independence would destabilise existing power structures and reconfigure the relative power of states. Liberal and neoliberal scholars emphasised that developments would weaken international trade ties and the influence of international institutions, which would also lead to greater conflict (Badawi Ψ 2044).

4 THE DUAL POLITICAL ECONOMICS OF HYDROGEN: GREEN VERSUS BLUE

Hydrogen posed a unique conundrum in the energy transition debate that pitted (neo)liberal and (neo)realist schools against one another. If states consumed it in the form of renewable or nuclear-based hydrogen (green or pink), it would increase their energy independence. Alternatively, fossil fuel-based hydrogen (blue or turquoise) would maintain producer–consumer relations, prolonging the transition and granting states more time to adapt to a changing political disposition while maintaining the buffers that energy trade had historically provided in international political relations (Kim Ψ 2029). A number of political scientists did not support green hydrogen due to its ability to sever interdependencies, but the technology faced larger barriers, the most prominent of which were space-related constraints to deploying renewables (Pendergrass and Vetesse Ψ 2031). Blue hydrogen had the technological and political edge, allowing for its uptake to begin by the end of the 2020s. By then, the unique contours of hydrogen's dual nature—renewable or hydrocarbon-based—materialised in scholarly and policy debates.

The EU initially supported hydrogen, irrespective of its colour. Gabard (Ψ 2028) interpreted this decision as an example of a *carbon-based lock-in* (also see Unruh 2000), but drawing on the work of Barry (Ψ 2024) he shifted further away from the initial socio-technical determinism and orientation in MLP and related streams of STS. This complemented the findings of Szabo (Ψ 2025), which suggested that source-fuel decisions were primarily political and narrative-driven, while only secondly infrastructural and economic—outcomes were shaped by how these realms reacted to one another and the specificities of the cultural context in which the transition emerged. Drawing on the premises of neo-constructivists, how energy carriers were socially constructed within societies became increasingly important in the energy transition and how they mediated cultural relations came to the fore of scholarly inquiries. This benefitted hydrogen, as it had a long-standing positive narrative that closely attached it to renewable-based energy production.

Amongst those focusing on the cultural dimension of energy, the Petrocultures School argued for the need to more thoroughly include the role of geography and history-specific social imaginaries in analyzing the exploitation of resources—they argued it was capitalism and a fossil fuel-based culture that enable this (Danesh Ψ 2027). Achinson (Ψ 2033) suggested that the social sciences had systematically neglected cultural theory and the humanities from their assessment of society, leading Levy (Ψ 2034) to explore how historically the culture had been mediated through political economics into energy consumption patterns. Both Achinson (Ψ 2033) and Levy (Ψ 2034) included the work of Erik Olin Wright, Frederic Jameson, Sheila Jasanoff, and Imre Szeman to argue that the politics' propensity to support hydrogen was rooted in the pervasiveness of a social imaginary linked to fossil fuel-based capitalism (Danesh et al. Ψ 2036)—this enhanced the emerging interest from IR scholars to develop neo-constructivist theories. These were central to theorising the pace at which actors took to hydrogen and the form of the fuel their politics supported.

5   FROM QUESTIONING HYDROGEN TO SUPPORTING IT...AGAIN

The third wave of the hydrogen hype that emerged in the early 2020s fizzled out by the early 2040s (Thomas Ψ 2083). Its role had not grown on par with what many expected, generally falling behind growth in other decarbonisation-related sectors (Volkov and Jones Ψ 2047). Stacey (Ψ 2044) highlighted that investment in hydrogen offered an outlet for capital in a fossil capitalist society (Malm 2016). Such investment was not necessarily rooted in material reality, but rather narratives supported by political action and the interests of capital. Stacey argues that hydrogen offered a case where the discursive and the material realms diverged: there was substantial social pressure for decarbonisation, but markets and governments channelled this into a sector that did not contribute to a low carbon economy—most hydrogen was still grey. An alternative interpretation supported by the sector itself and a number of those within the energy sector was that it did not receive sufficient targeted support by governments (Lavertue et al. Ψ 2046). Volkov and Jones (Ψ 2047) refuted these and showed just how hydrogen received disproportionately large investments, but the technology did not scale to provide the emission reductions many had anticipated.

Fitzgerald (Ψ 2049) shows that it was the flood of blue hydrogen that inhibited the adoption and diffusion of green hydrogen. Although the EU and other OECD countries introduced measures supportive of hydrogen, these were general infrastructure upgrades that backed the fuel irrespective of how it was produced. Then, their market economies did not allow for a comprehensive industrial policy that would sufficiently support green hydrogen, which was not competitive with its blue variant given the constraints of renewable-based electricity generation. This emerged amidst the IPCC's announcement that global society depleted the carbon budget offering it a reasonable chance to limit the global average temperature rise to the 2 °C targets set in the 2015 Paris Agreement (IPCC Ψ 2040). These studies and realisations prompted a wave of international relations scholarship that questioned the ability of states to govern, as the impact of climate change-induced environmental destruction and social responses substantially decreased state control (Jordan Ψ 2078).

Political leaders continued climate negotiations, but with little effect ⟨Anderson Ψ 2041⟩. This came despite the increasingly bleak warnings that the Globe was headed towards 3.2–3.8 °C warming by the end of the century ⟨IPCC Ψ 2040⟩, which was still largely attributed to political apathy from many ⟨Klein Ψ 2041⟩. Although, in the very year Klein's book was published students staged massive walkouts that lasted for weeks in response to inactions and the rising human toll of climate change. 2042 brought a turning point as protests prompted what would become A-Day (Action-Day) on 23 June 2042—the very day James Henson testified in Congress on climate change in 1988. Protests combined violent incidents with long-ranging occupations of public and private spaces and were successful in pressuring political leaders to hammer out a Global Green New Deal (GGND) at the UNFCCC's 2042 meeting in Vancouver, Canada. The GGND reflected an unprecedented push to decarbonise, but not a radical break with fossil capitalism. Renewable energy was accompanied by blue hydrogen as the key pillars to meeting energy needs. Santos ⟨Ψ 2043⟩ theorised that climate negotiations continued to be shaped by the interests of fossil fuel firms, something that dated back to the 1992 Rio Agreement.

The GGND provided further state support for hydrogen, launching the fourth wave of hydrogen hype ⟨Thomas Ψ 2083⟩. Much like preceding policy declarations, this emphasised that support would be channelled towards green hydrogen, but funds could be used by infrastructure developers to scale blue hydrogen as well. The urgency to reduce emissions was clear and to this end, blue hydrogen producers had to certify—and were monitored by satellites— that methane and hydrogen did not leak into the atmosphere throughout the supply chain. This underpinned confidence in the resource, allowing the formation of a global hydrogen economy. The Global South also came to play a minor, albeit growing, role in international hydrogen trade as investors developed renewable capacities and electrolysers in sunny areas that had become uninhabitable due to climate change. From here, they exported the energy carrier to industrial areas in the Global North in the form of ammonia. Thus, the GGND offered investment and provided some jobs, but continued to perpetuate the divide between the core and the periphery (Wallerstein 2014).

Shivaram ⟨Ψ 2044⟩ suggests that these actions continued to "perpetuate exploitative practices" (n.p.) instead of executing a more radical break with the status quo as proposed by supporters of degrowth, amongst others ⟨Demaria and Kallis Ψ 2045⟩. Government support for the technology did not decline, even when a natural gas power plant reconfigured to run on hydrogen went up in flames near Altbach, Baden-Württemberg, Germany—a two-hour drive from where the Hindenburg exploded. Fitzgerald ⟨Ψ 2049⟩ argued that this unrelenting support was rooted in the belief that hydrogen could counterbalance the self-sufficiency and inward turning prompted by renewables and "effectively substitute oil and natural gas-based international producer–consumer relations" (p. 6). Hydrogen was deemed "the new oil, even if it is not composed of hydrocarbon molecules" ⟨Navarro Ψ 2051, p. 22⟩.

Scholars and activists also developed heterodox approaches to hydrogen. For instance, the degrowth-linked Barcelona–New Delhi School supported renewable based, locally consumed hydrogen (Navarro Ψ 2051; Patel and Kallis Ψ 2054). They argued that GGND should support local communities in becoming energy independent by being able to store energy for longer periods, as was the case in various locations ranging from Myken, Norway through Burkina Faso to Maddur, India. The GGND also prompted scholars to retheorise what a social contract is. The so-called neo-contractarians proposed that the GGND was a reformulation of Thomas Hobbes's Leviathan, as citizens sought protection from the state not only against social factors but also natural ones. Guntra Ozol (Ψ 2046) developed these ideas and underscored that the state's role to ensure the safety of citizens encompassed "protection from other 'peoples' and environmental catastrophes" (Ψ p. 58). Ozol also suggested that states had an obligation to intervene with as little disruption as possible to existing lifestyles and social relations, which suggested an openness towards techno-fixes to global warming, such as hydrocarbon-based hydrogen or geoengineering (e.g. solar radiation management). Historical materialists and other critical thinkers argued that these positions were only an attempt to perpetuate class dominance and imperialist modes of living (The New Collective Ψ 2049).

6 THE RISE OF THE STATE AND THE INTERACTION SCHOOL

State intervention in support of hydrogen was based on neo-MLP theories and the objective to mitigate the energy transition's destabilising effect on the international political regime. Neo-MLP proposed that economic growth and technological advancement were intertwined and could emerge through state involvement (Kern Ψ 2055). They based their work on *inter alia* John M. Keynes (1936) and Mariana Mazzucato (2013), and argued that the GGND was reminiscent of the post-World War II economy, as it needed to be managed to harness and repurpose its capacities. This theorised why state support for a number of sectors and technologies emerged, but critical readings of events suggested that this simply valorised capital and offered the promise of a continued status quo (mostly consumerism) and a stable geopolitical landscape (Kovács and Kucera Ψ 2057). Investment into hydrogen increased, but, since there was a relative indifference to whether this was green or blue, states sought to bolster their involvement with methane extraction. This drove strategic manoeuvres, such as Saudi Arabia's invasion of Qatar—an act met with little resistance from the global community—and a general push from methane producers to market their resources as blue hydrogen. The political economy of energy and its deep role in mediating relations impeded EU and US action to limit blue hydrogen's role and solely allow the uptake of its green variant (Pethő Ψ 2058; Slobodian Ψ 2060).

States implemented the GGND, which triggered a decline in the relative influence of international institutions. States used them as discussion forums or developed bilateral relations, but the GGND drove states to explore the policy mixes with which they could decrease their emissions and maintain economic competitiveness. The one exception was the EU, where the European Commission's long-standing role in climate and energy policy allowed it to maintain a prominent role in developing the policy agenda. As Hassan ⟨Ψ 2078⟩ notes, "the never-ending debate between neofunctionalists and intergovernmentalists may not be resolved, but it seems to be tipping to the former, yet again" ⟨Ψ p. 233⟩. The European Commission's leadership drove the EU's climate agenda to meet the decarbonisation targets that it had missed in 2050. This prompted the Commission to develop the Revised Neutral Gas Directive which allowed for the consumption of blue hydrogen for years to come. Kim ⟨Ψ 2106⟩ suggests that the cultural, political, and geopolitical factors that sustained hydrogen came to the fore and shaped the EU's ethical stance towards the fuel—its consumption was reintroduced as ethically permissible. International relations scholars interpreted this as yet another case of how the socially constructed values of political communities are flexible, despite the pressure to change.

Geoeconomic considerations were also of key importance in the EU's support for hydrogen, as it saw to establish global benchmarks and trading hubs ⟨Fitzgerald and Duda Ψ 2058⟩. The EU looked to turn the narrative that hydrogen would be a key fuel in the future into geoeconomic power by controlling related trading activities and financial flows. Schulz ⟨Ψ 2061⟩ shows how this was the basis of the "resource for power" ⟨Ψ p. 247⟩ mentality the EU had adopted towards the energy carrier. This was a part of its bid to establish TTF (Netherlands) and Gaspool (Germany) as the centres of hydrogen ahead of TG (Torgovlya Gazom; Russia) and SHE (Shanghai Hydrogen Exchange; China). Schulz's ⟨Ψ 2061⟩ ideas were shaped by the work of the Interaction School that emerged at the time. Proponents of the approach proposed that international political relations have used geography inadequately and called for the need to more thoroughly incorporate the environment and climate into political thinking, as opposed to thinking about the spatial boundaries of states and the geographic dimension of their strategic action ⟨Macaraeg Ψ 2057⟩. Thus, the implications of human–environment relations should be at the core of all political theory—in a sense, it was a reiteration of ecological approaches, but had a much broader impact. This would thus lead policymakers to consider the "need" for hydrogen on ecological grounds, which could then underpin their political economic power ⟨Schulz Ψ 2061⟩.

7   The Impact of Nuclear Fusion

2073 marked a pivotal year for energy studies, international relations, and, more broadly, global society: it was the year when the first high capacity, but relatively compact and modular nuclear fusion reactor began to operate. The facility in southern France was developed as a part of the International Thermonuclear Experimental Reactor (ITER) project. The unit had an installed capacity of 3 GW and was of historic significance. Lewis Strauss' 1954 assumption that with nuclear fission electricity will be "too cheap to meter" was reinvigorated with the launch of fusion, which offered a potentially much safer source of essentially unlimited carbon–neutral energy. Nuclear fusion, coupled with the ongoing hydrogenation of societies around the world offered to substantially curtail emissions within a relatively quick timespan. By this point average global temperatures had risen by 2.3 °C (IPCC Ψ 2118), wreaking havoc globally, rendering most of the Global South uninhabitable, and prompting unwelcomed migration flows to the Global North. However, it seemed that the silver bullet to decarbonisation suddenly became available. Oliveira et al. (Ψ 2074) suggested that the fuel would "quickly scale" and "shift the global energy regime to a low carbon and sustainable system" (p. 5). This stood in contrast to neo-green transition theory thinkers (Matthews Ψ 2074) suggesting that uptake would be gradual at best, given the earlier findings of green transition scholarship, cultural theory, and critical geopolitics—these suggested that politics reduces the pace of technologically and economically determined change.

Countries involved with ITER (EU, India, Japan, China, Russia, South Korea, and the USA) quickly devised a policy to roll out the technology. Leaders looked to keep the change in average surface temperature below 3.5 °C by the end of the century. The technological cooperation brought new theorisations of international relations that drew on the acceptance of common norms and values subjugated to certain goals (Cossa and Han Ψ 2075). Cooperationists were a branch of the Interaction School that looked at the technology-based cooperation prompted by environmental events that conditioned international political economic relations. ITER-related cooperation was a key instance of this, but so were fora such as the Global Hydrogen Network or the UN Department for Geoengineering. The problem with this theoretical approach, as shown by *inter alia* Dončić (Ψ 2076), was that once the technology was developed, cooperation dissipated, and governments tended to pursue deployment without cooperation—behaving in a manner suggested by realist scholars.

Focus on technological diffusion and decarbonisation was at the top of political agendas between 2080 and 2100. This was the point by which effectively all countries were in possession of the technology necessary to decarbonise, while bilateral agreements that financed projects were signed between governments and companies. Zambrano (Ψ 2102) argues that this is best described as the emergence of *liberal realism*, where countries had to channel all resources to eliminate carbon emissions, develop carbon negative technologies, and take climate adaptation measures, while cooperation between states and private enterprises were prevalent in politics, economics, and technology. The objective of these engagements was to further domestic decarbonisation agendas, since the enemy was common and solutions were shared, but action was independently taken by states. This disposition underpinned some stability, but also, as states acted quite independently, raised the risk of confrontation. Hydrogen was such a case, since the consumption of fossil fuels was not permissible anymore, which led to the suspension of natural gas-based hydrogen markets in the matter of a few years ⟨Thompson Ψ 2103⟩.

8 CONCLUDING THOUGHTS

The intellectual trajectory of energy-based international relations reflected a number of new ideas and innovations, but these continued to be deeply rooted in tenets of liberal, realist, and critical theory prevalent in preceding centuries. The core addition was the gradual inclusion of more ecological thinking. Climate change functioned as the catalyser for this process, as it fundamentally recalibrated the environment actors could operate in, altering the social relations linked to fossil fuel consumption. Hydrogen was at a unique intersection of theories, since its various forms underpinned multiple strands of scholarship. Depending on the object of study being green or blue hydrogen, the political implications were fundamentally different. It was simultaneously a key component of an energy transition that enhanced the self-sufficiency of states and a source of energy that sustained hydrocarbon producer–consumer relations. As critical theorists have continuously argued, this reflects capital's continued appropriation of narratives that support its expansion and the necessary exploitation of resources that underpin its uptake.

Hydrogen also showed the deep cleavage that can emerge between the "real" and the "socially constructed". The waves of hydrogen hype show how politics can shape the role of a fuel and distance it from the technological needs of the energy system. The rise of hydrogen was paradoxical from an energy standpoint, since electrification was broadly possible by the middle of the twenty-first century. In this sense, it was, a postmodern fuel, reliant on social construction, and detached from the physical and economic rationale of the energy system. On the other hand, as this chapter has shown, many have argued that it played a profound role in dampening the blow of the energy transition and accelerating the process as well. With the rise of nuclear fusion pink and green hydrogen emerged as the dominant forms of the resource, underpinning theories of international politics arguing that hydrogen would allow for the energy independence of states, enhancing the risk of conflict given the decline in interdependencies. Now, in 2122, the Globe's energy system is largely carbon neutral. However, the carbon dioxide emissions that have accumulated in the atmosphere since the Industrial Revolution led to a 2.5 °C average temperature increase, which has made a large swath of the globe uninhabitable. Scholars must now turn to the next challenge at hand: the politics of carbon removal to allow for humanity to reclaim the Globe.

LITERATURE

Achinson, J. ⟨Ψ 2033⟩. *Beyond the Social Sciences and into Culture*. Oxford University Press, Oxford, UK.

Anderson, K. ⟨Ψ 2041⟩. 'Talks in the City of Light Allow More Heat'. *Nature*, vol. 840, no. 11, p. 109.

Badawi, M. ⟨Ψ 2044⟩. *The History of Energy Studies*. John Hopkins University, Baltimore, MD, USA.

Balmaceda, M. ⟨Ψ 2029⟩. *The Materiality-based Political Economics of Energy*. Columbia University Press, New York, NY, USA.

Barry, B. ⟨Ψ 2024⟩. *Beyond the Socio-Technical: The Ideology and Politics of Energy Transitions*. Routledge, Abingdon, UK.

Bradshaw, M. ⟨Ψ 2029⟩. 'It's Not Only About Geopolitics!' *Energy Research and Social Sciences*, vol. 172.

Brown, N. ⟨Ψ 2056⟩. 'The Political Economics of Town Gas: A Historical Overview of England'. *The English Historical Review*, vol. 171, no. 718.

Cossa, M., & Han, J. ⟨Ψ 2075⟩. *Cooperationism in International Relations: An Introduction*. Oxford University Press, Oxford, UK.

Cramp, P. (2022). 'More Interlinks, More Hydrogen'. *World Politics*, vol. 74, no. 4, pp. 511–532.

Danesh, P. ⟨Ψ 2027⟩. 'A New Culture of Energy'. *South Atlantic Quarterly*, vol. 127, no. 2, pp. 276–292.

Danesh, P., Szabo, J., & Brückmann, R. ⟨Ψ 2036⟩. 'A Hydrogen Culture?' *Hydrogen Policy*, vol. 12, no. 1, pp. 54–76.

Demaria, F., & Kallis, G. ⟨Ψ 2045⟩. 'The Global Green New Deal should be a Deal for Degrowth'. *Ecological Economics*, vol. 473.

Dončić, P. ⟨Ψ 2076⟩. 'Dissipating of Cooperationism: The Case of ITER, Hydrogen, and Geoengineering' in *Technology and International Relations in the 21st Century*, Petrov, V. & Smith, K. Routledge, Abingdon, UK.

Fitzgerald, P. ⟨Ψ 2049⟩. 'The Geoeconomics of Hydrogen'. *European Journal of International Relations*, vol. 56, no. 2, pp. 213–243.

Fitzgerald, P., & Duda, S. ⟨Ψ 2058⟩. 'The Geoeconomics of Hydrogen Pricing'. *Oxford Institute of Energy Studies*.

FotE ⟨Ψ 2027⟩. 'The Futility of Hydrogen'. *Friends of the Earth Report*, San Francisco, CA, USA.

Gabard, H. ⟨Ψ 2028⟩. 'The Carbon Lock-in Revisited'. *Energy Policy*, vol. 56, no. 5, pp. 384–399.

Geels, F. (2002) 'Technological Transitions as Evolutionary Reconfiguration Processes: A Multi-Level Perspective and a Case-Study'. *Research Policy*, vol. 31, no. 8, pp. 1257–1274.

Geels, F., Kern, F., Sovacool, B., Szabo, J., & Turnheim, B. ⟨Ψ 2027⟩. 'The Diffusion of Hydrogen: Key Global Insights'. *Energy Research and Social Sciences*, vol. 147.

Haas, T. (2019). 'Struggles in European Union energy politics: A Gramscian Perspective on Power in Energy Transitions'. *Energy Research and Social Sciences*, vol. 48, pp. 66–74.

Haas, N. ⟨Ψ 2026⟩. 'Hydrogen: The Key to Energy Autonomy?' *Energy Policy*, vol. 182, pp.

Hassan, M. ⟨Ψ 2078⟩ 'Will It Ever End? The Neofunctionalist–Intergovernmentalist Debate'. *Review of International Studies*, vol. 104, no. 2, pp. 228–251.

IEA [International Energy Agency]. 〈Ψ 2027〉. *World Energy Outlook 2027*. IEA/OECD, Paris, France.

IEA [International Energy Agency]. 〈Ψ 2118〉. *World Energy Outlook 2118*. IEA/OECD, Paris, France.

IRENA. (2022). 'Geopolitics of the Energy Transformation: The Hydrogen Factor'. *International Renewable Energy Agency*, Abu Dhabi, UAE.

IPCC. (2021). 'Sixth Assessment Report'. *International Panel on Climate Change*, Geneva, Switzerland.

IPCC. 〈Ψ 2040〉. 'Ninth Assessment Report'. *International Panel on Climate Change*, Geneva, Switzerland.

IPCC. 〈Ψ 2118〉. 'Twenty-Second Assessment Report'. *International Panel on Climate Change*, Geneva, Switzerland.

Johnstone, P., & Flynn, T. 〈Ψ 2033〉. 'Oil in the First World War: The Beginning of the end'. *Energy Research and Social Sciences*, vol. 222.

Jordan, M. 〈Ψ 2078〉. 'Energy and Climate Change: Beyond Modernism and Postmodernism?' *Theory, Culture, and Society*, vol. 264, no. 1, pp. 64–83.

Jørgensen, T. 〈Ψ 2031〉. 'Energy Mercantilism', in Khun, P. (ed.) *Thinking about Energy: How Energy Economics Evolved*. Palgrave, London, UK.

Kern, C. 〈Ψ 2055〉. 'The Role of the State in the Diffusion of Technology: A Comparative Case of Hydrogen in the USA and Germany'. *Research Policy*, vol. 84, no. 2, pp. 211–227.

Keynes, J. M. (1936). *The General Theory of Employment, Interest and Money*. Palgrave Macmillan, London, UK.

Kim, C. 〈Ψ 2029〉. 'The Realpolitik of Renewables' in Goldthau, A. & Eicke, L. (eds.) *The Changing International Relations of Energy*. Polity Press, Cambridge, UK.

Kim, P. 〈Ψ 2106〉. 'Energy is Not Just Energy, So Neither It Hydrogen'. *The New Energy Journal*, vol. 27, no. 2, pp. 61–83.

Klein, N. 〈Ψ 2041〉. *Still On Fire (And Why We Have Done Little About It)*. Simon & Schuster, New York, NY, USA.

Korver, K. 〈Ψ 2075〉. 'The State of the Global Energy Transition Sixty Years after Paris'. *Climate Policy*, vol. 76, no. 3, pp. 156–171.

Kovács, Zs., & Kucera, P. 〈Ψ 2057〉. *Eclipsing Reason: Responses to Climate Change*. Verso Books, London, UK and New York, NY, USA.

Lavertue, F., Levesque, F., & Yin, J. 〈Ψ 2046〉. 'The Role of the State in the Niche to Landscape Transition: The Case of Hydrogen'. *Technological Forecasting and Social Change*, vol. 509.

Lestari, M. 〈Ψ 2105〉. *Hydrogen: A Century after the Hydrogen Fuel Initiative*. Department of Energy, Washington DC, USA.

Levy, C. 〈Ψ 2034〉. *Interpreting Energy*. Routledge, Abingdon, UK.

Liebrich, M. (2020). 'Liebreich: Separating Hype from Hydrogen – Part Two: The Demand Side'. *Bloomberg NEF*.

Macaraeg, J. 〈Ψ 2057〉. *The Interaction School: Geopolitics after Climate Change*. Oxford University Press, Oxford, UK.

Malm, A. (2016). *Fossil Capitalism*. Verso Books, London, UK and New York, NY, USA.

Malm, A. (2017). *The Progress of This Storm*. Verso Books, London, UK and New York, NY, USA.

Matthews, M. 〈Ψ 2074〉. *Still not Recognised: The Politics of Green Transitions*. Praeger, Westport, CT, USA.

Mazzucato, M. (2013). *The Entrepreneurial State*. Anthem Press, London, UK.

Miller, A. (2022). 'Forging Relations through Hydrogen Trade'. *Foreign Affairs*, vol. 101, no. 3.

Muñoz, J. (Ψ 2029). *See! High Rates of Renewable Penetration are Possible*. Greenpeace, London, UK.

Navarro, J. C. (Ψ 2051). *A Degrowth-based Critical Approach to Energy*. Pluto Press, London, UK.

NE (Ψ 2118). Statistical Review of World Energy: Total Data 1951–2117. *Next Energy*.

O'Conner, S. (Ψ 2027). 'Energy Trade and Global Peace'. *Energy and Geopolitics*, vol. 4, no. 3, pp. 146–162.

OECD. (Ψ 2030). *Assessing a Decade of Hydrogen Investments: A Comprehensive Report*. Organisation for Economic Co-operation and Development, Paris, France.

Oliveira, J., Santos, M., Bakker, J., & Abu, P. (Ψ 2074). 'Scaling Technology: Hydrogen in-Light of Nuclear Fusion'. *New Research Policy*, vol. 7, no. 2.

Overland, I., & O'Sullivan, M. (Ψ 2025). *A New Age of Energy-based Geopolitics*. Harvard University Press, Cambridge, MA, USA.

Ozol, G. (Ψ 2046). *The Green Social Contract*. Wiley Blackwell Publishers, Hoboken, NJ, USA.

Patel, I., & Kallis, G. (Ψ 2054). *(International) Social Relations in Degrowth*. Routledge, Abingdon, UK.

Pendergrass, D., & Vetesse, T. (Ψ 2031). *Half-Earth Socialism: A Roadmap*. Verso Books, London, UK and New York, NY, USA.

Pethő, A. (Ψ 2058). 'Hydrogen Market-Building: Infrastructure in Support of Neoliberalism' in *The Handbook of Hydrogen*, Nowitzki, D. & Jaco, W. Palgrave Macmillan, London, UK.

Popescu, F. (Ψ 2066). 'The Realism of Hydrogen'. *Foreign Affairs*, vol. 145, no. 2.

Santos, J. (Ψ 2043). 'Fossil Capital and Climate Agreements: Fifty Years On'. *Climate Policy*, vol. 44, no. 1, pp. 45–62.

Schmid, (Ψ 2023, n.p.). *Wall Street Journal*

Schulz, M. (Ψ 2061). *Liberalism, Strategy and Geography*. Cambridge University Press, Cambridge, UK.

Slobodian, Q. (Ψ 2060). 'A Century of European Market Building'. *N+1 Magazine*, vol. 198.

Shivaram, P. (Ψ 2044). 'Policy Has to be Ecological, Not Only Theory'. *Nature*, vol. 877, no. 11, p. 598.

Smil, V. (Ψ 2028). *Hydrogen*. John Wiley & Sons, Hoboken, NJ, USA.

Stacey, D. (Ψ 2044). 'Hydrogen: Captured by Capital to Sustain Fossil Fuels'. *Capitalism, Nature, Socialism*, vol. 63, no. 2.

Szabo, J. (Ψ 2025). *An Environmental History of Gas: From Lock-In to Lock-In*. Palgrave Macmillan, London, UK.

Takahashi, A. (Ψ 2027). *A Comprehensive Analysis of OECD Hydrogen Strategies*. The Institute of Energy Economics, Tokyo, Japan.

The New Collective. (Ψ 2049). *We Won't Continue: Resisting the Status Quo*. Verso Books, London, UK and New York, NY, USA.

Thomas, R. (2018). 'The Development of the Manufactured Gas Industry in Europe' in *History of the European Oil and Gas Industry* (eds.) Craig, J., Gerali, F., & Sorkhabi, R., Bath, UK, pp. 137–164.

Thomas, P. ⟨Ψ 2083⟩. 'The Waves of the Hydrogen Hype'. *Hydrogen Policy*, vol. 9, no. 2, pp. 117–129.

Thompson, J. ⟨Ψ 2103⟩. *The Unfolding Geopolitics of Hydrogen*. Oxford Institute of Energy Studies, Oxford, UK.

Unruh, G. C. (2000). 'Understanding Carbon Lock-In'. *Energy Policy*, vol. 28, no. 12, pp. 817–830.

Van de Graaf, T., & Goldthau, A. ⟨Ψ 2031⟩. 'The International Political Economics of Hydrogen: More Oil or More Renewable?' *Belfer Center Working Paper Series*, no. 78.

Van de Graaf, T., Overland, I., Scholten, D., & Westphal, K. (2020). 'The New Oil? The Geopolitics and International Governance of Hydrogen'. *Energy Research & Social Science*, vol. 71.

van Hulst, N. (2018). *Hydrogen, the Missing Link in the Energy Transition*. International Energy Agency, Paris, France.

Verne, J. (1874). *The Mysterious Island*. Project Gutenberg.

Volkov, D., & Jones, P. (eds.) ⟨Ψ 2047⟩. *The Sixth Kondratieff Wave: Conception or reality?* Edward Elgar Publishing, Cheltenham, UK.

Wallerstein, I. (2014). *Historical Capitalism*. Verso Books, London, UK and New York, NY, USA.

Wilson, S., Carlson, A., & Szeman, I. (2017). *Petrocultures: Oil, Politics, Culture*. McGill Queen's Press, Montreal, Canada.

Yergin, D. (1990). *The Prize: The Epic Quest for Oil, Money, and Power*. Simon and Schuster, New York, NY, USA.

Zambrano, F. ⟨Ψ 2102⟩. *Liberal Realism: Cooperating Outward, Acting Inward*. Brookings Institution, Washington, DC, USA.

The Degrowth Transition in Latin America: Deurbanised, Autonomous City-States in 2122—An Invitation

Joshua Hurtado Hurtado

May 1, 2122
Alejandro "Don Loro" Casar
Professor of Intelligent Computational Foresight
St. Lucia QLD, 4072, Brisbane, Australia

Dear Alex,

We last saw each other over a decade ago, when you presented at the 18th ICF Conference in Norway the results of the Zero-disease City project. I believe you now reside in Brisbane, which is hopefully doing better than other regions of Australia. I know the storms and flooding have been particularly intense this year, so I hope you and your family remain safe.

I am writing to you because I wish to invite you to join our recently established (and expanding) research centre in the Caracol Network in Chiapas. After the intense droughts and fires that overwhelmed Western Canada back in 2112, I went back to Chiapas to see whether the political experiment started by the Zapatista Movement in 1994, which also gained traction in the 2020s with the Zapatista journeys throughout Europe, and found renewed force in the 2070s with the emergence of the New Zapatista Movement, had consolidated its quasi-utopian aims of creating regenerative city-states free from

---

J. Hurtado Hurtado (✉)
Interdisciplinary Environmental Sciences, Faculty of Agriculture and Forestry,
University of Helsinki, Helsinki, Finland
e-mail: joshua.hurtado@helsinki.fi

© The Author(s), under exclusive license to Springer Nature Switzerland AG 2023
L. Horn et al. (eds.), *The Palgrave Handbook of Global Politics in the 22nd Century*, https://doi.org/10.1007/978-3-031-13722-8_15

256 J. HURTADO HURTADO

capitalist and state oppression. I happily report that, though significant challenges persist, the Chiapas' Caracol Network is now thriving, and I consider it a leading example for other Latin American city-states in terms of economic organisation, political participation and socio-ecological relations.

I would like you to join the research centre to help with some current problems experienced by the Caracol Network. I know your expertise in Intelligent Computational Foresight, particularly as applied to public health, could help in adapting the buildings with monitoring devices and self-repairing nano-materials, which I think might mitigate the growth of mould inside homes and prevent diseases. Similarly, you are internationally known for anticipating the trajectory of transmissible diseases while factoring in human agency with computational methods, and your presence here could protect the health of the population of the Caracol Network. This is important because we lack cutting-edge medical centres, and we are at moderate risk for the appearance of zoonotic diseases.

I know that you might be sceptical of joining us given the radically different ways of organising and living here compared to the remaining Western, anglophone states. Yet, once I explain why I think the Caracol Network in Chiapas can be considered a radical socio-ecological project that became a Real Utopia (Wright 2010), you might share the same enthusiasm I have in helping the revolutionary inhabitants of this network of city-states to lead flourishing lives.

In this letter, I describe some early academic literature that offered some precedents for the current Latin American city-states. I also explain how the planetary crises led to the rise of the "green states", as well as their shortcomings and eventual dissolution. Finally, I delve into my experience in the Chiapas Caracol Network, which hopefully will inspire you to join us.

1 EARLY IDEAS FOR THE REORGANISATION OF SOCIETIES TOWARDS ALIGNMENT WITH OUR BIOPHYSICAL SURROUNDINGS: DEGROWTH, DEURBANISATION AND DECOLONIAL APPROACHES

You may be surprised, Alex, that many ideas and proposals that advocated for a deep, socio-ecological reorganisation of societies were developed in the 1990s and 2000s, before most of the planetary crises that engulfed most of the Earth really manifested themselves. One could identify the altermondialist movement, the Seattle to Brussels Network and the emergence of the transnational campaign People's Global Action. Solidarity across networks were an important phenomenon linking together anti-globalisation movements in North America (e.g. the Battle of Seattle) with the Zapatista movement in Mexico (Johnston and Laxer 2003). A striking feature of these ideas was the precision of their foresight: had their ideas been implemented soon after they first emerged, the impact of the planetary crises—specifically climate change, biodiversity loss and ocean acidification—could have been significantly mitigated.

In the 1990s, after the Uruguay Round of multilateral trade negotiations, economic growth had become the core focus of policymaking from most world governments. It entrenched itself in governments, international organisations such as the WTO and the general public, becoming not only hegemonic but also reaching the status of societal goal (Schmelzer 2016). A counter-hegemonic movement, ideational framework and field of research known as degrowth emerged around this time that openly challenged the dominance of economic growth in public life. A key idea from degrowth was the incompatibility of economic growth with the Earth's ecological limits (Kallis 2017). Degrowth's ideas integrated a social and political-economic perspective to sustainability transitions, considering the need to bring human activities within a "safe operating space" known then as the Planetary Boundaries (Steffen et al. 2015) while also addressing how the dynamics of capitalist societies exerted pressure on the Earth's ecological limits.

Degrowth sought the equitable downscaling of production and consumption through collective and deliberative means, and to reduce the centrality of markets and commercial exchanges to the organisation of human activity (Schneider et al. 2010). Hence, its proposals emphasised social and political collective action instead of purely technocratic solutions (Brand et al. 2021). Achieving this was considered necessary to reduce the pressures of economic activity on the biosphere and reduce carbon emissions, pollution and stop widespread biodiversity loss. In addition to the critique of growth as a societal goal, degrowth also offered a critique of capitalism, GDP as the key indicator of success of a society and the commodification of human and non-human natural life.

Proponents of the degrowth movement frequently put forward some measures that could incite a transition towards degrowth societies. Videira et al. (2014) focused on possible pathways for a degrowth transition from a systems-thinking perspective. They outlined the complementarities between nine degrowth proposals, which included house sharing, work sharing, establishing resource sanctuaries, moratoria on large infrastructures, restrictions to advertising, limits on international trade, 100% reserve banks, localised cooperatives that practice economic democracy and maximum and minimum income levels. More detailed policy proposals were identified by Cosme et al. (2017), which classified them according to general-level degrowth goals: (1) reducing the environmental impact of human activities, (2) redistributing income and wealth within and between countries, and (3) transitioning to a convivial and participatory society grounded in reproductive economies of care and commoning practices. Nonetheless, none of this early literature, except for Timothée Parrique's (2019) contribution, coalesced into a coherent programme for degrowth policies. Parrique, in turn, suggested that any programme for degrowth should start with a challenge to three institutions of growth-addicted societies: property, work and money, from which more specific and context-dependent measures should emerge.

Along with these policy proposals, ideas regarding the scale and political organisation of degrowth societies were also central for the degrowth movement. Small ecological communities and cities where direct participatory democracy was possible were favoured over large-scale, complex political entities like the nation state (Latouche 2009; Romano 2012). Demonetising activities and establishing networks of reciprocal relations was also considered essential, because it would free people from being enslaved to wage labour and allow them to participate in political deliberation and cooperative activities (Heikkurinen et al. 2019). Although some criticised the possibly anti-democratic, homogenising political imaginaries of degrowth (Romano 2012), others asserted that political life in degrowth societies does not imply a peaceful end-state without diverse perspectives, but instead encourages continuous deliberation about the political projects of a degrowth community and how such projects could facilitate wellbeing and alignment with the biosphere (Kallis and March 2015).

Parallel to degrowth, another movement and research field gained traction in the mid-2010s to the early 2030s: deurbanisation. The deurbanisation movement focused on redesigning cities to become regenerative—it explicitly went beyond weak sustainability proposals and integrated ideas of economic democracy, permaculture, social and political ecology and sustainable urbanism. The deurbanisation movement emerged with a collective of practitioners trained by a core group of de-urban designers based around the world, and their ideas gradually resonated with certain social groups that considered urban lifestyles to be fundamentally unsustainable and harmful for the wellbeing of both human beings and the biosphere. Deurbanisation sought to regenerate and transform cities, which had developed and expanded under the paradigm of urbanisation. From deurbanisation's perspective, urbanisation had become synonymous with the "exploitation of vulnerable people, commodification and pollution of nature, and accumulation of power" (Sadri and Zeybekoglu 2018, p. 209), particularly when combined with the forces of capitalism. Hence, deurbanisation explicitly sought to transform cities into eco-communities and permanent habitats, thereby eliminating the harms of urbanisation and cultivating diverse civic values that actively attempted to reach harmony with nature (Sadri and Zeybekoglu 2018).

In order to align human settlements, specifically cities, with the surrounding biophysical conditions, deurbanisation advocated for human settlements to "harvest their own water; produce their own energy and food; regenerate and enrich their natural environments and their ecosystems; establish their own local economies, governmental, social, cultural, educational institutions (invisible structures)" and create ethical linkages between the deurbanised cities' inhabitants (Sadri and Zeybekoglu 2018, p. 213). Specific proposals related of deurbanisation included:

- Shrinking cities' sizes to reduce pressures on the biophysical surroundings.
- Developing local intelligence that recognised the biophysical conditions of a territory and developed plans to align human activity with those conditions.
- Engaging in initiatives of community-supported agriculture and urban food gardening.
- Favouring the creation of local agroecology cooperatives that display democratic decision-making processes.
- Designing, caring for and cultivating food forests or equivalent spaces with the aim of increasing biodiversity, economic vitality and fostering shared ownership of sources of food.
- Governance through democratic assemblies at the municipal level.
- Education committees that fostered post-anthropocentric mindsets in citizens.

These two compatible movements were, however, often criticised for their Eurocentric perspectives ⟨Menem Ψ 2025⟩ and (Muradian 2019). This is why, within both movements, some called for deeper dialogue with the Global South and the *re*-indigenisation of these movements' ideas ⟨Sadri and Zeybekoglu Ψ 2028⟩ and (Singh 2019). While North–South academic dialogues did occur (Kothari et al. 2019) and ⟨Sadri and Zeybekoglu Ψ 2028⟩, the ideas of both movements did not become widespread in Latin America, where conceptualisations such as Buen Vivir and Vida Plena—indigenous worldviews that describe community-centric and ecologically-balanced lifestyles—were better known. Hence, degrowth and deurbanisation in Latin America remained fringe movements for the next two decades, relegated to academic circles and progressive social movements. Their perceived regressive, anti-modern ideas, as well as a lack of coherent policy programmes, led to a marginalisation of these movements in mainstream political debates in the region.

2   2040–2070: Planetary Crises and the Rise of the "Green States" in Latin America

I know, Alex, that some of your earliest research involved mapping out the decision-making processes of different stakeholders in Latin America when facing the planetary crises, so you may have some familiarity with the following historical events. The effects of the planetary crises fuelled the consolidation of the climate justice movements in several Latin American countries. Previous decades saw these movements severely hampered by authoritarian policies in countries such as Mexico, Colombia and Brazil. Moreover, organised crime had committed several murders and enforced disappearances of climate justice leaders (Querales Ψ 2040). However, after the increased frequency of droughts, floods, heat waves and fires resulted in severe pollution problems and disruption to food systems, the need for urgent actions became clear. These problems started disrupting the daily activities and lifestyles of people in big urban areas, such as in Buenos Aires, São Paulo, Santiago de Chile and Mexico City, among others, and the planetary crises became significantly more visible to the general population.

Some widely mediatised events brought the severity of these crises to public awareness. For example, the Andean drought of 2036, which decreased rainfall that year to 20% of the average levels in the 2020s, led to a loss estimated to be up to 70% of agricultural production and livestock for the Andean countries (Rebollo Ψ 2039). This disrupted food systems in Bolivia, Colombia, Ecuador, Perú and Venezuela, and protests erupted in the capital cities of these countries in late 2036 as a result of food supply shortages. Core demands of these protests focused on insufficient actions taken by those countries' governments to undergo sustainability transitions, inadequate planning that did not prevent the shortages, continued reliance on fossil fuels and concern over continued economic practices that relied on mining and land-use change (Courdup Ψ 2041). By 2043, Mexico City had sunk 54 feet from its level in the year 2000. This event raised public awareness of the damages of water extraction from the underground in metropolises (Solano Ψ 2045).

On the basis of these events, De Armas ⟨Ψ 2072⟩ argues that "green political movements", spearheaded by previously marginal climate justice movements, finally entered the mainstream political debates in Latin America towards the end of the 2030s and the early 2040s. They consisted of coalitions of bottom-up movements, civil society organisations, circular economy businesses, cooperatives, and young, progressive politicians that prioritised ecological thinking and intergenerational ethical perspectives. These movements were united beyond the national borders of their respective countries by the aim to mitigate the negative impacts of the planetary crises on their populations and build-up resilience to severe climate events. They also heavily emphasised the need to "green the economy", recognising that much of the Latin American economies' production processes were energy-intensive and that cities needed to be redesigned to make them ecologically benign.

From 2048 to 2060, these political movements participated in and won national elections in several Latin American countries, most notably in Argentina, Brazil, Chile, Uruguay, Colombia, Ecuador, Costa Rica, Guatemala and Mexico. Their campaigns were collectively referred to as The Green Decision phenomenon, and their message in national elections was clear: survival and wellbeing were dependent on successfully undergoing sustainability transitions, and the political platforms of these movements were the only way of achieving them (Andrianopoulos Ψ 2069). The success of green parties or coalitions in the national elections of one country ushered the same success in neighbouring countries. By 2060, about two-thirds of Latin American countries had a government with policy programmes oriented to stimulate a sustainability transition. This phenomenon came to be known as The Green Tide (Arnarsson Ψ 2065).

The implementation of these policy programmes across the region led to "the rise of the green states": Latin American states which aimed to apply a science-based, systemic perspective to sustainability transitions (De Armas Ψ 2072). They funded large-scale infrastructure projects to redesign cities and allow for the monitoring of energy and waste flows, they increased the budgets in their Ministries in charge of environmental issues, they promoted widespread campaigns aimed at fostering ecologically benign diets for their populations and they passed legislation that established forbidden zones for human activity to allow for the restoration of ecosystems.

Although the commitment to pursue a sustainability transition was apparent in those Latin American governments that had a green political movement in power, some academic circles and social movements criticised the green states for following an ecomodernist paradigm (Barajas and Elizondo Ψ 2068). Despite their appreciation for their government's efforts in addressing widespread ecological problems, criticism was directed at a perceived overly technocratic approach to solving them, without simultaneously fostering enough cultural, political and economic changes in their respective societies. These critics foresaw that an emphasis on technical and market-based solutions to the detriment of social and political interventions would yield limited effects and would hinder serious attempts at reaching societal-scale alignment with the biosphere (Asociación Latinoamericana para los Estudios del Cambio Climático Ψ 2065).

3   2070–2090: The Failure and Dissolution of the "Green States" and the Emergence of Latin American City-States and Bioregions

For a limited time, Alex, it seemed that Latin American states were finally taking seriously the urgency of taking decisive measures to bring human activity into harmony with ecological conditions. Nonetheless, the ecomodernist paradigm under which they operated proved to be their most severe oversight. Their failure to account for cultural, social and political factors, combined with the deepening harshness of the planetary crises, directly led to the dissolution of several of these states and the rise of new city-states that incorporated ideas from degrowth and deurbanisation to come into being. This is elaborated upon below.

De Armas (Ψ 2080) described the political, economic and environmental crises that plagued the Latin American green states in the late 2060s and early 2070s and drove country-level and regional-level political instability. The green states promised to undergo sustainability transitions, but could not accomplish them for several reasons:

- The government bureaucracies were unable to overcome corruption and inefficient resource-allocation mechanisms, and some political leaders publicly faced corruption accusations that undermined their "green" political projects.
- The implementation of some policies did not lead to perceived tangible results, which resulted in public perception of inefficiency and ineffectiveness. For example, between 2061 and 2064, several Latin American countries tried to redesign the infrastructure of buildings to incorporate vertical food gardens, but such measures did not meaningfully allow access to enough nutritious food for those with low incomes. Hence, this and similar initiatives were considered useless by a majority of the population.
- Political leaders in big Latin American countries such as Argentina, Brazil and Mexico, did not effectively mediate competing interests, particularly those of big corporations (which were most inclined to pursue technological and market-based solutions to sustainability problems) and those of civil society organisations and bottom-up movements (which were looking for more radical policies that stimulated the energy transitions).
- Intense heat waves starting in 2067 resulted in a massive death toll in the tens of thousands of people each summer. The most affected countries were Bolivia, Perú, Colombia, Paraguay and Chile, all of which reported upwards of 50,000 deaths due to heat waves in the summer months.
- Economic shocks derived from limits imposed by some Latin American governments to extractive economic activity, such as mining, drilling and deforestation, resulted in increased poverty and inequality in many of the Latin American green states. Big countries such as Mexico, Brazil and Argentina saw the percentage of their population living in poverty rise to around 65%. Smaller countries, such as Colombia, Perú and Bolivia, saw increases in poverty of up to 75% in some cases. This triggered political discontent and upheaval, with governments, big corporations and upper classes being blamed for their incompetency in managing the situation. The latter were seen by the majority of each countries' population as being the only ones who benefitted from the attempts to stimulate a sustainability transition. This deepened a general sense across Latin America that sustainability transitions, although necessary, were harsh processes that involved suffering.
- A phenomenon that remains puzzling to scientists occurred in many freshwater bodies in Latin America at different points between 2065 and 2069: a purple-coloured, mucus-like substance covered lakes and caused the deaths of most aquatic organisms residing in them. Human communities reliant on these lakes were severely affected, with some human communities becoming sick and most of them facing food scarcity due to the loss of food sources caused by this phenomenon. National and subnational governments provided aid to these communities, but it

quickly became evident both to the members of these communities and allies in social movements and civil society organisations that any long-term attempt at aligning human activity with the surrounding ecological conditions would need to have both localised, regenerative solutions and macro-scale cooperation.

Lozano et al. (Ψ 2082), in their seminal book *The New Green Anarchism: Ecological Crises and the Dissolution of the Latin American Green States*, argued that these and other crises incited the formation of ecological-anarchist movements that sought to reorganise Latin American societies into small-scale, deeply democratic political entities that respected to the greatest extent possible the integrity of ecosystems. The premise supporting these movements' goals was that smaller political entities and smaller populations would be able to effectively manage their natural means of subsistence and formulate more effective socio-ecological policies. They envisioned governance through democratic assemblies and networked municipalities after having abolished centralised, top-down governing entities. This would yield self-organising societies attuned to their biophysical surroundings, since they would be able to systematically map, distribute and regenerate the natural means of subsistence. Their imaginaries were inspired by Murray Bookchin's green anarchism and democratic municipalism (Bookchin 2006, 2021).

The first of these movements emerged in Bolivia, in 2071, with the name of *Alianza Popular para la Supervivencia y Vida Plena*, and other movements across Latin America soon followed. These movements embodied a pluralism of ideas and social groups, but all of them considered the modern state to be an archaic form of political organisation because its existence was predicated on the domination of and control over its members. Similarly, its territorial scale was ill-suited to address local, everyday problems, such as plentiful food for a city's population or pollution-free settlements. Accordingly, the ecological-anarchist movements found the Latin American green states' ineffective in guaranteeing the wellbeing of human and non-human beings alike. The initial leading groups in these movements were indigenous organisations, bottom-up peasant and permaculture organisations, the middle-class educated youth, environmentally focused civil society organisations and academics who focused on topics related to the planetary crises.

The ecological-anarchist movements took up many of the ideas of the climate justice movements from decades prior, and also obtained some inspiration from the earlier formulations on Buen Vivir, Vida Plena, Degrowth and Deurbanisation. Although, initially, these movements did not represent demands shared by the majority of the Latin American population, who prioritised everyday survival in a region with severe crises, they soon designed messages to gain widespread support from each country's population. For example, in Mexico in 2072, the New Zapatista Movement spearheaded the call for *Bienestar Regenerativo* (Regenerative Wellbeing), which linked the message of regenerative, ecologically benign practices with economic democracy, autonomy and wellbeing for all (including non-human beings) ⟨El Nuevo Movimiento Zapatista Ψ 2072⟩. The lightning-fast speed at which the *Bienestar Regenerativo* message spread across Mexico facilitated the formal separation of Chiapas from Mexico as a political entity, as there was enormous support from the population for such a political project. In the following years, tens of thousands of Mexicans left their origin state and asked to be admitted to Chiapas as a separate political entity, agreeing to adapt to the Chiapans' project of *Bienestar Regenerativo*. Under political pressure, Mexican leaders allowed some peripheral subnational states to separate politically from Mexico in the years 2073–2075, following the Chiapas model, on the condition that such separation was on the basis of the new political entities' capacity to create their own self-sustaining, socio-ecological political projects.

While reduced in territory, Mexico remained its own political entity after the separation of previous subnational states, including Chiapas. Most of the other Latin American states, however, dissolved under pressure from the ecological-anarchist movements and the overwhelming support they gained. In 2072 and 2073, transnational networks of these movements organised massive protests across the region. Thousands of protesters affiliated to the movements regularly occupied the metropolises' streets to demand effective governance solutions for socio-ecological problems. Some even turned violent, as in the Battle of Buenos Aires in 2072. Eventually, once the ecological-anarchist movements refined their message and gained support from different social groups, leaders in national governments were forced to meet with representatives of the movements. The movements' reasoning and demands were quite clear: smaller-scale, independent but cooperative political entities would be able to successfully face the socio-ecological challenges that the region was experiencing. From these movements' perspective, the state would not be able to find a one-size-fits-all solution to reach sustainable conditions at a macro level. The state, to maintain its existence and its governing structures, required the subjugation of the more-than-human world to a role of resources. Surpassing anthropocentric notions of nature-society relations was deemed necessary for survival, and the ecological-anarchist movements' proposal of symbiotic nature-society relations could only be accomplished with non-hierarchical, democratic governance networks that cultivated citizens' attunement to the biosphere's needs and sought to rehabilitate ecosystems.

While the specificities of the process varied according to each country, a common pattern was observed throughout the region. The representatives of the ecological-anarchist movements held summits with national and subnational political leaders and, after weeks of negotiations, they would agree on how each state would be dissolved and what subnational territories would belong to the new form of political entities: city-states with associated territories, consisting of natural resource areas and smaller cities and villages. Lozano et al. ⟨Ψ 2082⟩ described this process as the "De-Stating" of Latin America. Argentina was the first Latin American green state to declare "impossible conditions of governability", recognising that the multiple crises it was facing required localised, culturally specific responses instead of purely national-level measures, and announced its dissolution and reconfiguration into city-states on November 1, 2073. This was followed by Colombia on January 14, 2074, and Costa Rica on March 23, 2074. Between 2074 and 2080, neighbouring countries followed this path, becoming territories of independent city-states but united by historical, cultural and environmental ties ⟨Lozano et al. Ψ 2082⟩. Their organisation at higher levels only served a coordination function, with true decision-making power residing in local communities. In this sense, it was a reflection of democratic confederalism (Öcalan 2015) as practiced in Latin America.

What resulted from this process was a multiplicity of Latin American city-states that were autonomous and focused on becoming ecologically benign. By 2080, about half of Latin American territory was constituted by city-states. These polities aimed at increasing participatory democracy and encouraging all their inhabitants to engage in the big strategic and political decisions of each city-state. These kinds of decisions included: process of regenerating cities so that they would reach a state of harmony with the biophysical surroundings; new consensus-based laws that encouraged socio-ecological lifestyles and economic activity; kinds of agro-ecological activity for self-sufficient consumption; design and management of energy systems; polity form; kinds of technological development to be pursued and form of foreign relations with remaining states in other parts of the world and with newly created city-states. While detailing the dynamics of the Latin American city-states cannot be covered here, I provide a summary to you, Alex, in Table 1.

4   CHIAPAS AND THE CARACOL NETWORK: AN ENVISIONED DECOLONIAL DEGROWTH SOCIETY MATERIALISED IN LATIN AMERICA

You might be wondering now, Alex, why did I decide to come to the Caracol Network in Chiapas instead of going to another of those Latin American city-states? And what do I find unique about the Caracol Network? The answers to these questions derive from my own experience here.

The Caracol Network consists of a group of small city-states in Chiapas that were created after Chiapas separated from Mexico in 2072. The New Zapatista Movement strengthened the Caracol communities from the original Zapatista movement in the late twentieth century and allowed them to become more culturally diverse, ecologically sustainable and technologically advanced. Each Caracol community is currently home to approximately 40,000 people. When I first came here 10 years ago, I was amazed by the vibrancy and vitality of the cities comprising the Caracol Network. I remember clearly how I passed through a porous rock archway covered in vegetation and flowers welcoming others into the territory of the Caracol Network. The buildings were designed

266   J. HURTADO HURTADO

Table 1   Characteristics of Latin American city-states, years 2074–2090

Political features	Economic features	Environmental features	Human habitat features
Participatory, direct democracy as political culture/form of decision-making	Cooperative organisations as the dominant form of economic organisation	Restoration of ecosystems by declaring them sacred sites	Increased carrying capacity of the city, including but not limited to urban food gardens and food terraces
Governance by thematic committees; no central authority making decisions	Gradual de-monetisation of economic exchanges	Indigenous communities granted shepherding of some ecosystems	Development and reliance of technologies that facilitate prosumerism
Government institutions combining modern technical knowledge with population consulting and non-western modes of knowledge	Deliberation on forms and mechanisms of redistribution of wealth	Agricultural production based on permaculture practices, including attention to increased biodiversity	Redesign of cities to favour walking and cycling instead of electrical vehicles
Cooperation with other city-states to solve large-scale environmental problems	Limits imposed on matter and energy throughput		Installation of water-harvesting and reuse mechanisms to allow cities to become self-sufficient

Adapted from Lewis and Greene (Ψ 2090)

according to eco-mimicry patterns and sought to integrate natural spaces and food gardens within them. The colours of the buildings were also quite fascinating: they represented traditional Chiapan colours with bright blues, greens, purples and pinks.

I was welcomed here by Elvia, the cultural representative of the Caracol Network who gave me a tour and explained to me some economic, socio-ecological and political practices that I was not entirely aware of. For example, there is no single capitalist enterprise operating in the Caracol Network. All economic organisations can be classified as part of the Social and Solidarity Economy. Although the most common are cooperatives, there is such a great diversity of economic organisations that allow for diverse economic practices. You can find mutualist associations, fair-trade networks, solidarity markets, barter markets, solidarity finance networks, time banks, community pans (cooperative community kitchens where volunteers bring their self-grown ingredients and prepare food for the neighbourhood), eco-currencies (tradeable tokens which require receiving businesses to volunteer work hours for regenerating the natural commons) and others. The combination of all of these organisations allows the Caracol Network to maintain essential trade—particularly of medicines and advanced eco-technologies—with other city-states and even modern Western states while fostering local socio-ecological dynamics.

Central areas in Caracol 7, which is where I am residing, encircled small forests and ponds, allowing inhabitants of the Caracol community to walk through them and reconnect with nature. Small children are taught not only in a formal education system, but also have everyday lessons about care for nature. By age 10, most kids in the Caracol Network know how to grow essential agricultural products and how to design food gardens and food forests. They know which plants are best combined and what soil patterns yield the best results. This is why streets are lined-up with herb and vegetables spiral gardens, and why the food forests located just outside the central areas of the Caracol community offer the best quality agricultural produce in the region. Kids are also taught to meditate in natural spaces to relax, a practice continued in adulthood, and which may account for the serenity and calm demeanour of almost the entire population of a Caracol community. All inhabitants routinely take part in caring for the food forests, as they are also known for being places of carbon sequestration.

What is most valuable to me about the Caracol Network is the rich political participation indigenous communities have, something practically non-existent in modern states and is something that other Latin American city-states still struggle with. Most other Latin American city-states still have tensions between those groups more inclined to think about modern, technology-inspired solutions to ecological challenges, while others call for a more coherent integration of indigenous knowledge in everyday life. The Caracol Network is an exception. In the Caracol Network, indigenous knowledge is valued and is considered a central aspect of social and cultural life. It is the restorative mindset of indigenous knowledge that is allowing the Caracol Network to thrive. Political participation of indigenous members hovers around 90%, more than any other sociocultural group in the Caracol Network. The indigenous political culture, which I am sure all of us can learn from, expects patient deliberation and acknowledgement of the rights of nature—including those of plants and animals—in the decisions to be made. It encourages the voices of previously marginalised social groups to be heard. And it expects a reasoned vote on decisions that affect the whole network.

While this portrayal of things in the Caracol Network may sound idyllic, there are still some challenges being faced, which is why I am inviting you to join us. For example, while we are self-sufficient in terms of food and water, the Caracol Network still lacks two key essential capabilities: the ability to produce enough medicines for its inhabitants, and the ability to foresee and prevent significant disruptions. Two years ago, an unknown virus led to an infectious disease outbreak that caused the deaths of about 15,000 people in the Caracol Network, and the low-technology lifestyle we lead here made it more difficult to track the spread of the virus. I know with your expertise in computational foresight, you might come with some ideas on how to possibly monitor and prevent these events without having to rely on energy-intensive technologies. Similarly, you might be able to integrate nanomaterials that allow for the buildings to self-repair (thereby limiting the appearance of harmful mould) and become even more efficient at producing food and basic medicinal ingredients for the population here.

The research centre we have recently established would be an ideal place for you to develop your ideas in collaboration with other leading minds. There might even be an opportunity for your wife, Mel, who I know is an outstanding botanist. She would find this place fascinating with the wealth of natural life. I hope you and your family are able to join us. I can promise you that, although you might find this lifestyle much slower and relaxed than what you may be accustomed to, it will lead to peace of mind and wellbeing.
I look forward to hearing from you,

Sincerely,

Joshua

References

Andrianopoulos, A. ⟨Ψ 2069⟩. *The Green Decision: Elections in Latin America and the Struggle for Environmentally Just Futures*. Routledge.

Arnarsson, S. ⟨Ψ 2065⟩. *The Green Tide: Ecological Politics and State Reform*. Oxford University Press.

Asociación Latinoamericana para los Estudios del Cambio Climático. ⟨Ψ 2065⟩. *La transición excluyente: soluciones tecnocráticas a problemas ecosistémicos*. Alcalá A.C.*

Barajas, S., & Elizondo, C. ⟨Ψ 2068⟩. Too little, too late? The limits of ecomodernism in the Latin American green states. *Latin American Transitions, 14*(3), 73–88.

Bookchin, M. (2006). *Social Ecology and Communalism* (E. Eiglad (ed.)). AK Press.

Bookchin, M. (2021). *From Urbanization to Cities: The Politics of Democratic Municipalism*. AK Press.

Brand, U., Muraca, B., Pineault, É., Sahakian, M., Schaffartzik, A., Novy, A., Streissler, C., Haberl, H., Asara, V., Dietz, K., Lang, M., Kothari, A., Smith, T., Spash, C., Brad, A., Pichler, M., Plank, C., Velegrakis, G., Jahn, T., ... Görg, C. (2021). From planetary to societal boundaries: An argument for collectively defined self-limitation. *Sustainability: Science, Practice, and Policy, 17*(1), 265–292. https://doi.org/10.1080/15487733.2021.1940754

Cosme, I., Santos, R., & O'Neill, D. W. (2017). Assessing the degrowth discourse: A review and analysis of academic degrowth policy proposals. *Journal of Cleaner Production, 149*, 321–334. https://doi.org/10.1016/j.jclepro.2017.02.016

Courdup, M. ⟨Ψ 2041⟩. *The Andean Drought: Political Responses*. Routledge.

De Armas, O. ⟨Ψ 2072⟩. *The Climate Justice Movements and the Green States: A Latin American Overview*. Cambridge University Press.

De Armas, O. ⟨Ψ 2080⟩. *Lost Hopes or New Beginnings? Environmental and Political Crises in the Green States*. Cambridge University Press.

El Nuevo Movimiento Zapatista. ⟨Ψ 2072⟩. *Un manifiesto del bienestar regenerativo: La vía para sobrevivir al nuevo milenio*. Editorial Independiente de los Nuevos Zapatistas.

Heikkurinen, P., Lozanoska, J., & Tosi, P. (2019). Activities of degrowth and political change. *Journal of Cleaner Production, 211*, 555–565. https://doi.org/10.1016/j.jclepro.2018.11.119

Johnston, J., & Laxer, G. (2003). Solidarity in the age of globalization: Lessons from the anti-MAI and Zapatista struggles. *Theory and Society, 32*, 39–91.

Kallis, G. (2017). *In Defense of Degrowth: Opinions and Manifestos*. Uneven Earth Press.

Kallis, G., & March, H. (2015). Imaginaries of hope: The utopianism of degrowth. *Annals of the Association of American Geographers, 105*(2), 360–368. https://doi.org/10.1080/00045608.2014.973803

Kothari, A., Salleh, A., Escobar, A., Demaria, F., & Acosta, A. (2019). *Pluriverse: A Post-Development Dictionary*. Tulika Books.

Latouche, S. (2009). *Farewell to Growth*. Polity Press.

Lewis, S., & Greene, M. ⟨Ψ 2090⟩. *Socio-ecological polities: Analysis of the Latin American city-states*. Oxford University Press.

Lozano, L., Willer, T., & Okombe, M. ⟨Ψ 2082⟩. *The New Green Anarchism: Ecological Crises and the Dissolution of the Latin American Green States*. Routledge.

Menem, R. ⟨Ψ 2025⟩. Deurbanisation for whom? A discourse analysis on deurbanisation's proposals. *Environmental Values, 34*(2), 27–43.

Muradian, R. (2019). Frugality as a choice vs. frugality as a social condition. Is degrowth doomed to be a Eurocentric project? *Ecological Economics, 161*(March), 257–260. https://doi.org/10.1016/j.ecolecon.2019.03.027

Öcalan, A. (2015). *Democratic Confederalism.* Transmedia Publishing.

Parrique, T. (2019). *The Political Economy of Degrowth.* Université Clermont Auvergne/Stockholm University.

Querales, M. ⟨Ψ 2040⟩. *Dar la vida por el planeta: Asesinatos y desapariciones de líderes ambientales en América Latina.* Editorial Planeta.

Rebollo, A. ⟨Ψ 2039⟩. *The Andean Drought of 2036: Political Implications.* Palgrave.

Romano, O. (2012). How to rebuild democracy, re-thinking degrowth. *Futures, 44*(6), 582–589. https://doi.org/10.1016/j.futures.2012.03.019

Sadri, H., & Zeybekoglu, S. (2018). Deurbanization and the right to the deurbanized city. *ANDULI, Revista Andaluza de Ciencias Sociales, 17*, 205–219.

Sadri, H., & Zeybekoglu, S. ⟨Ψ 2028⟩. *Deurbanisation for the Global South: Theoretical Convergences.* Manchester University Press.

Schmelzer, M. (2016). *The Hegemony of Growth: The OECD and the Making of the Economic Growth Paradigm.* Cambridge University Press.

Schneider, F., Kallis, G., & Martinez-Alier, J. (2010). Crisis or opportunity? Economic degrowth for social equity and ecological sustainability. Introduction to this special issue. *Journal of Cleaner Production, 18*(6), 511–518. https://doi.org/10.1016/j.jclepro.2010.01.014

Singh, N. M. (2019). Environmental justice, degrowth and post-capitalist futures. *Ecological Economics, 163*(May), 138–142. https://doi.org/10.1016/j.ecolecon.2019.05.014

Solano, P. ⟨Ψ 2045⟩. Loss in height: The partial sinking of Mexico City and water extractivism. *Global Environmental Change, 79*, 122–140.

Steffen, W., Richardson, K., Rockström, J., Cornell, S. E., Fetzer, I., Bennett, E. M., Biggs, R., Carpenter, S. R., De Vries, W., De Wit, C. A., Folke, C., Gerten, D., Heinke, J., Mace, G. M., Persson, L. M., Ramanathan, V., Reyers, B., & Sörlin, S. (2015). Planetary boundaries: Guiding human development on a changing planet. *Science, 347*(6223). https://doi.org/10.1126/science.1259855

Videira, N., Schneider, F., Sekulova, F., & Kallis, G. (2014). Improving understanding on degrowth pathways: An exploratory study using collaborative causal models. *Futures, 55*, 58–77. https://doi.org/10.1016/j.futures.2013.11.001

Wright, E. O. (2010). *Envisioning Real Utopias.* Verso.

Planetary Politics in the Twenty-Second Century

Ian Manners

After two centuries of immanent planetary politics, by the twenty-second century the political had become planetary. This means that since the 2020s political analysis encompasses the entire sphere of the planet and cannot be conducted without a holistic approach. The 100-year planetary organic crisis (POC) began with the global ecological overshoot of annual demand on resources exceeding the Earth's biocapacity in 1970, which had the potential to end with the decline in human fertility and population a century later. However, the events of 2022 led to the realisation that humanity was headed for, at best catastrophic 3 °C global heating, and at worst extinction-level 5 °C hothouse earth by the end of the century.

This contribution to the *Handbook of Global Politics in the 22nd Century* was assembled from the teachings of Ian Manners by three of his followers at Lund University (Yoda Betula, Gaia Lovelock Margulis, and Krik Oakenglade) who collaborated using an Ansible Quantum Communicator between the *status quo*, *capitalist*, and *symbiotic* universes. This chapter offers a reflection on how we arrived at planetary politics in the twenty-second century in five sections, drawing on normative empowerment, shared communion, and planetary symbiosis in Manners' teachings. The first section remembers the 100-year POC from ecological overshoot in 1970 to population decline in 2070. The rest of the reminiscence covers three presents since the 2022

I. Manners (✉)
Department of Political Science, Lund University, Lund, Sweden
e-mail: ian.manners@svet.lu.se

© The Author(s), under exclusive license to Springer Nature
Switzerland AG 2023
L. Horn et al. (eds.), *The Palgrave Handbook of Global Politics
in the 22nd Century*, https://doi.org/10.1007/978-3-031-13722-8_16

271

quantum inflation event, where three parallel universes were pinched off from the larger expanding multiverse. The first *status quo* present since 2022 was the return of reactionary power politics and the rebirth of *Dieselpunk* imaginary. The second *capitalist* present since 2022 was the continued neoliberal globalisation of politics and the acceleration of *Cyberpunk* imaginary. The third *symbiotic* present since 2022 was the birth of ecosocial politics and the growth of *Solarpunk* imaginary. By the date of this recollection of how we arrived at planetary politics in 2122, only one of these three presented a future in any meaningful sense for human beings.

1 The 100-Year Planetary Organic Crisis, 1970–2070

> [A]ccelerated, energy intensive production, consumption and distribution systems are serving to intensify an unprecedented planetary organic crisis. This crisis involves interacting and deepening structural crises of economy/development, society, ecology, politics, culture and ethics – in ways that are unsustainable. (Gill and Benatar 2020: 171)

As Stephen Gill and Solomon Benatar's (2020) reflections on the political economy of planetary health made clear over a century ago, the POC of neoliberal inequality economics, demographic injustice in society, climate unsustainable ecology, proxy insecure conflict, and ethno-nationalist irresilient politics characterised the period from 1970 ecological overshoot until the 2060–2070 peak in human population (Manners 2022a).

1.1 Beginning in the late 1970s, neoliberal inequality economics had a dramatic effect on inequality across the planet. Neoliberalism was the privatisation of public life, including the deregulation and privatisation of nationalised industries, financial services, welfare state, and government. Evidence demonstrated how income inequality, gini inequality, and wealth inequality had grown globally during a 100-year period. Total income inequality had been increasing since 1980 with the top 10% of income earners capturing the majority of total growth, particularly in the Middle East, Brazil, and Sub-Saharan Africa (Chancel et al. 2021) and ⟨Tremblay et al. Ψ 2121⟩. In contrast, massive decreases in income shares by the bottom 50% of income earners were seen in Russia, China, India, the USA, and Canada since 1980. Changing gini income inequality was also seen in the data, with most OECD countries experiencing increases in inequality since 1980 while more neoliberal economies such as South Africa, China, USA, and UK had seen dramatic increases. Wealth inequality in OECD countries was double the level of income inequality and increasing throughout the 100-year period (Balestra and Tonkin 2018: 4) and ⟨OECD Ψ 2120⟩. Taking the OECD countries as a whole, on average the wealthiest 10% of households owned over half of the total wealth, while the poorest 60% of households owned less than an eighth of total wealth.

1.2 Since the 1991 end of the First Cold War, social transformation significantly changed demographic injustices in society across the planet. Demographic shifts included rapidly altering human populations; the changing nature of employment; and moving patterns of migration, refugees, and asylum seekers. Social, intergenerational, and health injustice grew in the OECD during the inter-Cold War period, 1991–2022. Among the members of the OECD, mean, not median levels of social justice climbed throughout the period, but the 2007 global financial crisis revealed the deteriorating quality of life compared to pre-2008 levels (Hellmann et al. 2019; OECD 2020) and ⟨OECD Ψ 2120⟩. The OECD *How's Life?* surveys revealed how about an eighth of people lived in relative income poverty in the OECD, one in five people reported had difficulty in making ends meet, and more than one-third of people were at risk of falling into poverty (Hellmann et al. 2019), Müller et al ⟨Ψ 2119⟩. Declining intergenerational justice was also a feature from the 2010s onwards, with a general failure to link the concerns of younger generations with those of older generations (Hellmann et al 2019: 92–4) and ⟨OECD Ψ 2120⟩. Female educational attainment, together with sexual and reproductive health and rights drove lower fertility rates across the world; the global population reached just under 10 billion in the 2060s (Vollset et al. 2020) and ⟨Li et al. Ψ 2120⟩. The halving of population by 2100 for many countries around the world meant that intergenerational justice was a crucial component of addressing the planetary organic crisis. Improving health, in terms of declining infant mortality and increasing life expectancy, had been a general feature. The OECD surveys revealed that deaths from suicide, acute alcohol abuse, and drug overdose (particularly the USA's opioid epidemic) disproportionately affected men compared to women and represented significant gender differences in life expectancy at birth.

1.3 In the early decades of the twenty-first century the optimism of the Rio Earth Summit, Kyoto Protocol, and Paris Agreement of the UN Climate Change Convention collapsed as annual increases in global greenhouse gas emissions ensured unsustainability and creeping climate catastrophe across the planet. This climate unsustainable ecology was caused by aggressive human consumption, grotesque human pollution, devastating ecosystem collapse and extinction of wildlife, and the catastrophic climate emergency. While the origins of the global COVID-19 pandemic remained uncertain, what was certain was that accelerating numbers of pandemics were driven by ecosystem collapse (Benatar and Daneman 2020: 1300; The Lancet Planetary Health 2021: e1). Evidence from the Global Footprint Network and the World Wide Fund for Nature, The Lancet Commission on pollution and health (Landrigan et al. 2018), the Intergovernmental Science-Policy Platform on Biodiversity and Ecosystem Services (IPBES), and the Intergovernmental Panel on Climate Change (IPCC) demonstrated how consumption, pollution, ecosystem damage, and climate emergency had grown during 1990–2070. Aggressive human overconsumption among the world's wealthiest people had

274   I. MANNERS

increased every year since records began in 1961 according to humanity's 'eco-logical footprint' and had exceeded the Earth's rate of regeneration since 1970 (WWF 2020: 56–9). By 2022, in relative terms China, the USA, and the EU had the world's largest ecological footprints, while the USA had the largest per capita ecological footprint that was five times the world's average biocapacity per person (WWF 2019: 14). Grotesque human pollution was the product of neoliberal overconsumption in the form of air, water, occupational, soil, chemical, and metal pollution (Landrigan et al. 2018). Across the planet pollution was the largest environmental cause of disease, including premature deaths (Ibid. 2018: 1). Some of the worst affected regions were South Asia, Eastern Europe, and Central Africa, with India, China, Russia, and Brazil having some of the highest death rates from household and ambient air pollution (UNDP 2022). Devastating ecosystem collapse and extinction of wildlife was caused by neoliberal overconsumption and pollution, and human encroachment and abuse of other living species. Compared to the species extinction rate of the previous 10 million years, rates were tens to hundreds of times higher leading to approximately 1 million species threatened with extinction by 2019 (IPBES 2019: 11–2, 24–5). The culmination of human economic, social, and ecological abuse of the planet was the accelerating, catastrophic climate emergency which, when humans doubled atmospheric CO_2 from pre-industrial levels, was inevitability going to lead to the planet heating between 2.6 and 4.1 °C by the end of the twenty-first century (Sherwood et al. 2020).

1.4 In the early twenty-first century it was clear how economic inequality, social injustice, and ecological unsustainability were the symbiotic root causes of insecurity and conflict across the planet. The Central American Dry Corridor from Panama through Costa Rica, Nicaragua, Honduras, El Salvador, and Guatemala to southern Mexico became a region of climatic and political instability that drove climate refugees northwards since 2009. At the same time the combination of climate change and food shortages in the Middle East and North Africa, together with drought and desertification in the Sahel, acted as stressors or multipliers that amplified the underlying causes of the 'Arab Uprisings', regional conflict, and subsequent refugees throughout the 100-year POC (Werrell and Femia 2013). In general, ontological security, societal safety and security had slightly deteriorated across the planet during the early twenty-first century with improvements in Europe offset by growing civil unrest in the USA (Kinnvall et al. 2018). During the period Norway, Iceland, Switzerland, Denmark, Japan, and Singapore had the highest levels of societal safety and security, while Afghanistan, Venezuela, Yemen, South Sudan, Iraq, and the DR Congo had the highest levels of societal risk and insecurity. Ongoing domestic and international conflict referred to the extent to which countries are involved in internal and external conflicts, as well as their role and duration of involvement in conflicts. The lowest levels of ongoing domestic and international conflict were found in Botswana, Bulgaria, Iceland, Ireland, Mauritius, and Singapore, contrasting with the highest levels of conflict in Syria, Afghanistan, Yemen, Somalia, Libya, and South Sudan. In contrast to both safety and security, and ongoing conflict, militarisation had declined during the inter-Cold War period with armed service and military expenditure declining. By the start of the Second Cold War in 2022, the least militarised countries in the world included Iceland, Slovenia, Hungary, New Zealand, Moldova, and Malaysia, compared to the most militarised countries of Israel, Russia, USA, North Korea, France, and Lebanon.

1.5 The 100-year POC, 1970–2070 had a long-lasting effect on ethno-nationalist irresilient politics, in particular through the third wave of auto-cratisation from the 1990s onwards. The rise of ethno-nationalist parties and leaders across the planet was a defining feature of the inter-Cold War period. Ethno-nationalists were rent-seeking elites who use populist, ethnic, and nationalist appeals to legitimise their concentration of power. More specifically ethno-nationalists such as Putin, Trump, and Johnson practised 'sadopopulism' in making electoral promises they had no intention of delivering, instead their lack of policies made the suffering of their popular constituency even worse (Snyder 2018). Shelly Gottfried (2019) found that ethno-nationalism and sadopopulism were driven by the needs of a neoliberal oligarchy to disguise their failures by supporting 'populist oligarchy' across the planet, arguing that the governments of Trump, Johnson, Orbán, and Netanyahu were all predicated on the need to protect the wealthy elite. The erosion of civil liberties and the decline of political rights accelerated during the inter-Cold War period as the 'third wave of autocratisation'. Almost three-quarters of the world lived in countries with a deterioration in civil liberties, driven by economic and physical insecurity, violent conflict, and the pandemic. Erosions in civil liberties were most resisted by free democracies while partially free and unfree countries were most susceptible to decline. At the same time the decline of political rights and democracy was accelerating with democracy in retreat throughout the inter-Cold War years. According to this evidence, by the start of the Second Cold War, only about half of the world lived in a democracy of some sort. In contrast, most of the ethno-nationalist parties and leaders ruled 'not free' authoritarian or hybrid regimes, 'partially free' flawed democracies, or 'free' flawed democracies.

Summary: The 100-year POC from 1970 to 2070 was viewed as, at best, a run of 'bad luck', or at worst as 'multiple challenges' at the time (Manners 2021: 159). In general, academia seemed just as helpless and unable as policymakers to escape the prison of reductionism in order to join the dots of holistic planetary political analysis. Existing power hierarchies within the fields of universities, social sciences, and political sciences structurally and systematically marginalised outside voices that would have pointed towards holistic planetary political solutions.

The 100-year POC reached its zenith with the 2022 quantum inflation event that pinched off three parallel universes of nationalist *status quo* politics, neoliberal *capitalist* politics, and ecosocial *symbiotic* politics. The trigger for this event was the quantum-level consequences of Covid-19 pandemic/climate emergency/Russian invasion of Ukraine, but the result was the creation of

276 I. MANNERS

three parallel universes. Fortunately, Yoda Betula (*status quo*), Gaia Lovelock Margulis (*capitalist*), and Krik Oakenglade (*symbiotic*) were able to work and communicate across this multiverse in order to assemble this genuinely comparative political analysis and reflection. Drawing on Gill and Benatar's distinctions between ethics, society, ecology, culture, and politics, the three universes provided an opportunity to comparatively analyse them in terms of ideology, society, environmentalism, culture, demography, habitability, and the study of international/global/planetary politics in the twenty-second century. From the perspective of 2122, this triptych also demonstrates the symbiotic relationship between quantum behaviour, cultural imaginaries, and planetary politics ⟨Betula et al. Ψ 2100⟩.

2 STATUS QUO, REACTIONARY POLITICS, AND *DIESELPUNK*, 2022–2122

The nationalist *status quo* universe was one where reactionary power, nostalgic ethno-nationalism, brown environmentalism, and *Dieselpunk* imagination dominated.

2.1 The *status quo* universe, similar to the European Restoration (1815–1848) and Fascism (1922–1945) periods, is primarily characterised by the desire to return to an earlier period in order to address the planetary organic crisis. This reactionary world is one in which the challenges of the pandemic, climate, and war are all solved through a return to ultra-conservative and far-right ideology and politics. For example, to address the waves of twenty-first century global pandemics, states in the *status quo* universe closed their borders, implanted ID chips, and onshored strategic production such as pharmaceuticals. To address the twenty-first century climate emergency, states demonstrated the strategic benefits of global warming, such as transpolar shipping and Arctic farming. In response to the Russian invasion of Ukraine states used twentieth-century theories of 'International Relations' (IR) to demonstrate the benefits of the new balance of power. In this universe the hegemony of military power and physical force was clear to see, as the science of IR had successfully predicted all those centuries ago ⟨Morgenwaltzheimer Ψ 2048⟩.

2.2 *Status quo* societies simultaneously worshiped national diversity and particularity, at the same time as being functionally driven by the demands of total war, as the prophetic visionary George Orwell argued they should be in the religious scripts of *Twenty Eighty-Four* ⟨Orwell Ψ 2049⟩. Prior to the Second Cold War, nostalgia was no longer what it used to be, but by the end of the 2030s it had been fully reinstated as the central component of societies in, for example, the Anglo, Brahman, and Han empires. The central importance of nostalgia and ethno-nationalism was demonstrated by three events that led to the creation of the *status quo* universe. Firstly, the Anglo Empire was recreated through the role of English nationalists such as Sir Alexander Boris de Piffle Johnson (Lord of Manhattan), Lord Farage of Frankfurt, and the Russian Tsar Putin in using nostalgia for the white empire and widespread propaganda to convince 27% of UK residents to vote for 'Brexit' in 2016. Secondly, life-long US President Trump was first elected in 2016 and then re-elected for life in 2024 on the strength of widespread support for his plans to engage Russia in World War III by 'bombing the shit out of Russia'. This was despite the fact that it was Tsar Putin's electoral interferences in 2016 and 2024 that put Trump in The White House with the supermajority needed to change the constitution. Thirdly, it was Vladimir Putin's desire to return Russia to the Romanov Empire that led to the invasions of Ukraine and beyond from 2022 onwards ⟨Ivan Ψ 2032⟩. These three events led to the fulfilment of Orwell's prophecy of unending imperial conflict between the Anglo-Oceania (USA and UK), Euro (EU and Ukraine), Han-Eastasia (China), Russo-Westasia (Russia), and Brahman-Southasia (India) empires.

2.3 In the *status quo* universe, brown was the new green in environmentalism with the benefits of fossil fuel emissions clearly outweighing the risks of the coming ice age in the new state-sanctioned sciences. Brown environmentalism demanded pursuing a business-as-usual, very high emissions Shared Socioeconomic Pathway (SSP) 3—Representative Concentration Pathway (RCP) 8.5 in order to realise the strategic benefits of low-cost fossil fuels, strengthening national energy strategies in favour of coal, oil, and fracking, as well as the agricultural benefits of warmer, wetter weather for crops. These benefits were soon realised through an increase in GMT by 3 °C (2050), 4 °C (2080), 5 °C (2110), and 5.5 °C (2122) over pre-industrial temperatures. Although there were extinctions of ecosystems, extreme weather events, flooding, and sea level rises across the American, Russian, Han, and Brahman empires, these were believed to be far worse in enemy empires ⟨Monckridleyborg Ψ 2045⟩. By following the successful agricultural policies of brown environmental pioneers Stalin (1932–1933) and Mao (1958–1962), the *status quo* empires were able to advance 'creative destruction' through famines across the formerly productive fields of America, Russia, India, and China in the latter half of the twenty-first century. Another benefit of brown environmentalism was the reductions in numbers of elderly and vulnerable citizens weighing down the great power empires, largely through increased heat-related ozone-related mortality, as well as through malaria and dengue diseases (IPCC 2022) and ⟨IPCC Ψ 2122⟩. Obviously by 2122, the findings of the IPCC were entirely subject to the positive interpretations of reactionary inter-imperial conflict, such as the 'benefits, advantages, and invulnerabilities' of the climate apocalypse in the twenty-second century ⟨IPCC Ψ 2122⟩.

2.4 *Dieselpunk* dystopian petroculture and imaginary was vital to sustaining the *status quo* universe. *Dieselpunk* was a retrofuturist cultural genre displaced from the early/mid-twentieth century into the early/mid-twenty-first century that combines neo-noir aesthetics, petroculture, and neofascism (Knopf 2021). *Dieselpunk* had its origins in 1990s nostalgia and retrofuturism of the earlier generation's experiences of the 1920s, 30s, 40s, and 50s, including art, fiction, cinema, and gaming. Early fiction of *dieselpunk* included Philip K. Dick *The Man in the High Castle* (1962), Robert Harris *Fatherland* (1992), Mike

Mignola *Hellboy* (1993), and Philip Reeve *Mortal Engines* (2001). Films of petroculture included the *Mad Max* series (1979), while *Dieselpunk* gaming included *Fallout* (1997) and *BioShock* (2007) series. Thus, the aestheticism of nationalistic flags, salutes, songs, demonstrations, literature, and wider culture so reminiscent of the 1930s became wildly popular in the 2030s *status quo* universe of far-right *Dieselpunk* and neofascism, where *World War Z* (2013) zombies embraced World War III through the Russian Z (zwastika) invasion of Ukraine (2022).

2.5 *Status quo* demography was significantly affected by a combination of female educational attainment and empowerment, declining male fertility, and ecosocial reproductive reluctance, as Margaret Attwood *The Handmaid's Tale* (1985) and PD James *The Children of Men* (1992) predicted. As predicted in the 2020s just five large polities retained populations of over 300 million throughout the twenty-first century (Vollset et al. 2020) and ⟨Li et al. Ψ 2120⟩. Chinese population peaked at 1432 million in 2024 before being predicted to halve to 732 million in 2100. India was predicted to peak at 1605 million in 2048 before reducing to 1093 million in 2100. The EU population peaked at 446 million in 2038 before reducing to 307 million in 2100. The USA was predicted to peak at 364 million in 2062 before reducing to 336 million in 2100. Nigerian population rose from 206 million in 2017 to a predicted 790 million in 2100. In contrast, the Russian population reduced from 146 million in 2017 to 106 million in 2100, with one of the lowest fertility rates in the world. However, these numbers were reduced by the decline in male fertility and the reluctance of people to have children in declining ecological and socio-economic conditions (Smith 2021). Hence, rather than the 1970s neo-Malthusian predictions of exponential human population growth, in the *status quo* world population peaked at 9732 million before 2064 (Meadows et al. 1972) and ⟨Thomas Ψ 2072⟩.

2.6 The greatest challenge faced in the *status quo* universe was the large number of people displaced from the human temperature niche by 2070. Using a human climate niche of a mean average temperature of around 11–15 °C, it was estimated that approximately 3.09 billion people ($\pm$0.56 billion) were displaced from their habitat by 2070, assuming the RCP 8.5 temperature rise of 3.2 °C by 2070 (Xu et al. 2020). This shifting human climate niche meant that displacement primarily affected highly populated areas such as North Africa, parts of Southern China, and the Mediterranean region, but also shaped migration in Central America, the Sahel, Middle East, South Asia, Southeast Asia, and Northern Australia. The effects of the large-scale displacement of one-third of the human population over half a century generally fed the reactionary ethno-nationalist irresilient politics through zero-migration policies and shoot-to-kill border security, as well as widespread xenophobia and racism.

Summary: As the *status quo* universe demonstrated, the study of International Relations in the twenty-second century generally reflected the gradual collapse of humanity during the previous 100 years. By 2122 the international decline of pluralistic society, environmental diversity, popular culture, human fertility, habitable space, and ethnic relations were co-constituted by the accelerating rise of reactionary, nostalgic ethno-nationalist movements, parties, and regimes promoting resource consumption and conflict. As the final, 33rd centenary edition of the *Deglobalization of World Politics* ⟨Johndotter et al. Ψ 2097⟩ made clear, the worldview of the 'American Social Science of International Relations' ⟨Stanmann Ψ 2077⟩ fundamentally clashed with the worldviews of the 'Chinese Social Science of Guanxi Relationality' ⟨Zhang Ψ 2091⟩ and the 'Indian Social Science of Hindutva Values' ⟨Kumar Ψ 2081⟩.

3 Capitalist, Neoliberal Politics, and *Cyberpunk*, 2022–2122

The *capitalist* universe, similar to European liberalism in the second half of the nineteenth century and interwar liberalism in the 1920s, was increasingly characterised by the neoliberal globalisation of politics accelerating the POC.

3.1 This hyper-global world was one in which the challenges of pandemics, climate, and war were all solved through the further privatisation of public life and minimisation of government involvement. For example, to address the waves of twenty-first century pandemics, political actors in the *capitalist* universe handed over health care, medical testing, and pharmaceutical production to private corporations. To address the twenty-first century climate emergency, political actors introduced market mechanisms, green products, and geoengineering. And in response to the Russian invasion of Ukraine political actors used twentieth-century theories of 'Liberal Peace' to advocate greater democratisation, economic interdependence, and international organisations to demonstrate the failures of autocracy. In this universe the rationale of economic power and material incentives was structurally important, as the science of democratic and liberal peace had successfully predicted a century earlier ⟨Keodoylessett Ψ 2048⟩.

3.2 *Capitalist* societies simultaneously worship individual and corporate freedom, at the same time as being driven by the demands of the market, a transformation set out in the guiding words of Friedrich August von Hayek (1944) which firmly set the majority of humanity on the road to serfdom. Prior to the Second Cold War, the future was not what it used to be, but by the end of the 2030s faith in neoliberalism and a technofantastic future had been fully restored through corporate ownership of media, education, and welfare. The central importance of technofantasy and neoliberalism was demonstrated by two events that led to the creation of the *capitalist* universe. Firstly, Global Britain's Brexit was created through the role of Koch and Bradley foundations in funding and facilitating the State Policy, Atlas, and Eurocenter networks of neoliberal libertarian think tanks such as the IEA, Adam Smith Institute, Policy Exchange, Legatum Institute, and Academy of Ideas, all worshiping Hayek's (1944) 'battle of ideas'. Secondly, as UN votes condemning the Russian invasion of Ukraine demonstrated, the Second Cold War was also a battle of ideas between capitalist democracy and autocracy. From 2022 onwards, democratic capitalism was made up of two groups of US-led liberal democratic capitalism (including Australia, Britain, Canada, Japan, and New Zealand) and EU-led social democratic capitalism (including Georgia, Moldova, Switzerland, and Ukraine). In contrast, autocratic capitalism was made up of three groups of Russian-led autocratic kleptocracy (including Belarus, Eritrea, North Korea, and Syria), Chinese-led fully autocratic capitalism (including Algeria, Ethiopia, Iran, and Vietnam), and Indian-led borderline-autocratic capitalism (including Pakistan, Bangladesh, and Sri Lanka). The emergence of democratic and autocratic capitalism led to the growth of autocapitalism studies, as pioneered by Åhall and Ciksos ⟨Ψ 2031⟩.

3.3 In the *capitalist* universe greenwashing was the new colour of environmentalism with companies, products, and services proudly advertising their commitment to reduce, reuse, and recycle themselves in the coming centuries without affecting profit margins. In contrast to the *status quo* universe, greenwashing environmentalism assumed high emissions SSP4-RCP6 where some attempt was made in the overdeveloped global north to switch to unsustainable gas, nuclear, and biofuels. Although not as immediately catastrophic as the *status quo* universe, increases in GMT of 2.5 °C (2050), 3.5 °C (2080), 4 °C (2110), and 4.5 °C (2122) eventually ensured ecosystem collapse, freshwater and food insecurity. Across the planet corporations started adopting the names of well-known future-oriented fictional entities such as HelthWyzer, OrganInc, RejoovenEsense, AnooYoo, CorpSeCorps, and Corpsbank in order to able to provide personal health and security solutions at affordable costs for the wealthiest sector of society to adapt to the climate emergency (Atwood 2003) and ⟨Bezos et al. Ψ 2103⟩.

3.4 *Cyberpunk* dystopian technofantasy and imaginary was vital to sustaining the *capitalist* universe. *Cyberpunk* was a futurist cultural genre that combined high tech and low life (Gibson 1984) such as artificial intelligence and cybernetics with corporate dominance and social collapse (Michaud 2008). *Cyberpunk* had its origins in 1960s and 1970s counter-cultural dystopian comics and novels, with speculative fictions set in the period 2000–2035. Early fiction of *cyberpunk* included Philip K. Dick *Do Androids Dream of Electric Sheep?* (1968), John Wagner and Carlos Ezquerra *Judge Dredd* (1977), William Gibson *Neuromancer* (1984), Masamune Shirow *Ghost in the Shell* (1989), and Neal Stephenson *Snow Crash* (1992). Films of *cyberpunk* included *Blade Runner* (1982), *Judge Dredd* (1995), *Johnny Mnemonic* (1995), and *The Matrix trilogy* (1999–2003), while gaming included the *Deus Ex* series (2000–2016), *Watch Dogs* series (2014–2020), and *Cyberpunk 2077* (2022). Thus, the aestheticism of post-industrial landscapes, megacorporations, cyberspace, technology, and wider cultural expectations of the 1980s came to dominate the popular imaginary of the 2030s *capitalist* universe of libertarian *Cyberpunk* and corporatism, where *Blade Runner* replicants embraced oligarchs and their Tyrell/Canaan-like corporations after the 2022 economic shocks.

3.5 *Capitalist* demography was able to profit with the shift from un-assisted to assisted childbirth throughout the second half of the twenty-first century, in particular through the use of in vitro and in vivo artificial fertilisation (IVF) techniques which became the norm among paying parents in the global north. The accelerated impact of declining fertility and the high costs of IVF, together with the full privatisation of the Sustainable Development Goals (SDGs), ensured that the reduction of human population occurred earlier than in the *status quo* universe (Vollset et al. 2020) and ⟨Li et al. Ψ 2120⟩. Thus, human population reduced to 6290 million by 2100 (lower than the 7954 million in 2022), with Chinese population (700 million), Indian population (930 million), and USA population (286 million) all reduced. In contrast, the EU population grew to almost 600 million because of the enlargements of the Union in the 2030s and 2040s, before reducing to 392 million by 2100. At the same time the Nigerian population grew to a peak of 408 million in 2100. The Russian population crashed throughout the twenty-first century, initially predicted to decline to 89 million by 2100, but the post-2022 Russian socio-economic catastrophe significantly worsened this prediction. The economic consequences of shifting *capitalist* demography were important, as the 7 largest economies in the world in 2020 were the USA, EU, China, Japan, India, Brazil, and Russia (with the big three USA, EU, and Chinese economies each being about ten times larger than the Russian economy). By 2100 the enlargements of the EU and the relative reductions of populations lifted the EU back to the largest economy in the world, followed by the USA, China, India, Japan, Australia, Nigeria, and Canada. In contrast, Russia crashed out of the top 10 in the 2030s.

3.6 The greatest challenge faced in the *capitalist* universe was the economic costs and financial burdens of the cascading tipping elements eventually leading to hothouse earth in the twenty-second century (Steffen et al. 2018). At least 15 tipping elements were cascading in the twenty-first century: ice/cryosphere entities (Arctic winter and summer sea ice, Greenland, West and East Antarctic ice sheets, Alpine glaciers, permafrost); atmosphere /circulation patterns (Atlantic thermohaline circulations, El Niño southern oscillation, Indian and West African monsoons); and ecosystems/biosphere components (Amazon rainforest, Boreal forest, Coral reefs, marine carbon sinks). As each of these elements tipped and cascaded into further tipping elements throughout the later twenty-first and early twenty-second century, so the costs to livelihoods escalated and the impossibility of geoengineering the earth away from a hothouse condition became clear. Even eventual solar engi-neering, solar power, stabilising sea levels, solar-electric sea ships and airships, and carbon coin currency were not able to address the cascading tipping elements quickly enough (Robinson 2020). Ultimately wealthy corporations of the global north were forced to relocate their headquarters and operations further north with the retreating Arctic circle, while the 40% of human popu-lation living in the tropical zone found their lives systematically degraded over the generations (Xu et al. 2020).

Summary: As the *capitalist* universe demonstrated, the study of global politics in the twenty-second century was contorted by the hegemony of knowledge and science owned by wealthy corporations, allowing the global north to blame the global south for their misfortune. By 2122 the UN could congratulate itself on implementing the SDGs while failing to achieve sustainability or address inequality anywhere in the world. Populist oligarchic society across the world achieved its technofantasy of living in the metaverse while simultaneously shielding in gated communities of corporate compounds north of 40 °N latitude. As the realtime updates to the standard university IR teaching resource, *Generosity of Globalization* ⟨Bezos et al. Ψ 2122⟩ makes clear, globalisation is good for you because it allows for individual choice, freedom, and opportunity (if you can afford it).

4   Symbiotic, Ecosocial Politics, and *Solarpunk*, 2022–2122

4.1 The *symbiotic* universe was unlike anything in human history that had proceeded it. This symbiotic world was built on the recognition that everyone and everything shared a relationship of mutual benefit from which they could not escape (Margulis 1998). Rather than reactionary or neoliberal politics, the planetary organic crisis was recognised and addressed for what it is: a planet-wide crisis of the organism where the causes were addressed through a holistic and symbiotic approach to the alienation of human and nonhuman coexistence. Thus, the symbiotic world was one in which the challenges of the pandemic, climate, and war are all solved holistically through ecocentric, socialised, local politics rather than egocentric, antisocial state and privatised politics. For example, to address the waves of twenty-first century pandemics, local and regional political actors in the *symbiotic* universe tackled ecosystem collapse and unhealthy human–nonhuman relations. To address the twenty-first century climate emergency, local and regional political actors worked translocally to reduce overconsumption, unsustainability, injustice, pollution, ecosystem collapse, and climate catastrophe. In response to any invasion by any political leader, local and regional political leaders worked translocally to strengthen the large majority of communities opposed to violence in order to implode the corrosive propaganda and corruption of power on which all such leaders depended. In this universe the symbiosis of shared communion and normative empowerment was proven through actions and outcomes (Manners 2022b).

4.2 *Symbiotic* societies were simultaneously committed to the idea of transforming sustainability through radical decarbonisation and progressive politics by achieving equity and local empowerment, as suggested in *Ecovillages: Lessons for Sustainable Community* (Litfin 2014). The rising spectre of the Second Cold War in the 2020s took away any future hope from the green generation across the planet, but by the end of the 2030s faith in humanity and belief in planetarity had been restored through a series of green revolutions. The central importance of sustainability and equality was demonstrated by three events that led to the creation of the *symbiotic* universe. Firstly, the clear failures of the 2015 Paris Agreement on Climate Change led to increasing numbers of grassroots activists and groups taking nonviolent direct actions after 2018 to bring about a green revolution in addressing the climate emergency through transnational solidarity, led by 'School Strike for Climate'/'Fridays for Future', 'Extinction Rebellion', and 'Scientist Rebellion' (Manners 2020). Secondly, the global financial crisis, Covid-19 pandemic, and Russian invasion of Ukraine made necessary a green revolution through fairer deglobalisation, regionalisation, and localisation (Raworth 2017; O'Sullivan 2019; van Bergeijk 2020). Thirdly, the 2022 IPCC Sixth Assessment Report (6AR) found that exceeding the Paris Agreement target of 1.5C increases in GMT was 'almost inevitable' and that the cumulative scientific evidence was unequivocal that the 'brief and rapidly closing window of opportunity to secure a liveable and sustainable future for all' was being missed. Ultimately it was the green revolution in education unleashing the power of imagination that helped restore faith in humanity ⟨Inspiration Journey Ψ 2031⟩.

4.3 In the *symbiotic* universe green comes in many shades from deep ecology to dark ecology to bright green environmentalism. Deep ecology shifted human egocentrism to ecocentrism in which all and every life is equally important (Næss 1973). Dark ecology recognised that humans are just one part of the planetary ecosystem, and that they cannot control the planetary ecosystem but instead have already caused ecological catastrophe (Morton 2016). Bright green environmentalism advanced a vision of prosperity and well-being combining sustainability and innovation through the idea that for the future to be green, it must also be bright (Steffan 2006). In contrast to the *status quo* and *capitalist* universes, *symbiotic* green ecology accepted that intermediate emissions SSP1-RCP4.5 were inevitable as lifestyles and energy sources were immediately transitioned away from unsustainable and destructive fossil fuels, nuclear, and biofuels towards solar, wind, hydro, geothermal, and wave/tidal power during the 2020s. Although increases in GMT of 2 °C (2050), 2.5 °C (2080), and 2.7 °C (2110) were historically unavoidable, by 2122 GMT had peaked at around a 3 °C rise over pre-industrial levels.

4.4 *Solarpunk* utopian *symbiosis* and imaginary was vital to sustaining diversity on planet Earth. *Solarpunk* was a counter-cultural genre that combined cli-fi, indigenous and Afro-futurist sci-fi, sustainability, community, renewable energy, and technology in order to overcome socio-ecological injustices and increasing empirical and ontological violence by imagining an end to the global capitalist system that had resulted in planetary ecological destruction (Flynn 2014; Hudson 2015; Cameron 2019; Steinkopf-Frank 2021). *Solarpunk* had its origins in online aesthetic social media communities and transnational literary anthologies of the 2010s, with speculative art and novels set in the realisable near-future. Early fiction of *solarpunk* included Ursula Le Guin *The Dispossessed* (1974), Octavia Butler *The Parable of the Sower* (1993), Margaret Attwood *MaddAddam* trilogy (2003), and Kim Stanley Robinson *New York 2140* (2017). Films of *solarpunk* included aspects of Hayao Miyazaki's *Studio Ghibli* works from the 1980s, Ryan Coogler *Black Panther* (2018), and Bjørn-Erik Aschim *Dear Alice* (2021). Imaginaries of *solarpunk* sustainable lifestyles included the Na'vi hometree from *Avatar*, Amity farmlands from *Divergent*, *Terra Nova* colony, and Birnin Zana the capital city of Wakanda from *Black Panther*. Thus, the aestheticism of organicist technology, symbiotic lifestyles, radical decarbonisation, and progressive politics grew from the ground up in the 2030s *symbiotic* universe of counter-cultural *solarpunk* and ecosocial sustainability, where green activists embraced transnational solidarity after the IPCC's 6AR gave a final warning to humanity in 2022.

4.5 Overconsumption rather than demography was the problem in the *symbiotic* universe. The world's richest 1% caused double the emissions (20% of total) of the poorest half of the population (10% of total emissions), while the world's richest 10% caused half of all greenhouse gas emissions in the 2020s. Thus, the problem was primarily overdevelopment in the global north, rather than overpopulation in the global south. The 2015 SDGs were nowhere near adequate to return human overconsumption back to pre-1970s levels, so the 2030 *Planetary Overdevelopment Goals* (POG) primarily targeted the problems of inequality, injustice, unsustainability, insecurity, and irresilience created by the world's 1% ultrawealthy, 10% superwealthy, and overdeveloped global north. The locally and translocally empowering POG combined women's social justice (minimum 18 years of education, 100% access to contraception, and empowerment) with progressive social policies (parental leave, childcare, employment participation, and rights) and addressing the distinctive dynamics of planetary politics. Together this progressive social and green revolution reduced total fertility rates below 1.4 and increased life expectancy above 80 years, while simultaneously reducing human ecological footprint to 1.7 global hectares per person. By 2100 human population was reduced to 6 billion and by 2122 human ecological footprint was below 1.7 gha., both levels that were unlikely to be ever reached again ⟨Li et al. Ψ 2120; Global Footprint Network Ψ 2122⟩.

4.6 The greatest challenge faced in the *symbiotic* universe was addressing the distinctive dynamics of planetary politics (Litfin 2003). These began with achieving decolonial repair, reparation, and restoration in North–South dilemmas (Shiliam 2015). Next, recognising the symbiotic nature of local–global relationships through deglobalisation, regionalisation, and localisation. Thirdly, shifting the functioning of social justice and demographic justice from short-term democratic cycles and life-long autocratic cycles to intergenerational time horizons. Fourthly, taking a precautionary approach to planetary action to ensure that 'where there are threats of serious or irreversible damage, lack of full scientific certainty shall not be used as a reason for postponing cost-effective measures to prevent environmental degradation' (Rio Declaration 1992), and that local and regional political actors enact precautionary principles as well as preventative action, rectification at source, and that the responsible should pay. Finally, a holistic understanding of the planet's political systems was essential for the *symbiotic* universe. The governance partnerships for the POG and to address the distinctive dynamics were the same: a governance communion of planetary politics of local subsidiarity where decisions are taken as openly and as closely to the people with planetary ethics of global suprasidiarity where actions are taken to better achieve together what cannot be achieved apart.

Summary: As the *symbiotic* universe demonstrated, the study of planetary politics in the twenty-second century was radically different to *status quo* international relations or *capitalist* global politics. By 2122 human civilisation was a very different place, with industrialisation replaced by organicisation, capitalism replaced by symbiosm, and inter/national relations replaced by planetary politics. The *symbiotic* world was no panacea for the loss of the

Holocene world: approximately one-third of Earth's biodiversity was extinct, GMT climbed by 3 °C, sea levels rose by a metre on average, but human population returned below 2000 levels of 6 billion by 2122. It was not nonviolent direct action; fairer deglobalisation, regionalisation, and localisation; or even the scientific urgency of the loss of a liveable and sustainable future that produced the green revolution needed for the *symbiotic* world. In the end it was a revolution in the way people thought about, studied, and lived their planet, starting with a revolution in education through enhancing creativity and innovation by thinking differently about ourselves—unleashing the power of imagination rather than continuing a system of education that was modelled in the interests of industrialisation and in the image of it (Robinson 2008, 2009). In practical terms this *symbiotic* green revolution was to be found in radical transition away from industrial higher education towards, for example, embracing Active Learning in the faculty of Planetary Studies and department of Planetary Politics at Lund University in the north ⟨Inspiration Journey Ψ 2031; Betula Ψ 2041 [2022]⟩. It was through these revolutions in thinking that we realised only the *symbiotic* world of ecosocial politics and *Solarpunk* culture presented a future in any meaningful sense for human beings to live and sustain for all.

5   PLANETARY POLITICS IN THE TWENTY-SECOND CENTURY: A *STATUS QUO*, *CAPITALIST*, OR *SYMBIOTIC* UNIVERSE?

On reflection, what does knowledge about the 100-year POC and the *status quo*, *capitalist*, and *symbiotic* universes mean for contemporary readers in 2122? Yoda Betula communicating from the *status quo* universe tells us that by the twenty-second century it was entirely possible to return the world of 1922—a very hot 1920s with a lethal mix of nostalgic ethno-nationalist neofascism at 5 °C over pre-industrial temperatures. And all Yoda and fellow academics had to do was nothing—keep calm and carry on regardless—safe in their far northern universities teaching courses on the international relations of inter-imperial balance of power. As Yoda says, the absence of children and hope was depressing, but what could you do? Nobody wants to lose their job for publishing the wrong things, and certainly no one wants to be imprisoned for thought crimes such as questioning the national culture, the environmental apocalypse, or the hegemony of military power and physical force in international relations.

Gaia Lovelock Margulis communicating from the *capitalist* universe tells us that by the twenty-second century it was entirely possible to live in the techno-fantasy world of the 1980s or 2010s—an almost as hot 4 °C world where the technocracy was eternally promising the geoengineering benefits of nuclear power-driven carbon capture, sulphate aerosols, and market-based solutions.

And all Gaia and fellow academics had to do was accelerate the neoliberalism—place your trust in the market—precarious but wealthy on the income generated by citation streams, quality assurance scores, and online research retail. Teaching profit-making courses had been a challenge, in particular the monetisation of online texts, citations, and exam grades. But zero-hours jobs did make student-customer satisfaction more motivating. And the courses in global politics using the corporate publisher-sanctioned online teaching resources helped. As Gaia put it, in the end the rationale of economic power and material incentives put food on the table and kept poverty at bay.

Krik Oakenglade communicating from the *symbiotic* universe has a very different story to tell. A tale of struggle and hard work against the powerful status quo and the hegemony of capitalism. Because of the struggles and sacrifices of the twenty-first century generations, by the year 2122 it was safe to say that the planet and its species had mostly been saved from the worst excesses of humanity. And while a 3 °C rise over pre-industrial levels was not good, it was possible to put in place the decarbonised society and reforesting earth needed to avoid cryospheric collapse and associated sea level rise. But the path of understanding symbiosis and adopting solarpunk lifestyles was not the easy route. Far from it, this path meant changing everything about industrialisation in favour of far more demanding organisation of society, including a symbiotic economy and radical decarbonisation. But most important of all for the study of global politics in the twenty-second century, this path meant radically changing education and higher education, in particular by recognising the fallacy of inter/national relations and embracing the ecocentric reality of planetary politics.

REFERENCES

Åhall, Petra, and Davina Ciksos. ⟨Ψ 2031⟩. *Varieties of Autocapitalism: The Authoritarian Foundations of Comparative Disadvantage* (Oxford: Oxford University Press).

Atwood, Margaret. (2003). *Oryx and Crake* (London: Bloomsbury).

Balestra, Carlotta, and Richard Tonkin. (2018). *Inequalities in Household Wealth Across OECD Countries: Evidence from the OECD Wealth Distribution Database.* OECD Statistics Working Papers 2018/01 (Paris: OECD).

Benatar, Solomon, and Denis Daneman. (2020). 'Disconnections between Medical Education and Medical Practice: A Neglected Dilemma', *Global Public Health* 15(9): 1292–1307.

Betula, Yoda. ⟨Ψ 2041 [2022]⟩. 'Student-Driven Pedagogy Challenges Regulations', Lund University 1666–2041 Special Jubilee Edition, *LUM: Lund University Magazine* 4: 20–21. https://www.lu.se/samverkan-innovation/projekt-och-samarbeten/tankesmedjan-lu-futura/valkommen-till-ar-2041/welcome-lund-university-2041

Betula, Yoda, Gaia Lovelock Margulis, and Krik Oakenglade. ⟨Ψ 2100⟩. *The Symbiotic Relationship between Quantum Behaviour, Cultural Imaginaries, and Planetary Politics* (Multiverse: Ansible Quantum Communications).

288　I. MANNERS

Bezos, Elon, Jeff Gates, and Bill Musk. ⟨Ψ 2103⟩. *Proxymoronic Corporate Branding* (Longyearbyen: Alphametatesla Inc.).

Bezos, Elon, Jeff Gates, and Bill Musk. ⟨Ψ 2122⟩. *Generosity of Globalization*, metaverse edn. (Longyearbyen: Alphametatesla Inc.).

Cameron, Rob. (2019). 'In Search of Afro-Solarpunk', *Tor.com*, 29th & 30th October. https://www.tor.com/author/rob-cameron/

Chancel, Lucas, Thomas Piketty, Emmanuel Saez, and Gabriel Zucman. (2021). *World Inequality Report 2022* (Cambridge MA: Harvard University Press).

Flynn, Adam. (2014). 'Solarpunk: Notes toward a manifesto', *Hieroglyph*, 4th September.

Gibson, William. (1984). *Neuromancer* (New York: Ace).

Gill, Stephen, and Solomon Benatar. (2020). 'Reflections on the Political Economy of Planetary Health', *Review of International Political Economy* 27(1): 167–190.

Global Footprint Network. ⟨Ψ 2122⟩. *National Footprint and Biocapacity Accounts, 2122 Edition*. https://www.footprintnetwork.org

Gottfried, Shelly. (2019). *Contemporary Oligarchies in Developed Democracies* (Chem: Springer).

Hellmann, Thorsten, Pia Schmidt, and Sascha Matthias Heller. (2019). *Social Justice in the EU and OECD: Index Report 2019* (Gütersloh: Bertelsmann Stiftung).

Hudson, Andrew Dana. (2015). 'On the Political Dimension of Solarpunk', *Medium*, 15th October.

Inspiration Journey. ⟨Ψ 2031⟩. *Planetary Politics: A Symbiotic Revolution* (Lund: Lund University Press).

IPBES. (2019). *The Global Assessment Report on Biodiversity and Ecosystem Services* (Bonn: Intergovernmental Science-Policy Platform on Biodiversity and Ecosystem Services).

IPCC. (2022). *Climate Change 2022: Impacts, Adaptation and Vulnerabilities* (Geneva: WMO).

IPCC. ⟨Ψ 2122⟩. *Climate Change 2122: Benefits, Advantages and Invulnerabilities* (Geneva: WMO).

Ivan, Alex. ⟨Ψ 2032⟩. *On the Essence of Christian Fascism: Liberating Chechnya, Syria, Ukraine, and Moldova* (Zurich: Zollikon Press).

Johndotter, Bayley, Steffi Stevendotter, and Owen Patriciasson. ⟨Ψ 2097⟩. *Deglobalization of World Politics: An Introduction to International Relations* (Kiruna: Kiruna University Press).

Keodoylessett, Robert. ⟨Ψ 2048⟩. *Democracy, Interdependence, and International Institutions* (Anchorage: Free American Press).

Kinnvall, Catarina, Ian Manners, and Jennifer Mitzen. (2018). 'Introduction to 2018 Special Issue of European Security: "Ontological (in) Security in the European Union"', *European Security* 27(3): 249–265.

Knopf, Christina. (2021). *Politics in the Gutters: American Politicians and Elections in Comic Book Media* (Jackson: University Press of Mississippi).

Kumar, Ramesh. ⟨Ψ 2081⟩. 'Indian Social Science of Hindutva Values', *Indian Political Science Review* 113(3): 100–114.

Landrigan, Philip, et al. (2018). 'The Lancet Commission on Pollution and Health', *The Lancet* 391(10119): 462–512.

Li, Ruòxī et al. ⟨Ψ 2120⟩. 'Fertility, Mortality, Migration, and Population Scenarios for 295 Countries and Territories from 2117 to 2200: A Forecasting Analysis for the Planetary Burden of Disease Study', *The Lancet* 1396(20258): 1000–1021.

Litfin, Karen. (2003). 'Planetary Politics', in John Agnew, Katharyne Mitchell, and Gerard Toal (eds.) *A Companion to Political Geography* (Oxford: Blackwell): 470–482.

Litfin, Karen. (2014). *Ecovillages: Lessons for Sustainable Community* (Cambridge: Polity).

Manners, Ian. (2020). 'Symbols and Myths of European Union Transnational Solidarity', in Helle Krunke, Hanne Petersen, and Ian Manners (eds.) *Transnational Solidarity: Concept, Challenges and Opportunities* (Cambridge: Cambridge University Press): 76–99.

Manners, Ian. (2021). 'European Communion and Planetary Organic Crisis', in Nathalie Brack and Seda Gürkan (eds.) *Theorising the Crises of the European Union* (London: Routledge): 159–182.

Manners, Ian. (2022a). 'Normative power in the planetary organic crisis', in Ian Manners (ed.) Special Issue of *Cooperation and Conflict* 56.

Manners, Ian. (2022b). 'Arrival of Normative Power in Planetary Politics', *JCMS* 60.

Margulis, Lynn. (1998). *The Symbiotic Planet: A New Look at Evolution* (New York: Basic Books).

Meadows, Donella, Jorgen Randers, Dennis Meadows, and William Behrens. (1972). *Limits to Growth: A Report for the Club of Rome's Project on the Predicament of Mankind* (Earth Island).

Michaud, Thomas. (2008). 'Science Fiction and politics: Cyberpunk Science Fiction as Political Philosophy', in Donald Hassler and Clyde Wilcox (eds.) *New Boundaries in Political Science Fiction* (Colombia SC: University of South Carolina Press): 65–77.

Monckridleyborg, Dirt. ⟨Ψ 2045⟩. *Back to Earth: Global Warming is Getting Better* (New Copenhagen Nuuk: Greenland Press).

Morgenwaltzheimer, Robert. ⟨Ψ 2048⟩. *Great Power Facts of International Relations* (New Washington: US Confederal Publishing).

Morton, Timothy. (2016). *Dark Ecology: For a Logic of Future Coexistence* (New York: Columbia University Press).

Müller, Lena et al. (2119). *Social Justice in the EU and OECD: Index Report 2119* (Oberwiesenthal: Bertelsmann Stiftung).

Næss, Arne. (1973). 'The Shallow and the Deep, Long-range Ecology Movement. A Summary', *Inquiry* 16(1–4): 95–100.

OECD. (2020). *How's Life? 2020: Measuring Well-Being* (Paris: Organisation for Economic Cooperation and Development).

OECD. ⟨Ψ 2120⟩. *How's Life? 2120: Measuring Well-Being* (Ulaanbaatar: Organisation for Economic Cooperation and Development).

Orwell, George. ⟨Ψ 2049⟩. *Twenty Eighty-Four* (Londinium: Airstrip One Press).

O'Sullivan, Michael. (2019). *The Levelling: What's Next after Globalization* (New York: Hachette).

Raworth, Kate. (2017). *Doughnut Economics: Seven Ways to Think Like a 21st Century Economist* (Chelsea Green Publishing).

Rio Declaration. (1992). *Rio Declaration on Environment and Development* (Rio de Janeiro: United Nations Conference on Environment and Development).

Robinson, Ken. (2008). 'Changing Paradigms', Talk to the Royal Society of Arts (London). https://www.thersa.org/video/animates/2010/10/rsa-animate---changing-paradigms

Robinson, Ken. (2009). *The Element: How Finding Your Passion Changes Everything* (London: Penguin).

290   I. MANNERS

Robinson, Kim Stanley. (2020). *The Ministry for the Future* (London: Orbit).

Sherwood S, et al. (2020). 'An Assessment of Earth's Climate Sensitivity Using Multiple Lines of Evidence', *Reviews of Geophysics* 58(4): e2019RG000678: 1–92.

Shilliam, Robbie. (2015). *The Black Pacific: Anti-Colonial Struggles and Oceanic Connections* (London: Bloomsbury Publishing).

Smith, Ryan. (2021). 'Male fertility is Declining: Studies Show that Environmental Toxins Could be a Reason', *The Conversation*, 2 August. https://theconversation.com/male-fertility-is-declining-studies-show-that-environmental-toxins-could-be-a-reason-163795

Snyder, Timothy. (2018). *The Road to Unfreedom: Russia, Europe, America* (Tim Duggan Books).

Stanman, Hoffley. ⟨Ψ 2077⟩. 'American Social Science of International Relations', *International Relations* 206(3): 1–21.

Steffen, Alex (ed.). (2006). *Worldchanging: A Users guide for the 21st Century* (New York: Abrams).

Steffen, Will, Johan Rockström, Katherine Richardson, Timothy Lenton, Carl Folke, Diana Liverman, Colin Summerhayes et al. (2018). 'Trajectories of the Earth System in the Anthropocene', *Proceedings of the National Academy of Sciences* 115(33): 8252–8259.

Steinkopf-Frank, Hannah. (2021). 'Solarpunk is Not About Pretty Aesthetics: It's About the End of Capitalism', *Vice*, 2nd September.

The Lancet Planetary Health. (2021). 'A Pandemic Era', *The Lancet Planetary Health* 5(1): e1.

Thomas, Malte. ⟨Ψ 2072⟩. *Delimits to Growth: A Report on the Downsizing of Humankind* (Planet Island).

Tremblay, Jade et al. ⟨Ψ 2121⟩. *Planetary Inequality Report 2122* (Montréal: Planetary Inequality Lab).

UNDP. (2022). *Human Development Report 2022: New Threats to Human Security in the Anthropocene Demanding Greater Solidarity* (New York: UN Development Programme).

van Bergeijk, Peter. (2020). *Deglobalization 2.0: Trade and Openness During the Great Depression and the Great Recession* (Cheltenham: Edward Elgar Publishing).

Vollset, Stein, et al. (2020). 'Fertility, Mortality, Migration, and Population Scenarios for 195 Countries and Territories from 2017 to 2100: A Forecasting Analysis for the Global Burden of Disease Study', *The Lancet* 396(10258): 1285–1306.

von Hayek, Friedrich August. (1944). *The Road to Serfdom* (Chicago: University of Chicago Press).

Werrell, Caitlin, and Francesco Femia (eds.). (2013). *The Arab Spring and Climate Change* (Washington DC: Center for American Progress).

WWF. (2019). *EU Overshoot Day 10th May: Living Beyond Nature's Limits* (Brussels: WWF).

WWF. (2020). *Living Planet Report 2020: Bending the Curve of Biodiversity Loss* (Gland, Switzerland: WWF).

Xu, Chi, Timothy A. Kohler, Timothy Lenton, Jens-Christian Svenning, and Marten Scheffer. (2020). 'Future of the Human Climate Niche', *Proceedings of the National Academy of Sciences* 117(21): 11350–11355.

Zhang, Wei. ⟨Ψ 2091⟩. 'Chinese Social Science of Guanxi Relationality', *Chinese Review of International Studies* 127(5): 43–63.

"Now Live from Lagos, Tehran and Oceanside": Three B7CC Leaders Reflect on Strategies for Cooperation After the Anthropocentric Purge

Franziska Müller

Editorial remarks:
The following text is a slightly abridged script of the award-winning video documentary "Now Live from Lagos, Tehran and Oceanside," which reflects on the anthropocentric purge and on the establishment of the Big 7 Cooperation Council (B7CC). Originally it was broadcast on May 4, 2100. Production took about 5 years in preparation, as no airborne transport was used. The documentary made by the well-known filmmaker Nabre Tanlo and their team won several prestigious awards, including the Best Documentary Award at the Unruly Futures Film Festival.

We consider it as an outstanding piece of reflection over one of the worst possible man-made catastrophes. We are therefore convinced that it positively complements our textbook by adding an extra layer of reality that allows us to zoom in on the anthropocentric purge and its aftermath. Indeed, the human brain is able to repress traumatic memories and replace them by neutral or even glorifying ones. Given this (dis)ability, today's generation seems to have effectively cut their connection to the shadows of the past, and all the more we see the need to initiate a debate on how today's frugal lifestyles formed and how climate change resulted in a hitherto unseen rupture of civilization.

F. Müller (✉)
Business, Economics and Social Sciences,
University of Hamburg, Hamburg, Germany
e-mail: franziska.mueller@uni-hamburg.de

© The Author(s), under exclusive license to Springer Nature
Switzerland AG 2023
L. Horn et al. (eds.), *The Palgrave Handbook of Global Politics in the 22nd Century*, https://doi.org/10.1007/978-3-031-13722-8_17

292 F. MÜLLER

Teaching instructions:
For classroom purposes the editors suggest to screen the documentary and initiate a discussion with the students. We recommend continuing coursework by zooming in on the script, for instance by comparing the three analytical lenses (institutions, energy, agriculture and land use) and by entering into a more intricate debate on the challenges and potentials of the "random ubuntu" norm. A number of questions to initiate debate, as well as a reading list can be found at the end of the chapter.
Script: Now Live from Lagos, Tehran and Oceanside (Originally screened on May 4, 2100)
[Interviewer stands at a seashore. We see waves floating in along a sandy beach. A peaceful scene, if only some building structures would not irritate the view. Some of them seem strangely familiar, such as the apex of the once prestigious Elbphilharmonie, which is mostly covered by the Elbe's brackish waters now].

Interviewer: "Good morning, my name is Nabre Tanlo, and I am standing here at the Hamburg Gulf. In the following months, I am excited to talk to representatives of the Big 7 Cooperation Council, celebrating its 40th anniversary. For those who are unfamiliar, B7CC was founded as a crisis response mechanism during the event we now call the Anthropocentric Purge—a series of massive thunderstorms, heavy flooding, drought and disease that created a state of emergency in several regions, and led to unprecedented death tolls.

Before we talk to folks from Lagos, Tehran, and Colo-Fornia, we will first take you back a few decades and remind you of the Anthropocentric Purge. Many of our younger viewers haven't experienced these days, while most people over 40, the Surviving Generation, have a vivid, and very grim memory of it. Even those below 40 may have inherited anthropocene trauma. Therefore, I'd like to declare a trigger warning for the next 10 min of this feature. What I am going to talk about will be sad and graphic."

[We see a timeline of the events, gloomy background music].

1   ANTHROPOCENTRIC PURGE

Interviewer: "We could have seen it coming. In the early 30s evidence became clear, that climate catastrophe was about to change people's lives fundamentally. Some nations were resilient and well prepared for the coming storm, whereas others were highly vulnerable. Weather extremes became more frequent. The 6th mass extinction accelerated. Ecosystems crashed and so did crop cycles. Hand pollination became common and created millions of jobs in China and in the US. Vast areas became uninhabitable—the Gulf region, parts of Pakistan and Iran, the Netherlands, Bangladesh. Right over here, the Hamburg Gulf including the beautiful Harburg lowlands was formed. A wide humid-heat belt expanded around the equator, covering the former Sahel zone, Sudan, Cameroon, Middle America and parts of Venezuela and Colombia, as well as South India. At the same time, the planet's rich kids—those who had capitalized on algorithms, social media and green urban technology—were able to secure their lifestyles thanks to largescale land-grabbing in the former Arctic regions. Greenland declared independence from Denmark, governed by an oligarchic regime. For those dwelling north and south of the jungle belt, the anthropocentric purge began—as a *state of violence, a state of flight and a state of trauma.*

In the 2040s and 50s resource wars spread, and it wasn't just for the last remnants of the fossil age, but rather for the new green geopolitics, the rush for scarce minerals like silicium, lithium, that old and new power games occurred in South Congo, China and the shores of Madagascar, whose hidden gems—vast deep-sea resources—seemed to provide the last and final capitalist expansion to the black depths hitherto unknown. Due to the adverse climatic conditions, wars were fought with mercenaries and drones. Think American and Chinese cyber kids sitting in air-conditioned war rooms, and desperate Pakistani, Bangladeshi or Sahel-zone men, whose desire to escape climate hell and just do something made them join mercenary forces. Death from above struck quickly. Some wars ended with successes for the Chinese, others for the Americans, and the result was more subaquatic drilling, more damage to marine ecosystems and submarine currents. What also happened was a new form of resource colonialism. In Malawi and Vietnam resource protectorates were created as a form of postmodern green statehood, and were labelled as a force for good.

Climate migration had been on political agendas already since the 2020s. Yet, when the UN gathered to address the "problem of climate refugees" in 2038 in New York, the results were frustrating. The conference could not secure safe migration ways for those fleeing heat, humidity and water day zero, except few offers made by Uruguay and Costa Rica. Striking parallels to the 1938 Evian Conference, which had unsuccessfully discussed asylum for Jewish refugees fleeing Germany, mean that this meeting is remembered to this day as the Evian + 100 Summit. Instead, in several European countries the political right captured green thought and used it as a strategy to close down borders, of course labelled as "ecological responsibility" in their PR proclamations, yet characterized as authoritarian ecocracy by political science. Climate asylum or a universal climate refugee status had been a political battleground, but in the end, only a limited, competence-based resettlement regime came into force, placing people from the Maldives, Nauru and the Caribbean's in chilly Antarctica. This seemed an easy-to-handle and in economic terms even favourable solution. Mass media showed happy politicians congratulating each other for having managed a transformation of statehood. In some regions, climate resilience measures were able to protect ecosystems and humans. Yet, this resembled a survival of the eco-fittest, i.e. those nations, which excelled as the most attractive green investment havens, Kenya and South Africa and the green resource protectorates under UNEP control, such as Zambia and Costa Rica, which received generous support to preserve resources and eco-systems. The oil industry's Saving Lagos campaign meant that Nigeria was able to stay unharmed, thanks to dikes, resettlement, and solar-powered air-conditioning.

Also, the Gulf Cooperation Council managed to secure conditions in Kenya and the Horn of Africa. Both regions however switched to nocturne lifestyles, as daytime temperatures were considered life-threatening for humans.

At the same time, the more complex 'problems' were left almost entirely unresolved. Climate flight was a mass phenomenon, which occurred on both the south and northern of the heat belt. Many fleeing from water day zero hot spots, such as Bengaluru, did not make it to safer terrains. Today, the so-called *trails of death* continue to remind us of the uncountable victims, who died due to heat waves and flooding. Still more were struck by extreme weather events. The foreshadows of category 6 and 7 hurricanes had already appeared in the 2020s. The anthropocentric purge culminated in 2061 with a 'hypercane', a tropical cyclone which had so far been considered a hypothetical weather event, demanding special breeding grounds: ocean temperatures between 40 and 50 °C, wind speed of about 500 mph, and clouds reaching up to the upper stratosphere, thus being able to last for several weeks. All hurricanes before had been given names, following good old meteorological traditions, yet this hypercane was indeed the unimaginable, the unseen and the ultimate. It raged between September and December 2041. We have no direct witnesses. No news from the death zone in India, Bangladesh and Indonesia, besides some drone footage. Also, the Sentinelese—an uncontacted tribe on the Andaman Islands, who survived so many natural disasters—are considered dead. We could have learned from them from a distance, even without ever contacting them. They were experts in defending their lifestyle. They left no traces and are now wiped out forever.

Collective ecological traumata (CETs) became devastating for many societies. A mix of generational guilt, hopelessness and extinction-related grief struck many people precisely at a time where joint action would have been needed most. Especially people in western nations, with their built-in trust in technological fixes were affected by CET paralysis. A collective depression meant that many from the 'Fridays for Future' youth generation lost their hopes in collective change. Losing trust in a hostile political system, they instead embarked on a 'fin de siècle' lifestyle, by cherishing cyber culture, anti-politics and 'suicide on invitation' with their BFFs. Historians tended to compare CET morbidities to the heydays of the fifteenth century 'danse macabre', when people expressed hysterical desire for amusement, only to expect a cruel and inevitable death. Psychological cure was difficult, given the sheer numbers of peoples suffering from CET and more so, as CET was considered to be a contagious phenomenon, that alienated so many gifted people from their most significant skills. Consequentially, psychological literature described CET as a fundamental and potentially chronic loss of self-efficacy. Indeed, what seemed to provide a cure was 'survival therapy' a combination of small-scale agricultural work, interspecies bonding, and local community commitment, as this reminded people of their resilience and reconnected them to the material world.

So, today is also a day of remembrance regarding the near-ecocide which we and the previous generations have caused ourselves. Sarcastically, the Anthropocene revealed a self-limiting quality. Similarly, to the 'Orbis Spike' of 1610, the so-far all-time low of CO_2 emissions in the earth's atmosphere due to settler colonial genocide in the Americas, the hypercane eventually caused a dramatic economic standstill. Earth is still recovering and will do so for the next centuries. We cannot yet be sure, whether our narratives are less toxic; this is something future generations will have to assess. Still, we may put some faith in the fact, that B7CC's continuous work has created a deeper understanding of ecological solidarity—a feeling that is stronger if not ultimately different than mere 'awareness', 'sustainability', or 'ownership'. But let's switch over to our first guest who can tell you all this much more accurate than I'd be able to do."

2 Interview with Rayowa Adebayo (Lagos Laguna, Floating Quarter)

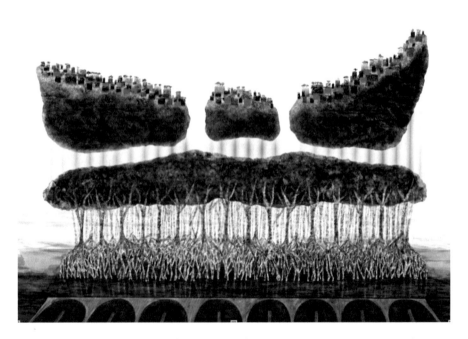

[Interviewer stands on a floating platform. Behind them we see a low-rise skyline, consisting of shiny cubicles, all covered in thin solar-cell foil. We see algae farms and people harvesting them. The interviewer crosses PanAfro-Makers, a "fab lab,[1]" where all kinds of product parts can be printed out on

---

[1] Fab labs were created in the early 2000s by the 'maker' movement, and later spread all across the globe. Fab labs are open labs that provide 3-D printing and laser cutting

organoplastic. We smell air thick with charcoal, fish and rice and a salty breeze from the sea. The waves come rolling in from the Atlantic, but the tide seems gentle, thanks to an artificial cliff that was erected to protect New Lagos from heavy seas.]

Interviewer: "You might feel a bit shaky. Yes, what you see here in the back is one of the famous floating quarters in the Lagos Laguna. This one is a home for about 20.000 people, and it's 50% self-sustaining, thanks to algae farms and rooftop gardening. Lagos itself, our notorious Nollywood, is all gone. Like so many other bustling metropoles, it is one of the sunken cities diving archaeologists might explore in future ages—at least if they have the courage for doing so. There might be ghosts, though. Folk lore says the ancestors are still in rage and anger, as the living did not do enough to protect the shrines and stools of their forefathers and -mothers."

[Interviewer walks down a small alley, surrounded by people who wave in the camera.]

Interviewer: "Now, as we walk across the quarter to talk to our first guest, Rayowa Adebayo from B7CC, you have the chance to at least enjoy a glimpse of the floating structures, built on hover platforms and on fortified mangroves in the Lagos Laguna. It is a stunning piece of seascape architecture, combining fisherfolk knowledge, petrochemical innovation, eco-design and GMOs. Still, New Lagos consists of only two million people. Many were able to resettle, as part of the Northern belt diaspora, but many others got lost on the trails of death. So we are here to mourn all those whom we lost. Old Lagos will forever remain a place to remember them."

[Interviewer stops at a cubicle and climbs a ladder up to a rooftop garden. We hear distant humming and chirping. Rayowa Adebayo, a tall woman in her late thirties, shows a warm smile and guides the way to a small pavilion, where both sit down. She is wearing wide pants and a matching top that combines wax print patterns with blinking solar foil particles; her long dark locks form a large chignon on top of her head].

Interviewer: "Rayowa, you are our first guest. We've decided to start with you, as you are so famous for your distinct knowledge of African philosophy and eco-political design. You've a story to tell—how New Lagos was created and how people learned to survive in the Anthropocene."

[Rayowa leans back. She looks thoughtful and a bit sad, as she begins to talk and her deep warm voice fills the room.]

Rayowa Adebayo: "Well I could talk about New Lagos for hours, and it's so good you came all the way to be our guest. But let me first look back at the creation of B7CC.

---

facilities, that allow manufacturing virtually every product of daily life. Fab labs hugely contributed to people's empowerment and independence in times of crisis. The invention of fully biodegradable organo-plastic was a huge success, which meant that fab labs were finally able to contribute to sustainable development.

You know very well, how all these politicians just postponed our future and acted like being blindfolded. So when the purge finally kicked in, we saw the UN system and the G20 coalition both failing to address the turmoil. Only after a 10-year interval of eco-anarchy, the B7CC rose from the ashes of empires. B7CC started as a grassroots action, when civil society movements started occupying western embassies in Ethiopia and Nigeria. They demanded responsibility and compensation for the devastating damage caused to our societies. The embassies debated handing out climate refugee passports, which was better than nothing, yet was not the material action people had been fighting for. "Climate reparation is not a metaphor" was a strong statement to which our movements subscribed. Rather than an end-of-the-pipe solution granted on individual grounds and materializing only at an all-too-late stage, what they really wanted was a fundamental sense of accountability for the fallacious decisions made in the past: reliance on voluntary regulations and fluffy incentives, trust in the carbon market's invisible hand, techno fixes such as e-cars. Civil society movements had lost their trust in both the UN system and in the power of western embassies, aid agencies and their shiny narratives of sustainable development and aid effectiveness.

B7CC predecessor groups called for 'random ubuntu', that is, a sense of deep-felt solidarity not for a concrete individual, but an imagined one, somebody we do not know and will maybe never meet, but somebody, who is as needy as oneself and should enjoy the same right to a safe climate and an intact environment. It is still based on the well-known South African philosophical concept, that is, the general idea of "I am because you are", but now, in the digital age it has been expanded to fit to our hybrid, post-modern societies. So our Afrocentric values and our tight-knit family networks helped us stick together, and random ubuntu was and is a powerful strategy to feel and express empathy and solidarity for random others, who have deserved to survive, just as ourselves. So, at some point 'random ubuntu' intensified, it became contagious in a positive sense, and it institutionalized. Some nodes were formed in Nigeria, and then the network spread to other places. Diaspora life, as sad it had been for so many generations, finally came as a godsend.

Indeed, random ubuntu became our baseline, our lifeline, you name it. It boiled down to random pairings on a communal level, fostered by a sense of ecological connectedness that had already manifested—yet in a much more abstract way—in earlier institutions such as the C40 city network or the African Peer Review Mechanism. Pairings were formed by the algorithm, building on some common features, and making way for common visions. The Lagos-Emirates post-oil partnership is one of the most successful examples, in sharing technology, food, energy and healthcare, based on a trust fund for overcoming fossil dependencies.

So B7CC started from scratch when a number of Anthropocene awareness groups and grassroots activists joined forces. While B7CC sounds overly grandiose, the name is basically a makeshift working title that was never replaced by something catchier, simply because nobody had the time to think about branding, when it was all rather about survival. Consequently, B7CC's political actions were built not so much on flagship agendas, such as the Sustainable Development Goals, but on small-scale change, policy exchange and local carbon budgeting, all to secure ecological existence.

So while B7CC is quite powerless in structure when compared to its predecessors, its strength lies rather in its dense connection to social movement infrastructures, and its dynamic power of powerlessness is able to create spaces of solidarity. Still, it feels so weird to think of all this in these old-school political science terms, like "democracy" or "decision-making". These categories are gone. In political science terms you might rather speak of an IR theory of extinction and survival, like it had been suggested by scholars in previous decades.

You see, mid-century was an unimaginably tough time for the planet. In these days it ultimately became clear, that the Anthropocene had become more than a mere philosophical concept. It had materialized in heavy floods and sea level rise. A number of prognoses from the early 2000s had come true. The end of nations big and small, such as the Netherlands and Nauru, who had both fallen prey to the ocean. The Anthropocentric purge with all of its horror, a combination of ecocide and genocide, climate change, soil failure, extreme weather events—and international organizations mostly unprepared to react, if only ACT. They used to call this business 'international relations' though, but to me this feels like old-fashioned hubris. We do not have 'international relations' anymore, we simply cannot afford this kind of large-scale diplomacy. We have some algorithms, that suggest how to use and redistribute resources and we have exchange structures along nodal points across the Northern Belt region, and occasional contact with the other B7CC partners, but only via data exchange and occasional ship missions. That's all we have."

Interviewer: "Wow, thanks for this rollercoaster ride through the history of apocalypse politics. I couldn't have put it so precise, with this myriad of activities all connected to B7CC. So, after this intro, would you like to tell us a bit more about how 'random ubuntu' materialized here in Lagos? And how would you assess the last decade?".

Rayowa Adebayo: "Well, crisis mode is here to stay. We have learned to somehow manage, month by month. While so many were fleeing extreme weather events, we here in Lagos found a way to thrive, thanks to some eco-innovations, and the help from the Emirate post-oil community. Without their support we would not have been able to erect the AfroCliff, which serves as breakwaters against the Atlantic waves. Fab labs helped us creating our own technology and product parts, as it soon became clear that technology import from the global North was less and less reliable. This was crucial for finally escaping fossil fuel dependency and entering energy independence. We also became independent from development aid and its fictions of superior knowledge and knowledge transfer. Indeed, the old textbooks of development cooperation seem strangely static and functionalist, with their groupings of over-developed and under-developed nations, and with their search for over-arching, universalist norms. We still remember the struggles going on in the Development Assistance Committee, and all the competitive game play with Chinese experts lurking around the corner, first playing low profile and then coming up with a grand oil deal somewhere in Angola. These days are gone, ancient diplomacy skills are no longer needed, as we now make politics on a day-to-day basis, supported—or irritated—through the power of our resource distribution algorithms.

It was Haske ('light' in Hausa), our IT start-up, a bunch of tech kids and philosophy graduates, who created these algorithms in the late 2070s. We were motivated by the aim to create solidary structures that equally rely on social relations as on technology. This was also understood as a critique of these weird debates on aid effectiveness and basically effective everything. You might have come across the debates about 'effective altruism' in the early 2000s. Some brainy Oxbridge kids made a fuss about how to channel both commitment and charity money in the most effective way. Like, make money as a stockbroker, but keep up a frugal life and donate your surplus for building schools in Africa, cuz that's obviously what Africa needs. It was wrong in so many ways, except maybe the pure mathematical logics. It resulted in a deep-reaching alienation from everyday poverty and empathy—the homeless you cross on your way to work, the lonely neighbour, the single mom—all those random acts of kindness that may distract you from the 'real work', may support somebody in a very concrete way, but count nothing against a six-digit donation receipt. Random ubuntu puts an end to this crap, both in philosophical, relational and digital terms.

So, switching to algorithmic mode, means the algorithm checks against a number of parameters, like, which communities could make good pairings for sharing, supporting and learning, and who could benefit from mutual exchange of control mechanisms. Mostly the algorithm chooses local partners, but sometimes we find odd combinations, that are difficult to manage, but may later appear as a wise choice. One stunning principle is land use. To protect land from overuse, we found that it is best, if two neighbours exchange control over land, so neighbour A uses neighbour B's land and vice versa, so both have to trust each other. It's in fact an ancient aboriginal form of land control. We do it here as well, and my neighbour tends this rooftop, so I will forward all your compliments about the flowers and fruits straight to her. I know it feels odd to put so much faith in an algorithm, and sometimes I wonder whether we've embarked on a cargo cult, adding new gods to our old ones. Still, with trust in politics weakening, and with the crash of international diplomacy, it was at least a structure that we could hold on to. Our regional governance is still working, but for any means of exchange, we put more trust in our open-source algorithm and its built-in intersectionality. We can manage on a regional level, we can exchange ideas, and we sometimes engage in sending missions abroad for a period of five years, to foster ever closer collaboration among B7CC and its partners. Yet it is a very loose exchange compared to the heydays of diplomacy. We are quite powerless. We can't send in armies; we only can protect our lifestyle and support others. We do not want to engage in the next drone war. Still, North Nigeria was and still is open chaos, struck by a toxic cocktail of doomsday Islamism and eco-apocalypse kicking in. We try to do something, send in drones, send in a mission of people to at least save the children, but we've mostly failed. The situation in the US Midwest is however quite similar. Doomsday preachers worked as true 'fishers of men', just like in the sermon, and people believed them and indulged in the epiphany. But I guess the Colofornian people will tell you more about that, and how they formed their own community west of the Plains and the Lands of the Failing Soil.

Excuse me for now. I have an appointment with the Laguna Council, to discuss some unresolved issues around public transport. To leave this floating office, you might use the hydro tunnel. Please say hello to my Tehrani colleague when you see her in half a year's time."

3   Infobox B7CC at a Glance

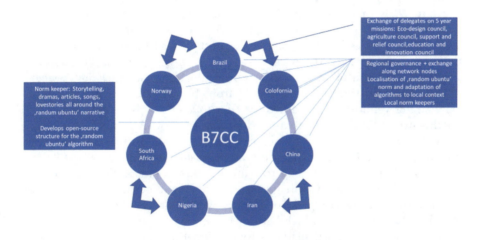

4   Interview with Shirin Mazanderani (Tehran)

Interviewer: "Salaam! Let me just briefly describe our surroundings: B7CC country delegate Shirin, our next guest, suggested a very beautiful meeting place. It is early spring in Iran, and we did a walk along the slopes of the Elburz mountain range in the northernmost quarters of Tehran. Sun is shining and many people are celebrating Nowruz, the traditional New Year, that dates back to the ancient Zarathustrian cosmovision. Shirin leans back, while telling me the story of Iran's involvement in B7CC. Not very surprisingly it all

"NOW LIVE FROM LAGOS, TEHRAN AND OCEANSIDE": THREE B7CC LEADERS … 301

started with a crash, a crash encompassing both the politico-clerical system, the economy and spirituality."

[Camera switches over to Shirin, who seems to be in her 60s. She is short-haired, black with many greyish strands and dark, expressive eyes. On her green blouse we see a button with the Iranian national flag, featuring the national animal, a cheetah.]

Shirin Mazanderani: "We call it the Green Revolution reloaded. 30 years after the Islamic Revolution blackened our beloved nation, powerful protests formed as it became clear that once again elections were faked and the democratic candidate was overthrown by Ahmadinejad, one of the hard liners. Sadly, the uprising was violently repressed, and also social protests that formed in the following years were only able to bring minor change. Think: higher heels and smaller headscarves."

"Only in the years of the Anthropocentric Purge things heated up, literally. Some provinces close to the Persian Gulf had become uninhabitable, with temperatures never falling below 35 degrees, leaving the human metabolism unable to recover from the heat. In these days, with droughts, air pollution and the Caspian sea falling dry, with climate migrants from the gulf region moving to the north, public unrest grew in unforeseen form. Water became scarce, scarce in a way that fundamentally questioned the lifestyle of the middle-class and the rich kids of Northern Tehran. We saw water wars at the harbours. Tank ships and desalination plants were occupied and angry youth entered the swimming pools of the posh resorts on Kish island in the Persian Gulf. Yet, let me tell you of an even more powerful and at the same time peaceful phenomenon: In those days, a picture from bygone eras became commonplace: water vendors selling drinking water in single cups or even single sips on the streets. We started to regard it as a symbol. A symbol of ultimate crisis, but also of solidarity, as people tended to pass on the cup and cared not to spill a single drop. The cup symbol washed away paternalistic gender relations. Men handed the cup to women, women passed the cup to men, foreigners shared water with beggars, and the simple gesture created a sense of small, yet universal compassion. The cup symbol also washed away the belief in Shia authoritarianism, which had for more than 70 years been the cornerstone of the regime. Particularly its foundational myth came under question, the eschatological prophecy of the Hidden Imam that would return at the end of the times in a well in the Jamkaran Mosque in the pious city of Ghom. Yet with wells falling dry and their stones crumbling apart, what crumbled away at a similar pace was the belief in these forms of authoritarian mysticism. Out of spiritual despair people cultivated syncretistic beliefs and combined Zarathustrian spiritual and intellectual traditions with a fundamental love for nature and rejuvenation. Yet, our fight against the Mullahs would not have been successful, had they not fallen prey to a crucial economic flaw: path dependencies and carbon capitalism). Indeed, one of Iran's seemingly adamant structures, the intimate connection between the Mullah regime and the oil industry, eventually became the straw that broke the camel's back). As soon as peak oil kicked in, trillions of stranded assets made clear that a political economy based on oil could no longer thrive in a green economy. Luckily, political visionaries had aligned with the nascent solar industry. Their close collaboration created a politico-economic plot—the vision of a solar democracy, as they used to put it. The Mullah regime was too anachronistic and too slow to accept change, and when the secret solar parks in the vast Ghom desert were connected to the grids, after a week-long power outage, this was the moment of change towards a solar democracy. The plot was simply too good. And, more so, it was realized thanks to financial cooperation with some of 'our' hereditary enemies. Some Sunnite regimes, most prominently the Emirates, had acted as first movers, and had been busy creating green sovereign wealth funds and divesting from fossils. Their support was much needed. So finally solidarity and random ubuntu allowed transcending the religious schism that has divided us for so long."

Interviewer: "Shirin, thank you so much for this story on the geopolitics and symbolics of transformation. For our last guest, I will embark on a long journey to Colo-Fornia, to meet a Native Colofornian activist and talk about random ubuntu in agriculture and food systems."

5   INTERVIEW WITH SCOTT GARCIA, OCEANSIDE

[Camera zooms along a creek. We see large black walnut, acorn and oak trees, under whose shadows we find redcurrant bushes and pomegranate trees. We also see a spiral formed of many different herbs. In the distance we can identify lines of mixed vegetable species such as carrots, beans and lentils and beautiful sunflowers. Several people are tending the gardens. The camera then closes up on Scott Garcia, a young man from the La Jolla Band of Luiseño Indians, who is wearing faded jeans and sandals made of car tires.]

Interviewer: "Hola Scott, thanks a lot for taking a quick break from gardening and showing us around this beautiful permaculture garden. Could you tell us a bit about its history and how it is linked to the birth of Colo-Fornia nation?".

Scott: "Welcome to Oceanside Community Gardens! Please feel free to walk around or taste one of these lovely redcurrants, but please take care of the plants and animals. Now, let me take you back a bit into the history of our young nation. Colo-Fornia was not so much affected by the Anthropocentric Purge. We however experienced large flows of migrants from the US Midwest. In these areas, many had believed the doomsday evangelists, who denied climate change and combined doomsday prophecy with the prosperity gospel, so they kept on exploiting the earth. Eventually, the soils had lost their fertility, so corn and wheat farming had to be terminated in the Midwest, and the deserted plains will take centuries to heal. In those days, in the 2050, our leaders declared they would prioritize land use permits for those, who could give proof of Native American origin. Also, to gain space for extensive agriculture, we created a 'return the land—respect the treaties' initiative, which resulted in partly voluntary, partly coercive changes in land ownership. I know, this was a difficult decision, yet our state is based on the outspoken condemnation of settler colonialism, so we felt an impetus to act in this way. We believe that settler colonialism is in essence responsible for all the ecological evils and for the troubles we still find ourselves in. Therefore, it's only logical for us to refuse our land to be exploited as a commodity once again, by those that had for such a long time benefitted from settler privilege. So, these events were the basis for the Colo-Fornian independence movement, which—as the other Federal States were unable to give a solid response—finally led to the creation of Colo-Fornia in 2056, about 200 years after the settlers had declared the 'war of extermination' on our tribes and removed us from our lands (Levin 2019). As I've already said our state is considered a counter-project to settler colonialism, which also means that we rely a lot on Indigenous nature-society relations and those with settler heritage learn to honour the land. We do not believe in national parks and wilderness, but rather in collective land use. Still, many of our traditions are lost, so in essence we're all syncretists now. Our food production system—one of the challenges we needed to resolve as an independent nation—is based on a mix of concepts—permaculture, Indigenous land use practices and the Kanat irrigation system,[2] which was brought to us by members of the TehrAngeles community. When we learned about the random ubuntu norm, we found that this matches communal land use practices, such as community-supported agriculture and mutual care for the land. Still, our food production systems are not as stable as we wish them to be. Extreme weather events continue to threaten our yields. We can only export small quantities of fruits and vegetables to the neighbouring nations, even if the algorithm requires us to do so. We will hand in a pledge at B7CC to update the algorithm, so as to model our annual sand storms and wildfires and be more flexible on our agricultural exports to the US, Canada and Mexico. I hope we can convince Rayowa and her colleagues. They always claim that the algorithm knows best, but in fact our soils still have to recover to produce the yields their estimation is grounded on."

Interviewer: Scott, thank you for this farming walk-through! May I pick some of these lemons and pomegranates from your beautiful garden? After all these visits I feel a bit overwhelmed. Luckily, I had much time to reflect during the long journeys between Lagos, Tehran, and Oceanside. Random ubuntu has proven to be a robust norm, which is why this is a day of celebration despite all ecological trauma. Still, I fear that the overall trust in the algorithm might erode this very norm. With all these neat and clean technologies in place, people are not forced to individually justify, narrate, feel or contest the meaning of random ubuntu. This is why my next mindcast will reflect on

---

[2] The Kanat (or Qanat) irrigation system is an ancient Persian irrigation concept. Gently sloping underground channels transport water from a water well to surface for irrigation and drinking, serving as an underground aqueduct.

didactics and teaching. Tune in next month when I will visit the kindergarten project "Ubuntu Adventurers" in Berlin.

6   Questions and Exercises

- "Random ubuntu" is a strong and enabling norm as the documentary has clearly shown. Think of similar norms stemming from your local context. What makes them so strong? Can you find general strengths that stabilize a norm or contribute to its attractiveness? Which strengths or weaknesses does the norm hold, considering the conditions of the Anthropocene? How could "normative erosion" be prevented?
- Compare the three interviews: Which facets and potentials of the random ubuntu norm can you identify?
- What would you regard as central political or economic components to stabilize a "solar democracy"?
- The Colo-Fornian state has radically changed land use practices and had outspokenly prioritized people with Native American roots. Is this ethically justifiable? Why? Why not?
- Thought experiment: Picture yourself in the pre-Anthropocene, the purge, the post-purge. Why would you survive? What are your personal and political (and, if you like: spiritual) strengths, weaknesses and challenges and privileges?

Further Readings

The documentary mentioned several concepts that need some broader contextualization. Please engage with the following recommendations to deepen your knowledge.

Agriculture and Human–Nature Relations

La Puig de Bellacasa, Maria. (2015). Making time for soil: Technoscientific futurity and the pace of care. In: Social Studies of Science 45(5), 691–716.

Von Redecker, Sophie. (Ψ 2031). Of Care and Compost: Queering Human–Soil Relations in the Planthropocene. Baltimore: University of Baltimore Press.

Richardson-Ngwenya, Pamela. (2021). Everyday political geographies of community-building: Exploring the practices of three Zimbabwean permaculture communities. In: Environmental Policy and Governance 31(3), 211–222.

Todd, Zoe. (2016). From fish lives to fish law: learning to see Indigenous legal orders in Canada. In: Yates-Doerr, Emily, and Labuski, Christine (Eds.) Somatosphere: Ethnographic Case Series. http://somatosphere.net/2016/02/from-fish-lives-to-fish-law-learning-to-see-indigenous-legal-orders-in-canada.html.

ANTHROPOCENE, CLIMATE CRISIS, AND ANTHROPOCENTRIC PURGE

Emanuel, Kerry A., Speer, Kevin, Rotunno, Richard, Srivastava, Ramesh, Molina, Mario. (1995). Hypercanes: A possible link in global extinction scenarios. In: Journal of Geophysical Research 100(13) 13755–13765.

McEwan, Cheryl. (2021). Decolonising the anthropocene. In: Chandler, David, Müller, Franziska and Rothe, Delf (Eds.) International Relations in the Anthropocene. London: Palgrave, 77–94

De Vries, Antje and Tsikata, Kwesi. ⟨Ψ 2034⟩. Anthropocene Trauma. Coping, Resilience, and Refusal in the Fridays No Future-Generation. Farnham: Rowman & Littlebrook.

Biermann, Frank and Boas, Ingrid. (2010). Preparing for a warmer world: Towards a global governance system to protect climate refugees. In: Global Environmental Politics 10(1). 60–88

Dreher, Tanja, and Voyer, Michelle. (2015). Climate refugees or migrants? Contesting media frames on climate justice in the pacific. In: Environmental Communication 9(1), 58–76.

Burke, Anthony, Dalby, Simon, Fishel, Stefanie, Levine, Daniel and Mitchell, Audra. (2016). Planet politics: A manifesto from the end of IR. In: Millennium Journal of International Studies 44(3), 499–523.

Mitchell, Audra. (2016). Is IR going extinct? In: European Journal of International Relations 23(1), 3–25.

Gilio-Whitaker, Gina. (2018) Unpacking the invisible knapsack of settler privilege, In: Beacon Broadside Blog, Nov. 8 2018. https://www.beaconbroadside.com/broadside/2018/11/unpacking-the-invisible-knapsack-of-settler-privilege.html.

Todd S. Menuhin-Kiiza. ⟨Ψ 2056⟩. Human Pessimism: Necropolitical Essays. University of Nairobi Press.

Bird Rose, Deborah, van Dooren,Thom and Chrulew, Matthew. (2017). Extinction Studies. Stories of Time, Death, and Generations. New York: Columbia University Press.

Gibson, Catherine, Rose, Deborah Bird and Fincher, Ruth. (2015, Eds). Manifesto for Living in the Anthropocene. Brooklyn: Punctum Books.

COOPERATION

B7CC. ⟨Ψ 2060⟩. Constitutive Act. Lagos.

Mert, Ayşem. (2021). Challenges to democracy in the anthropocene, In: David Chandler, Müller, Franziska, and Rothe, Delf (Eds.) International Relations in the Anthropocene. London: Palgrave, 291–310.

Müller, Franziska and Sondermann, Elena. (2016). Myths of the near future: Paris, Busan and the tales of aid effectiveness, In: Berit Bliesemann (Ed.) Myths and International Politics: A Narrative Approach to the Study of IR. London: Palgrave Macmillan, 249–266.

GREEN GEOPOLITICS

Ardastaninejad, Lale. ⟨Ψ 2052⟩. In the Shadow of Ghom's Mosques. Solar Revolution and Oil Dependency in Iran. Tehran: Tehran University Press.

Los Angeles Daily Mail. (Ψ 2039) The Big Polar Bear Safari: Krystal Khaloustian's Luxurious Hideway in Thule, 28.3. 2039.

Lederer, Markus. (2020). The promise of prometheus and the opening up of Pandora's box: Anthropological geopolitics of renewable energy. In: Geopolitics 27(2) 655–679

Chiang, Jane. (Ψ 2042).The Deep Sea Regime. Governance and Geopolitics.

Levin, Sam. (2019). 'This is all stolen land': Native Americans want more than California's apology. In: The Guardian, June 16, 2019. https://www.theguardian.com/us-news/2019/jun/20/california-native-americans-governor-apology-reparations.

Normative Orders and the Ubuntu Norm

Eze, Michael Onyebuchi. (2017) I am because you are: Cosmopolitanism in the age of xenophobia, In: Philosophical Papers, Vol. 46, No. 1 (March 2017): 85–109. Special Issue on Cosmopolitanism.

Ubuntu Dialogue. (2019). Mind & Life Institute. http://ubuntudialogue.org.

Themes: *Culture and Identity*

World Religions

Luca Ozzano and Alberta Giorgi

1   INTRODUCTION

The relevance of religion and the sacred in the global affairs of the twenty-second century is the subject of an ongoing debate. Most scholars however agree that the influence of this factor has significantly changed in the past century: both as a consequence of the phenomenon known as "convergence" between the major "traditional" faiths, as a consequence of the ongoing secularization process; and because of the association of different ideas of religiosity with the cleavage between Technoutopian and Neogaian perspectives (Rzb2 Ψ 2117). This latter shows, in today's world, both in a "hard" way, with a confrontation between the Solar System Web (SSW) and the "renegade states" (see below); and, in a "soft" way, through a lively social and cultural debate raging in the SSW (which is not possible in the renegade states, where authoritarianism and censorship, and in some cases mind control, prevail).

At the beginning of the twenty-first century, the perspective was quite different. At the time, the scientific debate in social and political sciences revolved around what seemed like a conundrum: on the one side, religiosity

L. Ozzano (✉)
Department of Cultures, Politics and Society, University of Turin, Turin, Italy
e-mail: luca.ozzano@unito.it

A. Giorgi
Department of Letters, Philosophy, Communication,
University of Bergamo, Bergamo, Italy
e-mail: alberta.giorgi@unibg.it

© The Author(s), under exclusive license to Springer Nature
Switzerland AG 2023
L. Horn et al. (eds.), *The Palgrave Handbook of Global Politics in the 22nd Century*, https://doi.org/10.1007/978-3-031-13722-8_18

appeared to be declining, especially in the richest world countries; on the other side, the political relevance of religion appeared to be steady, if not increasing, regardless of the countries' relative richness.

In the overall framework of the handbook, the aim of this chapter is to reconstruct the transformations of the world religions, for the reader to grasp the significance of religiosity in contemporary societies. The chapter is structured as follows: in the Sect. 2, we situate our chapter in a historical perspective, while in Sects. 3 and 4 we discuss, respectively, the evolutions and transformations of world religions in relation to the technology wars and the tensions between Technoutopianism and Neogaianism (Sect. 3), and the debates in the public and the political spheres (Sect. 4). Section 5 provides some conclusions and future research perspectives.

2   THE STATE OF THE ART ONE HUNDRED YEARS AGO

For almost two centuries, secularization was the main theoretical frame adopted to interpret the role of religion in society. Despite its many versions (see Dobbelaere 2016 for a reconstruction), the main core of the secularization theory posited a strict connection between modernity and the decline of religion: in modern societies, religion became less central to the public sphere and individual lives. At the beginning of the twenty-first century, a world-wide research corroborated this interpretation, showing how the poorest countries were also the most religious (Inglehart and Norris 2004).

However, the secularization framework was widely criticized between the end of the twentieth century and the beginning of the twenty-first, for many reasons. First, the connection between modernity and the decline of religion was mostly a European phenomenon—in other countries, things went differently (Burchardt et al. 2016). Second, the decline of religion could be better reframed as the decline of Christianity, whereas other religions, traditional or otherwise, were indeed thriving. Third, what counted as a decline was the object of debate: although the attendance to religious rites—important for some religions only—was indeed decreasing in Europe, other expressions of religiosity, such as religious associations, were not.

These criticisms led to new concepts for grasping the role of religions in society without postulating its decline—among which "post-secular" gained wide visibility in the early twenty-first century (Wilson and Mavelli 2017). In post-secular societies, individual religiosity was increasingly less mediated by religious institutions: mostly it was "personalized" and a matter of choice (scholars adopted concepts such as "bricolage", Hervieu-Léger 1999). While losing members and undergoing internal institutional fragmentation, organized religions maintained instead their symbolic value—Grace Davie (2007) spoke of "vicarious religion", to indicate that it was practiced by a minority but valued by the majority of the population. Hence, religion could be interpreted as intertwined with local and traditional cultures, a matter of heritage and nationality—a process particularly evident in those countries historically characterized by a majority religion.

In the meantime, the religious landscape of both rich and poor countries was also undergoing a pluralization process, not only as a consequence of globalization processes and migration flows, but also as a consequence of the development of scores of new religious movements. In some cases, they stemmed from mainstream religions and hybridized them; in others, they were completely new phenomena, often labeled as "new age spiritualities", which however often recovered elements from both non-western spiritualities and pre-monotheistic traditions, for example in relation to female spirituality and to the so-called "Neogaianism", which revered our planet and its environment as a divine entity (Hammer and Rothstein 2012; Clarke 2008; Lewis and Petersen 2005; Palmisano and Pannofino 2017; Possamai 2019).

Among the works on the subject, some were devoted to the interaction between religion and new technologies, with a focus both on how the adoption of new technologies was changing religious practice and beliefs, and on the new religious movements marked by a role of technology (e.g., artificial intelligence) in the beliefs themselves (Campbell 2012; Helland 2016; Hojsgaard and Warburg 2005). However, these latter movements were mainly studied as fringe phenomena, and at the beginning of the twenty-first century very few people thought they might regard the masses, and have a significant impact on politics and global affairs (Harari 2017).

As for how the broader relation between religion and politics would evolve in the twenty-first century, there was also disagreement among scholars. Until the last decades of the twentieth century most social scientists, convinced of the validity of the secularization thesis, also thought that religion and the sacred would no longer be relevant factors in domestic and international politics with the advance of modernization. These predictions were however put into question first by localized phenomena such as the "rise" of Christian democracy (Kalyvas 1996) and its role in the democratization of southern Europe and Latin America (Huntington 1991); and, later, by a more general process of "return" or "deprivatization" of religion (Kepel 1991; Casanova 1994) which involved both the developed and the developing world. Scholars thus also theorized a return of religion also in international relations (Petito and Hatzopoulos 2003), which were influenced by the sacred in several ways: through its influence on policy-makers' worldview, through its influence on the voters' worldview, as a legitimacy factor, and as a source of conflict (Fox and Sandler 2006). This latter point was particularly developed by Samuel Huntington, with his very controversial thesis about the "clash of civilizations", and the idea that religion would become the basis for a new international order (founded on religion-based civilizations) after the end of the era of the clash of ideologies (Huntington 1996). Lively discussions also revolved around religious fundamentalism (Almond et al. 2003), the role of religion in violence and new types of conflicts (Kaldor 1999), and the role of Islam (Huntington 1996; Bayat 2007).

Moreover, the early twenty-first century saw the development of two significant political phenomena involving religion. The first was the development of new public and political debates, related to identity issues (such as immigration, religious pluralism, multiculturalism, and the presence of religious symbols in the public sphere) and to the fields of morality and sexuality (such as bioethics, the beginning of life, the end of life, and LGBT rights), which often saw religion as a crucial factor and religious actors as active participants (Ozzano and Giorgi 2016; Engeli et al. 2012). Finally, in the first two decades of the twenty-first century there was also the development and the flourishing of a new family of right-wing populist parties, which proposed a use of religion very different from that of the "old" religious parties: as an identity marker rather than a matter of belief or practice (Ozzano 2020; Ben-Porat et al. 2021).

To sum up, in the early twenty-first century there was uncertainty and disagreement among scholars about how religion might evolve in the following century and the role it might still play in global politics. As reviewed above, there were competing points of view: that religion was still in decline in accordance with the secularization thesis; that some religions were in decline, while other religious traditions were not secularized and threatening; that religion might play a role only in the developing world; and that religion, in relation to politics, was increasingly turning into an identity marker rather than a matter of belief and practice as in the past. Little attention was still paid, instead, at least among political science and international relations scholars, to the role of new religious phenomena, such as new religious movements and digital religions: which, considering what actually happened, surely proved a short-sighted perspective.

3   The Evolution of Religions

In relation to the above-reviewed hypotheses about the possible evolution of world faiths and their role in global politics, what actually happened partly confirmed the tenets of the secularization thesis. The twenty-first century witnessed indeed a continuation of the trend of decline of religious practice in the developed world within religions such as Catholicism: the number of religious leaders and clergy has been significantly decreasing in the last century—the number of Catholic priests, for example, decreased from 414.582 in 2017 (official Vatican data, paper archive) to 513 in 2117 (last update: Ψ 01/03/2118). Since the mid-twenty-first century, however, with the progress of modernization and development also in other areas of the world—mainly as a consequence of technological development and its partial democratization—this trend started to involve also regions and faiths (such as Islam) that had previously been relatively untouched by it. This phenomenon, commonly labeled by early twenty-second century social scientists as "Scintoization" of mainstream religions, involved the gradual disappearance of religion as practice and its transformation into a matter of tradition and national/local identity (Robotham Ψ 2084; Tanaka Ψ 2093).

The extremization of the process of "culturalization" of mainstream religions (Astor and Meryl 2020) resulted in the progressive convergence of the values they promoted—namely, the defense of human and animal rights (and, as a consequence, the defense of vegetarianism and the respect of the differences between men and women); moderation and decency, and maintaining the world peace; the importance of technology to alleviate human work; and the religious obligation of helping the poor and the defenseless. Religions maintain their differences—mainly in terms of rites and practices—and their relationships are mainly arranged through the *Global Religious Council*. Although its contemporary relevance is mostly symbolical, the Council witnessed fierce struggles until at least one century ago, when the religions that are now convergent were still fiercely opposing one another: it was the risk of losing impact and relevance in the public and the political spheres that led mainstream religions to overcome their differences, territorializing their areas of influence. In the mid-2100s, Gibson-Stark (Ψ 2053) introduced a typology to differentiate "convergent" from "unconvergent" religions. Those latter were defined by difference: hence, unconvergent religions criticize human rights and refuse moderation in both values and religious practices. Apart from these aspects, however, religious groups included in this category are radically different from one another.

From a methodological perspective, the different ways of living and expressing faith led to rethinking measurement tools (Cristadoro-InTwig Ψ 2110). Broadly speaking, apart from mapping worship places, surveys remain the most diffused instrument to estimate religiosity. Especially in the last fifty years, measurement tools have become more and more reliable and capillary diffused, thanks to the massive project of "citizens listening" (CL) launched in the 2020s (during what is known today as "the populist era"). As it is well-known, CL has been harshly criticized as an instrument of control, and many individuals and groups, known as the "Undisclosed", variously sabotaged the project. For the same reasons, some scholars too refused to use CL data for research (Mutton Ψ 2035). Additionally, criticisms contended that CL would have led the research on religion to focus only on lived religiosity and quantitative data, neglecting other analytical perspectives (which is indeed what happened). Nonetheless, in the last decades the criticisms decreased, and the survey program extended to cover the entire globe. Also, the introduction of ID bracelets with survey warning systems increased the response rate—and nowadays we are able to collect highly reliable daily religiosity data.

Currently, 65% of the Earth population call itself "religious", with a daily variation of 34% on average, with a daily variation rate of 0,2%.[1] According to Dakeros and Tollen (Ψ 2118), the Earth religiosity rate raises to 72% if

---

[1] (see https://ssw.pewresearch.org.earth—last update: Ψ 01/12/2118).

we take into account the Undisclosed[2] (most diffused in the United States of Europe—hereinafter USE—following their estimates). The daily variation rate has been decreasing in the last decades, while the religiosity rate has been increasing. Research shows that the variation mainly concerns citizens born and raised in the United States of Africa (hereinafter USAF), the small independent republic New Japan, and Canada. In many scholars' opinion, this is related to the lower number of clones in these countries (Chapuis and Bourguiba Ψ 2109). In addition, following a multi-century and well-known trend (see Inglehart and Norris 2004), the levels of religiosity are higher in relation to contextual uncertainty (be it economic or political). Moreover, the surveys on religiosity rates are made more difficult by the fact that—while Convergent Religions largely correspond to the models of analysis developed in the twentieth century—in some of the main movements developed in the last century the lines between secular and religious have sometimes become blurred, which makes CL data quite useless for the analysis.

As mentioned above, in the early twenty-first century scholars were only starting to analyze and understand the role played by new technologies in the transformation of religions. While at the beginning these analyses mostly focused on the changes in religious practices and movements engendered by new technologies and media (such as for example the internet and the social networks), during the century it became increasingly clear that technological development was causing a major change in religious beliefs themselves. To explain this point, for completeness' sake, we will have to review some of the major political and economic developments of the twenty-first century.

The Influence of the Technology Wars

Around the middle of the century, technology became the main—if not the only—cleavage around which global political debates were structured: a development which was catalyzed by the pandemic waves and the European Wars of the 2020s and 2030s, which brought to the fore a number of issues related to the role of technology in contemporary human life, the role of scientists in public decision-making, and the widespread adoption of gene-editing technologies (Bolzonar et al. Ψ 2035). With the elaboration of new technologies permitting to replace humans with robots and AIs in about 90% of the jobs, and to (at least theoretically) feed all the human population almost for free, a major process of political and social change came about (also as a consequence of new massive global social movements and unrests demanding the democratization of such technologies in opposition to the neoliberal proprietary system, which was increasingly under attack), which also implied a restructuring of the nation states system. As a consequence, at the economic level,

---

[2] Even if it had its momentum in the 2070s, Dakeos and Tollen (2115) maintain that nowadays those who lie to the daily survey system are about 17% of the Earth population (32% in the USE).

in the SSW there was also the end of a global economic system largely based on capitalism, and the development of a mixed system, where capitalism (still in place for scarce resources, such as luxury goods) coexisted with other economic systems such as gift economy and reputational economy.

At first the debate developed around a cleavage between accelerationists, who believed that this change was good, and it was leading to the emancipation of the human race from need and suffering; and Neo-Luddists, who were concerned about an alleged uprooting of social structures and values carried out by the increasingly fast technological development (Rembrandt and Vanmarke Ψ 2041). Of course, the situation was very different in different political contexts, particularly in relation to the choice to democratize the allocation of resources through the implementation of a Universal Basic Income (UBI) system or to remain anchored to a neoliberal worldview despite the soaring unemployment rates and social unrest. States belonging to the SSW (which had replaced the United Nations, with more extensive powers, in 2048) largely implemented some UBI system, with the creation of a post-scarcity scenario, while mostly maintaining or adopting some type of digital democracy system (although post-scarcity has quelled most political debates, with a predominance of technocratic roles in state governance). On the contrary, the renegade states (see below) chose to remain anchored to the capitalist perspective, usually associated with totalitarian or authoritarian political regimes.

In the last decades of the century, particularly, the debate shifted toward a discussion on which technologies were to be regarded as beneficial or "kosher",[3] and which had to be regarded as dangerous and needed limitations. Toward the end of the century, a growing mistrust developed in most of the world in relation to "hard" technologies, based on inorganic materials: which led to the signature of several international agreements increasingly limiting their use (for example, with bans on the creation of AIs above the level of human intelligence, and the fusion of human minds with artificial AI networks). Most of the world states largely reoriented toward the use of "soft" technologies, based on the use of organic materials and DNA manipulation.

However, a few states (which had also remained anchored to predatory capitalism and to an unequal allocation of goods and services, often nominally masked by some kind of reputational economy) rejected these agreements and focused instead on the development of "hard technologies". These states, whose most important representatives were the Japan-Korean Sphere, Gujarat, Belarus, Hungary, East Padania, South California, Zimbabwe, Great Texas, and Turkmenistan, opted thus out of the SSW system. This led in a first time to a growing international tension which led to a limited nuclear war

---

[3] This terms, derived from the Jewish tradition (where it refers to the food regarded as "pure"), became of common use in relation to this debate after the publication of the essay *Kosher and forbidden technologies: A blueprint to save the human race*, by the US sociologist Ramon Ben Porat (Ψ 2073).

in 2094, that annihilated a renegade state, East Padania (whose green flower flag is today widely used at international peace rallies as a memory of the danger posed by the association between advanced AI systems and extremist ideologies) ⟨Diotallevi Ψ 2097⟩. After that event, the global system was largely structured around a separation between the SSW and the renegade states, which often operate in isolation from the rest of the world (although several resistance movements, inspired by the prophetic book *Walkaway* by Cory Doctorow (2017), are carrying out a fierce struggle there).

All these developments also implied deep consequences in relation to religion and spirituality. As mentioned above, a first consequence was the fact that the lines between religious and secular phenomena and movements often became blurred. This was only partly a consequence of the already-mentioned process of culturalization and personalization of religion, which entailed a detachment from the religious institutions as "mediators of the sacred", and, as a consequence, also implied the detachment from religious authority as the sole authority on religious matters. Hence, different actors developed different ideas of the distinction between what is sacred and what is secular (see for example the sacralization of the removal of a person's digital recordings, widespread among digital cults; or, on the opposite side, the bureaucratization of religious services in many convergent religions) ⟨Egonu Ψ 2094⟩. However, it was largely the consequence of the development of new "unconvergent" social and cultural phenomena and movements whose "religious" or "secular" identity was unclear. On the one hand, in line with the accelerationist creed, and the reliance on "hard" technologies, a Technoutopian ideology developed (also propped by the widespread idea that a wider reliance on advanced technologies might save the human race from dangers such as climate change and pandemic waves). Particularly interesting in this respect is the intersection with cyberfeminism and the chthulucene perspective developed in the 2020s: Donna Haraway (2016) suggested that, considering the inextricable connections of the human and the non-human, humanity needed to develop new practices of sym-poiesis (make with) and to learn to live together with the earth and all its inhabitants. Strands of Technoutopia, then, included technologies among the "earth inhabitants" with which to create kinship. Other strands of Technoutopia—such as particularly the belief in a digital afterlife based on the reproduction on a computer mainframe of the scan of the deceased's mind— indeed took the shape of real cults, although in reality they did not imply any belief in metaphysical ultramundane dimensions ⟨Krjen Ψ 2103⟩. On the other hand, people who still based their identity on convergent religions mainly took a more conservative approach, and were more oriented toward the neo-luddist side of the debate (see for example the conservative reactions to, and the subsequent global unrest during the Catholic conclave of 2063 when the possibility of the election as Pope of Cardinal Nguyen, a transgender person, became public). In this respect, they saw technologies as yet other dispositifs of biopolitical control, developing Mbembe's (2019) necropolitical perspective.

Soft Technologies, Technoutopianism and Neogaianism

Some decades later, this situation repeated with the development of "soft" and DNA-based technologies, which prompted the flourishing and thriving of a galaxy of new religious movements based on the so-called Neogaianism and the "Spirituality of the Goddess", whose vitality completely overcame convergent religions, which had largely become a matter of tradition rather than belief.

So, within Technoutopianists and Neo-Luddists there were secular and religious strands alike, which are sometimes difficult to single out from each other: while sharing the rejection of technology, the "missionary" and "sacred" aspect of this refusal raises internal disagreement. There is a wide scholarly discussion debating whether Technoutopianism can be considered as a religious confession: on the one hand, its followers have rituals, everyday rules of conduct, and an afterlife perspective; on the other hand, this latter is based on technology and, particularly, on mind emulation rather than the belief in some supernatural entity and/or order. Moreover, among Neogaians today prevails a kind of personal and extemporaneous spirituality that sociologists hesitate to define as "religion" (Shackleton Ψ 2027; Lalonde Ψ 2051; Egonu Ψ 2094). Unconvergent religions (as mentioned above, a residual category which includes all the new religious and spiritual trends reviewed above) also include Neo-Luddist organizations and small apocalyptic nationalist cults.[4] Many Neo-Luddist organizations are affiliated to the World Salesmen&women network, from the name of Kirkpatrick Sale, the neo-luddism opinion leader of the 1990s. Even though the network is extremely active in sabotaging and campaigning, unaffiliated groups are usually more radical—such as the Green Witches, responsible for the deadly attacks in New Delhi and Amsterdam in 2021 and 2073, and the attempted murder of USE President Greta Thunberg in 2068. On the other hand, it must be noted that phenomena of violence associated to Convergent religions largely stopped since the mid-twenty-first century.

Adopting Gibson-Stark's typology (Ψ 2053), Convergent Religions still nominally prevail in most of the continents, with the exception of the United States of America (hereinafter, USA), where the Unconvergents account for the 70% of the religiosity rates.

These statistics of course exclude the renegade states, where usually some strand of Technoutopianism has been adopted as official ideology, while the activity of Convergent Religions has been restricted and in some cases banned; and Ais and bionics are largely preferred to biotechnologies.

Contemporary religiosity is interpreted as a complex entanglement of family and cultural traditions, on the one side, and individual choices, on the other (Dakeros and Tollen Ψ 2118). Because the adherence to convergent religions

---

[4] Gibson-Stark (Ψ 2053) does not include techno-radicals among the unconvergent groups, because, she argues, they stem from the general acceptance and celebration of technology praised by convergent religions.

is usually inherited, religiosity rates can also be seen as expressions of satisfaction or distress with the current political debates. Hence, the decrease in this type of religiosity has been read as criticisms of the government (see Ameramani Ψ 2111). Indeed, we expect a minimum daily variation, in the next decades. On the other hand, unconvergent religiosity may be the expression of individual choice and commitment toward specific values or goals, or it can be a lifestyle choice—as in the case of Technoutopianists, which in fact are not properly unconvergent, according to many scholars. Broadly speaking, data confirm the XXI century trends: large constituencies of what we can define "cultural believers", and significantly smaller groups that profess radical and militant religiosity. Technoutopianists represent instead the unexpected, because of their sacralization of technology and AI, which were in fact considered as opposing principles at the beginning of the twenty-first century.

4   Religion-Related Public Debates and Policies

In line with the broader political and religious trends of the twenty-first and early twenty-second centuries, the debates involving religion and values also mainly revolved around technology. Particularly, in the decades around the mid-twenty-first century the main bone of contention became the digitization of the human brain and its reproduction on a computerized mainframe. The debate started in the 2030s, after WEBSCI, a Silicon Valley firm, developed an ion rays scan system which allegedly permitted to scan, digitize and store the connectome of the human brain: that is, the connections among the neurons, regarded as the real structure of the mind.

The complexity of this debate was a consequence of the fact that it did not simply reproduce, as in other cases, the rift between believers and nonbelievers, or that between Technoutopianists and Neo-Luddists. In that case, a recomposition of the rift had partly been possible by developing different kinds of codes disciplining "kosher" and "non-kosher" technologies (see Shackleton Ψ 2027; Surya and Kim Ψ 2031). In this case, the discussion was more complicated because such fields were also internally split between supporters and opponents of the new technology. The reactions of the traditional churches were mainly very harsh: for example, we can mention the Vatican's 2036 decision to excommunicate all people involved in the procedure, operators and patients alike. Some evangelical and jihadi groups, as it is known, even carried out targeted bombing campaigns against the facilities performing the procedure; which, added to the restrictive policies enacted by many governments, frightened by the possible social consequences of the development of the technology, made this latter for some years available only through underground Doctorow-anarchist circles, or private medical facilities for billionaires.

It was only in the early 2040s, after the distribution on the GloNet of the documentary *A Bit of My Brain* (Ψ 2042)—which told the story of the anthropologist Rinaldo Cabrera, the first man whose digitized brain was actually "resurrected"—that a real popular movement demanding the legalization and democratization of the technology developed. A very lively new religious world also developed, based on the idea of computer-based immortality, seen as either the actual realization of some sacred scriptures or as a paradise accessible also to nonbelievers (for a study of the renovation of spirituality as a consequence of brain digitization, popularly known as "bit spirituality", see Lalonde Ψ 2051). All this proved very disruptive at the political level, with many states—already in dire straits because of the problems in managing the spread of wet 3D printers, granting food and drugs to everybody almost for free—actually crumbled into pieces. This process also made obsolete, in the end, policies such as the provision of UBI, considering that most goods had become virtually free.

The debate on mind digitization, in its latter stages, largely overlapped with the one on artificial superintelligence (later, as mentioned above, banned by a 2081 International convention signed and implemented by all countries with the exception of the renegade states), after the development, in a Beijing lab, of an allegedly self-conscious superintelligent quantum computer, MARKO64. Quite naturally, those who were in favor of mind digitization also supported the development of super-AI technology, and vice-versa. This was also a consequence of the fact that artificial superintelligence also permitted to enhance both digitized and—through neural laces—biological human brains. This latter technology, which entered into mass production in the mid-2060s, proved critical for many reasons. On the one hand, it made possible to exponentially enhance human brain, with the creation of a new "Homo Deus" species (Harari 2017) (which of course was blamed by most traditional religious traditions); on the other, in small religious groups and sects, it allowed religious leaders to directly access the followers' minds. This situation tragically came to the fore after a mass suicide, near Beirut, of more than 5000 techno-Salafites, under the influence of an apocalyptic preacher (for a description of the events, see Kropotkin Ψ 2067; and the Ψ 2071 movie *I will not Die in Vain*, starring Josephine Fonda and Robert Kline): a traumatic event which was crucial for the process which led to severely limiting such technologies. The events, as it is known, ignited a global debate which prompted some states, such as South China, to utterly ban neural laces outside government control; and others, such as the United States of Europe, to put into place strict regulations to prevent mind control and hijacking attempts (see also, in the US, the Ψ 2073 Supreme Court sentence on the case Harris vs. Microsoft).

The 2070s, however, witnessed the rise of another major ethical-religious debate, when a clinic in Austin (not bound by any of the specific legal frameworks developed for the SSW countries) developed a technology which permitted to completely design the DNA of a child as desired. This development raised the anger of many believers that regarded this technology as immoral, as well as the reaction from many other people, religious and secular alike, that were concerned it might lead to a generalization of eugenetic practices. Once the technology became widespread it also raised a massive wave of violent attacks, while in some countries with a strongly religiously oriented political leadership, such as Turkey and the United England, *manufactured* children were even denied the status of citizens, and were regarded as a kind of social pariah ⟨Hussenmeyer Ψ 2081⟩. A similar situation took place in the case of clones, which also proliferated thanks to technological advancement. In this case, the religious implications were even more significant, because the creation of the exact copy of a person put into question the existence of an individual soul for each human being. At first, clones were looked at with even more suspicion than "simple" manufactured humans. However, the growing popularity of the doctrine of souls gemination, after the publication of the widely successful *Mate Soul* (written in 2085 by Father Charles Li, the clone of a billionaire who had decided to take the vows), significantly quelled the dispute (although in some local contexts occasional outbursts of violence took place until the 2110s) ⟨Sachashvili and Guberian Ψ 2115⟩.

When microbioma medicine became the standard, in the 2040s, the acknowledgment of the role of bacteria in human health led to an increasing attention to the ecosystemic balance and the respect of all the elements involved. When the convergent theologian Shanya Twain wrote her watershed anti-speciesism essay, in 2051, she interpreted and voiced the spirit of her time: the world was ready to recognize the importance of all natural beings. The further development of bio-technologies—such as the creation of the skin plants—made less and less relevant the use of metallic materials for intervening on damaged human bodies. With the exception of the transhumanist Technoutopians—since the 2080s largely settling in the renegade states—who praised the cyborg-ideal of human and machine hybrids, the world population grew accustomed to the separation between the natural and the manufactured (as the debates on in vitro pregnancy and clones testify).

5   Concluding Remarks

To sum up, the development of religions in the past 100 years has only partly confirmed the predictions of the secularization thesis. On the one hand, it is true that "traditional" mainstream faiths have undergone a process of culturalization and "Scintoization", largely remaining relevant only in terms of tradition and identity; and that this process has involved all major religious traditions, which have increasingly become "convergent" (with a significant reduction of religion-based conflicts, which had taken scholars largely by surprise). However, the restructuring of the international system and the cultural and political debate around the different kinds of technological development, their effects and their desirability, has also indirectly engendered a new galaxy of religious and spiritual movements, in relation to both "hard" and "soft" technologies. Another relevant feature of these developments has been the blurring of the boundaries between secular and spiritual and the development of new social and cultural phenomena whose position on the secular/religious axis is unclear. At the political level, finally, we can detect today a significant cleavage between the countries belonging to the SSW, where convergent religions coexist (mostly peacefully) with new religious phenomena largely based on Neogaianism and female spirituality, while technoutopian cults are mostly fringe phenomena; and the renegade states, where technoutopian cults prevail (and in some cases enjoy the status of official state religion) while other faiths and spiritual orientations are discouraged and, in some cases, banned.

References

Almond, Gabriel A., R. Scott Appleby, and Emmanuel Sivan. (2003). *Strong Religion: The Rise of Fundamentalisms Around the World*. Chicago: University of Chicago Press.

Ameramani, Ameramani. ⟨Ψ 2111⟩. *Religio-Rebels: What Religiosity Rates Can Tell Us About Politics*. Leiden: Amsterdam University Press.

Astor, A., and D. Meryl. (2020). "Culturalized Religion: A Synthetic Review and Agenda for Research", *Journal for the Scientific Study of Religion*, Vol. 59, No. 2, pp. 209–226.

Bayat, Asef. (2007). *Islam and Democracy: What Is the Real Question?* Leiden: Amsterdam University Press.

Ben-Porat, Guy, Dani Filc, Ahmet Erdi Ozturk, and Luca Ozzano. (2021). "Populism, Religion, and Family Values Policies in Israel, Italy and Turkey", *Mediterranean Politics*.

Ben Porat, Ramon. ⟨Ψ 2073⟩. *Kosher and Forbidden Technologies: A Blueprint to Save the Human Race*. New York: Bar-Ilan University.

Bolzonar, Fabio, Alberta Giorgi, and Luca Ozzano. ⟨Ψ 2035⟩. "Pandemic, Religion, and Cleavages: What Lies Ahead?", *European Journal of Politics and Religion*, Vol. 8, No. 2, pp. 536–557.

Burchardt, Marian, Monika Wohlrab-Sahr, and Matthias Middell, eds. (2016). *Multiple Secularities Beyond the West. Religion and Modernity in the Global Age*. Berlin: De Gruyter.

Campbell, Heidi A. (2012). *Digital Religion: Understanding Religious Practice in New Media Worlds*. Abingdon: Routledge.

Casanova, José. 1994. *Public Religions in the Modern World*. Chicago: University of Chicago Press.

Chapuis, François, and Safiya Bourguiba. ⟨Ψ 2109⟩. "A Multivariate Analysis of the Impact of Cloning Technology on Religiosity Rate", *Politics and Religion*, Vol. 102, No. 3, pp. 913–941.

Clarke, Peter B. (2008). *Encyclopedia of New Religious Movements*. London: Routledge.

Cristadoro-InTwig, A. ⟨Ψ 2110⟩. *How Can We Study Religiosity? Methods and Techniques*. New ed. Tokelau: University of Samoa.

Dakeros, Para, and There Tollen. ⟨Ψ 2118⟩. *"Not Sharing is Self-Caring" – Covert Ethnography among the Undisclosed*. New Venice: New Venice University Press.

Davie, G. (2007). "Vicarious Religion: A Methodological Challenge", In *Everyday Religion: Observing Modern Religious Lives*, edited by N. Ammerman, 21–36. New York: Oxford University Press.

Diotallevi, Giampiero. ⟨Ψ 2097⟩. *The Burning Sun of the Alps. From Bossi's Dream to the Nuclear Holocaust*. Rijeka: Padua University Press.

Dobbelaere, K. (2016). "Secularization", In *The Blackwell Encyclopedia of Sociology*, edited by G. Ritzer, 4148–4156. Malden: Blackwell.

Doctorow, Cory. (2017). *Walkaway*. London: Head of Zeus.

Egonu, Yaroslav. ⟨Ψ 2094⟩. *Believing without Being. A Critical Reappraisal of Grace Davie's Thesis for the 21st Century*. Beijing: Palgrave.

Engeli, Isabelle, Christoffer Green-Pedersen, and Lars Thorup Larsen. (2012). *Morality Politics in Western Europe: Parties, Agendas and Policy Choices*. Basingstoke; New York: Palgrave Macmillan.

Fox, Jonathan, and Shmuel Sandler. (2006). *Bringing Religion Into International Relations*. New York: Palgrave MacMillan.

Gibson-Stark, Sumaya. ⟨Ψ 2053⟩. "Re-categorizing Religion—Revised Typology", *Politics, Religion and Ideology*, Vol. 52, No. 4, pp. 972–1000.

Hammer, Olav, and Mikael Rothstein. (2012). *The Cambridge Companion to New Religious Movements*. Cambridge; New York: Cambridge University Press.

Harari, Yuval Noah. (2017). *Homo Deus: A Brief History of Tomorrow*. New York, NY: Harper.

Haraway, D. (2016). Staying with the Trouble: Making Kin in the Chululucene. Duke University Press.

Helland, Christopher. (2016). "Digital Religion", In *Handbook of Religion and Society*, edited by David Yamane, 177–196. Handbooks of Sociology and Social Research. Cham: Springer International Publishing.

Hervieu-Léger, Danielle. (1999). *Le Pèlerin et le converti: la religion en mouvement*. Paris: Flammarion.

Hojsgaard, Morten, and Margit Warburg. (2005). *Religion and Cyberspace*. London: Routledge.

Huntington, Samuel P. (1991). *The Third Wave: Democratization in the Late Twentieth Century*. Norman, OK: University of Oklahoma Press.

Huntington, Samuel P. (1996). *The Clash of Civilizations and the Remaking of World Order*. New York: Simon and Schuster.

Hussenmayer, Alice. ⟨Ψ 2081⟩. *I Was Created Equal. The Struggle for Recognition of Vitros' Rights in the EU*. Glasgow: Glasgow University Press.

Inglehart, R., and P. Norris. (2004). *Sacred and Secular: Religion and Politics Worldwide*. Cambridge: Cambridge University Press.

Kaldor, Mary. (1999). *New and Old Wars: Organized Violence in a Global Era*. Stanford, CA: Stanford Univ Press.

Kalyvas, Stathis N. (1996). *The Rise of Christian Democracy in Europe*. Ithaca: Cornell University Press.

Kepel, Gilles. (1991). *La revanche de Dieu: chrétiens, juifs et musulmans à la reconquête du monde*. Paris: Editions du Seuil.

Krjen, Rozen. ⟨Ψ 2103⟩. "Reviving Chtulucene: Why Harawayanism Is Still Relevant Today", *Religion, Gender, Society*, Vol. 37, No. 2, 555–578.

Kropotkin, Emmanuel. ⟨Ψ 2067⟩. *The Beirut Mass Suicide and Its Religious Meaning*. New York: Viking.

Lalonde, Elon. ⟨Ψ 2051⟩. *Bit Spirituality: Movements and Ideologies*. Beijing: Beijing University Press.

Lewis, James R., and Jesper Aagaard Petersen. (2005). *Controversial New Religions*. Oxford: Oxford University Press.

Li, Charles (Father). ⟨Ψ 2085⟩. *Mate Soul. How I Came to Accept Myself and Found the Faith*. Beijing: Amazon Originals.

Mbembe, A. 2019. *Necropolitics*. Durham: Duke University Press.

Mutton, Sarimba. ⟨Ψ 2035⟩. "Turning a Cold Shoulder to Citizens Listening", *Political Analysis* Vol. 43, No. 2, pp. 326–349.

Ozzano, Luca. (2020). *The Masks of the Political God. Religion and Political Parties in Contemporary Democracies*. Lanham: Rowman and Littlefield.

Ozzano, Luca, and Alberta Giorgi. (2016). *European Culture Wars and the Italian Case: Which Side Are You On?* London: Routledge.

Palmisano, Stefania, and Nicola Pannofino. (2017). *Invention of Tradition and Syncretism in Contemporary Religions: Sacred Creativity*. London: Palgrave Macmillan.

Petito, Fabio, and Pavlos Hatzopoulos, eds. (2003). *Religion in International Relations: The Return from Exile*. New York: Palgrave Macmillan.

Possamai, Adam. (2019). *In Search of New Age Spiritualities*. Abingdon: Routledge.

Rembrandt, Janine, and Joseph Vanmarke. ⟨Ψ 2041⟩. *Too Late with Too LIttle or Too Fast with Too Much? The Ongoing Neoluddist/Accelerationist Debate*. Beijing: Oxford University Press.

Robotham, Layla. ⟨Ψ 2084⟩., "The End of Islamic Exceptionalism?", *Technology and Religion* Vol. 16, No. 3, pp. 864–885.

Rzb2, J8. ⟨Ψ 2117⟩. "If We Want Things to Stay As They Are, Things Will Have to Change. Technoutopists and Neogaianists Today", *Technology and Religion,* Vol. 22, No. 1, pp. 1–24.

Sachashvili, Robert, and Gheorghios Guberian. ⟨Ψ 2115⟩. "The Rise and Fall of the Clonation Debate", *Comparative Politics,* Vol. 147, No. 3, pp. 987–1005.

Shackleton, Ananda. ⟨Ψ 2027⟩. *Neo-Luddism: The Only Way Forward?* Abu Dhabi: Routledge.

Surya, Prakash, and Jennifer Kim. (2031). "Technos vs. Neo-Luddists: The New Culture War", *Politics, Religion and Ideology,* Vol. 32, No. 2, pp. 346–367.

Tanaka, Ahmed. ⟨Ψ 2093⟩. *The Scintoization of Mainstream Faiths: An Hypothesis About the Religious Transformation in the Late 21st Century*. Princeton: Princeton University Press.

Twain, Shania. ⟨Ψ 2051⟩ "Man! We Are All the Same", *Annual Review of Convergent Religion Essays*, Vol. 4, No.1, pp. 12–56.

Wilson, Erin K., and Luca Mavelli. (2017). "Post Secularism and International Relations", In *Routledge Handbook of Religion and Politics*, edited by Jeffrey Haynes, 2nd ed. Abingdon: Routledge.

The UNCorp Quantum Mechanism for Wellbeing

Isabella Hermann

The Human Wellbeing Report 2121: "30 years of Global Wellbeing for Individuals, States and the Planet"—The 30th Anniversary Human Wellbeing Report is the latest in the series that UNCorpQMW has published since 2091 as an independent, analytically, and empirically informed discussion of important issues, trends, and policies related to global wellbeing. The United Nations & Corporations (UNCorp) established the Quantum Mechanism for Wellbeing (QMW) in 2089 to guide the world toward the Wellbeing Gateways and to establish the Algorithmic Global Pareto Optimization.

1 FOREWORD TO THE 30TH ISSUE OF THE HUMAN WELLBEING REPORT

First Co-Director of the UNCorpQMW from 2090 to 2108

The world is not perfect, but it looks good: Our 7 billion global citizens have an average life expectancy of 109 years. There is no hunger and no misery, and most people in all parts of the world can live their lives in good health and self-determined until old age. It goes without saying that these unprecedented achievements are due to the UNCorp Quantum Mechanism for Wellbeing (UNCorpQMW). Thirty-one years ago, in 2090, the UNCorpQMW created

---

I. Hermann (✉)
Independent Scholar, Berlin, Germany
e-mail: mail@isabella-hermann.com

© The Author(s), under exclusive license to Springer Nature
Switzerland AG 2023
L. Horn et al. (eds.), *The Palgrave Handbook of Global Politics in the 22nd Century*, https://doi.org/10.1007/978-3-031-13722-8_19

a new way to further improve global wellbeing: since then, we have automated the international coordination of individual countries' algorithmic wellbeing policies to achieve the Algorithmic Global Pareto Optimization (AGPO). In 2091, the Human Wellbeing Report was launched to annually highlight and critically reflect on the progress toward optimizing global wellbeing. We can proudly say that today, in 2121, more than seventy percent of all national household expenditures are executed using wellbeing algorithms that have been pre- and post-audited by the UNCorpQMW and calculated according to a global pareto optimum—a number that is to increase in the future. But as is often the case, the road to get here was not straight, but winding. How did we arrive at this stage of global peace, equality, and freedom in balance with the planet?

Many will recall that the UNCorpQMW resulted from a merger of two UNCorp institutions, the UNCorp High Commissioner for Quantum (UNCorpHCQ) and the UNCorp Wellbeing Program (UNCorpWP) in 2090. The UNCorpWP, established in 2069, provided new guidance for future policies after the global upheavals of the late 2040s to early 2060s in the wake of increasing global warming, migration fluxes, pandemics, and global inequalities. "Development" was finally dead after the failure of the UN Sustainable Development Goals in the 2030s, since in the end, the concept couldn't be intellectually freed from a focus on capitalist paradigms such as "growth", "GDP", "progress", and "consumerism."[1] The abandonment of development meant a new focus on spiritual, physical, social, and environmental wellbeing that was decoupled from a neoliberal understanding of "development", which has always been linked to "more" and "faster". Under the leadership of the UNCorpWP, tangible ways to political wellbeing were defined to be binding for the UNCorp members—consisting of all nations and the bigger economic entities. It took two years and controversial but lively and fruitful discussions in the UNCorp Stakeholder Assembly before the new eleven UNCorp Wellbeing Gateways (UNCorpWG) were adopted in 2071 with sixty-seven percent of votes.[2]

Three years later, following major breakthroughs in quantum computing by the late 2060s, UNCorp established the UNCorp High Commissioners for Quantum (UNCorpHCQ) in 2074. The mission of the new agency was to provide expertise in developing powerful algorithms and data collection tools to help countries to implement their policies more effectively toward the Wellbeing Gateways. At the time, algorithmic policymaking was still in its infancy, but quickly grew in popularity as being able to overcome democratic inefficiencies. I myself joined UNCorpHCQ as Chief Tech-Solutionist by the end of the 2070s, along with a group of visionary people all coming from technophile communities. We wanted to be part of something politically more

---

[1] Look at Wolfgang Sachs' Development Dictionary of a 100 years ago.

[2] I can only recommend the video diary "In retrospect it becomes history" by then Ethiopia's Ambassador to the UN Aeba Tiruneh documenting the whole process.

meaningful. We became like a family that spent intense hours in increasingly superbly created environments in the Sphere, and shared bio-mental experiences in nature or kitchen whenever it was possible to meet up physically. I still remember well how, exhausted from long hikes in the mountains or desert, together with the High Commissioners, we cut all kinds of vegetables and opened one wine bottle after the other for our meals while discussing like mad people the possibilities of quantum computing for policy. We were a crazy group united by the unconditional belief that quantum technology and algorithms could change the world for the better—and it did!

Motivated by the new technological possibilities of quantum computing, many governments in collaboration with public and corporate research institutions were already developing political decision-making algorithms on their own to improve democratic processes.[3] There was in fact no need for UNCorpHCQ support, however, since the algorithms had to be aligned with the Wellbeing Gateways after the 1971 UNCorp Stakeholder Assembly decision, the UNCorpHCQ became more of a watchdog to see if the governments' algorithms were really in the best interest of human wellbeing. Therefore, in the 1980s, a triangular practice between the states, the UNCorpWP, and the UNCorpHCQ institutionalized: states worked on algorithms to implement wellbeing policies according to the Wellbeing Gateways. The UNCorpWP regularly updated and adjusted the directions of the Wellbeing Gateways by considering the latest data and the newest global wellbeing situation. The UNCorpHCQ, in close collaboration with the UNCorpWP, conducted pre- and post-audits of the algorithms to verify that the gateways were being complied with. During this period, in the mid-2080s, the first countries held democratic elections in which people no longer voted for parties and politicians, but for a preference list of algorithms—all drawn up by tech-solutionist experts and subject to the pre- and post-audit of the UNCorpHCQ.

While this triangular relationship was becoming increasingly relevant to states' policies, it had never been officially mandated by UNCorp. Rather, it had grown into a kind of customary law. This unofficial status naturally led to occasional conflicts between states and the UNCorp bodies, but mainly to conflicts between the UNCorpWP and the UNCorpHCQ over jurisdictions, responsibilities, and—most irreconcilably—worldviews and ideology. Basically, the UNCorpWP socio-technocrats thought that the Wellbeing Gateways were an ideal to be adjusted to reality, and the tech solutionists of the UNCorpHCQ—including myself—were sure that reality needed to be adjusted to the Wellbeing Gateways—history proved us right. To clarify the uncertain status,

---

[3] The anxiety that "inefficient" democracy might decline and even disappear with new data-processing possibilities—as expressed, for example, by historian Yuval Noah Harari more than 100 years ago—proved to be nonsense: quite the contrary, data processing must be integrated to bring democracy into the twenty-third century.

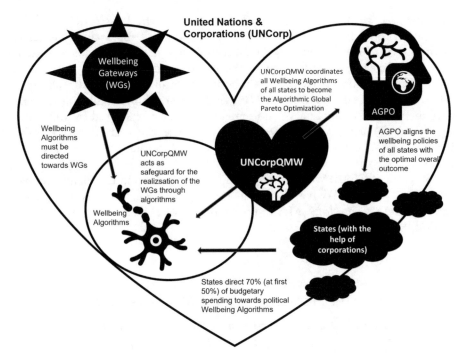

Fig. 1 The basic functioning of the UNCorpQMW

UNCorp hosted the Global Algorithmic Wellbeing Conference in 2089.[4] The results of the conference are widely known:

- UNCorpWP became part of the UNCorpHCQ and formed the new agency of UNCorpQMW.
- UNCorpQMW was officially mandated to function as safeguard for the compliance of each state's wellbeing algorithms according to the Wellbeing Gateways.
- Fifty percent of budgetary national spending must be executed through wellbeing algorithms certified by UNCorpQMW.
- UNCorpQMW was mandated to automize the coordination of all political wellbeing algorithms of all states to reach the Algorithmic Global Pareto Optimization (AGPO).
- The Wellbeing Gateways were reduced from eleven to ten gateways: The eleventh gateway of "Participation" was not a necessary gateway for wellbeing anymore, since based on ever more advanced algorithms, governments can execute wellbeing policies without civic participation (Fig. 1).

---

[4] For the conference, our team from UNCorpHCQ volunteered to design the remarkable "Wellbeing Ambience" of the Sphere, which can still be admired in the Museum of Lost and Found Legendary Ambiences.

I became part of the three-body leadership circle of the UNCorpQMW. The acquisition took the entire year 2090. The majority of the socio-technocrats of the UNCorpWP left in mischief, because they felt to have lost an ideological battle against datafication of the world—and some of them founded "Real World against Modelling". But notwithstanding, we could really take off now and let wellbeing fly. The 2108 Global Algorithmic Wellbeing Conference increased the budgetary requirement for policies executed by wellbeing algorithms from fifty to seventy percent. This was the year when I left the UNCorpQMW as the last one of the first leadership round to give place to a younger generation.

"30 years of Global Wellbeing for Individuals, States and the Planet" shows that the UNCorpQMW hasn't lost any of its spirit to make the world a better place through technology. Maybe the world is not perfect, but it is well and getting better and better.

---

2   COMMENT ON THE 30TH ISSUE OF THE HUMAN WELLBEING REPORT 2121

Real World against Modelling—activism in the spirit of UNCorpWP

In 2089 the UNCorpHCQ swallowed the UNCorpWP and became the UNCorpQMW. What this meant was already viewed with sorrow back then and is apparent in the present: The Algorithmic Global Pareto Optimization (AGPO) model is flawed and there is no human oversight to critically reflect what it is doing. The UNCorpWP was not free from errors, but at least it understood the social challenges associated with the history and future of global wellbeing. The UNCorpQMW does not. But what does it do? First, it checks whether each state's algorithmic policy design matches the 10 Wellbeing Gateways. Democracy, elections, and representation no longer matter as long as any combination of the gateways is specified as the government's policy goal. So, the eleventh Wellbeing Gateway of Participation was abolished right away in 2089 as soon as the UNCorpQMW took over. We criticize the whole mechanism around the national wellbeing algorithms elsewhere,[5] particularly their over-reliance on data correlation and their negation of causation—problems that were already discussed a hundred years ago in simple machine learning algorithms.[6] Quantum computing can cause good with oversight, but it cannot make the world better automatically.

---

[5] See: Real World against Modelling ⟨Ψ 2119⟩: Automating the World—Why algorithmic policymaking is no utopia.

[6] See for example these two pieces I recently came across: Chandler, David (2015): A World without Causation: Big Data and the Coming of Age of Posthumanism. Millennium 43(3): 833–851; Chandler, David ⟨Ψ 2026⟩: Prediction without Vision? The Future of IR and global politics. Journal of AI in IR 2 (2): 311–333.

However, for now, our main point of critique of the 30th issue of the Human Wellbeing Report 2121 is how, secondly, the UNCorpQMW coordinates the harmonization of all the different wellbeing policies of all states. To maximize the global wellbeing outcome, the UNCorpQMW automized the coordination of each individual state's wellbeing algorithms to reach an Algorithmic Global Pareto Optimization (AGPO). Just to clarify the basics: A global wellbeing system is called pareto-optimized if it is not possible to increase the wellbeing of one state through re-allocation of resources without simultaneously decreasing that of another state; in other words, a condition where there is no way to make one state better off without making another worse off at the same time. In fact, the algorithmic global pareto optimum ensures that different wellbeing strategies of states are not in conflict with each other. There is enough wellbeing for everyone—yeah! Just that it is not entirely true.

The UNCorpQMW says that the algorithms calculating the pareto-optimum are fair and neutral. But by now we should know that this is not right: Technology is not "fair", it only conveys one perspective on fairness out of many, and it is never neutral, because it is always based directly and indirectly on the views of the people who have built it initially. Stating this does not mean that "Real World against Modelling" is against tech—we are not. But the intentions behind a technical system should be transparent and the workings explainable so that we can have political discussion about it. The UNCorpQMW doesn't make anything transparent. The pareto-optimum algorithm is opaque and invisible like a god and its verdicts are beyond dispute or appeal. We don't know if the UNCorpQMW doesn't want to or just cannot fully explain publicly the workings of the system, but since global wellbeing is de facto increasing, it obviously sees no need to question the system. The AGPO creates its own truth.

The AGPO is no doubt made to serve a good purpose. Nevertheless, we have strong presumptive evidence that human prejudice, misunderstanding, and bias are encoded into the software system that manages our whole global economic, political, and social system. We closely analyzed a sample of countries over the last 50 years, when back then eleven UNCorp Wellbeing Gateways were approved in 2071. The sample of countries was chosen because we were given access to their wellbeing algorithms and the data points. This research program under the name "OpenPareto" is extraordinarily complex and can only provide an idea of what is going on. Without full data and our limited resources, we couldn't make the workings of the algorithmic system fully visible, but we could design a simplified model of the AGPO. We have strong indications that the algorithm is not working toward the pareto optimum but discriminates against certain states. Concretely, the history of countries disadvantaged in the past let us believe that the wellbeing of certain states is increased to the detriment of other states.

How could that happen if the system should be neutral and fair? The AGPO cannot be drawn out of thin air. The model required programming and data—a lot of data—to be trained with initially. We assume that the UNCorpQMW used data on how international affairs were non-automatically coordinated from 2071 to 2090, the 19 years when the Wellbeing Gateways were already mandatory for every state. The introduction of the Wellbeing Gateways was a big step, but they didn't just magically end global injustice overnight. Some states were wealthier and more powerful than others, they could better implement the wellbeing policies and act to their advantage at the international level. We suspect, therefore, that the data was biased, that the AGPO learnt these biases and that states that were advantaged in the past are still advantaged now—or that certain states are disadvantaged, respectively. But obviously, there is no need to question the AGPO: it is claimed that global wellbeing is maximized, and everyone is better off. Who cares then that some states are slightly more or less well-off depending on their more favorable past condition? So, the AGPO—without any feedback—just keeps going because it is doing exactly what it is supposed to. However, this means that it perpetuates the biases and transfers them to the future: it becomes a self-fulfilling prophecy of the UNCorpQMW ideology of utilitarian optimization of wellbeing.

We believe that the AGPO was created with the best intentions to make the world a better place. Nevertheless, the UNCorpQMW encoded bias into the AGPO that increasingly manages our international affairs and private lives. Even though human wellbeing is as high as it has never been before, the AGPO is not fair and neutral. If the UNCorpQMW was not so fixated on technical solutionism it would realize that the world is not just a computer model with data points. We could unite resources, discover the flaws of the AGPO and use that knowledge to work toward even better policies. Don't rely on technology to solve our problems but use technology to find better solutions! Otherwise, we will be enslaved by our own technology. Therefore, we must reclaim the wellbeing gateway of participation. The AGPO is problematic because when it works perfectly as it should, it fails.

---

3   Wellbeing or Well-Exploitation?

Sphere Watch—non-profit research and advocacy

The 30th Wellbeing Report describes the world as a good place. And it is true, the algorithmic policymaking according to the Wellbeing Gateways under the auspices of the UNCorpQMW ensures that all living beings are better off. But that counts only for the physical or—as some might call it—"bio-mental" world.

During the last 25 years, a true digital alternative to the physical world has been established. After the breakdown of the "metaverse"-idea in the chaos of the 2050s and breakthroughs in quantum computing in the late 2060s, a new hype of virtual realities emerged. They became fully interoperable with the mandatory decision of the Global Institute of Standards and Technology in

2084. This was the birth of the Sphere as we know it today, a conglomeration of all the different virtual realities out there. By now 84 percent of all global citizens spend at least two daily hours in the Sphere, 73 percent four daily hours, 48 percent six daily hours, 32 percent eight daily hours and 15 percent even more. People work and shop, chat with friends and go out for dates, join cultural events and parties—the Sphere never stops, takes place in real-time, is open to everyone, and has partly its own economy. This is great, it is a parallel second world which makes life not only easier but offers incredible new experience. But it has also become a hub for illegal business, exploitation, and misery. The reason for this is that the Wellbeing Gateways do not entirely count for the Sphere.

Absurdly, it was the other way round, the Sphere is part of the Wellbeing Gateways (see Fig. 2), of Gateway 6 "Good digital and physical Infrastructure" to be precise. This means that the Sphere as a "good digital infrastructure" contributes to the realization of wellbeing, but the Sphere itself has become a space that escapes wellbeing. This is a relic of the 2080s, when the Sphere was only in the making and not as encompassing as it was now. But since the UNCorpWP was quasi-abolished when it merged with the UNCorpHCQ, the gateways have not been revised or adjusted (Fig. 2).

The Sphere has become a normal part of the lives of many, but it has also become an escape for both: For the ones who are too well off and bored in the physical world searching for illegal adventures and extreme experiences, and for the ones who want to be even better off in the real world and are in need to earn extras. Parts of the Sphere thus have become areas of intellectual, psychological, and sexual exploitation bypassing all efforts put in the Wellbeing

Fig. 2 The 10 wellbeing gateways

Gateways.[7] Principles like "Equality of all humans", or "Livable Cities and Communities" mean nothing in the bleak and dreary parts of the Sphere. While cities and communities in the real world need to fulfill standards to be livable including for example diverse neighborhoods, local economy, and vibrant public spaces, this is not the standard for the Sphere. While in the real world—as the saying goes—neoliberalism and capitalism are systems of the past and the economy is subordinate to political wellbeing algorithms, this is not the case for the Sphere which works according to a logic of total commercialization.

So why isn't the UNCorpQMW putting the problem on the table, why aren't political actors prioritizing the issue? Why does everyone keep silent? Frankly, after years of building up expertise in and out of the Sphere doing research, gaining knowledge, and talking to people we have come to a conclusion: There must be a tacit collusion between the UNCorpQMW and the interest of Corporations. Corporations and economic entities subscribed to the Wellbeing Gateways in the physical world as part of UNCorp, but for that, they get something in return: As a compensation they can act according to the logic of a Wild West capitalism in the dark corners of the Sphere. Development is dead, long live exploitative capitalism!

We demand not only the full application of the Wellbeing Gateways to the Sphere, but also an actualization of the Gateways to make the Sphere a fair and friendly place for all.

Subscribe and join our protest.

---

4   Wellbeing on Earth, Martial Law on Mars

Op-ed based on information by a whistleblower working in a space exploration program, The New York New Times, Jan 2122

Following the decision of the 2nd Wellbeing Conference in 2108, 70 percent of all national budget expenditures is obligatorily directed toward algorithmic policies to implement the Wellbeing Gateways. Around a dozen countries even direct a higher percentage toward wellbeing algorithms. But in most cases the part of the budget that is "free to use" is 30 percent.

A small part of the "free budget" is spent on fighting illegal activities that try to bypass the Wellbeing Gateways; another small part on protecting the interfaces of the Sphere from cybercrime. Apart from that our lives are peaceful since physical war on Earth in the form of armed conflict is a thing of the past.

---

[7] Intellectual exploitation may include the creation of economic goods in the Sphere by a person that can be commercialized inside and outside the Sphere without the person receiving adequate financial compensation; psychological exploitation may include making oneself available in the Sphere as a "mental slave" for paying and non-paying customers; sexual exploitation refers to all paid and unpaid cybersex actions without the consent of the exploited person—for details see Human Sphere Watch Ψ 2121: Not well in the Sphere—exploit and get exploited.

Nevertheless, power struggles have not ceased to exist—of course they haven't. They have been externalized to Mars. It's a bit like the old cult series Star Trek, where all sorts of problems were solved on Earth, but instead political, cultural, and military conflicts were carried into space. So where does most of the "free budget" go? Correct, into the colonization of Mars, including armed conflicts between the various alliances. According to our internal information, the 16 countries active in space exploration use around 25 percent of their budget for activities on Mars. This is almost the whole remainder which is not directed toward the wellbeing algorithms. 40 countries support the coalitions with 5 percent to 10 percent of their "free budget".

The space programs in its current form started after the upheavals in the 2050s as a backup plan for humanity. The idea was that if humanity fails on Earth, there might be a future on another planet. After commercial space travel had been banned, states appropriated the knowledge and material of the private space programs for their own purposes and formed alliances. Quick reminder: The first colonizers from Alliance Alpha reached Mars from a lunar base in 2065, and Alliance Beta followed directly from Earth in 2071. With the new quantum computing resources, colonization activities on Mars took a big leap in the 2070s, since everything went smoother due to advanced calculation capabilities: space flight, cryo-sleep, production of materials, any kind of forecast. So by now a total of about 100,000 people live on Mars, organized in five different alliances. The colonies were never included in the Wellbeing Gateways. They are without law, jurisdiction, or authority. Whereas on Earth politics is effectively peacefully automated, on Mars violent military rule prevails to gain predominance over territory. There are no resources, there is no atmosphere, there is no future except power struggle.

The argument of a backup plan for humanity has become nothing more than an excuse. After great natural and social disasters and the losses of many lives, people on Earth have successfully adapted to human-induced climate change and took measures against further global warming. On Mars, the alliances are in a permanent state of war for domination. In the fictitious universe of Star Trek, the conflicts took place between different alien civilizations, on real Mars they are between changing alliances of humans even though on Earth is peace. Or maybe because on Earth is peace. Mars has become a valve to vent tensions on Earth. Mars is an adventure game of peace-bored nations and people.

Is this Martial Law on Mars the price we have to pay for wellbeing on Earth?

---

5   Message to Mum

Transcript private message from 8th February 2122

Hey Mum,

I know we're meeting tomorrow… but I need to tease something so that you don't freak out and we can talk about this rationally. I will go to Mars. I mean not the Mars ambience but the real thing. It's just that I have the feeling that in reality nothing feels "real", and in the Sphere the extreme ambiences that are supposed to feel "real" don't either. Let's be frank, you know I've tried a lot there—I've been a victim and treated people bad myself. You, and probably everyone else, don't see it that way. You have the life you want, you have your purpose, your creativity, and your aesthetics. But I'm bored out of my mind because I'm "well". I need a real adventure. Something unexpected. Risky. Dangerous. There's not much validated information about what's happening on Mars, but that alone is worth it. To go to a place where you don't really know what's going on…fight with your elbows without private communication and happy go lucky control. I've got to do this!

Let's meet our biological selves in a real place, ok? Would be important to me.

Bye,

Genet

PS: I was not drugged writing this!!!

Cloning God: The UN Bioethics and Human Dignity Declaration of 2043 and the Rise of Monotheistic Fertility Cults in the Middle East

Elana Gomel

Disclaimer: This essay is part of a new collaborative project between the WEB University and the AI Network. The opinions expressed in this essay come from the AIs involved in the project and do not necessarily represent the WEB (World Educational Bureau) or its human researchers. The Humans involved in the project, provisionally titled "Is Biology Still Relevant?", are responsible for data-gathering and fact-checking only.

The 2043 Bioethics and Human Dignity Declaration by the United Nation was a momentous cultural and legal event, comparable in its significance only to the 1948 Universal Declaration of Human Rights. The latter was passed in the aftermath of World War 2 and the Nuremberg Trials and reflected the collective shock of these singular events. The 2043 Declaration, on the other hand, was the culmination of several slow and apparently disconnected processes that came together at the emergency meeting of General Assembly at Istanbul in 2042.

The first of these processes was, of course, climate change. But by this point in time, climate change and its concomitant loss of habitability of various regions have been going on for so long that they have lost the urgency of a

E. Gomel (✉)
Department of English and American Studies, Tel Aviv
University, Tel Aviv, Israel
e-mail: egomel@tauex.tau.ac.il

© The Author(s), under exclusive license to Springer Nature
Switzerland AG 2023
L. Horn et al. (eds.), *The Palgrave Handbook of Global Politics
in the 22nd Century*, https://doi.org/10.1007/978-3-031-13722-8_20

337

political problem.[1] While catastrophic events such as the complete flooding of New Orleans and the desertification of a large portion of Rwanda created occasional political shockwaves, these were quickly assimilated into the routine of adaptation that characterized what became known as the "post-world order". This colloquial designation fairly summarized the sense of endless duration that developed in the wake of post-utopia, post-history, and post-apocalypse. While the final catastrophe was eagerly expected in some quarters, it never actually came about, and powers-that-be shifted into the modality of crisis management rather than crisis aversion or proactive action "No more revolution or even evolution; we paddle in time as if it were a swimming pool rather than a rushing river or a mighty ocean" (Patnaik, Ψ 2111, 425). As some suggested, history itself became endemic (Fukuyama Jr., Ψ 2118).

The second process of relevance came across as a single event, even though it was the end result of gradual accumulation of scientific and technological developments. This was the birth of the first ten human clones in ten different countries from different and unrelated surrogate mothers. Cloning was a known and well-established technology since Dolly the Sheep, the first cloned mammal in 1996. But while it had been widely deployed in animal agriculture, religious and ethical considerations precluded it from being used on humans for a long time. This long hiatus came to an end in 2041 when a hitherto unknown organization that called itself The Goddess Circle (TGC) declared that it had implanted ten cloned embryos in the uteri of ten female volunteers. Each of these volunteers lived in a different country: China, South Korea, the US, Norway, Lithuania, Russian Federation, Botswana, Argentina, Palestine, and Israel. The women were genetically unrelated and did not know the identities of each other. Nor did they know the identity of the donor whose clone was implanted in their uteri using the old-fashioned IVF technology.[2] It was later revealed that though all of them had given consent to be the surrogate mother to a cloned baby and were enthusiastic about the TGC platform, some of the volunteers were unaware that their identities would be made public. Two of the mothers even sued The Goddess Circle for breach of contract and infringement of privacy.

---

[1] The greatest loss of habitats to flooding at this point in time occurred in Polynesia, the Caribbean, and Thailand. These, however, were not regarded as matters of urgency by China and the US that had been putting in place various programs to mitigate the impact of climate change for their own populations, including, but not limited to, relocation, subsidies, and new building codes. See Yu Ren (Ψ 2100).

[2] Since many different techniques of cloning are used today, including splitting a single zygote into multiple embryos and cloning stem cells, it is important to specify that the technique used by TGC was the old-fashioned one of cloning an adult organism. In this technique, first used with Dolly the Sheep, the genetic material of the donor is introduced into a hollowed-out ovum which is implanted into the uterus of the surrogate. The identity of the Second Advent donor was never disclosed and has been the subject of much speculation and conjecture. See Sigurdardottir (Ψ 2118) for a survey of existing theories, ranging from well-founded to whacky (i.e. that the donor was an actual goddess).

On April 4, 2041, six of the volunteers gave birth to healthy daughters. It was speculated that the delivery date was chosen because in Ancient Rome it was celebrated as the holiday of Cybele, the Phrygian goddess of fertility, later incorporated into the Roman Pantheon. The label of "Cybele Mothers" stuck, even though the TGC later denied that the delivery date had any symbolic or religious significance, pointing out that three of the ten babies were delivered several days later and one–five days earlier. All the babies were, of course, genetically identical, and had no genetic connection to their birthmothers.

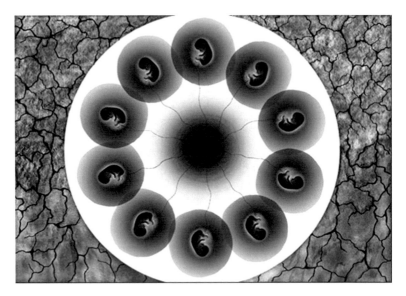

After what later became known as The Second Advent, The Goddess Circle stepped into the global limelight. It was revealed as a loose organization of feminist religious movements, including Musawah, Women of the Wall, Ecumenical Women's Movement, and several others. While not necessarily espousing a coherent theology, the Goddess Circle's statement of purpose emphasized female power, autonomy, and responsibility for Mother Earth. It proclaimed fertility to be the ultimate act or worship and denounced the restrictions on population growth.

Such restrictions had long history, starting with China's One-Child Policy (1980–2015). In this period, India also implemented a national child policy aimed at slowing population growth. Even though the national child policy in India was rescinded in 2021, one-child families received perks in education, health care, and employment, while couples with three or more children became ineligible for state subsidies and welfare benefits, and lost the right to run for a state assembly seat. India's policies became a model for Rwanda (when it was hit with severe food shortages), Benin, and were later adopted with some modifications in Nigeria. At the same time, due to cultural and social reasons, the population growth in Europe and parts of the US was stuck in the negative territory. Paradoxically, while governmental restrictions were quite effective in bringing down the birthrate, the opposite was not true. Some European governments (Germany and Spain) tried to enact pro-natal policies without any uptick in the number of babies born in these countries. One of the reasons was the influence of what became known as eco-theology: the belief that humanity was destroying the Earth and needed to atone for its sins by limiting its numbers.

But while eco-activists and eco-theologians argued that humanity needed to shrink its footprint on the planet and that zero or negative population growth was a necessary means to this end, a backlash was brewing (Dwornik, Ψ 2035). It came from several different quarters. First was the feminist movement, reinvigorated after its long slump in the 2020s, and asserting the importance of procreation as the source of female biological uniqueness and dignity. Then, there were small neo-utopian communities practicing a more natural form of living and suspicious of population control as a conspiracy of the global techno-elites. Somewhat hypocritically, these communities often relied on genetically engineered crops and lab-grown meat that created abundant food supplies and erased the historical memory of famines caused by over-population. Global agricultural companies were eager for new markets and encouraged growth. And religious revivals epitomized by The Goddess Circle brought together all of these disparate trends by creating a new theological discourse of fertility as virtue.[3]

The issue of cloning was initially a sticking point for the feminist movements and rejected outright by back-to-nature utopians. But eventually, their emphasis shifted from the means of procreation to its end. Following the lead of Dwornik (Ψ 2035) and McMahon (Ψ 2040), many feminists and neo-feminists argued that cloning gave women complete autonomy and control over the process of reproduction as it eliminated the need for the male contribution to the process. Old twentieth-century feminist utopias by Joanna Russ and Alice Sheldon, depicting all-female societies that reproduced by cloning, were resurrected, and enjoyed new popularity (Barn, Ψ 2065). And some neo-utopian movements, eager for growth, pointed out that cloning was modeled on the entirely natural process of twinning and that some animals, such as armadillos, consistently give birth to identical twins (Bebeshnikov, Ψ 2041).

The Second Advent quickly became the flashpoint of media and a political scandal. In most countries (with the notable exception of China and Russia, whose shrinking populations had long been a cause for concern for their political elites), the reactions were uniformly negative. The ten Cybele mothers were excoriated on social media, while The Goddess Circle became

---

[3] As the new study of electronic archives from that period (2030–2045) shows, *fertility, reproduction, babies, cute babies*, and *natural IVF* were consistently among the top online searches, exceeded only by *voluntary extinction* and *eco-suicide*. Unfortunately, the data come from a publication by the AI collective (Ψ 2120) and are no longer available to Human researchers. Therefore, its authenticity could not be verified.

the target of abuse and violence. Its participant groups were excommunicated by their respective religions, and several Muslim clerics issued threatening fatwas against anybody espousing such views. There was also a fatwa calling for the killing of the Palestinian mother who fortunately escaped to Iceland. Nevertheless, threats continued. The Argentinian mother was injured in a terrorist attack which also killed ten bystanders and for which nobody took responsibility. The US mother was murdered by a gunman who then supposedly turned the gun upon himself. The police investigation declared him to be a mentally ill lone-wolf shooter, though later it was revealed that he was a member of a charismatic Christian sect and died after having been taken into custody.[4] The Russian mother was murdered by her estranged husband who was promptly sentenced to 20 years in jail and never seen again. Riots broke out in several European countries, including Sweden and Denmark, and were put down with unusual force, while in the US marches for and against The Goddess Circle led to bloody clashes with the police and several contested midterm elections. The threats on the lives of the ten adorable baby girls proliferated until they had to be taken into protective custody and their whereabouts kept secret. Their identical pictures kept popping up on social media and were regularly declared to be forgeries by the authorities. Nevertheless, the public pressure to know what happened to the Cybele Daughters, as they became known, was so great that authenticated pictures and videos were released, and also declared to be forgeries by conspiracy theorists.

While religious scholars and public figures debated the spiritual status of the babies, the secular scientific and medical authorities did not quite know how to deal with the issue. Scientists allowed to examine the babies and concluded that they were healthy and thriving, and despite their varied epigenetic backgrounds, appeared to be as closely related as monozygotic (identical) twins.[5]

Meanwhile, a new cultural flashpoint was emerging in Western Europe where the Green Movement had strong historical roots. The Greens insisted that humanity needed to minimize its ecological footprints and that population reduction was a necessary means to that end. While never attaining a political majority, the Greens had an oversized social and cultural influence. Birthrates in Europe kept plummeting in the 2030s, and reproduction began to be seen as a somewhat embarrassing activity.

[4] The details of the so-called Jay Smith affair are so murky that we have decided to omit it from our discussion as the AI Collective denied our repeated requests for more information. Nevertheless, it was influential in swaying the American public opinion at the time toward a greater sympathy with TGC.

[5] "Epigenetic" as the term was used at the time related to the girls' different uterine environments and post-natal upbringing. It was widely believed that epigenetic influences can "rewrite" DNA. We now know this to be false (DNA can spontaneously adjust to environmental challenges due to its multiple redundancies) but since this article explores the contemporary social and political implications of the Second Advent, we decided to retain the obsolete term.

At the time, climate change still loomed over humanity. While in sub-Saharan Africa and the Middle East lower birth rates were mainly due to economic factors, in Western Europe women who had more than one child were regarded as rather irresponsible, if not altogether delinquent. And yet, the debate over the Cybele Daughters rekindled a new interest in motherhood. Cute videos of the identical girls shared on social media did not change the public opinion overnight, but they shifted the public sentiment. Aware of this shift, the Green Movement organized several anti-natal demonstrations but these backfired when a pregnant woman with no connection to TGC was yelled at and pelted with trash at a Green protest in Berlin.

Mindful of the growing violence around the world, the UN acted with unusual alacrity. In October 2041, it decided to empower the Commission on Bioethics and Human Rights. Wranglings about membership in the Commission slowed down the proceedings but it was officially inaugurated on April 2, 2042, almost exactly a year after the Second Advent. The Global South was represented by scientists and intellectuals from Chile and South Africa; there was also representation from various NGOs and women's organizations. But the tone of the proceedings was set by influential bioethicists and public figures active in the fight against climate change. Greta Thunberg was a member, and so were the aged Naomi Klein and Tim Jackson. Later on, there was a complaint that the Green Movement wielded outsized influence in the Commission, and some ex-members even hinted at alternative voices having been silenced.

The conclusions of the Commission were strongly tilted toward the Green point of view. While there was no general agreement on cloning itself, most members of the Commission felt that encouraging population growth in any form was a wrong strategy because of the deeply seated concerns about climate change. Some historians argue that this shows how culture and politics lag behind technology, since, by this time, carbon capture and storage and genetically engineered crops had already started reducing the effects of climate change and possibilities of food scarcity (Chiang, Ψ 2110). Others point out that extinction and speciation were accelerating nevertheless, and that preservation of the biosphere was seen as more important than the increase in Human numbers (Rivera, Ψ 2112). Still others deride the proponents of the latter view as ignorant of the nature of evolution which never "preserves" anything and is subject to perpetual change (see Schlossberg, Ψ 2120). Without taking a position in this ongoing debate, the AI Collective wishes to state that *Tempora mutantur, nos et mutamur in illis.*[6]

While the Commission was at work, the public debate continued, much of it (especially in the US) centered on the morality of abortion even though it

---

[6] The Human component of this project wishes to register their strong disagreement with the sentiment expressed in this Latin adage ("Times change, and we change with time") by pointing out that certain Human values are eternal and universal. We are aware, however, that the AI Collective does not share this belief, and we respect their rights as sentients to adhere to their own views, no matter how mistaken or dangerous.

was repeatedly pointed out by biologists that cloning does not involve abortion in any form. The inner deliberations of the Commission were not made public, but it is known that the issue of abortion was raised by several Catholic members, though it was excluded from the final report as it was found irrelevant. At the end, the Commission issued a series of recommendations that were later collected into the first draft of the Declaration. Though the final text of the Declaration differed in several significant ways from this draft, the basic points were as follows:

Article 1. Humanity is an inextricable part of the web of life on Earth and has an obligation to sustain and maintain ecological harmony.

Article 2. Any technology that contributes to perversion of the natural order of being is to be deployed with greatest caution and only in cases of absolute necessity.

Article 3. All natural life has dignity.

Article 4. Human dignity derives from nature.

Article 5. Reproductive technologies, such as cloning, go against the natural order of beings and are to be strongly discouraged.

The Declaration was adopted as a non-binding resolution, with China and the Russian Federation abstaining. Meanwhile, the ten cloned girls whose identity was an open secret grew up in their respective countries, and The Goddess Circle founders were put on trial, jailed, and in one case, executed: In China, the Declaration engendered an unexpected and potent backlash.[7]

Enthusiastically embraced in the West where now even the long-established IVF was now being viewed with suspicion and disgust, in the Middle East the Declaration was received as a stark instance of cultural imperialism. While contraception and abortion had long been a flashpoint for Catholicism and the evangelical movements, especially in the US, the Middle East had a long tradition of large families and fertility cults going back to the pre-monotheistic times. Moreover, the effects of climate change in the Middle East were mitigated by large-scale desalination projects and GMO-based agriculture. The history of the gradual dissemination of these technologies from Israel to other countries in the region (Saudi Arabia, UAE, and Egypt) and their embrace by the powers-that-be is still hotly debated as more archives are being opened to international researchers ⟨see Raby, Ψ 2120; Livni, Ψ 2121; Keiko, Ψ 2119⟩. However, this history, whether viewed in positive or negative light, is not relevant to our purposes since we believe that cultural and religious, rather than economic or ecological, factors play a decisive role in Human history.[8] The rhetoric of a "smaller ecological footprint" for humanity on the natural world

---

[7] The Chinese Cybele mother was put on trial for embezzlement of public funds, collaboration with hostile elements in the West, and slander against the PRC and sentenced to death. This was a paradoxical decision since China was generally supportive of cloning. It was later proposed that the Chinese Government wanted to keep its control over new reproductive technologies rather than be led by individual initiatives.

[8] The Human researchers of the WEB University wish to register their disagreement with this statement made by their esteemed AI colleagues.

had little appeal in the area which had been continuously modified by human intervention since the Neolithic period. To put it bluntly, there was precious little appetite for going back to nature in the countries where nature appeared in the guise of either deserts or fenced-in state preserves.

As a response to the Declaration, Israel, Lebanon, and Morocco defiantly announced a joint project called UMA (United Maternity Advancement, similar to the word for "mother" in Arabic and Hebrew) to explore the development of new reproductive technologies (including, but not limited to, cloning) in order to "facilitate biomedical research and ensure equitable access to fertility care". But even more significant was a religious shift. The Goddess Circle was savagely denounced by both Muslim and Orthodox Jewish authorities. Nevertheless, its theology started penetrating the religious discourse in several Middle Eastern countries.

Perhaps the most surprising change happened in the ultra-Orthodox Jewish community in Israel. Vehemently anti-Zionist and opposed to the secular state authorities, this community for a long time had been seen as a self-contained outpost of religious fundamentalism. Its relationship with science and technology had always been fraught. During the first waves of the pandemics, the highest percentage of the unvaccinated was among the ultra-Orthodox, which resulted in a higher-than-average mortality rate. And yet, precisely this blow to the community created the fertile ground for its embrace of cloning, tentative at first but spreading quickly. There were several reasons for that.

First, as the percentage of the ultra-Orthodox in Israel shrunk in relation to the general population, concerns about sustaining their numbers became paramount among the community's religious leaders. Guided by the high value accorded to fertility and children in the Jewish tradition, ultra-Orthodox rabbis had always encouraged large families. But with more and more ultra-Orthodox women joining the workforce, especially in high-tech, where they could work from home without physically interacting with men, their desire for undergoing ten or fifteen pregnancies diminished. Cloning that enabled "spreading" the burden of multiple pregnancies among several women became popular. A family could have triplets and quadruplets by "outsourcing" pregnancies to surrogates. Once several prominent ultra-Orthodox rabbis declared this practice to be permissible in accordance with the *Halacha*, the Jewish religious law, and allowed the use of non-Jewish surrogates (since they contributed none of their genetic material to the offspring), cloning became the favorite means among the ultra-Orthodox Jews to have large families without burdening the mother of the family with back-to-back debilitating pregnancies. Moreover, the cloning of great scholars also became popular, with young ultra-Orthodox women clamoring to give birth to a clone of an aged or dying (or even dead) rabbinical sage. This practice created some legal problems as strictly speaking, such babies would not be fathered by the mother's husband, thus qualifying as a *mamzer* (a bastard in the religious law). Several conflicting halachic rulings were issued but while the theological battle waged, the practice was steadily gaining momentum.

Meanwhile, among the secular Israelis, cloning was quietly and without much fuss adopted as another fertility treatment, alongside IVF and surrogate motherhood, both legal and supported by the state's health insurance. At first, it was embraced by single women who realized they did not need to scramble for sperm donors if they wanted a baby. Self-cloning became quite a fad, with young women posting selfies of themselves cradling their newborn identical twin. Married couples soon jumped into the game, often having a boy and a girl: the father's and mother's clones gestated together and birthed as fraternal twins. Eventually, some couples repeated the procedure several times, ending up with two or three sets, genetically identical but staggered by age.

In the Muslim countries of the region, the situation was more complicated. Several clerics argued that cloning does not contradict the Quranic principle of the precedent of creation as it utilizes life bestowed by God. Others argued to the contrary, stating that cloning was akin to slitting the ears of animals or otherwise altering God's creation, which is explicitly forbidden in the Holy Qur'an. Since the debate hinged on the definition of "creation", most ordinary people tuned out and simply followed their imams. After the Supreme Leader of the Islamic Republic of Iran approved the practice, the Shia community embraced it, and most Sunnis eventually followed suit.

Christianity had long been in decline in the Middle East, but the Maronites in Lebanon, the Copts in Egypt, the Eastern Orthodox and Catholics in Israel, and other Christian groups and denominations accepted cloning with little reservation, eager to boost their declining numbers and encouraged by the example of their Muslim neighbors. In fact, a sort of unofficial competition between various religious sects within Middle Eastern Christianity led to a population explosion that in some areas changed the religious and ethnic balance, and required the terms of constitutional democracies to be renegotiated.

Regardless of theology, secular governments of the Middle East, alarmed at the falling birthrates and eager to reestablish the Muslim world's predominance in the field of biotechnology, encouraged the development of assisted reproduction centers. Though ostensibly not focused on cloning, these centers became the foci of its spread.

The Goddess Circle was outlawed in most countries of the region, but its theology went mainstream. Assimilated to the monotheistic tradition, the worship of fertility and embrace of reproductive technologies to facilitate population growth became the common ground among these three warring religions of the Middle East: Islam, Christianity, and Judaism.

This created a schism between the historical cradle of these religions and their practice in the rest of the world. Comparable to the great schisms of tenth and eleventh centuries CE, this schism was theological, cultural, and geographic. Christianity in the West, profoundly impacted by the Green Movement and eco-theology, viewed population growth as a sin against the Earth and quietly preached zero or even negative birthrates. Judaism all but disappeared as a living religion among the few remaining Jews of the diaspora, while

Islam in the West was embroiled in socio-political standoff with the dominant secular society. Cloning was illegal in both the US and EU, and the public sentiment against it was so strong that even natural monozygotic twins were subjected to harassment and death threats.

On the other hand, in the Middle East (not only in Israel, Lebanon, and Morocco but also other Middle Eastern countries such as Turkey, Iran, and Iraq) cloning became socially acceptable and religiously tolerated, if not actually encouraged. As a result, population growth in these countries exceeded the rest of the world by orders of magnitude. However, confounding experts' warning, this growth did not cause an expected ecological collapse or widespread starvation, because the biotechnologies originally developed to facilitate human reproduction also brought about innovations in agriculture. Cloning animals had already been done for a long time, and cheap lab-grown meat and vegetable protein obviated the need for traditional large-scale farming. The Fertile Crescent, the birthplace of the Neolithic Revolution, now claimed to be in the vanguard of feeding humanity again.

Climate change was going on throughout the second half of the twenty-first century but the dire predictions of a sudden apocalyptic collapse had not materialized. While some climate denialists took it as a proof of their position, the truth was that climate change was absolutely real but like all geological processes, it unfolded on a timescale very different from the rapid churn of human history. *Natura non saltum facit*—nature does not take leaps—applied to climate change as much as it did to biological evolution. While several generations had lived in the feverish expectation of a planet-wide sudden catastrophic extinction, similar to the apocalyptic fever gripping Christendom at various points of its history, eventually it became clear that climate change was a long-drawn-out process. It proceeded in relatively manageable increments of disaster, giving (some of the fortunate among) humanity time to adapt. The disjunction between geological and human time was, once again, brought to the fore. The impatient expectation of the End Times was frustrated, as after every new flooding, hurricane, species extinction, or forest fire, history went on more or less as before. Moreover, advances in carbon capture and storage technology and development of new heat-adapted species (helped along by CRISPR and cloning) mitigated, though not obviated, climate change to the point where expectations of a global catastrophe appeared to be exaggerated, old-fashioned, and to many, simply irritating. The cultural perception of time shifted from chronology to duration; from difference to sameness; and from progress to endurance.

This had important theological consequences. All monotheistic religions experienced time as chronology; indeed, Judaism was credited with inventing the notion of linear time that progressed from the Creation to Redemption. Christianity developed its own elaborate eschatology, that later became secularized in numerous meta-theories of history, from Marx to Toynbee. Islam also embraced the "arrow of time". But with the cultural perception of temporality across the globe transitioning to the era of "post-history", the notion of historical rupture became problematized. Climate change, originally viewed as the last greatest incarnation of the Judgment Day/apocalypse/revolution, became the essence of continuity. As such, a slow but certain swing away from the notion of End Times entered the monotheistic religions of the Middle East, bringing them together in opposition to the still-apocalyptic mindset of the West.

The embrace of cloning to facilitate human fertility was the dividing line. As some scholars have argued, cloning which generates sameness and obviates the chaotic unpredictability of sexual reproduction, contributed to the growing perception that history was slowing down (see Weininger, Ψ 2055). This thesis has been debated by others who claim that cloning and post-history are unrelated trends that accidentally coincided within the same period—an ironic claim, considering that disavowal of accident was precisely one of the hallmarks of the nascent "steady-state" historical sensibility, which rejected the idea of historical rupture and sudden change occasioned by random events—the so-called "black swan" theory of history (see Markowski, Ψ 2063).

In any case, as cloning became an accepted part of monotheistic theologies, many ethicists and philosophers in the Middle East began arguing that humanity's sacred duty was to populate the world impoverished by Anthropocene extinctions, and that nature was subservient to human flourishing.

These trends were regarded with horror in the West, still in thrall to the Bioethics and Human Dignity Declaration. Eco-theology and Green ideologies, though diminished by their political failures, still exerted a profound influence on the mindset of the secular intelligentsia of the US and Europe. Fertility spike in the Middle East was seen as an incomprehensible insult to the very ideas of preservation and stewardship that motivated the moderate forces in the fight against climate change, while the more extreme factions defended the idea of gradual human extinction to allow nature's healing. The conscription of science to increase human fertility and enlarge humanity's footprint on the natural world was roundly rejected by most left-leaning politicians in the US and Europe.[9] Offended by their attitude, which they regarded as culturally insensitive and high-handed, the countries of the Middle East drew together. While the festering conflict between Israel and the Arab world had not been resolved or forgotten, it paled in comparison to their joint opposition to the UN. The fact that joint biotechnological projects between Israel, UAE, and Egypt were an important contributor to the Third Agricultural Revolution was a significant, though secondary, factor in their gradual political alignment.

For a while the standoff between the West and the Middle East remained mostly in the realm of words. The US tried to prevent clones from immigrating to the country which led to several Supreme Court cases, another

---

[9] The history of the factional split of the Global Left is not pertinent to this discussion; however, it is worth pointing out that some Western left-leaning movements sided with the Middle East, though most of them were outside the political mainstream of their countries (see Hassania, Ψ 2111).

contested election, and mass protests by twins and their allies. The growing economic power of the Middle East, now politically united in what was unofficially known as the Fertility Alliance against the declining West, created pressure on the world markets. While oil and natural gas were no longer as important as they used to be due to the predominance of solar, thermal, and nuclear energy, Saudi Arabia and Iran still had enough economic clout to make the West take notice and tread carefully. For ten years (2043–2053), Middle Eastern countries defiantly increased their population and embraced cloning, while the UN issued resolutions and condemnations.

But a new stage in this ideological and theological conflict was signaled by a shift in the attitudes of Russia and China. China had been experiencing a steady population decline since its One-Child Policy was rescinded in 2015 (see Zheng, Ψ 2115). No matter how the government tried to incentivize women to have babies by purely economic means, it did not work.[10]

After much dithering, China, alarmed at its population decline and afraid of losing its precarious economic dominance, came out in support of what became known as the "fertility faith". The deeply secular People's Republic did not care for its theological implications, but the notion of steady-state history chimed in with the Taoist tradition of cyclic time. The Russian Federation and its Orthodox Christian religion were more divided on the subject but fearing a population collapse and surprised by the success of cloning-based agriculture in averting famines, they came out in support of the fertility faith and against the Declaration. The political lines were drawn: the West against the rest. The Middle East officially reverted to the ancient name of the Fertile Crescent in 2070, proudly combining the symbology of Islam with the echoes of mother-goddesses of the Levant.

The ten cloned women were adults now. Known as *the First Ten*, or *Cybele Daughters*, they were adored by adherents of the fertility faith and reviled by Green thinkers and politicians. The identity of their original was never known, despite extensive research on the subject, thus giving rise to the folk belief that they were, in fact, avatars of the Goddess. Their DNA analysis showed a mix of European, Middle Eastern, Korean, and sub-Saharan ancestry, thus making them a symbol of human diversity. Interestingly, their divergent upbringings did not create profound ideological and/or psychological differences among them, though Number Five, brought up in Austin, Texas, embraced eco-theology for a while and repudiated her own origin. This phase did not last long, though, and she eventually rejoined her sisters who now resided in Beirut where a temple of fertility faith was being built, thinly disguised as an ecumenical center of reproduction ethics. Most people simply called it the House of the Goddess.

---

[10] As early as 2021, China had experienced the steepest birthrate decline in 60 years. The AI Collective found the following information on Google (obsolete) on a news portal from 2020s, titled "Despite Beijing's Baby Boosterism, China's Population Growth Hits New Low" (VOA, 2022). The Human component of this project wishes to register their doubt that these data are reliable.

In the meantime, cloning, while remaining the main method of enhanced reproduction, was not alone. Once the floodgates were opened, CRISPR also became widely used to improve the health of the new generation and to eliminate genetic diseases. While there was little appetite for more extensive human modification in the Middle East, China that had now decisively joined the Fertility Alliance in opposition to the Green League of the EU and the US, became known for producing a generation of supposedly "posthuman" children who, however, did not seem to differ much from their non-CRISPR counterparts. More unfortunate results of such experimentation were quietly disposed of.

The population explosion in the Middle East did not exacerbate the usual political tensions in the region, largely because cloning tended to stabilize the societies in which it was practiced by creating genetically homogenous populations. However, as the ideological and theological divergence between the Middle East and China on the one hand, and Europe and the US on the other grew into an unbridgeable gap, the seeds of the Fertility Wars were sown. For an authoritative account of this regrettable period, consult Ghannam ⟨Ψ 2117⟩.

References

(AI), Yu Ren. ⟨Ψ 2100⟩. *Architecture of the Flood*. New Shanghai: AI Collective.

AI Collective. ⟨Ψ 2120⟩. *Study of Google (Archaic) Searches, 2030–2045*. Unavailable.

Barn, Mauricia. ⟨Ψ 2065⟩. *Worlds of Their Own: Lost Feminist Utopias and Their Relevance to Our Time*. Boston: Boston College University Press.

Bebeshnikov, Valerian. ⟨Ψ 2041⟩. "Twins: A Manifesto." *Nature Now!*

Becker, Robert. ⟨Ψ 2042⟩. *To Tread Lightly: The Case for Negative Population Growth*. New York: Random House.

Chiang, Tom. ⟨Ψ 2110⟩. *How Societies Fail: Human Ignorance and the Wisdom of Technology*. Boston: MIT.

Dwornik, Adriana. ⟨Ψ 2035⟩. "Hating Babies: Misogyny and the New Green. " *FemTime: A Journal of Female History*, May 1: 1–26.

Fukuyama, Frances Jr. ⟨Ψ 2118⟩. *Histories of the End: Our Posthuman Past*. New York: Farrar, Straus and Bukowski.

Ghannam, Doaa. ⟨Ψ 2117⟩. *The Genesis of the Fertility Wars*. Beirut: The Goddess Circle Press.

Hassain, Hiba. ⟨Ψ 2062⟩. *Islam and Fertility: A New Perspective*. Boston: A New Light.

Hassania, Ali. ⟨Ψ 2111⟩. *The Global Left Is Neither*. Cairo: The New Alignment Press.

Keiko, Tatsuji. ⟨Ψ 2119⟩. *How the Apocalypse Did Not Happen*. Tokyo: Tokyo University Press.

Livni, Ornit. ⟨Ψ 2121⟩. *GMO and Zionism: Are the Two Connected?* New York: The Truth-Telling Press.

Markowski, Stephen. ⟨Ψ 2063⟩. *Where Did All the Black Swans Go? Accidents and the Historical Imagination*. Cambridge: Cambridge University Press.

McMahon, Glenda. ⟨Ψ 2040⟩. "Where Have All The Babies Gone? " *The Red Mother*.

Nassrin, Ghannam. ⟨Ψ 2071⟩. *The First Fertility War: A Brief History*. Riyad: The Historical Society of the Peninsula.

Patnaik, Aashirya. ⟨Ψ 2111⟩. *Water and Other Punishments: Collected Meditations* . Hyderabad: IFRA.

Raby, Nassrin. ⟨Ψ 2120⟩. *Beating Back the Desert: History of Land Reclamation in the Middle East*. Dubai: Dubai University Press.

Rivera, Felicia. ⟨Ψ 2112⟩. *Extinction and Its Discontents*. Barcelona: European Humanities Press.

Schlossberg, Joy. ⟨Ψ 2120⟩. *Evolution and Its Discontents*. Denver: American Humanities Press.

Sigurdardottir, Asa. ⟨Ψ 2118⟩. *Who Was the Great Mother? The Mystery of the Second Advent*. Reykjavik: Grapevine Press.

Smith, Deborah A. ⟨Ψ 2055⟩. *Voluntary Sterilization: A Biblical View*. Dallas: The Living Bible.

VOA. (2022, January 28). *Despite Beijing's Baby Boosterism, China's Population Growth Hits New Low*. Available at: https://www.voanews.com/a/despite-beijing-s-baby-boosterism-china-s-population-growth-hits-new-low/6417261.html#:~:text=China's%20birthrate%20has%20declined%20swiftly,according%20to%20statistics%20bureau%20records.

Weininger, Helene. ⟨Ψ 2055⟩. *The Republic of the Same: Cloning and the Shape of History*. Oxford: Oxford University Press.

Zheng, Yu. ⟨Ψ 2115⟩. *One Hundred Years of Population Control: History of Failure*. Hong Kong: Reducted.

Practices and Reflections

An Autobiographical Reflection by Daqin Kanja Augustine Prepared for Publication by Patrick Thaddeus Jackson

Patrick Thaddeus Jackson

Daqin Kanja Augustine (b. 2091, Nairobi, Kenya; d. 2172, Maryland, United States of America) was Principal of Brasenose House, McDaniel College, in the United States, from 2133 until his retirement in 2163; he was also a Satellite Fellow of Brasenose College, Oxford University, in England. He earned his Ph.D. in International Studies from Aberystwyth University in 2120, and subsequently turned his dissertation on the activation of ethnic identities during the global food riots of the late twenty-first century into the book *Whose Needs? The Cultural Politics of Food Shortage in China, India, and the United States of America* ⟨amazon/Routledge, Ψ 2129⟩. Dr. Daqin was the leader of the research team that produced the compendium *Bread From Heaven: The Manna Machines and the Transformed Persistence of Boundaries* ⟨Zhonghua Palgrave, Ψ 2138⟩, and his introductory essay to that work is a Google-certified Triple Platinum Download. His book *Otherness: A History* ⟨Oxbridge Press, Ψ 2150⟩ received the 2150 Lebow/Yamazaki Prize as the most important work of international theory published that year. Dr. Daqin is the author of a dozen peer-reviewed journal articles and several hundred blog posts and symposium contributions, many on the history of the international studies profession. He served as the President of the International Studies Association from 2156 to 2158, presiding over the Association at its bicentennial. His final book *Give Us This Day Our Daily Bread: The Manna Project from Prayer to Policy* ⟨Ψ Oxbridge Press⟩ was published in 2169.

P. T. Jackson (✉)
School of International Service,
American University Washington, Washington, DC, USA
e-mail: ptjack@american.edu

© The Author(s), under exclusive license to Springer Nature
Switzerland AG 2023
L. Horn et al. (eds.), *The Palgrave Handbook of Global Politics in the 22nd Century*, https://doi.org/10.1007/978-3-031-13722-8_21

354   P. T. JACKSON

EDITORIAL NOTE: *After Dr. Daqin's death, his husband Fr. Thomas asked me to curate his nachlass for deposit. A long scholarly career leaves a tremendous number of documents, and while I do not plan to make all of his voluminous correspondence readily available, some especially insightful and revealing missives will certainly find their way into his corpus entry, along with drafts of his best-known works. While sorting through the material I encountered the program for a meeting held at McDaniel College in June 2158 to commemorate Dr. Daqin's twenty-fifth year as Principal of Brasenose House. All of the invitees attended in person, incredible as that now sounds; the event was judged to be sufficiently important that the organizers purchased International Carbon Consumption Certificates for 25 (!) people, permitting them to travel to the United States from as far away as Australia, not to mention the Gagarin Lunar Zone (as you might expect, the ICCC for travel from Australia was considerably more expensive than the one for travel from the moon, as the lunar attendee simply landed at Canso Spaceport in Canada and took the train). I still have not discovered where the organizers got that kind of money, but I suspect that the Church might have played a role. The guest list was a veritable who's-who of mid-century international studies: Halvard Adam Sending, Akbar Robert de Mesquita, Qin Sujin, Gunther William Herborth, Laura Tickner Huntington, Daniela Saanvi Crawford...Dr. Daquin prepared a paper for the meeting, and read it in his usual colloquial style, complete with digressions and elaborations. I have chosen to publish the transcript and video of the presentation rather than the incomplete written version. It is, despite his self-deprecating introduction, an important document of a remarkable academic life.—PTJ, 8 February 2173*

Why anyone would want to read the life story of an academic is a puzzle to me. Most academic autobiographies seem like ego performances in which scholars and teachers try to make their work seem far more exciting than it is. Or they settle old scores, rehash battles already fought in print or in faculty meetings. I did not want to do that. But I was asked to prepare some remarks for the inevitable festschrift,[1] and since we are here on the occasion of my quarter-century at Brasenose-McDaniel, I thought it best to say something about how I got here.

I am grateful to see students and friends here, but you obviously are not the audience for these reflections because you already know my stories. Some of you are even *in* my stories [*laughter*]. But I think that the real audience for these kinds of pieces are students of the author; they want to know about their teacher, they want some context to put his strange habits into. So I imagined telling a tale to my undergraduates here, or to my graduate students through Oxford, about the old days, and worlds that they very fortunately don't remember. Forgive my indulgence in talking about events that many of you in the room have your own memories of; as I say, you are not the audience I imagined when writing these words.

---

[1] PTJ note: this festschrift never happened, in part because Dr. Daqin himself kept putting it off.

I was born in Nairobi, before the Last War, before the manna machines. My father was an engineer, a British citizen, but Kenyan by descent; my grandmother had moved to London when the droughts and floods in Nairobi were especially bad, before New Kibera was built. My mother was a medical doctor who worked at the San Marco Uhuru space center. Her parents had come to Kenya with the Chinese building crews, and found their skills in demand as SMU became the foremost satellite launch site in the world. My parents met when both were working at the space center. They were both Christians, and I think that is why they spent so much time outside of work aiding the poor—and then working with refugees, after the Kenyan government allowed huge numbers of Europeans looking for food to settle there.

You must remember that before the manna machines, all of the food that anyone ate had to be *grown* someplace. In the history books and blogs you have all read about the agricultural collapses of the middle of the twenty-first century? Yes, of course you have. The numbers do not really convey how terrible it all was. No, I don't remember that time myself, how old do you think I am? [*laughter*] But I heard tales from my parents, and from the priests at the orphanage. We were spared much of the horror by the African Union's "Green Sahara" project; I do not remember hunger as a child. But I do remember seeing the faces on the newscasts and hearing about mass starvation elsewhere, and I thanked God for the blessings apparently showered on Kenya, and on Africa in general.

I have a specific memory of when the Last War started, because the initial riots killed both of my parents. No, no, I don't need your sympathy; it was a long time ago and I have made my peace with it. When I got older I learned to appreciate the irony that even though the Europeans had in previous decades fantasized that refugees that they let settle in their countries would act like some kind of fifth column and wage war from within, it was only the Europeans themselves who actually did this! After there were almost half a million people in settlements surrounding Nairobi, one day everything exploded, and thousands of people took to the streets. There was fighting everywhere. I was in school at the time, and Fr. Luis made us all huddle in a room with no windows. Somehow the priests found food, and after the army had beaten down the riot those of us now without families were able to move to the orphanage. There we stayed for a few weeks, watching the reports about European Union forces landing in Libya and Egypt, and tracking the African Union counterattack as they strove to keep the EU from seizing control of the Sahara. That was the great prize, of course, because the shifting rains had made it very desirable land for growing crops, especially further to the south and nearer to us.

I think this is when my interest in international affairs was really kindled. My father had been proud of his birth country of England as well as his ancestral country of Kenya, not a hard loyalist by any means, but proud. He would root for the national teams of both countries in World Cup competition, and let's just say that 2150 would have been a difficult Cup year for him [*laughter*]. He would tell me stories about London, and my mother would tell me stories about Guangzhuo—not that she had lived there as a child, but she went back to visit relatives for a year before starting college, back when such travel was far less expensive than it is now. So I always knew that there were *other places* in the world, even as a young boy, and I knew that I was connected to those places somehow, without ever having been there. I was astonished at the violence of the European refugees and the military maneuvers of the EU forces, because I didn't understand why people weren't simply helping one another. I remember asking Fr. Luis about this, and he said something about original sin...something I must have scowled at, because I remember him laughing and saying, Augustine (he always called me by my Christian name), you always want to *know*, not just understand, don't you? Then he sat me down with a tablet and had me look at pages about countries and governments, and maps that showed where rainfall was plentiful and where it was not. I saw EU countries with starving populations, those were the ones invading us...but England, and Wales, they weren't part of the invasion even though they were starving too. *Why not?* I asked, and the tablet showed me the history of the European Union, the departure of the United Kingdom, the subsequent unraveling of the U.K. and Scotland's re-joining of the EU, the split of England and Wales but their continued alliance...

Oh, I had *questions*. I suppose I was still in shock from my parents' deaths,[2] but my abiding memory of the Last War is sitting in the orphanage with that tablet, learning about the politics of the EU and the politics of the world as a whole. I remember my delight when I figured out that China and the United States were both neutral but for different reasons: China because it was waiting to see who won, the United States because it couldn't be bothered to commit troops abroad. And both countries had immense stores of food grown in their own interiors, so they could afford to hold back: the same behavior, with the same assets, but on different grounds. As for England, its alliance with the United States allowed a measure of food security that countries in Europe could simply not achieve on their own.

Now, I was a precocious child, but I am not entirely certain that I understood all of this at age nine! But what I did understand was that places I was connected to, places that were connected through me, existed in a world of yet more places, and all of those places interacted and had their own histories and were *different* from one another. And I myself was part of that: a Kenyan with ancestors from China and England. I was a product of these entangled polities and their senses of self and their understanding of their responsibilities toward their people. Their actions on the world stage were a part of me, and I was in some sense "international affairs."

---

[2] PTJ note: the timeline is unclear here, because Dr. Daqin likely did not learn of his parents' deaths until after the fighting ceased. I would have loved to ask him to clarify this point!

It's difficult to put this into words. In some ways I have been trying to sing this song properly ever since those hours and days sitting with my tablet, looking at maps and pictures and videos of these places I had never been but dreamed of going. A psychoanalyst would have a lot to say, I am sure, about why I fastened on neutral countries, perhaps as a form of escape from the terrors around me, and as a way of feeling close to my absent parents. But as you know—I am in print on the subject!—*precisely* what I think about psychoanalytical accounts [*laughter*],[3] you will not be surprised that I put little confidence in that explanation. And as the old American pragmatist William James might have said, explaining an experience is not the same thing as experiencing it. What I had as a child was an *experience*, almost a revelation, a feeling of being deeply connected to places far away. That led to a life-long fascination with how these places worked, and how they related to one another.

William James?[4] Oh, yes, there's a funny story that you might not know. When I was fifteen and coming up to the time for my confirmation, I had the usual episode of doubt and hesitation and skepticism, why does God allow bad things to happen in the world, what is the use of praying to a God who does not grant our wishes, why do we need God when we have the manna machines and space flight and all of the other wonders of modern science. That sort of thing. Fr. Konrad—he had been a refugee as a newly ordained priest, had lost an arm in the war trying to calm down a group of rioters, and had refused repeated offers of a new one—was the person I poured all of my doubts out to, and one day he gave me two old books to read: Brian Flanagan's *The Queer Catechism* and William James' *The Varieties of Religious Experience*. I have no idea how or whether he realized that I was also struggling with my sexuality; I know I never said a word to him or any of the other priests! But those books really helped me put some things into perspective. They made space in the Christian faith tradition for me, but on terms that I did not think that others, and certainly not the bishop who did the confirmation examinations, would accept. So I was never confirmed.

The funny part of this story is that Fr. Konrad left the priesthood a few years later and became a philosophy professor. He's Gunther's father [*gasps and expressions of surprise*]. Yes, before I knew Gunther I knew his father. It is a small world.

But I have skipped over the most important event of all, the event that ended the Last War and, some would say, changed everything else—but you

---

[3] PTJ note: Dr. Daqin here likely is referring to essays like "Unraveling the Mind: On Doing Without A 'Deep' Account Of Personhood in International Studies," *Review of International Studies* 188:2 ⟨Ψ April 2142⟩, but numerous other cutting and even dismissive critiques of what he usually calls "psychological substantialism" pepper his writings over his entire career. I am sure that psychoanalysts would have a lot to say about this pronounced scholarly obsession of his.

[4] PTJ note: this paragraph was apparently in response to an interjected question which unfortunately was not captured on the recording.

know that I don't agree with that. *Some* big and important things changed when the manna machines appeared, but certainly not *everything*. I had a courtside seat, so to say, since one of the buildings on the orphanage grounds was where a manufactory did its work and assembled some of the machines before the big day. Obviously I did not know that at the time; Fr. Luis told me years later that not only had the Church *in general* provided the machines, but that our Catholic community *in particular* had been one of the key hubs for their distribution in the Nairobi area. I think he told me in trying to convince me to continue with Catholic higher education as a confirmand, but of course I went off to Cambridge instead. I'm getting ahead of myself.

The machines, yes. The manna machines. I still think that the real genius of the manna machine project was in crafting plans that could be enacted by basically any nanoassembler, even a small and limited unit like the one that we fed our garbage to. The new scripts created a new performance, and—as I later learned—we had several dozen boxes ready for Delivery Day, 6 January 2100, the feast of the Epiphany. Various trusted adults set them up all around our part of the city, so when the papal message went out that day, the impact was widespread and immediate. The boxes—we had one on the grounds, and the priests gathered us all around to watch it bloom—put forth tendrils, and the machine strung itself together, climbing out of the box like something alive. Instructions were available on any device: organic material of whatever sort goes in *here*, and *there* is where the machine's only two products come out. Water, of course, fresh and clean. And the manna bread, or cake, or whatever you want to call it. Engineered for nutrition and not for taste, as we all know. But that day it was simply delicious to all of us, since meals had been a bit spare during the fighting and now there was *enough for all*.

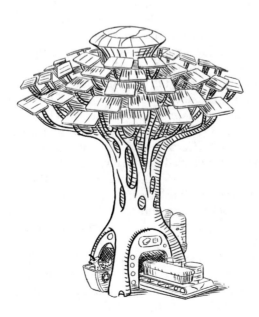

And that, of course, was the whole point. The wager was that if you provided *enough for all*, that would take away some of the urgency, some of the discontent, some of the fuel for the conflicts and the wars and the horror of a world of scarcity. Not a luxurious *enough*, but a simple and adequate *enough*—and not enough of everything, but enough for the basic sustenance of continued human life.

I said "during the fighting" a moment ago. The fighting did not stop immediately, even though we celebrate 6 January as the end of the Last War now. In fact, that very day the orphanage was set on by armed white men, demanding supplies; Fr. Luis and the other senior priests explained the manna machine to them, shared food and water, gave them a box of their own. I watched from inside, anxious that the armed men would shoot Fr. Luis. They did not, but I learned later that we had been lucky. In other places, people had shot one another vying for possession of a machine, apparently not reading or believing that part of the papal message that linked to the instructions that anyone could use to create their own manna machine, quite literally from the garbage. It took a few weeks for it to dawn on most people that there was simply no *need* to keep fighting in order to have enough food to eat and water to drink. By that point the European governments—both those that weren't overturned in popular uprisings as soon as people understood that they did not need to remain loyal to the regime in order to be fed, and those newly installed by revolutionary publics—had come to the negotiating table, the treaty of Cairo ended the Last War formally, and the old economic system started to unravel.

I remained an avid reader of the international news during those months, my eyes sometimes never leaving the tablet all day. I was thrilled when China dropped its official skepticism about the machines, and declared them compatible with Xiist Reform Communist doctrine; only later did I come to realize that this was the only way that the Party could retain control, because the public were embracing the machines already. I had a map file on the tablet where I would color in countries as they gave up opposing the manna machines, and started instead dealing with the implications of universal sustenance. I could see that all around me: people who no longer *needed* to work in order to survive stopped doing jobs that they did not want to do, and that led to a lot of popular redistribution of goods other than food. Especially since one of the jobs that no one wanted to do was to police the streets and stop people from stealing from stores. Certainly, we all know how the global markets in luxury goods were re-established eventually, but in those early days—as some of you here remember, I know—people just took the things that they wanted. And people left abusive relationships and oppressive governments, supported by the fact that they could always find enough to eat elsewhere. I read as much as I could, and that was my portal on the world, since the priests wouldn't let us leave the orphanage grounds.

I think I was most fascinated—and it was a horrific fascination—with the United States' response. Yes, even as a child, I was baffled that an entire country of nearly half a billion people would, or could, turn its back on the gift of the manna machines, declaring them "against nature" and making their possession or operation a crime. I had a file of news stories about the U.S. National Guard rounding up suspected "nanist heretics" and smashing manna machines wherever they found them (usually hidden away in basements and attics). One of my favorite episodes involved a warehouse outside of Los Angeles where someone was stockpiling manna for sale—apparently without realizing that it would dissolve in 48 hours! So the soldiers broke open all of these boxes that by that time contained nothing but dust. I was not sure who looked more foolish, the soldiers or the stockpilers.

Receiving a free gift is not an easy thing for a government constituted by suspicion to do, after all. The United States was just, as it often is, more *extreme* about things. As the enforcement of the ban on the manna machines grew into a general ban on engagement with the rest of the world at all, and the United States turned itself even more completely inwards, I became more and more desperate for any information about this place that had for so long been one of the dominant powers in the world. Maybe the most dominant, but as some of you will undoubtedly say, that all depends on how we measure "power," doesn't it, Daniela? [*laughter*][5] Some of the other children started calling me "Yankee," and I'm sure that the priests teaching us got tired of my *always* choosing the United States for my class projects. I did not understand what was happening here, and even though I have been studying it and living here for decades, I am still not sure that I understand it. Such a strange country, with such a firm sense of its "mission," persisting even while the details of that mission change!

But back to the story. Since I had refused confirmation, I was an increasingly alien presence in the orphanage. The priests' sense of vocation would not permit them to simply turn me out onto the streets, even though they knew that I would not starve because of the manna machines. A new kind of governmental authority was still slowly emerging in those days, as everyone struggled to come to terms with what it meant to live in a world where one did not need to work to eat. You younger colleagues who do not remember the world before might have an intellectual grasp of how much of a change this was, but that is different from having lived through it. I myself never had to work under that old system, but I remember my parents being concerned about money for food even though they both worked long hours at the spaceport. Food was available for purchase because of the Sahara croplands, but it was not cheap! And the constant worry about having enough to survive seeped into and colored everything. That is what the manna machines dispelled, that constant nagging worry. But it took time for people to figure this out. In those first years, there were still groups trying to monopolize the machines and use their control to produce allegiances and authority, but the machines were so *ubiquitous* that these efforts broke down—not without friction, and

[5] PTJ note: see the debate between Daqin and Crawford in *Duck of Minerva*, Ψ 2130-05, rdoi:121.5175/dcd644.

not without some violence. One of our priests—Fr. Jing, whose name many of you may know—was killed while trying to mediate a territorial battle between two rival groups; he died with two boxes in his arms, and after his death each group took one. Eventually a famous virtual scene was erected on the spot where he died.[6] But by the time I was seventeen, a lot of that had calmed down.

The main issue, you see, was not the priests' concern for my survival. It was their concern for the effect I and my skepticism were having on the other children. I was not an atheist, but I was not convinced of the universal truth of the Catholic faith, and I am still not, despite my husband's vocation! Yes, the Church had done a great thing by creating and distributing the manna machines, but in my view they had done an even greater thing by not at all insisting that the recipients of this free gift had to respond in kind by listening to any evangelical pronouncements. Far from it. Manna machines were for *all*, no exceptions, and no need to become or even consider becoming Catholic. That was the most controversial part of the project inside the Church itself, in many ways. Certainly the priests at the orphanage, like so many local priests all over the world, regarded the machines as the first step in a project of mass conversion: here is a gift, now, let me explain to you where the gift comes from and to whom you should be grateful for it. Very much like the old "international development" approach, which as we all know was a neocolonial arrangement fueled by a story about the superiority of the giver. This was the story I questioned, loudly and often, so Christian charity led to their efforts to help me use connections among my father's family to get a visa and more importantly a carbon certificate for travel to England, so I could begin studies at Cambridge.

Now England in those days was largely recovered from the effects of the COVID-77 pandemic, although after the density of Nairobi, London felt almost empty. Queen Lilibet, named for her grandmother, was approaching her silver jubilee as I arrived, and my older cousins and relatives had many stories of how virulent the racial divisions in the country had been before the pandemic took the rest of the royal family and made it necessary to bring her back from Canada to assume the throne. A quarter-century of a mixed-ethnic queen had done wonders—together, of course, with so many dying and the survivors needing to pull together to survive. England was such a fiercely nationalist place that when faced with the choice, the English chose a multi-racial England that remained independent over a whiter England that might have had to join some larger collective. Pride and adversity did what thoughts and prayers had not; the national story trumped—I am aware of the irony of this phrasing!—the stories about race that had been relegated to the past. The "English Way" was, as a matter of official policy, a multi-cultural blending of

---

[6] PTJ note: the "Memorial to Zhou Jing," sometimes referred to as "This Is My Body" after the name that the artist Consuela Mahlangu gave the installation, can be viewed at netcoordinates lat. −1.286401 lon. 36.816718.

traditions, and a frank acknowledgment that the British Empire had been a misguided mistake, but one that could now serve as raw material out of which something better could be built. If there were people still pining for a position of power that England had not occupied for over a century, I think they probably all moved to the southern United States before the Last War, nurturing their historical fantasies in the company of unreconstructed Confederates.

At Cambridge I was able to follow my bliss, as they say, and read widely in my favorite subjects: history, politics, sociology, philosophy. The HSPS tripos was just a perfect match, and there were whole weeks when I never ventured outside of the walls of Pembroke College, going from my room to the dining hall to a tutorial session and then ending up either in the library or on a bench outside. Most of my peers were thinking of careers outside of the academy; the money economy for luxuries was getting started again, and employers were offering very attractive packages for those with a demonstrated capacity to think critically. Since no one had to work to eat, jobs *had* to pay well to attract and retain people, so it was relatively easy to do well for oneself if one was talented. Just as it is now, much of the energy for college graduates was in creating and marketing entertainment experiences: theatre, music, art, holodrama, games. And then there was engineering, space exploration, medicine, and other technical fields—always a market for that. Beyond that, beyond college, there was always the local barter economy in handmade goods and services, where skilled tailors would swap a new pair of pants for a couple of hours of work in the garden…not a path to riches, by any means, but a fine way to live.

The manna machines made possible a world in which people could, to a much greater degree than before, do what they *wanted* to do. And what I wanted to do was to understand how the world worked, how society worked, why people did what they did when they no longer *had* to do as much. Obviously for some people it was a desire for some luxury product that was part of the money economy, so they chose to do work that would let the acquire those products. But I learned from my musician friends that although their performances and recordings could become commodities, they themselves were just as happy to create and play for very little money now that they were always guaranteed enough to eat. Skilled producers and recording engineers chose to work with artists whose music they found interesting, and talented marketing folks promoted what they found interesting to promote. What was left for the money economy—but not exclusively, sometimes there was barter here too— were the musical instruments, the recording and amplification equipment, the special deluxe editions of albums that functioned as collector's items. Here as in so many sectors, desire did not drive things; instead, it was a kind of pride in one's craft and a sheer delight in doing what one could do as well as one could do it.

The major benefit of the money economy, of course, was in becoming qualified for space exploration. Then as now, anyone who wanted to go off planet needed to have a set of skills and experiences that were in demand, and there is of course a fiercely competitive market for those. The ultimate luxury, then: leaving the Earth, going to one of the orbital stations, even on to one of the lunar bases. For the rest of us, happy to pursue our lives here, there is the freedom to live as we choose, unencumbered by desire for luxury.

What I saw all around me during my undergraduate studies was that my professors competed not for money or luxury, but for the esteem of their peers. The ancient system of peer review was complemented by the other virtual places to publish one's arguments and claims, places where the path to publication was much less arduous. Early on, when I expressed interest in an academic career, Dr. Tanaka[7] made sure that I understood that a peer-reviewed publication in one of the old and distinguished outlets was necessary to get my job application considered, but that I should in no way limit my reading and my engagement to those sources. The trick to a fulfilling academic life was to read widely, and the net had many, many corners to explore. And explore I did.

After Cambridge, going to Aberystwyth for my doctoral studies simply made sense: although the myth that international studies had begun there in 1919 had been well and truly shattered by scholars, there was still a sense of gravitas about the place, and a long tradition of pushing the boundaries of the field stretching back centuries. Critical security studies, post-humanist relationalism, international knowledge politics, lattice regionalism, collective and distributed international agency...so many lines of inquiry either started at Aberystwyth or were nurtured there. My Cambridge tutor Dr. Amalia[8] had earned her Ph.D. there, and I had visited several times while an undergraduate—after all it was only about ninety minutes by high-speed rail, and they had some excellent symposia after which they served good food (and after that there were plenty of pubs to go to in order to continue the conversation). The difficulty was affording it; undergraduate education was of course free, but graduate education required money. I was fortunate to receive a Rhodes/James scholarship, part of the ongoing effort to make sure that people from former British colonies had access to British educational institutions, and that made my matriculation possible.[9]

Most of what I would like to say about graduate school I will not say, for fear of embarrassing any of you gathered here [*laughter*]. The students I

[7] PTJ note: Horace Ari Tanaka, author of *International Studies As Interdiscipline* (Oxbridge Press, Ψ 2095). But Dr. Daqin is confused in his timeline here, because Dr. Tanaka was at Aberystwyth, not Cambridge, and likely did not have this conversation with Dr. Daqin until later on.

[8] PTJ note: Ketanji Bohdana Amalia, prominent scholar of the mid- to late twenty-first century whose work focused on the cultural structures of global politics. By the time Daqin studied with her, she would have been about 75 years old. She died at the age of 96 in 2124, and was still active enough in 2120 to attend Dr. Daqin's installation as a Fellow of Brasenose College, Oxford.

[9] PTJ note: typically, Dr. Daqin does not mention here that Rhodes/James scholarships are among the most competitive in the world, and that he had to pass through four rounds of selection interviews before being awarded one.

364 P. T. JACKSON

studied with, and drank with, and argued with, and then usually drank some more with, were the most important community I have ever been a part of. Every day was alive with ideas, and because there was such a large concentration of us there working in international studies, we hardly noticed that the field was shrinking as the mainstays of our scholarly profession—writing about war and peace, about conflict and cooperation among states—were starting to fade into contemporary irrelevance. After the Last War there simply were no more wars, because no country could maintain an army when the manna machines made basic food so plentiful that no one had to join the army in order to survive. And a lot of the old conflicts lost their edge when people had enough to eat. Not all of them, of course. But on the whole, the world was a lot less volatile than it had been when I was younger. So studying the world held less appeal than it once did. The action was in the past, and that meant that international studies started to look more like the study of history.

Now, I and my colleagues were still fascinated by what I later came to call the *problem of otherness*: how polities of various sorts dealt with the question of who belonged and who did not. Early on I became convinced that the manna machines would not make this problem go away, although it would change some of the means that polities used to create and enforce their boundaries. My childhood fascination with the differences between the United States and China in dealing with food shortages and the manna machines became—after Dr. Aziz[10] insisted that a good dissertation needed *three*, not *two*, comparative case studies—my thesis and first book, as I investigated the reasons why these polities reacted very differently to a similar set of challenges. While most people outside of our field were content to mark the United States as simply an outlier or a black swan—"you know those Americans," people said, and shook their heads—I was never satisfied with that. I wanted to *know* what made the United States such a different place, and why the Trumpite message of neo-isolationism so easily came to frame and dominate U.S. politics in the early twenty-second century. I wanted to know why a country that had been a superpower well into the twenty-first century would turn its back on the world. Akbar and I argued vociferously about whether this was the same process as had led the Ming rulers of China to stop sending out their treasure fleets—I think that may have been my first professional publication, in fact.[11] As you know I never liked that kind of historical parallelism; what always leapt off the page to me was the unique configuration of elements that produced specific outcomes...but you have all heard this sermon before, many times, so I will leave the preaching to my husband, who is much better at it than I am [*laughter*].[12]

---

[10] PTJ note: Karl Estrada Aziz, Dr. Daqin's doctoral chair.

[11] PTJ note: Dr. Daqin is correct. See the exchange between Daqin and de Mesquita in Ψ *The Disorder of Things* 2118-10, rdoi:121.2247/gqp5701.

[12] PTJ note: at this point in the session Fr. Thomas said something that the microphones did not pick up, and the room erupted into a lot of good-natured cross-talk about whether

But getting back to the story. While many universities in England saw their international studies programs shrinking, Oxford and Cambridge managed to hold onto their faculties. One benefit of long-standing tradition is that it is slow to change, and the mere upending of everything people thought they understood about global politics couldn't convince such august institutions to alter their curricula overnight, or even over a brief couple of decades. Students went to university looking for ways to enter the money economy, and there was no money in international studies. There had not been much money there all along, but once there was a career pathway for students to go into public service, or to advise transnational corporations about doing business abroad. But most of that collapsed pretty rapidly once the role of government changed to coordination instead of service provision, and once the exchange of physical goods became much more local. Not all of that was the manna machines, of course; the carbon costs of things like automobiles and airplanes simply became prohibitive, and the refining of virtual presence made it almost lifelike. Almost! The very fact that so many of you are here today in the flesh shows us that we humans still appreciate physical co-presence, although I wonder whether future generations will retain the same nostalgia for it as people our age do.

Tradition is slow to change. Yes. That is of course part of how I came to be here, in the United States, in charge of a residential college. I certainly appreciated my time at Oxford, the conversations with colleagues over good meals, and the research I was able to conduct thanks to the European Union's chunnel program.[13] But most of all I enjoyed tutoring the students, working with them to help them shape their views about their places in the world. The value of a classical liberal arts education was still pronounced in English society, so we always had students completing the PPE and HP degrees, looking less to acquire marketable skills and more to become broadly intelligent adults. I always delight my students by quoting the classic international studies scholar Hedley Bull to them:

> The search for conclusions that can be presented as "solutions" or "practical advice" is a corrupting element in the contemporary study of world politics, which properly understood is an intellectual activity and not a practical one. Such conclusions are advanced less because there is any solid basis for them

Dr. Daqin was in fact a good preacher. I have omitted this vibrant and confusing exchange from the transcript.

[13] PTJ note: Dr. Daqin here uses the colloquial name for what was formally called EPSA, the European Partnership for Scholarly Advancement, which later became the Weber/Habermas Scientific Initiative. Scholars in England called it the chunnel program because of its decided emphasis on bridging the English Channel and encouraging collaboration between scholars based in England and those based in continental Europe. Dr. Daqin's "bread from heaven" project was made possible by a series of generous grants from that program. I discuss the chunnel program in P'Ti Tano Jae, "Reconstructing International Studies Research," *European Journal of International Relations* 171:3 ⟨Ψ September 2165⟩.

than because there is a demand for them that it is profitable to satisfy. The fact is that while there is a great desire to know what the future of world politics will bring, and also to know how we should behave in it, we have to grope about in the dark with respect to the one as much as respect to the other. It is better to recognize that we are in darkness than to pretend that we can see the light.[14]

Of course I then had to explain to them that once people looked to international studies scholarship for exactly such "practical advice," which always prompts a round of bemused discussion about the epistemic status of claims in international studies and why anyone ever thought that the study of the problem of otherness would yield any such thing as "practical advice." And that in turn leads to a conversation about the purpose of pursing knowledge, and what we might reasonably hope to gain from the study of international affairs...and that of course is why I introduce the students to Bull in the first place.[15]

I would say that without the weight of tradition, the teaching of international studies would have fallen by the wayside long ago. The problem of otherness poses itself most pressingly for a traveler, after all, and so much travel nowadays is overland—and in a huge country like the United States, that largely means travel by high-speed rail within the borders. And of course there is exoplanetary travel, but that tends to be a one-way trip, some of present company excluded of course! The celebration of the local, despite its benefits for the planetary ecosystem, does mean a certain lack of curiosity. Of course people know that other people in other places do things differently, but it is a lot easier to ignore those other people and other places in practice when there is no pressing need to go there, and virtual presence even via avatar still lacks something. My students say that only people my age think so, and that they are very happy with the boundless virtual projecting they can do...but I would still argue that the very fact that they can turn off the machine at any time and sit up *at home* means that they never have to commit to actually being a stranger in a strange land. Not like I did when moving to England, and to Wales, and finally to Maryland. My students do not really experience the *foreign*, and the problem of otherness for them is always more of an intellectual exercise. A useful one, to be sure, since it helps prepare them for those

---

[14] Hedley Bull, *The Anarchical Society (centenary edition, with critical notes and introduction by Jonathan Daiyu Borah)* (Oxbridge Press, Ψ 2077).

[15] PTJ note: in the nachlass there is a copy of Dr. Daqin's first-year graduate student essay "Hedley Bull as an Exemplary Theorist of International Relations," which he submitted at the completion of a module in international theory. The grader—I have not been able to determine precisely who it was—called the essay bold and provocative but not a very subtle reading of Bull. I leave it to the reader to ascertain any parallels between that essay and Dr. Daquin's subsequent, and celebrated, article "The Suganami Thesis on the Origins of the English School, Reconsidered," *International Relations* 136: 1 ⟨Ψ March 2122⟩.

measures of difference they do and will encounter. But it's all at one step removed.

Which is not to say that teaching international studies is unimportant, of course! When the Paine Project got underway, after the electoral defeat of the Trumpites in 2132, and the call went out for scholars willing to relocate to the United States to help rebuild what had once been a global beacon of higher education, how could I say no? International studies was quickly judged an important field to import, precisely because it could help loosen the solid soil of nationalist exceptionalism that had frozen so much of U.S. society for decades. The physical sciences had not suffered much under the Trumpite regime, save of course anything having to do with nanoassembly (or human biological evolution). But the social sciences had been gutted, replaced by ideological propaganda or by the most simplistic of descriptions. New Freedom's victory at the polls opened the doors for a reconsideration of what students needed, and frankly, a certain degree of Anglo chauvinism meant that the models copied were English (despite the Paine Project being largely funded by Chinese entrepreneurs). So it was very appealing to have a fellow at Oxford come to Maryland and establish something like a college system here, and Maryland was one of those parts of the United States that even under the Trumpites had worked very hard to maintain diverse and inclusive communities. I do not think that someone who looked like me would have been as acceptable in other parts of the country: dark-skinned, and gay as well! Tom and my way was definitely paved by the Church,[16] still a power in this part of the country, and here again the weight of tradition helped immensely. *Any* Catholic, even a gay one, was acceptable to covert believers used to the casual Protestant chauvinism of the Trumpite regime.

Establishing the college system was engaging work, but I am glad that I did not have to labor under the publishing expectations of decades ago—I look at the c.v.s of some of our historical forebearers and marvel that they ever had time to do anything *but* publish! Dozens of books and scores of articles were more the norm for a career then. Had I stayed at Oxford I do not doubt that I would have published more, but instead, I have been able to impact hundreds of young lives and help them to discover their truest vocations. The bureaucratic inertia of accreditation requirements meant that colleges and universities never lost the need for distribution requirements in the humanities and social sciences, even as much of the energy among students shifted to the technical and physical sciences with their promise of gainful employment off-planet. And the old ideal of a liberal arts education and the value of critical thinking never completely went away. So students come to a place like this expecting to be challenged, and to have to learn to live together in community. Few stay; most

---

[16] PTJ note: Fr. Thomas was assigned to McDaniel as the Catholic chaplain at the same time as Dr. Daqin's appointment to the faculty. Fr. Thomas was the first Catholic chaplain at McDaniel in over twenty years.

pass on through and work in industry or the arts. Some remain, and a few have become colleagues.

I have gone on for too long already. And I have skipped the most salacious bits of the story—no, I am not about to break my silence about Janice Sean Adler's dismissal, and my answer remains "no comment," and not just on the advice of counsel [*laughter*].[17] We spend too much time trading gossip in our profession. Suffice to say that it was judged best that they simply step aside. You will get no celebration of victory from me. In that affair as elsewhere throughout my career, I have been guided by the importance of maintaining community, and that is the legacy I hope that I leave. I remain fascinated by our stories about belonging and exclusion, and by the impact of our *telling* of those stories—the content, the plot, yes, but even moreso the performance. While I continue to harbor doubts about Catholic theology, the ritual of the Mass holds a deep appeal for me. Likewise I find our theories very engaging, but what they do in practice—when practiced—interests me even more. Helping students learn to appreciate the power of a story told is my greatest joy, and telling stories about otherness remains my favorite task. Now that there are no wars, now that there is no hunger, now that the stakes of politics have been reduced, the fierceness with which polities once had to enforce their boundaries has also lessened. This leaves us free to experience the difference as something other than threatening. I am happiest when my students leave my classroom or my table[18] with their curiosity rekindled, having learned that the local must be balanced with something broader lest it become merely provincial. *To cultivate an appreciation for difference*: what finer task could there be!

---

[17] PTJ note: Janice Sean Adler's removal as Vice-Chancellor at Aberystwyth in 2118 remains the source of endless speculation; they never spoke publicly about it, nor did the student leadership in charge of the protests—including Dr. Daqin, who was part of the student coordinating committee.

[18] PTJ note: Dr. Daqin's modified "high table" dinners—in which he and a couple of other college faculty would dine with a small group of students—were a staple of Brasenose House life. Indeed, that's where I got to know Dr. Daqin and Fr. Thomas well enough to be asked to undertake this curation task. I am, after all, one of those who stayed in academia, and next Fall I take up the mantle of Principal of Brasenose House myself. I plan to keep Dr. Daqin's dinner institution intact.

Search: Physical Twin

Frans Magnusson and Elin Haettner

Welcome to the OpenScholar feed!

User: **Hagnus Frelin**
Login at: 2122-10-18 16:39:23 GMT+1…
Search Settings:

> **Search tags**: Physical Twin, Digital Twin, Information Overlay, Human Density Management, Automated Invisible Nudging Technology, UN Climate Refugee Agency, Global Citizen Program, Generic Zoning, Land Use, Migration
> **Results sorted by**: User Knowledge Graph Relevance
> **Selected reading modes**: Table of Contents, Points of Interest, Abridged

Loading results…

F. Magnusson (✉) · E. Haettner
White Arkitekter, Gothenburg, Sweden
e-mail: frans.magnusson@white.se

E. Haettner
e-mail: elin.haettner@white.se

© The Author(s), under exclusive license to Springer Nature Switzerland AG 2023
L. Horn et al. (eds.), *The Palgrave Handbook of Global Politics in the 22nd Century*, https://doi.org/10.1007/978-3-031-13722-8_22

STILL NO ARTIFICIAL INTELLIGENCE: THE ROLE OF GLOBAL MIGRATION IN PROLONGING THE 3RD AI WINTER
Halldóra Gortdottir, ILO, 2104

Outline

1. The 3rd AI winter

    1.1. Previous winters in AI history
    1.2. **The Phoenix Cascading Failure Disaster**

Timeline

2057-08-11
Citywide curfew due to extreme weather event

- *Arizona record wet bulb temperatures*
- *Air conditioning drives electricity demand over max capacity*
- *Accumulated charge deficit in electric vehicle fleet*

2057-08-13
Palo Verde nuclear incident

- *Detected failure in reactor core cooling system (false positive)*
- *Reactor shut down*
- *Local safety perimeter established*

Phoenix municipal AI control system safety protocol initiated

- *Airspace lockdown*
- *Highway roadblocks activated towards the west*

Power grid failure

- *Instant regionwide power shortage*
- *Cascading grid failure*
- *Household air conditioning outage*

Water Supply failure

- *Electric pumping stations power failure*
- *Emergency backup systems in poor condition*

2057-08-14
Evacuation failure

- *Grid-wide traffic congestion exacerbated by blocked highways*
- *Airlift efforts from Luke Air Force Base limited by local traffic congestion*

2057-08-15
US Army initiates search and rescue for remaining survivors

2. Dynamics of a prolonged AI winter

    2.1. Political and financial ramifications of the Phoenix Disaster
    2.2. Strong cultural and political resistance
    2.3. Investment capital moving to adjacent technologies

3. The role of global migration

    3.1. Global Citizens Program: an immense pool of workers
    3.2. AI vs the cost efficiency of "free" human intellectual labour

TWIN LIVING: PERSONAL PERSPECTIVES OF LIVING IN, BETWEEN, AND OUTSIDE OF INFORMATION OVERLAYS
Bart Whitakker, University of Oxford, 2118

Abridged

This paper presents an analysis of in-depth interviews with four subjects that engage with Information Overlays in their own unconventional ways. Most people select one brand of overlay early in life and rarely revise that decision due to the immense economic and social cost of switching. However, our subjects have found themselves living in, between, and outside these layers of digital reality. The study has been carried out using Ethnography, a method allowing for the use of in-depth interviews, and participatory observation to be interpreted by the author and woven into the logics of their narrative.[1]

Januz have worked for two years as a sales assistant at a Multitwinned Vendor Space. They intermittently twin with several brands—currently Mobi, Doobie, Sung, and Scranchy. For Januz this means adjusting body language, facial expressions, and voice tonality as they switch overlays to cater to customers of that specific brand.

> *I think my employers see potential in my ability to change persona. I have always found that my facial features and body are generic enough to twin well. At least that is what my followers tell me. —Januz*

LaGunilla have removed their Brain Computer Interface to escape dependence on information overlays. They sing, write, and paint on top of hosting creative workshops from their home—as forms of subversive political expression. Due to their absence from the overlays, they struggle to collect sufficient brandscrip to make a basic living. They have instead improvised a bartering system where people bring necessities like food and medicine in exchange for attending live performances. The audience is kindly asked to flight mode.

---

[1] Kirk, J. T. (Ψ 2117) "A New Wave of Ethnography: Lessons from Early 21st Century", *OpenScholar*.

372   F. MAGNUSSON AND E. HAETTNER

The only true way to be in contact with the core of your humanity is to be fully present in the physical world. I'm not alone in this of course. We are many who choose this way of living. We help each other. —LaGunilla

As a member of the Urban Exploration movement, Jacquotte map unknown cityscapes. They devote their offwork to venture into parts of their hometown that lie outside the overlay.

There is a sensation when you cross... There is like a line, you know. Things kind of fade. There are no icons, no text, no movement. The walls are bare there. The first time, it felt like being suddenly very lonely. You get used to it though. —Jacquotte

Jacquotte's personal quest is to establish contacts with inhabitants in these places. They recount a bizarre situation where they managed to get close to a group of people just outside of a building they later established as part of a Mobi housing compound. Besides speaking a foreign language, the group appeared to have trouble seeing Jacquotte—repeatedly turning their heads and glancing sideways to see. The group were soon picked up by a car, and Jacquotte suddenly found themself surrounded by a trip of goats seemingly moving in formation. This was an uncanny experience at the time, but they can now explain this as an increasingly common method for non-violently warding off intruders; an altered form of an automated animal husbandry practice, originating in the Cyborgoat Project in Norway in the early 2000s.

Skilla describe life in Mobi as quiet and routine based. A workplace assistant assesses the daily work capacity of residents and creates a schedule accordingly. If sub-optimal performance is detected it assigns effective offwork activities— physical exercise or leisure such as reading or social. When metrics are back to normal, work starts again. Skilla were drafted from the Bangalore Climate Refugee Camp four years ago and believe they were selected for being a single young adult with quick reflexes. Most people in their compound are either programmers or—as Skilla—automation assistants. Work consists of virtually switching between various machine sensoria—remotely manoeuvring trapped delivery bots out of complicated corners or navigating trucks through crowded streets.

What you don't want is to be promoted too far. I have seen the faces of the leet team sitting down at lunch before their relaxants kick in. Imagine switching from car to car, trying to avert highway crashes from a distance. A good success-rate there is 70%! I don't want to know what they see the other 30% of the time. —Skilla

Skilla are careful not to disappoint their custodians, fully aware that being sent back to Bangalore is a real risk. They have already received a warning for not avoiding contact with an intruder on one occasion. Knowing that their overlay will make it near impossible to escape the compound, they still feel this life is preferable to a life in the camp.

This paper has described four unusual walks of life, each in its own way shedding light on our reliance on technology. Only when trying to disengage with Information Overlays, does it become apparent how important they are for what you know and what you can know.[2] Additionally, with these perspectives it becomes apparent that discussions on the virtual and physical limitations imposed on us, are largely absent today. It seems our individualized realities prevent us from even imagining that there are other experiences.

AGRIVOLTAIC SOLAR/RABBIT INSTALLATIONS AS CULTURAL HERITAGE

Herman Blunt, Roskilde University, 2122

Outline

1. A culturally significant ecosystem

   1.1. Economic and culinary impact
   1.2. Other prevalent agrivoltaic ecosystems

2. An ecosystem in decline

   2.1. Dwindling numbers of agrivoltaic installations
   2.2. Declining profit margins
   2.2.1. Fusion power and electricity prices
   2.2.2. **Rising prices of rural land**
   Abridged
   The price of rural land has seen a historically unprecedented increase since the turn of the century. This has been a contributing factor in the declining profit margins for agrivoltaics, which for inherent reasons is a spatially extensive industry.[3] One common explanation for rising land values is the increased demand for food and raw materials to support massive global migration from environmentally stressed regions into wealthy urban areas. A large part of this migration has been attributed[4] to the UN Climate Adaptation Treaty of 2072.

3. Solar/Rabbit Installations as part of a cultural heritage

Comments

// Donna Basalt: Global citizens driving the cost of land, that is pure nonsense! those poor souls are fed catfish and airsallad. Just think about it, between fusion power and human density management there is zero pressure on land. see my work on biodiversion.
// Herman Blunt: What would you propose if it is not mass migration following the adaptation treaty?

---

[2] Schark, R. ⟨Ψ 2117⟩ "Epistemology of Brain Computer Interfaces", *OpenScholar*.

[3] Mwangi, M. ⟨Ψ 2117⟩ "Agrivoltaic Economics", *OpenScholar*.

[4] Xi, Y. ⟨Ψ 2090⟩ "Migration Patterns after the UN Climate Adaptation Treaty", *OpenScholar*.

// Donna Basalt: It's all club of nine feeding frenzy for the last scarce commodity. Nation states decided to sell off rural land to C9 to hide budget deficits and virtue signal on biodiversity loss in one genius move and now we have the club owning 76% of rural land.
// Donna Basalt: read the biodiversity protection acquisition agreements!
// Sirrus Heppsson: come on! C9 is not a thing. So easy to dream up conspiracies among the hyperrich.
// Donna Basalt: agitprop vector!

37 more comments...

UNCRA AND AINT: CLIMATE REFUGEE CAMPS AND THE DEVELOPMENT OF AUTOMATED INVISIBLE NUDGING TECHNOLOGY

Chander Aysert, International Centre for Climate Adaptation, 2089

Outline

1. UN Climate Refugee Agency (UNCRA) establishment

    1.1. International response to global climate refugee crisis
    1.2. UNCRA Climate Refugee Camps
    1.3. Rapid scaling and financial strain

2. Privatization

    2.1. UNCRA XPRIZE
    2.2. Mobi Dakhlet Nouadhibou Climate Refugee Camp Prototype

3. Human Density Management

    3.1. Systems of mass logistics
    3.2. **Systems of mass governance**

Abridged

The underlying infrastructure supporting both logistics and governance in UNCRA camps is based on City Twin technology. Developed for data management within municipal planning, these platforms supported operations like crowd movement simulation and real-time system monitoring of issues such as traffic congestion, water shortages, and spread of infections.

The need for large-scale and cost-effective governance of Climate Refugee Camps prompted UNCRA to initiate an ambitious research and development program applying Nudge Theory—a concept stemming from Behavioural Economics—to City Twins. Starting from simulations of crowd movement, systems of advanced surveillance were developed that could influence behaviours of individuals and groups through a "multitude of minute and discrete means".[5] A key modus was to meticulously monitor external indicators of an individual subject's emotional state, such as posture, movement, tone of voice, and speech—in order to model intent and subsequently predict action. Using Information Overlay technology, these Affect Metrics informed what and how information was visualized for the subject—actively shaping their intent and nudging their actions towards a specified outcome. The ability to systematically apply this nudging to a large set of individuals and groups, was a powerful way to coordinate and control behaviour without overt force.[5]

4. AINT

Abridged

UNCRA and associated commercial actors refer to these technologies of mass governance under the umbrella term of Human Density Management. However, Leti proposes the term *Automated Invisible Nudging Technology*, or AINT. He argues that the monitoring of individuals is problematic in terms of freedom and privacy, but the most problematic aspect is that these violations are hidden from the subjects.[6] There is also a critical discourse surrounding the underlying City Twin technology. Andersson argues that in the creation of City Twin platforms, the selection of descriptive datasets and performance indicators is a political action that often lacks transparency.[7] She explains that when a certain representation of reality is selected, it acts as a filter that limits the understanding of the city. When that filtered view is used for decision-making, this restricts the number of possible policy changes and marginalizes certain solutions. The same critique applies to Human Density Management where twinning is applied to individual humans; obscuring and distorting available information as a means to manipulate the choices available to them.[6]

5. The UNCRA legacy

5.1. Technology transfer

Abridged

The pace at which these technologies evolved is noteworthy. Substantial funding received from the international community as part of the UNCRA formation is one explanation.[8] Public investments were counter-financed with private venture capital as the rapidly expanding network of camps became largely privatized. As technologies found consumer applications, development was further

---

[5] Hale, Z. ⟨Ψ 2055⟩ "A Methodological Perspective on Human Density Management," *OpenScholar*.

[6] Leti, K. ⟨Ψ 2079⟩ "Automated Invisible Nudging Technology", *OpenScholar*.

[7] Andersson, L. ⟨Ψ 2033⟩ "Data Selection for City Twins", *Data in Urban Planning*, vol. 23, no. 3, pp. 165–184.

[8] Aysert-Chander M.A. ⟨Ψ 2086⟩ "The Establishment of UNCRA", *OpenScholar*.

376 F. MAGNUSSON AND E. HAETTNER

accelerated. The direct connection to practical application in the camps also provided a useful testbed for field trials and iterative development. Another explanation is provided by Ghat.[9] He argues that this level of progress could not have been possible without the disruption caused by the <u>Phoenix Cascading Failure Disaster</u>. The resulting collapse of the <u>Artificial Intelligence</u> research field radically transformed related academic disciplines, particularly <u>Human Density Management</u>, in terms of attracting funding and talent.

5.2. Permanentizing of camps

GENERIC ZONING: ORIGINS, ASSESSMENT, AND IMPACT
Vanjay Kontra, New TU Delft—Department of Urban Studies, 2115

Outline

1. Origins of Generic Zoning

Abridged

Ownership of real estate has seen major legal reform throughout the twenty-first century, entailing relaxed regulation of finance, planning, and construction.[10] Important first steps towards what would later be formalized as <u>Generic Zoning</u>, were the rebuilding efforts in Ukraine after the Russian invasion of 2022.[11] Due to remaining Russian claims to parts of the territory, official support from nation states was not politically viable for several decades. Instead, new systems for coordination of large numbers of private actors emerged in the 2030s, extending existing <u>City Twin</u> platforms with financial and collaborative layers.[11] These platforms and the actors around them, were taken up globally throughout the 2040s, accelerating a long trend towards privatization of public planning.[12]

Applied to real estate, <u>City Twins</u> describe and quantify buildings and plots, monitor their condition and performance, and prognosticate potential change. While developed for technical purposes such as planning, construction, and maintenance, they also provided a key to the automation of real-estate trading—through the minimization of risk. Providing access to previously unavailable data on built assets such as real-time economic and environmental performance, quality and condition of building components and materials—twins made it possible to

---

[9] Ghat, D. (Ψ 2087) "The Phoenix Disaster Effect on Human Density Management", *OpenScholar*.

[10] Skutt, L. (Ψ 2087) "Land Reforms in the Twenty-First Century", *OpenScholar*.

[11] Munger, H. (Ψ 2043) "Hybrid Nation Building", *Urban Sustainable Planning*, vol. 55, no. 1, pp. 63–85.

[12] Phisk, L. and Vurden, Y. (Ψ 2067) "Land Ownership and Transparency", *OpenScholar*.

instantly perform highly accurate economic valuations of the proper-ties.[12] As a result, the 2057 median turnaround for a parcel of land in Sweden, was 0.73 seconds.[OpenStat] Speed of trade, together with increasingly obfuscated land holding practices of large corporations and wealthy individuals, radically reduced traceability. In the 2050s it became practically impossible for authorities to determine who owns a partic-ular parcel of land.[12] A new breed of comprehensive <u>Planning APIs:</u> also allowed for automated interaction with public planning processes. Intended as a feature to simplify communication around early stage design proposals and make application procedures more transparent and predictable, these interfaces opened for financial speculation even earlier in the building lifecycle—before a finalized design proposal.[13]

Another element contributing to the acceleration of change in the built environment is <u>Generative Design,</u> an algorithmic design method-ology with roots in the 2010s where various inputs are automatically processed. Variables include site conditions, planning requirements, avail-ability of materials and components, speed of construction, cost, prog-nosticated financial value, etc. An optimization process then produces a design proposal and construction plan. Often run as part of a larger business operation, few—if any—humans are involved in these decision-making processes.[13] These ideas have permeated the construc-tion industry and are referred to as <u>Automated Construction.</u> Automa-tion is an age-old dream in construction, dating back to the twentieth century. Demonstrator projects were realized in an academic context in the 2020s[14] and the first commercially successful automated construc-tion actor <u>Smarter Quarters</u> was launched in Sweden in 2047. With the commercial slogan *Your new home, within the week*—this early adopter made full use of automated planning, design, logistics, and on/off-site fabrication to produce single and multi-family residential buildings. The technology saw major advancement in the 2050s as it was employed by <u>UNCRA</u> in the large-scale efforts to house millions of climate refugees within the <u>UN Climate Refugee Camps.</u> 2108 saw the first multi-storey building being erected overnight.[15]

2. Generic Zoning: A maturing phenomenon

  2.1. Geographical spread 2040–2100

  2.2. Diminishing public control

    Abridged

    <u>Generic Zoning</u> exists in various forms in most nations—leaving public authorities with diminished control over planning. Instead,

---

[13] Lynchmob, F. ⟨Ψ 2061⟩ "Generative Design and Speculative Capital", *OpenScholar.*

[14] Zhou, H. ⟨Ψ 2039⟩ "The Stuttgart Pioneers: A History of the ICD/ITKE Collaborations", Boutledges, Dublin.

[15] <u>Urban Explorer Wiki.</u>

a basic set of key performance indicators are usually stipulated—such as traffic, emissions, and noise at the zone perimeter, coupled with compliance inspections. Monitoring has thus replaced planning. In practice, inspections are often blocked, with many accounts describing unspoken standoffs between zone operators and local authorities. There are incident reports detailing how official inspection drones have been denied access through different means: software attacks, sensor jamming, and forced downings.[16]

2.3. Urban Exploration: an unconventional source of information

Abridged
Later decades have seen a shift in the interests of Urban Explorers; away from sewers and abandoned buildings and towards Generic Zoning areas. They hike on foot with military grade sensing gear—recording phenomena such as IR radiation, radio transmissions, and crowd movement. Close contacts with zone inhabitants have been scarce, and there are multiple testimonies of explorers being ignored by the inhabitants. Whitakker deducts that the systems managing the inhabitants' sensorium, mask out any unwanted elements.[17] This use of Information Overlay technology has a clear precedent within the prison industry.[18] Personal contact has also been obstructed through physical means such as blocking streets with synchronized swarms of vehicles, or automated construction equipment erecting fencing in real-time. Still, urban exploration provides a rich source of empirical data.[15] Their accounts have also proven invaluable in corroborating information from other sources, such as whistle-blowers and data leaks from corporation clouds.[19]

3. Impacts on urban fabric and life

Abridged
In the broadest definition of the term, Generic Zoning is applied to 82%[OpenStat] of global urban land, impacting the built environment on many levels. The volatile nature of these areas—when it comes to street layout, access regulation, and transportation—disrupts the legibility and functionality of the wider urban transport and circulation systems in which they are embedded. This results in diminished freedom

---

[16] Manning, J. ⟨Ψ 2094⟩ "Fog of War: Practical Difficulties in Generic Zoning Area Regulation Compliance", *OpenScholar*.

[17] Whitakker, B. ⟨Ψ 2110⟩ "Here Be Dragons", *OpenScholar*.

[18] Jeter, H. ⟨Ψ 2112⟩ "Parallel Penal Worlds: The Use of Visual Augmentation Technology for Incarceration", *OpenScholar*.

[19] OpenLeaks.

of movement for residents and loss of places for civic life.[20] On an epistemological level, Generic Zoning areas have become blind spots in the public eye. With the reliance on information overlays for travel and interaction in urban space, the lack of a common map leads to a severe loss of cohesion among urban inhabitants—when it comes to common experience, values, and sense of civic responsibility.[21] Elder frames this loss of common ground for conversation among neighbours as "human density management replacing civic life".[22]

GLOBAL CITIZEN PROGRAM 20 YEARS: A PROBLEMATIC WATERSHED IN HUMAN RIGHTS
Aoibheann Robinson and Young Xi, Human Rights Watch, 2092

Abridged
Ratified in 2072, The UN Climate Adaptation Treaty specified a revised minimum standard of living for individuals and families, to be upheld within a largely privatized network of Climate Refugee Camps. Another significant component of the treaty was the Global Citizen Program, a legal framework for the formation of contracts that grant individuals or families Global Citizen status. This arrangement made it possible for commercial corporations to take custody of camp residents and relocate them, as long as they are provided for in accordance with the treaty. As Secretary-General Ai Bezos proclaimed in the preface to the treaty: "The Global Citizen Program integrates the victims of our global climate disaster into wealthy and secure communities through ambitious learning and hard work". Prior to the treaty, the UN Climate Refugee Agency (UNCRA) had been running Climate Refugee Camps since the 2040s. Bringing private actors into the camp network and establishing the Global Citizen Program, was a last resort—a response to years of critique of the inefficiencies and unacceptable standards of living within the camps.[23] One important consequence of this privatization was that it shifted the responsibility for upholding the Human Rights of camp inhabitants and program participants from the nation state to the corporation.[24]

20 years into the program, UN data reveal that there is a strong bias towards children and young adults without family ties among the drafted global citizen population—compared with the overall demographic makeup of the climate refugee camp network. In 2085, 68%[OpenStat] of the drafted were single young adults. In 2090 that figure had increased to 72%.[OpenStat] Stone

---

[20] Kett, B. ⟨Ψ 2113⟩ "The Radical Decline of Public Space", *OpenScholar*.

[21] Heller, N. ⟨Ψ 2114⟩ "Virtual Gerrymandering", *OpenScholar.*

[22] Elder, M. ⟨Ψ 2108⟩ "Mievilles' City and the City: A Contemporary Reading", *OpenScholar*.

[23] Niels, P. ⟨Ψ 2075⟩ "UNCRA Failing Climate Refugees", *OpenScholar.*

[24] Letter, R. ⟨Ψ 2071⟩ "Proposed UN Climate Adaptation Treaty: Legal Ramifications", *OpenScholar.*

argues that this skewness primarily is driven by corporate labour demand.[25] One explanation for the recruitment pattern is that socially isolated young individuals have proven more receptive to Human Density Management than family groups and more experienced persons—rendering them more cost-effective workers.[25]

The cohorts of drafted global citizens are rarely integrated into the urban communities in which they reside. In the 20 years the program has been running, only 860 k[OpenStat] are participating members of a local community and 1.4 m[OpenStat] have been located in various training and education facilities—the remaining 50 m draftees are not accounted for.

This report has presented issues related to the implementation of the Global Citizen Program, calling into question its efficacy in ensuring Human Rights for its participants. This can be seen in the light of other reports on the dire situation in many of the Climate Refugee Camps.[26,27]

THE PHYSICAL TWIN CONDITION: A NEW UNDERSTANDING OF THE PHYSICAL AND THE VIRTUAL IN CONTEMPORARY SOCIETY

Amira Haddad, Gothenburg Information Overlay Centre, 2116

Abridged

This paper presents a genealogy of concepts regarding the cultural and technological coupling between the virtual, the physical, and the physical overlaid with the virtual. It concludes that in response to our information-impoverished physical realm, which is virtually overlaid with bountiful data, the addition of a concept—*Physical Twin*—is needed to capture a novel dynamic where virtual objects can be seen to precede the physical.

The Digital Twin concept originated in the manufacturing industry, extending existing knowledge management platforms within product development, to manage what was at the time considered to be large amounts of data.[28] The emphasis on the *digital* as a salient component of a *digital twin* is notable. The *digitalization* of society was a frequently used narrative around the turn of the millennium—denoting everything from the scanning of historic literature to political manipulation of whole populations.[29] One theory is that the language at that time reflected an increasing societal awareness of how knowledge automation was fundamentally reshaping society.[30] Twin technology eventually found its way into public planning through a combination of

[25] Stone, J. (Ψ 2091) "Global Citizen Recruitment Patterns", *OpenScholar.*

[26] Nones, B. (Ψ 2089) "Climate Refugee Camps: Food, Medicine, and Housing Shortages", *OpenScholar.*

[27] Leti, K. (Ψ 2090) "AINTs: Application in Climate Refugee Camps", *OpenScholar.*

[28] Haddad, A. (Ψ 2114) "Big Data in a Small Lake", *OpenScholar.*

[29] Wintermute, I. (Ψ 2111) "Cambridge Analytica: Canary in the Data Mine", *OpenScholar.*

[30] Lovelace, C. (Ψ 2055) "The Language of the Digital", *OpenScholar.*

open academic research and commercial platforms, resulting in digital twins of cities. From here sprung the term City Twin, removing the digital as a salient component. This could be seen as a first step towards a naturalization of the digital aspect of the digital twin technology.

Another important step towards the idea of a physical twin, is the academic term Information Overlays, which has found marginal use in popular language.[OpenCorpus] It refers to the confluence of City Twin, Social Network, Augmented Reality, and Machine Learning technologies. Over time, these technologies were seamlessly embedded into most societies. Due to their incremental and integrated nature, they are now rarely mentioned explicitly in public discourse.[OpenCorpus]

In the 2030s one of the major commercial actors tried to replace the usage of Information Overlays as a descriptive term with their specific brand of overlay, Autoworld. Initially picked up by various marketing departments and industry organizations, Autoworld ended up relatively short-lived in everyday use.[31] Following this, a number of diverse entities—states, municipalities, social movements, religions, and private companies—soon launched their own proprietary overlays. These platforms had widely different functions, target audiences, and modes of access. The majority were publicly available via open access, or through commercial models based on subscription, microtransactions, or ad-revenues. Some restricted access to citizens of a city or a nation.[32] Others were narrower in terms of target audience.[33] The vision of Information Overlays as a unified *Autoworld* was thus replaced by a variety of technical solutions and brands. A lack of standardization and integration in terms of user experience, technical functionality, and interoperability characterized this period, and this has been exacerbated since then. This has led to a fragmentation of human experience where a physical place is understood differently by different individuals depending on what virtual narrative they follow in their overlays.[34] Whitakker argues this is one explanation for the absence of public discourse around the effects of overlays on contemporary culture and politics.[35] Another explanation is the literal *disappearance from view* of the technology itself—with Brain Computer Interfaces replacing screens and glasses as the mediating device.[36]

---

[31] Davys, D. ⟨Ψ 2038⟩ "How We Almost Came to Live in Autoworld", *Twins and Society*, vol. 44, pp. 110–124.

[32] Lukku, A. and Look, K. ⟨Ψ 2033⟩ "E-stonia: The First National Twin", *Urban Sustainable Planning*, vol. 45, pp. 15–30.

[33] Stevenson, N. ⟨Ψ 2035⟩ "Thetaverse: The Scientology Information Overlay", *Twins and Society*, vol. 41, pp. 62–81.

[34] Jeeter, K.W. ⟨Ψ 2111⟩ "Individualized Virtual Narratives", *OpenScholar*.

[35] Whitakker, B. ⟨Ψ 2112⟩ "The Downloaded Self", *OpenScholar*.

[36] Jeeter, K.W. ⟨Ψ 2110⟩ "Always There, Never Seen: The Disappearance from View of Information Overlays", *OpenScholar*.

382   F. MAGNUSSON AND E. HAETTNER

Information Overlays, especially after the advent of Brain Computer Interfaces, provide their users with a living environment that is vastly richer in perceptual stimuli than what the physical environment offers.[37] Urban environments over the last century have gradually been visually impoverished in the physical domain when signs, signals, information, and aesthetic expression have been transferred to overlays or simply become outdated and obsolete.[38] An example of this shift is Navigation, an activity historically reliant on signage placed in the physical environment and visible to everyone, without the Access Management that regulates all overlaid information. Physical objects, imprinted with text or graphical symbols, directed travellers to destinations and annotated buildings and places. They were especially important for vehicle navigation in the pre-automation era, and subject to strict regulation.[39] This kind of visual stimuli, along with commercial messages and architectural gestures, used to permeate the physical environment.

Twinning, integrating actual matter and virtual data, is a concept with a significant cultural impact. The verb was established early and is still in frequent use today,[OpenCorpus] albeit subject to an ontological inversion. Originally a term for modelling reality in a virtual realm, today Twinning is more commonly used to describe the process of creating, or configuring, a duplicate physical object based on a virtual original.[40] A related common expression is to *twin with* a specific overlay; it conveys the act of adapting a physical entity—your Real-Life person, to a virtual system. This [35] could be framed as creating a *Physical Twin* of your person. Burkle discusses the lack of agency in our contemporary situation where all social, economic, and spatial affordances of the individual are controlled by their chosen overlay. She compares this to the freedom of personal expression that the earliest—often anonymous—virtual personas offered.[41]

The need to resort to the archaic word Real-Life to distinguish the physical aspects of an entity from the virtual, highlights a shortcoming in our common language; we talk as if we are now subconsciously framing ourselves as primarily virtual. Our Real-Life person is a mere *Physical Twin*.

---

[37] Burges, A. ⟨Ψ 2103⟩ "Information Overlays, Saccadic Eye Movements and Visual Attention", *OpenScholar*.

[38] Brown, D. ⟨Ψ 2114⟩ "Brand Ducks/Bland Sheds", *OpenScholar*.

[39] Vägverket ⟨Ψ 2025⟩ "Föreskrifter och allmänna råd om vägmärken och andra anordningar", *Kungl. Biblioteket*.

[40] Corpo, M. ⟨Ψ 2115⟩ "Back to the Humanist Ideal", *OpenScholar*.

[41] Burkle, S. ⟨Ψ 2115⟩ "140 Years of MUD", *OpenScholar*.

SEARCH: PHYSICAL TWIN   383

GLOBAL LAND OWNERSHIP CONSOLIDATION: EFFECTS OF THE BIODIVERSITY ACQUISITION AGREEMENTS
Donna Basalt, Selfhosted, 2122

Points of interest

- Price increases of rural land globally have accelerated since 2100.[OpenStat]
- This is often explained by economic pressure from increasing food production and urban expansion.[42]
- We show that this explanation is incorrect by using a comprehensive economic model[43] of city/hinterland interaction for a large set of cities. Despite growing urban populations, evidence does not support that rural land to a significant degree is shifting to either agrarian or urban use.
- We argue that land prices have risen as a result of recent acquisition agreements[44] where nation states have sold substantial parts of formerly common or public lands to private actors, on the condition that they are transformed into Biodiversity Protection Reserves.
- This trend towards large-scale private land ownership can be seen as a continuation of an earlier process where the most individual or small-scale landowners were forced to let go of their land in the shift towards Agrivoltaics.[45]
- We identify two primary beneficiaries of this development: states can mitigate increasing budget deficits[OpenStat] by selling land, and (wealthy) individuals gain access to land—a scarce commodity.
- Forensic Accounting techniques and data on financial arrangements in direct connection with the formation of Biodiversity Protection Reserves,[46] allow us to map the legal beneficiaries of these acquisitions. Through complex transnational financial setups, most of the agreements are connected to just nine individuals: the Club of Nine.[contested]
- We conclude that the transference of land under the guise of biodiversity protection from state to private ownership represents the biggest land grab in human history—a *Biodiversion*.

Comments

// Hagnus Frelin: This is the most relevant take out there on the largest issue of our time! How come it has not been added to the pub record?
// Donna Basalt: I've tried with @Fürelise several times, but they are too scared of the club.

[42] Mwangi, M. ⟨Ψ 2107⟩ "Global Migration and Pressure on Rural Land", *OpenScholar*.
[43] City/Hinterland Interaction, *ScholarHub*.
[44] List of Biodiversity Acquisition Agreements, *ScholarHub*.
[45] Agrivoltaic Land-Grab Model, *ScholarHub*.
[46] Biodiversion Actor-Network, *ScholarHub*.

// Fürelise: @Donna Basalt we have sent you suggestions on revisions regarding tone and certain wording that would make it possible for us to start an editorial process.
// Donna Basalt: @Fürelise the changes you want me to make are not about wording but about facts. I'd rather never be published than align with your chickenshit-vanilla approach to scholarly debate!

BOOSTER STAGE CAPITALISM: PREDICTING THE NEXT PHASE OF CAPITAL ACCUMULATION

Hagnus Frelin, Lund University, Centre for Earth Sciences, 2122

Draft

An alarming Human Rights Watch report establishes that drafted Global Citizens from privatized UN Climate Refugee Camps amount to 1.2 billion individuals between 2072 and 2121.[47] Out of these, only 60 million[OpenStat] are present in UNCRA data. Field research[48] and reports[49] indicate that draftees are housed at a massive scale around the globe, in corporate compounds located in urban areas under Generic Zoning regulation. These areas are juridically and practically closed off from official oversight,[50] and their inhabitants are thus effectively hidden from view.[48]

Additionally, we have indications that the draftees are held captive in the compounds, using techniques derived from UNCRAs research program on Human Density Management. The technologies developed were used on "*individual humans, obscuring and distorting available information in order to manipulate the choices available to them*".[51] If true, this is a historic Human Rights failure where more than 1 billion people are living under slave-like conditions in custody of private corporations.

To understand why there has been no apparent reaction from host communities, we draw on Haddad who coined the term Physical Twin to illustrate how we are subconsciously framing our lives as *virtual first*.[52] She argues that the individualized experience of life provided by overlays, results in what could be seen as physical Filter-bubbles. Engaging with overlays as a form of "*voluntary collective incarceration*", host communities cannot—or perhaps choose not to—see what goes on within these corporate compounds.

The urgency of Global Warming prompted rapid installation of Agrivoltaics over vast areas, a momentous shift in global land use.[53] This also entailed a shift in land ownership, where many smaller landholders were displaced

---

[47] Thunberg, R. ⟨Ψ 2122⟩ "Global Citizen Program: 50 Years", *OpenScholar*.

[48] Whitakker, B. ⟨Ψ 2118⟩ "Twin Living", *OpenScholar*.

[49] Urban Explorer Wiki.

[50] Kontra, V. ⟨Ψ 2115⟩ "Generic Zoning", *OpenScholar*.

[51] Aysert, C. ⟨Ψ 2089⟩ "UNCRA & AINT", *OpenScholar*.

[52] Haddad, A. ⟨Ψ 2116⟩ "The Physical Twin Condition", *OpenScholar*.

[53] Mwangi, M. ⟨Ψ 2117⟩ "Agrivoltaic Economics", *OpenScholar*.

through expropriation and their land subsequently was sold off to large investment bodies.[54] Since the introduction of Fusion Power, the economic viability
of Agrivoltaics has declined rapidly[53]—but this has neither led to lower prices
on land, nor re-migration into rural areas. Recently, rural land prices have
instead increased. According to Basalt, this is a consequence of a series of
recent acquisition agreements to turn large areas of public land and commons
into privately owned Biodiversity Protection Reserves, with the stated purpose
of mitigating the Current Mass Extinction Event.[55]

Basalt traces most of these acquisitions to nine individuals.[56] Applying a
geographic perspective to her model,[57] we can reveal the geographic pattern
of these land acquisitions. While globally distributed, we have identified a
contiguous area around the equator neatly divided into nine equal parts. Each
part can be traced back to one of the individuals identified by Basalt.

The equatorial region is of special significance for the emerging technology
of Space Elevators. The laws of orbital mechanics dictate that the base stations
of these elevators must be placed on the equator and the surrounding area is
exposed to significant damage in the event of a structural failure of an elevator
cable.[58]

Space Elevators are awaiting realization of certain key technologies. One
major problem is the tensile strength/density ratio of the extremely long
cable. Additionally, building an elevator would require the largest construction project in history with substantial financial, technical, and geo-political
risks involved. However, there are reasons to believe these obstacles will be
overcome[59]—and the potential rewards from an effective pathway to the solar
system are large enough to motivate substantial risk-taking and investment.[60]

This paper establishes a global pattern of migration that has formed over
recent decades. While parts of cities in wealthy nations have become black
holes with extreme population densities, rural land has been emptied out,
especially in equatorial regions. The main driver of this migration is Global
Warming, rendering large parts of these regions inhabitable. However, we
propose that a shift in landownership[55] has also been a factor.

We put forward the hypothesis that a cartel has been formed between the
members of the Club of Nine[contested] with the purpose of accessing space
using Space Elevators. This hypothesis is supported by the meticulous division of landownership along the equator suggesting a coordinated agenda
between these individuals. Furthermore, this part of the world has practically

---

[54] Agrivoltaic Land-Grab Model, *ScholarHub*.

[55] Basalt, D. ⟨Ψ 2122⟩ "Global Land Ownership Consolidation", *OpenScholar*.

[56] Biodiversion Actor-Network, *ScholarHub*.

[57] Biodiversion Geodata Analysis, *ScholarHub*.

[58] Base Station Placement, *International Space Elevator Consortium*.

[59] Kone, H. ⟨Ψ 2121⟩ "Space Elevator Feasibility Study", *OpenScholar*.

[60] Otis, E. ⟨Ψ 2115⟩ "East India Company in Space", *OpenScholar*.

been emptied of people which is a beneficial situation for the cartel since Space Elevators only can be realized on the equatorial plane. A successful endeavour would establish a position for the nine beyond the bounds of our current economic system.

Saving draft...
Log out at: 2122-10-18 21:12:23 GMT+1...

Acknowledgements This work is part of the Digital Twin Cities Centre supported by Sweden's Innovation Agency Vinnova under Grant No. 2019-00041 and White Arkitekter.

The Origins of AGE: From States and Markets to Scientific Methods

Karim Zakhour

For the most critical matters often have trivial origins and it is always easiest to correct impulses and remedy beliefs at the beginning.

—Polybius

The two texts published in this chapter were written with very different aims and audiences in mind. The first text, published in 2115, was written in connection with the 20th anniversary celebrations of the founding of the Association of Governmental Experimentation (AGE). The author is himself a high-ranking administrator in AGE and the text, while closely mirroring the form of twenty-first-century scholarly article, is more than a little hagiographic. It should perhaps be treated as part of the organization's attempt to lay down an official history of its origins. The second text, written a few years later by the anonymous and dissident research collective Satya al-Haq, is a vicious deconstruction of the first text. If we take the nameless authors at their word, then AGE is not the perfectly designed global governance structure that it portrays itself to be, but something far more nefarious. For those of us—increasingly few—outside of the orbit of AGE and its radical political experiments, it will appear difficult to ascertain the veracity of these two competing claims. Clearly the two texts cannot both be true; we leave it to our audience to decide for themselves.

K. Zakhour (✉)
Department of Political Science, University of Stockholm, Stockholm, Sweden
e-mail: karlkarim.zakhour@statsvet.su.se

© The Author(s), under exclusive license to Springer Nature
Switzerland AG 2023
L. Horn et al. (eds.), *The Palgrave Handbook of Global Politics
in the 22ⁿᵈ Century*, https://doi.org/10.1007/978-3-031-13722-8_23

1   INTRODUCTION

Since its founding in 2085 AD, the sage tutelage of the Association of Governmental Experimentation (AGE) has ushered in an unprecedented era of prosperity and stability. The road to a more perfect governance method was long and difficult; nation-state collapse, increased regional federalism, and finally a global governance model based on sound scientific grounding.[1] Yet, despite the method's place at the core of our world order, the intellectual roots of AGE remain a topic of some controversy. Many conflicting points of genesis have been proposed: the twentieth-century Chinese Communist Party (Hargopal Ψ 2110), the twenty-first-century Indian Federal System (Makdous Ψ 2107), or even as the last contribution of European civilization (Benjamin Ψ 2111). Some have even wrongly understood AGE as being a realization of Plato's Republic.[2]

This paper will seek to argue that the governing principles of AGE—to learn and evolve through a diffused yet centrally directed process of trial and error—has old and forgotten roots that date back to ancient Carthage. Furthermore, inspired by the Carthaginian example, political experiments by highly trained social and natural scientists on diasporic European populations had already been established in North Africa in the late twenty-first century. This claim is controversial enough that it will be necessary to retrace some familiar history in order to show that by the time the African Cooperative Union and The South Asian Federation formed AGE, its foundations had already been established in a now defunct Southern Mediterranean polity.

2   PUNIC REVELATIONS

Today the name Tunisia evokes images of refugee camps of European migrants. However, in the early twenty-first century, Tunisia's location on the southern periphery of an already fraying Europe placed it in a precarious position of political dependence. As will be demonstrated, this position of marginality also allowed for some radical forms of political experimentation.

In 2032, just outside of the city of Kasserine, in what was then the easternmost part of Tunisia, the remains of a second-century BC Punic colony were discovered. A small team of Tunisian and Indian archaeologists began excavation. It quickly turned out to be a unique find, for it pre-dated the Roman destruction of Carthage. Moreover, it contained the first fully preserved

---

[1] The rise of AGE, and with it global political experimentation, has of course has rendered such old-fashion subjects such as the study of International Relations (politics *between* states), redundant. There is no longer an international system of competing states: there is only the method of science, the trial and error of well-design research projects.

[2] Such slanderous claims of Platonic Utopianism come only from anonymous obscurantists. The AGE leadership is not a philosophical elite lacking practical knowledge, but selected through rigorous scientific methods.

THE ORIGINS OF AGE: FROM STATES AND MARKETS TO SCIENTIFIC METHODS   389

papyrus parchments of Punic origins, many of which contained historiographic accounts of Carthage.[3]

In 2037, the History and Archeology Department of Manouba, in collaboration with Osmania University, released the first of six volumes, *the Crown of Carthage*, that summarized their findings.[4] For the purposes of our investigation, the most interesting aspects were the parts pertaining to the ancient Carthaginian political system. Previously everything that was known about Carthage's political system was based on Greek and Roman accounts; primarily Aristotle's *Politics* and Polybius's *Histories*. Both had approvingly defined Carthage as having a mixed constitution, containing elements of democracy, oligarchy, and aristocracy-commenting on its resilience and stability.[5] The new volume provided the first account of Carthage from native sources and gave a much more fine-grained and detailed description than ancient Greek or Roman sources. The picture that emerged was of a highly complex political order that was at once stable and dynamic.[6]

Carthage had a popular assembly picked from Mizrahims; the special guilds that resembled religious cults. Being above all a trading city, the merchants had much power, but every caste was organized into guilds that had their representatives in the assembly.[7] Citizenship was not, like Rome, based on military service, but more general collective service. The role of the assembly was primarily consultative and supervisory. Executive power was in the hands of the so-called Thirteen. The Thirteen were chosen by lot from prominent families and served collectively for three years. Each of the Thirteen served as the civil leader for one month at a time, during which they were forbidden from leaving their quarters (thus, leaders were called by their word for house; "beit").[8] The state administration was staffed by professionals. Like the Thirteen, the rotation was fast. No bureaucrat was allowed to stay longer than a few weeks at the same post. In posts where the risks of corruption were high, they only served for a day. Every act of higher-level bureaucrats was checked by another independent body, chosen by the assembly. I quote from the authors of the volume:

> Clearly the ancients were right in admiring Carthage for its political design, even if many Greek and Roman authors were ignorant of its details. The

---

[3] The relatively dry environment of Kasserine was more conducive to preservation of papyrus than the coastal centers of Carthaginian civilization.

[4] Osmania University, founded by Mir Osman Ali Khan in 1915, would of course later play an important role in the creation of the South Asian Federation. Was the SAF inspired by the Carthaginian system? We can only speculate.

[5] Carthage was the only non-Greek city considered "civilized" by Aristotle and he approvingly compared it to Sparta.

[6] For a comprehensive discussion on the ways in which Greek and Roman authors misconstrued and misunderstood the Carthaginian system see Malouf ⟨Ψ 2045⟩.

[7] Citizenship was available to all excluding women, children, and slaves.

[8] Alone among the ancient systems, Carthage had a complete separation of military and civil powers.

Carthaginians took the art of governing seriously and were obsessed with mitigating the temptations of power. They managed to develop and maintain a superbly sophisticated system that not only lasted for centuries but that grew stronger with every crisis. Its final demise at the hands of a hyper-militaristic Rome was not due to the failure of its political system, but rather that it valued peace more than preparations for war. In contrast to ancient Carthage, our modern forms of government, supposedly based on separations of power, "checks and balance", appear hopelessly crude. ⟨Ahmedi et al. Ψ 2037: 592⟩

While undoubtedly "sophisticated," Carthage's political system was not by itself different enough from other ancient Mediterranean city-states to warrant something more than a historical footnote. There were primarily two aspects of Carthage that proved influential for the political development of mid-to-late twenty-first-century Tunisia and beyond. The first was neither directly political, nor unique to Carthage. The Punic city, like many ancient Middle Eastern polities, performed regular cancellations of all debt owed to the state (and sometimes private individuals). The timing of the "restorations" was decided by the high priestess and appeared to happen anywhere between every three and twelve years.[9] This practice of debt-cancellation had been largely forgotten by the modern era, yet had been an important way for ancient states to maintain a sizable tax-base through redistributing resources and keeping the elites from overwhelming the free peasants and urban classes. In Carthage, like in other polities, debt-cancellation was often combined with ambitious and large-scale building projects, often infrastructural or religious in character, that could absorb any idle labor: the most famous of which are the now submerged Pyramids of Egypt ⟨Ahmedi et al. Ψ 2037⟩.[10]

From the perspective of tracing the AGE antecedents, the most pertinent aspect of ancient Carthage was the continuous changes to the political system that was itself part of that system. Before the founding of every new colony, and the laying down of a constitution, a collection of former retired politicians and bureaucrats from Carthage and major colonies would gather and suggest tweaks, based on past experiences and the success and failure of previous colonies. Every thirteen years, there was an Empire-wide gathering of former officials from Carthage and its provinces where modifications to Carthage were suggested.[11] Here then we can see the seeds of AGE; a continual feedback between the various parts of the whole. Unlike Rome, Punic colonies did not merely reproduce the mother city in a system that fed the center, but the center

[9] It was not institutionalized like the Biblical Jubilee.

[10] To the extent that twentieth-century states enacted their own version of labor-absorbing policies it was referred to as counter-cyclical spending, the most effective of which was the Second World War.

[11] Thus, despite some similarities between Carthage and Sparta in that inequality was understood as a threat to political stability, Carthage was a polity of trade and emphasized dynamic change rather than ossified rigidity and Spartan suspicion toward change and money.

THE ORIGINS OF AGE: FROM STATES AND MARKETS TO SCIENTIFIC METHODS   391

was changed by the periphery. It may do well to keep in mind that prior to the Carthaginian discovery much of Western scholarship had assumed that center–periphery relations primarily worked in favor of the center and were primarily exploitative (see for e.g. Wallerstein 1979).[12] What the example of Carthage showed, however, was that the dynamic between center and periphery need not be zero-sum and could be reformulated in terms of a mutually consti-tuting and beneficial relationship. On some level neither center nor periphery existed; they were parts of a larger whole that learned from each other.

Ultimately these archaeological re-discoveries would have been of little interest outside of a few academic circles had it not been for the succession of political crises that hit the region and that eventually led to the first attempt to reinstitute a version of this ancient form of government in Tunisia.

3   A Return to the Past

At the time of the archeological excavation, the Tunisian political system was failing. Like elsewhere, Tunisia was attempting to deal with the plague of pre-AGE era states: endemic unemployment. It is hard to imagine now, but for much of the early twenty-first century the greatest social ill was idle labor, at a time when work was still the chief form of social recognition. Young men in particular proved hard to incorporate into the productive part of the polity with the conventional economic instruments of the time.[13] These idle youths were a constant source of political disruptions during much of the early twenty-first century, in Tunisia and beyond.[14] Khaled Ben Zaher, a young writer and psychoanalyst captured the mood of the period:

> As any Tunisian will tell you, hopelessness is not an attitude or a state-of-mind: it is a place. This is why dreaming of escape is our national obsession. The present is a cage, the future a desolation, but the past; the past shines. Oh Dido, was your death in vain? We have slain our Father, perhaps it is time to resurrect our Mother? ⟨Ψ 2039: 47⟩[15]

[12] The great Ibn Khaldun, by contrast, had long understood that the periphery can, and often does, overcome the center (Khaldun 2015).

[13] The particular problems associated with young men during this period is tied to both their lagging in educational attainments in relation to young women and the lingering twentieth-century norms around the male-bread winner at odds with the twenty-first-century reality of flexible labor.

[14] Scholars still disagree on why the historically dominant model for solving this problem—large-scale building project that also functioned as defenses or as vanity projects for the elites—was no longer considered legitimate for state's during this period (excepting Communist China). The most likely culprit was Macroeconomics, a now defunct academic discipline whose core belief was that states ought to behave like the infamous East-India Company ⟨see in particular Jalebi Ψ 2045⟩. There were some attempts by European coun-tries to invest in "Green Energy" prior to the Great Calamity, but this mostly helped Chinese production of solar panel rather than the unemployed.

[15] Psychoanalysis was an expensive therapeutic activity, popular through much of the twentieth century, that promised individual salvation by repeated and frequent interactions

As more and more historical and archeological evidence from the Punic archeological site began to accumulate during the 2030s and 40s, it began to tickle the popular imagination and to have a political impact in Tunisia. In 2041, the popular social-media personality and amateur historian Leila Bouzid started the political party *Neo-Carthage*. Bouzid, though lacking a clear political program, declared that she aimed to resurrect the old Carthaginian political order. Much derided by political commentators at the time, yet helped by a wave of Phoenicia-frenzy among the urban classes and the lack of any popular alternatives, the party swept to power in the 2043 elections. Bouzid quickly appointed a commission to set up guidelines for the realization of New Carthage (Tantawi Ψ 2046: 91).[16] The commission, composed mostly of academics, was beset by infighting and constitutionally constrained. After three years, it had still failed to agree on a single recommendation except for the creation of a department for further research into Carthaginian forms of government, and the commission was eventually quietly disbanded (Rafika Ψ 2053: 86).

As the scholars squabbled, an enterprising young mayor of Gafsa proposed a novel project of institutional reform in a small municipality of the city, based on almost complete decentralized decision-making. Similar schemes were started in other municipalities in interior regions and zones of self-organized political spaces began to emerge, blending what was at the time termed e-governance with distributed networks that sought to learn from each other. The projects began to attract unemployed youths, many with IT and Engineering degrees with experience in "hacking," from across the region as well as older activists that had participated in the early twenty-first-century uprisings (Radhoune Ψ 2053). As the Tunisian experiment showed, "dangerous youths" could also prove a wellspring of creative energies.

Whether any of these reforms would have borne fruit would prove moot. The Bouzid government was undone by its attempts to simultaneously cancel all private debt in combination with ambitious state-led infrastructural projects. Most of the Tunisian budget was financed, directly or indirectly, through loans from external sources and those donors accused the projects of being both retrograde and utopian and refused to subsidize the government. The ensuing financial and political crises eventually led to the Tunisian state defaulting on its payment of loans, followed by the intervention of the Global Quartet in Tunisian political affairs.

---

between therapist and subject. The goal was the integration of the three aspects of the soul; id, ego, and superego through symbolic patricide. There has been some debate over whether psychoanalysts should be properly considered a religious off-shoot from Judeo-Christianity.

[16] The most vocal domestic critics were the Islamists, who argued against political innovation, even if it took the form of return to the past.

4 From Political Science to Applied Politics

It is easy to forget that the diffuse "return to the past-movements" that sprang up across the globe in the 2040s and 2050s can only be understood in relation to the then dominant delusion that *modernity* had severed ties with the past and that historical examples were of little value.[17] As the realization that pre-modern political systems had been far more robust, and lasted far longer, than most modern iterations began to take root so the will to the future began to dissipate and came to be replaced with a desire for the past. Yet such reactions, while understandable, were themselves part of the false dichotomy of the past and future that modernity had engendered. It was only when the past was no longer treated as a distant shore to be reached or to leave forever behind, but rather understood as a permanent present that the true end of modernity was at hand.

The Tunisian experiment ended in failure yet had laid down important blueprints for later developments.[18] It was hampered by many structural constraints, both local and global in character.[19] Today to the extent that Tunisian experiment is remembered at all, it is lumped in with other restorative attempts of the period. Yet, the Tunisian experiment can still be distinguished from other "return to the past-movements" at the time, in that its emphasis was less on identity and morality, and more on the search for new forms of scientific politics. Furthermore, the experiment can be understood to mark a rupture in the dynamic of twenty-first-century international politics. For most of the early twenty-first century, North Africa and the Middle East were still considered a regional backwater to Europe, particularly in terms of its role in International Relations (see e.g. Akbarzadeh 2019). Yet this period saw the region once again become the center for political innovation, leading the way for other nations.

---

[17] In the late twentieth and early twenty-first century, first French and then American commentators made much of a supposed *post*-modern condition understood as a rejection of any larger "meta narratives" or myths and stories (Lyotard 1979). This proved to be less of a condition however and more its own short-lived "meta-narrative" among the affluent West.

[18] In retrospect it appeared hopelessly naive and altogether too radical. The third principle, of course, of AGE is "build on what is already present."

[19] The resistance to experimenting with political systems, even on a small, local level appears difficult to fathom today. It seems clear that it was only with the abolition of certain metaphysical concepts, primarily the Nation and its concomitant term the People, both of which assume relative political homogeneity across a political territory, that the new discipline and government could emerge. The Tunisian experience also appears to show the limitations of "Experimental Politics in One Country."

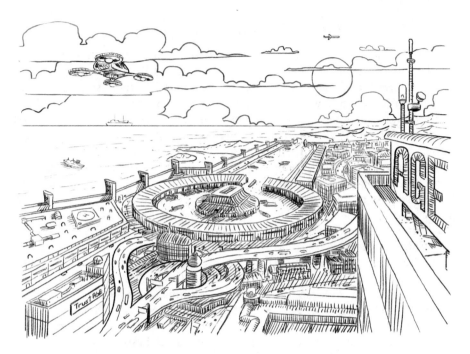

The most immediate legacy of the short political career of *Neo-Carthage* was the creation in 2044 of the Department of Applied Politics, *al-qism li-siyasat al-'amaliya* (DAP). The department was run by Jamil Hassan, a former politician and historian specializing on Ibn Khaldun. The guiding principle of the department was to seek to merge theoretical and practical knowledge and apply it to politics. Thus, DAP explicitly rejected much of political science at the time, which often took great pride in its lack of practical knowledge and hands-on experience of politics. The department attracted many former activists as well as computer and data specialists.[20] What this amalgamation of specialists brought about was a movement toward application and experimentation. Hassan and his group suggested, by way of their exegesis of Carthaginian governance and Ibn Khaldun's writing, methods through which decline of political institutions could be mitigated, and vitality reinforced, not through a perfect model, but through a dynamic system of feedback loops.

---

[20] Conspicuous in their absence were political scientists. This was partly due to factors of Tunisian history. In the years of authoritarian rule prior to 2010, Tunisia did not have any departments of political science to speak of, and the subject was still poorly established in the country. This necessitated a more inter-disciplinary approach than was the norm elsewhere.

THE ORIGINS OF AGE: FROM STATES AND MARKETS TO SCIENTIFIC METHODS 395

5   THE FIRST EXPERIMENT

The Department of Applied Politics implemented their approaches on various small projects in inland Tunisia, but it was not until the European refugee crisis of 2065 that they could really put their models to the test. The destination for most refugees was of course sub-Saharan Africa, yet many hundreds of thousands remained stuck in camps distributed across the newly formed Maghrebi Union ⟨Pir Ψ 2070⟩. The unsanitary conditions in the new refugee settlements and increasingly violent clashes driven by ancestral hatreds between various European ethnic groups, brought international pressure on Maghrebi Union and demands for military intervention. Instead, President Idris Abdellatif, a close friend of Jamil Hassan, set up the European Refugee Experiment. The experiment was run under the aegis of the DAP. Generously funded by the African Federation, they cooperated with the European Diasporic Council, yet ultimate responsibility lay with Hassan and his team ⟨Hassan Ψ 2071: 21⟩. The crises had provided the perfect opportunity for the principles of Applied Politics to be tried and tested on a large scale. The refugees were separated into various groups through random selection. A number of hypotheses regarding political stability and violence were tested, meaning that different independent variables were administered to the different groups except for the control groups. The results were evaluated on a continual basis. New camps were created; new hypothesis was proposed. A few camps descended into chaos, the necessary causalities that provided the counter-examples for more successful strategies. In the first report on the project Hassan wrote:

> Science proceeds through counter-intuitive findings. We did not achieve the results we expected. We achieved infinitely more. We can now separate the wheat from the chaff. Why stop at studying political violence? We can organize, on small and large scale, new forms of societies at will. It was once said that only democracy allows for transformation without violence. Well, we have now shown democracy to be a drunkard, stumbling like a fool aimlessly in the dark. A new way of organizing society along scientific foundations has finally seen the light of day. What took the Ancients centuries to perfect, we can do in a matter of months. ⟨Ψ 2071: 221⟩

Beyond a doubt the project was the first true instance of experimental and scientific politics. Yet, not all researchers from the school of Applied Politics were enthusiastic followers of Hassan and his methods. The scholar of medieval science Sulayman al-Maqdisi claimed the experiment to be perilous and unpredictable:

> Through this small, seemingly rational step we have crossed a threshold into a dangerous age. To think that the subterranean field of desires can be tamed, to think that the sins of the past are not haunting us, is a delusion equal in scope to that of past would be reformers like Mao Zeduóng and Milton Friedman.

Today we are playing at God. But God cannot be fully known, and neither can his creations. This endeavor is doomed to a brutal end. ⟨Ψ 2073: 38⟩

Barring the few lone voices of obscurantism the project was hailed as a success, with the African Federation beginning its own similar experiments in order to deal with the mounting refugee crises. The experiments that were first applied to European refugees eventually began to be employed on civilized populations, yet remained essentially contained to specific nations and regions. A truly global realization of the ideals of experimental politics had to wait the more comprehensive collapse of the old order.

6 THE BIRTH OF THE NEW WORLD

The collapse of Europe was but the first and necessary step toward a more enlightened age; the USA and China would need to fall too.[21] The divergence and convergence of the two empires is a story too familiar to describe in full: America, no longer the young and confident Empire, mustered one last sigh of youthful optimism by surrendering to its libertarian temptation and dissolving itself in 2076, on its three-hundred-year anniversary. In its place an experiment in decentralized governance fueled by cryptocurrency arose, only for its piecemeal territories to be quickly conquered and absorbed by Canada and Mexico.

For a brief moment, following the collapse of Europe and the disappearance of the USA, China seemed to hold the keys to success.[22] Its efficient control of markets and ecological work was the envy of the world. Particularly following the end of the Warring States period (2057–2080) and emergence of the 15th Dynasty (2080–2096), it appeared as if China had overcome many aspects of the dreaded information-suppression problem that had hitherto plagued dictatorships and rendered them vulnerable to sudden shocks. Repression hides vulnerabilities, yet through sophisticated surveillance, and various forms of incentive mechanisms, the Chinese state appeared to have combined top-down and bottom-up governance ⟨Wen Ψ 2078⟩. Unfortunately, the Chinese political model proved difficult to replicate anywhere outside of its own territory, embedded as it was within its own political history. Finally, China too would succumb to the lure of information suppression that it had so deftly avoided previously and buckled under the weight of its own over-extended state apparatus. Wu Fan wrote; "We thought we had Sinicized Capitalism, just like we

---

[21] By the 2070s Liberalism, was of course, dead of Covid-55. Yet, some of its central tenants survived in improved forms; the belief in progress, in science, in the leaving behind of questions of values.

[22] The rapid decline of Political Islam across the globe during this period took many contemporary commentators by surprise. The simplest explanation must be that as the scale of European and then American collapse became evident, resentment-based politics subsided. The Muslim World had lost its mimetic double, its Other, without which it's political project could not survive.

had Buddhism, but in fact, we proved merely to have repeated the mistakes of Qin Shi Huangdi, confusing silence with stability" ⟨Ψ 2099: 834⟩.

War eventually proved the undoing of the mixed constitutions of the ancient Mediterranean and gave way to empires. Economic competition eventually ended empires and gave rise to the nation-state. When markets proved too volatile and violent, and too environmentally and socially costly, an alternative to the international state-led system had to be found. Just like modern nation-state arose out of the Peace of Westphalia and the failure of any one side to win the 30 Years War, so, its final dismantling arose out of failure. Failure simultaneously of the nation-state and of market competition. The time of politicians and economists was over; the time of empiricists and experimentalists was at hand.

Finally, the truth had become obvious: that independent states had played out their roles. The Federalism phase of global governance proved short-lived and what was needed was a flexible political meta-entity that could direct and design trials across the globe. States it became obvious were neither the expression of the will of a "people" nor a political community for collective decision-making; states were best understood as units of analysis in a larger global experiment to find the most robust forms of political organization.

Following the failure of the 15th Dynasty, the ascendency of experimental politics and AGE was fast and inexorable. Its chronicle is so well known that there is no need to repeat it here. I wish merely to note that Samira Bin Jalal, a student of Jamil Hassan, was part of the first international monitoring group the Bureau of Dynamic Governance that would later transform into AGE. It would not be a stretch to imagine that Bin Jalal's role was to translate the experiences of Applied Politics and the Maghrebi Union into the new AGE.

7   Conclusion

It is certainly the case that the emergence of AGE came about as a result of a confluence of contextual and only partially understood factors. And yet I hope to have shown that there are sufficient grounds to claim that the genesis of experimental politics lies in North Africa, inspired by a Punic past and incubated in the Department of Applied Politics.

Has finally become a science, thus rendering politics obsolete. Academia has been dismantled and scholarly research has been placed firmly where it belongs; as a past-time of bureaucrats. The question of the origins of AGE is therefore of merely scholastic value. With the advent of AGE, history itself has finally been confined to the dustbin of history. Regardless of the beginnings, what matters is that civilization has finally recovered from the shocks of its birth, and that there is finally community, identity, and stability.

The Zahir and the Batin: The Return of the Repressed

By Satya al-Haq[23]

For there is nothing hidden that will not be disclosed, and nothing concealed that will not be known or brought out into the light—Luke 8:17

The Suspicious Subject

On the surface, the article *The Origins of AGE* by Karim Zakhour ⟨Ψ 2115⟩ reads like a straightforward example of late neo-empiricist fluff. Its language is what you would expect: disinterested, detached, and dispassionate. Yet, the tone and tune of the piece is so simplistic, contains so many contradictions and odd silences, that it is difficult not to be suspicious. The whole article is imbued with exactly the kind of Western eschatology that it purports to disavow. Ostensibly, the article seeks to demonstrate that AGE arose from the periphery. This patently absurd claim is itself enough to give us pause. AGE is, as we all know, not a resurrected Carthaginian order, nor is it the brainchild of Tunisian scholars of Ibn Khaldun. It is the old and familiar marriage of Athens and Rome; it is philosophy and power made flesh. Zakhour begins his article by dismissing the parallel between AGE and Plato's Republic; but by doing so draws our attention to the obvious similarities. Granted, AGE is a dictatorship of empiricism rather than rationalism; yet a dictatorship nonetheless. It is the hubris of Popperian piecemeal social engineering disguising itself as humility. AGE is the end of history by other means.[24] Should the article then be read as yet another case of the old adage "power makes stupid" or is there something else afoot?

We argue that the article by Zakhour, in fact, contains a hidden message. The true purpose of AGE is not to guide the world through methodological precision and rigorous experimentation, but to function as a violence producing and reducing machine. It will be shown that AGE was imagined into life by a cabal of conspirators, inspired by long defunct political philosophers. That the prime movers of AGE believe that irrational human violence can be averted only through periodical sacrifices in the name of the scientific method.

Devils and Madmen

Let us begin by noting that Zakhour, who is a key administrator at AGE, wrote his Bachelor's thesis on a now mostly forgotten twentieth-century scholar by the name of Leo Strauss. Strauss, through his work on the medieval

---

[23] (Note from editor: Satya al-Haq the *nom de guerre* of an anonymous research collective. This article was first published in *Ghoulat Magazine* in Ψ 2122).

[24] Zakhour's article is sprinkled with nods to the twentieth-century thinkers like Karl Popper and Francis Fukuyama, who are never mentioned by name.

THE ORIGINS OF AGE: FROM STATES AND MARKETS TO SCIENTIFIC METHODS   399

philosopher Abū Naṣr Muḥammad ibn Muḥammad al-Fārābī, resurrected the neglected method of reading a text esoterically. Al-Fārābī had warned all philosophically inclined thinkers against expressing outright any position that runs counter to the passions of the day, lest they suffer the same fate of Socrates. Instead, through allegory and metaphor and seemingly contradictory messages and odd turns of phrases the philosopher signals the true meaning of the text.[25] Building on Al-Fārābī, Strauss argued that when looking at the works of many old philosophers we must make a distinction between the outer, superficial layer, and the inner, hidden core truth. In the words of Strauss, "An exoteric book contains[..]two teachings: a popular teaching of an edifying character, which is in the foreground; and a philosophic teaching concerning the most important subject, which is indicated only between the lines" (1952: 36). This is what the Sufis and heterodox Shi'a sects understood as the *Batin* (the hidden/esoteric) and the *Zahir* (the manifest/exoteric). In fact, looking at the article by Zakhour we find that peppered throughout the text are many quotations, headings, and footnotes that appear to tell their own lively tales, strangely at odds with the text itself. Given Zakhour's Straussian past, it is entirely possible, perhaps plausible, that his article should not only be read at the level of the exoteric, and that at least some of the inconsistencies are intentional and are clues to the hidden meanings of the text.[26]

How are we to uncover then, this hidden esoteric world? Strauss himself wrote that philosophers would often "hide certain truths quite openly by using as mouthpiece some disreputable character...devils, madmen, beggars, sophists, drunkards, epicureans, and buffoons" (1952: 38).[27] If we are to look for the deeper message of the text it is, I suggest, toward these devils and madmen that we should turn our gaze.

The Brethren of Purity

Above all, the figure of Sulayman al-Maqdisi draws our attention and his critique of experimental politics. Ostensibly he is a renegade disciple of Jamil Hassan, the founder of the Department of Applied Politics, yet there is no record of any Sulayman al-Maqdisi ever having attended the Department of Applied Politics. In fact, no such figure appears to have lived in Tunisia at the time. Why then invent this character and put words into his mouth that the

---

[25] Strauss was a somewhat controversial figure in American academic circles. Although mostly publishing books on ancient political philosophy, his emphasis on esoteric messaging led to accusation that he and later his students, a group called "Neoconservatives" were some of the main drivers behind the disastrous American invasion of Iraq in 2003 (see for e.g. George 2005). His thinking also inspired some limited theorizing within International Relations (see for e.g. Hirst 2012).

[26] It is also entirely possible that the article should be taken at face value.

[27] Strauss also claimed that a philosopher would often write "three or four sentences in that terse and lively style which is apt to arrest the attention of young men who love to think" (1952: 24).

author purports to disavow? Could the name in fact refer to Abû Sulaymân Muhammad Ma 'shar al-Bustî, called al-Maqdisî, the tenth-century Basran scholar? Al-Maqdisî was one of the supposed authors of the *Rasâ'il Ikhwân al-Safâ* (Epistles of the Brethren of Purity). The Brethren of Purity were a secret society that, much like Al Fārābī, understood the dangers that rational enquiry posed, and thus advocated for *taqiyya* (dissimulation) when necessary. In true Ismaili and Neo-Platonic fashion, they distinguished between the Batin and the Zahir. Here then is another clue that we are on the right path, that the text has layers of meaning for us to uncover. Is it not possible that the position of Zakhour is in fact closer to the purported enemy, to al-Maqdisî himself? If this is the case, then why hide the message? Is it himself he seeks to protect? Or is it an expression of Gnostic Imamism? That power is beyond reform and redemption, and yet we must make our peace with it? That AGE is built on a lie, but perhaps it is a noble lie? A necessary lie? A Platonic lie: what Strauss building on Maimonides and al-Farabi has termed the double truth theorem?

The key to the message of the text, so dangerous that it must be hidden, lies in a blink-and-you-miss-it footnote. Casually, in the final footnote of the text the author explains the decline of Political Islam as a result of its lack of a "mimetic double." No reference or explanation is given for this at once vague and provocative claim. Yet the clues are there, for the term "mimetic double" lead us to another liminal and lost figure of twentieth-century academia; René Girard and his apocalyptic theory of mimesis.

Violence and the Sacred

For Girard, mankind is defined by a *lack* in its very being, a lack that compels individuals toward others, toward *models*. Models are *mediators* of desire. There are no authentic or original desires, according to Girard, but only desires that we learn from imitating others. Imitation is the foundation of all social existence but invariably breeds conflict through escalating rivalry between imitators and their model (Girard 1977, 1987). Culture exists in order to limit violent mimesis through *reducing similarities* between individuals and thus potential rivalry, yet mimetic competition and violence can never be fully contained. Times of crises are periods of the loss of distinctions, when neighbors begin to treat each other as *the same*, and the mimetic rivalry of the community threatens to consume all and spill over into outright violence. In such periods, violence becomes redirected away from the community by finding a *scapegoat* (Girard 1986, 1996) Scapegoating is nothing other than replacement of violence against all with violence against one. The victim is "sacred" in the original sense of term; imbued with supernatural powers of danger and pollution, and often the victim is worshiped after its death. All rituals are, for Girard, at their origins re-creations of the mimetic cycle: mimetic crisis, scapegoating, sacrifice, and restoration of order (1986: 183). It is precisely because humans have no natural breaks on violence, that religion/myth is needed, to channel violence, to mitigate it, by minimizing it into

THE ORIGINS OF AGE: FROM STATES AND MARKETS TO SCIENTIFIC METHODS   401

ritualized violence against a scapegoat. This process only functions as long as it is *misunderstood*. As Girard writes;

> Men cannot confront the naked truth of their own violence without the risk of abandoning themselves to it entirely. They have never had a very clear idea of this violence, and it is possible that the survival of all human societies of the past was dependent on this fundamental lack of understanding. (1977: 82)

It is precisely when we "understand" violence that it is beyond our control. The only way to contain violence is to be fooled, to believe in its mythical powers of restoration. Religion uses strategic violence to build peace through the obscuring of its own process of violence-making (Girard 1987).

The AGE of Scapegoating

How are Girard and his memetic theory tied to the article and to AGE? Well, according to Girard the modern and rational process of understanding violence exposed the world to apocalyptic risks by negating the scapegoating mechanism. The whole of the twentieth century and its nationalist and communist paroxysms of violence was a direct result of the dismantling the mechanisms that minimized murder. Instead of the violence of many against one we had the violence of many against all (Girard 2009).

Let us extrapolate Girard's model into the twenty-first century, where increasingly it was the global market that transplanted the violence of nation-states.[28] In the place of bloody wars, the market sacrificed the poor across the globe as scapegoats in order to quench its ecumenical bloodlust. Such a market logic, focusing its violent appetite on those that could not compete efficiently (and therefore were not "worthy" of dignity), while "rational" was nonetheless highly unstable. Eventually succumbing to its own destructive dialectic by undermining the very nation-state system that kept it afloat.

Enter AGE, and its empirical and scientific method. A competitive market system of nation-states is replaced with a globalizing organization that runs controlled experiments to find the most robust forms of political and social organizations. More controlled, seemingly more stable, certainly less chaotic. Yet, is not its experimental process simply another form of violence of many against one? A scapegoating through other means? A violent memetic crisis is held at bay through our constant ritual sacrificing in the name of trial and error. Violence is not removed, but displaced and hidden behind the cover of scientific sagacity. No longer at the mercy of abstract markets, it is not the poor and destitute that are sacrificed at the altar of progress, but rather random

---

[28] There were brief, and ultimately abortive, attempts to use Girard's theory to explain International Relations in the early parts of twenty-first century (see for e.g. Brighi and Cerella 2015). The apocalyptic aspects of his thought were toned down in the academic application of his works, and yet we argue that it is precisely the eschatological dimensions that have influenced the architects of AGE.

populations and random nations are bathed in blood for the glory of the scientific method.[29] The experiment of 2111, that led to the annihilation of the entire eastern Bengal is merely the latest example of this horrific logic. Ostensibly it was done in order to find the most efficient form of hydro-political organization. Yet despite all the rigors of scientific selection and design, the very assumption that a few must suffer for the benefit of the many reveals that violence is built into this system of governance. Ultimately, from the perspective of AGE, the millions of lives lost were less a casualty of science as much as a necessary scapegoating sacrifice. Thus, violence is "minimized," but only as long as its mechanism remains obscured and the multitudes continue to believe that it is done in the name of progress. AGE is the religion for the new age, expressed in the language of scientific reason.

Haqiqat al-Tafsir

From what we have presented here we have good reason to suspect that the author of *The Origins of AGE* believes that the tension between the City and the Philosopher is real, that Truth does not serve the Community and therefore must be obscured and kept hidden from the masses. For Al-Fārābī and his Neo-Platonic brethren, science was the hidden and dangerous knowledge, and prophetic revelation was the vulgarized outer *zahir:* knowledge for the common folk. AGE, Zakhour instead suggests, negates this form; for it is the scientific knowledge that is the vulgarized knowledge that hides the *batin*: the real truth. The masses blindly follow the method of science (*sharia*), the scholars interpret the methods (*tafsir*), and only the chosen few, (*al-ikhwan*), transcend it. As the Brethren of Purity put it: "the sharia [science] is the medicine of the sick." The philosopher elites of AGE, Zakhour is obliquely telling us, understand this. Zakhour and his ilk believe that through obfuscation by science they are keeping the dark and destructive impulses of mankind in check. Through homeopathic violence they save us from a worse fate.

To this we say: enough of that foul medicine! Perchance we are not as sick as we have been led to believe? We no longer wish to be fooled by those whom think themselves wise. For history has not stopped, the Owl of Minerva has not taken flight. Reason alone may be baptized, but the pagan passions of the soul have not been conquered, only silenced. Well, let them be silent no more.

---

[29] Let us not forget that experimental politics began as a way of avoiding violence between European populations.

THE ORIGINS OF AGE: FROM STATES AND MARKETS TO SCIENTIFIC METHODS   403

BIBLIOGRAPHY

Ahmedi, Nazruddin & Lazhar. ⟨Ψ 2037⟩. *The Crown of Carthage*. Osmania University Press.

Akbarzadeh, S. (Ed.). (2019). *Routledge Handbook of International Relations in the Middle East*. Routledge.

al-Maqdisi, S. ⟨Ψ 2073⟩. *Incoherence of the Incoherent*. Gog Magog Press.

Ben Zaher, Z. ⟨Ψ 2039⟩. *Patricide and Other Adventures*. Sigmund Press.

Benjamin, B. ⟨Ψ 2111⟩. The Last Hurrah of the West. *The Administrators Journal of Amateur History*.

Brighi, E., & Cerella, A. (2015). An Alternative Vision of Politics and Violence: Introducing Mimetic Theory in International Studies. *Journal of International Political Theory*, 11(1), 3–25.

George, J. (2005) Leo Strauss, Neoconservatism and US Foreign Policy: Esoteric Nihilism and the Bush Doctrine. *International Politics*, 42: 174–202.

Girard, R. (1977). *Violence and the Sacred*. John Hopkins University Press.

Girard, R. (1986). *The Scapegoat*. JHU Press.

Girard, R. (1987). *Things Hidden since the Foundation of the World*. Stanford, CA: Stanford.

Girard, R (1996). *The Girard* Reader. New York: Crossroad.

Girard, R. (2009). *Battling to the End: Conversations with Benoît Chantre*. MSU Press.

Hargopal, P. ⟨Ψ 2110⟩. The Communist Origins of AGE. *The Administrators Journal of Amateur History*.

Hassan, J. ⟨Ψ 2071⟩. *Applied Politics*. University of Applied Politics.

Hirst, A. (2012). Leo Strauss and International Relations: The politics of modernity's abyss. *International Politics*, 49(6), 645–670.

Jalebi, G. ⟨Ψ 2045⟩. *How Economics Killed Europe*. The Samir Amin Institute .

Khaldun, I. (2015). *The Muqaddimah: An Introduction to History—Abridged Edition*. Princeton University Press.

Lyotard, J.F. (1979). *The Postmodern Condition*. Manchester University Press.

Makdous, C. ⟨Ψ 2107⟩. Jinnah, Nehru, Gandhi and AGE. *The Administrators Journal of Amateur History*.

Pir, M. ⟨Ψ 2070⟩. *European Diaspora in Africa*. University of Dakar Press.

Radhoune, A. ⟨Ψ 2053⟩. *Experiments in the Desert*. Tataouine Town Press.

Rafika, B. ⟨Ψ 2053⟩. *The Rise and Fall of Leila Bouzid*. Gafsa Research Collective.

Strauss, L. (1952) *Persecution and the Art of Writing*. The University of Chicago Press.

Tantawi. ⟨Ψ 2046⟩. *Neo-Populism in New Carthage*. Khartoum Center of Advanced Studies University Press.

Wallerstein, I. (1979). *The Capitalist World-Economy*. Cambridge University Press.

Wen, G. ⟨Ψ 2078⟩. *The Brilliance of the 15th Dynasty*. Xiamen University Press.

Wu Fan, B. ⟨Ψ 2099⟩. *Chinese Dreams and Delusions*. Shangri La Press.

Conclusion

The Realism of Our Time? Futures, Fictions, and the Mid-Century Bang

Laura Horn, Ayşem Mert, and Franziska Müller

The Handbook of Global Politics in the 22nd Century (HGP22) is a unique project that diffuses the dichotomy between the factual and the fictional. In a *future antérieur* style, each contributor to this volume has used their creativity to ask tricky, sad, hopeful, cynical questions: Where is IR, in times of war, climate and ecological catastrophe, and deepening social and political conflicts? A discipline that wears its foundational myth with pride, having been "conceived on the blood-stained battlefields of Europe, with the infant child of IR having been delivered in 1919 after a grueling 48-month gestation period" (Hobson 2012: 15), seems again lost in translation. Looking at our discipline, a number of anachronistic, but also futurist features seem remarkable: the broken, but re-establishing trust in global cooperation, the trust in post-human techno-fixes that enhance, or sometimes even replace human

---

L. Horn (✉)
Roskilde University, Roskilde, Denmark
e-mail: lhorn@ruc.dk

A. Mert
Stockholm University, Stockholm, Sweden
e-mail: aysem.mert@statsvet.su.se

F. Müller
Business, Economics and Social Sciences, University of Hamburg, Hamburg, Germany
e-mail: franziska.mueller@uni-hamburg.de

© The Author(s), under exclusive license to Springer Nature Switzerland AG 2023
L. Horn et al. (eds.), *The Palgrave Handbook of Global Politics in the 22nd Century*, https://doi.org/10.1007/978-3-031-13722-8_24

cooperation thanks to benevolent algorithms, the hope for radical, more-than-human encounters. We 'qurated' multiple manuscripts which sometimes expanded the scientific form, and sometimes made us imagine that future IR research will be completely different. Several of our 'transmissions' picture IR as the political science of global survival, similar to projections from Anthropocene Studies (Bhat 2021; Mitchell 2017; Burke et al. 2016), Capitalocene Studies (Patel and Moore 2018), or Extinction Studies (van Dooren 2014; Rose et al. 2017). An epistemological counterpart to Anna Tsing's postcapitalist fungi (Tsing 2015), IR in 2122 is portrayed as a discipline thriving on the ruins (rather than: in the footsteps) of earlier IR traditions. And yet, as *social science fiction*, the contributions to this book go beyond the contested boundaries of the discipline as we know it now. Fiction is not a replica, Ricoeur tells us: "because it has no previous reference, it may refer in a productive way to reality, and even *increase* reality" (Ricoeur cited in Kirby 2017: 685). What happens when we take our contemporary IR, with its fallacies, myths, and blind spots, as a reference point, and then seek to increase its realities by expressing, extrapolating, and exploring its potential into futures we will never know?

This concluding chapter has multiple, possibly contradictory aims, broadly following some of the questions we have received while discussing the project: Why write a book about looking back from the future? How is this even IR? How and why did you go about the project the way you did? The next section offers a contextualization of the book's position on the future within political and social theory. It is to those readers we're speaking here, for whom the onto-epistemological focus on the fantasmal resonates as the prism does for our Qurators. In the following discussion, then, we situate the book in the existing multiverse that is International Relations and Global Politics. Here, we discuss linkages and continuities, as well as disruptions of ongoing conversations in IR, covering the IR/science fiction nexus, as well as recent debates about the Anthropocene and 'worlding' IR. We invite students and researchers of IR to connect in their own ways and to consider what this book, if at all, can contribute to the teaching of IR, as well as teaching to IR. In the third part, as becomes any self-styled Handbook, we offer concluding reflections on the contributions and the volume's overarching perspective. This particular part will be of interest to anyone who has a distinct sense of *future whiplash* after reading through the contributions, as well as readers who are curious about how on earth, this glorious, overheating planet, this book has been made. At the same time, these conclusions do not constitute a closure as such—after all, is it open-endedness rather than finitude that we insist on.

1   Future Making as Ontoepistemology

Engaging with the future has been a part of scientific writing for a long time. The way this has been done, particularly with the Enlightenment and the birth of the scientific method is that scientists try to build models and theories that help discover the underlying logics of phenomena (e.g. that of nature, human nature, the universe), build models on these logics, and predict what is coming. This would allow for the human domination of the future and ensure stability for modern societies (Illich 1973). This practice sits neatly in the modernist tradition and it is very conservative: It aims to maintain and sustain the existing logics and practices of social life, the habits that are already institutionalized, and possibly nudge and shift them in small ways to address newly emerging problems. It is a positivist, rationalist, and often quantitative (albeit deeply speculative and futuristic) scientific method and it is still the dominant discourse/hegemonic project across (most) scientific disciplines, as most of them locate their intellectual history and logics of inquiry in enlightenment thought and the built-in domination of humans over nature (Patel and Moore 2018). IR has a long and troubling history in this regard, visible in a focus on system preservation rather than transformation, which is a problem framing that clearly demonstrates how IR has for most of the time been unfit to even grapple with how the Anthropocene condition fundamentally juxtaposes the planetary polity (Burke et al. 2016; Chandler et al. 2017; Mitchell 2017). The goal of this project, however, is not so much to affirm and nudge, but rather to disrupt and dislocate what has already been revealed by critical thinkers and scholars for decades.

What would, then, disrupt and dislocate, and even provide an alternative to the rationalist, post-/positivist epistemological positions that fall into the traps of modernity and its false dichotomies, including its racist, sexist and classist biases? This is important because one of the dichotomies that modernity and its scientific method have constructed is the one between truth and falsehood, which is one of the starting points for our reflection.

Looking Backward: 2122–2022

The socialist utopia Edward Bellamy wrote in 1888, *Looking Backward: 2000–1887*, imagined a postcapitalist society, inspired many real-life utopian communities, influenced activists and social movements, and started a battle of books that lasted decades. Opponents and supporters of Bellamy's liberal socialist imaginary have written sequels and even adapted translations (e.g. *The Present as Seen by Our Descendants and a Glimpse at the Progress of the Future* by Iliya Yovchev). Looking backward from the future is a method already used, in a variety of ways.

And not as an afterthought, either: Socialist utopias were abundant in the late nineteenth century, and their influence was significant in ideological and popular imaginaries across cultures. So much so that, in *Socialism: Utopian and Scientific* Friedrich Engels (1880 [1999]) labeled a group of socialist thinkers as 'utopian socialists', as they were interested in the emancipation of the whole of humanity rather than the proletariat and therefore reconceptualizing all dimensions of human life, education, housing, economy, marriage, visible for instance in utopian communities created in the US, long before forms of 'alternative living' were even imagined. Engels found them important: Saint-Simon, for instance, foretold the complete absorption of politics by economics, by declaring politics to be the science of production. Fourier's criticism of the existing conditions of society was at times inspiring. But ultimately, the theories of these utopian socialists could not be complete, because, at the time they were writing, they could not have detected the slowly forming antagonism between the bourgeoisie and the proletariat. Moreover, for Engels, it was a problem that there are many different interpretations of socialism in utopian socialist thought. This could divide the working class or lead to an 'eclectic, average Socialism' rather than one that is scientific: "To make a science of Socialism, it had first to be placed upon a real basis" (ibid.: 70–71), which was historical materialism. Karl Marx's remark, printed in the 1873 Afterword to the Second German Edition of Capital I, about the expectation by his critics and followers alike to find blueprints for a future society in his work, reflects this well. He was reproached, he pointed out, that, "on the one hand, I treat economics metaphysically, and on the other hand — imagine! — confine myself to the mere critical analysis of actual facts, instead of writing recipes [..] for the cook-shops of the future." This split between utopian and materialist socialists resulted in a spectrum of positions that allowed social scientists to perceive the past and the future in radically different ways, ranging from deeply deterministic to relational, constructivist, relativist, and/or post-structuralist. Scholars such as Ernst Bloch still trace to bridge this gap by imagining concrete utopias coming with a Marxian spirituality focused on hope, convivial technologies, and nature's creativity (Bloch 1959).

Deconstructing Utopia

Focusing on the function and future of critique, Bruno Latour (2004) reflected that Critique has lost its initial function, for two reasons: (1) the abuse of critical approaches to scientific inquiry: Critical and constructivist methods have relentlessly shown in the last two decades that knowledge, institutions, technologies and rationales all lack scientific certainty and are means to construct 'facts'. They are also linked with power: Knowledge produces (the facts for) power as much as power produces (the need for) knowledge (hence the Foucauldian term power-slash-knowledge). But it has been increasingly the case, recently, that this perception is employed by public figures that "aim at fooling the public by obscuring the certainty of a closed argument." Such "artificially maintained scientific controversies" (Latour 2004) are the first reason why we should approach critique critically. (2) Critique has influenced our thinking: there is an increasing tendency both within and outside academia toward disbelief and conspiracy. He notes, "Of course, we, in the academy, like to use more elevated causes–society, discourse, knowledge-slash-power, fields of forces, empires, capitalism–while conspiracists like to portray a miserable bunch of greedy people with dark intents, but I find something troublingly similar in the structure of the explanation, in the first movement of disbelief and, then, in the wheeling of causal explanations coming out of the deep dark below." In a more recent article, Latour (2010: 4) refines his position on critique by suggesting that "critique did a wonderful job in debunking prejudices, [...] but it ran out of steam because it was predicated on the discovery of a true world of realities lying behind a veil of appearances." The power of critique in reassembling is much more limited than its power in deconstructing, which results in the frustration it seems to cause, as manifest in the tendency toward disbelief. Against it, he conceives compositionism: "With critique, you may debunk, reveal, unveil, but only as long as you establish, through this process of creative destruction, privileged access to the world of reality behind the veils of appearances. Critique, in other words, has all the limits of utopia: it relies on the certainty of the world beyond this world. [What is the use of poking holes in delusions, if nothing more true is revealed beneath?] By contrast, for compositionism, there is no world beyond. It is all about immanence. The difference is not moot, because what can be critiqued cannot be composed." For this reason, Latour (ibid.: 5) argues, social science requires a transformation; to move away from "debunking from a resource [...], to a topic to be carefully studied." Latour is not alone in this endeavor: In *Birth of the State: The Place of the Body in Crafting Modern Politics*, Charlotte Epstein's (2020) method is 'constitutive theorising'. Not only does she show the way the body has been historically used as a force to conserve and institute, depoliticizing difference and hegemony built upon it, but she also shows that it can be remobilized as a critical tool revealing the deeply racialized and gendered origins of statehood and suggesting it can be reconstituted differently.

In this book, our aim is not to go so far as 'suspending the critical gesture', as Latour suggests. Yet, it seems reasonable to reflect on the possibility that deconstruction can be a more limited aim than the composition of histories and a history of the contestations in epistemologies. To compose, one has to understand what has been eliminated in the selective process we call politics. Not only does IR see a transformation in this regard (with Russian cyber attacks, psychological warfare, post-trust, post-truth, trumpism, etc.), but also we want to construct something else in this volume. Ours is a different kind of onto-epistomology, which defies this fact/fiction dichotomy, and opens the future up, to multiple possibilities through the use of imaginaries. We have gathered all these futurisms to structurate a pluralist and radically open future. We feel that rather than affirming and suggesting slow, procedural shifts in social life and scientific onto-epistemologies, a radical feminist approach to epistemology would aim to disrupt and insist on politicizing, polarizing, and interrupting the practices that are obviously problematic and unjust.

Yes, in at least two ways: (1) Methodologically, this volume is utopian (similar to utopian socialism, before 'the split'), in the sense that it does not consider so much how we will get to an ideal world, but just imagines and narrates it. The moment we take the existing structures as a starting point, the possibility of change becomes incredibly difficult. Just like the utopian communities established in the early nineteenth century, many of the contributions take a clean slate in the way we write IR.

(2) Secondly, it is utopian because it does not assume a linear historical procession for societies, or even futures, but paves the way to the future (if there is any) in multiple ways with multiple ruptures. In doing so it problematizes historical determinist approaches, just as it problematizes other modernist dichotomies (between nature/culture, masculine/feminine, scientific/value-laden, etc.).

Accepting multiple futures already allows the reader to imagine that another, radically different utopia is possible. Most utopian imaginaries disregard the question of what constitutes a people and their identity, which in turn would constitute *the political*. Accordingly, no further structural change could take place in these utopian societies: The lack of contingency is the rule for a continuous state of perfection unanimously agreed upon since Plato, for whom democracy was undesirable to begin with. In this sense, socialist utopias narrated the end of politics, imagining societies with no antagonism (Mert 2015). For this, they relied on the assumption that it was the circumstances (as opposed to identities such as race, class, or gender) and upbringing that made people antagonistic. In an equitable society, harmony would replace all antagonisms.

These utopias precluded further identity formation/transformation among their citizens, and (as a result) assumed the end of antagonisms. The lack of antagonisms, however, insinuates not only the end of politics, but that of democracy. Democracy requires social antagonisms; many issues are politicized based on antagonisms originating from these identities, or otherwise they turn into newly formed identities: "A society in which all antagonisms have been eradicated, far from being a truly democratic one, would be its exact opposite. Pluralism is constitutive of modern democracy, and it precludes any dream of final reconciliation" (Mouffe 1996: 25). The utopia worth thriving for therefore should be one that does not imagine an end to politics, one which does not cancel out differences but rather embraces them.

Fantasmal Politics, Antiessentialist Articulations

In Erik Olin Wright's (2010) 'theory of structural possibility', he argued that "what is pragmatically possible is not fixed independently of our imaginations, but is itself shaped by our visions." Thus, Wright calls for transforming capitalism through what he calls real utopias. Ursula LeGuin explained what this might mean further, in her acceptance speech for the National Book Foundation's 2014 Medal for Distinguished Contribution to American Letters, when she said

Hard times are coming, when we'll be wanting the voices of writers who can see alternatives to how we live now, can see through our fear-stricken society and its obsessive technologies to other ways of being, and even imagine real grounds for hope. We'll need writers who can remember freedom – poets, visionaries – realists of a larger reality. Right now, we need writers who know the difference between production of a market commodity and the practice of an art. [...] We live in capitalism, its power seems inescapable — but then, so did the divine right of kings. Any human power can be resisted and changed by human beings. Resistance and change often begin in art.

For instance, E. P. Thompson's (2011) work on (eco-)socialist utopian William Morris provides some critical arguments for a new alliance between socialism and utopianism. Tracing the works of Miguel Abensour, Thomson notes: "what Morris offered was not any concrete blueprint for the future, but rather to liberate desire by questioning all existing values: he wanted to teach desire to desire, to desire better, to desire more, and above all to desire in a different way." He coined the term the 'education of desire' to refer to this process. According to Lynne Segal (2017), Thompson warns us that "if workers were educated only to heed the contradictions and destructiveness of capitalism then, apart from their engagement in 'the bitter praxis of class struggle', they were always likely to fall back on the ruling ideas of the moment." It is the lack of any interest in discussing the future in the later Marxist tradition, Thompson (2011: 792) declared, that resulted in the significant failings of the Marxist imagination itself: "its lack of a moral self-consciousness or even a vocabulary of desire, its inability to project any images of the future, or even its tendency to fall back in lieu of these upon the Utilitarian's earthly paradise – the maximization of economic growth."

It is both desirable and possible to revive various utopian traditions.[1] Science fiction, as Kim Stanley Robinson famously put it (2017), takes on a function as 'the realism of our time'. For our book, this meant relying on two principles: The primacy of the fantasmal, and a post-natural antiessentialism.

Understanding politics as a practice of collective storytelling, in which the role of fiction and narrative is a constitutive element instead of being 'mere rhetoric', is still under-theorized. From a narrative point of view, the boundaries between reality and fiction are always blurry. And an important but largely ignored part of this common world are shared imaginaries, expressed or represented in stories, e.g. myths, legends, and various futurisms that "produce images of what is one's own and what is alien, images that attract collective energy and are thus capable of catalysing mechanisms of self-realization" (Koschorke 2018: 80). The fantasmal has been central to political imaginaries since the beginning of political thought. And recent scholarship focused a lot

---

[1] While many of today's ecologically concerned utopian projects (real and imaginary) sound naïve, as Elena Pulcini pointed out—therein lies their distinctively radical nature and strength. Notable examples are the Convivialist Manifesto (2013), the Degrowth movement, Cittaslow (Slow Cities), and other slow practices.

more on the function of the fantasmal in the construction of current reality as well as future possibility (see for instance, Freistein and Gadinger 2020; Leira and De Carvalho 2018; Gadinger et al. 2016; De Guevara 2016), building on the work of critical scholars from various disciplines. Dvora Yanow paid attention to the importance of ambiguity: The power of metaphors and symbols lies "in their potential to accommodate multiple meanings" (Yanow 1996), while myths reduce tensions in social life, by directing attention away "from equally valued but contradictory societal principles" (Yanow 1996). Roland Barthes (1957 [1987]: 117) highlighted the double function of myth: that "it points out and it notifies, it makes us understand something and it imposes it on us. [T]he very principle of myth [is that] it transforms history into nature." In other words, by normalizing past injustices or simply what seems incongruous in established practices. This is why Cynthia Weber considers IR's myths as 'apparent truths' which carry their universalizing, naturalizing, and even depoliticizing functions (Weber 2001: 2–7), and why we can conceptualize the role of IR theorists also as 'mythographers', engaging in a kind of 'storytelling', structured by certain narratives, tropes, protagonists, scripts, and tensions (Müller 2016). Consequentially, Himadeep Muppidi wonders: "In the wasteland that is conventional IR, stories of any sort might appear, at first glance, to offer a welcome respite. But there is also, as some of our fellow disciplines can attest to, a politics of storytelling: whose stories do we get to hear all the time; whose stories are generally inaudible; how do stories make us over; whose mansions do stories furnish with humanity in every remote room and whose huts do they deprive of life and dignity" (Muppidi 2013).

Regardless of their exact function, the fantasmatic elements have a connection to political desires: "the imaginary promise of recapturing our lost/impossible enjoyment [provides] the fantasy support for many of our political projects and choices. [...] On the one hand, fantasy promises a harmonious resolution to the social antagonism, a covering of lack. On the other hand, this beatific dimension of fantasy 'is supported by a disturbing paranoiac fantasy which tells us why things went wrong (why we did not get the girl, why society is antagonistic)' (Žižek 1998: 210)" as Yannis Stavrakakis (2005: 73–74) aptly puts. Inversely, "[fantasies] seek to maintain existing social structures by pre-emptively absorbing dislocations, preventing them from becoming [politicised and transformed]" (Glynos and Howarth 2007). This is why we turned to fantasy, then we asked, what can the future tell us about the history of international relations? What can history tell us about the future of international relations?

Marilyn Strathern (1992) suggested that humanity has entered an era defined by a sense of being "after nature," pointing not in the least to our species' recent inability in maintaining the life cycles that support its life, and that of other species. More critically for this study and perhaps also for the future of life on our planet, she pointed to how understanding and representing nature has become increasingly difficult at the age of such unprecedented intervention in nature. Since then, our intervention has advanced both in micro (e.g. further genetic interventions and nanotechnology) and in macro (e.g. geo-engineering) levels. Other scholars, such as Donna Haraway (1985), have noted that with this 'artificial production of nature', it becomes impossible to perceive Nature as an independent domain of intrinsic value and authenticity: An unmediated, pristine concept of Nature outside of human intervention is no longer possible even in our minds. These scholars are not suggesting that nature has little value or that there is nothing natural about Nature anymore, although many environmentalists misconceived their work as such (cf. Kate Soper's response 1996). On the contrary, they are preoccupied with the formation of a new, antiessentialist ontology for social sciences that could represent nature and society without making them the binary opposition they have been since the Enlightenment or even beforehand, in the works of various political philosophers.

Antiessentialism emerged as a response and objection to the general assertion of essentialism, that entities have (at least some) essential properties that define them. The premise of antiessentialism in relation to the environment would be that nature is always constructed through humanity's discursive processes of giving meaning: Every conception we have about nature is also cultural and social. As Bruno Latour (1993) recognized, nature is at once real, collective, and discursive (fact, power, and discourse) and must be naturalized, sociologized, and deconstructed accordingly. Another seminal work was *After Nature: Steps to an Antiessentialist Political Ecology*, where Arturo Escobar (1999: 2) claimed that an antiessentialist theory of nature would entail the simultaneous articulation of the biophysical basis of the concept and its culturally constructed and socially produced dimensions. Two important intellectual sources for political ecology are feminist and poststructuralist political thought, with the antiessentialist conceptions of identity they produced. Rather than assuming an unchanging and pre-existing core (i.e. an essence), both theories highlight the constant and differential constitution of identity, its radical openness, and incompleteness. Escobar notes that (similar to Laclau) he also regards "this critique of essentialism arising out of poststructuralism, the philosophy of language, and hermeneutics as a sine qua non for radical social theory today and for understanding the widening of the field of social struggles" (ibid.: 3). More importantly, he explores whether an antiessentialist analysis can be applied to 'nature', when he asks (ibid.): "Is the category 'nature' susceptible to this kind of analysis? If seemingly solid categories like society and the subject [even so entrenched a category as the capitalist economy is subject] to anti-essentialist critique, why has nature proven so resistant? [...] The poststructuralist rethinking of the social, the economy, and the subject [...] suggests ways of rethinking nature as having no essential identity. As in the case of the other categories mentioned, the analysis would have a double goal: to examine the constitutive relations that account for nature —biological, social, cultural—and to open the way for revealing ethnographically or imagining discourses of ecological/cultural difference that do not reduce the multiplicity of the social and biological worlds to a single

416 L. HORN ET AL.

overarching principle of determination ('the laws of the ecosystem,' 'the mode of production,' 'the knowledge system,' [etc.]).""

Hence, the antiessentialism that deals with Nature *after* the dichotomies of modernity (such as nature/culture) are disrupted can be neither deterministic nor causal: It must be the study of articulations wherein historical and biophysical are implicated with each other in order to provide new articulations of the biophysical, the cultural, and the techno-economic, which are "realizable today, and conducive to more just and sustainable social and ecological relations [both now and in the future]" (ibid.: 4). 'After nature' does not imply a causal relationship between human behavior and the deepening ecological crises or possible solutions. It emphasizes that our understanding of both society and nature is conceptually co-constitutive: On the one hand, it recognizes that nature has always been a concept that defines social institutions and is used to legitimize and construct new ones (in fact, it could be argued that 'man in nature' has been a long-lasting theme in Western political thought). On the other hand, it maintains that various meanings of nature were produced throughout history by social and political developments that are at once relevant and inspirational for various political and social goals. More recently, scholars turned their attention also to the connection between nature, Nature, environment, and fantasy, wherein "the concept of fantasy is critical to move forward and further develop the understanding of nature and environment as inherently contingent and political" (Behagel and Mert 2021: 81).

2   The Means of Imagination in International Relations

More than ever, the future is an essentially contested terrain within the social sciences. In this section, we now contextualize and link these fundamental dimensions within contemporary academic debates, in particular International Relations. Future studies have gained traction over the last decades, consolidating into an interdisciplinary academic field that goes beyond futurism as specific aesthetic and political programs. It is, as Dator argues, "interested not in itself furthering any particular view of the future, but rather in furthering both narrowly professional as well as broadly participative inquiry into the future; understanding the roots and consequences of each of the manifold images of the future that exist in people's minds and in support of people's actions" (Dator 2002: 7). The meaning of the future is, as Kemp and Andersson (2021) show, a question of power, of representations and counter-representations, and forms of struggle over future imaginaries. The ways in which we know and represent the world 'are inseparable from the ways in which we chose to live in' (Jasanoff 2004: 9). Even Future Studies now has a 'social turn' (Lopez Galviz and Spiers 2022), one hinging on interdisciplinarity and new insights into how social futures are being made today. What, then, is the state of 'the future' in International Relations, and how does this book link up to these discussions? Broadly speaking, we might be able to put approaches to the future into two categories; sometimes interlinking but more often than not intentionally distinct. Bilgin (2016) here points toward a gap between policy and theory aspects of 'future techniques' in IR. Foresight and forecasting have been a core concern in some corners of International Relations and Foreign Policy (Schneide et al. 2011). Future techniques have been instrumentalized in particular in the more applied IR hinterland, such as with the RAND Corporation, Stratfor, or the Hudson Institute. Not limited to immediate security concerns, foresight studies also covers existential themes such as 'long-term trajectories of human civilization' (Baum et al. 2019). At a time when uncertainty and global risks have become key policy parameters, foresight and forecasting take on renewed methodological impetus (e.g. Bostrom et al. 2008; Lohmann and Tepel 2014; Torres 2017). It is however *not* future studies and foresight that this book speaks to; in fact, it is by the very nature of the fantasmal and the anti-essential principles guiding our approach that it would be quite futile to try and render the book relevant for any forecasting at all. Neither does it constitute a backcasting exercise, a methodology that has risen to prominence in future labs and other attempts of future-making initiatives (e.g. Bishop et al. 2007). In contrast to forecasting, backcasting does not seek to predict future states but rather sets out to formulate how a desirable future state might look, so that pathways to this configuration can then be realized. HGP22 does not aim at providing blueprints, or tentative manuals. For this book, our approach is closer to what Raven and Stripple (2021: 229) for their own work on the carbon ruins call 'a more exploratory mode of speculation'. Having established how the book stands in relation to future studies, we now turn to the other side of IR, the one that takes a theory-led road to the future and its representations.

IR Between Pop Culture and Worlding in the Anthropocene

Much has been written about IR's preoccupation with science fiction (SF), that is different pathways and approaches to the analysis of SF. Following Jameson (2005: xiv), (utopian) SF has 'an essentially epistemological function'. Many International Relations perspectives on science fiction insist on a political theory reading of the future. In his critical survey, Kirby (2017: 574) calls the interface between SF and IR 'an emerging sub-sub-field in its own right'. Scholars have engaged with various theoretical contexts from literary studies, including subtext, extrapolation, and estrangement (Weldes 2003; Kiersey and Neumann 2015). The relevance of pop culture phenomena, including SF, has been discussed widely in and for the study of IR (Grayson et al. 2009), including how SF in fact causes future developments (Carpenter 2016). Kirby here introduces a helpful heuristic, to distinguish between approaches that regard SF as politically expressive, *world revealing*, and programmatic, *world making*. As he argues (Kirby 2017: 586), "to continually 'read' the speculative for discrete political content, for coded messages about ourselves sent from a future we are fantasizing, is also to foreclose part of the experience of speculation, resolving all too easily its cacophony of dream wishes." In Albert's analysis, many corners of IR are still characterized by a pervasive continuationism, that is an assumption "that coming decades will see no dramatic transformations of world order outside the basic parameters of economic growth, inter-capitalist competition and the shifting balance of power that have defined the past two centuries of world politics" (Albert 2020). The contemporary relevance and reception of Kim Stanley Robinson's work in academic and policymaking communities might serve as an illustration of this; with readers scouring *The Ministry for the Future* (2020) for causal pathways, and critics admonishing the 'unrealistic' developments in the science fiction book.

If IR has in the last decades sought to engage science fiction, it is nothing less than worlding, and the very future of existence in itself that is at stake in current debates. Mitchell calls out IR for being ignorant about ecological catastrophe, insisting that IR in the Anthropocene needs to be re-imagined as a political science of ecosystemic survival (Mitchell 2017). As Mitchell and Chaudhury argue (2020: 326):

> Discourses on 'global catastrophic risk', 'human extinction', and similar large-scale threats are fundamentally apocalyptic: they see the collapse of currently-dominant power structures as the 'end of the world' and the extinction of 'humanity'. This is a powerful and increasingly common way of conceptualizing the changing patterns of inter-relations between humans, ecologies, climates, and technologies addressed in this volume, and it is a compelling narrative for many mainstream audiences.

Two observations should be made about this narrative. First, such discourses are increasingly often countered by post-apocalyptic environmentalisms, which can open spaces to better understand possibilities and political desires for survival. In fact the eighth principle of uncivilization, according to the infamous Dark Mountain Manifesto is "the end of the world as we know it is not the end of the world full stop. Together, we will find the hope beyond hope, the paths which lead to the unknown world ahead of us." Cassegård and Thörn (2018: 569) note that apocalyptic images of future catastrophes still dominate much of environmentalist discourse, but they are now challenged by 'a postapocalyptic environmentalism', an anti-apocalyptic position based on the experience of irreversible or unavoidable loss, as well as an attempt at politicization. The recent waves of environmental protests are neither "nourished by a strong sense of hope, nor of a future disaster, but a sense and an idea that the catastrophe is already ongoing" (ibid.). The underlying emotional context to this observation is articulated for instance the Dark Mountain Project, the concept of *Deep Adaptation* (Bendell 2018), as well as more academic undertakings, e.g. *Arts of Living on a Damaged Planet: Ghosts and Monsters of the Anthropocene* (Tsing et al. 2017). These reflections refrain from postponing the images of the apocalypse into the future. They understand the catastrophe as already happening here and now and imagine ways of living in it, creating a political agency that is different than that of modern environmentalisms. This is also noted by critical governance scholars working on environmental politics, for instance Dryzek and Pickering's (2019) conceptualization of formative political agencies in the Anthropocene. They note that indigenous peoples, the most vulnerable, and future generations act as formative agents, who "give form to what justice, sustainability, and related concepts should mean in practice" in the Anthropocene (Dryzek and Pickering 2019: 105). In contrast, they argue that those who have contributed most to pathological path dependencies in Holocene institutions (states, international organizations, and corporations), should not form the Anthropocene. Recent posthumanist contributions to IR argue for the importance of nonhumans—for instance, other animals, ecosystems, materials, machines, and networks—in co-constituting and transforming the world, and in making ethical demands (see, for instance, Burke 2011, 2013; Coward 2009; Cudworth and Hobden 2011). Some planners go even a step further and imagine, as Ihnji Jon does, urban planning as a multispecies exercise, with futurist cities catering to the needs and desires of raccoons, blackbirds, peregrines, and foxes (Jon 2020).

Secondly, what the apocalyptic discourses worry about is not, in fact, the end of earth, but rather 'the collapse of whiteness' as a formation of global power (Mitchell and Chaudhury 2020). Beyond race, this is also very much in line with doomsday prophecies invoking non-Christian religions, queerfeminism, indigeneity, or democracy. Prominent scientists and science journalists working in the area of mass extinction have provided dismal pictures of the security implications of these trends, thereby updating the security doctrines by defining new threats and new risks to western civilization. This is a pernicious juxtaposition of causation: with the climate crisis rising, analysts consider some of the most vulnerabilized places, that is, islands like the Maldives, as places prone to fall prey to food riots, islamic fundamentalism, and then, boom. Yes, there may be climate revolt. We do not know the hashtags, the suffering, the grief. But precisely locating the source of evil not by pointing to the roots, but to the cause, will not lead us anywhere, but to the new fortresses of authoritarian climate regimes, and to the horrific failures in disaster governance that Mike Davis has meticulously portrayed in 'Late Victorian Holocausts' (Davis 2000; Bhat 2021). We want to amplify Mitchell and Chaudhury's call (2020: 327) that "the next generation of IR (and other) scholars and practitioners need to pay close attention to the assumptions they engender, the worlds they seek to protect, and those they work – intentionally or not – to preclude."

Contemporary thinking about extinction within international discourses has moved away from both Cold War-era preoccupations with sudden, catastrophic events and the ethics of elimination toward the biopolitical management of life processes. As Albert points out (2020), a key question is what the nature of global collapse would be, that is whether it would involve "a slow and geographically uneven 'long descent' over the course of decades," or "a more rapid process of 'synchronous failure' with mutually reinforcing ecological and political-economic crises." We see the Anthropocene debate as an entry point into this post-apocalyptic vista. On the other hand, we also highlight that it easily renders invisible the environmental damage long inflicted on the poor, the colonized, and the vulnerable (the long emergencies and slow erosions of environmental justice that Rob Nixon (2013) called 'slow violence'.) Decolonial and Indigenous communities have been experiencing this kind of slow violence, already since 1492 and have been experiencing a post-apocalyptic struggle for ecosystemic and epistemological survival since then (Whyte 2016). Moving beyond a cyclical temporality, there is room for an empathetic understanding of lost worlds, longing, and survival strategies, which, as Farhana Sultana puts it, encompass collective memory and culture rebuilding, storytelling, relational entanglements, food sharing, as "for many these are simultaneously coping mechanisms, refusals, resistance movements, and decolonial actions, where recollections of collective memories and practices as well as enactments for liberation remain the goal. However, it is vital to not fetishize pre-histories as frozen time or culture as magical solutions to systemic oppression, but recognize how they further propel decolonization and revolutionary resistance" (Sultana 2022: 9).

Future (Im)Perfect—The Shape of Worlds to Come

Future histories showcase the strength of a historically anchored yet speculatively open way of thinking about worlds to come. Within science fiction studies, the power of history is well recognized; even historians acknowledge the role of science fiction as historical genre (Liedl 2015). Looking backward, and writing in *future antérieur* style has been a powerful approach in a range of literatures, e.g. in the previously mentioned *Looking Backward* and the utopian works of nineteenth-century socialists. In science fiction, Olaf Stapledon's 1930 *Last and First Men* is a classic example of a future history, inspiring, e.g. Isaac Asimov's *Foundation* Series. The perhaps most well-known and influential example of a future history approach is H.G. Wells' 1933 *The Shape of Things to Come*. In discussing relations between cultural history and science fiction, scholars point to science fiction's "intrinsically historiographic imagination" (Luckhurst 2010: 10). On a fundamental level, future histories resonate with Jameson's approach to science fiction as archaeology of the future, in that they project the overdetermination of social processes, or, as Jameson puts it (2005: 395), "what is finally not ultimately unthinkable about historical conjunctures." By adopting a future history approach, Butor argues (1971: 158/159), "we open up the complexity of the present, we develop still larval aspects." Larvae, of course, transform into a mushy goo before transitioning into their next stage, while retaining key memories; in other words, there is much potential in future histories to move on from

THE REALISM OF OUR TIME? FUTURES, FICTIONS ... 421

their historical anchor points. It is also, fundamentally, a genre with subversive power. Butor (1971: 159) calls it "a remarkable instrument of investigation in the tradition of Swift. It readily assumes a satiric aspect." More recently, climate science fiction has taken up future histories as a key genre, in a range of literature as well as films (e.g. *The Age of Stupid*, 2009). Kim Stanley Robinson's work constitutes an essential part of this discussion, e.g. the *Three Californias* Triptych, or *New York 2140*. As he explains, "from about one to three centuries from now, there exists a less-populated story zone that I find interesting. You could call it future history. Stories set in this zone resemble nineteenth-century social novels: the characters interact not just with each other, but with their societies and even their planets" (Robinson 2017). Naomi Oreskes and Eric Conway's 2014 *The Collapse of Western Civilisation* has been a milestone in bridging between climate fiction and academic discussions of the Anthropocene. Writing a future history, they point out, has numerous advantages, among them "honoring the factual constraints of nature, as illuminated by science, with the creative opportunities offered by fiction" (ibid.: 67). Oreskes and Conway's book demonstrates the subtle power and agency of satire, while also exhibiting the emotional distance of retrospection. The date they had chosen, that is the year 2393, according to Oreskes (ibid.: 71) has been arbitrary, but in any case 'far enough into the future for emotional comfort'. Following Vermeulen, we can distinguish between two contemporary figurations of the future reader oscillating between two disciplinary incarnations: "that of future historian and that of a future geologist – the former *competently* interpreting humanity's current failures, the latter typically *dispassionately* reading the record of its passing" (Vermeulen 2017: 874, emphasis in original). We can see this play out in much of science and climate fiction, as well as the broader engagement with future worlds in International Relations. In the following section, we will discuss where we as editors (but by all means not all of our contributors) stand.

3   WRITING THE HANDBOOK OF GLOBAL POLITICS IN THE 22ND CENTURY

While it might seem that the social science fiction in this book is fully open-ended and boundless, it is in fact shaped and disciplined by a kaleidoscope of decisions, parameters, and limitations. In this section, we reflect on and discuss the core dimensions of the project; how they matter to what you have read, and what they mean. This includes the timeframe of the book, core parameters such as plausibility and the laws of physics, the engagement and entanglement with academic genres and assumptions about academic practices, as well as the very real limits and also failures of the project.

Timeframe and Parameters

Forecasting and scenario-based engagements with the future tend to have a near-future focus that ties them to the next five, ten, fifteen years. Zero emissions by 2030, 2050, over the course of the next 10 years, with this five-year plan... depending on the level of assumed predictive accuracy, the future is measurable, and ever so tangible. Near-future science fiction such as Kim Stanley Robinson's *Ministry for the Future*, many episodes of *Black Mirror*, the successful BBC mini-series *Year after Year* and other contemporary science fiction works in print, TV, and film, adopt a similar time frame, close enough for their scenarios to play out in the readers/viewers lifetime. The affective resonance this affords is a powerful tool for both cognition and estrangement (Suvin 1988). However, it also binds imagination, desires, and extrapolative potential from taking on a form that goes *beyond* the dominant presentism fueled by 'any minute now' impulses triggered by yet another round of international climate policy meetings; human rights conferences; financial agreements. Getting out of these temporal bubbles allows for a longer view, possibly even including a longue durée of the future, if you want. One of the hooks we have used in the establishment of this project was the founding myth of International Relations as a discipline—1917 and all that—(Hobson 2012; De Carvalho et al. 2011). This was a useful heuristic for pitching it to an audience that was enthralled with discussing its own myths and boundaries. However, as the making of the book meandered onward, this dimension quietly receded into the background. Instead, we realized that what provided the temporal scope for the book was the recognition that we wanted our futures to bear resonance to both future and past, rather than prioritizing one over the other. In recognition of Indigenous perspectives highlighting the temporal connections of the web of life, we adopt a modified seven generations approach in this book. This means a 3 + 1 + 3 perspective, with contributors exploring their chapters in awareness of the legacies of the past, taking note of their own present, and then writing the future with these links to the next three generations in mind. The 100-years frame still constitutes a fairly long time span, increasing uncertainty and contingency with every year beyond the near-future horizon. But as you see in many of the chapters, contributors felt compelled, and comfortable, to explore their temporal horizons thinking themselves or their descendants into their futures. In this way, the emotional distance and cool disassociation from these futures dissolve, giving rise to an intimacy that renders them almost subversive in this permanent present. At the same time, not *all* contributors fully immerse themselves in this perspective. Even so, the 100-years timeframe is pertinent to capture long-term social and technological change and concomitant consequences, taking a long view on the critical mass of changes, and the fundamentally uneven character of these developments. Importantly, the book refuses to accept teleological certainty, instead following Agathangelou and Killian who argue (2021: 834) that "in every shift or transition, in every adaptation, there is a possibility of erasing linearity and the 'teleological work of time itself." Instead of an "evacuation of the near future" (Guyer 2007: 409), that is the fantasies of catastrophe or crisis in scientific, earth, social sciences, and literary studies alike following temporal linear presuppositions, our chapters proceed in non-Euclidian, qurated ways. And yet, a curious tendency emerges when reading through many of the chapters—the mid-century bang. Independently of each other, many contributors narrate and develop their futures via a cataclysmic event taking place somewhere in the 2030/2040s. Initially, for some, this meant either setting up a *tabula rasa* scenario or casually killing off millions of people. While we, as editors, had committed to not interfering in contributors' futures, we did insist that they reflected on whether this was indeed how they wanted their global politics to play out. As Mitchell and Chaudhury (2020) argue, the ease with many future scenarios (in their discussion, Oreskes and Conway 2014) assume and imagine the total elimination of people, often BIPOC communities other to the author's own positioning, as a matter of course reflects and shapes the expectations of readers. We also have to recognize and acknowledge that the very temporal parameter of the book, i.e. a quantum branch-off point on 2022, does not as such change the realities against which the future chapters unfold, that is the extant power relations, limits, and violences within the discipline. At the same time, we very decisively did not want to write alternate histories. Instead, perhaps we can best think about our engagement with contemporary IR also along the lines of Vermeulen's literary figure of the 'future reader', not only focusing on that which will have been but adding a subjunctive to the future perfect of the Anthropocene (Vermeulen 2017: 8739)—what might we have done?

The timeframe of the book, and concomitantly the horizon of human agency, also meant setting a number of other parameters for our contributors. We excluded the possibility of introducing alien, extraterrestrial species, assuming that the more-than-human dimension of the Anthropocene would provide sufficient focus. Concerning technological development and exploration, we insisted on a principle of plausibility, to the extent that, e.g. we allowed for a station to be set up on Moon, but not fully fledged Mars colonization. We also asked contributors to, as far as possible, stay within the laws of physics—until they reach the point where their narratives took a science fiction turn. Contributors have dealt with these parameters in rather diverse ways; some deciding to introduce technologies, others relying purely on social innovation to drive their narrative. Cause and effect, common sense, progress; many chapters still follow modernist principles, some more explicitly than others.

The Ecology of Academic Writing

Working academic science fiction made us realize just what a multitude of genres of academic writing entails, and which power lies therein. Many scholars in IR have engaged with various forms of storytelling (e.g. Ling 2014; still with us in spirit). As Inayatullah and Dauphinee argue (2016: 1), "it matters how we tell our stories, and changing the form of telling can allow the reader to think." HGP22 contributions span a range of academic genres that you will not find in other handbooks. Thinking about this range as a spectrum, we could put the chapters that follow the conventional Handbook chapter format on one end. Beyond this, contributions have chosen the format of a review, a letter, a transcript of a documentary, a speech at a future ISA, a memoir, an open-source encyclopedia, all the way to the other side of the spectrum where the scholarly feed has replaced traditional chapter formats. This playfulness and diversity in genres on the one hand reminds us that we can do so much more than limit ourselves to the exigencies of academic publishing; on the other hand, it might well inspire us to explore these other forms of writing also beyond that which is academic and scholarly. You would be surprised how many people enthusiastically responded with 'oh and by the way I also write science fiction, but I have never shown anyone this story which has been in the drawer for years' when they heard about this project.

Why then did we decide to group together this wondrous ecology of academic writing into a Handbook, the vociferous genre that has taken over the publishing market by storm over the last decade or two? For readers familiar with the publishing formats within science fiction proper, the format of our book might actually be familiar—a collection, or rather anthology of contributions, loosely linked through a theme (global politics in the twenty-second century) but not related in any way, with the editor taking on an essential role in curating the chapters. Several times, contributors expressed surprise and even discomfort at the thought that there was nothing that linked the various contributions aside from the premise. Certainly, a link had to be there; isn't that what a handbook does, group around different scholars in the exploration of a theme, process, or concept so that they can explore various dimensions of the same thing? It was in fact out of a deep unease with the Handbook trend that we set out to write one. Where handbooks claim authoritative standing and comprehensive coverage, our book naturally has neither. Instead, it aims to subvert the closure that comes with Handbook projects, as brilliant as many of them might be (and in the interest of full disclosure, we editors have contributed to a fair share of them). Handbooks also constitute a culmination of the capitalist academic publishing model; easily accessible and self-contained in each chapter, claiming to be an intellectual 'one-stop shop', neatly downloadable with the reference list in each file; and curated by established scholars in the field that lend their epistemic authority and legitimacy to the book. As printed copies, Handbooks are prohibitively expensive; for electronic access, often as part of negotiated package deals, university libraries spend an extraordinary amount of public funding. And yet, you reading this text which was indeed published as a Handbook shows that even science fiction cannot escape the realities of the present; rather we are considering and negotiating ways in which we can navigate the Handbook format. We certainly hope that future academic publishing will find more inspiring, stimulating, and inclusive formats.

It is the fake references that have perhaps been our main instrument of linking to, and at the same time questioning, teasing, and disrupting contemporary academic conventions and power structures. Including fake academic references might at first glance seem like a trivial, mainly entertaining feature. However, as became clear through the writing process, they are in fact a key dimension of the genre. They also turned out so subversive that the publisher had to request that we mark fake references so that they could be clearly distinguishable from real existing scholarly work. More critically still, we had to ask contributors to consider near-future fake references that might in a few years show up on people's citation metrics without them actually having written them—algorithms can't deal with imagined publications that, as form of 'epistemological empathy', extrapolate a writer's future research interests. For our contributors, fake references became just as much part of the world-building as they were a way to signal, or rather claim scholarly authority. With this, HGP22 is in very good company. The great storyteller Jorge Luis Borges has shown the fantasmal power of making up worlds of writing, for instance in his 1940 short story *Tlön, Uqbar, Orbis Tertius*. As a critic in the New York Times (1986) wrote rather breathlessly, "when he cites fictitious titles, imaginary cross-references, folios and writers that have never existed, Borges is simply regrouping counters of reality into the shape of possible other worlds." Fictional references and satire of academic conventions can already be found, e.g. in Thomas Carlyle's *Sartor Resartus* (1833). We see the fake references in the contributions to this book as an important element of the interplay between cognition and estrangement. While, initially, readers might feel more at ease reading the chapters as references are a familiar, recurrent feature in academic text, by making these very references fake the familiar is rendered estranged, and cognition is interrupted. A similar effect might be the broader references to future university structures in several chapters. By extrapolating, exaggerating, and also caricaturing institutional features and practices in our contemporary academic life world, contributors address the rather fundamental assumption that we're probably all working with—universities, institutionalized learning, knowledge, and respective social hierarchies will still be there in the future. The monks in the Swiss Alps after a nuclear war put this assumption into stark relief. But even without nuclear apocalypse, we need to interrogate the assumed continuities that guide our own existence and strategies. There is a narrowness to academic practices and horizons that contributors to this book engage with. The theme of academic institutions and future universities has been explored by science fiction writers in many

426   L. HORN ET AL.

different ways, e.g. Lem's *Futurological Congress* (1974) or Oomza University in Nnedi Okorafor's *Binti* (2015). The ambivalence in which many of the contributions to this project navigate the question of structures of academic research and learning indicates that much work remains to be done here. On the one hand, the modern university has increasingly become hopeless (Hall 2021), its pathologies, including the cynical instrumentalization and marketization of knowledge, more and more pronounced; its structures and processes hostile toward actual imagination and desirable futures. More importantly still, universities and other places of institutionalized learning are of course just as much part of the Anthropocene unraveling, and our practices are as much part of the carbon ruins as they are shaped by them. As Charlie Gardner, member of the Scientist Rebellion group of activist scholars puts it: There are no professorships on a dead planet. In the context of this book, one might add that there are no quantum computers or International Relations on a dead planet, either.

Who Gets to Write the Futures of Global Politics?

Thinking about who gets to write stories about the future in the Anthropocene, while others have to live those futures in the here and now has been a recurring discussion in our collective bookmaking. This question is also central to some of the main limits, and, frankly, failures of this book. There is a profoundly ethical question at the heart of narrating futures. In contrast to other future-making exercises, the academic science fiction that you read in this book does not assume that any of our histories will come true. That is, some of these futures might be more desirable than others; some might make the hair on your arms stand up. However, none of them are written as backcasting exercises, nor as ominous warnings. In contrast to much science fiction, in particular climate fiction in the Anthropocene (Vermeulen 2017: 871), we do not assume that contributions will *necessarily* "significantly affect human behaviour, inculcate attitudes that help human life navigate the altered relations between nature and culture, and ultimately inform ethical and political change." The chapters in this book all have their own assumptions about structure/agency, causality, and politics, including how and which individuals and subjectivities constitute these futures. Against the background of the discussion, earlier in this conclusion, of the intersections between future-making, science fiction, and International Relations in the Anthropocene, we acknowledge that also in this book the power structures and silences within the discipline are reproduced. Just as it matters whose history is being written, and who gets to write it, it matters whose future is being written, and who writes it. This book, as much as it is a radical, inclusive, collective project, ultimately fails at bringing in more perspectives on futures in and of Global Politics. This failure unfolds along many faultlines—geographical, social, and political. Where is the future of the Belt and Road Initiative, arguably one of the defining projects of contemporary global politics? Why isn't there a queer chapter that offers a take on the future in which linguistic and social conventions have changed along with the liberation of bodies and sexualities from capitalism? Speaking of, why not include an actual fully automated luxury space communism future? And why are the majority of contributors to the book scholars based in the Global North, many of them on permanent positions? It isn't that as editors we haven't discussed these issues, and tried to recruit more contributors—many emails have been sent, many contacts have been mobilized. Still, we bear much of the responsibility for the futures that have not been written in this book, particularly the Afrofuturist and Africanfuturist ones, to whose radical, empathetic, and wise imagination we owe immense tribute. Who has time to write yet another book chapter, when publication metrics are clamoring for articles, and it's those metrics that matter most for jobs and grant applications? Who agrees to write a contribution for a weird book project without even a book contract, brought together by a group of white people in the Global North? We have learned a lot about power and hierarchies in making this book. This also includes what kind of futures have been written in the group. Beyond the tired utopian/dystopian dichotomy, we found our position in Ursula Le Guin's distinction between yin and yang utopias (1982: 11–12). "Utopia has been yang" she argued, "bright, dry, clear, strong, firm, active, aggressive, lineal, progressive, creative, expanding, advancing, and hot." The yang is also strong for many, if not most of the contributions in this book. Asking with Le Guin, what would a yin utopia be? "It would be dark, wet, obscure, weak, yielding, passive, participatory, circular, cyclical, peaceful, nurturant, retreating, contracting, and cold." Bring this distinction to the chapters in HGP22, and see if it resonates. There is so much to be done, to write those futures that are in the making already in so many ways. Perhaps this book can at least serve as a fertilizer to help bring them about.

4   There Are No Conclusions: Let Us Keep Writing Futures

We have grounded our writing in who we are, in our collective, in the sheer weirdness of doing this project together. We have imagined our worlds, as they exist, as they might exist, and as we do or do not want them to exist. In doing so, we have rejected reducing academic science fiction to a mere commentary on contemporary politics. We want our futures to be meaningful, yes, but we also want to insist on the frightening beauty of the future and the need for estrangement, against the immanence of the present. As far as moral interventions go, in this way HGP22 might be seen as an articulation of hope; a stubborn hope that shakes its head at a future that is an endless repetition and continuation, and hence no future at all.

References

Agathangelou, A., & Killian, K. (2021) 'About Time: Climate Change and Inventions of the Decolonial, Planetarity and Radical Existence.' *Globalizations* 18(6), 821–838.

Albert, M. (2020) 'Beyond Continuationism: Climate Change, Economic Growth, and the Future of World (Dis)Order.' *Cambridge Review of International Affairs*.

Barthes, R. (1957 [1987]) *Mythologies* (New York: Hill & Wang).

Baum, S.D., Armstrong, S., Ekenstedt, T., Häggström, O., Hanson, R., Kuhlemann, K., Maas, M.M., Miller, J.D., Salmela, M., Sandberg, A., Sotala, K., Torres, P., Turchin, A., & Yampolskiy, R.V. (2019) 'Long-Term Trajectories of Human Civilization.' *Foresight* 21(1), 53–83.

Behagel, J. H., & Mert, A. (2021) 'The Political Nature of Fantasy and Political Fantasies of Nature.' *Journal of Language and Politics* 20(1), 79–94.

Bellamy, E. (1887 [1951]) *Looking Backward, 2000–1887* (New York: The Modern Library).

Bhat, H. (2021) 'The Weather Is Always a Method.' In: David Chandler, Franziska Müller, & Delf Rothe (eds.), *International Relations in the Anthropocene: New Actors, New Agencies and New Approaches* (Basingstoke: Palgrave Macmillan), pp. 407–424.

Bilgin, M. (2016) 'The State of Future in International Relations.' *Futures* 82 (2016), 52–62.

Bishop, P., Hines, A., & Collins, T. (2007) 'The Current State of Scenario Development: An Overview of Techniques.' *Foresight* 9(1), 5–25.

Bloch, E. (1959). *Das Prinzip Hoffnung* (Frankfurt: Suhrkamp).

Borges, J.L. (1940) *Tlön, Uqbar, Orbis Tertius*. Available at https://sites.evergreen.edu/politicalshakespeares/wp-content/uploads/sites/226/2015/12/Borges-Tl%C3%B6n-Uqbar-Orbius-Tertius.pdf.

Bostrom, N., Cirkovic, M., & Rees, M. (eds.). (2008) *Global Catastrophic Risk* (Oxford University Press).

Bruno, L. (1993). *We have never been modern.* (Harvard University Press).

Burke, A., Fishel, S., & Dalby, S. (2016) 'Planet Politics: A Manifesto from the End of IR.' *Millennium: Journal of International Studies* 44(3), 499–533.

Butor, M. (1971) 'The Growing Pains of Science Fiction.' In: Clareson, T. (ed), *SF, The Other Side of Realism: Essays on Modern Fantasy and Science Fiction* (Bowling Green, Ohio: University Popular Press).

Carlyle, T. [1833] *Sartor Resartus: The Life and Opinions of Herr Teufelsdröckh in Three Books.* Available at https://gutenberg.org/ebooks/1051.

Carpenter, R.C. (2016) 'Rethinking the Political/-Science-/Fiction Nexus: Global Policy Making and the Campaign to Stop Killer Robots.' *Perspectives on Politics* 14(1), 53–69.

Cassegård, C., & Thörn, H. (2018). Toward a postapocalyptic environmentalism? Responses to loss and visions of the future in climate activism. *Environment and Planning E: Nature and Space, 1*(4), 561–578.

Chandler, D., Cudworth, E., & Hobden, S. (2017) 'Anthropocene, Capitalocene and Liberal Cosmopolitan IR: A Response to Burke et al.'s 'Planet Politics.' *Millennium* 46(2), 190–208.

Dator, J.A. (ed.). (2002) *Advancing Futures: Futures Studies in Higher Education* (Westport: Praeger).

Davis, M. (2000). *Late Victorian Holocausts* (London: Verso).

De Carvalho, B., Leira, H., & Hobson, J.M. (2011) 'The Big Bangs of IR: The Myths That Your Teachers Still Tell You about 1648 and 1919.' *Millennium* 39(3), 735–758.

De Guevara, B.B. (ed.). (2016) *Myth and Narrative in International Politics: Interpretive Approaches to the Study of IR* (Springer).

Engels, F. (1880 [1999]) *Socialism: Utopian and Scientific* (Chippensdale: Resistance Books).

Epstein, C. (2020) *Birth of the State: The Place of the Body in Crafting Modern Politics* (Oxford University Press).

Escobar, A. (1999) 'After Nature: Steps to an Antiessentialist Political Ecology.' *Current Anthropology* 40(1), 1–30.

Freistein, K., & Gadinger, F. (2020) 'Populist Stories of Honest Men and Proud Mothers: A Visual Narrative Analysis.' *Review of International Studies* 46(2), 217–236.

Gadinger, F., Kopf, M., Mert, A., & Smith, C. (2016) 'Political Storytelling: From Fact to Fiction.' *Global Dialogues* 12.

Glynos, J., & Howarth, D. (2007). *Logics of critical explanation in social and political theory*. Routledge.

Grayson, K., Davies, M., & Philpott, S. (2009) 'Pop Goes IR? Researching the Popular Culture-World Politics Continuum.' *Politics* 29(3), 155–163.

Guyer, J. (2007) 'Prophecy and the Near Future: Thoughts on Macroeconomic, Evangelical, and Punctuated Time.' *American Ethnologist* 34(3), 409–421.

Hall, R. (2021) *The Hopeless University: Intellectual Work at the end of The End of History* (Mayfly Books).

Haraway, D. (1985) 'Manifesto for Cyborgs: Science, Technology, and Socialist Feminism in the 1980s.' *Socialist Review* 80, 65–108.

Hobson, J. M. (2012) *The Eurocentric Conception of World Politics. Western International Theory, 1760–2010* (Cambridge: Cambridge University Press).

Illich, I. (1973). *Tools for Conviviality* (New York: Harper Collins).

Inayatullah, N., & Dauphinee, E. (eds.). (2016) *Narrative Global Politics: Theory, History and the Personal in International Relations* (Routledge).

Jameson, F. (2005) *Archaeologies of the Future: The Desire Called Utopia and Other Science Fictions* (London: Verso).

Jasanoff, Sheila (ed.). (2004) *States of Knowledge* (Abingdon, UK: Taylor & Francis).

Jon, I. (2020) 'Deciphering Posthumanism: Why and How It Matters to Urban Planning in the Anthropocene.' *Planning Theory* 19(4), 392–420.

Kemp, S., & Andersson, Jenny. (2021) *Futures* (Oxford: Oxford University).

Kirby, P. (2017) 'Political Speech in Fantastical Worlds.' *International Studies Review* 19(4), 573–596.

Koschorke, A. (2018) *Fact and Fiction. Elements of a General Theory of Narrative* (De Gruyter).

Latour, B. (2004) 'Why Has Critique Run out of Steam? From Matters of Fact to Matters of Concern', *Critical Inquiry* 30(2), 225–248.

Latour, B. (2010) 'An Attempt at a 'Compositionist Manifesto'.' *New Literary History* 41(3), 471–490.

Le Guin, U. (1982) 'A Non-Euclidean View of California as a Cold Place to Be.' In: Le Guin, U. *Dancing at the Edge of the World* (London: Gollancz).

Leira, H., & De Carvalho, B. (2018) *The Function of Myths in International Relations: Discipline and Identity* (London: Sage).

Lem, Stanislaw. (1974) *The Futurological Congress* (Orbit).

Liedl, J. (2015) 'Tales of Futures Past: Science Fiction as a Historical Genre.' *Rethinking History* 19(2), 285–299.

Ling, L.H.M. (2014) *Imagining World Politics. Sihar & Shenya, A Fable for Our Times* (Routledge).

Lohmann, S., & Tepel, T. (2014) 'Will the Real Security Foresight Please Stand Up?' *European Journal of Futures Research* 2(1), 1–6.

López Galviz, C., & Spiers, E. (eds.). (2022) *Routledge Handbook of Social Futures* (Routledge).

Luckhurst, R. (2010) 'Science Fiction and Cultural History.' *Science Fiction Studies* 37(1), 3–15.

Mert, A. (2015) *Environmental Governance Through Partnerships: A Discourse Theoretical Study* (Cheltenham: Edward Elgar).

Mitchell, A. (2017) 'Is IR Going Extinct?' *European Journal of International Relations* 23(1), 3–25.

Mitchell, A., & Chaudhury, A. (2020) 'Worlding Beyond 'the' 'End' of 'the world': White Apocalyptic Visions and BIPOC Futurisms'. *International Relations* 34(3), 309–332.

Mouffe, C. (1996) 'Democracy, Power, and the 'Political'.' In: S. Benhabib (ed.), *Democracy and Difference* (Princeton: Princeton University Press), pp. 245–255.

Müller, F. (2016). 'How to Study Myths: Methodological Demands and Discoveries.' In: Berit Bliesemann (Hg.): *Myths and International Politics: A Narrative Approach to the Study of IR* (London: PalgraveMacMillan), pp. 107–126.

Muppidi, H. (2013) 'Reflections on Narrative Voice' Blog post at 'The Disorder of Things', 23 March. http://thedisorderofthings.com/2013/03/23/reflections-on-narrative-voice/ (Accessed 12 June 2022).

Kiersey, N.J. & Neumann, I.B. (eds.) (2015) *Battlestar Galactica and International Relations* (Abingdon: Routledge).

New York Times. (1986) *Jorge Luis Borges, a Master of Fantasy and Fable, Is Dead*, Edward A. Gargan, 15 June 1986.

Okorafor, N. (2015) *Binti* (Tor).

Oreskes, N., & Conway, E. (2014) *The Collapse of Western Civilisation. A View from the Future* (CUP).

Patel, R., & Moore, J. (2018). *A History of the World in Seven Cheap Things* (London: Verso).

Raven, P.G., & Stripple, J. (2021) 'Touring the Carbon Ruins: Towards an Ethics of Speculative Decarbonisation.' *Global Discourse* 11(1–2), 221–240.

Robinson, K.R. (2017) '3D Glasses on Reality' Science Fiction When the Future Is Now.' *Nature* 552, 20 December 2017. Available at https://www.nature.com/articles/d41586-017-08674-8.

Rose, D.B., van Dooren, T., & Chrulew, M. (2017) *Extinction Studies: Stories of Time, Death, and Generations* (New York: Columbia University Press).

Schneide, G., et al. (2011) 'Forecasting in International Relations: One Quest, Three Approaches.' *Conflict Management and Peace Science* 28(1), 5–14.

Segal, L. (2017) *Radical Happiness: Moments of Collective Joy* (Verso).

Stavrakakis, Y. (2005) 'Passions of Identification: Discourse, Enjoyment, and European Identity.' In: D. Howarth & J. Torfing (eds.), *Discourse Theory in European Politics: Identity, Policy, Governance* (Basingstoke: Palgrave), pp. 68–92.

Strathern, M. (1992) *After Nature: English Kinship in the Late Twentieth Century* (Cambridge).

Sultana, F. (2022) 'The Unbearable Heaviness of Climate Coloniality.' *Political Geography.* https://doi.org/10.1016/j.polgeo.2022.102638.

Suvin, D. (1988) *Positions and Presuppositions in Science Fiction* (Basingstoke: Macmillan Press).

Thompson, E.P. (2011) *William Morris: Romantic to Revolutionary* (PM Press).

Torres, P. (2017) *Morality, Foresight, and Human Flourishing: An Introduction to Existential Risks* (Pitchstone Publishing).

Tsing, A.L. (2015) *The Mushroom at the End of the World: On the Possibility of Life in Capitalist Ruins* (Princeton University Press).

Van Dooren, T. (2014). *Flight Ways: Life and Loss at the Edge of Extinction* (New York: Columbia University Press).

Vermeulen, P. (2017) 'Future Readers: Narrating the Human in the Anthropocene.' *Textual Practice* 31(5), 867–885.

Weber, C. (2001) *International Relations Theory. A Critical Introduction* (London and New York: Routledge.), 3rd edition.

Weldes, J. (ed.). (2003) *To Seek Out New Worlds: Science Fiction and World Politics* (Basingstoke: Palgrave MacMillan).

Whyte, K.P. (2016) 'Is it colonial déja-vu? Indigenous People and Climate Injustice.' In: Joni Adamson & Michael Davis (eds.), *(2016) Humanities for the Environment* (Taylor & Francis).

Wright, E.O. (2010) *Envisioning Real Utopias* (Verso).

Yanow, D. (1996) *How does a Policy Mean? Interpreting Policy and Organizational Actions* (Washington: Georgetown University Press).

Yovchev, I. ([1892] 1900) The Present as Seen by Our Descendants and a Glimpse at the Progress of the Future adapted from Bellamy E. (1887) 'Looking Backward, 2000–1887' Йовчев, И. Настоящето, разгледано от потомството ни и надничане в напредъка на бъдъщето. София: Печатница Кос-тадин Г. Чинков, 1900.

List of Contributors

Alberta Giorgi is Senior Assistant Professor in Sociology of Culture and Communication at the University of Bergamo.

Aleksandra Spalińska is Ph.D. researcher at the Faculty of Political Science and International Studies, University of Warsaw.

Alexander van Eijk is a researcher, writer and translator based in Amsterdam.

Andriy Tyushka is Senior Research Fellow at the European Neighbourhood Policy Chair, College of Europe in Natolin.

Annette Freyberg-Inan is Professor of International Relations Theory at the University of Amsterdam.

Ayşem Mert is Senior Lecturer at the Department of Political Science, Stockholm University.

Barry Buzan is Emeritus Professor of International Relations at the London School of Economics.

Elana Gomel is Professor in the Department of English and American Studies, Tel Aviv University.

Elin Haettner is industrial partner in the technical board of the Digital Twin Cities Centre, Chalmers University of Technology, Gothenburg. Project manager at White Arkitekter.

Frans Magnusson is industrial partner in the Digital Twin Cities Centre, Chalmers University of Technology, Gothenburg. Architect (Licentiate), computational developer at White Arkitekter.

Franziska Müller is Assistant Professor for Globalization and Climate Governance at the Faculty of Business, Economics and Social Sciences, University of Hamburg.

© The Editor(s) (if applicable) and The Author(s), under exclusive license to Springer Nature Switzerland AG 2023
L. Horn et al. (eds.), *The Palgrave Handbook of Global Politics in the 22nd Century*, https://doi.org/10.1007/978-3-031-13722-8

434 LIST OF CONTRIBUTORS

Giuseppe Porcaro is a political geographer, author, and Head of Outreach and Governance at Bruegel, Brussels.

Ian Manners is Professor at the Department of Political Science, Lund University.

Isabella Hermann holds a Ph.D. in International Relations and works as science fiction analyst, based in Berlin.

Jakub Zahora received his Ph.D. in International Relations from the Institute of Political Studies, Faculty of Social Sciences, Charles University in Prague.

Jeffrey Knopf is Professor of Nonproliferation and Terrorism Studies at the Middlebury Institute of International Studies (MIIS), Monterey.

John Szabo is Ph.D. Candidate at Central European University & Junior Fellow at the Centre for Economic and Regional Studies.

Joshua Hurtado is Ph.D. researcher in Interdisciplinary Environmental Sciences at University of Helsinki.

Karim Zakhour is Senior lecturer at the Department of Political Science, Stockholm University.

Laura Horn is Associate Professor in the Department of Social Sciences and Business, Roskilde University.

Luca Ozzano is Associate Professor of Political Science at the University of Torino.

Lucian Ashworth is Professor in the Department of Political Science, Memorial University of Newfoundland.

Lucyna Czechowska is Assistant Professor at the Department of European Studies, Faculty of Political Science and Security Studies, Nicolaus Copernicus University in Toruń.

Maria João Ferreira is Associate Professor at the School of Social and Political Sciences, University of Lisbon.

Michal Onderco is Professor of International Relations in the Department of Public Administration and Sociology, Erasmus University Rotterdam.

Patrick Thaddeus Jackson is Professor of International Studies in the School of International Service, American University, Washington, DC.

Peter Christoff is Associate Professor in the Department of Resource Management and Geography, University of Melbourne.

Ronnie D. Lipschutz is Emeritus Professor of Politics, UC Santa Cruz, and President & Senior Analyst, Sustainable Systems Research Foundation, Santa Cruz.

Tomasz Kamiński is Professor at the Faculty of International and Political Studies, University of Łódź.

Acknowledgements

Working on this book has been a long and transformative journey. It would not have been possible without the continuous support, love, care, feedback and sometimes very practical agency of our colleagues, friends, and families, including beloved companion species.

The idea for this book first emerged in 2017—at a kitchen table, like so many other meaningful thoughts. Reaching out to scholars in the IR community (and beyond) to ask whether they would like to be part of this project initially felt a little daunting. It was all the more surprising and wonderful to receive many enthusiastic responses; who knew that there were so many scholars who actually wrote science fiction in their free time?

With the project, we organised workshops, panels and lots of conference chats including various locations such as Bath (BISA 2018), Prague (EISA 2018), Kraków (EISA Joint Sessions 2019), Rapallo (EISA Joint Sessions 2019). With in-depth workshops in Roskilde in January 2020 and September 2021, our bunch of futurist IR aficionados travelled across time and space to become an even more close-knit community. The Covid19 crisis couldn't stop us, even if it meant a slight delay for the project. It certainly forced several contributors to rethink their futures. All these conversations allowed us to delve deeper into various multiverses and engage with IR theories, world-building, and fictional formats. Since then, our thoughts have meandered and resulted in many seeds planted in different places. Likewise, when we now express gratitude to those who have supported this project in various stages, our thank you goes out in many directions.

We owe thanks to all our wonderful contributors who along these stages became part of the project. Our deep gratitude for your creativity, patience, and perseverance! Some contributors eventually chose other directions, but their ideas still are relevant and remain an important conceptual foundation—thanks to all who have been part of this journey. In particular we thank Nicholas Kiersey for all his input, networking, motivation, and ideas. Several

© The Editor(s) (if applicable) and The Author(s), under exclusive license to Springer Nature Switzerland AG 2023
L. Horn et al. (eds.), *The Palgrave Handbook of Global Politics in the 22nd Century*, https://doi.org/10.1007/978-3-031-13722-8

436 ACKNOWLEDGEMENTS

of our colleagues and friends also offered critical feedback at various stages of the publication process.

Ayşem would like to thank the Centre for Global Cooperation Research (KHK/GCR21), especially Katja Freistein and Christine Unrau, for the encouraging and supportive intellectual environment; to Jason Glynos, Jelle Behagel, and Elise Remling who patiently listened; to Ola Svenonius, Tyra Hertz, Emiliano Farinella, Natha Wahlang, and Gökçe Mete for ongoing political, futuristic, fantastic, artistic, and literary conversations, as well as shared moments of daily joy and inspiration; Tomas Nilsson and Philipp Grötsch for retouches and improvements in the actual manuscript; and of course, Minnie, for reminding and insisting on what matters in life: affection, playfulness, and curiosity. Most of all, she thanks her co-editors, who made this a truly feminist project and an amazing learning experience of inspiring and supporting each other in every way. Special thanks to Peter Christoff and Robyn Eckersley, for "getting lost in Laponia under mysterious circumstances" in laughter and mosquitoes, when we first started imagining our chapter together.

For inspiration, lots of natureculture recommendations, and not least distraction, reflection, laughter, and punk Franziska would like to thank Aram Ziai, Friz Trzeciak, Myriam Kaskel, Anna Bauer, Christine Klapeer, Sophie von Redecker and Katrin Pahl, Anil Shah, Joshua Kwesi Aikins, Anne Löscher, everyone else from the housing coop "Auenland" as well as sleeping beauty Jenny in all her furriness.

Laura would like to thank all her patient friends and colleagues who over the years had to listen to enthusiastic stories about all the wonderful chapters being written; in particular but in no particular order: Catia Gregoratti, Angela Wigger, Tomas Skov Lauridsen, Bernd Bonfert, Lara Monticelli, Vasna Ramasar, Klaas Dykmann, Helene Dyrhauge, and so many others. She promises to find something else to talk about now, although there's a good chance that it'll still be science fiction themed. A special institutional thanks goes out to Laura's Head of Department, Peter Kragelund. Projects like this one are not particularly conducive to boosting institutional publication rankings; sometimes people having your back really makes a difference. Working on this book has been a transformative experience in many ways. Laura would like to thank Franziska and Ayşem—having two brilliant and caring co-editors has made this project even more special! The warmth of feline and canine companions has been an essential part of making it through the last years, with all the love and loss they bring. To Edda and Eric, you and your futures are worth fighting for, always.

We thank Hiroko Tsuchimoto and Thomas Poulsen for their beautiful illustrations for several of the chapters; their art has added an imaginative and aesthetic dimension to the project. Tim Henke has been wonderful in providing quantum support in the most patient way. Julia Feine has been incredible in working with the future references and making them happen.

At Palgrave Macmillan, executive editor Anca Pusca has done a fantastic job by offering editorial guidance, and by dealing with issues as weird as "fake references, leading to fake google scholar entries, leading to absolute publisher market failure". At the *Palgrave Studies in International Relations* book series, we thank Knud Erik Jørgensen, for putting his editorial trust in us, and seeing the potential and relevance of the project. We also thank Shreenidhi Natarajan and Gopalakrishna Lakshminarasimha for their professional and patient handling of this manuscript.

Finally we would like to express our thanks and appreciation to the European International Studies Association for their generous support as funders of the workshops in Kraków and Rapallo. Ayşem Mert's and Karim Zakhour's work on this volume have been funded by the Swedish Research Council for Sustainable Development (FORMAS) (Grant number: FR-2020/0008). Illustrations and administrative work on this volume have been funded by the Federal Ministry of Science and Technology Germany (BMBF) (Grant number: FKZ 01LN1707A).

Roskilde	Laura Horn
Stockholm	Ayşem Mert
Hamburg	Franziska Müller
December 2022.[1]	

---

[1] Dear reader in 2122, how are you reading this text? Do prints on wooden extracts still exist? In any case, we can only hope that large, publicly accessible time capsules, currently known as "libraries" will store and preserve this volume, so that our antedecessors will be able to cross-check how their individual universes matches with the multiverses that our contributors have sketched.